Connecticut Historical and Industrial

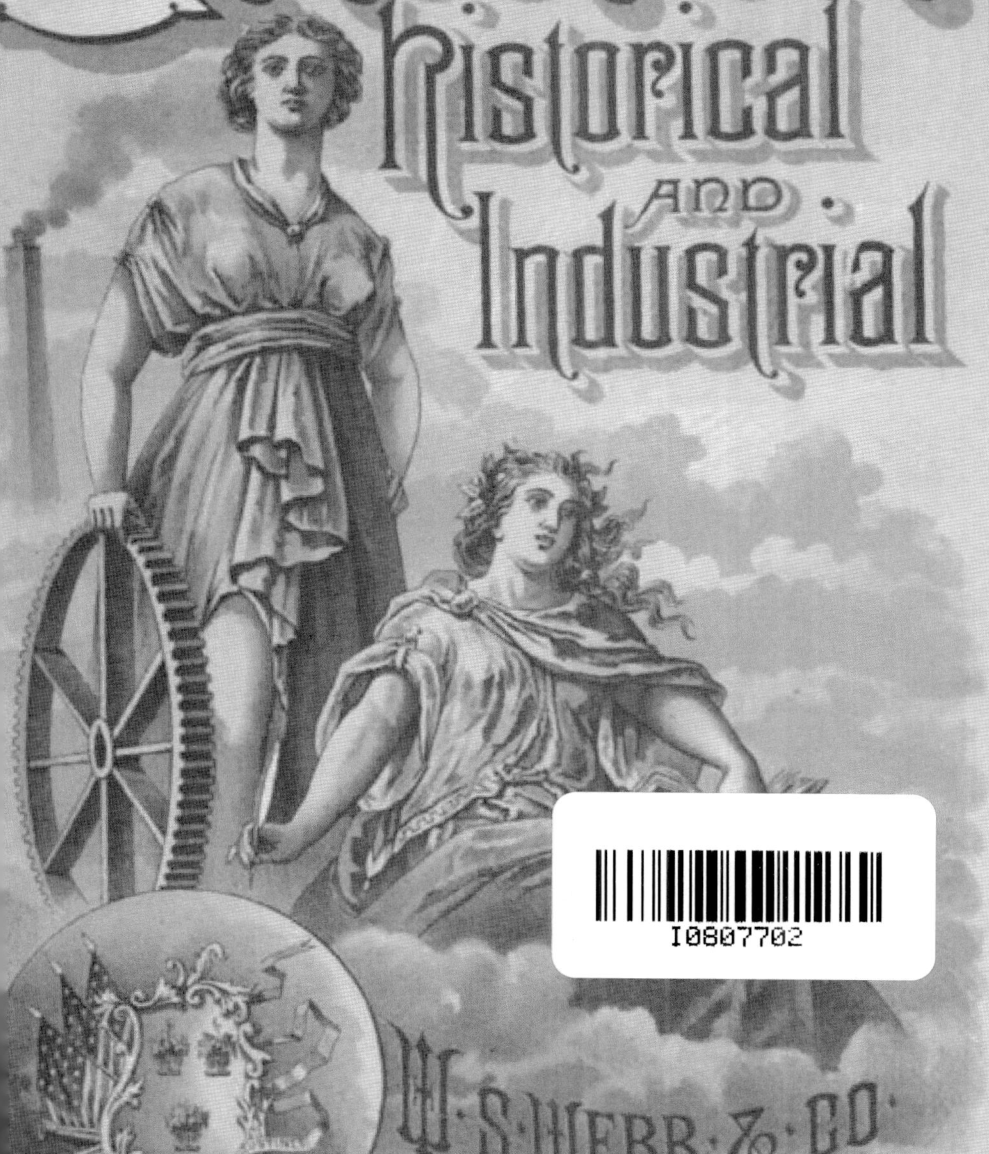

W. S. WEBB & CO

PUBLISHERS

49 & 51 Park Place, New York.

Marula

An imprint of Arcadia Publishing

The Historical, Statistical and Industrial Review of the State of Connecticut
W.S. Webb & Co.

A Marula Historical Reprint
Originally published in 1883

Published by Arcadia Publishing
Charleston SC

ISBN 978-0-7385-9461-3

Printed in the United States of America

For all general information contact Arcadia Publishing at:
Telephone 843-853-2070
Fax 843-853-0044
E-mail sales@arcadiapublishing.com
For customer service and orders:
Toll-Free 1-888-313-2665

Visit us on the Internet at www.arcadiapublishing.com

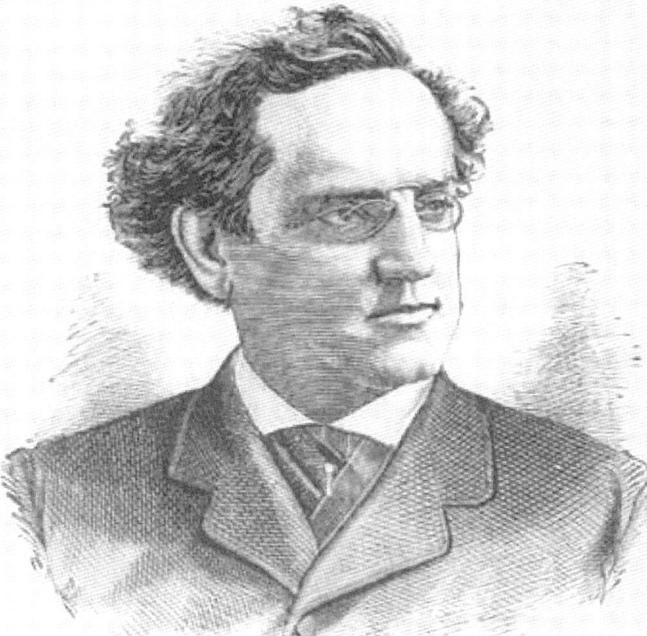

THOMAS M. WALLER, GOVERNOR OF CONNECTICUT.

THE HISTORICAL,

Statistical and Industrial Review

OF THE

STATE OF CONNECTICUT.

PART I.

"There is no other land like thee,
No dearer shore,
Thou art the shelter of the free;
The home, the port of liberty
Thou hast been and shalt ever be,
Till time is o'er."
—*Anon.*

ILLUSTRATED.

THIS ISSUE IS COMPLETE IN ITSELF AND IS A PORTION OF A LARGE VOLUME NOW IN PROGRESS, REPRESENTING THE INDUSTRIES OF CONNECTICUT.

PRICE, ONE DOLLAR.

NEW YORK:
W. S. WEBB & CO., PUBLISHERS, 49 & 51 PARK PLACE,
1883.

PREFACE.

The following pages, which represent the constant labor of a corps of reporters, writers, editors, and printers for several months, is presented to the public.

The general idea of a history is a large expensive volume, bound in heavy board covers, associated with a library and accessible only with more or less trouble. That of the publishers is to furnish a History of Connecticut and its representative industries at a low price and in such a portable shape that "he who runs may read." In order to do this at a profit, large editions are printed, enabling the publishers to furnish each part at a price so low that all who wish can possess it.

It has been the aim to mention representative mercantile houses and manufacturing establishments in the cities and villages of which this part especially treats, that would be of interest to present and future generations.

Not a line within the covers of this work has been paid for as an advertisement and no expense has been spared in its typographical execution—facts which will go far toward its favorable reception by the general public and those residing in this and foreign countries to whom it will be sent, informing them of the great prosperity of Connecticut. Acknowledgments are especially due to the proprietors of the Hartford *Evening Post* for permission to use illustrations of the State Capitol and the Governor, together with biographical sketches of the general State officers, which will be found in the first pages of this work; to Messrs. Crocker & Co., publishers of the Popular History of New England, a work which has generally been consulted and that portion relating to Connecticut largely reprinted, when occasion required.

Among authorities consulted have been Mansfield's History and Description of New England, Hayward's Gazetteer of New England, and Webb's New England Railway and Manufacturers' Statistical Gazetteer. With sincere thanks to those who have received the representatives of this work in a spirit of courtesy, to the public for its generous support, to the press for its wise discrimination that induced its hearty aid and the expression of a hope that this work will be received favorably and its usefulness felt generally,

The public's obedient servants,

THE PUBLISHERS.

CONTENTS.

CONNECTICUT.

BY FITZ-GREENE HALLECK.

"The woods in which we had dwelt pleasantly rustled their green leaves in the song, and our streams were there with the sound of all their waters."—MONTROSE.

I.

——still her gray rocks tower above the sea
That crouches at their feet, a conquered wave;
'Tis a rough land of earth, and stone, and tree,
Where breathes no castled lord or cabined slave;
Where thoughts, and tongues and hands are bold and free,
And friends will find a welcome, foes a grave;
And where none kneel, save when to heaven they pray,
Nor even then, unless in their own way.

II.

Theirs is a pure republic, wild, yet strong,
A "fierce democracie," where all are true
To what themselves have voted—right or wrong—
And to their laws denominated blue;
(If red, they might to Draco's code belong.)
A vestal state, which power could not subdue,
Nor promise win—like her own eagle's nest,
Sacred—the San Marino of the West.

III.

A justice of the peace, for the time being,
They bow to, but may turn him out next year;
They reverence their priest, but disagreeing
In price or creed, dismiss him without fear;
They have a natural talent for foreseeing
And knowing all things; and should Park appear
From his long tour in Africa, to show
The Niger's source, they'd meet him with—we know

IV.

They love their land, because it is their own,
And scorn to give aught other reason why;
Would shake hands with a king upon his throne,
And think it kindness to his majesty;
A stubborn race, fearing and flattering none.
Such are they nurtured, such they live and die;
All—but a few apostates, who are meddling
With merchandise, pounds, shillings, pence, and peddling;

V.

Or wandering through the southern countries, teaching
The A B C from Webster's spelling-book;
Gallant and godly, making love and preaching,
And gaining by what they call "hook and crook,"
And what the moralists call over-reaching,
A decent living. The Virginians look
Upon them with as favorable eyes
As Gabriel on the devil in paradise.

VI.

But these are but their outcasts. View them near
At home, where all their worth and pride is placed;
And there their hospitable fires burn clear,
And there the lowliest farmhouse hearth is graced
With manly hearts, in piety sincere,
Faithful in love, in honor stern and chaste,
In friendship warm and true, in danger brave,
Beloved in life, and sainted in the grave.

VII.

And minds have there been nurtured, whose control
Is felt even in their nation's destiny;
Men who swayed senates with a statesman's soul,
And looked on armies with a leader's eye;
Names that adorn and dignify the scroll,
Whose leaves contain their country's history,
And tales of love and war—listen to one
Of the Green-Mountaineer—the Stark of Bennington.

VIII.

When on that field his band the Hessians fought,
Briefly he spoke before the fight began:
"Soldiers! those German gentlemen are bought
For four pounds eight and sevenpence per man,
By England's king; a bargain, as is thought.
Are we worth more? Let's prove it now we can;
For we must beat them, boys, ere set of sun,
OR MARY STARK'S A WIDOW." It was done.

IX.

Her clear, warm heaven at noon—the mist that shrouds
Her twilight hills—her cool and starry eves,
The glorious splendor of her sunset clouds,
The rainbow beauty of her forest leaves,
Come o'er the eye, in solitude and crowds,
Where'er his web of song her poet weaves;
And his mind's brightest vision but displays
The autumn scenery of his boyhood's days.

X.

And when you dream of woman, and her love;
Her truth, her tenderness, her gentle power;
The maiden listening in the moonlight grove,
The mother smiling in her infant's bower;
Forms features, worshipped while we breathe or move,
Be by some spirit of your dreaming hour
Borne, like Loretto's chapel, through the air
To the green land I sing, then wake, you'll find them there.

BIOGRAPHICAL SKETCHES.

THOMAS M. WALLER,

Governor of Connecticut.

The career of the present Governor of this State ot an uncommon one, in a country which affords ple opportunities for men of natural genius and orable ambition to push their way in spite of y obstacles; but in the case of Thomas M. ller, there is something more of romance than rdinarily furnished in the lives of many men have attained merited distinction in public business affairs. It is a matter of note that a ority of the Governors of this commonwealth e been the architects of their own fortunes. They e been "poor boys," and have encountered hard s in the struggle which finally gave them onal and financial success.

ov Waller, now forty-three years of age, was in New York. His parents were Thomas stopher and Mary Armstrong. Both his mother his father and his only brother, who was his er, died before he was nine years old, and he d himself alone in a great city. Obtaining e assistance he was able to buy newspapers, to n the life of a newsboy. His life from that has been filled with work, and every step of way toward his exalted position has been won is own devotion to duty and cheerful submis- to the law of labor. Of his occupation then History of New London County, which contains ches of the distinguished residents of that on, says: "For some months he carried papers e lower parts of the city, finding his best mers, in the Tammany Hall of those days, and than one night, while he was following this he pillowed his head on the steps of the old une building." In a speech, made during the ampaign in this State, Gov. Waller himself, that anybody who knows him, will justify in saying: "Since I was a newsboy in New many years ago—ever since I was selling, "Herald," the "Tribune," the "Sun" and rning Star"—up to the moment I accepted omination of Governor of the great Democratic of this Commonwealth, I have been endeavor- n an honest way, by skilled labor and careful ght, to build for myself a reputation that I d not be ashamed of, and that five boys of should not be ashamed of either."

gave up selling papers to go to sea, and was oyed on several fishing vessels, as cabin-boy cook's mate, until in 1849 he had made gements to ship to California, on the "Mount n," from New London. It was at this time he late Robert K. Waller, of New London, the lad, and becoming interested in him ed him, and thereafter he assumed the name aller. He was treated with all the considera- tion of an own son, and in after years was able to show a son's kindness, to those who had protected him. He attended the public schools of New London, and was graduated at the Bartlett High School, with honors. In 1861, he was admitted to the bar, and very soon after, entered as a private in the Second Regiment, Connecticut Volunteers, and was chosen fourth sergeant of Company E. He went to the front with the regiment, but was compelled, owing to a painful affliction of the eyes, to leave the service. His spirit-stirring addresses in behalf of the Government during the dark days of he war, did much to promote loyalty and strengthen the power of the government.

Upon his return he entered actively into the practice of his profession, and from that day has successively filled honorable public positions, and continually become more and more favorably known to the people of the State. In 1867, 1868, 1872, and 1876 he was elected to the lower branch of the Legislature from New London, and in the latter year was Speaker of the House, a position he filled with distinguished ability. In 1870 he was chosen Secretary of State on the Democratic ticket, headed by Gov. English, and in that service made an honorable record. In 1873 he was elected Mayor of New London, and filled that office in a business-like and most acceptable manner for six years. In 1875 he was chosen by the Judges of the Supreme and Superior Courts to be State's Attorney for New London County, and up to the time of his election as Governor he held that position.

Gov. Waller has been consistently a Democrat in politics, but has never possessed the least bigotry as a politician. He has been frankly independent on many occasions in conventions of his party, and in other places of partisan debate. As an orator he is impressive to a degree which, on occasions of party strife in important gatherings, has given him a magnetic hold of men, and no man of his party in the State has so often carried convictions by the power of eloquence or any other influence. In personal manner Gov. Waller is a gentleman of many attractions. Pleasant and fluent in conversation, easy of approach, strong in his friendships, he is greatly loved by his friends, of whom he has multitudes in all political parties and among all classes.

GEORGE G. SUMNER,

Lieutenant-Governor.

The family of the Lieutenant-Governor of Connecticut lived at the time of his birth, January 14, 1841, in the north part of the society of Gilead, in the town of Hebron. He was named after his mother's father, George Gleason, who lived near the Manchester line in Glastonbury. His grandfather on his father's side was Henry Peterson Sumner, a Methodist preacher in Gilead. When he was about six years of age, his father, John W. Sumner, moved to Collinsville, where the latter was superintendent in the axe factory established by the Collinses, whose enterprise has resulted in the building up of a great manufacturing industry. In 1852 the family moved to Bolton and has lived there since. George, the son, attended the district school, and when about fourteen years of age was sent to the Bartlett High School, at New London, where he studied for a year and a half, and there met for the first time Thomas M. Waller, who was in the same school, laying foundations for the professional and public life which both he and Mr. Sumner subsequently entered. Before reaching the age of sixteen Mr. Sumner became the teacher of a district school in Andover, which he successfully conducted, and then went to Williston Seminary, at East Hampton, Mass., and fitted for college; but his purpose of obtaining a university education was defeated by impaired health, and with the good mental equipment which he had obtained he returned to the farm in Bolton, working in the summer time and teaching winters for about four years. During this period he was Town Clerk for three years, Probate Clerk, and Acting School Visitor. The kindness and favors of the people of Bolton in those years have often been the subject of Mr. Sumner's conversation with his friends, and he frequently expresses his pleasure in renewing old associations there upon his repeated visits to his home. In 1864 he began the study of law with Hon. David M. Calhoun, the present Judge of the Hartford County Court of Common Pleas, then living in Manchester, and afterwards came to Hartford and entered the law office of Waldo & Hyde, and in 1866 was admitted to the bar. In 1867 he was elected a Representative in the Legislature from Bolton, and in the same year Mr. Waller was for the first time a member of the House. He was chiefly instrumental that year in securing the passage of the bill for a public act which gives the accused in a criminal trial the right to testify in his own behalf. In the same year Mr. Sumner established his residence in Hartford, and in 1868 was elected to the Board of Aldermen from the Fifth Ward, and served four years. He was City Attorney for one term, Associate Judge of the City Court, and Police Commissioner for three years, and Recorder of the City Court for four years. In these positions he served the public with zeal and fidelity, and there was a manifest appreciation of his worth as a public servant when, in the third year of his membership, a Republican Common Council refused to accept his resignation, and increased the salary of his office as an inducement for him to remain.

Mr. Sumner had been prominently named for the Democratic nomination for Governor at the last election, but he encouraged no active movement in his behalf, and cordially concurred in the nomination of Mr. Waller. By common consent he was named for the second place. The high school boys in New London in 1855, and the young legislators in 1867 had come together again, each in the pursuit of an honorable ambition.

Mr. Sumner is one of the rising men in his party and in the State. He has in every place of public trust so justified the confidence of the people that his place in public affairs is the honorable reward of faithful service. Besides the integrity of his character, he is a man of most kindly disposition, of generous impulses, a true and manly friend, broad in his sympathies, and fair in his judgment. While consistently a party man, yet he is so broad in his views, and so tolerant of the convictions of those who entertain opposing opinions, that party lines furnish no measure of the esteem in which he is popularly held.

D. WARD NORTHROP,

Secretary of State.

Hon. D. Ward Northrop, of Middletown, Secretary of State, was born in the town of Sherman, Conn., February 19, 1844, and is of Scotch descent, the family being among the best citizens in the western part of the State. On his maternal side he is a descendant from the Rogers family, straight down from the first martyr, John Rogers, in Queen Mary's reign. His grandmother, Lucrecia Rogers, was an own cousin of the late Gideon Welles. Judge Northrop spent his early life on a farm, and attended the district school. He prepared for college at Amenia Seminary, in Duchess County, N. Y. After finishing his academic education he entered Wesleyan University, in the class of '68, graduating with honors in that year. For a year after graduating, Judge Northrop taught languages in the Fort Edward Institute, N. Y., at the same time reading law. He then entered the Albany Law School and completed the course there in 1870. In the fall of 1870 he was admitted to the bar o[f] this State in Middlesex County, settled in Middletown and has remained there since. In 187[illegible] Judge Northrop was elected Judge of Probate for the district of Middletown, and served in tha[t] position faithfully and honorably until 1881, receiving at each re-election a considerable numbe[r] of Republican votes. In 1881 he declined to be a candidate for re-election. In 1871 Judg[e] Northrop was elected to the General Assembly and was Chairman of the School Fund Committee. He was again elected in 1881, and wa[s] a member of the Judiciary Committee, also o[n] the committees on Engrossed Bills and Stat[e] House Grounds. He was a member in 188[illegible] served on the Judiciary Committee, and was als[o] Chairman of the Committee on Engrossed Bill[s]. On the floor of the house Judge Northrop wa[s] the recognized leader on the part of the Dem[ocrats] and well earned the title. Locally, Judg[e] Northrop has been many times honored. H[e] has been a member of the Common Counci[l], member and Secretary of the Board of Educa[tion] of the City School District, Assistant Cler[k] of Courts for ten years, member of the Board o[f] Trustees of Wesleyan University and of its Exe[c]utive Committee, and in other minor position[s]. He was for a number of years a member of th[e]

Democratic State Central Committee. Is a member of the Psi Upsilon Chapter located in Middletown, and has continued his interest in the fraternity since he left college, rendering much assistance in the erection and maintenance of the elegant chapter house on Broad street.

Judge Northrop's grandfather, David Northrop, represented the town of Sherman in 1810 as a member of the House of Representatives, and his father, David Northrop, served in the same capacity in 1835, thus he is the third in the line of succession as member of the General Assembly.

Judge Northrop's family have always been among the best and most honored citizens of Sherman and the western part of the State.

Judge Northrop's advancement to office since he graduated from college in 1868 has been rapid, and shows a rare estimation of his abilities and the esteem in which he is held among all classes of citizens in the community where he resides.

ALFRED R. GOODRICH,

State Treasurer.

Hon. Alfred R. Goodrich, State Treasurer, is a direct descendant of Ensign William Goodrich, who, with his brother, John Goodrich, settled in Wethersfield about the year 1636. His grandfather, George Goodrich, served in the Revolutionary war, and after its close removed to the town of Gill, Mass., where he died at the advanced age of ninety-two years. A large family of children survived him, but his wife, Lucinda Wells, died in 1814. Alfred Goodrich, the father of Alfred R. Goodrich, was born in Gill in 1787, and occupied the old homestead, where he also reared a large family of children. He died in 1866 at the age of seventy-nine. His wife was Abigail Howland, daughter of Solomon Howland, of Greenfield, Mass. She died in 1821, leaving three sons, of whom the subject of the present sketch was the youngest. He was born in Gill in 1818. At the age of nine years he was installed in the family of a near relative at Vernon, and has since resided there. Mr. Goodrich was educated at the Deerfield Academy. Subsequently he became an associate teacher and principal in the institution. In 1843 he commenced the study of medicine under the instruction of the late Alden Skinner, and graduated in 1846 with distinction from the Berkshire Medical College. He practiced for some time in New York City, and remained there during the terrible epidemic of ship fever. Dr. Goodrich was himself prostrated by the disorder, but finally recovered from the attack. After his restoration to health he returned to Vernon, and has since been engaged in his profession there, entering also into mercantile and manufacturing interests. In 1870 Dr. Goodrich was elected as the first Democratic Representative from his town, receiving, as he has invariably done when a candidate for public office, a very flattering vote from his political opponents. In 1871 he was the Democratic nominee for Congress in the first district, and came very near securing his election. Dr. Goodrich was elected State Comptroller in 1873, and was re-elected for the three succeeding terms, discharging the duties of the office with fidelity and honor. He was successful in largely reducing the expenses of the State. Since 1874 he has been President of the Mutual Benefit Life Company of Hartford. Previous to 1874 he was Vice-president of the Company. In 1879 Dr. Goodrich was elected President of the Connecticut State Medical Society, but he declined a re-election. He is also a member of the State Board of Agriculture. He is a director in the Rockville Savings Bank, and in the Hartford Spring and Axle Company. In addition to his business associations, he is still engaged in the practice of his profession. Dr. Goodrich married Charlotte Dobson, daughter of the late Hon. Peter Dobson, the founder of cotton manufacturing interests in Vernon. In politics Dr. Goodrich is a Democrat.

FRANK D. SLOAT,

State Comptroller.

General Frank D. Sloat, of New Haven, State Comptroller, was born at Fishkill, New York, September 28, 1835. His ancestry were Hollanders, and his mother's English. After a few years of clerkship, the latter portion of the time in New York City, he became identified with the New York Steam Heating Company as salesman. He continued in this position two years, and was then invited, in 1859, to become the manager of the company's manufactory, located at New Haven, Conn. In 1862 he enlisted in a company then recruiting for the Fifteenth Regiment C. V. Being too late to enter that regiment, his company was assigned to the Twenty-seventh Regiment C. V. At the election of company officers, General Sloat was made Second Lieutenant, and before leaving the post rendezvous for the seat of war he was appointed First Lieutenant. The term of service of the regiment having expired, it returned to New Haven, where General Sloat was offered the position of bookkeeper and confidential secretary for Mr. C. S. Bushnell. He was also while thus employed President of the Steam Heating Company.

General Sloat, when absent from home in 1864, was nominated for the important office of Town Clerk of the Town of New Haven by the Republicans, and was elected.

From 1867 to 1870 he resided in Wisconsin, and later was an officer of a manufacturing company in Middletown, Conn. With the exception of a year or two, General Sloat has resided in New Haven. The exception was a residence in Middletown, where he was elected a member of the Common Council of that city by a flattering majority.

General Sloat is a veteran Mason for one of his age, having been a member since his majority. He is a member of the Knights of Honor, and has been Grand Dictator of the Grand Lodge, etc., etc.

He is a prominent member of the Grand Army of the Republic, and there is no society of which he is a member that has a warmer place in his heart.

A Republican in principle, he is in no sense a partisan. No man can be more sensitive and careful than he that politics shall not cloud his friendships and social ties. Many of General Sloat's warmest friends are Democrats, and it would cause him great unpleasantness to know that political differences had lost him a friend.

THE STATE GOVERNMENT, 1883.

vernor—Thomas M. Waller, New London.
utenant-Governor — George G. Sumner, Hartford.
cretary of State—D. Ward Northrop, Middletown.
easurer—A. R. Goodrich, Vernon.
mptroller—Frank D. Sloat, New Haven.

SENATE.

op, Joseph W.
ker, Tallmadge
rnes, Chester W.
rrows, Clark E.
ss, Eugene S.
rk, William J.
t, Robert
oke, Lorrin B.
Forest, Robert E.
nnis, Ebenezer C.
on James S.
bert Ralph P.
nn, George M.
ls, John R.
g, Owen B.
rthrop, William N.
nkett, Joseph D.
hardson, Milo B.
field, Edwin L.
encer, Richard P.
ickland, Rial
rtevant, Charles P.
lch, Elisha N.
e, Charles D.

HOUSE OF REPRESENTATIVES.

ll, Charles J., Lebanon.
nander, Pardon M., Groton.
en, Charles N., Putnam.
adon, William Perry, Stafford.
lrews, Charles H., Darien.
lrews, Charles S., New Britain.
old, Titus E., Chatham.
r, E. Eugene, Franklin.
bitt, Isaac, Bridgewater.
ley, Ezra B., Windsor Locks.
er, George H., Ashford.
dwin, Herbert C., Beacon Falls.
ncroft, Horace M., East Windsor.
tle, Jacob, Glastonbury.
rows, Royal R., Hebron.
tlett, Prescott, Putnam.
ton, Merrick, Chaplin.
s, Waterman C., Scotland
Beard, James H., Huntington.
Beebe, William H., Lyme.
Bell, Charles W., Norwalk.
Benedict, Abel, Sharon.
Bennett, Charles, Canterbury.
Bentley, John S., North Stonington.
Bentley, William H., Col., New London.
Bindhammer, Henry, Vernon.
Blackman, Samuel A., Newtown.
Blackwell, John, Bloomfield.
Bliss, John F., New Canaan.
Bowman, George A., Rev., South Windsor.
Bradley, Edward E., Gen'l., Orange.
Branch, Levi J., Sprague.
Bristol, Freeman, Cheshire.
Bronson, Ely, Middlebury.
Brown, Frank T., Norwich.
Brown, Frederick J., Waterbury.
Brown, Wm. J., Ledyard.
Bulkley, Stephen, Wethersfield.
Bunnell, Norris W., Burlington.
Burnham, James A., Hampton.
Burr, Myron St. Clare, Killingworth.
Butler Horace B., Middletown.
Carlisle, Elihu, Goshen.
Carrier, Ralph T., Colchester.
Carroll, Patrick, Newtown.
Carter, Calvin H., Waterbury.
Carter, Henry B., Wolcott.
Carter, Ruel, Warren.
Case, Fredus M., Windsor.
Catlin Lyman S., Stratford.
Cheney, Frank M., Manchester.
Child, John, Saybrook.
Clark, Thos. G., Canterbury.
Clark, Wm. H., Jr., Chester.
Cleveland, Edward S., Hartford.
Coleman, Marvin P., Coventry.
Cook, James N., Voluntown.
Cook, Marcus E., Wallingford.
Cook, Reuben T., Meriden.
Couch, E. P., Stonington.
Cowdery, Oliver P., Hartland.
Cowles, Geo. R., Norwalk.
Cowles, Horace, Morris.
Cressey, R. I., Norfolk.
Cundall, Edward L., Brooklyn.
Curtiss, Wallace K., Harwinton.
Daggett, S. Henry, Andover.
Davis, Clinton B., Haddam.
Davis, Noah Chapin, Stafford.
Delano, Thos. H., Greenwich.
DeWolfe, Roger W., Old Lyme.
Downes, William E., Derby.
Doyle, William H., Litchfield.
Drake, Samuel D., Windsor.
Durand, George G., Bethel.

Durand, Wm. Cecil, Milford.
Eaton, Arthur W., East Hartford.
Edwards, Geo. W., M. D., Granby.
Eldredge, Geo., Groton.
Eno, Luman B., Somers.
Essex, Charles C., Willington.
Fitts, Thos. K., Ashford.
Fleischer, Hermann, New Britain.
Fonda, John E., Colebrook.
Foote, Charles, North Branford.
Forbes, Alex. W., East Haven.
Fowler, Amos T., Windham.
French, Wm. G., Watertown.
Gardner, Washington R., Waterford.
Gates, Wm. F., Lebanon.
Gay, Erastus, Farmington.
Geib, Henry P., Stamford.
Gillette, Rufus M., Prospect.
Gilman, Ashbel, East Hartford.
Gladwin, Richard H., East Haddam.
Gorham, Frank, M. D., Weston.
Griswold, Edward, Guilford.
Griswold, Rufus W., Rocky Hill.
Grover, Lester K., Somers.
Grover, Wm. B., Fairfield.
Hart, Lewis D., Winchester.
Henry, E. Stevens, Vernon.
Hilliard, Elisha C., Manchester.
Hitchcock, Roland Judge, Winchester.
Horace, M. Bancroft, East Windsor.
Howe, Andrew J., Bozrah.
Hoyt, Albert B., Danbury.
Hubbell, James T., Wilton.
Humphrey, Lucius C., Farmington.
Hungerford, L. Beach, Sherman.
Hurd, Samuel S., Monroe.
Hurlbut, Hiram H., Bristol.
Husted, Nehemiah H., Greenwich.
Hyde, Fred'k, Pomfret.
Jackson, Alfred, Durham.
James, Coley, Torrington.
Johnson, John P., Clinton.
Jones, Flavel, Marlborough.
Kellogg, Henry A., New Hartford.
Kirtland, Ozias H., Old Saybrook.
Law, Geo. H., Killingly.
Law, Wm. H., New Haven.
Lockwood, David B., Bridgeport.
Loomis, Geo. H., Columbia.
Lucas, Aaron, Preston.
Luther, Linus A., Lyme.
Lyman, Charles P., Washington.
Lyon, George N., Eastport.
Mahan, Bryan F., New London.
Main, Charles H., North Stonington.
Mann, Bela A., Hamden.
Markham, H. P., Chatham.
McCarty, Thomas, Lisbon.
McLean, George P., Simsbury.
McNamara, Timothy B., Plymouth.
Mead, Henry J., North Canaan.
Merrill, Henry C., New Hartford.
Merwin, Nathan P., Milford.
Middleton, John, Enfield.
Miller, Edward D., Glastonbury.
Miller, James E., Redding.
Mills, Gustavus D., East Granby.
Miner, Edward S., Torrington.
Miner, William C., Madison.
Minor, Chas. William, Stamford.
Mitchell, Nelson W., Southbury.
Mix, John W., Cheshire.
Mooney, Patrick, Wallingford.
Morehouse, Chas. B., Jr., Ridgefield.
Morgan, Daniel N., Bridgeport.
Morse, John, Meriden.
Morse, Nathan C., Woodstock.
Morton, Arthur J., Tolland.
Munger, Elisha, East Lyme.
Neal, Elisha J., Southington.
Newcomb, Loren, Tolland.
Newton, William C., Durham.
Nichols, Geo. H., Thompson.
Nickerson, Leonard J., Cornwall.
North, Geo. P. Thomaston.
Odell, Wm. T., Washington.
Osborn, Newton, Newington.
Osborn, Orlando O., Oxford.
Palmer, Alex. S., Jr., Stonington.
Pease, Lorin H., Enfield.
Perkins Charles C., Bethany.
Perkins, John S., Salisbury.
Perkins, Orlando, Cornwall.
Perry, Wilbert Warren, Hartford.
Pine, Charles H. (Speaker of the House, Session of 1883), Derby.
Pomeroy, Newton S., Suffield.
Porter, Charles, Redding.
Post, John A., Westbrook.
Rathbone, George B., Colchester.
Richmond, Henry A., Preston.
Rindge, Thomas, Union.
Robbins, Edward Denmore, Wethersfield.
Rogers, Frank L., Fairfield.
Rogers, J. Randolph, Montville.
Rosebrooks, Geo. L., Mansfield.
Rossiter, Henry M., Guilford.
Rouse, Willis D., Plainfield.
Ruggles, Sidney B., Southington.
Russell, Charles A., Col., Killingly.
Russel, Charles T., Harwinton.
Ryder, James, Gen'l, Danbury.
Savage, Geo. P., Cromwell.
Sedgwick, Timothy, West Hartford.
Sevin, N. Douglass, Norwich.
Shailer, Orrin, Haddam.
Sherwood, Moses, Westport.
Simonds, William E., Canton.
Sisson, Wm. M., East Haddam.
Smith, Guilford, Windham.
Snow, O. M., Norfolk.
Southworth, Jabez, Saybrook.
Spencer, Thomas B., Colebrook.
Sperry, Norman, Seymour.
Sprague, Albert B., Plainfield.
Squires, Aaron H., New Milford.
Starkey, Horace W., Essex.
Starr, E. Ratchford, Litchfield.
Stevens, Daniel K., Killingworth.
Still, James S., Willington.
St. John, Edward F., Simsbury.
Street, Gilbert S., Salisbury.
Strong, Newton B., Portland.
Sumner, Edwin G., Mansfield.
Taylor, Charles, New Milford.
Terrill, Moses W., Middlefield.
Thomas, Albert N., Ridgefield.
Thompson, Joseph Abbott, Ellington.

iffany, Stephen, Griswold.
iffany, Timothy C., Barkhamsted.
odd, F. Hayden, North Haven.
olles, Fremont W., Naugatuck.
owne, Edward S., Rev., Plainville.
owne, Eli M., Woodbury.
roup, Alexander, New Haven.
ieto, Henry G., Granby.
adhams, Wilbur H., Goshen.
aite, Silas A., Sterling.
ales, Andrew J., Union.
alker, Charles T., Woodbridge.
alker, Fred'k A., Woodbury.
alsh, John T., Middletown.
ard, James J., Easton.
ard, John E., Bristol.
ard, William M. W., Hartland.
arner, Charles C., Suffield.
arner, Elihu S., Berlin.
ells, Lewis G., Woodstock.
ells, Philip W., Roxbury.
heeler, John R., Coventry.
hite, Jabez Lee, Bolton.
hitehead, James S., New Fairfield.
ilbur, Thomas, Thompson.
illiams, Amos L., Brookfield.
illiams Charles G., Pomfret.
Williams, Joseph Hanford, Trumbull.
Williams, Nelson N., Salem.
Wilson, James Martin, Avon.
Winchester, Edwin M., Sharon.
Winegar, Linus B., Kent.
Wolcott, Charles E., Canaan.
Wood, Jonathan Nichols, Hebron.
Wootten, Jonathan, Bethlehem.
Wright, William Alvin, Branford.
Youngs, Wilfred D., Barkhamsted.

UNITED STATES SENATORS.

Orville H. Platt, term expires 1885.
Joseph R. Hawley, term expires 1887.

REPRESENTATIVES IN CONGRESS.

Term began March 4, 1883.

Wm. W. Eaton, First District.
Charles L. Mitchell, Second District.
John T. Wait, Third District.
Edward W. Seymour, Fourth District.

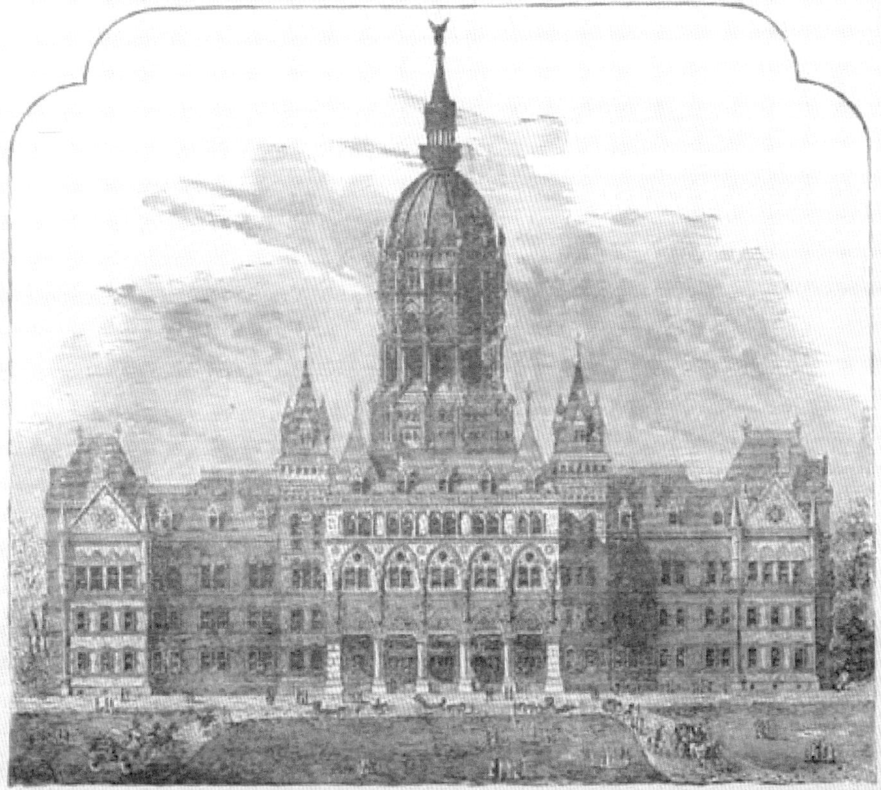

STATE CAPITOL, HARTFORD, CONN.

CONNECTICUT.

THE State of Connecticut derives its name from its most beautiful natural feature, the chief river of New England, which, entering its northern borders from Massachusetts, divides the State, east and west, into two unequal portions, and empties into Long Island Sound between the towns of Old Lyme and Saybrook. The river's name, in the original Indian tongue, was Quinnituk, which, as has been ascertained by that Connecticut scholar, Dr. J. Hammond Trumbull, who is the foremost authority in this country on Indian language, signified, "The long, tidal river." This river is at this day navigable for steamboats only as far as Hartford, its capital, some fifty miles from its mouth, and it was only to a point a short distance above Hartford that the first white explorers of the river attained.

It was in 1614 that this first exploring expedition was made, under command of Capt. Adrian Block, commander of an Amsterdam ship, one of five vessels sent out from the New Netherlands, who, having entered Long Island Sound from the eastward, coasted along until he found the river, up which he sailed, as stated. Block Island, near the entrance of the Sound, still preserves the name of this discoverer, upon whose voyage, most glowingly reported at home, the Dutch laid their claim to the territory now known as Connecticut.

The English claim to this same land was based primarily upon a patent granted, in 1631, to Lord Say and Seal, Lord Brooke, Sir Richard Saltonstall and their associates, by Robert, Earl of Warwick, who derived his title from the patent of New England granted by James I. in 1620.

In 1633, the rival claimants each made their first lodgments on the soil of the State, the Dutch building a fort on the river at Hartford, and one William Holmes, of Plymouth Colony, a house at Windsor, some seven miles north. For a few years there was contention between the two nationalities, but ere long the Dutch yielded, sold out to the English, and retired.

In 1635 and 1636, Rev. Thomas Hooker, who had won a reputation in England and Holland as one of the ablest of the non-conforming clergy, emigrated, with nearly his whole congregation, from Cambridge, Mass., where he had been settled, and founded the towns of Hartford, Wethersfield and Windsor.

The motive for the wholesale emigration of Mr. Hooker and his church, including his associate teacher, Samuel Stone, and, a little later, John Haynes, who in 1635, was governor of Massachusetts, has been a matter of some speculation.

In 1635, also, John Winthrop the younger, son of the Massachusetts governor, built a fort at Saybrook under direct commission from the English proprietaries.

It is a satisfaction to record that Hartford, then a tract of six square miles, was honorably purchased of the Indian tribes who inhabited it.

In 1636, the first General Court was held at Hartford.

In 1637, the new Colony found itself, in its very beginnings, involved in war with the powerful Pequod Indians—a war which threatened its very existence, but which ended in 1637 with the virtual extermination of the tribe, consequent upon two crushing defeats inflicted upon them by colonial troops led by Capt. John Mason.

New Haven was settled in 1638 from Boston by English settlers, headed by Theophilus Eaton and Rev. John Davenport. These adopted a constitution of their own, without warrant or sanction from England, and, purchasing the land from the Indians, proceeded to lay out the beautiful Elm City in regular squares, upon a plain as level as Runnymede, with a fine harbor opening into the Sound. The site was chosen with reference to its facilities for trade and commerce, avocations in which the settlers had been engaged in England. The inhabitants of this Colony were greatly annoyed at the consolidation with Connecticut Colony by order of the crown in 1665, especially as in New Haven, suffrage had been restricted to church-members, a restriction that did not prevail in Connecticut. From 1701 to 1872, the legislature met alternately in Hartford and New Haven; but, in 1872, the people of the State voted that Hartford should be the single capital, and a very large and handsome State capitol building was completed in 1879, and occupied in that city. It is built of marble, and cost, site included, more than \$3,000,000.

In 1639, the people of the State adopted their first constitution, of which that ripe student of New England history, Dr. Leonard Bacon, of New Haven, has said that "It is the earliest precedent of a written constitution proceeding from a people, and in their name, establishing and defining a government."

The first governor chosen under the constitution was John Haynes, who alternated in the office with Edward Hopkins for many years; for until 1659, it was not the custom to allow a governor to serve two consecutive years, although in the alternate years he might be, and generally was, elected "deputy governor," an office equivalent to that of our modern lieutenant-governor.

In 1643, Connecticut joined the New England Confederation—a creation, in the main, of Haynes and Hooker, for the purpose of combining the strength of the Colonies against Indian wars and Dutch aggression.

In 1657, ex-Governor Hopkins died in England, leaving handsome legacies to executors in the

Colonies "for the breeding up of hopeful youths both at the grammar school and college, for the public service of the country in future times." These funds were the foundation of the present Hopkins grammar school, of New Haven, and the Hartford high school. In 1657, John Winthrop was elected governor of Connecticut, a position to which, after the year 1658, he was annually re-elected until his death in 1676. Few names in the New England annals are comparable to that of this gentlemen, scholar, traveler, and physician of note, whose name is preserved in many parts of the State, notably in New London, which he founded in 1646.

In 1662, Governor Winthrop made a visit to England in the interests of the Colony. He found in Lord Say and Seal, the only survivor of the original patentees, a warm friend, through whose influence he was enabled to gain audience with Charles II. At this interview, Winthrop, with his wonted tact, first presented the king a ring that had been given by Charles I. to his grandfather, and then presented a petition from the Colony of Connecticut for a royal charter. This charter, freely granted by the king, can still be seen in the office of the secretary of state at Hartford, framed with wood from the Charter Oak. Based, as this instrument was, upon the colonial constitution of 1639, it was indeed a royal gift, and proved of great value to the young Colony, as evidenced by the many subsequent attempts to revoke it on the part of the successors of Charles II.

Upon the death of Gov. Winthrop, in 1676, William Leete—who had served a term of six years as governor of New Haven Colony—was chosen his successor, Connecticut thus showing that the union with New Haven was complete and cordial. In 1683, Maj. Robert Treat succeeded to the gubernatorial chair on the death of Gov. Leete. He was a son of one of the original patentees of the Colony, and at the time of his election a resident of Milford. He was one of the few men in that section who dared to favor the union of New Haven with Connecticut, in face of the opposition of Davenport, and was instrumental, with Winthrop, in bringing about that union. Like his predecessor, Gov. Leete, he was one of those who helped to harbor, conceal, and assist the regicides, Goffe and Whalley, during their concealment in New Haven Colony. He won his military rank during King Philip's war in 1675-6, in course of which he distinguished himself in command of the Connecticut troops serving in Massachusetts.

In 1687, during the administration of Gov. Treat, came the usurpation of Sir Edmund Andros, who, having been appointed governor of New England by James II., assumed sway over the Colonies until the news of the fall of his royal master reached America in 1689. The tale of Andros' futile efforts to get the charter of Connecticut, and of how it disappeared, to reappear after his downfall, has made the name and fame of the Charter Oak synonymous with that of the State.

In 1690, and again in 1693, the State furnished its quota of troops for the war against the French and Indians.

In 1693, Gov. Fletcher, of the New York Colony, demanded of Connecticut that its militia should be put under his orders, under powers conferred upon him by William and Mary. The assembly and the people declined to accede to this demand, and sent Fitz John Winthrop—son of the late governor—to England to remonstrate. He was successful in procuring a revocation of the order, and was rewarded therefor by the assembly with a present of three hundred pounds sterling, and in 1697, was chosen governor.

In 1701, the college was founded at Saybrook, that, seventeen years later, was removed to New Haven, and christened Yale College in honor of its first private benefactor, Elihu Yale.

During the reign of Queen Anne (1702-14), another futile attempt was made in England to force Connecticut to give up its charter, the failure of which was due, as in prior cases, to the cool-headed obstinacy of the colonists.

In 1707, Fitz John Winthrop died while governor. He was succeeded by Rev. Gurdon Saltonstall, a gentleman of marked nobility of carriage and character, who left the ministry to become governor—an office to which he was re-elected for seventeen years. During his administration, "election sermons were inaugurated, it being enacted by the legislature that, on the day appointed by law for choosing rulers, the ministers of the gospel should preach to the freemen a sermon proper for their direction in the work before them." This custom was observed, almost without intermission, until 1830, when it was finally abandoned. A companion custom of baking "election cake" for the same ceremony, whose origin is venerable, but unknown, lasted until the abandonment of spring elections in 1876.

In 1708, the "Saybrook Platform" was adopted by the clergy of the State assembled in council at the College Commencement. This furnished a uniform standard or confession of faith for the churches of the State, and a guide for the instruction of the college which was then designed chiefly for the education of the young men for the ministry. As all the churches first formed were Congregational, this platform was a matter of such importance that, when the churches had ratified it, the Assembly passed a vote expressing its gratification thereat.

In 1710, the Saybrook Platform was published in book form by Thomas Short—the first book printed in Connecticut. Short soon died and was succeeded by Timothy Greene, who settled in New London as State printer—a position held by himself and heirs till after the Revolution. The first newspaper in the State was the "Connecticut Gazette," published in New Haven in 1755; the second, the "New London Summary," was started by Greene in 1758, and the third, the "Connecticut Courant," begun in Hartford in 1764, has been continuously published there ever since, its principal editors at this date being Gen. Joseph R. Hawley, and the equally well-known Charles Dudley Warner.

In 1724, Gov. Saltonstall died, and was succeeded by Joseph Talcott, who, like his predecessor, was elected every year until his death in 1741. A touching incident of his gubernatorial career was the sudden death of his wife during the legislative session of 1738. Custom then required the presence of governor, or deputy governor, at all sessions of the assembly, and as the latter was absent

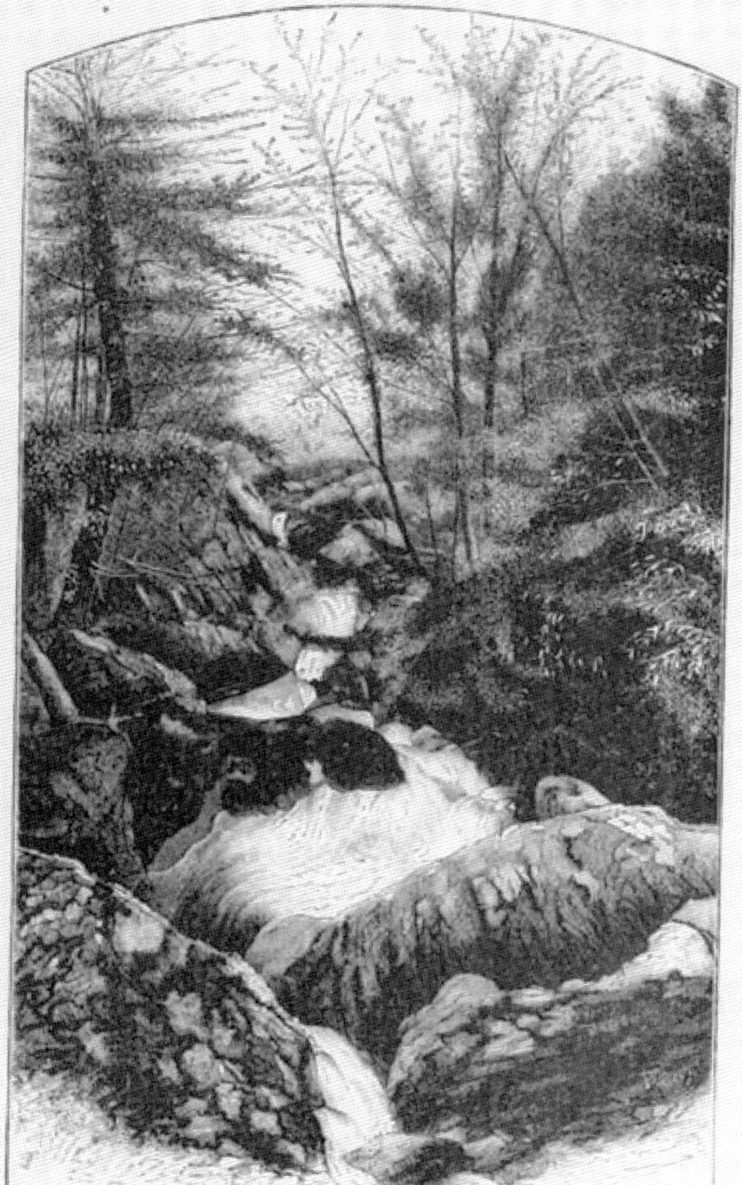

SCENE AT HIGH ROCK GROVE, A SUMMER RESORT ON THE NAUGATUCK RAILROAD

from the city, and his wife had died after the morning session, Gov. Talcott was compelled to leave her dead body to preside over the afternoon session, which was, of course, made as short as possible. His conduct on this occasion is spoken of in an address of condolence made by the assembly, as betokening "greatness and presence of mind."

In 1750, the towns of Enfield, Suffield, Woodstock and Somers, which since 1713 had been governed by Massachusetts, were returned to Connecticut. It is owing to a confusion that then occurred as to the correct boundaries of the town of Suffield that a tract of land of two miles square on the west of that town, and east of Granby belongs to Massachusetts, making that queer jut that appears on the northern boundary of Connecticut. As the Southwick ponds, projecting well into Massachusetts, cover most of this space no recent attempts have been made to rectify the line.

In 1751, Gen. Roger Wolcott, who had won his rank in the French war, became governor. A scion of a family that had held office in the Colony from its first settlement, he was the first to attain the chief magistracy, an honor afterwards held by his son, Oliver, in 1796 and 1797, and grandson, Oliver 2d, from 1818 to 1827; while his daughter, Ursula, who married Gov. Matthew Griswold (1784), and was the mother of Gov. Roger Griswold (1811), was related and connected with twelve governors and thirty-two judges, as shown by an interesting paper prepared by Prof. E. E. Salisbury, of New Haven, for the "New England Genealogical Register."

In 1756, Connecticut furnished 2,000 men for operations against Canada in the English war against the French, and 5,000 more after the disaster at Fort William Henry. It was in this war that Israel Putnam and Benedict Arnold won their first laurels as Connecticut soldiers.

In 1763, a small band of Connecticut emigrants settled the beautiful Wyoming Valley in Pennsylvania—a section of country over which Connecticut claimed jurisdiction under its original patents—a claim disputed, however, by Pennsylvania. The settlers suffered much annoyance from the disputed proprietorship, but maintained their position in the valley, although in 1778, during the Revolution, a band of 400 British and 700 Indians overran the valley, the latter putting to the torture so many of its inhabitants, that the "Massacre of Wyoming" has passed into history and legend as an example of barbaric cruelty. The title to the land was finally awarded Pennsylvania, to whose government the Connecticut colonists then submitted.

When in 1765, the "Stamp Act" went into force, all Connecticut was ablaze with indignation, and Jared Ingersoll of New Haven, the stamp-master appointed by the crown, was forced to resign the post, in peril of his life, by a body of some 500 farmers, all bearing staves, who overhauled him in the streets of old Wethersfield, as he was on his way to Hartford to put himself in communication with Gov. Fitch (himself of Tory proclivities), and the assembly. The clergy of the State, headed by that earnest patriot, Rev. Stephen Johnson of Lyme, were active in inciting the people to opposition, and when in October Gov. Fitch, despite the earnest remonstrance of two-thirds of his council, took the oath to enforce the Stamp Act, seven of the eleven councilors—among whom were two of his successors in the executive chair—Jonathan Trumbull and Matthew Griswold, left the room rather than witness the humiliating spectacle. The assembly and people indorsed this protest and, in the ensuing election in 1766, replaced Fitch, the Tory, with William Pitkin, the patriot, with Trumbull as deputy governor.

In 1769, Jonathan Trumbull, who was the famed "Brother Jonathan" of the Revolution, was promoted to be governor, a post to which he was annually re-elected till 1784, when, at the age of seventy-three, he refused further service, after having held one public office and another in the State for fifty-one years. The friend and counsellor of Washington, who bestowed upon him that name, "Brother Jonathan," that has since come to be applied to the United States as a nation, the honor of having been the great war governor of the Revolution belongs to Trumbull, as did a similar honor to his townsman Wm. A. Buckingham, in the war of the Rebellion. As in the case of Wolcott, a son and grandson of Trumbull became governors of the State.

In 1774, Connecticut prepared for hostilities, ordering New London fortified, and the towns to lay in ammunition.

In 1775, the assembly commissioned David Wooster a major-general, and Israel Putnam, a brigadier. With the first news of Lexington, Putnam rode post-haste to Cambridge, whither he had ordered his troops to join him. In the words of Bancroft, who is no partisan of Putnam, "He brought to the service of his country, courage which during the war was never questioned, and a heart than which none throbbed more honestly or warmly for American freedom." From all over Connecticut volunteers were pushing for the seat of war, when the assembly voted to raise six regiments of 1,000 each. The total number of men raised by the State during the whole war was 31,959, out of a population of 238,141, a larger number than were enlisted in any other State except Massachusetts, although Connecticut was but seventh in population of the Old Thirteen. At Bunker Hill Gen. Putnam was certainly present, and useful, however the question of who held command may be settled.

At the disastrous repulse of the Revolutionary troops at Quebec, Arnold, who had been in service from the outbreak of the war, was in command, with Montgomery, and had his leg shattered.

In June, 1776, the assembly instructed its representatives in Congress to "give their assent to a Declaration of Independence." The Connecticut signers of the great document of July 4th, 1776, were Roger Sherman, Samuel Huntington, William Williams and Oliver Wolcott, two of whom, Huntington and Wolcott, were afterwards governors of the State.

In August, 1776, Putnam commanded the Americans in the battle of Long Island, a defeat for which the latest and most careful writers on the subject acquit him of the responsibility.

It was soon after this that Nathan Hale, a gallant young officer of a Connecticut regiment, a native of Coventry, but twenty-one years old at this time, met the sad fate of a spy, owing to his capture by the British, while returning from their camp on Long Island, whither he had been sent by Washington to procure intelligence and plans of the enemy's works, in which he had entirely succeeded. The story of his brutal execution, denied both a Bible and clergy and of these memorable words of his, "I only regret that I have but one life to lose for my country," has enrolled his name among heroes as the young martyr of the American Revolution.

In April, 1777, Gov. Tryon, Tory Governor of New York, raided into Connecticut, burned a portion of Danbury, and, when his troops were attacked on their retreat by Gen. Wooster with a small force, repulsed their assaults, Gen. Wooster being shot and killed. Arnold, who commanded another detachment of Americans, narrowly escaped a similar fate, his horse being shot under him; yet he succeeded in harrassing Tryon's retreat to such an extent that the latter lost one hundred and seventy of his men, killed and wounded.

May 21st, Col. Meigs, with 200 men, retaliated for Tryon's visit by a raid in boats from New Haven to Sag Harbor, Long Island, where they burned thirteen British vessels, captured ninety prisoners, and returned scatheless.

This year Arnold was made a major-general, and did splendid service at the battle of Saratoga.

In February, 1779, Tryon made another raid over the border. Putnam tried to stop him, at Greenwich, with a few old field-pieces and sixty men, but seeing that his position could be easily flanked, galloped off to Stamford for reinforcements, taking the famous ride down the rugged hill of Horseneck, the centennial anniversary of which has but lately been appropriately celebrated at Greenwich.

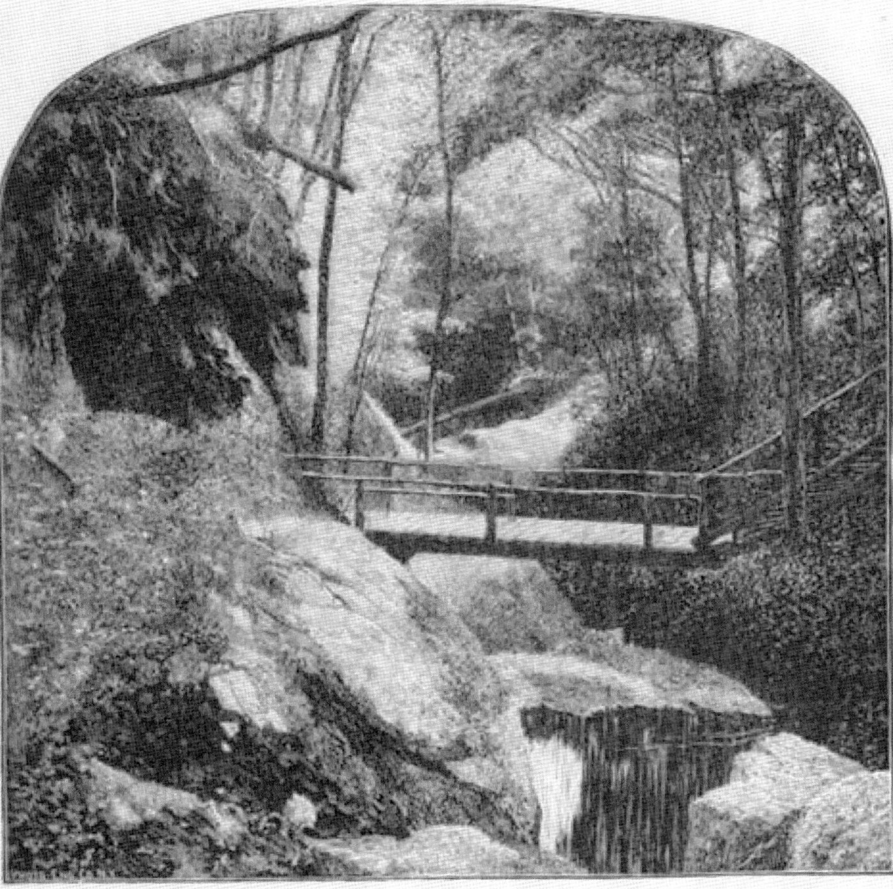

SCENE AT HIGH ROCK GROVE, A SUMMER RESORT ON THE NAUGATUCK RAILROAD.

July 5th, 1799, a British fleet landed 3,000 troops at the entrance of New Haven harbor, who after a stern resistance from the few patriots that could hastily be gathered, burned a number of stores and private houses, pillaged others, murdered several prisoners, and insulted and stabbed Rev. Dr. Daggett, president of Yale College, who was only spared at the intercession of a Tory guide of the British, who had been an old pupil of the Doctor, who, for his part, told his captors that he should take arms against them whenever opportunity offered. The British embarked on the 6th, but on the 8th landed at Fairfield, where they plundered and burned the village to ashes, inflicting the same fate on Norwalk on the 11th.

In 1780, Benedict Arnold turned traitor to his country, and in September, 1781, appeared off New London with a British fleet of twenty-four ships. Capturing the city and Fort Trumbull, on the 6th of September, with little difficulty, a portion of his force attacked Fort Griswold on the Groton bank of the Thames river, which was most bravely defended by Colonel Ledyard and the Americans under his command. Overpowered at last by the greatly superior number of the enemy, who were pouring into the fort, Ledyard surrendered, but was brutally murdered with his own sword by the British officer to whom he gave it up. Eighty-five Americans were killed in the assault, whose bravery is commemorated by a handsome granite monument one hundred and twenty-seven feet high, which was erected close by the fort in 1830. In New London, sixty-five dwellings and eighty other buildings were destroyed by fire, and damage done to the extent of $500,000.

A native of Norwich, which is but fourteen miles from New London, it is not to be wondered at that Arnold has ever been especially execrated in Connecticut, that once had high hopes of him.

This was the last act of the Revolution on Connecticut soil, and the State eagerly welcomed the honorable peace and independence that followed the surrender of Cornwallis in October, 1781.

Connecticut came out of the Revolutionary war with an untarnished reputation, and, as appears from the Silas Deane correspondence, in the files of the State Historical Society, and other sources, with the reputation of having a model governor, and a constitution that was "superior to any other," and which served a high purpose in furnishing a pattern for that soon adopted for the nation.

At the convention that formed the Constitution of the United States, in 1787, the Connecticut delegates were Roger Sherman, Oliver Ellsworth (later Chief Justice of the United States), and William S. Johnson. Originally a poor shoemaker, Roger Sherman won such a reputation as a statesman, that it is his statue, with that of Jonathan Trumbull, that Connecticut has put up in the National Capitol, "as the two of her deceased citizens illustrious for their historic renown, or for distinguished civil or military services." So successful were Sherman and Ellsworth in their efforts at harmonizing and compromising the varied and dissenting elements in the convention that adopted the Constitution, that no less an authority than John C. Calhoun has said that it is to these two men and Judge Patterson of New Jersey that "we are indebted for the National Government." Connecticut ratified the Constitution in January, 1788.

Gov. Trumbull, who retired in 1784 and died in 1785, was succeeded as chief magistrate by Matthew Griswold, who had been lieutenant-governor for fifteen years. He in turn was succeeded in 1786 by Samuel Huntington, one of the signers of the Declaration, who governed until 1796. It was during these administrations that national parties began to take fixed shape throughout the country, the masses of Connecticut folk and the governors being stanch Federalists.

In 1796, Oliver Wolcott, Sr., became governor, to be succeeded in 1798 by Jonathan Trumbull, a son of "Brother Jonathan," who continued to be chosen till his death in August, 1809. Early in that year President Jefferson called upon Gov. Trumbull to designate special officers of militia, upon whom the United States customs collectors could rely for aid in carrying out the Enforcing Act, which was designed to put in force the celebrated "Embargo," of Jefferson's administration. The governor declined to comply, on the ground that Congress had overstepped its authority, and called a session of the Legislature, which adopted a protest to Congress against the embargo, which contributed greatly to the repeal thereof in February, 1809.

In 1812, Roger Griswold, a son of the first Gov. Griswold, who was then governor, adopted a similar course when called upon to furnish detachments of the State militia to Maj. Gen. Dearborn for service in the war just declared against Great Britain. He based his non-compliance with the President's request upon the grounds that the constitutional contingency in which the militia of the State could be called into the Federal service did not exist, and, moreover, that the militia could not be constrained to serve under other than their own officers, except under the President of the United States personally in the field. Gov. Griswold's position was sustained by his council, and by the large Federal majority in the State.

In 1813, Commodore Stephen Decatur, with his little fleet of American vessels, was blockaded in New London Harbor and the river Thames, and so closely watched by the British that, in his vexation at being unable to get out at sea, the commodore charged that "blue lights" had been burned by the Federalists on the shores of the harbor to advise the enemy when he sought to run the blockade, compelling him to abandon the project. This story was long used to stigmatize the anti-war party as "Connecticut blue-light Federalists"; but neither the gallant, but hasty sailor, nor any one since his day, has been able to substantiate the charge.

April 7, 1814, a detachment of two hundred sailors and marines from the British fleet off New London, made an expedition up the Connecticut River to Essex, where they burned some twenty-five vessels, destroying some $200,000 of property.

On the 9th of August, Capt. Hardy of the blockading fleet, with five of his vessels, began a bombardment of Stonington, which continued some forty-eight hours, but was so bravely resisted by a small force of militia, gathered behind a little battery of three guns, that he finally retired with damaged ships, and a loss of seventy-five men killed and wounded, while the Americans had none killed, and only six wounded.

Dec. 15, 1814, the New England discontent with the war came to a focus in the "Hartford Convention," whereat twenty-six delegates, appointed by the New England legislatures, assembled together. After a session of twenty days, the convention adjourned, having adopted a report making a respectful protest against certain acts of Congress in originating and carrying on the war. This protest was adopted by the legislatures of Connecticut and Massachusetts, but was rendered useless by the conclusion of peace Feb. 17, 1815.

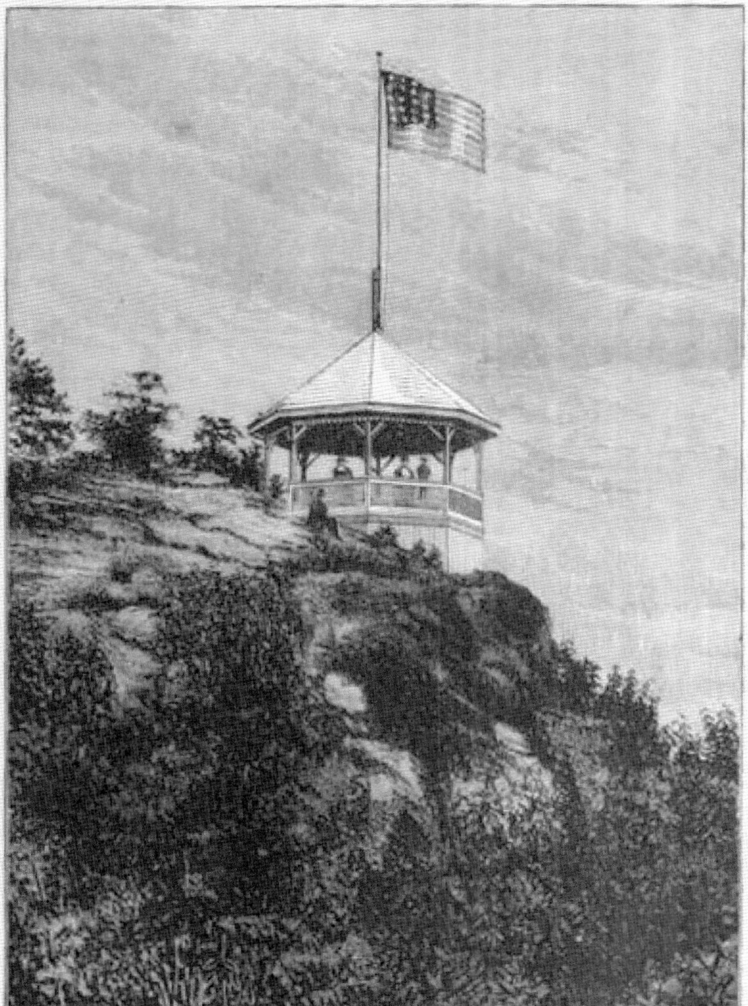

SCENE AT HIGH ROCK GROVE, A SUMMER RESORT ON THE NAUGATUCK RAILROAD.

The return of peace not only put an end to the dissatisfaction with the war, but, in a short time, to the old Federal party that had held continuous sway in the State; and in 1817 Oliver Wolcott, 2d, son of the last Gov. Wolcott, was elected governor by a combination of the opposition elements. In 1818 the same combination elected a legislature in favor of a constitutional convention, which was speedily called, met in August, and formed a constitution, which was ratified by the people in October. Under this constitution, with but few amendments, the State is still governed. It is no light tribute to the value of the charter obtained by John Winthrop, that the Colony and State had needed no other constitution for 150 years, and that the present constitution is based in the main upon that old charter, but few changes being necessary even in the direction of wider religious toleration and suffrage.

The most important of recent amendments to the constitution of 1818, beside such as conform to changes in the Federal Constitution, is that of 1875, extending the governor's term to two years. Another amendment recently submitted to the people providing for biennial sessions of the legislature was defeated.

In 1824 Trinity College was started at Hartford, under control of the Protestant Episcopal Church. In 1872 the college grounds were sold to the State for $600,000, as a site for the new Capitol building, and a new location, a mile south, purchased for the college, where fine buildings of Portland freestone have been erected for its use.

In 1831, Wesleyan University, the oldest and best known American college under control of the Methodist Episcopal Church, was organized at Middletown, where it now occupies a number of handsome buildings on a commanding knoll.

In 1847, Connecticut furnished a company for the New England regiment in the Mexican war, a regiment of which Thomas H. Seymour, of Hartford, returned as colonel, having distinguished himself in the war. He was subsequently (1850-54) governor of the State.

Connecticut continued greatly to increase and prosper until the outbreak of the war of the Rebellion in 1861. This event found in the governor's chair William A. Buckingham of Norwich, who, like his great prototype, Trumbull, was a native of Lebanon. Fortunate it was for the State that this courtly, Christian gentleman, of devoted patriotism, undeviating integrity, great generosity, and large wealth was at its helm. It was in great measure owing to him that Connecticut was among the first to get her troops to the front, that her regiments were, as a rule, admirably officered, that her soldiers never lacked attention from the State during his term of office, as the writer can testify from personal experience. The total number of men credited to the State during the whole war was 54,882, which, reduced to a three years' standing (the terms of enlistment varying a little), equals 48,181, an *excess* of 7,000 over its quota, of whom but 263 were drafted men. As Trumbull was the friend of Washington, so Buckingham was a tried and trusted friend of President Lincoln.

The Connecticut troops raised during the war of the Rebellion consisted of twenty-eight regiments of infantry (two colored), two of heavy artillery, a regiment and squadron of cavalry, and three light batteries. These were so distributed among the different Union armies, that there was hardly a battle of moment during the war in which Connecticut troops were not engaged, and some of the infantry regiments, notably the 7th, 8th, 10th, 11th, 14th, 16th and 21st, had a list of battles to show at its close rarely ever equaled in the same space of time. To enumerate these battles, or to specify instances where Connecticut men distinguished themselves therein, would be to write a history of the war, for which we have no space. In the navy, too, which was presided over during the whole contest by a Connecticut man, Gideon Welles, who was throughout Mr. Lincoln's administration Secretary of the Navy, Connecticut won new glory and renown.

A few of the more prominent officers of the army and navy who were sons of Connecticut, who lost their lives in the contest, were Generals Lyon, Sedgwick and Mansfield, Admiral Foote and Captain Ward. The following-named attained distinction and the rank of general officers in the volunteer service, in nearly every instance winning their rank by hard and gallant field service: H. G. Wright, J. A. Mower, A. H. Terry, R. O. Tyler, H. W. Birge, H. W. Benham, J. R. Hawley, R. S. Mackenzie, H. L. Abbot, Alex. Shailer, A. S. Williams, J. W. Ripley, Daniel Tyler, W. S. Ketchum, O. S. Ferry, H. W. Wessells, H. D. Terry, Edward Harland, H. B. Carrington, A. C. Harding and L. P. Bradley.

At home the State nobly sustained its grand and good governor, and its legislators never faltered in voting men and money in response to every call he made upon them.

In May, 1866, Governor Buckingham's last term expired, he refusing longer service now that the war had ended. He was succeeded as Governor by General Joseph R. Hawley, who had won his way up from captain to general in the volunteer service, and has, since the war, won a reputation as one of the leading Republican statesmen of his day, and as president of the Centennial Commission of 1876, and lately as United States Senator. Governor Buckingham was elected a United States Senator from Connecticut in 1868, and died while holding that office in 1875. Governor Hawley's successors in office have been James E. English, Marshall Jewell, Charles R. Ingersoll, Richard D. Hubbard, Charles B. Andrews, Hobart B. Bigelow and Thomas M. Waller, the present incumbent. To Governor Hubbard, confessedly one of the first statesmen and lawyers, as he is one of the first orators in the country, is due the credit of many reforms in the legislative and legal practice of the State, all in the line of retrenchment, reform and simplification of methods. As he served but a single term of two years, much of the work that he began fell upon his successor, who, though of another political party, showed such zeal and judgment in the same direction, that it is clearly evident that in Governor Andrews the State added another to its long list of distinguished and able governors.

Connecticut has an area of 4,750 square miles. Its population in 1880 was 622,683. It is bounded on the east by Rhode Island, north by Massachusetts, west by New York, south by Long Island Sound. Its climate is changeable but healthful; its soil, especially in the valley of the Connecticut River, good, but, as a whole, best adapted for grass growing. Its woods are abundant and valuable, while its fruits are excellent and plentiful. Tobacco is extensively raised, especially in Hartford County, along the Connecticut river, and has in years past been a most profitable crop, though at the low prices which have prevailed since 1873, it has been much less so than of old.

The mineral resources of the State are varied and extensive, the most valuable quarries being those of red sandstone or freestone, found in abundance at Portland on the Connecticut. At Canaan is found the white marble of which the new State House is built; at Bolton, a micaceous slate, useful for flagging; while at Salisbury and Kent iron ore is found in such abundance that iron production has become the chief interest of that section of the State. Granite and limestone are also abundant in various sections, and of excellent quality; while cobalt, feldspar and copper are found in lesser quantity, with clay in abundance for bricks.

But it is in manufacturing that the State is pre-eminent, the proverbial ingenuity of the Connecticut Yankee, which has been satirized in the mythical wooden nutmeg, winning most of its triumphs in this sphere of action. The reports of the patent office shows the proportion of patents granted to Connecticut to be in excess of those of any other State, being one to every 829 inhabitants. Clocks, India-rubber goods, carriages, cotton and woolen goods, hardware, britannia and nickel-plate ware, table silver, cutlery, machinery, sewing silk, cotton warps and shoddy are among the principal productions. Insurance and banking employ much of the capital of the State, Hartford being especially interested therein, and famed all over the world for the number and strength of its life and fire insurance companies of large assets.

The common-school system of the State has been perfected in recent years to such an extent that 95 per cent. of the children of the school age are school attendants.

The State possesses a "school fund" of $2,-021,346, the principal of the fund being derived from the sale of the so-called "Connecticut Reserve" in the northern portion of Ohio, in 1786, for $1,200,000. This "Reserve" consisted of 3,300,000 acres of land, received by Connecticut at the time of its cession to the general government of its share of vacant lands in the unoccupied territory of the West. The State granted 500,000 acres of this reserve to such of the citizens of New London, Groton, Fairfield, Norwalk and Danbury as had suffered from British depredations during the war, and sold the remainder. The high schools of most of the larger towns and cities fit pupils for college or business life, while the universities within its borders send forth graduates all over the world.

In literature, theology and science the State has always maintained a high reputation, giving to the world, or claiming as residents, such poets as Trumbull, Percival, Brainard, Halleck and Stedman; such philologists as Noah Webster and J. Hammond Trumbull; such theologians as Horace Bushnell, Leonard Bacon and Noah Porter; such antiquarian students and historians as C. J. Hoadley; such writers on educational topics as Henry Barnard; such political economists as Theodore Woolsey, D. A. Wells and W. G. Sumner; such writers of fiction and essayists as Harriet Beecher Stowe, Charles Dudley Warner, Donald G. Mitchell, Samuel L. Clemens (Mark Twain), and many others; and in science, the elder Silliman, Clarence King, and many more.

In legal circles such names as Ellsworth, Waite (the present chief justice is of Connecticut birth), Gould, Goddard, Storrs, Seymour, Waldo, and many others have been famous; while at the bar, a very long array of men of talent could be named. Of living members of the profession who have attained more than local fame are Hubbard and Robinson of Hartford, Harrison and Ingersoll of New Haven, Seymour of Litchfield, and Halsey of Norwich.

Of orators there is also a long array, including such names as Sherman, Griswold, Baldwin, Deming, Stuart, Harrison and Hubbard.

In art, Col. John Trumbull of Connecticut was the finest painter of the Revolutionary era, and Fred. E. Church ranks among the first today.

. . . .

The early settlers of Connecticut were men of education and enterprise, as well as of character and piety. Hooker at Hartford, and Davenport at New Haven, meant to implant free commonwealths of God-serving people. The seed they planted brought forth such fruit that the distinguishing name of the State has long been "Land of Steady Habits."

Its State seal, which has been in use with but slight modification since 1656, bears, "Argent, three vines supported and fruited;" with the legend, "*Qui transtulit sustinet*"—"He who transplanted will sustain." In this faith the citizens of the State have seen their grand old Commonwealth increase and prosper year by year; in this faith they fought French and Indians, Mother England herself, and treason against the Union. So long as loyalty to this motto inspires her people, so long may they hope for prosperity.

FAIRFIELD COUNTY.

It was six years before the landing of the Pilgrims at Plymouth Rock, nineteen years before the first frame house was erected at Windsor in Connecticut, and about twenty-three years before we have any knowledge of Europeans setting foot on the soil of the State west of the Housatonic River in what is now Fairfield county, that the adventurous Adrian Block, a Dutch explorer, sailed into Long Island Sound, from the little settlement of his own countrymen on Manhattan Island, comprising only about four houses, in his ship of state, the "Restless," and made the discovery of the shores of Fairfield county; first observing the Norwalk Islands, which he named the Archipelagoes, and then sailing to the mouth of the Housatonic River, its eastern boundary, which he named the river of the Red Mountain; and thus, as early as the year 1614, this county and the Connecticut River, and the entire coast of the State, for the first time became known to a race of beings different from the aborigines. The first knowledge of the desirable situation and great natural advantages of this county for future settlements, was obtained by the English colonists while pursuing the retreating Pequot Indians westward to the "great swamp" in the present town of Fairfield, where, July 13, 1637, a decisive battle was fought. In a short time thereafter the formation of settlements and towns commenced.

In 1639, Mr. Ludlow, a distinguished lawyer, of Windsor, who was at the Indian swamp fight about two years before, when he became most favorably impressed with the locality, commenced a settlement at Fairfield, called by the natives Unquowa. He brought about ten families with him, and settlers joined them from Watertown and Concord, Mass. The territory was generally purchased of the natives; and the settlers soon formed a township, and came under the jurisdiction of the Connecticut Colony. The same year Mr. Fairchild came from England and purchased a plantation at Stratford, comprising Pequonnock and Cupheag, as they were known by the Indians, situated between Fairfield and the Housatonic River; and settlements were commenced immediately, although William Judson is said to have settled here in 1638, and to have erected a stone house. John and William Eustice and Samuel Hawley came from Roxbury, and Joseph Judson and Timothy Wilcoxson from Concord, Mass. A few years later Samuel Wells came from Wethersfield, and some others from Boston. The first clergyman at this place was Adam Blackman, an eminent and greatly beloved preacher, formerly of the Church of England, who came directly from Derbyshire. Many of his admirers followed him to these shores, declaring that "thy people shall be our people and thy God our God."

On this early settled territory, and within a comparatively recent period, Bridgeport, the third city in size and importance in the State, has sprung into existence. The exact date of the commencement of the settlement in this latter locality seems to be in doubt; but, in 1650, it is evident that a few families were residing in this section of Toilsome Hill, where Capt. David Sherman, a leader in matters of church and state, was born and resided; and that, although the population has changed in locality, this was the germ of the future city. In 1694 a parish was formed named Fairfield Village. In 1701 Fairfield Village was named Stratfield by the General Court; and, after a period of seventy-five years contained only about 1,000 inhabitants. With the gradual increase in population, the business began to centre at the head of tide-water, and down the harbor or river east of Golden Hill, and near the east side of Pequonnock River, in the town of Stratford, when it was named Newfield. In 1765 the present Main street of the city was merely a cart-path, and there was a small ferry to the point on the east side of the harbor. In 1820 Newfield proper contained only about 800 inhabitants. This place became an incorporated borough in the year 1800, and was then named Bridgeport, although, as a town, it had no legal existence until 1821, when a tract of territory of about ten square miles on the harbor and river was organized as a town, then containing not far from 1,700 inhabitants. The borough was organized under a city charter in 1836, with a population of about 3,400.

The next section of the county occupied by whites, after the territory covered by Fairfield and Stratford, was Stamford, the Indian name of which was Rippowams. Capt. Nathaniel Turner made the purchase of the place of the Indians for the New Haven Colony, for the consideration generally of a dozen each of coats, hoes, hatchets, and knives, two kettles and four fathom of white wampum. In the latter part of 1641 about thirty-five families had made this their place of residence; and the next year, John Whitmore and Mr. Mitchel were admitted members of the General Court of the New Haven Colony, from the new plantation, when it received its present name. The first minister at this place was Richard Denton.

The town of Greenwich was purchased of the natives in the year 1640 by Robert Feaks and Daniel Patrick, with the expectation that it would adhere to the New Haven Colony; but New Amsterdam, in the New Netherlands Colony, was so near, and its influence so potent, that the purchasers betrayed the confidence of the Colony, and commenced the settlement under the Dutch government, in which course the inhabitants seem to have acquiesced. The unfriendly relations between the

Indians in these parts, and the Dutch, and their intrusions upon the settlers, whose lands were their frequent and bloody battle-fields, were undoubtedly the chief reasons why, in the year 1657, they freely yielded to the jurisdiction of the New Haven Colony. The dividing line between the States of New York and Connecticut, as fixed in 1664, brought the plantation of Rye into the Colony of Connecticut, and that town was admitted to the jurisdiction in 1665; but in 1683, the dividing line between the two colonies at Greenwich was so changed at to leave it nearly as it is at present.

The first authentic settlement of Norwalk was in the year 1651, although it is probable that there were some scattering inhabitants here the year before, and perhaps some in 1640, after Mr. Roger Ludlow of Fairfield purchased the eastern part of the place from the Norwalk Indians on the 26th of February of that year, as worded in the deed, "from the sea a day's walk into the country." In April Captain Patrick purchased two islands and the meadows and uplands on the west side of the Norwalk River "as far up in the country as an Indian can go in a day from sun rising to sun setting." In June, 1650, Nathan Ely, Richard Olmsted and others, secured permission from the Connecticut Colony to commence a plantation at Norwalk, and obtained a deed of the territory from the Indians, February 15, 1651; and in September, 1651, the General Court organized it into a town. Thomas Hanford was the first minister at this place. The name of the town was derived from the Norwalk River, although there is a common tradition that it was taken from the day's "North-walk" which fixed the northern boundary in the Indian deeds. The surnames of Benedict, Raymond, Fitch, Lockwood, Betts and some others of the first settlers are quite common in the city and town at the present day. Norwalk was made a borough in 1836, and the village of Old Well, named from an ancient well where vessels were supplied with water, was incorporated as a city in 1868, and named South Norwalk two years afterward.

In 1684, a settlement at Danbury called Pahquioque by the Indians, or Paquiage in the Colony records, was commenced. The pioneer settlers were Thomas Taylor, Francis Bushnell, Thomas Barnum and others, who were mostly from Norwalk. Dr. Wood and Josiah Starr came from Long Island, and Joseph Mygatt came soon after from Hartford; and men of the name of Picket, Knapp and Wildman were among the earliest settlers, of whose names are a number still common in the town. The settlement was called Danbury, from a village in Essex, Eng., and it was laid out six miles square. The town patent, from the General Court, was given in 1702, and it was made a borough in 1822. The Rev. Seth Shove, probably ordained in 1696, was the first minister.

The next section occupied by the English settlers was at Pootatuck, the Indian name of Newtown. In May, 1708, several persons petitioned the General Court, or Assembly, as it began to be called, for a committee to survey the land and consider what number of inhabitants the tract would accommodate, and determine where the settlement should be; and in 1711, the town was incorporated.

The town of Ridgefield was purchased of the Indians in 1708 by John Baldwin and others, and a second purchase was made of the natives in 1715. In October, 1709, Maj. Peter Burr of Fairfield, John Copp of Norwalk, and Josiah Starr of Danbury reported a survey of the tract to the General Assembly, and the grant of the town was then made; but the patent was not signed till the year 1714. After the Assembly, in 1714, gave the inhabitants of the town the right to settle an orthodox minister, it is probable that the Rev. Thos. Hawley became the first settled minister at this place.

Several inhabitants of Fairfield secured a grant of the present town of New Fairfield in 1707. The territory was purchased of the natives in 1729, but it does not appear to have been settled until the next year. It was organized as a town in 1740. The boundary line between New York and Connecticut on the western limit of this town was settled in 1731, when, for lands on the Sound, the section known as Oblong was granted to New York. The first minister was the Rev. Benejah Case, ordained in 1742.

In 1761, a township which is said to have been named Reading, after Col. John Read, one of the early settlers, was incorporated and taken principally from the old town of Fairfield.

Weston, originally a parish in the town of Fairfield, was granted town privileges in 1787, about fifty years after the locality was first settled.

Brookfield, originally a part of New Milford, Danbury, and Newtown, and known as the society of Newbury, was incorporated as a town in 1788. It is said to have been named after its first minister, the Rev. Thomas Brooks, who was ordained Sept. 28, 1758, when the church was formed.

Huntington, comprising the parishes of Ripton and New Stratford in Stratford, was created a town in 1789. The Rev. Jedediah Mills, ordained in 1724, was probably the first clergyman.

Trumbull, a part of the old town of Stratford, was organized in the year 1798.

New Canaan was formerly Canaan parish in Norwalk and Stamford, and was made a separate town in 1801. The parish had existed since 1731, when the Rev. John Eells of Milford became the first minister.

Sherman was made a town in 1802, and was formed from the north part of New Fairfield; and Wilton was also incorporated the same year, having formerly been a society in Norwalk from the year 1726.

The year before Bridgeport was given town privileges, Darien, in the year 1820, was taken from Stamford and made a town, having before been known as the Middlesex parish.

Monroe, formerly the parish of New Stratford in Huntington, was formed into a town in 1823.

Westport, on the Saugatuck River, was formerly a part of Fairfield, Norwalk and Weston, and was granted town powers in 1835.

Easton, formerly a parish with Weston in the town of Fairfield, was taken from the eastern part of Weston, and made a town in 1845; and Bethel, the 23d and the last town formed in the county, was incorporated in 1855, having been a portion of Danbury.

The county was constituted in the year 1666, and Fairfield was made the shire town. Bridgeport, however, was given that honor about the year 1854. Danbury was created a half shire town in May, 1784.

The Indian history of the county, though not as thrilling, perhaps, as the history of the great savage tribes living to the east and north, is interesting, however, as showing the complaints, struggles, and gradual extinction of the race of red men here. At the time of the settlement of the county, the principal tribes within its borders were the Paugusetts, who inhabited Stratford, Huntington, and the adjoining towns, and the Norwalk tribe, which was nearly a clan; but there were some considerable clans at Newton, New Fairfield, Ridgefield, Greenwich, Stamford, Fairfield, and Bridgeport. They were more numerous, however, along the sea-coast, at the mouths of the rivers and along their courses; and the inland tribes visited those on the coast and were treated to oysters, clams, and other sea food, the entertainers returning these civilities, to secure lamprey-eels and the privilege of indulging in better hunting. In 1659, eighty acres of land at Golden Hill, Bridgeport, were made a reservation by the General Court for the Pequonnock Indians; and it was ordered that when they desert their land it shall revert to Stratford plantation, which shall pay Fairfield one half of the consideration received. All the Indians residing within the limits of this county were, with the exception perhaps of those living at Greenwich and Stamford, friendly to the early settlers, who always made honorable purchases of their lands before attempting to take possession; but the natives and first settlers were greatly harrassed by the fierce and very powerful Iroquois or Mohawks, the mere rumor of whose appearance created the wildest alarm. Coming annually to collect tribute of the natives, their natural ferocity was exercised in killing and destroying on every hand, if their demands were refused. They were defeated, however, eventually (1647) by the Paugussetts in one battle, while attempting to take the fortress, near the mouth of the Housatonic River. The war with the Pequots closed with the fight at Sasco Swamp, near the sea shore, in the town of Fairfield, about two years before the county was permanently settled, when 700 warriors were killed and captured; and as this tribe then became broken and discouraged, they were not a source of danger to the early inhabitants.

The Fairfield County Indians participated in a war which sprung from selling intoxicating liquors to an Indian by some Dutch traders of New Amsterdam in 1642. The Indian, while intoxicated, killed two whites; and, in retaliation, by consent of the Dutch governor, some eighty natives were slain. Several tribes on the Hudson River having been defeated by the Mohawks, the remnant fled to New Amsterdam for protection, but the governor again had his revenge, and about one hundred of them were killed. In 1643, the Indians on Long Island, on the Hudson and in Connecticut, arose to avenge their wrongs, and the territory of Greenwich and Stamford was the theatre of many bloody conflicts.

A united body of more than 1,500 warriors had their encampment on this territory, and the tomahawk did its work of massacring women and children as well as men. Even animals were driven into buildings and destroyed by fire. In February, 1644, a battle was fought at Strickland's Plain, in this county, between the Dutch and Indians. After a tedious march, the former came upon the Indian village in the light of a brilliant full moon, after a heavy snow-storm, when, after a fierce conflict of an hour, a victory was achieved, and the blood of one hundred and eighty warriors crimsoned the snow. This put an end to the war, and in April, the Indians consented to a peace; but there were some murders of settlers in Greenwich and Stamford after this time.

This county has sustained its share of the loss of life and treasure in the colonial wars as well as in those of later times.

There were said to be twenty-five wigwams on Golden Hill, Bridgeport, in 1710; and only three women and four men remained in 1765. They were ejected from their reservation in 1760, and after it was restored to them, they gave it all up for thirty bushels of corn, blankets worth £3, twelve acres of land on the west bank of the Pequonnock River, and eight acres of woodland on Rock Hill. About the year 1810 their lands were sold; and the fund secured, in 1842, amounted to $1,175, of which sum $500 was used to purchase a house and twenty acres of land in Trumbull. In 1850 there were two squaws and six half-breeds living. Their family name was Sherman.

In 1774 there were thirty-five Indians in Stratford, Monroe, Huntington, Trumbull and Bridgeport, only eight in Greenwich, nine in Norwalk and Stamford. It is quite probable that the Pootatuck clan in Newtown, had many years before joined the tribe in Southbury, and afterwards the Weantinogues at the Great Falls on the Housatonic River in New Milford.

With the early settlers the train-band of independent military companies was as much of a necessary institution in each town as the church, and was compelled to be on the watch at all times, and to train one day in the first week of March, April, May, September, October and November.

In 1709, the militia was made more effective, and a committee of war for Fairfield County was appointed to provide for the defense of the frontier towns in the county. In the French and Indian wars this county furnished about 3,000 men to maintain the honor of the mother country. The war of the Revolution, however, called forth all the patriotic ardor of its people, and although not having the war-spirit at the Lexington alarm in April, 1775, as had the counties nearer Boston, on account of its nearness to New York, with which was its principal trade, yet fifty men marched from Fairfield and fifty-eight from Greenwich for the relief of Boston at that time, and thirty-three also went from Stamford to defend New York.

There were three regiments formed from this county in 1776, and its quota was kept up during the war. Lying on Long Island Sound, the county was particularly exposed to the incursions of the enemy. On Sunday, the 27th of April, 1777, a force of more than two thousand of the enemy, under command of Gov. Tryon of New York, arrived in Danbury for the purpose of destroying the large quantity of military supplies stored there.

The few American troops in the place being forced to withdraw, the supplies, and all the dwellings and buildings belonging to the patriot inhabitants but one or two, were destroyed by fire. The individual losses were estimated at more than £16,000. The town records were burned, but the probate records were saved by being taken to New Fairfield. Gen. David Wooster took command of the few American troops at his disposal, and followed the enemy to Ridgefield, where he was mortally wounded. Gen. Arnold took immediate command, and followed them to the mouth of the river, where they re-embarked. The only real fight was where the gallant Wooster was fatally shot; and, on the evidence of an eye witness, sixteen British and eight Americans were killed and several wounded. Several dwellings, and other houses at Ridgefield, were burned and plundered.

July 8 and 9, 1779, Gov. Tryon's troops plundered and burned two hundred and twelve houses, barns and stores, three churches, and two school-houses. The court-houses at Fairfield, and Green's Farms were also consumed. The Rev. Dr. Daggett was one of the wounded. The loss of the British was about eighty. Tryon landed at Norwalk in the evening of July 11, and destroyed the vessels in the harbor, magazines, and stores, with the whole village of one hundred and ninety dwellings. Gen. Putnam was stationed with his army at Reading in 1779, to support the garrison at West Point if attacked, and also cover the Sound, and while here quieted a discontent in his army by a short, sharp speech. Greenwich became famous as the town where he made his celebrated plunge down a steep precipice at "Horseneck" to save his life, one shot of the many going through his hat. On Sunday, July 22, 1782, at Darien, the British troops, made up of Tories mostly, residing in this neighborhood, took Moses Mather, D. D., and his congregation, prisoners. Thus this county, from its situation, suffered heavily during the war, but was amply compensated for its losses pecuniarily by the State, which, in 1792, granted to those in this and New London County, whose property was destroyed by the invasions of the British, in addition to what they had already received, 500,000 acres of land of the western part of the reserve in Ohio, known as the Fire Lands.

During the war of 1812, the county furnished its full proportion of troops to defend the State, and a small fort erected at Black Rock Harbor, Fairfield, was manned by a small force of militia, to protect the coasting trade of the Sound, which was almost entirely suspended by the partial blockade of the ports. A British privateer captured the sloops "Minerva," Capt. Baldwin, and "Victriss," Capt. Pennoyer, both of Bridgeport, packets plying between this port and New York. Whale-boats of light draft were used in the trade between New York and Bridgeport. Commodore Isaac Chauncey of Black Rock commanded our forces on Lake Ontario; and the privateer "Scourge" of Stratford, commanded by Capt. Nichols, took so many prizes in the North and Baltic seas that two English frigates attempted to capture her, but unsuccessfully. One afternoon, towards the close of the war, Bridgeport was startled by the appearance of two British men-of-war coming to anchor in the harbor, with port-holes open, and great activity on board, as if intending to immediately shell the town. The inhabitants remembered the burning of neighboring towns in the Revolutionary war, and there was no sleep that night. The church bells were rung, valuables and the money in the bank were removed to a place of safety; the militia were called out, and messengers sent for re-enforcements, and the wildest alarm prevailed; but long breaths were taken in the morning when it was known that the war-ships had disappeared.

During the war of 1861, this county furnished about 8,000 men.

The first church of Bridgeport was formally organized in 1695, and Rev. Charles Chauncey, a grandson of the president of Harvard College, became the first minister. In 1706, the Rev. George Murison, an Episcopal missionary in the town of Rye, and the Hon. Caleb Heathcote made a tour from Greenwich to Stratford, where about twenty-four persons were baptized. The next year they were organized into a parish. The first Episcopal church edifice in the Colony was erected here, and opened for divine service on Christmas Day, 1724. From this beginning Episcopacy soon spread to Fairfield and other towns. The Rev. Samuel Seabury, consecrated in 1784, in Scotland, the first bishop of Connecticut, formerly under the jurisdiction of the Bishop of London, made his first visit to the church at Stratford. There are now thirty-four Episcopal parishes in the county.

Stratford is also the parent of Methodism, not only in this county but in the State. It was here that, in September, 1789, the first society was organized; the second one was established at Reading. At the town of Weston, in this county, "Lee's Chapel" was the first house of worship erected by this denomination in New England. This building stood until 1813. There are now nearly fifty Methodist churches in the county, within the jurisdiction of the New York East Conference.

The first Baptist church in the county was constituted at Stratfield, now Bridgeport, in the year 1751. There are at present fifteen churches of this denomination in the county.

From about 1830 to 1840, the Roman Catholic Church commenced organizing in the county, and, in 1838, the first service was held at Danbury. From these beginnings it has increased till there are ten churches in the most central places in the county. A Sandemanian church was formed at Danbury in 1765, by Robert Sandeman, a native of Scotland, who was buried at this place in 1771, and in 1798 there were three of these churches in the town.

The early settlers seemed to be as desirous of promoting the cause of education, as of establishing the church, and it may be said that the school and state were as united, nearly, as church and state. In many of the petitions of the settlers in this county for church privileges, their needs of a school were also set forth. A little more than thirty-three years after the first settlement of the county, six hundred acres of land were granted by the General Court to Fairfield County, as well as the others, for a grammar school, to be established at the county town forever, which should be maintained so as to fit young men for college, which, it is believed, was accepted by this county; so that, in those early times, the people had not only the advantages of the common schools in the county, but of a grammar or Latin school also. There are now two hundred and forty common and forty-seven graded schools in the county.

In 1819 the Brookfield Union Library Association was organized, and since that time there have been ten of these institutions formed in the county. William Augustus White of Brooklyn, N. Y., who died in 1868, left $10,000 by will, in trust, for a public library at Danbury, and afterwards the old White homestead was deeded by Alexander M. and Granville White for the same purpose. In 1876 they made a gift of about $25,000 for the erection of a library building, which was commenced in 1877.

There was an academy established by President Dwight of Yale College at Fairfield, which sustained a very high reputation, and was subsequently a seminary for young ladies. Afterwards, such institutions were established at several other towns in the county, but they have been on the decline since our admirably perfected common-school system has become so popular.

For the promotion of agriculture, manufactures and commerce, perhaps this county was more favorably situated than some other portions of the Colony, because of its nearness to New York. Near the beginning of the present century, the Fairfield County farmers commenced improving their lands by systematic drainage, when hundreds of acres of swamp lands, in the towns of Greenwich, Danbury, Westport, Ridgefield, and other towns were reclaimed and were made vastly more productive than before.

The farmers, having become awake to the benefits of agricultural societies, four have been organized in the county, the oldest of which, the County Society at Norwalk, was organized about forty-five years ago. In 1869 the first cattle show and fair of the Danbury Agricultural Society was held.

Since the days of railroads, most of the grain comes from the West, and the only grain elevator on the sea-coast between New York and Boston was erected by Messrs. Crane & Hurd in 1871, at Bridgeport. The grain is transported by rail or water, and 1,500,000 bushels have been landed in it in a year.

The manufacturing industries of the county have grown up mainly since the Revolution. Hats were first manufactured at Danbury in 1780 by Zadoc Benedict, who, with one journeyman and two apprentices, made about three in a day. About 1790, Messrs. Burr & White built the first hat factory in the town, employing thirty hands and producing fifteen dozen per week. There were produced in 1800, at this place, 20,000, fur hats mostly, surpassing any other town in the United States in the annual manufacture. About forty years ago there were fifty seven hat factories here, making about 270,000 annually, with a capital of about $290,000. There were eleven hat factories in Norwalk forty-five years ago, making about 36,000 hats annually. Besides these, there were numerous factories in other towns of the county. This county stands first in this branch of business, having manufactured nearly twice as many hats as all the other counties of the State. Machinery of all kinds, steam-engines and boilers were first made in the county at Bridgeport more than fifty years ago. In 1792 a paper-mill was carried into successful operation at Danbury, which produced about 1,500 reams annually; fifty years afterwards Fairchild's Mill at Bridgeport was the only one in the county. Carriages were manufactured extensively at Bridgeport at an early day by Mott & Burr. Fifty years ago there were fourteen tin factories in the county, employing a capital of over $40,000. Combs were largely manufactured in Newtown in 1834; and in 1845, there were nineteen factories engaged in this business in the county. In the early part of the present century the boot and shoe business gave employment to many men, and the most extensive business in this branch of manufacture in the county has been done at Norwalk. About 1830 there was over $20,000 capital employed in the manufacture of felt-cloth at Norwalk, and the business has been largely prosecuted since that time. For some twenty years the manufacture of rubber-belting has been carried on at Newtown on an extensive scale. In the early growth of Bridgeport the manufacture of saddles and harnesses was an important industry.

Among the more recent manufacturing industries of the county has been that of patent leather. In 1845, Mr. S. J. Patterson commenced this business at Bridgeport, and soon after the Bridgeport Patent Leather Company was formed, which has done a heavy business. The first practicable machine for sewing was patented by Elias Howe, Jr., in 1846, and consisted, generally, of a needle with the eye in the point, and a shuttle to unite two edges in a seam, forming the stitch by interlocking two threads. In 1862, he established his business at Bridgeport, and erected a large factory, where the Secor Company also have their works. In 1857 the world-renowned Wheeler and Wilson Sewing-Machine Company established their works at Bridgeport. One of the heaviest and most successful industries of Bridgeport has been the steel works, from which the Union Car-Spring Company of Jersey City, N. J., were supplied with bar steel; but, about 1874, this company removed their works to Bridgeport, and both are now under one management in the making of car-springs not only for their own, but for foreign markets. The manufacture of cartridges of all kinds was commenced at Bridgeport in 1860. The makers of the celebrated Sharp's rifle located their armory here in 1875.

In 1680, when there were but twenty-six towns in the Colony, the little commerce of this county was managed at Fairfield, where ships of about 300 tons burden could come into the barbor of Black Rock. The principal centre for the trade of the county for a long period prior to the rise of Bridgeport, was at Norwalk, from which place regular lines of passenger and freight sloops sailed to New York. The first incorporated steamboat company in the county was formed at Norwalk in 1824; and soon after the first regular line of steamboats made trips to the metropolis; and, about 1825, commenced to run from Stamford. It was not, however, till 1832, that the first steamboat connection was made with Bridgeport and New York, and about thirteen years since with Port Jefferson on Long Island. For the past forty years Bridgeport has taken the lead as a commercial centre, and the commerce has been confined mostly to the coasting trade, as the export trade is still in its infancy. This place was a grain mart up to 1832; and extensive commerce was carried on from here with eastern and southern ports. Prior to 1840, the West Indian trade was very considerable, and made good business for millers and coopers. Three ships were at one time engaged in the whale-fisheries from here, and a company pursued cod-fishing on the banks of Newfoundland; and, for the last few years, a large trade in ice has been developed. There are six light-houses on the coast of this county. The Penfield Reef light-house at Black Rock harbor, erected in 1873, has a flashing red light, with a fog-bell. The Bridgeport light-house, completed in 1871, has a fixed red light.

The first board of trade formed in the county was organized at Bridgeport in 1875, for the purpose of giving every possible impetus to commercial and manufacturing enterprises.

In 1687, roads leading from one plantation to another were first designated as king's highways or country roads. The first road of this character in the county was laid out from Stratford over Golden Hill at Pequonnock, for horses and carts, which afterwards became a section of the regular stage-road and post-route through the county from New York to Boston.

At the commencement of the present century, it took thirty hours to travel by the mail-stage on the route from Hartford through Danbury, the half-way place, to New York, not including the time required to stop over-night at Danbury; and the stage-fare alone was $6.90, with fourteen pounds of baggage, and a single fare extra, if it weighed over one hundred pounds. In place of the old king's highway, the New York and New Haven Railroad Company, incorporated in 1844, and consolidated with the New Haven and Hartford Company in 1872, but which commenced business in this county in 1839, was a great stimulus to all kinds of industry in the towns along the seacoast. The Housatonic Railroad, incorporated in 1836, running through the western part of Connecticut, and fully opened for business in 1842—the result of the great perseverance and energy of Alfred Bishop—placed Bridgeport in as favorable a position as any other seaport town in New England in its railway connections with the West; and was the germ of the rapid growth of the manufactures and commerce of that city. Hardly less important, however, has been the effect of the Naugatuck Railroad upon this part of the county, which, incorporated in 1845, to run from Winsted to Bridgeport, and not fully operated till 1849, has opened up to this county, and to Bridgeport in particular, the advantages that flow from the extensive manufacturing interests in the Naugatuck Valley. From the time of the opening of the Danbury and Norwalk Railroad in 1852, Danbury has grown rapidly in population and business activity. The New York and Housatonic Northern Company, chartered in 1868, since 1870 has been run from Brookfield to Danbury by the Housatonic Company. The New Canaan Railroad commenced operations in 1868, and runs to Stamford. The New York and New England Railroad Company runs through Danbury from the west to Boston, and has become a grand trunk line through the county, making more direct communication with New England and the West.

The first savings bank was organized at Bridgeport in 1842, from which time there have been seventeen monetary institutions of this kind formed in the county, with deposits amounting to nearly $14,000,000.

The first newspaper published in the county was the "Fairfield Gazette," ninety-six years ago, at the county seat. The oldest newspaper published in the county is the "Republican Farmer," still a flourishing paper, with a large circulation. The "Farmer's Journal" was established at Danbury the same year (1790). The "Norwalk Gazette" was first brought out in 1818, and still maintains its leading position in the southwestern part of the county.

In 1829 the "Stamford Advocate" was first published. The "Republican Standard" of Bridgeport first made its appearance in 1842. The "Evening Standard" was the first daily paper published in the county; its initial number was issued in 1854. The next daily paper successfully established was the "Evening Farmer," also of Bridgeport. The "South Norwalk Sentinel" was issued in 1870. The world-renowned "Danbury News" was established in 1870, having grown out of the consolidation of the "Danbury Times" and the "Jeffersonian." The centennial issue of the "News," printed in blue ink, gave a graphic account of the great celebration in Danbury July 5, 1876, when the people rejoiced for the final victory which was achieved over the torch of Gov. Tryon.

The other papers are the "Greenwich Graphic," "Stamford Herald," "New Canaan Messenger," "South Norwalk Republican," "Norwalk Hour," "Westport Westporter," "Bridgeport News," "Bridgeport Leader," "Ridgefield Press," "Newtown Bee," "Danbury Democrat," "Danbury Republican," and "Danbury Item."

The population of Fairfield County has increased, next to New Haven and Hartford counties, with greater rapidity than any other in the State. In 1669 there were only about 165 freemen in the county, which then comprised the four plantations of Stratford, Fairfield, Norwalk, and Stamford, not including that of Rye. In the year 1756, the population was 19,849; in 1870, 95,370; and in 1880 the county had a population of 112,044.

Towns.

Bridgeport, most favorably situated on Long Island Sound, fifty-eight miles from New York, has a population of about 30,000. This thriving city is in first-class railroad communication with New York and Boston, with the West from Albany, and with the Naugatuck Valley; and there are seventy arrivals and departures of trains daily at this point. Its facilities for commerce are unsurpassed, having within its limits the Bridgeport, and one-half of the Black Rock, harbors. That part of the city known as East Bridgeport is connected with the other part by four free public bridges across the Pequonnock river; and there is an ample foot-bridge on the New York, New Haven, and Hartford Railroad bridge.

A large portion of the population are skilled artisans, who are employed in a great variety of manufacturing; and among the long list of productions, which may be named to show the extent of this industry, are machinery, steam-engines, boilers, and castings of all descriptions; cast-steel and car-springs, springs, perches and axles, brass ware, pumps, locks, hardware, cutlery, Sharp's rifles and sporting guns, bits and braces, silver-plated goods for carriages, saddlery and horse trimmings, and electro-plating in gold, silver and nickel; and sewing machines, for which the Wheeler and Wilson Company occupies four entire blocks, with a capital stock of $1,000,000, employing 1,400 hands, with a monthly pay-roll of $100,000 and producing about 600 machines per day; while the Howe Company, with a capital of $1,000,000 also, and having a branch house in Glasgow, Scot., is doing an enormous business. There are here two patent-leather companies of $100,000 each, of which the Patent Leather Company handles and finishes about 20,000 hides per annum, and the John S. Way & Company produces russet grain leather to the amount of 35,000 sides annually; and besides annually dresses 9,000 buffalo robes, running two factories and employing about eighty men. Cartridges are also manufactured here, with $300,000 capital, and a working force of 450 men; also percussion caps, and paper and metallic shells, paper and paper boxes, carriages and coaches, coach-lace and coach-lamps, hats, furniture, shirts (employees numbering about 300, with about 400 who take work outside the factory), ornamental wood, wood-finishing goods, novelties and toys (employing several hundred hands), saddles and harnesses, cement, sewer and drain pipes, having branches in many places in western Connecticut; silk, ribbon, varnish of a superior quality, soap, water-motors, jewelry of a cheap grade, boots, shoes, etc.

The commerce of the city is mostly in the coasting trade. The business of the Custom-house for the Fairfield district is located here. The Bridgeport Steamboat Company dispatches two first class steamers, the "Bridgeport" and the "Laura," to New York daily. The monetary institutions consist of five national and three savings banks and a mutual fire insurance company. There are seventeen most attractive public school buildings, one of which will accommodate over 1,000 pupils, a high school, a young ladies' seminary, and numerous private schools. The Bridgeport Library contains over 9,000 volumes.

The city has three daily, two weekly, and three semi-weekly newspapers. Its water supply is ample. The streets and avenues are kept in a cleanly condition; are well curbed and thoroughly lighted with gas; the walks are mostly of stone and concrete, and the system of drainage is effected by over eighteen miles of sewer pipes. A well-equipped horse railroad and its branches accommodate the people from the centre to the suburbs of East Bridgeport and Fairfield, and to the cemetery and the parks. Mountain Grove Cemetery, on the extreme western limits of the city, covers about eighty acres. It is laid out with most exquisite taste, and is adorned with massive and costly monuments. This city cannot be surpassed for its favorite drives and popular pleasure grounds. Seaside Park is a most charming place for recreation and pleasure. Here, in this most appropriate spot, has been erected an imposing and costly granite monument, adorned with marble statues and bronze medallions, to the memory of the soldiers and sailors who fell in the late war. Washington Park, in East Bridgeport, containing a fine grove of old forests, is also an attractive place.

The city is not deficient in fine blocks of buildings and public edifices. Some of those that attract attention are the Bridgeport and People's Savings Bank buildings, the City National Bank; the Court-house, built of freestone at a cost of $75,000; Wheeler's Block, which contains the Public Library; the Standard Association Building, and two opera-houses, one of which is a fine structure.

The churches of the city are twenty-nine in number. St. Augustine's Roman Catholic Church is a massive Gothic edifice, built of granite at a cost of about $150,000. St. Mary's Catholic Church, in East Bridgeport, is of a striking architectural design. St. John's Episcopal Church is of handsome Gothic design, and cost about $100,000.

The First Presbyterian Church edifice is of a peculiarly novel design throughout. It is of undressed blue stone, trimmed with light granite, with a tower about 150 feet in height.

Nathaniel Hewit, D.D., an eminent pulpit orator and reformer, was born at New London, Conn., in 1788. He graduated at Yale College, and studied law, which he abandoned for the ministry. He was installed over the Second Congregational Church at Bridgeport in 1830, and over the First Presbyterian Church in 1853. He died in February, 1867.

Hon. William D. Bishop, a native of Bridgeport, has been a member of Congress and Commissioner of Patents. He was a long time President of the New York, New Haven and Hartford Railroad Company.

Hon. P. T. Barnum, born in Bethel, Conn., in 1810, is not only the greatest showman of the age, but a good lecturer and a popular temperance advocate. He has also been mayor of Bridgeport.

The city of South Norwalk, and the borough and town of Norwalk.—The city, situated on the west side of Norwalk harbor, is one of the most important stations on the line of the New York, New Haven and Hartford Railroad. It has an estimated population of about 6,000. The manufacturing interests at this point are quite extensive; its nearness to the great metropolis, and its first-class water and railway communications rendering it one of the most desirable locations for carrying on the great industries. Among some of the most important manufactures are locks, knobs and bronze ware; steam-engines and the celebrated Earl's steam-pump at the Norwalk Iron Works; fine hats by several different companies, also straw hats; boots and shoes on an extensive scale, and paper boxes. There are also two large planing-mill companies doing a heavy business. Attention is also largely given to shipbuilding and the cultivation of the oyster.

The situation of the city renders its commerce of great importance to its growth. Besides the large number of vessels built and owned here, and others, engaged in the coasting trade, the transportation lines of steamers are continually engaged in a profitable business. Twenty passenger trains arrive from and depart for New

York daily, and five to and from Danbury daily. A line of freight propellers runs regularly to and from New York, and large and commodious passenger steamers make daily trips all the year round, conveying passengers at the low fare of thirty-five cents a distance of forty-five miles, or the trip to New York and return, ninety miles, for fifty cents. The sail is delightful, and connections are made with the New York and New Haven and Danbury trains. Vessels drawing twelve feet of water discharge their cargoes at the wharves. Boats are also run by the Steam Freighting Company.

The city is growing rapidly, having about doubled its population during the last decade. It has some fine blocks of buildings and church edifices, and a handsome opera-house. The school facilities are excellent. The religious interests are represented by five churches. The water works are among the most complete in New England.

The borough of Norwalk is situated in the centre of the town, on the river, nearly one and a half miles north of the city. It contains about 7,500 inhabitants, and has five banks, six churches, and several manufacturing establishments. There are two academies in the borough, and four newspaper offices.

The town of Norwalk contains about twenty square miles of territory, and had a population of 13,956 in 1880. There are five national, two savings banks and ten churches.

Hon. Thomas Fitch was born about 1697; was deputy-governor of the Colony for four years from 1750; governor for twelve consecutive years from 1754. He was a lawyer, distinguished for great abilities and large acquirements. He died July 18, 1774.

Hon. Thomas Belden Butler was born August 22, 1806; graduated at the Yale Medical School, and settled at Norwalk in 1829, as a physician, but on account of his nervous temperament abandoned that profession, studied law, and was admitted to the bar in 1837. He was a member of Congress one term; was elected a judge of the Superior Court in 1855; of the Supreme Court in 1861, and was made chief justice in 1870. He resigned this office in 1873, because of ill health. He was the author of an elaborate work on the atmospheric system; an inventor, and obtained several patents, and took an active interest in agriculture. He died June 8, 1873.

Clark Bissell, LL.D., was governor of the State, and a judge of the Supreme Court of Errors from 1829 to 1839.

Hon. Orris S. Ferry was born at Bethel, Conn., August 15, 1823; graduated at Yale College, and settled at Norwalk in the practice of law. He was a member of Congress one term, and colonel and brigadier-general of volunteers in the late war. He took his seat as United States senator in 1867, and was re-elected in 1872 for a six years' term. He died in 1876.

Danbury, the northern terminus of the Danbury and Norwalk Railroad, had a population in 1880 of 11,669. No town in the State manifests a more lively interest in education, and the ample school buildings and grounds are made most attractive.

Although the central part of the town is not yet a city, it is an incorporated borough, containing a population of about 9,000, and is one of the most attractive, as it is also one of the most enterprising places in New England.

The religious denominations are represented by eight churches. The newspapers, besides the "News," are the "Democrat," "Republican" and "Item," which are ably-conducted journals. The borough contains two national banks.

One of the places of interest is Deer Hill, the location of beautiful residences. There are two delightful lakes, Neversink and Kenosha, the last of which is a fashionable resort for picnic and excursion parties, about two miles west of the centre, and is the source of Still River, which runs through the borough, and affords a good water power. The Wooster Cemetery, embracing an inclosure of about 100 acres, with its evergreens, tastefully laid out mounds, walks and drives, its artificial lake, and costly and attractive monuments, is a fit and handsome place of sepulture. Near the entrance, on a sightly elevation, stands the monument erected to the memory of Maj. Gen. David Wooster. It is of freestone, and about forty feet high. The coat of arms of Connecticut is carved on one side of the shaft; his deeds of valor are recorded on another; and on the third the fact of his having organized the first lodge of Freemasons in Connecticut at New Haven.

Rev. Ebenezer Baldwin, born July 3, 1745, and a graduate of Yale College, was ordained at Danbury in October, 1770. He was a chaplain in the Revolutionary army at New York in 1776, and, amid the hardships of the camp in attending the sick and suffering, contracted the disease of which he died. He was a man of great talents and culture. He died October 1, 1776.

Stamford had in 1880 a population of 11,298. The borough is situated on Mill River. The commerce is principally with New York. Steamers make daily trips to and from New York, and the freight of the transportatiom companies is heavy.

The manufacturing interests are somewhat varied, and among them may be noticed the production of iron, brass and copper ware. A large business is carried on in the manufacture of stoves, hollow ware, hot-air and cooking ranges and castings. There are also camphor refineries, and dyewoods of all kinds are quite extensively manufactured, as are boots and shoes, edge tools and wire, locks, carriages, woollen goods, billiard-tables, fire-brick, drain-pipes, marble, granite and flagging-stone.

This is one of the most popular localities for residences of the business men of New York, and those who wish to retire to live in wealth and luxury; and the town is believed to have more elegant private residences than any other of its size in the State. About twenty passenger trains leave here on the N. Y., N. H. and H. R. R., and as many arrive daily from New York. The town is one school district, having seventeen common and several private schools. There are also four graded schools and two academies. The religious interests are maintained by twelve churches. Some of the church edifices are models of architecture.

The town hall, of brick and Ohio stone, with a tower 100 feet high, was built at a cost of $140,000.

Woodland Cemetery is an attractive spot. The drives in the vicinity of Stamford are charming, and the views of the Sound and the surrounding country from the adjoining hills are magnificent.

Abraham Davenport, grandson of the Rev. John Davenport, the founder of the New Haven Colony, was a resident of Stamford. His true Christian integrity, vigor and uncommon firmness of mind, were prominent traits of character. In the legislature of Connecticut, May 18, 1780, on the famous dark day, which was thought to be the judgment day, on a motion to adjourn, he said: "I am against an adjournment. The day of judgment is approaching, or it is not. If it is not, there is no cause of adjournment; if it is, I choose to be found doing my duty. I wish, therefore, that candles may be brought." While sitting as chief justice of the Court of Common Pleas at Danbury, after being struck with death, he heard a portion of a trial, charged the jury, and retired for the night to be found with life extinct soon afterwards.

Charles Hawley, born June 15, 1792, graduated with honor at Yale in 1813, and opened a law office in Stamford about 1816. He left an estate probably larger than any lawyer has accumulated from his profession alone in the State, and stood in the first rank of the profession. He was lieutenant-governor from 1838 to 1842, and died Feb. 27, 1866.

The remaining towns of Fairfield County are Greenwich (population, 8,000), having several business centres, whose local newspaper needs are served by the "Greenwich Graphic"; and is noted principally for its fine villas and residences of men doing business in New York. On the eastern limit of the town is the hill noted as the place of the daring feat of Gen. Putnam in the Revolutionary war. Fairfield (4,000), embracing, in its extreme southwestern part, at the mouth of Mill river, Southport, which, like Greenwich, is a most charming suburb of New York, and has a small though deep and commodious harbor. In the western and upper part of the town is Greenfield Hill, one of the most sightly elevations of the region. From the church steeple here twenty-eight church spires in Bridgeport, Stratford, Milford, Reading and other places can be seen, also about half a dozen light-houses from Stratford Point to the Norwalk islands. A public avenue now runs over the celebrated "Saco Swamp" of earliest Indian warfare fame, near Southport. Newtown (4,000), an agricultural town, yet favored with the business of the New York Belting and Packing Company, the oldest manufacturers of vulcanized rubber fabrics in the country, as also with the manufacture of car-springs, solid emery vulcanite wheels, antiseptic linen hose, rubber-lined linen hose, etc. Stratford (4,500 situated on Long Island Sound, at the mouth of the Housatonic river, a level township for the most part, whose meadows at the mouth of the river are of very rich alluvial formation; and its village is characterized by one long, fine street, pleasantly lined with elegant residences, and well shaded with a variety of ornamental trees. Westport (3,500), a town noted, like several of the foregoing, for its beautiful residences of those still in business in New York city, as also of those who have retired from active life.

On a bend of the river, at a point near the Sound, is the elevation known in Revolutionary history as Compo.

New Canaan (2,800), a mountainous, yet growing town at the terminus of the New Canaan Railroad, whose manufacturing interests are in boots and shoes, and whose local paper is the well-esteemed "New Canaan Messenger." Bethel, an incorporated borough of 2,800 inhabitants; a growing, prosperous place, whose leading industry is the manufacture of hats, and whose admirably constructed water-works are justly the pride of the town. Ridgefield (2,000), lying in the western part of the county bordering on New York, the principal street of whose village, with its lawns, walks and shade trees, imparts to the place a wonderful home-like appearance, and whose newspaper, the "Ridgefield Press," has deservedly an excellent circulation.

Some parts of this township are so elevated that a view can be had of Long Island Sound at a distance of fourteen miles, and of East and West Rock at New Haven, and of the Highlands of the Hudson.

Darien (2,000), a small township situated on Long Island Sound, a favorite resort for purposes of residence of New York business men, and withal of gentlemen of leisure. Wilton, an agricultural town of 1,900 inhabitants. Reading, a sparsely settled, strictly agricultural township, with a population of about 1,600. Huntington (2,500), having quite extensive manufactures of silver-ware and paper, and a growing place. Trumbull (1,300), its people being largely given to husbandry, though shirts are quite extensively manufactured here; as also paper, at Beers' Mills. Monroe (1,200), an agricultural township, with an uneven surface, though quite productive soil.

Tashua Hill, in this town, is a signal-station of the United States Coast Survey, and is the first land visible when approaching this coast.

Easton (1,200), an irregular township lying north of Fairfield; a farming and eminently "well-to-do" community. Brookfield (1,200), a farming town, though giving some attention to the manufacture of lime, hats, etc. Weston (1,000), which has an iron foundry and machine-shop at Valley Forge; a plough and hay-cutter manufactory, and a flour and plaster mill at Lyon's Plains. New Fairfield (800), an agricultural town lying adjacent to the New York State line. Sherman (800), the most northern town in the county, wedged in between Litchfield County and the State of New York, and whose people are nearly all farmers.

All these towns have the usual complement of churches, quite all being of the so-called Evangelical order, the Congregationalist and Methodist, perhaps, predominating; and of schools.

Rev. Isaac Lewis, D. D., born Jan. 21, 1746; Yale College, 1765; settled at Greenwich Oct. 18, 1786; was a fervent Revolutionary patriot, and at one time a regimental chaplain. In the only house left standing at the burning of Norwalk, he preached an appropriate sermon from Isa. lxiv. 11-12, the inhabitants having assembled on the occasion for the purpose of fasting and prayer. He died Aug. 27, 1840.

Joel Lindsley, D. D., (1793–1868), was long the esteemed pastor of the Greenwich Congregational church.

Hon. Gold Selleck Silliman, born at Fairfield in 1732; Yale College, 1752; a distinguished lawyer, and a brigadier-general of militia in the Revolution; was the father of the late Benjamin Silliman, LL.D., of Yale College. His death occurred July 12, 1790.

Philo Shelton, A. M., former rector of Trinity Church of Fairfield (1754–1825; Yale College, 1778), is believed to have been the first Episcopal clergyman ordained in the United States.

Roger Minott Sherman, LL.D., a native of Fairfield, one of the most eminent lawyers of his day, and son of Roger Sherman, one of the signers of the Declaration, was one of the judges of the Supreme Court of Errors of this State from 1839 to 1842.

The Rev. Samuel Johnson, D. D., one of the founders of Episcopacy in Connecticut (1696–1772; Yale College, 1714), an author of note, a man of great talents and personal dignity, was settled at one time over the church in Stratford.

Maj.-Gen. Daniel Wooster, a native of Stratford (1711–1771; Yale College, 1738), having entered the military service, was captain of a company in the expedition against Louisburgh in 1745. He was a general in the French wars; commander of the troops sent to guard New York in 1775; went to Canada, and was chief in command after the death of Gen. Montgomery. He was appointed major-general of the State militia about 1776; and, in 1777, learning that the British had landed at Compo, pursued them to Danbury, and was mortally wounded at Ridgefield, April 27, 1777.

Hon. David Plant, a native and life-long resident of Stratford, a graduate of Yale in 1804, was a member of Congress from 1827 to 1829, and died Oct. 18, 1851.

The Rev. Jonathan Ingersoll, installed pastor of the Ridgefield church Aug. 8, 1739, was a chaplin in the Colonial army on Lake Champlain. Died Oct. 2, 1778, in the 65th year of his age, and the 40th of his ministry.

The Rev. Samuel Goodrich, father of the renowned Peter Parley, was, for upwards of twenty-five years, the faithful pastor of the Ridgefield church.

The Rev. David Ely, D. D., settled at Huntington, Oct. 27, 1773 (1749–1816; Yale College, 1769), was so zealous in the patriot cause during the Revolutionary war, that the Tories in this section threatened to hang him, when the rebellion should have been crushed, on an oak tree in the public square.

The Rev. James Beebe, pastor of the Congregational church at Trumbull for thirty-eight years, took an active part in the capture of Ticonderoga during the French and Indian wars, and was very instrumental in stirring up the enthusiasm of the people during the Revolutionary war.

Mr. Samuel Staples, a noted man of his time, founded the celebrated academy in Easton, by giving a fund which made it a free school, and a number of acres of land for the benefit of the school.

Rev. Samuel Sherwood (1730–1783; Yale College, 1749), was ordained at Weston Aug 17, 1757. Espousing the colonial cause in the Revolutionary war with such zeal as to become obnoxious to the British and Tories, it was not deemed safe for him at one time to sleep in his own house. A published Fast-day sermon, delivered by him in 1774, was some years ago deposited in the library of Yale College.

Rev. Maltby Gelston (1766–1856; Yale College, 1791), was installed pastor of the church in Sherman April 26, 1797, at a salary of £100, and a few cords of wood. He was proverbial for his wisdom, elevated piety, industry and punctuality. After an active ministry of forty-five years in this town, where he always resided after his installation, he died at the advanced age of ninety years.

HARTFORD COUNTY.

At the time of discovery, the Connecticut River Valley was inhabited by several small tribes of Indians, allied to the Narragansetts and the Nehantics, and, like them, subject to the constant attacks of the more powerful and warlike Pequots. They were also in a condition of enforced vassalage to the mighty Iroquois or Mohawk confederation, which bounded them on the west, and whose warriors levied arbitrary tribute upon the Connecticut tribes, and in case of resistance devastated their villages. Many of the river Indians had been driven from their original homes and had migrated to eastern Massachusetts, where they were found by the Plymouth settlers. Within the limits of Hartford County were several fortified villages, where the remnants of these tribes were intrenched as a protection against their numerous enemies. At Pyquag, now Wethersfield, Capt. Block held an interview with "Sequin," sachem of a tribe resident there; and he also makes mention of a village a few miles farther north, inhabited by the "Nawaas" tribe. Upon the Tunxis River was located the tribe of that name, and the Podunks occupied the eastern shore of the Connecticut, opposite Hartford. Suckiage, the location of Hartford, had probably been seized by the Pequots, as the Dutch, who were first to make a purchase of land at this place, treated with a Pequot sachem.

In the spring of 1631 Wahquimacut, a sachem of one of the river tribes, evidently impressed with the idea that the English would prove powerful allies against his relentless foes, the Pequots and Mohawks, visited the Massachusetts settlements and invited emigration to his country, extolling its natural advantages and guaranteeing reasonable terms for the land and bounties to actual settlers. Gov. Winthrop of Massachusetts Bay seems not to have been favorably impressed by the proposition, and took no action, but Gov. Winslow of Plymouth deemed the matter of sufficient importance to warrant a journey to the Connecticut. He was soon followed by other explorers, and projects for emigration were warmly discussed by the Massachusetts colonists. As the early settlers were anxious to remain near navigable water, the towns in the vicinity of Boston were already complaining of overcrowding, and the Connecticut Valley was regarded with longing eyes, although the government of Massachusetts Bay continued to discourage the proposed migration. But advocates of the measure were continually arriving from England, and the government soon found itself in the minority.

In June, 1633, Jacob Van Curter, an agent of the Dutch West India Company, purchased about twenty acres of land at what is still known as Dutch Point in Hartford, and erected thereon a fort and trading-house, which he named the "House of Good Hope." In October, 1633, Plymouth Colony, having in vain endeavored to secure the co-operation of Massachusetts Bay, dispatched a vessel to the Connecticut River, under command of William Holmes, who established, near the mouth of the Tunxis River, on the site of the present town of Windsor, a trading-post.

During the summer of 1634, a company from Watertown settled at Wethersfield. It seems certain that a portion of this company remained through the winter, thus constituting this the first actual settlement of Hartford County. June, 1635, the church at Dorchester, of which the Rev. John Wareham was minister, located at Windsor, near the trading-post established by Holmes. The Plymouth government regarded this as an invasion of their rights, but took no active measures to dispossess the Dorchester people. The matter was compromised several years later by a grant of land and the payment of a stipulated sum of money. Among the Dorchester emigrants was Roger Ludlow, lieutenant-governor of Massachusetts Bay, and several other men of distinction. During this summer the colony at Wethersfield was greatly strengthened by new arrivals. After erecting the necessary buildings, the Windsor settlers returned to Massachusetts for their families. October 15, a party of about sixty started from Dorchester to travel overland to their new home. Winter closed in unusually early, and the journey was accomplished with great difficulty, a portion of their live stock perishing on the way. Before they reached their destination snow fell to a great depth, and the Connecticut River was covered with thin ice, rendering crossing extremely difficult. They had taken but a limited stock of provisions, their winter's supply, together with their household goods, having been shipped by water. Many of the vessels were wrecked, while others were compelled to return to Boston. The situation of the little band of colonists was truly deplorable. The severity of the weather frustrated all attempts to obtain provisions, and they were destitute of the blankets, etc., necessary as a protection against the intense cold. Many of the settlers, after suffering incredible hardships, found their way through the wilderness back to Massachusetts, while those who remained in many instances were forced to subsist on nuts and acorns. But spring opened early, and with the return of mild weather matters improved very rapidly. Those who had been driven away by cold and starvation returned, bringing with them large reinforcements. A fort was erected at the mouth of the river to prevent the encroachments of the Dutch, and the permanency of the Colony seemed assured. A third settlement was commenced at Suckiage, and was named

Newtown, the colonies at Wethersfield and Windsor, respectively, taking the names of Watertown and Dorchester. April 26, 1636, the first court was held at Newtown, Mr. Ludlow presiding. The present names of the towns were given by the General Court in February, 1637. The name of Hartford is taken from that of Hertford, Eng.

During the spring of 1636 the Rev. Thomas Hooker and his assistant, the Rev. Samuel Stone, pastors of the church at Newtown, now Cambridge, Mass., headed a party of about 100 persons, including women and children, in an overland journey to the valley of the Connecticut, and laid the foundation of the city of Hartford. At the close of the year 1636 the total population of the three settlements was about eight hundred.

The Pequots early manifested symptoms of hostility against those who had wrested from them their possessions on the river, and had either restored these lands to their rightful owners, or had purchased them from such owners. They viewed with alarm the rapid increase of the Colonies, and conceived the plan of uniting all the tribes in a common war upon the English. Fortunately they were but partially successful in this. During the winter of 1636-7, a number of the settlers were murdered by the Pequots, and in April, 1637, a large body of savages descended upon the outskirts of Wethersfield, killed nine persons, and carried two girls into captivity. The captives were subsequently redeemed by the Dutch and returned to their former homes. At the General Court in May it was determined to wage a war of extermination against the Pequots, as the only means of self-preservation. A force of ninety men was raised, of which Hartford furnished forty-two, Windsor thirty, and Wethersfield eighteen. The command of the expedition was given to Capt. Mason, an experienced soldier, and the Rev. Mr. Stone was appointed chaplain. The force was accompanied by seventy friendly Indians, under the famous sachem Uncas, and sailed from Hartford May 10. The movement was entirely successful, resulting in the total rout of the Pequot tribe, with scarcely any loss to the colonial forces.

The bravery of Capt. Mason and his companions had saved the infant Colony, but its future prospects were far from flattering. The campaign had entailed a large debt, which it was but poorly prepared to meet, and had greatly augmented the effects of the prevailing scarcity of provisions. It had been found impossible to get the ground prepared the previous year in season to raise a sufficient supply of corn, as the colonists were almost entirely without ploughs or other agricultural implements. Many cattle had perished during the winter, and, the war having taken away a large share of the able-bodied men during planting time, a famine seemed imminent. A supply of corn was fortunately obtained from the Indians farther up the river, and the subsequent winter was passed in comparative comfort, although the Indians continued troublesome, rendering necessary the utmost vigilance. The "train-band" of Hartford organized in 1638, still exists as the Governor's Foot Guard.

Up to this time the colonists upon the Connecticut had continued to submit to the authority of the Massachusetts governments, but, finding that they were outside the limits of those patents, it was determined to form an independent government. A convention of delegates from the three settlements assembled at Hartford, and on Jan. 4, 1639, adopted a preamble and constitution for the government of the Colony of Connecticut. For nearly two centuries this constitution remained unaltered, a monument to the wisdom and sagacity of its framers, and with the exception of a few months, when a royal governor claimed authority under protest, Connecticut has always been ruled by officers chosen by the ballots of her freemen. John Haynes was the first governor under the constitution. At the spring session of the General Court the towns were vested with authority to conduct their own affairs.

In the autumn of 1639, Gen. Mason conducted a second successful expedition against the Indians. Subsequent to this it does not appear that Hartford County suffered to any extent from the depredations of the savages, although for many years the inhabitants dwelt in continual terror, and maintained a vigilant guard day and night. Having in all cases paid the former owners liberally for the land taken, they secured, if not the friendship of the local tribes of Indians, at least a passive acquiescence in the rapid growth of the Colonies. During the later bloody Indian wars, many of the members of the river tribes disappeared, probably allying themselves with the various hostile tribes, with whom they perished. For a long period, however, the settlers in the western part of the Colony were harrassed by occasional raids, and the territory east of the Connecticut River was not deemed safe until about 1670. In the last mentioned year the Simsbury settlers became so alarmed that they abandoned the settlement, and fled to Windsor. Their buildings were burned, and when they returned, six years later, they were unable to find the precise location of their former dwellings. The towns in Hartford County furnished a large number of men during King Philip's war, but were fortunately spared the horrors of savage warfare in their own midst. Numbers of friendly Indians remained in the county for many years. The sachem Uncas was a powerful ally of the colonists, and greatly assisted them in subduing the Pequots.

The members from Hartford County of the New England Confederation, formed in 1643, were men of great ability and influence.

A settlement on the Tunxis River, in the western part of Windsor, was incorporated as a town in 1645, under the name of Farmington, which name was thenceforth also applied to the river.

In 1654, England being at war with Holland, the Dutch property in this section was formally sequestrated by the colonial authorities, thus ending the occupation of this region by the Dutch.

In 1662, Gov. Winthrop, who had gone to England for the purpose, obtained from King Charles II. a charter for the Colony of Connecticut, conveying ample privileges. By the terms of this charter, Connecticut extended from the Narragansett river on the east to the sea on the west, and under this grant the Colony subsequently laid claim to portions of New York and Pennsylvania, giving rise to protracted and bitter discussions. Although this charter included New Haven Colony within the limits of Connecticut, it was not until 1665 that the former would consent to the union.

tion of Wethersfield, lying east of the river was incorporated in 1690, under the name of Glastonbury.

In October, 1687, Sir Edmund Andros appeared at Hartford, where the General Court was in ses-

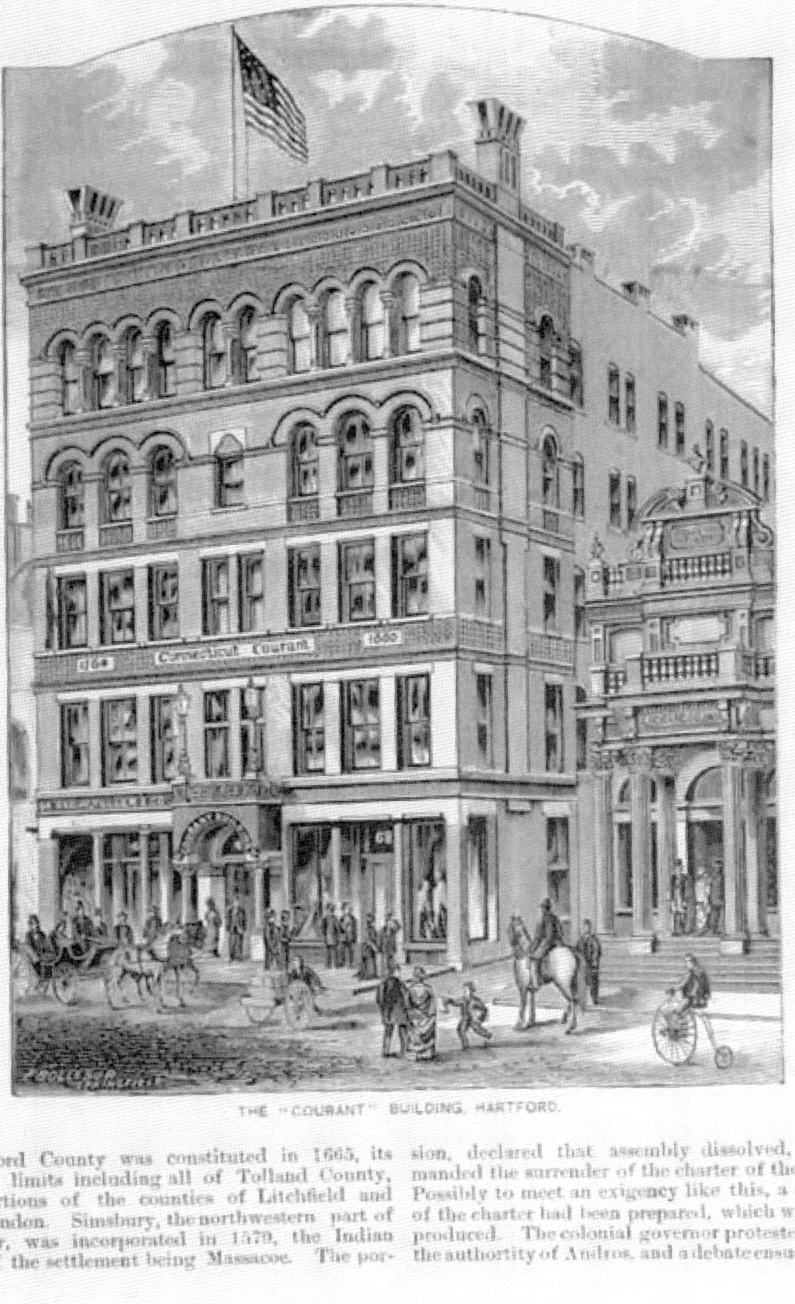

THE "COURANT" BUILDING, HARTFORD.

Hartford County was constituted in 1665, its original limits including all of Tolland County, and portions of the counties of Litchfield and New London. Simsbury, the northwestern part of Windsor, was incorporated in 1570, the Indian name of the settlement being Massacoe. The por-

sion, declared that assembly dissolved, and demanded the surrender of the charter of the Colony. Possibly to meet an exigency like this, a duplicate of the charter had been prepared, which was finally produced. The colonial governor protested against the authortity of Andros, and a debate ensued, which was prolonged until dark. Candles were called for and upon their arrival it was discovered that the copy of the charter had disappeared. It had been taken by Capt. Joseph Wadsworth, who conveyed it to the south part of the city, and concealed it in the hollow trunk of a large oak, in front of the residence of Hon. Samuel Wyllys, where it remained until less troublous times. The tree which was pointed out as having been the depository of the precious document was one of the chief attractions of Hartford until Aug. 20, 1856, when it was destroyed by a furious storm, while its name is perpetuated in various ways, Hartford itself being called, by common consent, the Charter Oak City.

Until 1701, Hartford had been the sole capital of the united Colony, but in that year New Haven was made a semi-capital, and from that time until 1873, the sessions of the General Court were held alternately in the two cities.

During the almost continual wars with the French and Indians from 1689 to 1763, Hartford County, being on the frontier so far as its western towns were concerned, was in a continual state of uneasiness owing to the atrocities committed in New York and Pennsylvania. Fortified houses were erected at various exposed points, including four in Hartford, while the ferries at that place and at Windsor were placed in a condition of defense. In 1704 the General Court resolved that the frontier towns must be held, as a measure of public safety, and that the inhabitants of these towns must remain, under penalty of forfeiture of their lands. This county had her full proportion of men in the military service, and during the 100 years next preceding the war of the Revolution, many of her citizens were either killed in battle, or died of disease contracted in camp. In the successful expedition against Louisburg, in 1745, Roger Wolcott of Windsor, lieutenant-governor of the Colony, commanded a brigade of Connecticut troops. The principal officers under Wolcott were from Hartford County. During the war, which began in 1755 and ended with the treaty of Ryswick in 1763, Hartford County had at various times from 500 to 2,000 men in active service.

The first code of laws for the Colony was compiled in 1650, and was composed almost entirely of extracts and adaptations from the Mosaic code. The odium of the so-called "Blue Laws"—if, indeed, there be any ground for such odium—rests rather with the New Haven Colony than with the Hartford.

The early history of Hartford County, like that of all the New England Colonies, must necessarily be somewhat ecclesiastical in character. The settlements at Hartford and Windsor were made under the guidance of the same faithful shepherds who had led their flocks across the sea in search of religious liberty, and a list of the early settlers of these towns is, in each case, an almost complete roster of the membership of some Massachusetts church. It is claimed that the First Church at Windsor is the oldest religious organization in New England. At first, under the ministrations of Rev. John Wareham, assisted by Ephraim Henet as teacher, there was great harmony and prosperity in the church; but Mr. Henet died in 1644, and as Mr. Wareham was advanced in years he felt unable to perform the pastoral labor without a colleague, over the appointment of whom arose an exceedingly bitter and protracted controversy. Appeal was finally made to the General Court, which ordered that an election of assistant pastor should be held. This was done, but the minority refused to acquiesce in the result, so that nothing was accomplished. Mr. Wareham died April 1, 1670, and for many years there was no settled pastor. Rev. Samuel Mather was settled in 1682, and remained until his death in 1726. The dissensions culminated in 1694 in the organization of the Second Church, with Rev. Timothy Edwards as pastor, an office which he retained for the remarkable term of sixty-four years.

The church at Hartford, upon the death of Mr. Hooker, in 1647, remained under the guidance of Mr. Stone, but he found it impossible to control a dissatisfied and controversial feeling which had sprung up in the church, and which rapidly increased. Several councils of the neighboring churches were called, but to no purpose; and several general councils, in which the New Haven and Massachusetts churches united, also failed to effect a reconciliation. But many of the disaffected members moved to other places, and comparative peace was at length restored. Mr. Stone died July 20, 1663, and was succeeded by Joseph Haynes. A division of the church took place in February, 1670, Samuel Whiting taking the pastoral care of the Second Church.

The Watertown people were not accompanied by their pastor in their migration to Wethersfield, but Rev. Henry Smith was settled soon after their arrival in their new home. This church, like its neighbors, soon became involved in disputes, and very early in its history sent out a colony to Milford. Upon the death of Mr. Smith, in 1648, the Rev. Jonathan Russell succeeded to the charge. Various disagreements finally led to an open rupture, and Mr. Russell removed to Hadley, Mass., taking with him a large number of the congregation. This seems to have ended the troubles in this church.

A church was gathered at Farmington Oct. 13, 1652, with Rev. Roger Newton as pastor. Rev. Timothy Stephens was installed at Glastonbury in October, 1693. The first minister at Simsbury was Rev. Dudley Woodbridge, settled March 3, 1696.

With the exception of a few Quakers, who were promptly banished, no dissenting sect made its appearance in Hartford County until more than 100 years after the first settlement. This county sent its due proportion of delegates to the convention which, in September, 1708, adopted the religious constitution known as the Saybrook Platform, which, by subsequent legislative confirmation, became the rule of faith for the entire Colony. Under strict repressive measures the growth of so-called "Separatist" churches was but slow until after the Revolution; and to-day Congregationalism is still the leading form of belief in Hartford County, although it has been much modified since the days of Hooker and Wareham.

When in 1715 to 1718 the proposed removal of Yale College from Saybrook was under consideration, Messrs. Woodbridge and Buckingham, the

Hartford County members of the board of trustees, warmly urged its location at Wethersfield, and so dissatisfied were they with the action establishing it at New Haven, that at the time of the first commencement after the removal, they held independent graduating exercises at Wethersfield, and conferred degrees upon several undergraduates. Subsequently, however, these gentlemen became for refusing to satisfy a judgment against him. On the day mentioned, an armed party of about sixty from Coventry and vicinity visited Hartford, forcibly entered the jail and liberated the captain. The party were pursued by Sheriff Whiting and a posse, but made their escape, after severely beating the sheriff and his assistants. The ringleaders were subsequently fined £20 each. In

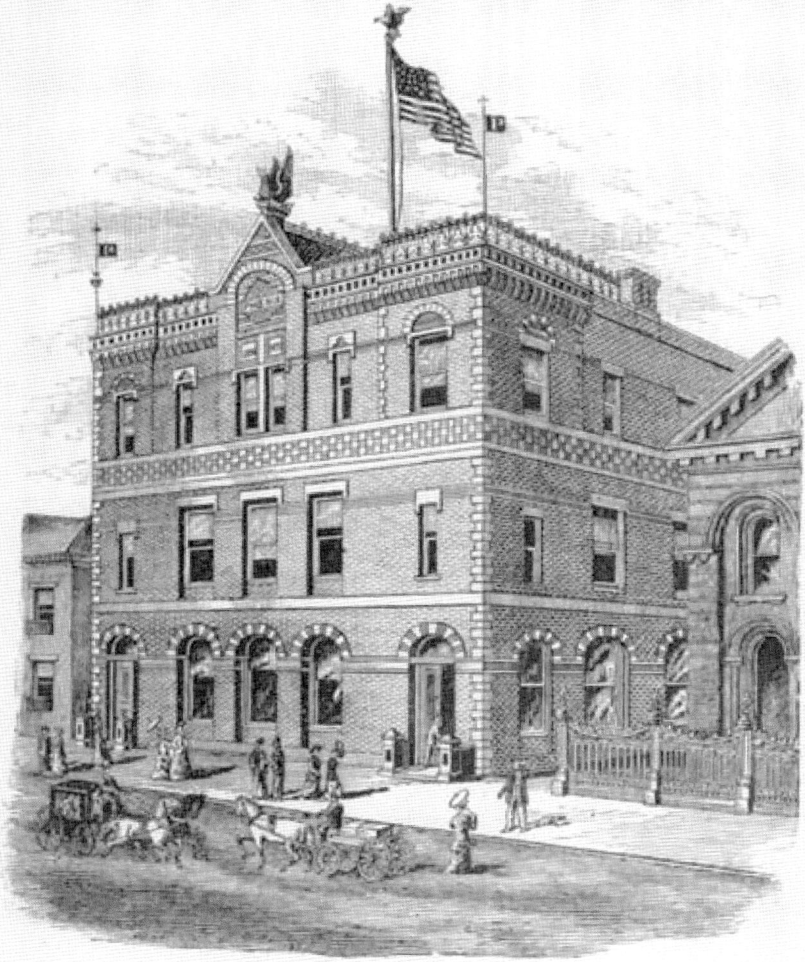

BUILDING OF THE PHŒNIX INSURANCE CO., HARTFORD.

econciled to the location of the college, and took art in its management.

In consideration of the distinguished services of en. Mason and his soldiers the General Court ade extensive grants of land to them. The locaon of these grants gave rise to heated controersies, resulting, in some cases, in actual conflict. ut of these land troubles arose the riot of Oct. 2, 1722, at Hartford. Capt. Fitch, a resident of oventry, had been committed to Hartford jail, 1761 the town of Hartland, then in Litchfield County, having been adjudged to be the property of Windsor, was annexed to Hartford County.

During the first years of the eighteenth century the limits of Hartford County, as defined by act of the General Court in 1665, were enlarged by annexing several towns which had been organized in the outlying districts. The portion of Windsor lying east of the Connecticut River was incorporated in 1768 as the town of East Windsor. At the commencement of the Revolution there were fifteen towns in the county, but its present territory was included within the limits of ten towns; namely, Hartford, Windsor, East Windsor, Wethersfield, Glastonbury, Farmington, Simsbury, Enfield, Suffield and Hartland.

The inhabitants of Hartford County were firm in their resistance to the oppressive measures of the British Government, and when, in May, 1766, the news of the repeal of the Stamp Act was received at Hartford, the General Court, then in session there, appointed a day of general rejoicing.

Although this county was spared the actual horrors of war in her midst during the Revolutionary struggle, her citizens bore a prominent part in that conflict. Owing to the inland location of the county, on a navigable stream, and having an abundance of water power, it became an important depot of supplies and prisoners, while arms, equipments and ammunition were manufactured in large quantities. Major Clarke's Farmington company, which passed through Hartford July 30, 1775, was entirely equipped by local industry. Farmington appears to have been thoroughly imbued with the patriotic fever, the Boston Port Bill being publicly burned in 1774, by the common hangman "in the presence of a large number of respectable citizens."

Early in the summer of 1774 the several towns held meetings and passed resolutions condemnatory of the action of the British Government, and pledging a hearty support to the sister Colonies. The militia was immediately reorganized, every person capable of bearing arms being enrolled, and during the winter frequent drills were held. September 15, 1774, a county convention was held at Hartford, which adopted an agreement for the non-consumption of British goods, and appointed a committee of inspection.

The expedition for the capture of Ticonderoga, in May, 1775, had its origin in this county, and seems to have been first suggested by General Samuel H. Parsons. April 26, Captains Noah and Elisha Phelps of Simsbury, and Epaphras Bull, William Nichols, Elijah Babcock, John Bigelow and Bernard Romans of Hartford, started for Vermont, where they met Ethan Allen. The party was subsequently joined by Captain Edward Mott of Preston, to whom the importance and feasibility of this movement had also occurred. The successful result of the expedition was largely due to the sagacity and shrewdness of Captain Noah Phelps.

When the news of the battle of Lexington was received in Hartford County, ten companies, numbering some four hundred men, were immediately raised and put in motion for the scene of action; but their services were not immediately required. Five regiments of militia were located in this county.

The county jail was soon filled with Tory prisoners, and many avowed sympathizers with the British were kept under close surveillance at their homes. Prisoners of war were also continually arriving, and it became necessary to provide a more commodious and secure place of confinement. This led to the use of the "Newgate of Connecticut," as the prison at East Granby has always been termed, which was an abandoned copper-mine, first discovered about 1707. The first use of the excavation as a prison appears to have been in 1773. In 1775 the mouth of the mine was inclosed in a palisade, and a block-house was erected, while the interior to some extent, was partitioned into cells, a place of confinement suggesting the famed Bastille and the castle dungeons of feudal times.

To more thoroughly disgrace the prominent Tories, the county committee of inspection, in April, 1776, adopted the plan of publishing their names in large capitals upon the first page of the Connecticut "Courant," as "enemies of their country."

During the Revolution there were five military executions in Hartford. March 19, 1777, Moses Dunbar was executed for high treason, in the presence of a "prodigious concourse of people," to whom the Rev. Nathan Strong delivered a lengthy and solemn discourse, which was afterwards published in pamphlet form. It does not appear that the other executions were thus solemnized.

March 21, 1781, Alexander McDowell, adjutant of Col. Welles's Connecticut regiment, having been found guilty of desertion, by a court-martial, was executed in the jail-yard, Gen. Washington, then in Hartford, having signed the death-warrant on the preceding day.

The defense of Hartford was not neglected, as the records show that on July 29, 1777, the selectmen ordered a cannon to be mounted, although it does not appear that it was ever used. Troops were occasionally quartered in the county during the war. In 1779 Gen. Gate's division was located in East Hartford for a time, and in November, 1782, the French allies occupied the same camping-ground.

When Count Rochambeau landed at Newport in September, 1780, he proceeded directly to Hartford, where he met Washington and other prominent American officers. September 26, the distinguished visitors were received with due honors. And thus Hartford, where was conceived the attack on Ticonderoga, at the very opening of the war, was also the scene of the formation of the final plans which carried the contest to a successful termination.

Immediately after the close of the war, Hartford County was reduced to nearly its present limits by the formation of Middlesex County on the south, and Tolland County on the east. Southington had been set off from Farmington in 1779. In 1784 that part of Hartford lying east of the Connecticut was incorporated as East Hartford, and May 29 of the same year, the city of Hartford received its charter, the population within the city limits at that time being about 3,000. In 1785 the southwesterly parish of Farmington was incorporated as Bristol, and a new town, named Berlin, was formed from portions of Farmington, Wethersfield and Middletown. This town included the parish of Kensington, which has retained that designation to the present time. Granby was formed from Simsbury in 1786. Marlborough, incorporated in 1803, included the southeastern part of Glastonbury, and portions of New London and Windham counties. The northern part of Bristol was incorporated as Burlington in 1806, and the same year Canton was formed from portions of Simsbury and of Litchfield County.

After the close of the war of the Revolution, Hartford County enjoyed a season of quiet, and her citizens devoted themselves to the development of her internal resources. June 28, 1784, the first city election was held in Hartford, Thomas Seymour being chosen mayor.

In common with the rest of New England, Hartford County was firmly opposed to the war of 1812. This county, however, was brought into especial prominence in connection with the war by the famous "Hartford Convention," which assembled in that city Dec. 15, 1814.

The first fair in the county was held at Wethersfield, Oct. 22, 1784, and was repeated several succeeding years. The first exhibition of the Hartford County Agricultural Association was held at Hartford in 1817.

To Hartford belongs the credit of sustaining one of the oldest newspapers in the country, "The Connecticut Courant," which was first issued Oct. 29, 1764, by Thomas Green, and has appeared regularly every week since that time, with the exception of four issues in December, 1775, and January, 1776, which was omitted on account of the failure of the supply of paper. This want of paper led to the development of an important branch of industry in East Hartford, where Mr. Green, in connection with other parties, established a paper-mill. There was great difficulty in procuring the quantity of rags necessary to keep the mill in operation, and the early files of the "Courant" abound in urgent appeals to the ladies to furnish the necessary material.

A mill for the manufacture of woolen cloth was established in Hartford soon after the close of the Revolutionary war, and when Gen. Washington visited the city, in October, 1789, he inspected its operations. At his first inauguration as president, he was dressed in an entire suit of Hartford manufacture. This mill was not the first established in the county, however, as one had been erected at Windsor Locks in 1768. In 1788 a bell-foundry was established at Hartford by Doolittle & Goodyear. It is supposed that the first manufacture of tin ware in the United States was by a Mr. Patterson, who settled at Berlin in 1740, and who peddled his wares from house to house in a basket. A powder-mill was built in East Hartford in 1775, believed to be the first in the country, and was a most important establishment during the Revolution. The first cotton-mill in Connecticut was erected at Manchester in 1794. In 1797, or thereabouts, a steam locomotive was invented by Dr. Kinsley, and appeared on the streets of Hartford. A patent for a lever printing-press was issued to John I. Wells of Hartford in 1819.

As early as 1787, there were lines of packets, chiefly sloops, between Hartford and New York, but there was little certainty or regularity in their trips. In November, 1818, the first steamboat constructed on the Connecticut was launched at Dutch Point in Hartford. It was a small propeller, intended for towing purposes, and was named the "Enterprise." The Connecticut River Steamboat Company was incorporated in 1824, and soon after purchased the steamer "Oliver Ellsworth," which arrived at Hartford on her first trip from New York, May 7, 1824. The "Experiment" had plied between Hartford and New London during the summer of 1823, and was probably the pioneer in steam navigation of the Connecticut. During the year 1824, work was commenced on the canal between New Haven and Farmington, and water was first let in in June, 1828. This canal was subsequently extended to Northampton, Mass.

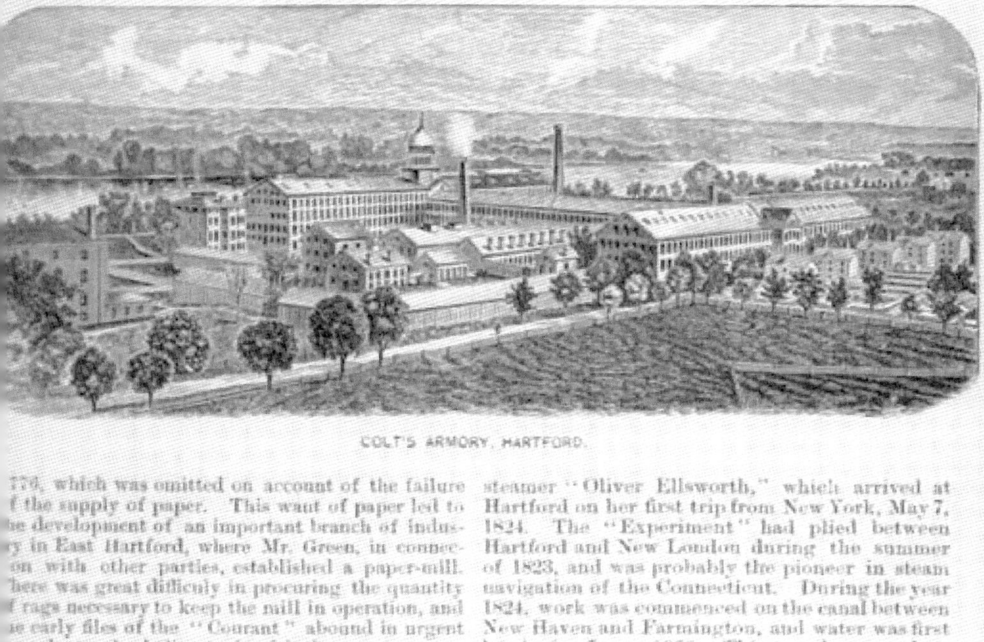

COLT'S ARMORY, HARTFORD.

The navigation of the upper Connecticut, prior to the construction of railroads, was regarded as a measure of great importance to the citizens of this county, and large sums were expended upon various projects for the improvement of the channel of the river. November 26, 1826, the little steamer "Barnet" left Hartford, and succeeded in going as far north as Bellows' Falls, Vt., returning the following week. The falls at Enfield were found to be a serious impediment to navigation, and in 1828 a company was formed in Hartford, which dug a navigable canal, some five miles in length, avoiding the falls, and furnishing the valuable water-power at Windsor Locks. Steamers continued to ply between Hartford and Springfield until the completion of the railroad, and Charles Dickens, in his "American Notes," gives a graphic description of this short voyage.

Shipbuilding was carried on for many years at Hartford and Glastonbury, and in 1833 a packet of 600 tons burden was launched at the former place.

In May, 1835, the legislature granted charters for railroads from Hartford to New Haven, and also to Worcester. The following year, the construction of the New Haven road was commenced, and it was opened for travel in December, 1839.

The New Haven and Northampton Railroad, which follows the route of the old canal, was opened for travel in 1848. The New York and New England Railroad Company, in December, 1878, took possession of the Hartford, Providence and Fishkill line, which crosses the county from east to west, and was completed in 1853. In 1871, the Connecticut Western, running northwest from Hartford and the Connecticut Valley, following the river south from Hartford, were opened for travel. In 1876, the Connecticut Central, from East Hartford to Springfield, was completed. In addition to the foregoing lines, there are branches of the New Haven road from Berlin to New Britain and Middletown, and from Windsor Locks to Suffield. The line from Manchester to South Manchester is leased to the New York and New England Company.

March 2, 1854, occurred the most fatal accident with which Hartford County has ever been visited. Shortly after noon on that day, the boiler in the car-manufactory of Fales & Gray, where some four hundred men were employed, exploded with terrific force, nearly demolishing one of the large shops. Nineteen were killed, many of them heads of families, and about forty others were injured.

The breaking out of the civil war in 1861 found the inhabitants of this county engaged in the vigorous development of the manufacturing industries which have given to many of its towns a world-wide fame. The news of the attack on Fort Sumter summoned the busy workmen to the defense of their country, and, as in the olden time, Hartford County was prompt in sustaining the government.

April 16, Gov. Buckingham issued his proclamation, calling for a regiment of volunteers. The next morning, Joseph R. Hawley, editor of the Hartford "Press," Albert W. Drake, and Joseph Perkins, met in the office of the "Press," and signed their names to an enlistment paper, as members of a rifle company for the first regiment. Many names were added during the day, and the company was completely filled up at an enthusiastic meeting held in the evening. George H. Burnham was chosen captain, and Mr. Hawley first lieutenant. The Hartford Light Guard, Capt. J. C. Comstock, also promptly volunteered, and a third company was also recruited under Capt. Ira Wright. In the first regiment, which rendezvoused at New Haven, in addition to the companies already mentioned, was a company from New Britain, under Capt. F. W. Hart, and a company composed of men from Windsor Locks, Enfield and Simsbury, under command of Levi N. Hillman, of Windsor Locks. The regiment left New Haven May 9, on the steamer "Bienville," and proceeded directly to Washington, arriving there on the 13th, and going into camp at Glenwood, two miles north of the Capitol.

In addition to the various Connecticut organizations, Hartford County was represented in many regiments from other States, and also in the navy, Capt. Ward of Hartford being the first victim of the war in that branch of the service. Among the distinguished leaders of the army, this county had many notable sons. The names of Gens. Joseph R. Hawley, Theodore G. Ellis, Griffin A. Stedman, and Robert O. Tyler of Hartford, John Loomis and William O. Pierson of Windsor, and John L. Otis of Manchester, attest the honorable part taken by this county; and Gideon Welles of Hartford, as secretary of the navy, was one of the President's most trusted counselors. About 800 citizens of the county were killed in battle, or died in the service. And those who served their country at home during the long conflict with signal ability—perhaps even more than if they had gone to the front—must not be forgotten. Prominent among these was J. Hammond Trumbull of Hartford, who, as secretary of state, was a most efficient assistant to Connecticut's noble war governor, William A. Buckingham. Many private citizens consecrated their wealth and their best energies to the equipment of the soldiers and the maintenance of their families. David Clark of Hartford contributed to these objects not less than $60,000, and his name is held in grateful remembrance by numerous widows and orphans.

The series of religious meetings held in January, February, and March, 1878, by the evangelists, Moody and Sankey, and Pentecost and Stebbins, were without a parallel in the history of Hartford. They were held in the skating-rink, which has a seating capacity of over three thousand, and which was filled twice every day for many weeks. These meetings resulted in large accessions to the churches, and their influence was felt throughout the county. The religious interest was undoubtedly deepened by the sad accident of January 15. On that day, a large number of excursionists from the towns along the line of the Connecticut Western Railroad had visited Hartford to attend the meetings. The returning train, consisting of nine cars, and drawn by two engines, had reached the bridge over the Farmington river, just west of the Tariffville station, when the entire western span of the bridge gave way, precipitating four cars into the river. Fourteen persons lost their lives, and many were badly injured.

In addition to the towns already mentioned, others have been formed, as follows:—In 1823, the eastern part of East Hartford was incorporated as Manchester. Avon was set off from the north end of Farmington in 1830. The parish of Wintonbury, in Windsor, became the town of Bloomfield in 1835. Rocky Hill parish, in Wethersfield, was made an independent town in 1843. South Windsor was incorporated in 1845. In 1850, New Britain was incorporated as a town, and in 1870 received a city charter. West Hartford became a separate town in 1854, and in 1857 the northern part of Windsor was incorporated as Windsor Locks. East Granby was set off in 1858. Newington parish, in Wethersfield, was made a town in 1871, and Plainville in 1869, having been part of Farmington. The territory included in Hartford County, which, at the close of the Revolution, was comprised within the limits of ten towns, is now divided into twenty-seven towns and two cities.

TOWNS.

Hartford, see page 98.

New Britain, see page 98.

Enfield, population 7,000, lies in the north-east corner of the county. The Connecticut River forms the western boundary, and the Scantic crosses the southern part of the town. dred buildings, covering an area over a mile long and half a mile broad, and is capable of producing upwards of $1,000,000 worth of powder annually. During the Crimean war it had an extensive contract with the British government, and furnished some 10,000 barrels, while during the civil war in this country the works were taxed to their utmost capacity. Several of the buildings have names suggested by the late war, as "Harper's Ferry," "Bull Run," and "Fortress Monroe."

A tract of about 1,200 acres in the north-eastern corner of the town is occupied by the

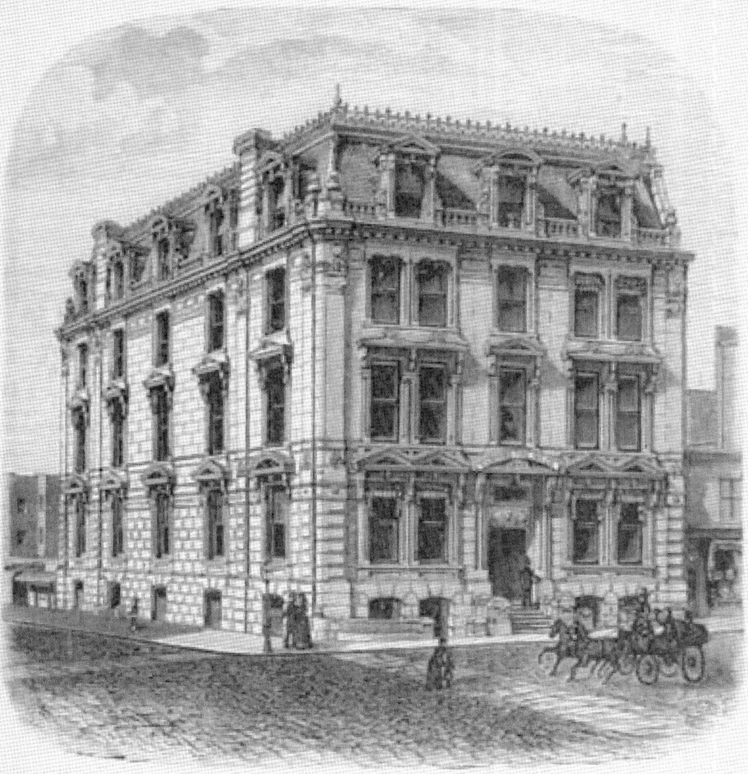

BUILDING OF THE HARTFORD FIRE INSURANCE CO.

bridge over the Connecticut, 1,000 feet long, nnects the town with Suffield. This bridge as originally erected in 1808, and was the first idge across the river within the limits of this ate. The principal village is Thompsonville, cated in the north-western corner of the town. his thriving village has grown up around the orks of the Hartford Carpet Company, which nploy about 1,400 hands, and have an annual pacity of about 3,000,000 yards of different ades of carpeting. This village has four urches, and contains many elegant residences. Hazardville are the works of the Hazard Powr Company, among the most extensive in the untry. This company occupies over one hun- Shaker community, founded here in 1787. The society is divided into six families, forming nearly a circle, with the central or church family as a radiating point. Their lands are in a high state of cultivation, and their buildings present the neat and thrifty appearance common to this sect. They are largely engaged in the cultivation of garden seeds, and also produce agricultural implements, etc., to some extent.

The New York, New Haven and Hartford and Connecticut Central Railroads pass through the town.

James Dixon, United States senator from Connecticut from 1857 to 1869, was born in this town in 1814.

Southington in an important manufacturing township in the south-western corner of Hartford County. The Quinnipiac River runs nearly through the centre of the town, from north to south, the New Haven and Northampton Railroad following its course. The two villages of Southington and Plantsville are located on this river. Among the most important of the manufacturing industries here carried on are tinmen's tools and general hardware, machine-forged nuts, carriage hardware, screw bolts of every description, tinsmiths' machines, sausage-fillers, paper bags and cutlery. There are seven churches, representing all the leading denominations, and an academy. At Hitchcock's Station and at Marion, in the southern part of the town, are manufactories of bolts and of jewelry. Population about 5,000.

Dr. Edward Robinson, the distinguished biblical scholar, Col. Charles Whittelsey, a gallant soldier of the civil war, and Rev. Levi Hart, for sixty-nine years minister at Preston, Conn., were born in this town.

Bristol is in the south-western part of the county, eighteen miles from Hartford. Good water-power is furnished by the Pequabuc River and branches, which has been well improved. The principal or centre village is divided into two portions, the north and south villages. About two miles north of the north village is Polkville, and about the same distance to the east is Forestville. There are in all seven churches and twelve school-houses. Two of the schools are graded. Bristol has a national, and a savings bank. The most prominent industry is the manufacture of brass clocks. Other manufactures are brass in all its varieties, spoons for plating, gray iron castings, trunk hardware, furniture knobs, augur bits and stockinet fabrics. The population is about 5,000, of which over 1,100 are employed in the various manufactories. The town is traversed from east to west by the New York and New England Railroad.

Manchester, an important manufacturing town, lies next east of East Hartford. The New York and New England Railroad crosses the northern part of the town, and is connected with South Manchester by a branch, about two miles long. Union Village, or North Manchester, is located at the railroad station on the main line. There are nine school-houses, including an excellent graded school at South Manchester, and seven churches. The silk manufactory of Cheney Bros. at South Manchester (Cheneyville), employs nearly 1,000 hands, producing dress silks fully equal to those of foreign manufacture. In fact, this company has revolutionized the silk trade in this country. The village of Cheneyville is a model of neatness and good taste, and in summer, with its abundant shade and spacious lawns unbroken by fences, is a most attractive place of residence. The Union Manufacturing Company, at North Manchester, produces an excellent quality of ginghams. Paper is manufactured in large quantities in this town. The population is about 6,500.

Glastonbury is the largest town in the county, being nine miles long, from east to west, and six miles broad. An excellent water-power is furnished by Roaring Brook, which rises in the northeast corner of the town, and empties into the Connecticut a little north of South Glastonbury village. Good mill-privileges are also located on Salmon Brook, in the northern part of the town. Granite of excellent quality is quarried in the town. This granite abounds in feldspar, and there are two mills for grinding this article for potters' use. There are eighteen schools, a private academy, and, in the various villages, eight churches. Perhaps the most widely known industry of the town is the manufacture of soap, by J. B. Williams & Co., whose works are located east of Glastonbury village. Near these works is Brodhead's tannery, one of the oldest in this region. On Salmon Brook are located the satinet mill of the Eagle Manufacturing Co., and also the Glastonbury Knitting Co., manufacturers of underwear. At Buckingham village is a manufactory of horse hoes and cultivators. On Roaring Brook are the paper mills of Case & Co., and the Roaring Brook Paper Co., Pratt & Post's anchor forge, Hollister & Glazier's woolen mill, Greene Bros.' cotton mill, and a twine factory. Population of the township, 3,800.

Glastonbury has acquired a national reputation through the determined resistance of the Smith sisters, Julia and Abby, to the payment of taxes, they holding that taxation should carry with it the right of suffrage. They have refused to pay their taxes for many years past, compelling the town authorities to seize upon and sell personal property belonging to them. They have annually appeared before the legislature as petitioners for redress, and have been regular attendants upon woman's rights meetings. Miss Abby Smith died in December, 1878, leaving her sister to fight the battle single-handed.

Gideon Welles, Secretary of the Navy, was born in this town (see Hartford). Alonzo B. Chapin, D. D., a distinguished clergyman of the Episcopal Church, was rector of St. Luke's Church from 1850 to 1855, and was the author of a bi-centennial address in 1853, a valuable contribution to the history of the town.

Suffield is eminently an agricultural town, the only branch of manufactures ever pursued to any extent being that of cigars and tobacco, for which the town at one time had an extended reputation. Here is located the Connecticut Literary Institute, founded in 1835 under the auspices of the Baptist Education Society. This institution occupies three large brick buildings, located on rising ground just north of the centre of the village, the most modern of which was completed in 1876. The present average number of students is about 100. Suffield village lies in the eastern part of the town, along a broad street, on elevated ground, affording fine sites for residences. There are three churches in this village. The canal around Enfield Falls is mostly located in this town. At the west village are two churches. The estimated population is 3,000.

Phineas Lyman, a native of Durham, Conn., and a celebrated officer in the French and Indian war, was long a resident of this town.

Among the natives of Suffield who have achieved distinction may be mentioned Gideon Granger, member of Congress from New York, and postmaster general; Sylvester Graham, vegetarian, and founder of the celebrated "Grahamite" system; Timothy Swan, musical composer, author of the favorite church tune, "China;" and George Tod, a distinguished lawyer and jurist of Ohio. This town has produced several clergymen of note, among them Rev. S. Dryden Phelps, D. D., now editor of the "Christian Secretary;" Rev. David N. Sheldon, who was excommunicated from the Baptist denomination for heresy, and afterwards became a Unitarian preacher; and Rev. Cotton M. Smith, who was settled at Sharon, Conn., from 1755 to 1806.

East Hartford is a valuable agricultural township on the east side of the Connecticut River, opposite Hartford. It contains some of the finest river meadows in the State. The Hockanum river passes through the central part of the town. The manufacture of paper is carried on at Burnside, and the Hazard Powder Company have a branch mill near the eastern boundary of the town. The New York and New England Railroad crosses the northern part, having two stations. Large quantities of tobacco are raised. The town contains six churches and a population of about 3,800.

East Hartford has furnished two distinguished professors to Yale College, Denison Olmsted, the astronomer, and Anthony D. Stanley, the mathematician. William Pitkin was one of the first settlers of this town. He held many important offices, and was governor of the State from 1766 until his death in 1769.

East Windsor is a rectangular township, bounded on the west by the Connecticut River. The Scantic River crosses the town from north to south, and, with a tributary, Broad Brook, furnishes good water-power. Although the surface of the township is somewhat broken, the soil is generally productive and well improved. The town contains several woolen manufactories, seven churches and twelve school districts. Population about 3,000. The Connecticut Central Railroad passes through the eastern part of the town.

John Fitch was born in East Windsor, January [illegible], 1743. He married unhappily, and separating from his wife, went to New Jersey, where, during the Revolutionary war, he pursued various vocations. In 1786 he successfully completed a small steamboat, which attained a speed of eight miles an hour. He was unable to secure funds to carry out his projects, government lands in Kentucky which he had pre-empted, were taken by squatters, and he died in Bardstown, Ky., July 2, 1798, in circumstances of poverty, leaving the advantages of his important invention to be reaped by others.

Thomas Robbins, a noted Congregational divine and historian, who was born in Norfolk, Conn., August 11, 1777, was pastor of a church in this town from 1809 to 1827. During the later years of his life he resided in Hartford; was one of the founders of the Connecticut Historical Society, and for many years its librarian. Although his income was limited, he accumulated an exceedingly valuable library, which he bequeathed to the Historical Society. A well-authenticated anecdote of Dr. Robbins is to the effect that when a young man he began the accumulation of his library, when the question of marriage was brought to his serious consideration. His income was so small that he thought it would be impossible to support a wife and at the same time indulge his passion for books. He decided the question by the very simple method of tossing up a penny, and remained a bachelor! He died in Hartford Sept. 13, 1856. His library is particularly rich in early editions of the Bible.

Other natives of East Windsor were Oliver Wolcott, one of the signers of the Declaration of Independence; John W. Barber, author of many historical works; and Danforth Marble, the comedian, celebrated for his delineations of Yankee character.

Windsor, or "Old Windsor," as it is commonly called, is an irregularly-shaped township, lying on both sides of the Farmington River, and bordered on the east by the Connecticut. The river meadows are large and productive, and the town also contains many valuable tracts of upland. At Poquonnock and Rainbow villages, in the northwest part of the town, are falls in the Farmington River, which have been extensively improved for manufacturing purposes. The main village is situated near the mouth of Farmington River, and runs along the Connecticut Valley for some distance, forming what is known as "Windsor street," which is broad and well-shaded. There are many substantial residences, some of these, like the Ellsworth mansion, dating back to the Revolutionary period. Like many of the towns in the county, it is largely interested in the growth of tobacco. The Hartford Paper Company has mills at Poquonnock and Rainbow. There are two mills at Poquonnock, producing cassimeres and fancy cloths. At Rainbow are located the paper-mills of the Springfield Paper Company, Hodge & Son, and House & Co.; Hodge & Son making a specialty of tissue papers, and House & Co. of press-boards. Population about 3,000. The New York, New Haven and Hartford Railroad passes through the eastern part of the town.

Oliver Ellsworth was born in Windsor April 29, 1745, and graduated at the College of New Jersey in 1766. He was a representative in Congress from 1777 to 1780; a member of the Council in 1780, and judge of the Superior Court in 1784; was a delegate to the convention for framing a constitution, and United States senator from 1789 to 1795. In March, 1796, he was appointed chief justice of the United States Supreme Court. In 1799 he was one of the envoys sent to France to adjust the differences between that government and the United States. In 1802 he again entered the Council, and in 1807 was elected chief justice of the State, an honor which he however declined. He died November 26, 1807.

William W. Ellsworth, son of the preceding, was born at Windsor, November 10, 1791, and graduated at Yale in 1810; studied law, and was professor of law in Trinity College over forty years; member of Congress from 1829 to 1833; governor of the State from 1838 to 1842, and judge of the Superior Court from 1847 to 1861. He twice declined an election to the United

States Senate. He died at Hartford January 15, 1868.

Henry L. Ellsworth, twin-brother of William W., graduated at the same time; studied law at Litchfield, and practiced for several years in Windsor and Hartford; was appointed resident commissioner to the Indian tribes of Arkansas, and was commissioner of patents from 1836 to 1845. He devoted himself especially to the development of the agricultural interests of the country. On his retirement from office, he settled in Indiana, and engaged in real estate business. He died December 27, 1858.

Henry W. Ellsworth, son of Henry L., was born at Windsor in 1814; studied law, and was counsel for S. F. B. Morse in telegraph suits; removed to Indiana, and published a book, entitled "Sketches of the Upper Wabash Valley," and was a contributor to various periodicals. He died at New Haven in August, 1864.

The ancestors of ex-President Grant, and of ex-President Hayes, at one time resided in Windsor. John S. Newberry, the geologist; John M. Niles, Postmaster General; Oliver Phelps, the enterprising purchaser of the Western Reserve; and the Rev. Henry A. Rowland, the author, were natives of this town.

Wethersfield lies on the west side of the Connecticut River, next south of Hartford. Since Newington parish was made a separate town, in 1871, the area of Wethersfield is much contracted, and it now contains only about eleven square miles. The village which lies in the northeastern part of the town, near the river, resembles most of the villages in the Connecticut Valley in having broad streets, lined with large shade trees. There are four churches, one of which, the Congregational, was erected in 1761, and is one of the most ancient church edifices in New England. The town supports six district schools, and an excellent high school. The state prison, removed here from Granby in 1827, is located at the north end of the village. The main buildings and wall of the prison are of Portland brownstone, and were, some years ago, improved at large expense, making this the equal of any penal institution in the country for convenient arrangement and thorough ventilation.

The leading industry of Wethersfield is raising and putting up garden-seeds for market. This business has been pursued for nearly a century. The onion crop, for which this town has always been noted, is much less than formerly, the farmers having turned their attention to tobacco and other crops. The Hopson & Brainard Manufacturing Company manufactures iron brackets and other light castings. Their works were destroyed by fire in November, 1878, but have been rebuilt.

At Griswoldville, a small village in the southwestern part of the town, is a Congregational church, and a factory which has been used for the manufacture of edge-tools. The Connecticut Valley Railroad passes through the eastern part of the town, and there is a steamboat landing near the village. Population, about 2,000.

Silas Deane, a native of Groton, Conn., and one of the ambassadors to France in 1776, was for some years a merchant in Wethersfield.

Calvin Chapin, D. D., born in Springfield, Mass., in 1763, was settled over the Congregational church in Wethersfield from 1794 to 1847.

Among the natives of Wethersfield who have attained distinction may be mentioned John Chester, an officer of the Revolution; Stephen M. Mitchell, U. S. senator; Elizur Goodrich, the astronomer; Harvey D. Little, western editor and poet; Ashur Robbins, U. S. senator from Rhode Island; Royal Robbins, the historian; and Gen. Samuel B. Webb, a distinguished hero of the Revolution.

Canton is a large township in the western part of the county. The Farmington River flows through the southwestern part of the town. The principal village, Collinsville, is situated on this river, and was formerly partly within the limits of Burlington. This village is named from the Collins Company, whose extensive manufactory of edge-tools was established here in 1826, and gives employment to several hundred men. The axes produced by this company have a world-wide reputation for superior quality and finish. A branch connects Collinsville with the Canal Railroad at Farmington, and it is also a station on the Connecticut Western Railroad. Canton village, about one and a half miles northeast from Collinsville, was the location of the first settlement within the limits of the town. The town contains five churches and a population of about 2,500.

Rev. Heman Humphrey, D. D., president of Amherst College from 1823 to 1845, and Rev. Hector Humphreys, president of St. John's College, Annapolis, from 1831 to 1857, were natives of Canton.

Farmington occupies a comparatively level valley, about four miles wide, and lies north of Plainville and west of West Hartford. There is much excellent farming land in the town. Farmington River enters the township near the northwest corner, flows southeast to the centre, and then makes an abrupt turn to the north. At Unionville, where the river enters the town, there is an excellent water-power, which has been well improved. The principal manufacturers are the Union Nut Company, the Platner & Porter Paper Manufacturing Company, and the Cowles Paper Company. This village is very neatly laid out, and contains several elegant residences. The main village is situated on an elevated plain, about seventy-five feet above the river. The soil in its immediate vicinity is very fertile, and flowers and vegetables are grown in profusion. Before the completion of railroads Farmington was an important trading point, it being on the favorite route from Vermont and eastern New York to the seaboard; and its trade in West India goods at one time exceeded that of Hartford. The village is substantially built, and contains many comfortable and attractive houses. The Congregational Church was built in 1771, and is still in a good state of preservation, being, next to that at Wethersfield, the oldest church in the county. The American Board of Commissioners for Foreign Missions was organized here, and held its first meeting in the Congregational parsonage, September 5, 1810. Population, 3,000. The New Haven and Northampton Railroad passes through the central part of the town.

John Treadwell, governor of the State, and the first president of the American Board of Commissioners for Foreign Missions; James Kilbourne, a member of Congress; Rev. Philip Milledoler, D. D., the distinguished Dutch Reformed clergyman; Rev. Asahel S. Norton, D. D., one of the founders of Hamilton College, at Clinton, N. Y.; Rev. Noah Porter, D. D., president of Yale College; Rev. John Richards, D. D., a noted Congregationalist clergyman and editor; and Timothy Pitkin, a leading Federalist politician—were natives of Farmington.

Berlin lies in the southern tier of townships in Hartford County. The Mattabeset River rises in the southwestern corner, flows north and east, and then turning south forms the eastern boundary. The New York, New Haven and Hartford Railroad runs through the centre of the town. Berlin village is about one and a half miles southeast from this station. Here are located several churches and an academy. Kensington village is a short distance to the west of the station. The works of the Hart Manufacturing Company, makers of coach and general hardware, are in this village. East Berlin village has a station on the Middletown branch. Here are manufactories of corrugated iron and tinmen's tools. Population of the township about 2,500.

Jonathan Hart (or Heart, as the name was originally spelled), a graduate of Yale in 1768, a gallant soldier of the Revolution and in the regular army, killed in a severe battle with the Indians; John Kilbourne, western author and publisher; the Rev. John Eliot, for thirty years settled at East Hampton, Conn.; James G. Percival, the poet; and Mrs. Emma C. Willard, the celebrated teacher and authoress—were natives of Berlin.

Windsor Locks is a small township, lying about three miles along the Connecticut River. The village is situated on the river in the northeast part of the town, at the locks by which the canal around Enfield Falls descends to the Connecticut, hence the name of the town. The surface is generally hilly and broken, most of the population being concentrated in the village, and employed in the various manufactories. There are four churches and two public schools. The town has a variety of manufactures, including paper, school furniture, spool silk, etc.; and a population of 2,500. The New York, New Haven and Hartford Railroad passes through the eastern portion of the town, crossing the Connecticut River on a substantial iron bridge, one mile north of the village.

Simsbury is an irregularly shaped township, containing about twenty-eight square miles, and is intersected by a spur of the Taconic mountain range. The Farmington River runs northerly through a portion of the town, and is bordered by spacious meadows; but, making an abrupt turn to the southeast, it breaks through the range of hills, and its course where it leaves the town is almost exactly the opposite of the first direction. Simsbury village is situated in the broadest portion of the valley, near the centre of the township. It contains two churches, and a safety-fuse manufactory. At Tariffville, in the southeast part of the town, and at one time an active manufacturing point, are three churches. The Canal Railroad crosses the Connecticut Western Railroad at Simsbury village. Population about 2,000.

Alexander V. Griswold, presiding bishop of the Episcopal Church; Hon. Greene C. Bronson, chief justice of New York; and Anson G. Phelps, were natives of Simsbury.

West Hartford is relatively one of the wealthiest towns in the State. The surface of the town is gently undulating or level, except in the western portion, where it rises to a considerable elevation, known as Talcott Mountain, separating it from Avon. There are three churches and eight schoolhouses. The New York and New England, and the New York, New Haven and Hartford railroads pass through the southeastern corner of the town. The manufacture of pottery is carried on at this point. Population about 1,800. Assessed valuation $2,117,000. The average valuation of the real estate is nearly $63 per acre.

Nathan Perkins, D. D., a native of Lisbon, Conn., was settled over the Congregational Church in West Hartford from October, 1772, to his death in January, 1838. Among the eminent men born in West Hartford were Theodore Sedgwick, judge the Massachusetts Supreme Court; Harry Crosswell, politician, editor and clergyman; Noah Webster, the lexicographer; and Lemuel Haynes, the celebrated colored preacher.

The remaining towns of the county are South Windsor (population 1,900), Granby (1,400), Bloomfield (1,400), Plainville (1,900), Burlington (1,200), Rocky Hill (1,100), Avon (1,000), East Granby (750), Newington (950), Hartland (650), and Marlborough (400). Most of these towns are agricultural, but Newington, Granby, Plainville and South Windsor have some manufactures. Avon contains Talcott Mountain, upon whose summit, some 900 feet above the ordinary level of the Connecticut River, is a lake of great depth. Near this lake is a stone tower fifty-five feet high, from the summit of which an extensive view is obtained.

A part of Massachusetts about two miles square projects into the town of Granby; this territory was long in dispute, but was finally ceded to Massachusetts in 1804.

South Windsor is noted as the birth-place of the great metaphysician, Jonathan Edwards, who was born in a house on the river road, about one mile north of South Windsor village.

Leonidas L. Hamline, a celebrated Methodist bishop, was born in Burlington. Walter Forward, secretary of the U. S. Treasury from 1841 to 1843, was a native of East Granby.

HARTFORD, a port of entry, the capital of Connecticut and of Hartford County, is situated on the west bank of the Connecticut River, at the head of sloop navigation, fifty miles from its mouth. It is built for the most part on elevated ground, and its site is eminently picturesque and healthful. It was settled in 1635, by people directly from what is now Cambridge, Mass., and indirectly from Essex, England. It was first named Newtown, but in 1636 it was changed to Hartford. The latitude is 41 deg. 45 min. 59 sec.; longitude, 72 deg. 40 min. 45 sec. from Greenwich. The distance to Boston by rail is 124 miles, to New York, 110 miles; 26 miles to Springfield, 110 to the Hudson River, and 90 to Providence. The city was incorporated in 1784. Bushnell Park, containing forty acres, lies in the central part of the city.

The new capitol, unquestionably one of the most satisfactory public buildings in the country, occupies an elevated site in Bushnell Park, in full view of passengers arriving in the city by railroad.

The building, which was completed in 1879, at an expense, including the site, of more than $3,000,000, is in the modern secular Gothic style, at once massive and ornate, and is constructed of white marble quarried at East Canaan, Conn. In the centre of the building is a twelve-sided tower, surmounted by a dome, on which stands a colossal ideal figure in bronze, representing the Genius of Connecticut. The total height from the ground to the top of the crowning figure is 257 feet. The legislative halls are very elaborately finished in gold and colors, and the various offices are replete with every elegance and convenience.

In Bushnell Park are bronze statutes of Israel Putnam, by J. Q. A. Ward, and of Dr. Horace Wells, by T. H. Bartlett. The new buildings of Trinity College are situated about one mile south of the former location. The college grounds contain about eighty acres. Trinity College was founded in 1826, and was originally known as Washington College. The faculty is composed of fifteen members, the Rev. Thomas R. Pynchon, D. D., being president.

The public schools of Hartford are unexcelled by any in the country. The high school, which has acquired an excellent reputation, will occupy an imposing brick building, costing $250,000.

There are thirty-six churches in the city, many of them models of tasteful architecture.

Hartford is a centre of the insurance business of the country. The assets of the various insurance companies—fire, marine, life, accident, and steamboiler, are in the rough, $150,000,000. The capital, properly speaking, cannot be even roughly approximated, because most of them are mutuals, with no capital at all except the accumulations from business; the stock companies are a small minority, and their nominal capital bears little relation to their business. There are twelve banks with a capital of $11,000,000; and also eight savings banks and trust companies, with deposits of $15,000,000. Sixty-four manufacturing companies, representing a capital of $20,000,000, have their principal offices in this city, although many of their works are located elsewhere. Hartford has some of the largest manufacturing establishments in America, their productions finding a market in all parts of the world.

The main water supply of the city is from four reservoirs in West Hartford, which are fed from small streams and springs, having a total capacity of 1,200,000,000 gallons. There is also a pumping-engine on the river which supplies the lower part of the city in times of drouth. The city has a paid fire department, a fire-alarm telegraph, telephone company, and electric lights. Its railroad facilities are ample, it being on the through line from New York to Boston, and about midway between the two cities. The New York and New England Railroad has been completed to the Hudson River, giving Hartford a new route to the West. By its connections at Millerton and Canaan, the Connecticut Western line affords a convenient route to western Massachusetts and Albany, while the Connecticut Valley brings the seashore within easy reach. The Connecticut Central furnishes a route to Springfield. The New York, New Haven and Hartford line has extensive construction and repair shops at this point. During the season there is a daily line of steamers to New York.

The Opera House is one of the most commodious and best-appointed places of amusement in New England, its seating capacity being equal to that of the largest metropolitan theatres. There are also several large halls, well adapted for lectures, concerts, etc.

The population of Hartford in 1880 was 42,551. Assessed valuation, $46,992,000. Probably a fair estimate of the total wealth of the city, invested here or elsewhere, would be $175,000,000.

It has the reputation of being the wealthiest city according to its size of any in America.

NEW BRITAIN.—This growing manufacturing centre is situated about ten miles southwesterly from Hartford on the line of the New York and New England Railroad. It has been a city since 1870, and a borough since 1850. In the latter year it contained a population of 3,029. In 1880, 13,978. The present population is about 17,000. There are excellent water works owned by the people. Gas is $2.50 per thousand. There are over 1,800 dwelling houses and numerous large manufacturing establishments of world-wide reputation. The real estate is assessed at $5,000,000. Macadamized streets are a feature of the city. The State Normal School is located here; an illustration of the new building will be found on another page.

There are two national and one savings banks, three hotels, four newspapers, including a daily, an opera house, said to be the most beautiful of any in New England, outside the larger cities, and having superior acoustic properties. There are also a complete telegraph, telephone, and electric fire-alarm systems. A branch of the New York, New Haven and Hartford Railroad connects with the main line two miles away at Berlin. The city is about 130 feet higher than the track of the New York, New Haven and Hartford Railroad, and occupies a natural amphitheatre among the surrounding hills, a situation beautiful in the extreme. New Britain can be justly classed among the prosperous and pleasant places with which Connecticut abounds.

LITCHFIELD COUNTY.

The first white settlers of Litchfield County in the State of Connecticut, came from Stratford, on Long Island Sound, in the spring of 1673, and took possession of the fertile valley of the Pomperaug River, named after a chief of the Pootatuck tribe of Indians. Their emigration to this place resulted from ecclesiastical controversies between the Rev. Israel Chauncy and the Rev. Zechariah Walker, ministers of Stratford. At length Gov. Winthrop advised Mr. Walker and his church and people to remove to a tract of land which should be allotted to them for the settlement of a new town. In the spring of 1672, accordingly, the General Court having granted to Mr. Samuel Sherman, William Curtiss and others, liberty to erect a plantation at Pomperaug, subsequently named Woodbury, some of Mr. Walker's church-members came to the new town in the wilderness, and he, with most of his followers, removed there the next year. Following the Ousatonic River, formerly called the Pootatuck, till they came to a large river flowing into it from the north, they finally reached a sightly elevation overlooking the beautiful valley of their search.

The increase of population at the new settlement was rapid, and a few years after it commenced, in 1686, the town was incorporated by the General Court, the first in the county. The new town was represented in the General Court for the first time, in 1684, by Capt. John Minor and Lieut. Joseph Judson; while the first meeting-house built in the county was erected here in 1681.

Col. Robert Treat, Thomas Clark, Jonathan Baldwin, and 110 others, chiefly of Milford, Conn., by authority of the General Court at the October session in 1703, purchased of the Colony, at a cost of about $484, a tract of 84 square miles of land, called by the Indians Weantinogue, and situated in the southwestern part of the present county on the Housatonic River, which was at that time named New Milford by the General Court.

The first white person who came to this place, not a proprietor, was John Noble, in 1707, from Westfield, Mass. The town was incorporated in 1712, with a population of about seventy persons, the first minister settled here being the Rev. Daniel Boardman of Wethersfield, the same having been ordained over the Congregational Church and society in 1716. The second meeting-house built in the county was erected here in 1719. Col. John Read had studied for the ministry in his youth, and the first sermon the settlers heard here was preached by him. This town was first represented in the General Court, in 1725, by John Bostwick and Capt. Stephen Noble; and it may be remarked that the first bridge built across the Housatonic River was erected here in 1737.

When the first white people came to this county in 1672, the Indian tribes occupied the valley of the Housatonic River chiefly. Here they found congenial places for their wigwams and villages, and good opportunities for fishing, and for the culture of maize and beans, their chief vegetable food. At this time the Pootatucks were the most powerful tribe in the western part of the Colony, with clans in the present county at Nonnewaug, Bantam, Weantinogue, and on the Pomperaug River. Their principal seat, however, was on the northeast side of the Housatonic, just below the present line of this county, at Southbury, in New Haven County, with a central point at Woodbury. But this tribe soon commenced to migrate to the north and west, either to escape their enemies, or to find better fishing and hunting grounds, until they became absorbed in other tribes, and finally utterly disappeared. The chief Pomperaug was buried in Woodbury, as was his brother, a powwow, and the places are designated by heaps of stones. The last chief of the tribe was Mauquash, who died about the year 1758, and was buried in Woodbury.

About the year 1735, Weraumaug, or Raumaug, a Pootatuck chief, and a great councillor at the principal council-fires of his people, was visited, during his last sickness, by the Rev. Mr. Boardman, who took great pains to instruct him in the doctrines and principles of the Christian religion. The great sachem died shortly after, and was buried in the Indian ground a short distance from his residence. His grave is now plainly distinguishable. His tribe has entirely passed away, and the only traces of its existence are the arrow-heads, pipes, and other relics that are very often unearthed by the ploughshare, as is the case in other parts of the county where the Indians once lived.

This chief had his wigwam on a high bluff near the Great Falls on the Housatonic River, near the present village of New Milford. The abrupt bluff at these falls is now known as Lover's Leap. The most authentic tradition of the origin of the name is, that the lovely daughter of the chief had given her affections to a white settler, while her father had, with great care, selected a brave warrior to receive her hand, whom she, however, did not love. One fine day, the lovers remained on this cliff till long after sunset, and she successfully besought her father to allow her suitor to lodge at the palace that night, which so excited the jealousy of the warrior that, in the morning, he told her he would have the scalp of his rival before nightfall. The two lovers met again at the same romantic place, where they were found by the enraged warrior, and, to make a sure escape, with clasped hands they leaped from the giddy height into the surging waters.

A tribe of Schaghticoke Indians, occupying an interval on the west side of the Housatonic River, came under the influence of the Moravian missionaries about the year 1742, and Gideon, their chief, was the first convert, and was baptized in 1743, as were 150 others very soon afterwards, and many hundreds still later.

There are now about fifty who are considered as belonging to this tribe, scattered around in different towns, and are the only remnants of the red-men left in this county. Eunice, a grand-daughter of their renowned chief, died in 1860, at the great age of 103 years. They now possess about 300 acres of land situated on the Schaghticoke Mountain, and a fund of $5,000; and are under the charge of an overseer appointed annually by the District Court in the county.

At the time of the first settlement of Salisbury there was an Indian village at Weatog, the Indian name of the town, consisting of about seventy wigwams. Their trail through Cornwall to the Bantam clan at Litchfield was well known

Chaugum, the last man of a small tribe in New Hartford, lived till near the close of the last century; and his decendants in the female line kept up the council-fires till quite recently. The descendants of his married daughter are the only representatives of the race in Winchester and Barkhamstead.

The lands of this county were generally purchased of the Indians by the settlers, together with the Colony title, as appears by the names of the chiefs appended to deeds on the records of many, if not all, of the earlier settled towns. The Indians were friendly to the first settlers, and supplied them with provisions in many instances, and defended them from hostile attacks.

The next settlement by whites in the dense western woods of the county was at Bantam in 1720, by a grant from the Colony to John Marsh of Hartford, and John Buel of Lebanon, and fifty-seven associates, of a tract of land ten miles square, and named Litchfield by the General Court in 1719, and incorporated a town in 1724. None of this tract appears to have been purchased of the Indians, and, in consequence, the early settlers had some experience of the ferocious native character of the red man.

Captain John Griswold, in 1722, was suddenly rushed upon, pinioned, and carried far away into the thick woods. While his enemies were asleep around a fire, however, he disengaged himself, and seized their guns, his arms still pinioned, and made his escape safely to his home. That same year, Joseph Harris, while at work in the woods, was attacked and shot by the Indians. There was a monument erected to his memory in 1830, in the town, not only to perpetuate his name as a martyred citizen, but to record the first death among the early settlers.

Rev. Timothy Collins was ordained the first minister of the people here in 1723, and the first house of worship, the third in the county, was finished in 1726.

About the time that Litchfield was settled, three families—one English, and the other two Dutch—settled at Weatog, or Salisbury, in 1720. In 1740, eleven English and five Dutch families settled in different parts of the town. In 1732, most of the township was surveyed. It was sold by the Colony at Hartford in 1737, and the charter was given in 1745. The town took its name from a man named Salisbury, who lived in about the centre of the purchase. The Rev. Mr. Lee was their first settled minister, and a meeting-house was built about 1748. In this house there were two watch-towers, with sentries placed in them on Sundays, to guard against the Indians. These first settlers came from the manor of Livingston, in the Colony of New York.

Harwinton, which derived its name from Hartford, Windsor and Farmington, was settled in 1731, was named a town in 1732, and was incorporated by the General Court in 1737. Their first minister was the Rev. Andrew Bartholomew, who was ordained about 1736. John Watson and others came from Hartford in 1733, and settled at New Hartford, which was named and incorporated a town that year. The Rev. Jonathan Marsh, their first minister, was ordained in 1739. It was an evergreen region, where there were extensive forests, called the "Green Woods." One of the seven companies of the inhabitants of Windsor that bought townships in 1732 was the Torrington Company named after a hamlet in Devonshire, England. The patentees were Matthew Allyn, Roger Wolcott and Samuel Mather, Esqrs. A survey of the town was made in 1734, and there were three divisions of land. The last one was completed in 1750, in which two hundred and twenty acres were appropriated for schools. Ebenezer Lyman, Jr., was the first permanent settler of the town, and came from Durham about the year 1737. Torrington was made a town in 1740; and, becoming an ecclesiastical society, the Rev. Nathaniel Roberts was ordained in 1741, when there were but fourteen families in the place. Wolcottville may be said to have been commenced in 1751, when Amos Wilson purchased of the town the mill privilege on the west branch of the Naugatuck River. Its great business prosperity may be said to date from about 1813, when manufacturing first began.

A considerable area of territory on the Housatonic River was sold at auction at New London in 1738, and settled by John Franklin and others. The town was named Canaan by the General Court that year, and incorporated in 1739. Their first clergyman was the Rev. Elisha Webster, ordained in 1740. The tract of land known as Kent was sold in 1738, and settled that year by Mr. Platt and others from Colchester, Mr. Comstock from Franklin, and Mr. Slausen and others from Norwalk. The town was named in 1738, and incorporated the following year. The first minister was the Rev. Cyrus Marsh. Goshen was settled, named and incorporated in 1738. The Rev. Stephen Heaton was their first minister. The territory of Sharon was purchased in 1738, and settled and incorporated the following year. The first settler was Daniel Jackson, from New Milford. In 1740, thirteen families moved into Cornwall from Massachusetts, and from Colchester and Litchfield in this State. It was named in 1738, and incorporated two years afterward. The Rev. Solomon Palmer was their first minister. Settlers from Windsor came to Norfolk in 1744. When incorporated, in 1758, there were thirty-seven families within its limits. The Rev. Ammi R. Robbins was their first pastor. The first settler in the present town of Barkhamsted came in 1746, and was the sole inhabitant for more than ten years. The town was incorporated 1779. The Rev. Ozias Eels was their first minister.

Winchester was incorporated in 1771, and the next year the Rev. Joshua Knapp was ordained minister. Ebenezer and Joseph Preston, and Adam Mott, from Windsor, were the first settlers. In 1799, there were only about twenty families within the present limits of Winsted. In 1832, the west village was incorporated as the borough of Clifton. In 1858, the two sections of Winsted became united, and the place has since been known as Winsted.

The first settlers of Colebrook came there in 1765, and others soon followed. The town was organized in 1786, and the Rev. Jonathan Edwards, son of the renowned minister of that name, was their first pastor.

The ecclesiastical society of Northbury was organized in Waterbury, New Haven County, in 1739, and was organized a town by the assembly in 1795, named Plymouth, and annexed to this county. The first settlement in Plymouth was made in the centre of the new town of Thomaston. In 1728, Henry Cook came there with a family and settled. The first child born in Plymouth was Samuel How.

The first settlement in Waterbury was in Wooster Swamp, as Thomaston and the western part of Plymouth were called. Many settlers preferring to locate on higher land up the river, above the fogs and malaria of the swamp west of the river, the Northbury community was established. Roxbury was created a town in 1801, and taken from Woodbury; and Bridgewater Society was taken from New Milford and made a town in 1856. Two years later, North Canaan was separated from Canaan. Morris, from the town of Litchfield, was incorporated in 1859; and the twenty-sixth and last town in the county was taken from Plymouth, made a town, and named Thomaston, in 1875.

The increase of population and rapid colonization were such that in the year 1751, after about ten years of agitation in town meetings and in the assembly, a new county was created and named Litchfield, with Litchfield as the shire town. The territorial area was the same as at present, with the exception of the towns of Hartland and Southbury, and a portion of Brookfield, all of which then belonged to the county. Watertown and Plymouth, with Thomaston, have since been annexed. William Preston, Esq., of Woodbury, was the first chief justice; Isaac Baldwin, Esq., first clerk. Samuel Pettibone, Esq., of Goshen, was chosen king's attorney, and Oliver, Walcott, Esq., sheriff. For nine years from 1774, the valley of Wyoming, Pa., belonged to this county.

It was declared by a convention held in this county February 11, 1776, and represented by most of the towns, that the Stamp Act was unconstitutional, null and void, and that business should go on as usual; and town meetings were held quite frequently to consider the public safety. When the war cloud burst, Litchfield County was thoroughly aroused for any emergency. At the time of the Boston alarm, September 3, 1774, quite a number of soldiers went from Woodbury, where there was the most population, and joined companies from other towns. Col. Ethan Allen, claimed to have been born in three towns in the county, and at all events to have been a native of this county, and Col. Seth Warner, a native of Roxbury, with nearly 100 volunteers, assisted in the capture of Fort Ticonderoga May 10, 1775. Col. Hinman, of Woodbury, commanded 1,000 men sent to garrison this fort and Crown Point. After the Lexington alarm a full company was sent from Woodbury. The thirteenth regiment of militia was formed from that town, New Milford and Kent, at the commencement of the war. By an order of June 10, 1776, a draft was ordered, which, with former calls, had made such a drain upon the laborers that there was hardly sufficient provision to supply the people during the winter. Upon a sudden call for troops at Danbury in April, 1777, the militia of this county marched to the scene of conflict. Soldiers from this county participated in the battle of Bennington in 1777, under Col. Seth Warner, and others fought at Saratoga and White Plains. Woodbury being the oldest and largest town in the county, with a population of 5,313 in 1774, was represented on all the battle-fields of 1777. There were eight companies of militia in the town ready to rally at a moment's warning. New Milford furnished the next largest quota of men for the war. The old Indian warrior, Tom Warrups, a Schaghticoke, and a resident of Cornwall in his early life, participated in the battle of Long Island. Gen. John Sedgwick, of Cornwall, Cols. Canfield and Starr, of New Milford, Tallmadge, of Litchfield, and many others, were brave officers in the war.

There were, however, some Tories within the borders of the county; and committees of inspection were formed, who summoned before them those who were suspected of disloyalty to the cause of liberty. The Rev. John R. Marshal, of Woodbury, was one of these, and was put on the limits. The riflemen, passing through the county, took a man in New Milford, made him walk before them twenty miles, and carry one of his geese; they then made him pluck his goose, and, after tarring and feathering him, drummed him out of the company, and required him to kneel and thank them for their lenity.

Party spirit ran so high in this county during the war of 1812, and the administration at Washington met with such opposition from the State-rights or Federalist party, that enlistments into the regular army were greatly discouraged; and the conflict between the national and State governments, as to which should have the command of the drafted militia, caused riots in some places in the county, where efforts were made to fling the State flag to the breeze, and to cut down the liberty poles flying the stars and stripes. This opposition caused Congress to refuse the necessary appropriations and supplies for the maintenance of the militia of Massachusetts and Connecticut for the year 1814, thus forcing these States to defend their own coasts from invasion, which resulted in the Hartford Convention of December, 1814, of which the Hon. Nathaniel Smith, of Woodbury, and others, of the most distinguished and upright characters were members. The whole number of men who served in the war from this county was about 2,000.

At the commencement of the late Rebellion volunteer companies were immediately formed at Winsted and the other large towns in the county, which soon rendezvoused at New Haven. During the war the county furnished nearly 4,000 men. The nineteenth regiment, enlisted principally in this county, and reorganized into the second heavy artillery in November, 1863, experienced some very severe service in the Army of the Potomac; and it was at the head of the assault at Cold Harbor, Va., June 1, 1864, that its gallant commander, Col. Elisha S. Kellogg, lost his life.

A short time after the close of the Revolutionary war in 1784, the first law school of any note in the United States was founded in the town of Litchfield. Its projector was Tapping Reeve, of Long Island, a brother-in-law of Aaron Burr. There were then no professors of law connected with any American college, nor was the science treated as a liberal one. Judge Reeve, after having conducted the school from the commencement until his appointment to the bench of the Supreme Court of the State in 1798, then invited James Gould, Esq., a graduate of Yale College, who was in the practice of law at Litchfield, to take part in the instruction of the school. These gentlemen carried it on together, as partners, for a period of twenty-two years, when, on account of advanced age, Judge Reeve retired. Judge Gould continued the school until a few years before his death, when he associated with himself Jabez W. Huntington, afterwards a United States senator and Judge of the Supreme Court of the State. Prior to 1833 there had been educated at this school men from all parts of the county, more than one thousand in all, and as many as one hundred and eighty-three from the Southern States. They numbered fifteen United States senators, five cabinet officers, ten governors of States, fifty members of Congress, forty judges of the highest State courts, and two judges of the Supreme Court of the United States. This long list embraced the names of John C. Calhoun, of South Carolina, John M. Clayton, of Delaware, John Y. Mason, of Virginia, Judge Levi Woodbury, Marcus Morton, and many others of national renown. The school was discontinued in 1833.

As soon as the first settlement of towns in the county commenced, and a minister had been settled, attention was turned to the common schools. The ancient school-house in this county was a very rude affair, consisting of but one room, with but little furniture. The writing-desks fronted inward from the sides of the house, and there was a large shelf in one corner for the use of the scholars. The teacher's table was made of rough boards. The seats for the larger scholars were made of slabs supported with three or four legs of round wood.

Schools were carried on in the earlier times entirely under the district system. Afterwards for very many years they were managed under the jurisdiction of school societies, formed from towns and parts of towns. In 1869 the schools were made free by a general law, and since that time, in this county, the attendance and appropriations have greatly increased. There has been more uniformity of text-books; better school-houses have been erected; the terms have been lengthened; all pay their share of the taxes; while the improvements in the schools over the old method have been very great. There are now in this county 277 districts, and 275 schools, employing 625 teachers. Among the first of the academies established in the county was one in the town of Morris—then Litchfield—in 1790, by James Morris. Afterwards two were opened in the town of Sharon; and there have been many others since those early times. The first female seminary established at Litchfield, in 1792, was the resort of young ladies from all parts of the country for more than forty years. The first foreign mission school in this country was established in the county, at Cornwall, in 1817, to educate foreign youth to become missionaries, schoolmasters, interpreters and physicians among heathen nations. A farm was purchased and suitable buildings were erected; but the school was abandoned in 1827, because, after this time, the heathen could be educated at home, and also because of local opposition caused by two Cherokee Indians marrying respectable white girls of the town.

The Connecticut School for Imbeciles, located in Salisbury, was incorporated in 1861.

For nearly seventy years after the first settlement of the county, the only churches within its limits were of the Congregational order, the result of an ecclesiastical statute of the Colony that no church administration should be set up contrary to the order already established; but finally, in 1708, and afterwards, acts of toleration were passed, till all religious denominations were put upon the same common ground of equality, although all were for some time taxed to support the regular order. The oldest church in the county of the established order is in Woodbury, and was organized in 1670, at Stratford; and the next oldest one is in New Milford, and was organized in 1716. The church at Litchfield was organized in 1721; the church at Bethlehem in 1739; and the churches at Cornwall, Goshen and Sharon in 1740; and there are now forty-one churches of this order in the county.

The first Episcopal parish in the county was organized by the Rev. Mr. Beach of Newton, in 1740. There are now twenty-five parishes.

The first of the Baptist churches in the county were in New Milford and Colebrook, about the year 1788, when a church was organized in the first-named town. There are very few churches of this denomination in the county at the present time.

In 1790 a circuit of the Methodist Episcopal Church was formed at Litchfield, which then probably comprised the whole county and more, and Jesse Lee was appointed elder by the New England Conference. The circuit was traveled at this time by Samuel Wigton, Henry Christie and Freeborn Garritson. There was but little sympathy, however, between the Congregational and Methodist denominations in the county in these early days. The circuit preacher discoursed against pitch-pipes, steeples, ribbons and all gay equipages, to say nothing of the "five points" of Calvinism. The denomination during the nearly ninety years of its existence in the county, has, in number and membership, increased with great rapidity.

The first Roman Catholic church in the county is believed to have been erected at Cornwall about the year 1850, though there is no church there now. Public worship was instituted in Winsted in 1851 by the Rev. James Lynch; and in 1852, the Rev. Thomas Quinn commenced the erection of St. Joseph's Catholic Church, and entered on his pastoral duties. The Rev. Thomas Hendricken, since bishop of Rhode Island, came here in 1854; and there are now five churches in the county.

This county is the only section of the State in which rich and productive iron mines are found. The ore is found in vast beds, principally in connection with mica slate, and exists in the towns of Sharon, Salisbury and Kent. The oldest iron mine is the Old Ore Hill in the town of Salisbury, and it has been worked over 150 years, and since the year 1732. The site of this mine was purchased by a man named Bissell, several years before the town was incorporated. When this mine was first opened, Thomas Lamb bought fifty acres of land in the southeast part of the town, at Lime Rock on Salmon River, and erected the first forge in the county at that place as early as the year 1734. In 1762 Col. Ethan Allen, of Ticonderoga fame, Samuel Forbes and others, built the first blast-furnace in the county. During the Revolutionary war this property was taken possession of by the State; and Col. Joshua Porter having been appointed agent, large quantities of cannon, cannon balls, shot and shells were manufactured for the government. John Jay and Gouverneur Morris, agents of Congress, came here frequently at this time to oversee the casting and proofs of the cannon. The war ships "Constitution" and "Old Ironsides" and the New York Battery were armed with the Salisbury cannon; and this iron has been used since the war in the manufacture of guns and anchors for the navy, and chain cables, and has also furnished material for the uses of the government armories.

The never-failing resources of the mine, the facilities and means of smelting the ore, with its rich quality of forty per cent. of pig iron, have brought it into general demand for manufacturing purposes. Forty years ago there were in Salisbury four blast-furnaces, five forges, two puddling establishments, one anchor-shop and two cupolas for castings. This mine covers an area of several acres, and there are six principal pits. For the first forty years of this century the average amount of ore taken from this bed annually was 5,000 tons; and its bottom has not been reached. There are also important iron mines in Sharon and Kent. Salisbury iron was first used in 1840 for railroad purposes. Its great tensile strength, with its superior chilling properties, soon led to the manufacture of car-wheels at Salisbury, which are now in general use, not only in the United States, but in most civilized nations.

Spathic iron-ore, commonly known as silver steel, is found in this county at Mine Hill in Roxbury, on the eastern line of New Milford, in a mountain about 350 feet high, at the base of which runs the Shepaug River; and it is the most remarkable deposit of the kind in the United States. The mine, however, has never been profitably worked.

The first mill in the county was built in Woodbury in 1674, for grinding flour, the mortar and pestle having been used for pounding the grain prior to this time. Fifty years since there were thirty-four flour mills in the county. The first wheelwright was Samuel Munn, who built a cart and cart-wheels for the Rev. Mr. Walker of Woodbury, in 1688; and the business of making coaches and wagons was carried on in the county after their invention, till there were as many as forty of these establishments. In 1700, forty-four inhabitants of Woodbury gave Abraham Fulford ten acres of and to come there and comb wool, and weave and full cloth, and he accepted the offer. At this early period some of the outer clothing of the people was made of skins of deer and other animals; and in 1677, very large wooden shoes were made and used by the settlers. The first blacksmith came to this county in 1708, and he was given ten acres of land to remain and carry on the business. The tannery was one of the earliest industrial establishments of the county. Long since there have been as many as fifty of these, almost every town having its place for tanning leather. Boots and shoes were made by the shoemaker, who, "whipping the cat," went around to the houses with his own tools and wax, depending upon his customers for leather, shoe-thread, and pegs. The saw and shingle mill were a very early necessity to the settlers, and there were as many as nineteen in the county at one time; but they have begun to disappear somewhat since the days of railroads. Over 2,300,000 bricks were made annually in the county thirty-seven years ago; and there were seventeen hat factories and as many furniture establishments. Sixty years ago there were a very large number of manufactories of distilled spirits; 169 in the county, and twenty-six in New Milford alone. Soon after the commencement of this century a discovery was made in the latter place of porcelain clay by a goldsmith. The bed covers an area of about ten acres. Mr. Lyman Hine commenced the making of the common porcelain furnace and fire brick about the year 1828; and these articles for stoves, furnace-linings in brass-kettle establishments, and puddling furnaces, enjoyed a deservedly high reputation. From an early date, magnesian lime has been burnt from quarries in the county.

In 1792, Jenks & Boyd erected the first establishment at Winsted, for welding, drawing, and plating the scythe by water-power under trip-hammers, and grinding it on geared stones; which before had been made by hand, wrought in smiths' shops, and ground on stones turned by hand. Before the year 1800, the first cementing steel-furnace in the county was built at Colebrook by the Rockwell Brothers.

The making of axes as a distinct trade was first commenced in 1804; and about the year 1828, a factory was established at Winsted. The business of clockmaking commenced in a very small way at Thomaston, about the time Plymouth was annexed to the county. Eli Terry established himself at Plymouth, and commenced making the old hang-up wood clock with a foot-lathe, knife, and other hand-tools, and peddled them himself on horseback. In 1803, he had a shop with water-power; and he started a shop at Hoadleyville, and made 4,000 clocks in two years. In 1807, Riley Whiting commenced making wood clocks at Winsted, and made numerous improvements in them and in clock-cases. The manufacture of cutlery was commenced at Salisbury, and in 1852, at Winsted. The production of pins first began in the county at Winsted in 1852, and of plated-ware, coffin trimmings, and carriage-springs, within the past fifteen years. The manufacture of vegetable-ivory buttons, with new and greatly improved machinery for mottling and coloring, commenced in the county at New Milford about twelve years ago. In 1834, the first effort to make brass kettles in America, by the battery process, began at Wolcottville. The rolling process succeeded this in 1842. Meantime, with these new and greatly increased developments of manufacturing on the lines mentioned, there has been a corresponding decline in certain other branches; notably in the manufacture of leather, and of woollen goods.

From the time of the first settlement of the county when it was a dense forest of white oak, chestnut, and hickory, the general occupation of the people has been that of agriculture. The nature of the soil is such as to be quite well adapted to this, and particularly to the growth of Indian corn, wheat, rye, and oats. Turnips, beans and pumpkins were the principal vegetables; and, for the first hundred years, potatoes were comparatively unknown. The cattle were generally small, brindle and brown colors being favorites, and the sheep were long-legged and hardy, with thin, coarse wool. The wood plow, wooden-tooth harrow, and forks too heavy almost for men to lift, were samples of the farming tools of those early times, and the kitchen stove was unknown for years. Noxious weeds, like the Canada thistle, had not been heard of, and most of the insect pests of the present day were unknown, although as late as 1791 and the year after the orchards in some parts of the county, on all kinds of light, dry soil, were ravaged by the canker-worm. The early settlers were for many years greatly harassed by the depredations of wild beasts, ravaging their crops and flocks and putting themselves sometimes in personal peril. Wolves abounded as late as 1786 and wolf-hunts were very common sports in the Indian-summer days. Bears and panthers were common also in those early times, and were not unfrequently shot by the settlers.

The activities of agriculture, as well as of every other kind of business, were at one time materially impeded by the serious difficulties in the way of intercourse with the market towns—the roads being generally over steep hills and along miry and untrodden bottoms, and where the snow, in the winter, lay deep and drifted, while the means of communication were of the most primitive and incommodious character. The farmer saw but little money in those days, taking their farm products annually to the trader at the distant village and being supplied, in return, with whatever their necessities demanded.

Farming continued to be carried on in this primitive way, to a great extent, for more than 150 years after the settlement of the county—indeed until the railroad penetrated our borders, and the era of labor-saving tools and machines was introduced, and the people began to organize societies and clubs for the diffusion of agricultural and horticultural knowledge. These symbols of a more progressive civilization have, meanwhile, almost if not quite revolutionized the principles of farming. In 1846 T. L. Hart and six others met and organized the farmers' club in Cornwall. Meetings were held quite often, addresses delivered, and the public mind thus became better informed on the science of farming, and other organizations of the kind have since been formed in the county. In 1851, the Litchfield County Agricultural Association was incorporated. Fairs have been held since that time annually at the county seat. In 1859 the Union Agricultural Society was organized at Canaan, and the next year societies were incorporated at New Milford and Woodbury; and a like society has been formed in Torrington.

In 1849, it is believed, the first crop of tobacco was raised in the county to any extent for the market. At present it is grown quite extensively, and there is probably an annual average production of 1,800,000 pounds.

In 1784 the first newspaper was established in the county. This paper, the "Weekly Monitor," was published at Litchfield by Thos. Collins for many years. In 1824 the "Litchfield Enquirer" was established; and for about thirty years it was the principal paper in the country. The "Winsted Herald," established in 1853, has held a leading position among the influential papers of the State.

There are now nine newspapers of first-class character published in the county: "Winsted Press," "Herald," "Argus," and "Advocate" (the latter monthly), "Torrington Register," "Thomaston Express," "Connecticut Western (Canaan) News," "New Hartford Tribune," and "Litchfield Enquirer."

As early as 1789, thirty-six persons signed a temperance pledge in the county, agreeing to discard the use of distilled liquors; and among the number were Ephraim Kirby, Moses Seymour and Tapping Reeve. It is believed that the first modern temperance society was formed in the county at Salisbury, among the iron laborers. The Rev. Dr. Porter delivered temperance lectures in Washington in 1806, and Dr. Lyman Beecher delivered discourses and lectures on the same subject about 1812, and probably earlier, at Litchfield. Since then, societies to promote the cause of temperance have been very generally formed in the county; and a society was organized at Torrington as early as 1827.

August 13 and 14, 1851, the one hundredth anniversary of the organization of the county, was observed at Litchfield with appropriate ceremonies. An oration by the Hon. Samuel Church, LL.D., Chief Justice of the Supreme Court; a poem by the Rev. John Pierpont, LL.D., of Medford, Mass.; a sermon by Rev. Horace Bushnell, D. D., of Hartford; and speeches by Hon. D. S. Dickinson, of New

York, and many others, were among the interesting features of the occasion.

Towards the close of the last century, the legislature authorized the construction of turnpike roads, with power to erect gates at fixed distances, and to collect tolls from travelers for the maintenance of the road, some of which yielded very good dividends. From the year 1797, for a period of about forty years, there were some twenty-three charters of this character granted by the legislature for these roads; and no portion of the State was more improved by them than this county.

The Housatonic Railroad Company, incorporated in 1836, built the first railroad that was operated in the county. It was completed to New Milford in the spring of 1840, and the first train of cars ran into that place in February of that year. The track was made of wood and ties laid upon sleepers, with thick strap-iron, spiked down, upon which the wheels ran; and many fatal accidents occurred by the ends of the iron becoming loose and springing up and shooting over the wheels, when in motion, through the floor of the cars, when they were called "snake heads." The Naugatuck Railroad, running from Bridgeport to Winsted, was the second built in the county, and was incorporated in 1845. Within twelve years a branch road has been built from Waterbury to Watertown. The new impetus this road gave to manufactures in Winsted, Wolcottville, Thomaston and Plymouth was very marked. The Hartford, Providence and Fishkill Railroad Company was first incorporated in 1849. The Connecticut Western Railroad Company was chartered in 1866. The first passenger train passed over the road from Hartford to Millerton, on the Harlem road in New York, Dec. 21, 1871. In 1866, the Shepaug Valley Railroad Company was incorporated, to run from Litchfield to some point on the Housatonic road; and in December, 1872, trains were making regular trips over the whole line.

Until the beginning of the present century, the people of the county had carried on their business transactions without the aid of any banking institution; but, upon the incorporation of the Phœnix Bank of Hartford, in 1814, and within six months after it commenced to discount, a branch bank was started at Litchfield for the purpose of discount and deposit. The Iron Bank was established at Canaan in 1847, and was the first regular chartered bank in the county. All the banks in the county went into business under the national banking law during the late war, and have since been eminently prosperous.

The courts in the county have generally remained unchanged in the general organization, the Superior and Supreme courts sitting at stated times at the county town.

Towns.

Winchester and the Borough of Winsted.—The interval lands along the streams of this town are shut in by high hills and mountain ridges. The highest elevation is in the old Winchester parish, where mountains in Massachusetts and New York can be seen. The town is situated in the greenwoods district of the county, thirty-five miles by rail from Hartford. Long Lake, extending from the Torrington line northerly about three and one-half miles, is the largest body of water. Its surface is 150 feet above the centre of Winsted village near by. Still and Mad rivers are the principal streams. Lake Stream, running from the lake through a wild and narrow ravine into Mad River, furnishes a water-supply for many factories.

Winsted, situated on Lake Stream, Mad and Still rivers, is the largest place in population, and in the extent of its industrial interests, in the county, and contains about 5,500 inhabitants. These three streams afford a great supply of water-power, which is used extensively for manufacturing purposes; there being, on Mad River, one dam to about every twenty rods in its course through the borough. A very large variety of establishments are in successful operation, using both steam and water power. Among the manufactures are scythes and agricultural implements, brass clocks and cases, carriages, springs, undertaker's hardware and furnishing goods, bar-iron, railroad axles, pocket cutlery, pins, hardware and carpenter's tools, spool silk, machine screws, castings, mill gearing and pulleys, leather, etc. There are five churches, a Catholic literary and theological seminary, and a Catholic academy for young ladies, with a parochial school and convent. The town has three national banking institutions and two savings banks. Music Hall, a capacious brick and iron structure, contains a fine public hall. Another hall, lately constructed, is used for town and borough purposes. Water for extinguishing fires, and for domestic purposes, is obtained from Long Lake. Park place, a beautiful green, is adorned with evergreens, maples, and elms.

James Boyd, a man of indomitable energy and perfect integrity — who, with his partner and brother-in-law, Benjamin Jenkins, was the pioneer manufacturer of the place—died February 1, 1849, aged seventy-eight. Solomon Rockwell, Esq., one of the founders of Winsted, and an active promoter of its business interests, died August 1, 1838, in the seventy-fifth year of his age. Wm. S. Holabird, a lawyer by profession, was U. S. district attorney for four years, and lieutenant governor in 1842 and 1844. He died May 22, 1855, at the age of sixty-one. Other prominent natives are Gideon Hall (1808–67,) a judge of the Superior Court; John Boyd (1799–), for three years secretary of state; George Dudley, Roland Hitchcock, and F. D. Fyler.

New Milford, one of the most important towns in the county in the diversity of its industrial interests, is situated in the south-western part of the county, ninety miles by rail from Hartford. It has a population of about 4,000, and is the largest town in the county. The township is mountainous, and its agricultural interests predominate largely in the production of milk and tobacco.

The principal centres of intercourse outside of the village are at Northville on the Aspetuck River, Gaylordsville and Merwinsville in the north part of the town on the Housatonic, and Lanesville in the south part on Still River, were there is the best water-power in the town.

The town has nine religious organizations, eighteen public schools and one academy. One national and one savings bank accommodate the business of the locality.

The Housatonic Agricultural Society occupies fine grounds near the village. Agriculture is not the entire occupation of the inhabitants, there being important manufactures of manila and wrapping paper, vegetable-ivory buttons, plough castings, iron fences and castings, refrigerators, cigars and fire brick.

The village is one of the most beautiful and thriving in New England, having most of the conveniences of a city organization. There are two weekly newspapers published here. There are also a number of tobacco warehouses in the village, with several outside, employing about four hundred men in the season of assorting and packing. There is an elevator in the village, and the business of supplying the surrounding towns with all kinds of grain, flour and feed, shipped from the West, is extensively carried on. The Housatonic R. R. runs through the town. More business is done from this point than at any other in the county on the road. The village is supplied with water from a reservoir on Cross Brook. Concrete walks, some of them eight feet wide, have been laid in the village. There are some fine buildings and residences in the place, including the two bank buildings and the town hall, the latter standing on the spot where Roger Sherman once resided, and being a fine brick building, with high red sandstone basement, erected at a cost of about $45,000.

Rev. Nathaniel Taylor, born Aug 27, 1722, and a graduate of Yale, was ordained second pastor of the New Milford Church in June, 1748. During his ministry he prepared many young men for college. He died here Dec. 9, 1800, after having been ordained fifty-two years. He was chaplain of a Connecticut regiment at Ticonderoga and Crown Point in 1759.

Elijah Boardman, a successful merchant, was a United States Senator at the time of his death. August 18, 1823. His brother, Hon. David S. Boardman, a graduate of Yale in 1793, and chief justice of the county court, died December 2, 1864, in the ninety-sixth year of his age.

Roger Sherman, signer of the Declaration of Independence, came to New Milford on foot from Massachusetts, with his shoemaking tools on his back, in 1743, when he was twenty-two years of age. He was clerk of the first ecclesiastical society, and a deacon of the church for several years. He was admitted to the bar in 1754, and removed to New Haven in 1761.

Orange Merwin, one of the most influential men of the town, and at one time member of Congress, died September 4, 1853.

Perry Smith, a United States Senator during the administrations of Jackson and Van Buren, died in 1852, at the age of sixty-nine years.

David C. Sandford, a native of the town, born in 1798, and at the time of his death in 1864, a judge of the Supreme Court of Errors, was long a prominent and influential man.

George Taylor, M. D., Rev. Charles G. Acly, a retired Episcopal clergyman, and Hon. A. B. Mygatt, United States bank examiner for Rhode Island and Connecticut, are among the distinguished and honored residents of the town.

Torrington, one of the most regularly laid-out townships in the county, with a hilly surface and fertile soil, is forty-five miles from Hartford. The water-power is principally on the east and west branches of the Naugatuck River. The business centres are the Hollow, Newfield, Torringford, Wrightville, Burrville, Daytonville, and Torrington, formerly Wolcottville, in the extreme southern part of the town. The latter is a place of about 2,200 inhabitants, and one of the most important manufacturing centres in the county. The manufacturing industries are varied, and among the goods produced are hardware, notions, American scissors, upholsterers' brass and iron goods; black doeskins; ribbed and diagonal goods are also produced. Rolled and sheet brass and copper, for cartridges especially, brass, copper, and German-silver ware are extensively manufactured. The last-mentioned manufactures are carried on in buildings covering not less than three acres. Two hundred and fifty men are employed here, and the annual aggregate of the business amounts to about $1,250,000.

Sewing-machine needles for the Wheeler and Wilson Company are also made. Skates, leather goods, iron and brass ferrules, employ about one hundred men. Carriage and Furniture establishments are in successful operation. There are seven churches in the town, a savings bank and a weekly newspaper. A beautiful granite Congregational church edifice has been erected at Torrington at a cost of $32,000. The Naugatuck Railroad runs through the town. This place is supplied with water from Mine Brook. The reservoir has an area of five and one-half acres of surface, capable of holding 16,000,000 gallons of water. The whole population of the town, including Torrington, is about 3,500.

Prominent among the notable characters connected with Torrington in times past may be mentioned General Russel C. Abernethy, merchant, manufacturer and general of State militia; Mr. Owen Brown, a tanner, and the father of John Brown of Kansas and Harper's Ferry (Va.) fame, who was also born in Torrington in 1800; Dr. Samuel Wodward (November 8, 1750—January 26, 1835), a beloved physician, and an exceptionally noble man; Rev. Samuel J. Mills (May 17, 1751—May 11, 1833), pastor of the Torringford church for fifty years, and who to rare humor and deep sensibility united great strength of intellect and originality of mind; William Batelle, Esq., an old-time successful merchant, and Israel Coe, who established the battery manufacture of brass kettles at Wolcottville, the first of the kind in the county, and who was justice of the peace after he was eighty years old. Hon. Lyman W. Coe is actively identified with the interests of the town.

Salisbury is of importance as being the locality of the celebrated iron of that name, and is also one of the best agricultural towns in the county. The northwestern town in the State, having the Housatonic River as its eastern boundary, it has an area of about fifty-eight square miles. The population is about 3,700. It has five churches, three graded and several district schools. At Lakeville is a well-managed school for imbeciles. Lakes Washining and Washinee are the largest and most beautiful sheets of water in the town. The business centres are at Salisbury, Lakeville, Lime Rock and Falls Village; the latter on the Housatonic River, where the extensive building and repair shops of the Housatonic Railroad Company are located. The business of manufacturing cast-iron car-wheels is carried on here extensively. The foundry is at Lime Rock, and about 10,000 railroad wheels are produced annually. There are about six hundred men employed at the furnaces and the wheel factory. There are extensive grounds at Falls Village, used for agricultural fairs. The Connecticut Western Railroad runs through the town.

Among the notables of Salisbury have been William Ray, a naval officer and author; Samuel Church, LL.D. (1785—1854), an eminent jurist; Rev. Jonathan Lee (1718-88), pastor in the town for forty-five years; Gen. Elisha Sterling, a distinguished lawyer; and Colonel Elisha Sheldon, a Revolutionary officer.

Litchfield, the shire town of the county, is fifty-eight miles from Hartford, by rail, and has a population of about 3,500. The township is on high land, with strong soil. Bantam Lake, the largest body of water in the county, is situated partly in this town. The village commands a beautiful and extensive prospect, and has a fine park in the centre, in which stands a monument to commemorate the lives of those who fell in the late war. The prominent buildings are the old Court-house, with its turret and bell; the jail, and a Congregational church edifice costing about $30,000. With its beautiful shade trees, the village, at present, is a most delightful resort for those in quest of pleasure and recreation. The city of New York, distant about one hundred and fifteen miles by rail, is reached by the Norwalk, Housatonic, Shepaug and Naugatuck railroads. The churches in the town are six in number; and there are two banks, one newspaper, and twenty public schools. Manufacturing is carried on to a greater or less extent at East Litchfield, Bantam Falls, Milton and Northfield.

Among the eminent men of Litchfield have been Oliver Wolcott (1726-97), the commander of a company in the French war, first sheriff of the county, delegate to Congress in 1775, and signer of the Declaration of Independence, and governor of the State at the time of his death; Benjamin Tallmadge (1754-1835), a colonel in the Revolutionary war, serving with distinction in many battles, several times a representative in Congress, and instrumental in causing the capture of Maj. Andre; Gen. Uriah Tracy (1755-1807), congressman and U. S. senator; Hon. O. S. Seymour, LL.D., former member of Congress and chief justice of the State; George C. Woodruff, formerly a member of Congress; Gideon H. Hollister, author of a standard history of Connecticut; and Charles B. Andrews, late governor of the State.

New Hartford is a thriving mountainous town, containing about 3,500 inhabitants, and having five churches. There are in the place several saw-mills, while heavy duck and cotton goods, brass, and iron casters, furniture casters, paper, carriages, coaches and sleighs, and carpenters' tools are manufactured here.

Among the more prominent citizens of this place, past and present, may be named: Hon. William S. Williams, an eloquent advocate, and connected with the distinguished Williams family of Massachusetts (his father being a nephew of Col. Ephraim Williams, the founder of Williams College); Roger Mills, Esq., a lawyer of note; Hon. Jared B. Foster; John Richards, Esq.; and Hon. Edward M. Chapin.

Sharon, situated on the west side of the Housatonic River, is seventy-one miles from Hartford, and contains about 2,800 inhabitants. The eastern part of the township is mountainous, while the western section is part of a large and beautiful valley. The soil is fertile, and agriculture is the principal occupation of the people; the chief productions being grain, tobacco, and milk for the New York market. The three most thickly settled places are Sharon Valley, Sharon Village, and Hitchcock's Corner, all on the New York State line, and Ellsworth, in the south-eastern part of the town. The churches are five in number. There is a furnace for smelting the Salisbury ore at Sharon Valley.

Noted men: John Williams, town clerk for forty years; Rev. Cotton Mather Smith (1731-1806), pastor of the Sharon church for fifty-two years; John Cotton Smith, LL.D., son of the foregoing, member of Congress, judge of the Supreme Court of the State, and governor from 1813 to 1817; John Cotton Smith, son of the governor, a popular orator and author; Anson Sterling, at one time a member of Congress; and Gen. Charles F. Sedgwick, an able lawyer.

Woodbury, forty-five miles from Hartford, has a population of a little more than 2,000. The village is surrounded by high hills. The main street, running lengthwise of a charming and fertile valley, extends into Hotchkissville, so that the places are now really one. The localities of interest in the town are Weekeepeemee, Flanders, Nonnewaug Falls, of more than 100 feet descent; Castle Rock, one of the Indian guarding heights; Orenaug Rocks, near the lightning's play-ground; Deer Rocks, Middle Quarter, and some others that still retain the old Indian names. Shot-bags, belts, cassimeres, shears and cutlery are made in this town. The Masonic Hall, with pillars around it, built on a bluff of trap rock, about thirty feet above the street, is the best in the county, and is a prominent object of admiration upon entering the village.

Eminent men: Jabez Bacon (1731-1806), a native of Middletown, and a very successful merchant; Dr. Daniel Munn (1684-1761), probably the first native physician of the county; Russel Abernethy, M. D. (1774-1851), a celebrated physician; Judge Noah B. Benedict (1771-1831); Judge Nathaniel Smith (1762-1822), congressman and judge of the Supreme Court of the State; and Judge Charles B. Phelps (1788-1858), an eminent jurist.

The remaining towns of the county, mostly devoted to agriculture, with their respective populations, are Plymouth (2,500); Thomaston (2,500), so called for Seth Thomas, the founder of the extensive manufactoy at that place of the clocks known by his name, who was born about 1817, and came from Wolcott about 1808 to Hoadleyville for the purpose of making clocks, and moved to Plymouth Hollow in 1812, where he began the clock-making business on a large scale. From this beginning a new era in the history of the town, which now bears his name, may be dated.

Watertown (1,900), a favorite summer resort; Washington (1,600), in the southern part of which is a wild and rugged chasm, about six hundred feet high, where a wonderful echo is formed. On the eastern side of Lake Waramaug is a pinnacle supposed to be the highest point in the State. The lake just mentioned, romantically situated among the hills, is much frequented, during the heated term, by tourists and pleasure-seekers.

Canaan (1,200). The Housatonic Falls, at this place, are sixty feet high. The whole descent, including the rapids, above and below the falls, is one hundred and sixty feet.

North Canaan (1,600); Cornwall (1,600); Kent (1,700); Norfolk (1,500); Barkhamsted (1,300); Goshen, (1,100), where in one of the streets the rain-fall on the front roof of the houses is said to run into the Housatonic River, to the west, while that on the back roof of the same houses, finds its way into the Naugatuck.

Colebrook (1,200), a mountain town; Roxbury (1,000), famous as having been the birth-place of Col. Seth Warner, who was born in 1743, and with only a common-school education of the times, early became distinguished for his energy and perseverance. He was the commander during the contest of the Colony with New York, and although rewards were offered by the governor of New York for his arrest, he always evaded their vigilance. He was in command of the party that took Crown Point, and was in several engagements in the war of the Revolution, but had to be relieved on account of sickness. He was more than six feet tall, well proportioned, and was a gallant officer. He died Dec. 27, 1784.

Harwinton (1,000); Bridgewater (800); Bethlehem (700), like Bridgewater an agricultural hill-town; Morris (650); and Warren (600).

Rev. John Trumbull, an eminent divine, after a ministry of forty-eight years at Watertown, died Dec. 13, 1787.

John Trumbull, son of the foregoing, born April 24, 1750, educated at Yale, admitted to the bar in 1773, was the author of McFingal. He died at Detroit, Mich., in 1831.

Gen. John Sedgwick, an officer of the war of the Revolution, and born in 1742, was a man of frank, familiar, and most estimable qualities. He died Aug. 18, 1820, aged seventy-seven years. His remains repose in the Cornwall Hollow Cemetery.

Major Gen. John Sedgwick was a native of the town of Cornwall, born Sept. 13, 1813, and graduated at West Point Military Academy with honor in 1837. He was engaged in the Seminole war in Florida; was employed under Gen. Scott to remove the Cherokees to their western reservation; fought in Mexico under Generals Worth, Scott, and Taylor; called to the Army of the Potomac, he fought at Fair Oaks, Antietam, Fredericksburg, and the battles of the Wilderness; was killed near Spottsylvania C. H., Va., May 9, 1864, and was buried in the Cornwall Hollow Cemetery.

Rev. Joseph Eldridge, D. D., the settled minister of Norfolk for over forty years, died in 1876, at about seventy years of age.

William W. Welch, M. D., an eminent physician of Norfolk, has been a member of Congress.

Hon. Truman Smith, born in Roxbury, graduate of Yale, was an eminent lawyer, also U. S. senator, and argued a case in court in his eighty-sixth year.

Rev. Joseph Bellamy, D. D., born in Cheshire in 1719, graduated at Yale in 1735, was ordained in 1740, and continued to serve as pastor of the Bethlehem Church for fifty years. He was greatly distinguished as a theological instructor, and as an educator of young men. He held high rank also both as a preacher and as a writer on theological subjects.

MIDDLESEX COUNTY.

THE legislature of Connecticut in May, 1785, formed the county of Middlesex by taking the towns of Middletown, Chatham, Haddam, and East Haddam from the county of Hartford, and the towns of Saybrook and Killingworth from the county of New London. In May, 1790, Durham, from the county of New Haven, was annexed to Middlesex. An English settlement was commenced in Saybrook in 1635, in Middletown in 1650, and in Haddam in 1662, all on the west side of the Connecticut River. From these, in due time, proceeded the towns on the opposite side of the Connecticut. The settlement in Killingworth began in 1663, and that in Durham in 1698.

The settlers, in some instances, came direct from England, but the greater number from older settlements in Connecticut and Massachusetts.

This region was, in general, a wild, irregular tract of country, mountainous, and covered with forests, the alluvial soil being found on the banks of the river and on the shores of Long Island Sound. Some parts afforded comfortable means of settlement; the rest afforded the Indian a place of retreat after he had sold his patrimony to the white man.

The glory of the county is its noble stream. The granite formation begins just below the city of Middletown, at a place called the Straits, where the river, hemmed in by bold hills, is only thirty-five rods wide, and runs nearly to the mouth at Saybrook. The scenery in this part is positively beautiful, green with wealth of trees in summer, and literally reveling in brilliant colors in the fall. This charming region is classic ground. During the profligate and unlicensed reign of Charles I., several gentlemen of distinction contemplated a removal to America. They obtained from the Earl of Warwick, March 19, 1631, a patent of all that territory "which lies west from Narragansett River, a hundred and twenty miles on the sea coast; and from thence in latitude and breadth aforesaid to the South Sea." John Winthrop, son of the governor of Massachusetts, who was then in London, was appointed their agent, and was instructed to build a fort at the mouth of the Connecticut, and to erect houses for himself and his men, and for the reception of persons of quality. To enable Winthrop to carry out their designs, they constituted him governor of Connecticut River, and of the harbor and places adjoining, for one year after his arrival. Thus commissioned and furnished with men and supplies he arrived in Boston on October 8, 1631, where he discovered that some people had just left Massachusetts and settled upon the Connecticut river within the patent granted by the Earl of Warwick. Being assured by the governor of the Colony and the magistrates that the settlers should remove or satisfy the patentees, he dispatched his men to the mouth of the Connecticut and superintended their labors until the expiration of his commission. The level tract of ground west of the river known as Saybrook Point was the place of the new settlement. On this several streets were laid out with some pretensions to a town, and the fortification was intrusted to the care of Mr. David Gardiner, an engineer whom the patentees had procured for the purpose in England. The whole was secured by a palisade stretching across the landward side of the point. "In 1639 Col. George Fenwick, one of the patentees, arrived from England, and gave to the tract about the mouth of the river the name of Saybrook, in honor of Lord Say and Seal, and Lord Brooke, his principal associates." He governed the inhabitants until 1644, and then disposed of his jurisdiction to the Colony of Connecticut, as his associates in the patent had abandoned the idea of seeking a home in the wilds of America on account of the trouble to be apprehended from the Indians and the opposition in high quarters to their leaving England. Owing to this disaffection, the little colony was driven back on its original resources. These were strengthened by a few more arrivals from Hartford, and thus the nucleus of a river population was formed under the protection of the friendly fortification. The settlement at Saybrook was intended as the residence of Oliver Cromwell, Pym, Hampden and Hasselrigg, four of the great Commoners of the day, and it is said that they actually embarked in the Thames. They remained at home to do a greater work than the narrow field of Saybrook afforded, but it would be well to ask: were not the early settlers of this county men of the Cromwell stamp? They were simply battling for the same cause under different conditions.

These early settlers did not escape the ferocities of the Indians. It was not long before the utility of the fort at Saybrook was demonstrated. The Indians who roamed the territory in the vicinity of the fort were subject to a warlike and powerful nation, known as the Pequots, who inhabited the region of the mouth of the Thames. They were inveterate in their malignity against the English, and influenced other tribes against them. In 1634 they murdered Captains Stone and Norton with their crew, consisting of eight men, just above Saybrook Point, plundered the vessel, burnt and sunk her. Yet they held a treaty with Winthrop, and conceded to the English their right to Connecticut River and the adjacent country. This was merely a cunning expedient to secure confidence, for all the while they meditated treachery; for early in October, 1636, a band of Pequots concealed in the grass at Calves' Island, four miles north of the fort, surprised five men who went there to get the hay, caught one of them named Butterfield and put him to death by torture. The place was named from this circumstance Butterfield's Meadow. The rest escaped to their boat, one of them being wounded with five arrows. A few days after Joseph Tilly, master of a bark, anchored off the island, and taking one man with him, went on shore for the purpose of fowling. A large number of Pequots, concealed as before, waited until he had discharged his piece, killed his companion, and captured him. They barbarously cut off his hands and his feet. In this tortured state he lived three days, exciting the admiration of his inhuman captors by his stoical endurance, not allowing a groan to escape him. This single but horrible incident demonstrates but too clearly the moral and physical courage of the settlers. The place has ever since been called Tilly's Point. The enemy still maintained his system of surprises. Within a fortnight a force of 100 strong, suddenly attacked a house erected two miles from the fort, and held by six of the garrison. Three of them were fowling near the house, although the lieutenant had strictly forbidden the practice. Two of these were taken; the third cut his way through them, wounded with two arrows, but not mortally. During the ensuing winter the fort was in a constant state of siege, all their outlying property was destroyed, and no one could leave the fort without hazard. The Pequots, emboldened by their successes, became more troublesome as the spring advanced. In the month of March, 1637, Lieut. Gardiner, with a dozen men, went out to burn the marshes. Just as they had got clear of the palisades the enemy killed three, and wounded a fourth, who died in the fort next day. Gardiner was slightly wounded, but was enabled to retire with the rest of his men. The Indians then surrounded the fort, till the guns, loaded with grape-shot, caused them to retreat. Their next exploit in their design of extermination was to attack a shallop with three men on board. They shot one of them through the head with an arrow, who fell overboard; they ripped the other two completely open, split their backs, and then suspended them on trees. One of the Indians concerned in this barbarity named Nepanpuck, a famous Pequot, for this and similar atrocities, was beheaded at New Haven in 1639. The Colony of Connecticut became very apprehensive for the safety of the little band of settlers in the fort. The fort commanded the river. It had already beaten off a Dutch war-sloop, and so far had checked the ravages of the Indians, but the Pequots were not only warlike, but numerous, and swayed the neighboring tribes. Unless they could be subdued, it was quite evident that the settlement must succumb and the general safety be endangered. Capt. John Mason (a great colonial celebrity) was sent from the Hartford settlement with twenty men to re-enforce the garrison. He was strengthened by twenty men under the command of Capt. John Underhill, sent by the Colony of Massachusetts. On the 1st of May, the General Court of Connecticut Colony, seriously alarmed at the hostile attitude of the Pequots, resolved upon immediate and vigorous war. Massachusetts and Plymouth Colonies, alive to the necessities of the occasion, resolved to aid the sister Colony. Capt. John Mason was appointed commander of the Connecticut troops, ninety men in all, the whole number that Hartford, Wethersfield and Windsor could furnish. Uncas, sachem of Mohegan, his ally, contributed seventy men. The whole force embarked at Hartford, in three small vessels, and fell down the river for Saybrook fort. Arrived at what is now Chester, the Indians left the boats and proceeded on foot. They fell in with forty of the enemy, killed six, and took one prisoner, whom they murdered.

In five days from their departure they reached Saybrook fort, having been delayed several times by one or other of the vessels getting aground. Captain Underhill, with nineteen men belonging to the garrison, joined the expedition, and twenty of Mason's men were sent back to protect their friends up the river. An account of the expedition to the Pequot fort, and the subsequent extermination of the tribe, is elsewhere given.

With the close of these hostilities, the importance of the fort began to decline. Lieutenant Gardiner, who commanded the garrison, removed in 1639 to Manchanoc, now Gardiner's Island, and became the first English settler in the State of New York. His descendants reside on the Island to this day, the patent being granted by the crown. His son David was born at Saybrook, April 29, 1636, and is supposed to have been the first white child born in the territory which now comprises Middlesex County. In the year before George Fenwick sold the jurisdiction of Saybrook, his wife, Lady Anne Butler, commonly called Lady Fenwick, died. The tomb, an ungainly structure of brown stone, without inscription, isolated and neglected, remained until very recently. Captain John Mason, at the request of the settlers, took up his abode at Saybrook in 1647, and was appointed to the command of the fort. He resided there for thirteen years, and then removed to assist in the settlement of Norwich. The country to the west of Saybrook became known to the colonists by means of the pursuit of Sassacus in that direction; it opened up fine sites on the Sound, and these were speedily occupied. Other settlements were formed up the river in a few years, but Saybrook must be considered the parent town of Middlesex County, and its historical fort the preservation of all the country within its influence.

The first inhabitants of Saybrook, who endured the trials peculiar to the early settlers, sat under the ministrations of the Rev. John Higginson, whose teachings were "suitable, seasonable and profitable, according to the then present dispensation of Providence." He arrived in this country from England in 1629. After three or four years' ministry in Saybrook, he removed to Guilford. The first church was established there in 1643. He remained there until 1660, and then removed to Salem, and died on December 9, 1708, in the ninety-third year of his age. The first church in Saybrook was organized in 1646. Among the early inhabitants distinguished for learning and piety, or for some excellence, may be mentioned the Hon. Robert Chapman, ancestor of the Chapmans in Saybrook, East Haddam, and other parts of the

State. He arrived there in 1636, and was a particular friend of George Fenwick while he remained in the country. He died in October, 1687. Mr. John Tulley came into the town a lad; he was possessed with a mind original and ingenious; became a teacher of arithmetic, navigation and astronomy, and published the almanacs of New England from 1681 to 1702. Mr. David Bushnell, another genius, was the inventor of several machines destined to annoy the British shipping in the Revolutionary war. He served during the war as a captain in a company of sappers and miners.

The first building in the county designed as a collegiate school was erected here, since named Yale College. It was of one story, eighty feet long. Fifteen commencements were held here, and more than sixty young men graduated from it. Here, also, a confession of faith was instituted, upon the principles of which the college was to be conducted. This was the origin of the famous Saybrook Platform in 1708. The college was removed from this place to New Haven.

Encouraged by the security in which Saybrook seemed established, and by the Constitution of 1639, which was superseded by the more liberal charter of Charles II., a committee was appointed to explore the lands in the Indian territory of Mattabeset. Sowheag, its great sachem, who appears to have been a peaceable man for an Indian, ruled the tribes who dwelt within a considerable circuit on both sides of the river. His stronghold was a hill about one mile west of the river—a position dominating the surrounding country. Before any settlement had commenced, Sowheag negotiated with Gov. Haynes for the sale of his territory. The Indian title did not, however, become extinct until about twelve years after, when certain chiefs, aware of the deed of Sowheag, for a further and full consideration disposed of all that land "to run from the great river the whole breadth east six miles, and from the great river west as far as the General Court of Connecticut had granted the bounds should extend;" reserving a tract on the west side of the river for Sawsean forever, and three hundred acres for the heirs of Sowheag and Mattabeset Indians on the east side.

On Oct. 30, 1646, the General Court appointed a Mr. Phelps to join a committee for the planting of Mattabeset. Few settlers came at first, but more towards the close of 1651; for in September of that year the General Court ordered that Mattabeset should be a town. In 1652, the town was represented in the General Court, and in November, 1653, the General Court further approved "that the name of the plantation commonly called Mattabeseck should, for time to come, be called Middletown." The name was probably given to it on account of its lying between the towns up the river and Saybrook at its mouth. It has been considered that the name was taken from a place in England endeared to some of the settlers. This we consider as not very probable. Who the first settlers were we have not the means of ascertaining; the first few pages in the town records are lost, and others are nearly obliterated. The number of taxable persons in 1654 was thirty-one, and sixteen years after they had only increased to fifty-two. The planters—as they were called in colonial phrase—came from the mother country, Hartford and Wethersfield, and a few from Massachusetts. A large number of the inhabitants of Middletown, at this day, are direct descendants from these planters. It may truly be said, that in a population of 12,000 persons, their names largely predominate.

The occupation of these settlers was in fact that of planters; they had no other source of living but the products of the soil; they manufactured their garments for the family very imperfectly, owing to their deficient means; they were scantily supplied with farming implements, and had but few mechanics in the community. They reserved a lot worth one hundred pounds as a temptation for a blacksmith to cast his lot among them. In September, 1661, one appeared, who agreed to do the necessary smithing for the town for four years. The conditions of their lives never reached ordinary comfort for half a century. Trade was carried on by barter. In 1680, they only owned one small vessel of seventy tons; only one other was owned on the river, and that at Hartford, of ninety tons. Half a century later, two vessels only were owned here; their united tonnage, 105 tons. There was only one merchant here in 1680, and only twenty-four in the entire Connecticut Colony. They are mentioned in Gov. Leete's Report to the Board of Trade and Plantations in England, as doing but little business. Their condition must have been hard and difficult indeed, but they were neither better nor worse than the colonists of New England in general. The settlement was divided into two parts, with the Little River, a narrow stream falling into the Connecticut, between them. That portion to the north of the stream was called The Upper Houses; that to the south, The Lower Houses. The Upper Houses of those days is now the town of Cromwell. On February 2d, 1652, it was voted by the town that a meeting-house should be built; it was only "twenty feet square, ten from sill to plate, and was inclosed by palisades. In May, 1680, the second meeting-house was erected, "thirty-two feet square, and fifteen feet between joints."

The population of the Upper Houses increased so much that in January, 1703, "the town agreed they might settle a minister and build a meeting-house, provided they settled a minister within six, or at most twelve months from that time." In May of the same year, the Upper Houses were incorporated as a parish. By slow degrees, the inhabitants began to spread out over the neighboring country; a settlement was begun in Middlefield in 1700, and in Westfield in 1720. The former did not become a parish until 1744, and Westfield not until 1766. On the east side of the Connecticut, now the site of Portland, no parish was formed until May, 1714, although the land was of good quality. It was then called East Middletown. Middle Haddam, in the southeastern part of the township, was not formed into a parish until May, 1749. It was mostly settled by people from East Middletown. East Hampton, another settlement in the southeast corner of the township, was incorporated in May, 1746.

The next township in the order of date, and that a very interesting one, is Haddam, settled in 1662.

It covered that tract of country lying between the confines of Middletown to the north, and Saybrook to the south. Some individuals contemplated this settlement two years before. The legislature appointed a committee to purchase the tract from the Indians. This was completed in 1662 for the consideration of thirty coats, probably worth $100, the Indians reserving Thirty-mile Island, so called from being that distance from the mouth of the Connecticut, as the river runs, and forty acres at Pattaquonk, now Chester meadows; also the right of fishing and hunting where they pleased, provided they did not injure the settlers. Twenty-eight young men settled upon these lands; but they soon discovered that they were interfered with by their northern line encroaching upon the territory confirmed to Middletown, and a considerable tract to the south encroached on that claimed by Saybrook, owing, no doubt, to the loose manner in which the Indians held their original right. The legislature settled the difficulty, in 1668, by advising the contestants to divide the disputed territory equally, and the division was made accordingly. The settlers do not seem to have been fully satisfied by this reduction of their purchase, for the legislature, in 1673, granted them as compensation all that tract of land on the east side of the river, now the township of East Haddam. They came from Hartford, Wethersfield, and Windsor, and the descendants of most of them are in the town or its vicinity to this day.

Town privileges were accorded them in 1668, and the settlement was called Haddam, after a place in England. Shortly after this, Richard Walkley from Hartford, John Bates, William Scovill and others joined the settlement. On February 11, 1686, a patent was granted to the town by the Assembly, confirming the settlers and their heirs forever in the possession of all the lands, appurtenances and privileges previously granted. The growth of population was exceedingly slow; for forty years the inhabitants were confined to the western bank of the river.

The ancestors of the families of Dickinson, Hubbard and Ray settled here about the commencement of the last century; and at later periods, those of the families of Lewis, Hazleton, Tyler, Higgins, Thomas, Knowles and Burr. The Indians appear to have had no specific name for the township at large; the northern part they called "Higganompos," since changed to Higganum. The western part they called "Cockaponset," since changed to Punset. They remained on their reservation at Pattaquonk and Thirty-Mile Island for many years; a few had a place of resort in a hollow on Haddam Neck, within the township on the east side of the river. Some were in existence within the memory of people who were living in the early part of the present century. With that due regard for the maintenance of public worship, which ever distinguished the early colonists, the proprietors reserved one right for whoever should be their first minister, and another right for the support of the ministry forever. David Brainerd, the missionary, direct descendant of Daniel Brainerd, one of the original settlers, was born in this town in 1716. His efforts to Christianize the Indians in different parts of North America have been highly praised. In Great Britain he was considered a model missionary.

In October, 1663, it was resolved by the legislature that the tract of ground to the west of Saybrook, known by the name of Hammonasset, should be formed into a township. Twelve planters moved into it the same month; in two or three years they were joined by sixteen others, and the town was divided into thirty rights, viz.: one each for the settlers, one for the first minister who should be settled there, and the last for the support of the ministry forever.

In 1667, the new township was called Kenilworth, after the celebrated Kenilworth in England; according to tradition, the first settlers emigrated from there. The name is so written in the early records of the town and Colony. By corrupt spelling, or worse pronunciation the romantic Kenilworth has been changed into the unmeaning Killingworth.

The Indians were very numerous in the southern part of this township; they dwelt on the shores of the Sound, and on the banks of the small streams, immense masses of shells now indicating their places of resort. While Col. Fenwick lived at Saybrook he bought up most of their lands. On Nov. 20, 1669, Uncas, the Mohegan sachem, disposed of the remainder of his lands in the township to the settlers, reserving six acres on the east side of the harbor, and the usual liberty of hunting and fishing. They lived here in great numbers to 1730 or 1740.

"On the 26th of January, 1686, the Assembly granted to the inhabitants of this town the lands north of their bounds, and of the bounds of Guilford, and west of Haddam up to Cochincaug swamps; which, by agreement, were surrendered to the township of Durham in 1708."

Durham being an outlying section was very difficult of settlement. The lands were purchased from the Indians by Samuel Wyllys and others on January 24, 1672.

The colonists do not appear to have been very expert surveyors; the grants from the legislature when measured in some cases encroached upon others, and in the case of Durham the grant was not sufficient—a large tract being left out. The legislature granted many lots or farms in it to persons who had rendered distinguished services to the Colony, and in this way 5,000 acres became the property of people who were not resident there. The difficulty was ultimately adjusted by the patent granted by the legislature in May, 1708.

The colonists soon manifested their maritime inclinations. It has already been said that in 1730 only two vessels of small tonnage were owned on the river. Shipbuilding began on the eastern side of the stream in the neighborhood of Middletown and the settlement of Haddam. "The first vessel built in Chatham parish was launched in October, 1741; this was a schooner of ninety tons," supposed to have been built at Lewis' yard, where many vessels have since been built.

Shipbuilding was begun at Churchel's yard in 1795. From the beginning of 1806 to the close of 1816, 12,500 tons of shipping were built here. In this parish were built, during the Revolution, the "Trumbull" of 700 tons, thirty-six guns, and the "Bourbon" of 900 tons. Other war vessels of large capacity were subsequently built.

In the yards at Middle Haddam eighteen ships, nine brigs, eleven schooners and one sloop were built from 1805 to 1815, amounting to 9,200 tons. Shipbuilding appears to have been done on the west shore of the river—at Middletown, Higganum and Haddam. Out of this shipbuilding enterprise grew the West India trade. Prior to the Revolutionary war the shipping was mostly employed in West Indian adventure. Several merchants at Middletown embarked in the trade, exporting mules, cattle, corn and meal, and importing, in turn, molasses, sugar and rum. This trade not only enriched the firms who were engaged in it but stimulated commerce in the county generally. By this time the best parts of the lands had been gotten under cultivation, the necessary stock could be raised for exportation, and the growth of cereals was more than the inhabitants could consume. Everything favored the West Indian trade. Articles of the most useful description were brought to the doors of the colonists. Large numbers of families were maintained by the necessary labor to pursue the trade—the county alone did not present a field large enough to consume the valuable imports, so by opening up the roads they carried the cargoes across the mountains to distant places in New England; the merchants became their own carriers, and an ordinarily quiet agricultural community soon became transformed into enterprising merchant adventurers. They were on the highway to wealth, and many attained it.

The Revolutionary war suspended but did not destroy this trade. It was resumed with great vigor after the war, and did not finally decline till 1812. Small as the population of Middletown, Haddam and the other towns must have been at the breaking out of the war of independence, yet they appear to have contributed their full quota of men and means, and to have borne a most distinguished part in the military achievements in which they were engaged. The passage of the Boston Port Bill by the British Parliament, and the arrival of Gen. Gage in May, 1774, to enforce it by stopping the trade of the town, caused the patriots of this county to rise in righteous indignation. On the 5th of June of the same year, five hundred inhabitants of the township of Middletown assembled and passed ringing and patriotic resolutions.

It is not known whether the other towns passed such resolves, but the evidence is sufficient that they shared the same sentiments, and were faithful in sustaining them. The delegates from Massachusetts on their way to the first Continental Congress, stopped at Middletown. Dr. Rawson, Mr. Alsop, Mr. Mortimer, Mr. Henshaw and others, called upon them to pay their respects. They assured the delegates that they would abide by the decision of the Congress "even to a total stoppage of trade to Europe and the West Indies." Nothing could be more patriotic, as the gentlemen who made the assertion were very deeply interested in the West India trade. Whatever laws were passed by the Colonial Assembly for the safety or governance of the people, committees were immediately formed to ascertain if they were attended to or to see their provisions carried into effect. One thing they particularly did; to see that the inhabitants took the oath of fidelity to the State, and the records of the towns of Middletown and Chatham, year after year, abound with such subscriptions. It was discovered, early in the war, that Washington required regular soldiers and not militia, and Continental battalions were ordered by the State. The towns of this county filled up their quota cheerfully; they did much for the support of the families of the soldiers by assigning them to the care of committees or of individuals. Chatham and Middletown, in 1777, voted that the selectmen distribute to the officers' and soldiers' families the salt belonging to the town as they should think it needed. In 1779, Middletown voted that every man in the town that has a team be desired to furnish the light dragoons with wood.

Return Jonathan Meigs raised a company of light infantry in Middletown in 1774, and in 1775 he was appointed captain. Immediately after the news of Lexington he marched his company, "completely uniformed and equipped," to the environs of Boston. Captain Sage was there with his troop, and Captain Silas Dunham with a military company from Chatham. At this time the militia companies in Middletown and Chatham were formed into a regiment. In May, 1776, "large detachments of militia were ordered to hold themselves in readiness to march at the shortest notice for the defense of any portion of Connecticut or other adjoining Colonies." In June, seven regiments were ordered to join the army in New York; James Wadsworth, Jr., of Durham, was appointed brigadier-general, and among the seven colonels then appointed was Comfort Sage, of Middletown, who went with his troop to Boston the year before. Middlesex County not being the theatre of war, her inhabitants never ceased in their efforts, military or commissary, to contribute their utmost to the common cause. The drafts of militia ordered to New York in August included the militia of Middletown and Chatham. The brigades were commanded by Major General Joseph Spencer, of East Haddam, by Brigadier General James Wadsworth, of Durham, and Samuel H. Parsons, of Middletown. "They signalized themselves in all the achievements," and were distinguished as well for their sufferings as their valor. So great was the strain upon the resources of the country in 1776 that no less than five drafts were made upon the militia of the State. If we begin with the inquiry: who went to the war from the towns in Middlesex County? we would end by inquiring: who did not go?

The towns of this county endured also their share of privation and captivity, and suffered their proportion of loss in killed and wounded. The prisoners who were kept on board the horrible prison ships in New York were largely from these towns. Many living on the Connecticut River embarked in the tempting but hazardous business of privateering. The sloop-of-war, "Sampson," built at Higganum, was commissioned for this purpose. She was captured, and the officers and crew, one hundred in all, were consigned to the old prison-ship "Jersey." The commander, Capt. David Brooks, Lieut Shubael Brainerd, and several men died there.

Middlesex County produced a distinguished soldier, Gen. Return Jonathan Meigs, born in Middletown. In 1775, he accompanied Arnold's expedition up the Kennebec to Quebec, and has left the best account of that perilous and ill-starred undertaking. He was taken prisoner, and on being exchanged in 1777, was appointed lieutenant-colonel, with power to raise a regiment. He was then selected to undertake what proved to be one of the many dashing minor exploits of the war, no less than the surprisal and capture of a body of the enemy stationed at Sag Harbor, L. I. He crossed the Sound with 230 men in thirteen whaleboats, and arrived within three miles of Sag Harbor at one o'clock at night.

They attacked the enemy at five different places. Having come within twenty rods of them in the greatest silence and order, they rushed upon them with fixed bayonets and captured the whole; another company meanwhile securing the wharf and the shipping. Six of the enemy were killed, ninety taken prisoners, twelve vessels destroyed and a large amount of forage and provisions. Col. Meigs recrossed the Sound with his prisoners, and arrived at Guilford in twenty-five hours from the time he left it, without the loss of a man. Congress presented the brave commander with an elegant sword. He afterwards commanded one of the regiments which assisted in capturing Stony Point. It is worthy of mention, showing the spirit in which non-combatants supported the war, that the people of Durham sent two oxen to Gen. Washington at Valley Forge. They were driven through a country almost exhausted by the war, yet one of them weighed 2,270 pounds, after a journey of nearly 500 miles. After the war the county greatly suffered from the depreciation and finally the total collapse of the Continental script or paper money. The mercantile portion of the population returned to their West Indian trade, which flourished as vigorously as ever until the war of 1812.

Ship-building was carried on energetically, and the fisheries were extended; farms began to multiply, and the population soon repaired the waste of war. The numerous streams running into the Connecticut and the Sound were utilized as means of manufacture, and another interest destined in the future to assume large proportions was coming steadily into favor, viz.: the Portland quarries. The towns we have been describing were taken to form the county in 1785, just after the close of the war, Durham being added in 1799.

Of the naval force employed by the United States in the war of 1812, the citizens of the river towns of Middlesex County contributed largely in men and material, and although the Connecticut was not within the field of general operations, it was the scene of a foray by vessels from the enemy's fleet then blockading New London. On the 7th of April, 1814, two of these anchored off Saybrook bar in the evening, and dispatched two launches, each carrying nine or twelve-pound carronades and fifty to sixty men, and four barges with twenty-five men each. They were seen to enter the mouth of the river at eleven o'clock, and many of their men entered the old fort, which was altogether abandoned and neglected. They rowed between five and six miles, and arrived at their destination, Pautapong Point, at four o'clock in the morning, when the work of conflagration was immediately begun. Pickets of the enemy searched the houses for arms and ammunition, while the main force was busy setting fire to the vessels in the river and those on the stocks. At ten o'clock, Friday the 8th, they retreated, taking with them a brig, a schooner and two sloops. The wind shifting directly contrary, they set fire to the brig and the sloops, and anchored the schooner a mile and a quarter from where they had taken her. Twenty-two vessels and other property, computed in all at $160,000, were destroyed. The British were all day in the river, and did not succeed in gaining their shipping until ten o'clock at night.

With the close of this war, the last remnants of the West India trade, which had been carried on so long and so prosperously, died out. The merchants principally engaged in the business at different periods of its rise and decline were, Richard Alsop, George Phillips, Matthew Talcot, Elijah and Nehemiah Hubbard, Lemuel Storrs, George and Thompson Phillips, Gen. Comfort Sage, of Revolutionary renown, and Joseph W. Alsop, all of Middletown. The growth of the county from this period partakes of the growth of the age. Quarrying and carrying the brown stone of the celebrated Portland quarries became an immense business, quite a large fleet until very recently being employed in it. Quarrying another kind of stone at Haddam, largely increased the industry of the river. Small steamboats began to ply between Hartford and Saybrook, and a line of first-class Sound steamboats now maintains the traffic between Hartford and New York. The southern part of the county is cut by the Shore Line Railroad between New Haven and New London, crossing the Connecticut between Saybrook and Lyme, by a magnificent bridge with a large draw in the centre. The Valley Railroad skirts the western shore of the river from Hartford to Saybrook Point. The direct Air Line Railroad from New Haven to Willimantic crosses the river at Middletown over a magnificent structure constructed with a draw.

Churches, colleges, schools, agriculture and manufactures flourish equal to the requirements of the day. The population of the county at the last census of 1880, was 35,587. Middlesex is but a small county in a small State, which has nobly answered to the calls of duty in all cases of national exigency, and especially in the late civil war. The several towns sent their hundreds to the field of honor, where they ever distinguished themselves whether in moments of victory or in periods of disaster. They contributed their utmost in material as well as in men, and were never behind the larger cities in their efforts to promote the welfare of the national cause. Direct descendants of the early settlers have laid their lives on the altar of liberty in 1776, 1812 and 1861; they have assisted in creating and sustaining other Territories and States in the far West, true to the motto of Connecticut, that "he who transplants still sustains."

Towns.

Middletown, a half-shire town of Middlesex County, and a port of entry, is one of the most beautiful of New England cities. It stands on a large bend of the Connecticut, on its western shore, and runs backward to the hill-tops for the distance of a mile. The traveler can see but little of the city from any of its approaches by land or water, so completely is it embosomed in the foliage of the maple and the elm, which has given to it the well-merited name of "The Forest City" of New England. The population of the town is 11,731. It was incorporated as a city in 1784. Its colleges and schools, its numerous spires, its enterprising industries and numerous banks, all tell the story of the collected wealth of two centuries. High street, 180 feet above the river, is built up of costly and elegant residences, set in the most cultivated horticultural grounds. The arching sweep of the elms forms a superb vista of enchanting foliage. The view from this street is surpassingly beautiful. The Wesleyan University fronts on High street. The buildings which comprise it stand a little distance from the street, and in a straight line; the intermediate space of lawn, trees and gravel walks forming a fine campus. The buildings are chiefly of brownstone from the adjacent quarries at Portland. The most modern of these, erected at the expense of Orange Judd, Esq., is the Orange Judd Hall of Science. Its museum of natural history and ethnology is very extensive and remarkably well arranged under the supervision of Prof. W. N. Rice. The Scientific Association of Middletown holds its meetings here once a month. The library contains about 30,000 volumes, and is endowed with a fund for its continued increase. The Memorial Chapel is enriched with a graceful spire, which makes quite a landmark for miles around. The observatory is furnished with a splendid telescope by Clark. There are about 200 students and a large body of professors. Rev. John Wesley Beach, D. D., LL.D., is the efficient president.

The Berkeley Divinity School, on Main street, is designed for the training of young men for the ministry of the Episcopalian Church. The Right Rev. John Williams, D. D., bishop of Connecticut, is the president and dean. Attached to the school is a beautiful Gothic chapel, the gift of Mrs. Thomas D. Mutter, as a memorial of her husband, in which services are held daily.

Middletown has long been famous for her schools. The high school draws a large number of scholars from all parts of the county, and every year graduates a large class. The building is most convenient and substantial, built of brick with brownstone facings, and having two wings. The Catholics maintain a good parish school, which is well attended, and a most excellent convent school, under the charge of the Sisters of Mercy. The private schools of Middletown contribute their share to the educational reputation of the city.

The churches compare well with those of larger cities. The first church was established in 1661, and for a century the people were chiefly Congregationalists. Other denominations gradually crept in, and at the present day, the leading religious orders are well represented. The town is improved by four church edifices of considerable architectural pretensions; one of them, the most modern, the First Congregational Church—known as the North Church—is as graceful and as imposing a church edifice as any in the State. Its spire, reaching to a great height, is beautiful in its proportions. The South Congregational, the Episcopal and the Roman Catholic churches are also of fine architectural design.

Middletown is the centre of the monetary institutions of the county, and contains seven banking institutions and two flourishing insurance companies.

On a commanding eminence in the southeast part of the town, overlooking the river and city, and embracing a wide and varied prospect, stands the State hospital for the insane. No site could be more appropriate or better adapted for the humane purposes of such an institution. The building, of Portland brownstone, is a most imposing one, and a conspicuous feature in the landscape for many miles.

On an eminence in the western part of the town is another State institution; the Industrial School for Girls, established in 1870, designed for the care and education of homeless and neglected girls from eight to twenty-one years of age.

The educational facilities of Middletown are considerably enhanced by the Free Russell Library, the generous gift of Mrs. Samuel Russell, in memory of her husband.

Middletown has several cemeteries and old burying grounds. In an old cemetry in the south part of the town the grave-stone can be seen of Capt. Return Jonathan Meigs and his family. In another is the tomb of Commodore McDonough, the hero of Lake Champlain. The principal cemetery, and one of the most beautiful in the State, is situated on Indian Hill. The prospect from the summer-house on the crest commands the amphitheatre of hills which surround it at a distance of four miles. Above these can be seen the ranges of the more distant hills until they gradually lose themselves in the dim forms of Mount Tom and Mount Holyoke in Massachusetts. A wide sweep of the river is in full view in the midst of a most charming pastoral country. The smoke of distant cities may be seen, and although Middletown lies at its feet, nothing more than the spires are in sight, on account of the trees. The cemetery is beautifully laid out in gravel walks; the monuments are elegant, and many of them very costly, several being made of the polished Scotch granite. There is a fine monument in memory of Maj. Gen. Mansfield, U. S. A., who fell leading his brigade at Antietam. A brownstone chapel, Gothic in design, which all denominations can use, is another of the gifts of the benevolent Mrs. Samuel Russell.

Middletown has extensive and varied manufactures. Among the leading establishments may be mentioned the Russell Manufacturing Company, which makes heavy cotton belting and hose for mill purposes, suspenders and webbing; Messrs. W. & B. Douglas, the oldest and largest pump-makers in the word; the Middletown Plate, Co., and the Stiles & Parker Press companies. Beside these there are manufactures of silk, hardware, saddlery and harness trimmings, articles from bone and ivory, etc.

The city is a central point for railroad communication, and has considerable coasting trade in coal, iron and other heavy materials. Straddle Hill, an outlying district of Middletown, contains the largest waterfall in the county, and several factories.

Chatham, so called, from its shipbuilding, after Chatham in England, embraces the villages of Middle Haddam, Cobalt and East Hampton. It has a population of about 2,000. Cobalt takes its name from a mineral discovered there in 1762. East Hampton is the great seat of industry of Chatham township. In this small place, nestled among the bold and rugged hills of the granite formation, is made nearly every sleigh-bell which now tinkles throughout North America. Those made in other places are manufactured by men from East Hampton. It was not until 1743 that East Hampton was settled, the great attraction being the beautiful sheet of water known as Pocotopogue Lake, one of the prettiest in the State. In the same year a forge was established at the outlet of the lake.

Iron was in great demand at this time for shipbuilding and for other purposes, and for the first forty years the business done at this forge was considerable. The village owes its importance, however, to the fact that William Barton moved here in 1898, and introduced the manufacture of sleigh and hand bells. He had worked with his father in the armory at Springfield during the Revolutionary war, and had acquired considerable experience in the casting of metals, to which he added great mechanical skill. The business he introduced expanded; others shared the benefit of his industry, and thus the founder gave to East Hampton its peculiarly distinctive character. He died in East Hampton July 15, 1849. It may be taken for granted that almost every house and hand bell and gong bell in use comes from this village. Toy bells are also made on a large scale.

Pocotopogue Lake is resorted to in the summer months by many tourists, attracted by the fishing for which this sheet of water is famous. The landscape is grandly set off by a beautiful island in the centre of the lake, covered with a crown of foliage, and once a great resort of the aborigines, as shown by the numerous Indian relics which have been discovered there.

Middle Haddam, a place of landing on the river, is a highly respectable village, once the busy scene of a large shipbuilding industry. It formerly sent great quantites of cordwood to New York.

Portland, with a population of 4,156, so called after Portland, Eng., on account of its famous quarries of brown sandstone, is invested with national interest. The township is mostly agricultural. Shipbuilding is carried on at Gildersleeve's Landing on the Connecticut, where many vessels of large tonnage have been constructed. Its world-renowned and unrivaled quarries are situated on the banks of the river, occupying a frontage of nearly two miles. They yield a hard and durable brown sandstone, similar in grain and color to the stone quarried at Portland, Eng. There are three companies, whose property is contiguous. These quarries have been in operation for two centuries. The excavations, reaching in many instances to a depth of 150 feet from the original surface, cover forty acres. It was ascertained by means of the diamond drill that at a depth of 313 feet below the deepest point of excavation, the stone still ran downwards. In seasons of ordinary trade, the three companies employ 1,500 men, work 250 cattle and 100 horses, and, with their own and chartered vessels, make quite a fleet, which conveys the stone to all the principal cities on the Atlantic seaboard. The gravestones of the early settlers for miles round the country, and even on Long Island, were made of stone from these quarries. The oldest stone we know in the old burying-ground of Middletown bears the date 1698, as clear and legible as when it left the hand of the mason. Portland stone resists the effects of atmosphere and fire better than any other building-stone. This was proved by the great fires of Chicago and Boston.

Portland maintains very good schools and churches of the different denominations. The Episcopalian church, built of the quarry stone, is one of the most complete and handsome in the State.

John Stancliff was the first white man who lived among the Indians on the Portland side of the river. He took up his residence here in 1690.

Haddam, population, 2,500, is the other half-shire town of Middlesex County. It possesses a very fine granite quarry, which has been in operation for several years. The landscape is rugged and mountainous, but the wealthy growth of trees which covers the surface, even to the mountain ridges, gives it a most romantic and charming aspect. The granite is quarried from the hill-tops, just a little below the surface, and, in busy seasons, is the principal source of wealth of many families. It is harder than the brown sandstone of Portland, and not so well adapted to the finer operations of the chisel. It is in great demand for pavements and curbing, also for steps and other portions of buildings. Vessels in connection with the quarry convey the stone to the different Atlantic ports.

Haddam has long been noted for its academy, founded by one of the many Brainerds. It is a fine structure of gray stone, and has done great service to the community in its time.

Higganum, quite a large village in the township, enjoys great manufacturing facilities on account of the stream of the same name which falls into the Connecticut. Here are made the ploughs by the Higganum Manufacturing Corporation, which have contributed so much to the fame of American agricultural implements at home and abroad. The Russell Manufacturing Company has quite an extensive mill here, and Seoville Brothers make a hoe which has acquired some celebrity. Haddam Neck, a mountainous strip of land across the Connecticut, also belongs to this township. It was organized in 1740.

East Haddam is a township of about 3,000 inhabitants, on the east side of the Connecticut, embracing the villages of East Haddam, Moodus, Leesville, Millington and Johnsonville. It is built on a high bank of the river, dense with foliage, and the village is consequently hid from the traveler on the river It has two landing-places; the upper landing to the north and Goodspeed's Landing to the south. The latter takes its name from a gentleman of most active business enterprise, who materially enlarged the influence of the town by his spirited undertakings. He was a principal proprietor in the line of steamboats running between Hartford and New York, maintained by three handsome and powerful Long Island Sound boats, Goodspeed's (in local parlance) being their headquarters. Mr. Goodspeed erected a palatial-looking structure on the landing. The surface of the township is rocky, hilly and romantic, being in the very heart of the granite formation. Tobacco is grown in large quantities. Luther Boardman & Son conduct a plated-spoon manufacture on a large scale, which furnishes employment to a great many hands. The vicinity of the landings is the central point for all the business of the town, the products of the interior being brought here for shipment. The Maplewood Seminary has attained a great and well-deserved degree of celebrity. Students from all parts of the Union come here to receive a thorough musical education. In connection with the Seminary is an extensive opera-house.

Moodus is quite a thriving manufacturing village, and noted for its cotton-mills. Any sketch of this village would be considered incomplete without some reference to the loud noises proceeding from some, as yet, unexplained natural causes. They appear to issue from a mountain near the village, and have been heard more or less frequently from the time of the early settlers. The Indians called the place Mackimoodus, meaning the place of noises. Mr. Hosmer, the first minister of the town, says in a letter to Mr. Prince of Boston, dated Aug. 13, 1729: "I have myself heard eight or ten sounds successively, and imitating small arms, in the space of five minutes." He states further that he has heard them by several hundreds within twenty years, some more or less terrible; that they first imitate slow thunder, come nearer, and then exploding with a noise like cannon shot, "shake houses and all that is in them."

Ordinary grumblings they called Moodus noises; the heavier explosions of sound they called earthquakes. They were terrific in 1791, and since then appear to have gradually subsided.

Old Saybrook, the parent of the county, with a population of only 1,300, is the headquarters of the shad-fishery, the home of the retired sea-captains and private families, and a great resort of excursionists and tourists in the summer. Its principal street is broad, and the houses indicate respectable and wealthy owners, which give the place a very retired, but very aristocratic air. The tomb of Lady Fenwick, which has stood for two centuries on the point of Saybrook, in the vicinity of the old fort, and which was visible from the river, has at last disappeared. It was removed, we believe, to make room for the railroad from Hartford, which has its terminus here, and a handsome modern monument was erected on another spot in lieu thereof. A company has built a very fine hotel on the point, called the Fenwick Hotel.

A light-house is close to the mouth of the river, the bar which forms just outside being dangerous to vessels of heavy draught. The bar was a great source of danger and discouragement in the times of the early settlers.

Essex, a riverside town, with 1,855 inhabitants, was formerly a parish of Saybrook. It enjoys considerable commerce, and has every convenience for coasting vessels and fishing craft laying up for the winter, by means of two large coves connected with the river. The strip of land between the coves is known as Pantopoug Point, the scene of the destruction committed by the British in the war of 1812. The spires of the churches built close together on the hill-top, which commands the town, are well-known objects to travelers on the Connecticut. The granite formation begins to lose itself here, and the scenery to change; the wooded heights giving place to a more level landscape.

Centre Brook, or Ivoryton, a village in the township, two miles inland, boasts a national reputation on account of its extensive and exclusive business in the manufacture of articles in ivory. Cheney, Comstock & Co. employ a very large capital in the enterprise. The machinery used for cutting and preparing the ivory for work, and for executing the delicate processes of manufacture of which ivory is capable, is of the most costly and ingenious description. The glass sheds, with their roofs sloping to the south, would extend the length of an ordinary city street. In these, the thin strips of ivory are placed for the purpose of bleaching in the sun. Both faces are bleached and also the sides; this process alone is a work of time. The ivory is received direct from Africa by the importer in New York, and every tusk finds its way into this district. Cheney, Comstock & Co. run two extensive establishments, one for the manufacture of combs, and other small articles, such as billiard balls, fans, paper-cutters, rules, and such fancy ornaments as fashion may demand; the other exclusively for the manufacture of keys of pianos and organs, and also for the keyboard complete.

Cromwell, a small town of nearly 1,700 inhabitants, lies to the north of Middletown, and was known as Upper Middletown until it was made a separate township in 1851. The strata of the Portland quarries, on the opposite side of the Connecticut, run under the bed of the river and crop out again in the centre of the village, where a large brownstone quarry has been excavated, and has materially enhanced its interests. Toys and other hardware, and lamps are manufactured here on a large scale. A private asylum for the insane has recently been established in this town. The first cotton goods ever shipped to China were made here by Henry G. Bowers, about the time of the second war with England.

Middlefield, a parish of Middletown, but recently formed into a separate township, contains a population of about 1,000. It is a very fertile part of the county, containing large level and undulating pasture-lands. Some of the best cattle in the State are bred here.

In the most elevated parts of the town a large reservoir, secured by a dam of powerful construction, has been constructed to supply the city of Middletown with pure water. Clothes-wringers and other articles of wooden ware have been made here for years The settlement of this part of Middletown began in 1700 by three settlers from the first or parent society. The late David Lyman of this town, was one of the earliest and most energetic projectors of the Boston and New York Air Line Railroad.

Durham, adjoining Middlefield, has a population of 1,000. It maintains a good academy and several churches. A very respectable tin-ware manufactory furnishes employment to many; but the pursuits of the community are mainly agricultural. The scenery is very pastoral, exhibiting long stretches of land under the most careful cultivation, and bears in many respects a similarity to the best husbandry in Old England.

Killingworth, Chester, Deep River, Westbrook, and Clinton, the remaining towns of the county, have a respective population of 800, 1,100, 1,200, 900, and 1,400. At Deep River is the piano key and ivory works of Pratt, Read & Co., John H. Edmonds, Superintendent, the largest and oldest of its class in America. The oyster fisheries of Clinton have risen into importance. The town contains a fine high school, founded and liberally endowed by Mr. Morgan, a native.

NEW HAVEN COUNTY.

NEW HAVEN COUNTY has special interest for its colonial history. It was the youngest of the four Colonies that formed the New England Confederation. The men who came hither acted under no commission and had no connection with any chartered company or commercial association in England or elsewhere. They felt at liberty to form for themselves such government as should, in their opinion, be best suited to the ends they had in view when they came to this country. The original Colony, or jurisdiction, embraced colonies beyond the present limits of the county, and indeed of the State. The Colony of New Haven was composed of six plantations,—New Haven, Milford, Guilford, Stamford, Southold (L. I.) and Branford. Of these the first three, and Branford, lie within the limits of New Haven County and come under the notice of this narrative.

The first three of these were the fruit of a simultaneous exodus from three contiguous counties in England,—Yorkshire, Hertfordshire and Kent. The Yorkshire men came to New Haven, the Hertfordshire men to Milford, the Kent County men to Guilford. They came first to Boston in two ships; thence to New Haven in April, 1638. Here they remained some fifteen months before they made any formal civil or ecclesiastical organization. These months were by no means dormant. They selected their lands and made purchase of them from the Indians. Each company acted for itself, although they remained together. The Indian deed of New Haven, at first called Quinnipiac, was made to Theophilus Eaton, John Davenport and others, November 24, 1638; that of Milford to William Fowler, Edmund Tapp, Zechariah Whitman and others, February 12, 1639; that of Guilford to Henry Whitefield, Robert Kitchell, William Leete and others, September 29, 1639. Branford was not organized as a civil community until much later, in 1644.

The New Haven Colony was the first to take possession of its purchase and organize its political and ecclesiastical government. There seems to have been some sort of agreement entered into by those forming the Colony before coming to New Haven. This compact appears to have been entered into either before leaving England, or while tarrying at Boston. It is hardly supposable that men of such character and intelligence would have risked such an amount of capital, £36,000, and their own safety and welfare, without some articles of agreement binding them together. This compact they call the "Planters' Covenant."

Whatever it may have been, they seem to have been in no haste to be rid of it, for it was not until the 25th of October, 1639, that a civil government was instituted and installed. A meeting was called June 4th (commonly known as the meeting in Mr. Newman's barn) "to consult about settling civil government according to God, and about nominating persons that might be found of all fittest for the foundation work of a church." The result of that meeting, one of the most remarkable ever held in a barn, surely, is thus stated: First, the free planters without a dissenting vote, after a free discussion, adopted this "Fundamental Agreement:" "that church members only shall be free burgesses —and they only shall choose among themselves magistrates and officers to have the power of transacting all public, civil affairs of this plantation, of making and repealing laws, dividing inheritances, deciding of differences that may arise, and doing all things and business of like nature." Secondly, twelve men were chosen to designate among themselves, or from others whom they should publicly nominate as candidates for that trust, the seven founders of the Church and of the State. These seven, by this act of founding the church, became free burgesses of the commonwealth, the nucleus of the civil organization. They were to choose other free burgesses "out of like estate of church fellowship."

On the 25th of the following October, these seven men, "who were in the foundation of the church," viz., Theophilus Eaton, John Davenport, Rob't Newman, Math. Gilbert, Theo. Fugill, John Punderson and Jeremy Dixon, assembled to form the new government. This was to be permanent, and to supplant all former contracts. The term "Court" is applied to this body—these "*Septemvires*," as the old Romans would name them. Once organized, after most solemn prayer to God, they proceeded to ordain:—

1st. "All former power, or trust, for managing any public affairs in this plantation, into whose hands soever formerly committed, is now abrogated, and is henceforward utterly to cease."

2d. "All those who have been received into the fellowship of this church since the first gathering of it, or who, being members of other approved churches, offered themselves, were admitted as members of this court." That is, became citizens of this commonwealth. Sixteen members were thus admitted. As these new members came in they took the oath of allegiance "to the civil government here settled." They owned no allegiance as due to the king of England, or any other government on the footstool. This is worth remembering.

They then proceed—after Mr. Davenport expounded to them two texts—Deut. i. 13, Ex. xviii. 21: "Take ye wise men, and understanding, and known among your tribes, and I will make them rulers over you;" "Moreover, thou shalt provide out of all the people able men, such as fear God, men of truth, hating covetousness, and place such over men,"—to nominate and elect officers. Mr. Theophilus Eaton—the chief man of the Colony, one answering the above description—was chosen magistrate for one year. Four deputies were chosen. Each received a solemn charge on being inducted into office.

Thus the commonwealth was launched. Their laws were all summed up in the simple enactment, "That the word of God shall be the only rule to be attended to in ordering the affairs of government in this plantation." This is further explained later in their records, "as the judicial law of God, given by Moses, and expounded in other parts of the Scripture, so far as it is a hedge and fence to the moral law, and is neither ceremonial nor typical, nor had any reference to Canaan; this hath an everlasting equity in it, and should be the rule of their proceedings." All other systems of jurisprudence, civil or canon law, were excluded from this Colony. On this unique and model foundation they built their civil state.

This "Fundamental Agreement," as it was called, continued, with small modifications, to be the organic law of the colonies, which, on October 23, 1643, were united under one jurisdiction. After the combination, the name magistrate disappears, and that of governor is substituted. The colonies of Milford, Guilford, Stamford, Branford and Southold sent delegates to the General Court at New Haven. Besides this, they had their own magistrates and magistrates' courts. They had also a planters' court, corresponding to our police and justices' courts.

This same year also, 1643, a combination was formed between the four colonies of Massachusetts, Plymouth, Connecticut and New Haven, called the "United Colonies of New England." This combination was entered into for purposes of mutual defense, and was of great value to the several Colonies, especially in King Phillip's war, which threatened at one time to wipe out in blood and carnage all the English settlements.

Under this simple government, built upon the word of God, administered by wise, generous, good men, without charter or patent from any king or any body corporate under heaven, they continued to thrive. As the two colonies of Connecticut and New Haven, being contiguous and having so many interests in common, grew, it became, to wise men in both of them, more and more apparent that their union under one government was desirable. Governor Winthrop, of the Connecticut Colony, went to England to procure a royal charter for this and other purposes. The charter was secured in 1662. The Connecticut Colony claimed that this charter covered New Haven jurisdiction, and they, *nolens volens*, were part of Connecticut. This was stoutly resisted as absurd, as it was. No one had any authority to bargain them away, or put them under the control of anybody, against their will. After a few years it was clearly seen and felt, on all hands, to be best that the union should be consummated. This was done January 5, 1665. The government of the Colonies was so modified as to fit this new relation. The modification was merely technical, touching in no essential particular the "Fundamental Agreement" of the earlier colonists. The story of this charter, and its preservation when Andros came to Hartford to secure and destroy it, is told elsewhere.

Would space admit, we should speak with real enthusiasm of the government of New Haven Colony. So much ignorant aspersion has been cast upon it, that when the writer began this examination, he did so with much prejudice, expecting to find those blue laws that have haunted so many persons' brains. He found instead, laws that would seem somewhat strange to us, printed on blue paper, and so called "blue laws"; but the laws themselves were generous, and just adapted to the ends and times they were made to serve. One constantly marvels that a government so simple, so democratic, so equitable, so efficient, and, on the whole, so humane and kind, should have been framed here in the wilderness, without a precedent to go by, or any guide but the Word of God. We read the record of their courts, on which everything is spread out, and marvel at the scrupulous fairness, and painstaking candor, and gentle firmness which which their laws were administered. True, there were things punished as crimes which we should not think of punishing now. But we must not compare their times and legislation with our own, but with the times and governments that preceded them. We shall then find occasion to admire.

No witches were hanged or burned here; no man suffered persecution or punishment for his religious faith, if he kept the peace, and did not disturb the "settled order of things." They purchased all their lands, paying a fair equivalent. They protected the Indians from the violence and rapacity of the settlers, and lived in peace with them all their days—more than our government now does. No house was burned, no life taken by the red-men of the forests. They limited, it is true, the right of suffrage, but only so far as to secure the ends for which they exiled themselves from their homes in the Old World. They fled from persecution, and meant only to secure and protect themselves against its repetition. It remains yet to be seen which committed the greatest folly, they by narrowing, or we by extending, the right of suffrage.

When the struggle for our independence from England came on, the New Haven Colonies were found among the foremost and bravest. They furnished their full quota of men and means, and suffered all the privations and losses sustained by any of the thirteen Colonies. This has been eminently true of them ever since. We have been called upon to bear no strain, or to endure any loss or privation, that New Haven County has not stood nobly in her lot and place.

This historical sketch would not be complete without some mention of the churches, which were the real nucleus of the commonwealth. The church was the first care of all the New England colonists. In some few instances, the church, as an organization, came along with them across the waters. Where this was not the case, one of their first cares was to found one, that the foundations of civil and social order might be laid upon God's truth.

They were godly men, seed-corn sifted from the very best. They came for liberty to worship and serve God as they pleased. They kept this end in view at every step.

The churches at New Haven and Milford are supposed to have been formed on the same day. The method was the same in all the colonies constituting the New Haven jurisdiction. After some discussion between Mr. Davenport and Mr. Samuel Eaton, his colleague, on the nature of a "civil government in a New Plantation, whose design is religion," it was determined, on the 14th of June, as we now reckon (on the 2d of June, old style), to hold a public meeting of "all the free planters" "for the purpose of laying with due solemnities the foundations" both of church and state. This meeting was held in Mr. Newman's barn. The first church in this wilderness land, like its head, was born in a manger. The result of their deliberation and voting was to select twelve of their best and most approved men, who were to confer and consult together and select from their own number, or elsewhere, seven men who were "fit for the foundation-work of the church." The seven hewn pillars chosen were the same seven who laid the foundation of the state—Eaton, Davenport, Newman, Gilbert, Fugill, Punderson and Dixon. These seven persons first covenanted together, and then received others into their fellowship. Thus the first church of New Haven was founded on the 22d of August, 1639.

It is in place to say here, that although church and state are twin-children of the same womb, and have the same parents, they are entirely distinct. It was never the purpose of these men, who had fled into the wilderness from a state church and hierarchy, that the church should govern the state. They never allowed that the church, as such, had any power to choose civil magistrates. Indeed, church officers were ineligible to civil office. There was no confusion of church and state, and no purpose that the one should transact the business of the other. "Many could debate and vote in church-meeting who could have no vote at all in the government of the civil state." They affirmed and insisted that ecclesiastical and civil order must have different laws, different officers, and different powers. Though they may have the same ultimate end, they have different proximate ends, one the "preservation of human society," the other "the conversion, edification and salvation of souls." Although the right of suffrage was limited to church-members, and none could be freemen and eligible to office who were not members of some acknowledged church, there was no blending or confusion of the two. For this we have every reason to be grateful.

Mr. Davenport, whose strong and marked impress is seen in all the ecclesiastical and civil framework and management of both church and state, a man to whose clear head and sound heart, and broad views and Christian firmness, we owe so much for the cast and character of our government, our New England type of civilization, was the first pastor of this wilderness church. He continued to serve both it and the state, when occasion called for it, until the Colony he had so much to do in planting and training became a part of the Commonwealth of Connecticut, much to his grief.

He was followed in this office by a succession of men, who were distinguished alike for their scholarship and virtues—Pierpont, Whittlesey, and Dana.

One thing demands especial notice. Much denunciation has been lavished upon the New England fathers for the compulsory support of their churches, levying taxes to pay the salaries of their ministers and other current expenses. The New Haven Colony, to its honor, is an exception to this evil rule. It should be remembered, to their credit, that for many years after the settlement of their Colony, the church was supported by voluntary contributions, which were made on every Lord's day at the close of service. Not as now, by passing the contribution-box, but every one came up to the deacon's seat and deposited his own contribution, returning quietly to his place. It was not until a much later day, when perhaps men had become less godly and conscientious, that it was thought necessary to compel men, by assessing them, to support an institution so obviously for the public weal.

It must seem strange to us in our quiet, tranquil times, to recall the fact, that in all those early years the people never met for public worship without a complete military guard. We find in 1640 this order upon their records: "Every man that is appointed to watch, whether masters or servants, shall come every Lord's day to the meeting completely armed; and all others also are to bring their swords, no man exempted save Mr. Eaton, our Pastor, Mr. James, Mr. Samuel Eaton, and the two deacons." Seats were placed on each side of the front door for the soldiers. A sentinel was stationed in the turret. Armed watchmen patrolled the streets. Twice before each service the drum beat from the turret and along the main streets. When the congregation came together they resembled more a garrison than a congregation of worshippers.

Yet how peaceful and sacred these Sabbaths. From evening to evening no noise, no business, the whole population in church. Thus the years went on with changes, trials, sorrows, death, until the fathers slept and others rose in their stead, upon whom their mantles fell and who stood in their places.

The New Haven colonists were intense lovers of learning. Here the free school found a welcome and rose to prominence. For many years the people contributed annually to the support of Harvard College, sending up their wheat and wampum to keep it alive, and sending their sons to enjoy its privileges and bear away its honors. This, however, did not satisfy Mr. Davenport, who, during his latter years, urged again and again upon the Connecticut Colonies the importance of founding a college of their own. He was a scholar and student himself, and early saw the necessity of education of every grade to the life and perpetuity of the commonwealth, as well as the Christian religion. Although he did not live to see a college founded, he certainly was father of the thought. The seed he sowed sprang up in later years, and bore fruit in the noble institution, without a rival, if not without a peer in our land.

The Hopkins Grammar School, to-day one of the best preparatory schools in the country, is the oldest school in the State. The literary atmosphere of New Haven, its fine culture and excellent schools are no new things, but they have been true of it from the beginning. May it never cease to be the home of learning, refinement, and real Christian worth and excellence.

A few words of biography need to be appended to this sketch of colonial times.

Foremost among the great names of the colonists is Theophilus Eaton. He was born at Stratford, England, 1591, and was the son of a clergyman. He came to this country, first to Boston in 1637, then to New Haven in 1638. He was chosen first governor of New Haven Colony, and remained in office until his death, January 7, 1658. Mather calls him "the Moses of New Haven." "He carried in his very countenance a majesty which cannot be described." He was a magistrate of strict impartiality and inflexible honor. He had clear views of civil government far in advance of his times; he had a singular love of justice, and very decided opinions of the divine nature of human government as built on the Word of God. To him the New Haven Colony owed its existence, and to him and Mr. Davenport all those features which distinguish it from the other Colonies, its zeal for education, its impartial administration of justice, its freedom from frivolous and extravagant legislation. He was wont to say: "Some count it a great matter to die well, but I am sure it is a greater matter to live well." This is the key to his character, than which there is not a nobler in all our colonial history.

John Davenport, one of the two chief men in founding New Haven Colony, was born in Coventry, Eng., 1597. He was educated at Oxford; became vicar of St. Stephen's Church, Coleman street, London; soon became a non-conformist; resigned his benefice and fled to Holland, to escape the warrant that was out against him; preached to the English Church at Amsterdam for a season; became involved in difficulties about the indiscriminate baptisms of children, and resigned, when he emigrated to New England, reaching Boston on the 26th of June, 1637. The following spring he came with his company to New Haven. He and Mr. Eaton built their houses opposite each other on the same street, and became the leading spirits in the Colony.

He continued pastor of the church, as well as a directing and controlling power in the state, until near the close of his life. He lost hope somewhat when, against his decided opinion, the New Haven jurisdiction united with the Connecticut Colony. He saw a growing disposition on the part of the state to get control of the churches, a most serious evil, from which Connecticut suffered for many long years. Just at this time came a call from Boston. He made up his mind that "Christ's interests in New Haven Colony were miserably lost." His roots were loosened, and he was ready to leave his home and the child he had done so much to rear. Besides this, the action of the synod in establishing what was called "the half-way covenant," he opposed with all the vigor and ardor of his soul. The battle was to be fought in Boston. He wanted to be in the thickest of the fight. These considerations determined his removal to that city in 1668, thirty years after his settlement in New Haven, when he was more than seventy years old. The "dead line" was not quite so near in those days. The church in Boston was divided. The odious and mischievous "half-way covenant" prevailed. He died on the 11th day of March, 1670. A fine scholar, an able preacher, a clear-headed, far-seeing man, his views and opinions found an ample vindication in subsequent experience. The measures he maintained were just; those he opposed proved disastrous in the extreme.

Stephen Goodyeare, from the organization of the government until his death, was associated almost uniformly with Gov. Eaton, as Lieutenant-Governor. He was a fine business man and of great service to the Colony.

Thomas Greyson was another of the leading men, and was intrusted with much important public business.

Francis Newman, whose barn figures so largely in the early records of the Colony, deserves mention. He succeeded Gov. Eaton in office, the Joshua who came after Moses.

Thomas Fugill, secretary of state, John Punderson and Jeremy Dixon were among the seven pillars, both of church and state. Master Ezekiel Cheever, the father of New England schoolmasters, shines in the Colonial records. The boys had good reason to remember him.

Thomas Leete of Guilford, lieutenant-governor under Francis Newman, and first governor of the united Colonies of Connecticut and New Haven, was a man of wisdom and executive ability.

Goffe and Whalley, commonly known as the regicides, from their participation in the execution of Charles the First, found a retreat and an asylum in New Haven. On the accession of Charles the Second, they were compelled to flee the country. They came to Boston July 27, 1660, first, and resided for sometime openly in Cambridge. Their situation there becoming too exposed, they fled to New Haven March 7, 1661, and were concealed for awhile in Mr. Davenport's house. A royal proclamation was issued for their arrest. They were sought for by officers in New Haven, but could not be found. Fearing lest they should bring trouble upon their friend, Mr. Davenport, and others, they offered to surrender themselves to Lieut.-Gov. Leete. He was in no haste, however, to arrest them. After showing themselves openly in the streets of New Haven, so as to clear their friends from any complicity with their concealment, they fled to a cave near the summit of West Rock, known as now Judges' Cave, where they remained for awhile. They occupied another place near by, called the Lodge. They left New Haven and went (August 19) to Milford, and in 1664 to Hadley, where they remained until they died. It is believed that their bodies were brought to New Haven and buried by Dixwell, their companion in exile.

John Dixwell, the other regicide, came to New Haven in 1672, under the name of James Davids. He lived here in quiet security for seventeen years. The last years of his life he became very intimate with Mr. Pierpont, the minister. There seemed to be a strange and wonderful friendship between them. At his death he revealed his true character, and requested that a plain stone should mark his grave, with the initials J. D., Esq., inscribed on it. This was done as he wished.

Three avenues in the northwestern part of the city perpetuate the names and memory of the regicides.

Yale College was founded in 1700, and, traditionally, in this wise: ten eminent clergymen, roused to the importance of providing some means for a more liberal and thorough education for their sons, and others who were to become leaders in church and state, met at New Haven to consult concerning a collegiate school. At a subsequent meeting in Branford, these men brought forty folio volumes, and laid them down on a table with these words: "I give these books for the founding of a college in this Colony." This body of men, acting for the churches and ministry of the Colony of Connecticut, by this act founded the institution now known as Yale College.

In October of the following year, a charter was obtained from the legislature. In November, the trustees met for the first time in Saybrook, and passed this order: "That there shall be, and hereby is, erected and founded a collegiate school, wherein shall be taught the liberal arts and languages, in such place or places in Connecticut as the said trustees shall from time to time see cause to order."

Why found another college so near Harvard? It has been affirmed that a distrust of the theological soundness of this college was the real root-cause of the founding of Yale. But when you recall that the number of the Connecticut colonists was now 20,000, and also that the territory was an almost unbroken wilderness, the distance to Cambridge, and inconvenience and expense of travel were so serious, you will find the real reasons which moved these good men to found a college in their own Colony. This, and not bigotry, is the seed-thought of this noble university. The plan differed in some very essential particulars from that of Harvard. It was more unique and original having less of the European type. It was more indigenous, and more in accord with the spirit of the times. It was homogeneous, having all its board ministers; though this last is a doubtful advantage, and gave rise to disaffection in later years.

After a protracted and somewhat heated controversy, the new college was finally located in New Haven in 1717.

In 1718, came the great benefaction of Gov. Elihu Yale, a donation of books and other goods to the amount of £800. As a compliment to him the new building, recently erected, was named for him. This name passed by degrees from the building to the whole institution in 1745. The college passed through colonial times with various and alternating success. It came near extinction, however, during the Revolution. Its students and officers were dispersed, and its functions in a measure, suspended. The irregularities of the times, financial embarrassment, difficulties of subsistence, and the actual occupation, at one time, of New Haven by English troops, reduced the college to the lowest point.

In 1792 a change took place in the charter, which gave it a new lease of life, and brought it more closely into sympathy with the popular heart. Its prosperity was now assured.

Great changes have transpired in college customs since those early provincial days. It was no uncommon thing for derelict youths then to have their ears soundly boxed in the presence of the faculty and students. The formality and respect at that time demanded on the part of president and faculty, seems to us almost ludicrous. The freshmen, in those earlier times, held an almost menial position, being mere errand-boys for the upper classes. With the incoming of more democratic ideas, however, these old country notions and customs have long since naturally and happily disappeared.

From these small and adverse beginnings, Yale College has grown to its present commanding position. Its power in every department, in church and state, science and art, in literature and philosophy, has been wide and beneficent. Its graduates are everywhere. They nobly sustain and fulfil her proud yet modest motto—"*Lux et veritas.*"

The first president, or rector, of Yale College was Abraham Pierson, son of Rev. Mr. Pierson, one of the first settlers and first minister of Branford. He graduated from Harvard College in 1668. He was a good student, an able divine, a wise, judicious man. He instructed and governed the infant collegiate school, with general acceptance, from 1701 until 1707.

The subsequent presidents of Yale have been Rev. Timothy Cutter, S. T. D., chosen 1719; Rev. Elisha Williams, 1726; Rev. Thomas Clap, 1739; Rev. Naphthali Daggett, S. T. D., 1766; Rev. Ezra Stiles, S. T. D., LL.D., 1777; Rev. Timothy Dwight, D. D., LL.D., 1795; Rev. Jeremiah Day, D. D., LL.D., 1822; Rev. Theodore D. Woolsey, D. D., LL.D., 1846; Rev. Noah Porter, D. D., LL.D., 1871.

Presidents Stiles and Clap were men of exceptionally great learning; while Dr. Dwight, a grandson of Jonathan Edwards, was one whose powers as a thinker, gifts as a poet, and eloquence as a preacher were surpassed only by the fervor of his piety and the urbanity of his conversation and manners.

The present incumbent of the presidential chair, Rev. Noah Porter, D. D., LL.D., was born in Farmington, Dec. 14, 1811, and is considered to be one of the ablest of American metaphysicians.

Besides the presidents there have been professors of world-wide fame and splendid and varied acquisitions; Dana, Fitch, Goodrich, Marsh, Silliman, Packard, Hadley, and many others, have adorned their departments and added to the power and fame of the college. Many of its graduates have filled the highest offices of trust and honor. No institution has exerted a wider and more positive influence upon the culture and political character of the country.

The buildings are many, and some of them of great excellence. Battell Chapel is one of the finest buildings in design, materials, and solid elegance in the land, for that purpose. The Art School building, on the south-west corner of College Square, is one of considerable pretension and is admirable for its purpose. The Peabody Museum, named in honor of George Peabody, of London, its most liberal benefactor, one wing of which is completed, stands on the corner of High and Elm streets, just across the street from the College Square. It is an imposing building. The various cabinets and specimens are among the best, as far as they go.

The East and West Divinity halls, with Marquand Chapel between them, a gem in its line, the gift of the gentleman whose name it bears, are substantial and elegant buildings, affording fine accommodations for this department of the university. The Sheffield Scientific School, an institution of great merit and thoroughness, founded by Joseph Sheffield, Esq., constitutes another department of the university, and has substantial and commodious buildings at some distance from the College Campus, on the homestead of Mr. Sheffield. The departments of law and medicine have accommodations in other sections of the city.

Towns.

New Haven, the chief seat of the New Haven jurisdiction, is situated on a plain lying between two ranges of hills, on the east and on the west, and is limited, partly, on the northern side, by two mountains, called East and West rocks, which terminate abruptly at this point and form a marked feature of the scenery. It is at the head of a shallow harbor, between West and Mill Rivers, including also the neck between Mill River and the Quinnipiac, where a part of the town called Fair Haven is situated.

The town was originally laid out in nine squares. The central one is open and is styled the Green, the upper half of which is a beautiful slope, and was formerly a burying-ground; but, in 1831, the monuments were removed and the ground leveled. The lower, or level half, is surrounded by stately elms. It is divided in the centre by Temple Street, on which the churches are situated. Magnificent elms on either side of this broad street form a perfect arch, and make it one of the grandest in the world. There are three churches and the Old State House on the Green. Altogether it is one of the finest spots in the United States or Europe. The original squares, which cluster about the central square or Green, are divided each into four squares by streets running from northwest to southeast, and from northeast to southwest. The same general features have been measurably preserved in the extension of the modern city.

The city and town have distinct organizations and separate officers, a feature which has come down from colonial times, a sort of two-headed concern, not at all satisfactory or equitable in its representation in the legislature. The administration of justice is in the hands of a city court, while other courts, both of the State and the United States, hold sessions in the city.

The city is well supplied with schools of a high order. Many of the school-houses are commodious and elegant. The Hillhouse High School is one of great excellence. There are various private schools, which, together with Hopkins Grammar School, the oldest in the State, and Yale College, in its various departments, furnish the highest educational advantages.

New Haven is a port of entry, and has considerable coastwise and some foreign commerce. Manufactures are the principal source of its prosperity, and carriages, guns, builders' hardware, rubber goods, articles from iron, clocks, etc., are made.

There are many fine public buildings. Among these are several church edifices, college and seminary buildings, and elegant city hall and court-house, a commodious and well-managed State hospital, insurance building, music hall and opera houses. There are about forty churches of all denominations.

Many fine streets and handsome residences adorn the city. Hillhouse Avenue, Whitney Avenue, Prospect, Orange and Chapel streets are among the finest. The new, or lower Green, is a gem of beauty, surrounded with elegant houses. The old cemetery, on Grove Street, contains the ashes of Eaton, Clap, Stiles, Humphreys, Dwight, Eli Whitney, and many others of world-wide and national fame. Evergreen Cemetery, on the banks of the West River, is one of more modern pretension, and is an ornament and honor to the city.

Six daily and as many weekly papers keep the people well posted on current events. There are also several college papers as well as ponderous quarterlies.

New Haven is the largest city in the State, and the third in New England. Few cities in location, in historical interest, in educational institutions, in wealth, beauty or culture surpass it.

Among the most distinguished residents here is Leonard Bacon, D.D., for fifty years pastor of the First Church, and now professor in the theological department of Yale College, a man of great culture, an able preacher, a fine debater, and thoroughly versed in the colonial and ecclesiastical history of New England. Ex-Governors English, Ingersol and Bigelow also have their homes here. Mr. Sheffield, the founder of Sheffield Scientific School, is among the most honored citizens.

Waterbury was viewed by a colony from Farmington with reference to a settlement in 1673. August 21, 1674, land was purchased, on both sides of the Naugatuck, of the Indians "for £39, and divers other good causes." King Philip's war put a check upon its immediate settlement; but after peace was established the settlers returned to their purchase and commenced work in earnest. In 1684 they made a new purchase of land from the Indians, making in all a territory eighteen miles in length and ten miles in width, containing the present towns of Waterbury, Watertown and Plymouth, together with most of Middlebury, half of Wolcott, and a small part of Oxford and Prospect. This large, fine territory was gravely reported to the General Assembly "as capable of supporting thirty families." One wonders at the size of the families of those days, since the same territory now supports more than 20,000 persons, and is not half occupied.

The orignal town was located on an eminence on the western banks of the river, about a mile from the present location of the city.

For ten years the settlers were without a minister and the regular ordinances of religion. In 1689 Jeremiah Peck was settled among them, and remained until his death in 1699. Their first house of worship had no glass until 1716, a dark place in which to preach a gospel of light and life.

Waterbury is located on the Naugatuck (which runs its entire length) and the Mad Rivers, both of which furnish fine water-power. Hills rise on either side, forming an amphitheatre, in which the present city is mainly located, although many fine residences are creeping up the slopes of the hills. It has extensive and widely celebrated manufactories, with a capital of more than $6,000,000, seven churches, some of them among the finest in the State, two national banks, besides other banking institutions, a fine city hall, a hall for public amusements that seats 1,400 people, and is altogether one of the thriftiest and most energetic communities in the State. The Bronson Library contains 18,000 volumes, the gift of Cyrus Bronson of New York. The water-works are among the best in New England. It has a handsome park and fine cemetery. There are also several schools of considerable note located here. St. Margaret's Diocesan School for young ladies, the Academy of Notre Dame (Convent School), and Waterbury English and Classical School for boys. It has one daily and two weekly newspapers. To such a goodly city, the fifth in the State, has the wilderness settlement grown.

Rev. Samuel Hopkins, D. D., of such wide fame and remarkable powers, was a native of this town. He began life as a farmer's boy. At the age of fifteen he commenced his studies in Woodbury. He entered Yale College at the age of sixteen, and graduated in 1741. After graduating he went immediately to Northampton, Mass., where he studied theology with Jonathan Edwards. After he was licensed to preach, in 1642, he remained still at Northampton, pursuing his studies and occasionally preaching. He was settled in several small towns in Massachusetts and Connecticut. In April, 1770, he went to Newport, R. I., where he remained until the war of the Revolution interrupted his labors. In December, 1776, when the British took possession of Newport, he retired to Great Barrington. In 1780, he returned to Newport, only to find his old church and congregation too much diminished to provide for his support. He, however, continued to preach for them for what they could collect by a weekly contribution and the aid of generous friends, until he died, Dec. 20, 1803. Few men more influenced the religious thinking of his age. His writings were numerous, bold and forcible. He was author of a system of divinity, that bears his name and perpetuates his memory.

Lemuel Hopkins, M. D., was also another of Waterbury's great sons. He was as renowned in medicine as Samuel in divinity. He was founder of the Connecticut Medical Society, and also the author of several poems of considerable note.

Guilford was one of the colonies constituting the New Haven judisdiction. The first settlement was commenced in 1639, the next year after New Haven. The first settlers were Mr. Henry Whitefield, and several members of his church and congregation in England, to the number of about forty persons. They were drawn to this spot from the resemblance it bore to the homes they left behind them in England. They secured the land by peaceful purchase from the Indians. As a place for the security of all, a stone house was built, and is now standing, probably the oldest house in the United States. The first marriage in this town was solemnized in this building. The sumptuous marriage feast consisted of pork and peas. The government was first administered by four leading planters. When a Congregational church was formed in 1643, all power and authority was formally passed over to it, and the church, as in so many New England towns, became the nucleus and germ of the town. The government was in nearly all respects similar to New Haven, church-members alone being freemen and allowed to vote.

Guilford is situated (population about 3,000) fifteen miles east of New Haven, on Long Island Sound, and on the Shore Line Railroad. Farming and fishing are the principal pursuits. There are five churches and a fine stone school-house. Sachem's Head, a picturesque point of land, reaching out into the Sound, is a favorite summer resort, as are many other places in this noble old town. Off the coast is Leete's Island, named from Gov. Leete, one of the most distinguished men of colonial times, and the first governor of Connecticut. His house on this island was set on fire during the Revolution. This place was also the home of the famous Chittenden family.

Derby is situated (population about 12,000) nine miles northwest of New Haven, at the confluence of the Naugatuck and Housatonic rivers. About the year 1653, Lieut.-Gov. Goodyeare and others, of New Haven, purchased the land, and the year ensuing some few settlements were made.

It was incorporated in 1675, and the name changed from Paugassett into Derby. Derby Landing is at the head of navigation on the Housatonic River. Humphreysville, four miles above Derby Landing, is famous as the home of Gen. David Humphreys, who established here a large woollen factory, one of the first in the United States. He was a warm personal friend of Gen. Washington, one of his aids, ambassador to France under Jefferson, and afterwards to the court of Portugal. The modern township is divided into Derby Village, Birmingham, and Ansonia, named from Hon. Anson G. Phelps, of Phelps, Dodge & Co., who have large iron-works here.

North Haven (1,800) on the N. Y., N. H. and Hartford R. R., was formerly a part of New Haven. It lies on both sides of the Quinnipiac River. The gardens of North Haven are celebrated for early vegetables and fine small-fruits. The extensive salt-meadows produce immense quantities of grass.

The first settler of North Haven is believed to have been William Bradley, who had been an officer in Cromwell's army. He lived here soon after 1660, on land owned by Governor Eaton. The settlement was slow, and for nearly forty years the people attended church and buried their dead at New Haven. The women usually went on foot, attended two long services and returned, model pedestrians as well as model Christians. The Indians were numerous, but harmless, serving only to frighten women and children, never to injure them. The fine fishing and hunting grounds about the rivers drew them into this region. They swarmed at times along these streams, holding their "powwows," much to the terror and disgust of the people.

North Haven is the birthplace of Rev. Ezra Stiles, one of the most celebrated of Connecticut's great men, and for more than half a century the home of Dr. Benjamin Trumbull, the historian of Connecticut. He was born in Hebron in 1735; graduated at Yale in 1757; settled in North Haven in 1760, where he remained nearly sixty years. He wrote 4,000 sermons, published able essays on the inspiration of the Scriptures, wrote a history of Connecticut, and also of the United States. He received high honors from his *alma mater*, and was widely known and esteemed as an able divine and accurate historian.

Milford (3,500) was one of the settlements of the original New Haven Colony. The purchase of land was made from the Indians about the same time as those of New Haven, and settled in 1639, purchase price being six coats, ten blankets and one kettle, together with a number of hoes, knives, hatchets and glasses. The Indians, however, made a reservation of about twenty acres, which was subsequently bought in 1651, for six coats, two blankets and two pairs of breeches.

The original settlers were from the counties of Essex and York, and came over with Messrs. Eaton and Davenport's company, and remained with them one year before making a permanent settlement. They located themselves on either side of Mill River and West-end Brook, for convenience of themselves and cattle. The town was named Milford in commemoration of their native town in England.

A court of five judges was directed to set out a meeting-house lot in such manner as they should judge most convenient for public good. The site was the one occupied by the present meeting-house of the First Society, where it stood until 1727.

The first settlers being godly men and women, they formed themselves at once into a church, according to their peculiar views. It was formed in New Haven on the second of August, 1639. Peter Pruden was the first minister. In 1741, forty-seven persons, being dissatisfied with Mr. Whittlesey's moderate opinions, declared their dissent from the established church, professing themselves to be Presbyterians, according to the Church of Scotland. They were stoutly opposed by the First Church, having, in this respect, a common experience with all new churches in both the River and Sound colonies, and a protracted and bitter opposition, sometimes persecution even, followed. They were not invested with their full legal rights for nineteen years.

In 1648 a famous battle was fought near the town between the Mohawk and Milford Indians, resulting in the utter defeat of the former. In all the wars in which the county has been engaged, Milford has furnished her full quota of brave men.

There is a quarry of beautiful serpentine marble in the eastern section of the town. The harbor, never deep, has been gradually filling up since the first settlement. Milford Island, containing ten acres, is about three-fourths of a mile from the shore. Milford Point, at the southwest extremity of the town, is a place of some note, and also a summer resort.

There are five houses of worship, three Congregational, two Episcopal. The first church was organized in 1727, under Rev. Jonathan Merrick. The general intelligence of the people is evidenced from the fact that it has furnished more young men, who have been liberally educated, than any other town of its population in the State.

Wallingford formerly belonged to the original purchase made by Gov. Eaton and John Davenport, in 1638. The settlement was projected in 1669, and called New Haven Village. The first minister was the Rev. Samuel Street. The houses were fortified during King Philip's war, and much anxiety felt for the safety of the people. It is watered by the Quinnipiac River, and lies on the N. Y., N. H. and Hartford Railroad, twelve miles from New Haven. It contains nine churches, five schools, one hotel, extensive manufactories of britannia and silver ware, one newspaper, boot manufactories, and machine shops.

The Wallingford Community, a branch of Oneida Community, was founded here in 1850, by John H. Noyes and Henry Allen. It comprises 340 acres, 150 of which is covered by a valuable water-power belonging to the Community. Their business is agriculture, horticulture, job-printing, and book-making in all forms.

Lyman Hall, one of the signers of the Declaration of Independence, was a native of this town. He graduated at Yale in 1747, and first studied theology, but afterwards medicine. He subsequently removed to Georgia, and was a delegate to the general Congress in 1775, and afterwards became governor of Georgia.

One of the most remarkable tornadoes ever known visited Wallingford August 9, 1878. A large number of houses were caught up and whirled from their foundations, and crushed into fragments. One church was demolished, the upper story torn from the fine new high school house, the large trees were twisted and uprooted along the track of the whirlwind. Several persons were killed, others maimed for life, and much property destroyed. The scars of the terrible tornado still remain. It will not soon pass from the minds of those who witnessed its power or looked upon its desolation. It awakened much interest in scientific circles, and a careful study of this strange and unusual phenomenon.

The remaining towns of New Haven County are Bethany, originally a parish in the town of Woodbridge, and famous for being the scene of the celebrated Dayton Robbery, committed by a company of Tories from Long Island; Branford, which owes its final settlement to religious controversy and dissension at Wethersfield, beautifully situated on Lake Saltonstall, much frequented as a place of summer resort, and off the sea coast of which is a fine cluster of islands in the Sound called Thimble Islands, among which is Money Island, where Capt. Kidd is said to have concealed large sums of money. In this town also was once the home of Montowise, an early Indian chief. The place is the summer residence of several wealthy gentlemen.

Cheshire, originally a part of Wallingford, the seat of an Episcopal academy, founded in 1801; East Haven, incorporated and taken from New

Haven in 1735, and noted as being a favorite place of resort of the Indians, as also on account of the first iron-works in Connecticut having been established here in 1655; Hamden, also originally a part of New Haven, embracing several manufacturing villages, among them Whitneyville, so named from Hon. Eli Whitney, the inventor of the cotton gin, where is located Mount Carmel, one of the most elevated eminences in the State; Madison, formerly a part of Guilford, and sharing in all the colonial glory of that old town—a favorite summer resort. The famous regicides, Goffe and Whalley are said to have stopped in their wanderings on the banks of the stream west of the churches, and gave it the name of Pilgrim's Harbor—a name it still bears.

Middlebury, in which town is Break-Neck Hill, on whose summit the army of Gen. Lafayette, while on their way to the Hudson, is said to have encamped; North Branford, and Orange (so called for William, Prince of Orange, King of England), noted as the place where the British landed when they invaded New Haven in 1779; Orford, famous for its mineral spring, called the Pool, whose waters are said to heal salt-rheum and other kindred complaints, and which are reported, moreover, never to freeze, even in the coldest weather, nor even to fail in times of the severest drought; Southbury; Woodbridge named for the first minister, Benj. Woodbridge, settled here in 1742; Prospect and Wolcott. Some of the most charming scenery in Connecticut is found in the valley of the Naugatuck at a celebrated pleasure resort called High Rock Grove, owned by the Naugatuck Railroad Co., and visited annually by thousands. Illustrations of the same are given in this work.

Meriden—This city occupies a natural amphitheatre among the surrounding hills, midway between the cities of Hartford and New Haven, eighteen miles distant on the New York, New Haven & Hartford Railroad. No place in Connecticut has sprung into existence so quickly as a manufacturing centre. The ground on which the city now stands was, twenty years ago, a farm. The comparison to-day is bewildering, and a transformation scene is enjoyed.

The refinements of civilization and the resistless tide of manufacture have taken possession, and the result is churches, schools, immense manufacturing establishments, elegant private residences, and a city of twenty thousand people. In 1870, Meriden had a population of 10,495. To-day it is one of the most enterprising cities of New England, with public water-works, gas, electric lights, telephones, banks, insurance companies, daily and weekly papers, modern built hotels, and all the requirements to meet the demands of modern civilization. Silver and plated ware, lamps and lamp trimmings, house furnishing hardware, agricultural implements, machinery, hand-bells, spectacles, hammers, vises, butts, lanterns, coffee mills, spoons, faucets, scissors, shears, breech-loading guns, dies, hardware and sheet metal goods, forks, coffin trimmings, punching-presses, pewterer's machinery, glassware, paper boxes, lathes, furniture casters, piano stools, japanned and tinware, brass screws, butcher and shoe knives, fine cutlery, door locks and knobs, door bells, corsets, etc., are made in Meriden.

The growth of this city and the success of its manufacturing establishments is a commentary on the skill, financial ability and enterprise of her people.

Orville H. Platt, United States Senator. Among the list of Connecticut's public men, the name of Orville H. Platt stands foremost as a Christian and philanthropic statesman. He was born in Washington, Litchfield County, Conn., July 19, 1827. His father, Daniel G. Platt, was a farmer and the son learned his first lessons in life on the farm and at the district school until he was nearly twenty-one years of age. Later he studied law and was admitted to the bar in his native county in 1849. For a time he was a resident of Towanda, Bradford County, Pa., associated with Hon. Ulysses Mercer, now Judge of the Supreme Court of Pennsylvania. In 1851 he returned to his native State and located in the then village of Meriden, in which he saw great possibilities. Here he entered into the practice of law, and has since been identified with its interests and prosperity. His first public office in connection with the State Government was clerk of the Senate in 1855-6. In 1857 he was Secretary of State. He was a member of the Senate in 1861-2, and a member of the House in 1864 and 1869, in the latter year serving as Speaker. From 1877 to 1879 he was State Attorney for New Haven County, which office he held until he was elected in the latter year United States Senator to succeed Hon. William H. Barnum.

Mr. Platt is tall in person, and has a genial, popular but commanding presence. He is an able lawyer, making a specialty of patent cases. In private life he is known as a Christian statesman, interested in all the movements for the general good of society. His term will expire March 3, 1885.

NEW LONDON COUNTY.

NEW LONDON COUNTY, as originally constituted by the General Court in 1666, embraced territory extending from Pawkatuck River on the east, to the western bounds of Homonasset Plantation on the west, and from the interior settlements on the north, to Long Island Sound on the south. As now constituted, New London County is bounded north by Tolland and Windham counties, on the east by Windham County and Rhode Island, on the south by Long Island Sound, and by the Connecticut River and Middlesex County on the west. Its average length from east to west is twenty-six miles, and it has a medium breadth of twenty miles.

The face of the country is diversified by hill and dale, and is well supplied with streams of water. The soil is of varied fertility, but generally adapted to grazing and fruit growing, and moderately to general agriculture. Its navigable waters are extensive, and unsurpassed, for maritime purposes, by those of any section of equal extent upon the coast.

Notwithstanding these natural advantages, which rendered it an inviting locality for the early English settlers to improve, more than one-fourth of a century elapsed after the planting of a Colony at Plymouth before an attempt was made by the emigrants to settle upon any portion of this domain. A principal cause of this delay was doubtless the fact that the territory was pre-occupied by the Pequots, a tribe of Indians belonging to the widespread Algonquin race. This powerful tribe of savages had, by their cruelty, become the dread of the whites, far and near. It had, in fact, grown into a settled conviction on the part of the colonists, that it was only by their complete overthrow that eastern Connecticut could be colonized. This tribe inhabited a broad extent of territory, but their central seat was between the Thames and Mystic rivers in the eastern part of the present town of Groton. Their principal hamlets were overlooked and guarded by two fortifications, the one on Pequot Hill, and the other on Fort Hill. The Colony of Massachusetts had already failed in her attempt at their subjugation. At this juncture a company of ninety men was raised in the vicinity of Hartford, and placed under the command of Maj. John Mason, to chastise and subjugate the offending tribe. He was accompanied by Uncas, the Mohegan chief, and friend of the white man, at the head of seventy warriors. After a circuitous and well-planned march, Capt. Mason reached their fortress on Pequot Hill on the morning of June 5, 1637, undiscovered by the Indians till too late to make a successful defense. The English won a decisive victory over their savage foes. Their fort was destroyed, their dwellings consumed, and half the entire nation slain. By this single contest, in the overthrow and annihilation of the Pequot nation, the fate of eastern Connecticut and the adjoining country was decided. Unlike what till then had taken place elsewhere, eastern Connecticut was obtained by conquest.

New London County was the arena of military events scarcely less exciting during the Revolutionary period. On the 6th of September, 1781, a large part of the town of New London was laid in ashes by that infamous traitor, Benedict Arnold. The British troops burnt sixty-five dwellings, containing ninety-seven families, thirty-one stores, eighteen shops, twenty barns, and nine public edifices, including the court-house and several churches.

Fort Griswold on Groton Heights, after an obstinate resistance, surrendered to the enemy. The valiant Col. Ledyard was, after the surrender, slain with his own sword. Seventy officers and privates were also murdered.

During the war of 1812, the southern portion of the county was again menaced by the enemy. At this time the attack was made upon Stonington. On the 9th of August, 1814, Sir Thomas Hardy, in command of the British squadron, approached Stonington and bombarded the place vigorously for several hours. The attack was renewed each day till the 12th, and then as all their efforts to burn the town had proved abortive, the enemy withdrew.

In possession of rare maritime advantages and railroad facilities, the county of New London has, during the past half century, greatly prospered, its population having increased from 35,943 in 1820 to 73,137 in 1880.

TOWNS.

New London, as originally organized, included all the territory extending four miles on each side of the "Mohegan River," reaching north six miles from the sea. The Indian name of the prospective township was Pequot. A settlement was commenced here in 1646. The place was then known as Nameaug. In March, 1648, the General Court recommended that the town from that date should be called New London, and the river named Thames. New London was constituted a town in 1649.

The names of John Winthrop, Jr., Esq., Rev. Richard Blinman, Samuel Lathrop and Robert Allen were prominent among the early settlers.

The town is situated on the west bank of the Thames, three miles from Long Island Sound. It is four miles in length from north to south, and has an average breadth of three-fourths of a mile. New London was constituted a city in 1784. By the act of incorporation the entire township is included within the city limits. New London is also a half-shire town and a port of entry. Owing to the unevenness of the site, the city is, for the most part, irregularly laid out. Yet it contains many handsome public and private structures. Possessing as it does, one of the finest and most capacious harbors on the coast, it occupies a prominent rank among the commercial cities of New England.

The maritime surroundings of New London have had a marked influence in developing the business of the place. The whale and seal fisheries have at times constituted an important branch of commerce. The place is defended by Fort Trumbull, which stands upon the west side of the Thames, about one mile below the city.

Richard Law, LL.D., son of Gov. Jonathan Law, was born at Milford, March 17, 1733; graduated at Yale 1751; was admitted to the bar, and settled in New London, where he died Jan. 26, 1806. He held successively the offices of representative, member of the council, judge, and chief justice of the superior court, member of the Continental Congress, judge of the district court, and mayor of New London. This last municipal office he held twenty-two years.

Rev. Gurdon Saltonstall, son of Col. Nathan, and grandson of Sir Richard Saltonstall, was born at Haverhill, Mass., March 27, 1666, graduated at Harvard in 1684, and was ordained, Nov. 25, 1691, minister at New London, where he continued to discharge the duties of his sacred office in a most satisfactory manner till elected governor of the Colony in 1708, which office he held until his death in 1724.

John Winthrop, F. R. S., son of Gov. Winthrop of Massachusetts, was born in Groton, Eng., Feb. 12, 1605. His fine genius was improved by a liberal education at the universities of Cambridge and Dublin, and by travel on the Continent. He first came to New England in 1631, but three years later returned to Europe. While there he was empowered by Lords Say and Brook to make a settlement upon Connecticut River, and was commissioned as governor of the plantation. On his return to the New World in 1635, he did not press his claim to the chief magistracy, but caused a fort to be built at Saybrook, and otherwise gave aid to the settlers. New London is the home of Governor Waller.

The first settlers of Stonington in 1646 began their plantation under the direction of the younger Winthrop. He continued to reside at New London, and was identified with the public affairs of the town until elected governor of the Colony in 1657. Subsequently he resided in Hartford. He held the office of governor of Connecticut and of the united Colonies to the time of his death in 1676.

Fitz John Winthrop, son of the preceding, was born March 14, 1639. In 1689, he was, with the rank of major-general, commander of the army sent to operate against Canada. Subsequently he was an agent of the Colony to Great Britain, and rendered such service that the legislature presented him with £500 sterling. In 1698 he was elected governor of Connecticut, and was annually re-elected to the office till the time of his death, November 27, 1717.

Norwich—The domain lying between the Yantic and Shetucket rivers was by the Indians termed "Mohegan." In May, 1659, the General Court authorized the planting of a colony in the Mohegan country, and in the next month Uncas and his brother Wawequn, for the consideration of £70, ceded to the English a portion of their territory nine miles square, including within its limits the present towns of Norwich, Franklin, Bozrah, Lisbon and Sprague, with portions of other towns. In the spring of 1660 thirty-five proprietors, under the guidance of Maj. John Mason and Rev. James Fitch, removed from Saybrook hither, and established themselves in the locality now known as Norwich Town. The name Norwich was given to the settlement in 1662, in honor of Norwich in England. In the old Saxon language it signifies North Castle, and the towering rocks found here might easily suggest the idea of battlements.

The township has an average length from north to south of seven miles, and a medium breadth of three miles. The surface is diversified by hills and plains, which give to the place a picturesque appearance. The prevailing soil is dark-colored loam, which is generally fertile. Norwich is favored with excellent water-privileges. The Shetucket from the northeast, and the Yantic from the northwest (after dashing over high rocks at Norwich Falls, and rushing through a narrow, winding chasm in the cove below), unite, and in their union become the Thames. The entire length of the Thames, thus constituted, to Long Island Sound, is fourteen miles.

Norwich Town is situated about two miles above the navigable waters of the Thames. This place for two-thirds of a century was the principal centre of business in the town. It was also the seat of the courts till comparatively a late date. The buildings, though not modern in style, are quite respectable in appearance. The location had good natural advantages for the planting of a town at that date. Norwich City was incorporated as such in 1784. At an early day it was known as Chelsea or the Landing, being situated at the head of the Thames. Although the locality possessed rare maritime and other advantages, they remained unimproved till about 1726. At first it required great labor to remove the rocks and ledges, and reclaim the low, swampy grounds before eligible sites for the streets and for their dwellings could be secured. But by unremitting effort these obstacles have been overcome, and now a pleasant, romantic city crowns these rugged hillsides. The public buildings include the court-house and jail, the free academy, and several elegant churches. Almost the entire distance from the town plot to the city is studded with elegant and substantial residences.

The vast water-power of Norwich has, to a large extent, been brought into use. The Shetucket has been dammed at Greenville, at Taftville, and at Occum, and large mills have been erected at each of these villages for manufacturing purposes. Greenville is particularly distinguished for its mammoth paper mills. The waters of the Yantic River have been utilized at the Falls, and at other villages higher up the stream.

The Yantic Cemetery, on the east bank of the Yantic River, was consecrated in 1844. It includes an extensive area of ground, agreeably diversified, in a romantic section, and already contains many elegant and costly monuments.

The ancient Indian cemetery was located at the head of the cove. It contains a granite obelisk that commemorates the name of Uncas. The corner-stone of this monument was laid by President Jackson in 1833. The history of Norwich from its first settlement to the present time has been characterized by steady improvement. The population of the town and city in 1880 was 21,141.

Samuel Huntington, LL.D., born in Windham in 1731, was admitted to the bar, and settled in Norwich, where he soon rose to the front rank in his profession. In 1775, having previously held the office of judge of the Supreme Court, he was chosen a delegate to the Continental Congress, and, on the 4th of July, 1776, he appended his name to the Declaration of Independence. In 1779 he was chosen president of Congress, and was re-elected to the same office in 1780. In 1783 he was re-elected to Congress, and during the following year he was appointed chief justice of the Superior Court. In May, 1786, he was elected governor of the State, and was annually re-elected until his death in 1796.

Gov. Huntington, though not a graduate, had received honorary degrees from Dartmouth and Yale.

Rev. Nathaniel Whitaker, D. D., was born in 1710, graduated at Harvard in 1730, and was installed as the first minister of Chelsea, in Norwich, in 1761. As Mr. Whitaker was a man of fine talents and of prepossessing appearance, and had also manifested a deep interest in the welfare of the Mohegan Indians, he was, in 1766, selected to accompany Occum in his mission to England and Scotland. The selection proved to be judicious, for the collections from this source amounted to more than £10,000. His publications were quite numerous, consisting of sermons, tracts, etc. He died in Virginia in 1795.

Rev. James Fitch was born an Boking, Eng., in 1622, and came to New England 1638. He was for seven years in Hartford under the instruction of Messrs. Hooker and Stone. In 1646 he was ordained over a church at Saybrook, where he remained until 1660, when he removed, with the bulk of his people, to Norwich, and in that town passed the remaining active days of his life. When the infirmities of old age obliged him to cease from his public labors, he retired to the home of his children in Lebanon, where he died November 18, 1702. He became acquainted with the language spoken by the Mohegan Indians in the neighborhood of Norwich, and often preached to them in their native tongue. For his second wife he married Priscilla, daughter of Major John Mason, by whom he had seven sons and one daughter.

Benjamin Huntington, LL.B., was born in Norwich, in 1736, graduated at Yale in 1761, and, being admitted to the bar, settled in his native town, and soon rose to eminence in his profession. He was a member of the Continental Congress from 1780 to 1784, and from 1787 to 1788, and a representative to Congress from 1789 to 1791. He was a judge of the Superior Court from 1793 to 1797. On the incorporation of Norwich City in 1784, he was chosen its first mayor, in which office he served until 1796. He died in 1800.

Maj. John Mason, the military leader of the early settlers of the Colony of Connecticut, was born in England about the year 1600, and was bred to arms in the Netherlands under Sir Thomas Fairfax. During the civil disturbances in England in Cromwell's time, Fairfax requested him to join his standard, and assist those who were contending for the liberties of the people, but he did not comply with the request.

Mason arrived at Dorchester, Mass., in 1630, in company with the Rev. John Wareham and others, and in 1635, he removed to Windsor, Conn., and assisted in laying the foundation of a new Colony. The history of the part he acted in the Pequot war in 1637 is given in detail elsewhere. He removed from Windsor to Saybrook in 1647, and from thence to Norwich in 1660, where he died in 1672. He was successively commander-in-chief of the militia of Connecticut, a magistrate from 1642 to 1660, and deputy governor of the Colony until he retired from public life in 1670. He was wise and prompt in planning and energetic in executing whatever he deemed best for the general good. At the request of the General Court, he drew and published a brief history of the Pequot war which has since been reprinted.

Benedict Arnold descended from an honorable Rhode Island family, where one of his ancestors, bearing the same name, held the office of governor for fifteen years. Two brothers of this family—Benedict and Oliver—removed from Newport to Norwich in 1730. The elder Benedict, the father of the traitor, soon became engaged in business, and not long after his arrival in Norwich, married Mrs. Hannah King, whose maiden name was Lathrop. Benedict was born in Norwich January 3, 1741. Early in life he was apprenticed to Dr. Lathrop, a druggist in Norwich, with whom he remained during his minorty. He subsequently embarked in the same business in New Haven, and while there became captain of a company of militia. After the battle at Lexington he made a hasty march to Cambridge at the head of his company, and volunteered his services to the Massachusetts Committee of Safety. With the rank of colonel in the Continental army he joined Ethan Allen and assisted in the taking of Ticonderoga. Having been wounded at Quebec and at Saratoga, and so rendered unfit for active field service, he was placed in command at Philadelphia, after that place had been evacuated by Carleton, in 1778. He was at this time a major-general in the Continental army. While in Philadelphia, Arnold married the daughter of Judge Shippen, a Tory. At his own earnest solicitation he was, in August, 1780, appointed by Washington to the command of West Point. His eternally infamous act of treachery soon followed. Arnold received from the British government the stipulated reward of his perfidy. He was made a brigadier-genaral in the British service, which rank he held throughout the war. In childhood Arnold was quarrelsome, untruthful, and disobedient; and in manhood was ambitious, perfidious, dishonest, and revengeful. He died in disgrace at Gloucester Place, London, in June, 1801.

Stonington.—Southerton, or Stonington, was for a time claimed by Massachusetts by virtue of assistance rendered to Connecticut in the conquest of the Pequots. And further, this place was supposed to be included in a grant to them by the Earl of Warwick and Council for British America, December 10, 1643, and was settled by persons who went thither under John Winthrop, Jr., in 1646. It was assigned to Connecticut by commissioners of the United Colonies July 26, 1647. This order being revoked, the settlers at Southerton petitioned to Massachusetts that they might be a township, which was granted October 25, 1658, and they were united with Suffolk County. They continued to sustain this relation, and entered into a voluntary compact on the 30th of June to govern themselves and conduct their own affairs. But after Connecticut obtained the Royal Charter in 1662, the town, being included in the grant, was re-annexed to Connecticut.

In October, 1665, the General Court gave to the settlement the name of Mystic. In May, 1666, the name was changed to Stonington. The Indian name was Paweatuck.

The water-privileges of the town, including the Mystic River on the west, and the Paweatuck on the east, with the several intermediate streams known as Copp's Brook, Stony Brook and Anguilla Brook, are of great value. All these streams discharge their waters into the Sound, thus affording excellent manufacturing and maritime privileges. Add to these natural advantages the "Point," with its harbor, breakwater and railroad, and it will be made clear how so many large and self-sustaining villages have grown up within the township. These are the Borough, on Fisher's Island Sound, which was incorporated as such in 1801; Mystic Bridge, Greenmanville and Mystic on Mystic River; and Stillmanville and Paweatuck Bridge, on the Paweatuck River. These have in the past been largely dependent upon shipbuilding and other maritime interests for their prosperity, and have in turn been efficient nurseries for the production of an able body of seamen. The population in 1880 was 7,353.

Capt. Thomas Miner, born in England in 1608, came to New England in 1630, and was one of the original settlers at New London, being associated with Winthrop, in 1647. In 1653 he removed to Stonington and made that place his future home. He was for a long period engaged in civil affairs, and during King Philip's war rendered efficient service as a military leader. He died at Stonington Oct. 23, 1690.

Thomas Stanton, "The Indian Interpreter," came to this country in 1636, and with almost unparalleled facility, acquired the mastery of the dialects spoken by the aborigines in New England. In 1638 he was appointed to the office of interpreter by the General Court of Connecticut. He also received the appointment of interpreter-general from the Commissioners of the United Colonies. His peculiar qualifications as an interpreter rendered his services quite indispensable throughout New England. He was one of the early settlers of Stonington. His long-established residence was on the Connecticut side of the Paweatuck River, where he died in 1678.

William Cheesborough, the first permanent settler of Stonington, was born in Boston, Eng., in 1594. He came to New England with Gov. Winthrop and first settled in Boston. In 1649 he settled in Stonington. He held the office of first selectman of that town for a succession of years till his death in 1667.

Capt. George Denison, born in 1618, came to New England in 1631, in company with the Rev. John Eliot, and settled first in Roxbury, Mass. In 1651 he became a resident of New London and there remained till 1654, when he removed to Stonington, where he became permanently established. From 1671 to 1694, he represented Stonington in the General Court. As a military leader he became distinguished. He participated in the Narragansett Swamp fight in 1675, where he rendered important service. In March, 1676, he, with others, made an incursion into the Narragansett country and made Canonchet, the chief sachem, a prisoner. The savage, when offered his life on condition of living in peace, said, "he chose to die before his heart grew soft." The prisoner was shot at Stonington by Oneco, son of Uncas. During the year 1676, Capt. Denison and his volunteers killed and took as prisoners two hundred and thirty of the enemy. He died at Hartford in 1694, while attending a session of the General Court.

Groton was constituted an ecclesiastical society in 1703, from the section of Pequot country lying east of the Thames River. It was incorporated as a town in 1705, from territory which originally belonged to New London. It was named in honor of Groton, Suffolk County, Eng., the birthplace of John Winthrop, Jr., the first governor of Connecticut after the union. The township is uneven, being hilly and abounding in rocks. A narrow tract extending along the Sound, and another extending up the Thames to a considerable distance from its mouth, are pleasant and fertile, but the remainder is difficult of cultivation. The town is watered by the Mystic and Poquonoc rivers, which discharge their waters into the Sound.

There are five villages in the township, in each of which is a post-office—Groton Centre on the north, Mystic River on the east, Noank and Poquonoc on the south, and Groton Bank on the west.

Mystic River is navigable for vessels of 400 tons burden to Mystic Bridge. Shipbuilding has been carried on to some extent at the head of Mystic.

A monument has been erected on Groton Heights in memory of those who were slain in Fort Griswold in 1781. Its foundation stone is 130 feet above tide-water, and the monument itself rises 127 feet above its base.

The population in 1880 was 5,127.

John Ledyard, the distinguished traveler, was born in Groton in 1751. He sailed with Capt. Cook on his third voyage of discovery, and witnessed the tragical end of the great circumnavigator at Owyhee. After extensive travel in the sparsely inhabited provinces of Europe and Asia, he was finally employed by the African Association, which had been organized under the direction of Sir Joseph Banks, to make a thorough exploration of the interior portions of the African continent. He engaged in the service of this company with great enthusiasm and sailed from London on his tour of discovery June 30, 1788. After repeated delays at Cairo, he died at that place, greatly lamented, Jan. 17, 1789.

Col. William Ledyard, brother of the above, was also a native of Groton. In 1781 he was military commander of the district which included Fort Griswold on Groton Heights. The fortress was not strong nor sufficiently manned to resist a large force. When a detachment of British troops, numbering about 900 men, under the command of Col. Eyre were advancing toward the heights, the brave Ledyard remarked: "If I must lose to-day honor or life, those who know me best can tell which it will be." With only one hundred and fifty men he made a brave but ineffectual resistance, for, overpowered by numbers, the fort was carried by assault with the bayonet. Col. Eyre and Maj. Montgomery, having been slain, the command devolved upon Maj. Bloomfield, who inquired who commanded. Ledyard replied, "I did command, sir, but you do now;" and presented to him his sword. The ferocious officer instantly ran him through with his own sword. All the Americans in the fort, numbering about seventy, were brutally slain after they had surrendered.

Silas Deane was born in Groton, graduated at Yale in 1758, and became a resident of Wethersfield. In 1774 he was chosen a member of the Continental Congress, and while acting in that capacity was appointed as an agent from his own government to the Court of France to enlist the sympathies and secure the co-operation of the French people in our struggle for independence. He arrived in Paris in July, 1776. Through his influence Lafayette, Rochambeau and others were induced to aid the patriot cause. With Dr. Franklin and Arthur Lee, he was commissioner for negotiating treaties with foreign powers. He died at Deal, in England, in 1789.

Sprague was incorporated as a township in 1861, from the territory of Franklin and Lisbon. It is well supplied with streams of water, which afford extensive manufacturing privileges. It is washed by the Shetucket the entire extent of its territory from the northwest to the southeast boundary. Little River waters the eastern section of the town, and Beaver Brook the western. Sprague was organized principally as a manufacturing town. In the village of Baltic, in the central part of the town, upon the Shetucket River, is located a mammoth cotton mill. In the same village are two woolen mills on Beaver Brook, which there unites with the Shetucket. At the village of Hanover, two miles northeast of Baltic, is located a woolen mill, on Little River; and at the village of Versailles, two miles southeast of Baltic, is another woolen mill on the same stream. The population in 1880 was 3,207.

Colchester.—The General Court, in October, 1698, enacted that a township should be organized at or near the place called Jeremiah's Farm, on the road to New London. This locality was then in Hartford County. In October, 1699, it was called Colchester, and annexed to New London County. Some of the names prominent among the original planters were those of the Rev. John Bulkley, Samuel Gilbert, Michael Taintor and Joseph Pomeroy. The face of the township is uneven. The soil is a gravelly loam, of medium fertility. The borough of Colchester was incorporated in 1824.

The borough contains a pleasant village, centrally situated upon elevated ground, of perhaps fifty or sixty houses. Bacon Academy is located in this village; also a Congregational church. The extensive works of the Hayward Rubber Company are located a short distance east of the village. The population of the town in 1880 was 2,974.

Rev. John Bulkley, first minister in Colchester, was a son of Rev. Gershom Bulkley, who had been pastor of the churches in New London and Wethersfield. His mother was a daughter of President Chauncy of Harvard College. He graduated at Cambridge in 1699, was ordained in 1703, and died in June, 1731. He was regarded as one of the most profound and learned men in New England. He was thoroughly versed in theology, law, medicine, and science in general. Griswold was constituted the North Society in Preston in October, 1716. It was incorporated as a town in 1815, and received the name of Griswold. The Indian name of the settlement was Pachaug. The surface of the township is uneven. The prevailing soil is a gravelly loam, of medium fertility. Jewett City is the principal village in the town. It is located on the east side of the Quinebaug River, and contains about 1,000 inhabitants.

Hopeville is a small manufacturing village, situated on the Pachaug River, about 2½ miles east of Jewett City.

Doaneville and Glasko are two manufacturing villages located quite on the eastern border of the town. Glasko contains the Griswold paper-mill.

The population in 1880 was 2,745.

Montville was constituted the North Parish in New London in May, 1714. It was incorporated as a town in 1786 from territory which originally belonged to New London, and received the name of Montville.

Montville was originally the royal seat of Uncas, the Mohegan sagamore, and continued to be the residence of the royal family till it became extinct. In the eastern part of the town was located a large Indian reservation, which was held by the Indians in common till 1790, when it was divided among the families by the legislature of Connecticut. Since that period they have been under the care of guardians. Their interests have been carefully guarded, and much has been done to improve their condition. Still, the tribe is wasting, and but a remnant now remains. This reservation has for some years been favored with a convenient church edifice. Though agriculture is the principal business of the inhabitants, there are yet two manufacturing villages on the Oxoboxo River, in the southern part of the town. These are Uncasville and Montville, and each has a post-office.

The population in 1880 was 2,666.

William Hillhouse was the son of the Rev. James Hillhouse of New London, now Montville, where he was born August 25, 1728. He was for more than fifty years a member of the legislature, and for forty years a Judge of the Court of Common Pleas. From 1783 to 1786 he was a member of the Continental Congress. In 1792 he received the honorary degree of A. M. from Yale College. He died January 12, 1816.

James Hillouse, LL.D., son of the above, was born in Montville, October 21, 1754, and graduated at Yale in 1773. He was an officer in the war of the Revolution; in 1791 was chosen a member of Congress; from 1796 to 1810 was a member of the United States Senate; from 1810 to 1825 was Commissioner of the School Fund of the State; and from 1782 to 1832 was Treasurer of Yale College. He died at New Haven, December 29, 1832.

Rev. Sampson Occum, an Indian preacher of the Mohegan tribe, was born in the present town of Montville in 1723, and received his education from the Rev. Dr. Wheelock, the founder and first President of Dartmouth College. From a roving savage he became a humble Christian, and for about ten years was employed as a teacher among the natives of Long Island. In August, 1759, he was ordained by the Suffolk Presbytery. In 1766 he was sent on a mission to England by Mr. Wheelock to promote the interests of Moor's Indian charity school. From February, 1766, to July, 1767, he preached nearly four hundred sermons in various parts of England and Scotland, and everywhere immense throngs of people flocked to his meetings. Large contributions were made to the school, which was soon transplanted to New Hampshire, and formed the germ of Dartmouth College. He was often employed as a missionary among the different tribes of Indians. He died near Utica, N. Y., in July, 1792.

Uncas, sachem of the Mohegan Indians, was a Pequot by birth, and of royal descent. To the English he was uniformly friendly from the first settlement of the country. The triumph of Major Mason over the Pequot Indians in 1637 was largely due to the support of Uncas and his warriors, and to the information which he imparted. He was shrewd to plan and brave to execute, and generally the victor. After a lapse of forty years from the victory on Pequot Hill, and at a time when all the Indian tribes in New England were banded together under the leadership of King Philip for the utter extermination of the whites, Uncas, at the head of two hundred warriors, accompanied Major Talcott to western Massachusetts, and rendered important service to the settlers. He died in 1683, probably not less than eighty years of age, and was buried in the royal Indian burying-ground in Norwich.

Lebanon.—It was ordered by the General Court in October, 1697, that the new plantation situated west of Norwich be called Lebanon. Lebanon was originally constituted of four distinct proprieties, known as the five-mile purchase, the one-mile purchase, the Clark and Dewey purchase, and the Whiting purchase. These different tracts were united by agreement, and on their union obtained an act of incorporation as a township in 1700. Windham County, constituted in 1726, included Lebanon within its jurisdiction. It was annexed to New London County in 1824. Agriculture is the principal business of the inhabitants. The town has three flourishing parishes, known as Lebanon Proper, Goshen and Exeter. These have church edifices of the Congregational order, and high schools.

This historic town has given birth to six distinguished individuals, each of whom has risen to the rank of chief magistrate of a State in our Republic. Of these, five became governors of our own State, and the sixth of a State in the far West, as will appear from the annexed biographical sketches. The population in 1880, 1,845.

Jonathan Trumbull, son of Captain Joseph Trumbull, was born in Lebanon in 1710, and graduated at Harvard College in 1727. Early in life he consecrated himself to the ministry, but the exigencies of the times called him to a different if not a higher sphere of public exertion, and consequently he served as Governor of the Colony and State for fifteen years, commencing in 1769. He was the only governor of a Colony that remained true to his people during the war of the Revolution. In Revolutionary times he was almost universally known as "Brother Jonathan," having been so called by Washington in token of his filial regard and confidence. He died August 17, 1785.

Jonathan Trumbull, son of the preceding, was born in Lebanon, March 26, 1740, graduated at Harvard College in 1759, and settled in his native town. From 1775 to the close of the campaign of 1778, he was paymaster to the army in the northern department. In 1780 he was appointed secretary and first aid to Washington, in whose family he remained till the close of the war. In 1789 he became a member of Congress, and two years later was elected speaker of the House of Representatives. In 1794 he was elevated to a seat in the Senate of the United States, and in 1798 became governor of Connecticut, which position he continued to hold for eleven years. He died August 7, 1809.

Joseph Trumbull, LL.D., grandson of the senior Gov. Trumbull, was born in Lebanon, December 7, 1782, graduated at Yale in 1801, was admitted to the bar in 1802, and 1804 removed to Hartford, where he became permanently established. He was a member of Congress from 1839 to 1843, and in 1849 was elected governor of Connecticut. He died in Hartford August 4, 1861.

Clark Bissell, LL.D., was born in Lebanon in 1784, graduated at Yale in 1806, was subsequently admitted to the bar and became established at Norwalk, where he soon rose to eminence. He was a judge of the Superior Court, from 1829 to 1839; governor of the State for the years 1847 and 1848, and professor of jurisprudence in Yale College, from 1847 to 1855. He died in 1857.

William A. Buckingham, LL.D., was born in Lebanon in 1804. Early in life he became successfully engaged in business in Norwich, represented that town in the State legislature, was for a long period mayor of the city of Norwich, and from 1859 to 1866 was governor of the State. From 1869 to the time of his death in 1875, he was a member of the United States Senate. He was honorably known as the "War Governor of Connecticut."

Nelson Dewey, son of John Woodward Dewey, was born in Lebanon early in the present century. Removing to the West, he became a resident of Lancaster, Wis., and, during the years 1849 and 1850, served as governor of his adopted State.

William Williams, son of the Rev. Solomon Williams, D. D., was born in Lebanon, April 8, 1731, and graduated at Harvard in 1751. In 1755 he participated in the battle of Lake George, being then a member of the staff of Col. Ephraim Williams. After protracted service in the legislature of his own State, he was, during the years 1776 and 1777, a member of the Continental Congress, and as such signed the Declaration of Independence. He made great sacrifices for the cause of his country. He married a daughter of the elder Gov. Trumbull. Mr. Williams died at Lebanon, August 2, 1811.

Preston.—Permission was granted to Thomas Parke, Sr., and others, by the General Court in January, 1686–7, to make a plantation east of Norwich bounds. In October, 1687, it was by the same court named Preston. Preston was incorporated as a town in 1786, just a century after its first settlement. The Indian name of the locality was Poquetannock.

There are three villages in the township. Poquetannock is situated at the head of a cove of the same name about two miles east of the Thames. It contains about forty dwellings and several stores. Preston City is a village located in the eastern part of the town, which contains about thirty dwelling-houses and two churches. The other village is situated upon the south bank of the Shetucket, opposite to the city of Norwich. Laurel Hill, situated near the junction of the Shetucket and Thames rivers, was, till recently, included within the Preston limits. It now constitutes an inviting section in Norwich city.

The population of Preston in 1880 was 2,519.

Lyme.—The General Court authorized the division of Saybrook in May, 1649, the section east of Connecticut River to be known as East Saybrook. It was first settled in 1663, and was incorporated as a distinct township with the name of Lyme in 1667. The Indian name of the locality was Nehuntic. The surface of the township is rocky, and parts of it hilly and mountainous. The soil is hard, and does not admit of a general cultivation of crops, but affords tolerable grazing. Farming is the principal business of the inhabitants.

The principal villages in the town are at Hamburgh and North Lyme. Both are situated upon Eight-mile River.

The population in 1880 was 1,025.

Matthew Griswold, LL.D., was born in Lyme, March 25, 1714. After serving as a representative, member of the council, chief judge of the Superior Court, and lieutenant-governor, he was from 1784 to 1786, governor of the State. In 1788 he was chosen president of the convention which adopted the Constitution of the United States. He died April 28, 1799. His mansion was located at Black Hall, near the mouth of the Connecticut River.

Roger Griswold, LL.D., son of the above, was born in Lyme, May 21, 1762. He graduated at Yale in 1780, and being admitted to the bar, located in Norwich, and soon rose to eminence as an advocate. In 1811 he was elected governor of the State, having previously held the offices of judge of the Superior Court and lieutenant-governor of the State. He remained in office until his death, in October, 1812.

East Lyme was constituted the East Parish in Lyme in October, 1721. The Indian name of the locality was Neanticut. A moiety of the territory now constituting East Lyme was an Indian reservation for the Western Nehantics, when the towns of New London and Lyme were incorporated. This reservation was afterwards claimed by each town, but by mutual agreement the ownership was decided by a pugilistic contest between two combatants from each town in the field. Lyme became the winner, and the territory was annexed to that town. The surface of the township is diversified. Hills and rocks prevail in the northern portion, while on the Sound the grounds are low and marshy. The village of Flanders is located at the head of Niantic River, while Niantic Village is seated at the mouth of the same river on the Sound.

Population in 1880, 1,731.

Old Lyme was re-incorporated as a township in 1855, wholly from the territory of Lyme. At first the new town was called South Lyme. This name was subsequently changed to Old Lyme. The settlement of East Saybrook, at the mouth of the Connecticut River, primarily led to the early incorporation of the town of Lyme. Agriculture gives employment mainly to the inhabitants.

Lyme Village is situated about twelve miles from the Sound, and one mile east of Connecticut River. The main street runs parallel with the river, and contains a Congregational church edifice and the Lyme post-office. Black Hall, the ancient seat of the Griswold family, lies directly upon the Sound, near the mouth of the Connecticut River. The population of Old Lyme in 1880 was 1,387.

Franklin was originally included in the territory of Norwich. It was constituted the Second Ecclesiastical Society in Norwich in October, 1716, with the title of West Farms. Its settlement was almost coeval with that of the present township. In 1663 measures were taken to apportion the territory within the present town limits to the original proprietors then residing at Norwich town. Soon thereafter settlements actually commenced on the hillsides and up and down the streams, and shortly a thriving community occupied the most desirable portions of the new settlement. Among the early settlers are names that still honor the town, as Ayer, Huntington, Kingsbury, Mason and Tracy. It was incorporated as a town in 1786, and received the name of Franklin. Its population in 1880 was 686. The face of the township is diversified by hills and valleys. The soil is a loam, well adapted to grazing, grain-growing and fruit-culture.

There is no village within the limits of the town, and but one church edifice, and that a Congregational. Agriculture has been the principal pursuit of the inhabitants, which has been successfully conducted, but not to the neglect of more important interests. The common school has ever had the watchful, fostering care of the inhabitants, and to the credit of the community it may be said that, with a limited poulation, more than forty of her sons have graduated with honor at the different colleges in our country.

Rev. Samuel Nott, D. D., was born in Saybrook, January 23, 1754. He graduated at Yale in 1780, and was settled in the ministry at Norwich, now Franklin, May 13, 1782, where he remained until the close of his long and useful life. His ministry covered a period of more than seventy years. His death occurred May 26, 1852, from the effects of a burn. He published a large number of sermons.

Hon. Uriah Tracy, born in Franklin, February 2, 1755, graduated at Yale in 1778, read law with Judge Reeves of Litchfield, and settled in that town in the practice of his profession. He often represented Litchfield in the legislature, and in 1793 was speaker of the House. From 1793 to 1796 he was a representative in Congress, and from 1796 to 1807 was a member of the Senate, and in 1800 was president *pro tem.* of that body. He rose to the rank of major-general of militia. Gen. Tracy was a leader of the Federal party, and an intimate friend of Hamilton, Ames, Morris, and their associates. He died at Washington, July 19, 1807, and was the first person interred in the congressional burying-ground.

North Stonington was constituted the North Parish in Stonington, in October, 1720, and was by the General Court named North Stonington in May, 1724. The Indian name of this locality was Wequetequock. It was incorporated as a town in 1807, from territory which was originally a part of Stonington. It is an agricultural town, and is watered by the Shanock and Pawcatuck rivers, which afford sites for mills.

The only village in the town is now known by the name of North Stonington. This place was anciently called Milltown. It contains about thirty dwelling-houses, half a dozen stores and two churches.

The population in 1880 was 1,769.

Ledyard was made the North Parish of Groton by the General Court in October, 1725. It was then known as North Groton. It was incorporated as a town in 1836, and named from the hero of Groton Heights. Agriculture is the principal business of the inhabitants. A small remnant of the Pequot tribe of Indians still remains in the northeastern section of the town. The principal village in the town of Ledyard is at Gale's Ferry, on the east bank of the Thames, which consists of about thirty dwelling-houses.

The population in 1880 was 1,373.

Salem.—In May, 1728, a parish was constituted from sections of the towns of Colchester and Lyme, to which the name of New Salem was given. This was incorporated as a town in May, 1819, and received the name of Salem. There is no village in the township of magnitude. There are three houses of public worship—Congregational, Methodist and Episcopal. Agriculture is the principal business of the inhabitants. The population in 1880 was 574.

Bozrah.—Bozrah was constituted a society within the limits of Norwich in May, 1737, with the name of New Concord. It was incorporated a town in 1786, with the name of Bozrah. Among the early settlers the names of Waterman and Hough and Fox were prominent; names not uncommon at this date. The face of the township is generally uneven, consisting of hills and valleys; its geological character is granitic; the soil is gravelly loam, moderately fertile.

Fitchville, located near the centre of the town, and Bozrahville, two miles above, are both manufacturing villages, and both situated upon the Yantic River. The central part of the town is fourteen miles from New London and thirty-three from Hartford. The population in 1880 was 1,155.

Lisbon was originally included within the limits of Norwich. It was constituted the northeast parish of the parent township in May, 1718, and received the name of Newent in October, 1722. It was incorporated as a town in 1786, and given its present name. The Indian name of the locality was Shetucket.

Agriculture is the leading business of the inhabitants. The population is consequently scattered. The number of inhabitants in 1880 was 630.

Waterford was incorporated as a township in 1801, including all the remaining territory of New London except the city. The Indian name was Tawawang. A valuable quarry of granite is extensively worked in the southwestern section of the town. A small village, to which the name of Graniteville has been given, is located near the quarry. Agriculture is the principal business of the inhabitants. The population in 1880 was 2,701.

TOLLAND COUNTY.

TOLLAND COUNTY, the youngest and the least in area, except one, of the Connecticut counties, was incorporated by the General Court, at New Haven, in October, 1785, and included Tolland, Stafford, Bolton, Somers, Hebron, Willington, Union and Ellington. The act establishing the county was conditioned upon the building of a suitable court-house and jail in the town of Tolland. In May, 1786, the General Court re-enacted the act of 1785, and added Coventry to the lists of towns. This number of towns has been increased to thirteen by the creation of Vernon out of Bolton in 1808; by the transfer of Mansfield and Columbia from Windham County in 1827, and by the organization of Andover out of Coventry and Hebron in 1848. All of the towns were settled long before the county was organized, and most of them were incorporated before its organization.

About one-quarter of this county was bought of Indians—Joshua, a Mohegan sachem, and others. Some of it was sold by the Colony. The county lies, a small part of it, at the base, and a larger part among the hills which rise out of the Connecticut Valley about twelve miles east of Hartford, and extend beyond the eastern border of the county.

Many of the early settlers came from Norwich and vicinity, and from the Connecticut Valley, as those regions became more thickly populated. Among the earliest were many from eastern Massachusetts. The original settlers were of the Pilgrim and Puritan stock, and brought with them the purpose to make their settlements religious communities. Their first care, after finding habitations for themselves, was to establish the regular weekly worship of God, and to provide a house for this worship. The next public care was to open a school.

The earliest industries of the county were principally farming—clearing tracts of land and getting the soil in proper condition to raise produce for the maintenance of the family—and the manufacture, in each home, of hand-spun and hand-woven woolen and linen cloth for the wear of the family.

The streams of this county give numerous facilities for manufacturing, and, in later years, they have utilized, and have furnished water-power for factories which have drawn to themselves that domestic manufacture which before was scattered over the hills, and gave activity to every household. It may be said of this county, as a whole, that it has well improved its manufacturing facilities. In 1870 there were only two counties—Windham and New Haven—that had a larger ratio than Tolland County of capital invested in manufacturing, in proportion to the total valuation of property.

The brooks and rivers of the county gather a portion of the waters that unite at Norwich to form the river Thames. The Willimantic is the principal river in the county, and has contributed much to the support of the inhabitants. In early times shad and salmon were caught in large quantities up as far as Tolland, and probably higher.

Large tracts of heavy woodlands remained in this county thirty years ago, especially in the eastern part of it. It is estimated that full one-half of the forest trees then standing have been since cut off.

The New York and New England, and the New London Northern are the principal railroads in the county. The Boston and New York Air Line runs into the borders of two of the southern towns, and there are besides two or three short branch roads.

The people of Tolland County have always been law-abiding and orderly. There have been less crimes and fewer criminal trials than in any other county in the State. Only one person has ever been executed for murder in the county, and only four capital trials have occurred from its organization to the present time. The first of these occurred about thirty-eight years after its incorporation. The criminal was convicted of murder, and publicly hung in the presence of a vast concourse of people, who had come from every town in the county to witness so unusual a spectacle. The execution took place on an eminence near the county jail.

The county in Connecticut has no legislative functions. It is empowered to establish roads, and to prosecute offenses against the laws. As a county it has no representative in the General Assembly, and has no political life. The town is the unit, and it is not county-wise but town-wise that the people act as citizens of the Commonwealth of Connecticut. The history of the county is therefore to be found in the town records, and we turn to the towns for the history of the civil and religious life of the county. These were so much one in the colonial period, that any history of Connecticut would be partial and incomplete which should attempt to separate the civil from the religious history, and give one without the other. Indeed, the dominating religious purpose of the Colonies necessarily makes any faithful history largely a religious history.

The population of the county in 1790 was 13,106, and in 1880, 24,112.

TOWNS.

Mansfield, was originally a part of Windham. Settlements began to be made as early as 1690, several years earlier than any other town in the county. From that time the inhabitants gradually increased in numbers until they began to petition the General Court of the Connecticut Colony to make them a distinct town, on account of the great difficulties and hazards to which they were exposed by reason of the "deep and dangerous river" between them and the meeting-house in Windham. In May, 1703, the Court granted the petition, and the town was incorporated.

Among the original grantees are the names of Shubael Dimmock, Joseph Hall, Samuel Storrs, Robert Fenton, Peter Cross, John Royce and Peter Crane, nearly all of whom have lineal descendants in the place at this time.

Mansfield was incorporated on condition the petitioners should settle over them an "able and orthodox" minister of the gospel. Worship was regularly held and a pastor sought continuously until, in 1710, Mr. Eleazer Williams, son of Rev. John Williams of Deerfield, Mass., accepted a call to settle. The church was organized and the pastor ordained the same day. The second pastor was Dr. Richard Salter, whose ministry extended into and through the war of '76, and who helped to give the tone of patriotism which distinguished eastern Connecticut in the early days of that conflict.

Mansfield was divided into two parishes—the north and south—in 1737; and in the same year that Mr. Salter was ordained over the first church, Mr. William Throop was ordained the first pastor of the second church, Sept. 19, 1744. It is noteworthy that the second and third pastors of the second church were father and son—Daniel Welch and Moses Cook Welch—whose united ministry covered seventy years. It is an interesting fact that another member of the Welch family—Moses Cook Welch—a grandson and namesake of the second Mr. Welch, has been in recent years a pastor of the same church. He served as chaplain during the civil war.

About the time that Mr. Salter and Mr. Throop were ordained Mansfield had its experience of troubles produced by the Separatist movement. This peculiar religious movement was the natural outcome of several causes, some which lay far back in the history of the Colony. There had first been brought into the churches, gradually, through the half-way covenant, an element which loosened the discipline and led to decline in the piety of the churches. Along with this, and perhaps a result of this, there grew a demand for a closer union of the churches, and some judicial authority outside of the individual church. This desire found expression in the Saybrook Platform, which organized the *Consociation*. This was a court of judicature over Congregational churches. The General Court was in sympathy with this feeling and made the Platform the rule of the churches. Then came, in 1735, '41 and '42, powerful revivals, which awakened an earnest spirit of active piety mingled with self-confident enthusiasm. New proofs of being in a state of grace were demanded, and censorious judgments were pronounced upon such church-members as were not in sympathy with the revival. Churches were divided into parties. The "New Lights," or promoters of the revival were disciplined. Laws were enacted restraining liberty of worship outside of the "established order." Many of the "New Lights" paid no regard to these laws, but withdrew from the established churches and organized churches of their own.

A Separatist church was organized in Mansfield consisting in large part of members of the two established churches in town; but as it was the first church of the kind in that section of the State, seceders from the established churches in adjoining towns united with them, and Mansfield gained a certain notoriety as being the headquarters of the Separatists in that vicinity. This church called itself Congregational. It was not in any sense an active protest against Congregationalism; it was a protest against the want of tolerance in the colonial laws and in the spirit of the churches. But the protest, as is usual in such cases, was urged with an intolerance which emulated the intolerance of which they complained. This Separatist Church maintained its organization an uncertain number of years, and was disbanded sometime before the end of the century.

As early as 1793 there began to be Methodist services in town, and a Methodist meeting-house was built in 1797, in the eastern part of the north parish.

A Baptist society was organized in this town in 1808, and the society erected a meeting-house in the centre of the town the same year.

Tolland County, together with the rest of eastern Connecticut, was profoundly stirred by the arbitrary proceedings of the British Parliament in the Boston Port Bill and the Quebec Bill, and previously in the Stamp Act. In town meeting, October, 1774, the citizens of Mansfield expressed their affliction at the oppressive measures which threatened the inhabitants with total loss of liberty, and declared it to be their duty to oppose cruel and unjust measures, and to maintain *freedom*; and resolved that they would be faithful subjects of King George the Third, so long as the crown maintained inviolate the stipulated rights of the people; and that they would defend with their lives and their fortunes their national and constitutional rights.

As early as February, 1775, Mansfield directed her representatives to move in General Court that a proper number of men be levied and equipped for the defense of the Colony; and in October they were directed to move the Court to dispose of lands belonging to persons inimical to the cause of liberty.

Mansfield has been from a very early period a manufacturing town. There is record of a fulling-mill in 1731, and of a spinning-mill in 1734. The early raising of silk-worms, principally by women and girls, and the manufacture of silk by hand, gave distinction to the town. In 1788, thirty-two persons of this town petitioned the General Court to be incorporated for the manufacture of silk. The request of the petitioners was allowed, and silk-culture gradually became a leading industry in Mansfield. Nearly every farmer raised mulberry trees, and his wife and daughters fed the silk-worms, and spun the silk.

The introduction of machinery run by water-power, for spinning silk, made a revolution in domestic silk manufacture. The first experiments in this new method were made by Rodney Hanks, and his nephew, Horatio Hanks, in 1810, with machinery invented by themselves, and made with their own hands. The Hanks family, in several generations, has been noted for its inventive genius, which has, from time to time, produced various new machines and implements for facilitating labor in different branches of industry. It was several years, however, after the Messrs. Hanks began to spin silk by water-power, before a silk-factory of considerable dimensions was built in the town. Before that time, two cotton-spinning factories were erected in the western part of Mansfield, on the Willimantic River, and the women in the town were employed to take home the factory-spun yarn, and weave it into shirting and sheeting in hand-looms. After the use of water-power had become successfully established for weaving as well as spinning, the household manufacture of sewing-silk, and of woolen and linen cloth, gradually declined, and many of the girls left their fathers' houses, and worked in the mills. Then began a great change in the social life of the town; the girls began to leave the hillsides for the manufacturing villages, the young men and boys also sought business away from their homes, and few besides the elderly people remained by the old firesides. Farms were less widely cultivated; agriculture declined; the long-established churches diminished in numbers and wealth, and the inherited customs and old New England habits were so changed as to forever separate the modern from the old New England life.

The oldest burying-ground in Tolland County was laid out in 1696, in what was then called the Ponde-place—now the first parish of Mansfield—seven years before Mansfield was made a distinct town. Here was buried Samuel Storrs, who came from England, and who was one of the original proprietors of the town—the great ancestor, not only of the families of Storrs in Mansfield, but of Rev. Mr. Storrs, of Longmeadow, Mass.; of Dr. Richard Salter Storrs, of Braintree, Mass.; and Dr. R. S. Storrs, of Brooklyn, N. Y. In fact, he is the common ancestor of nearly all of the numerous families of Storrs in the United States.

The second parish of Mansfield, through the munificence of Mr. Charles Storrs, of Brooklyn, N. Y., has an unusually large and beautiful cemetery, inclosed by a substantial stone wall. From the rear of this cemetery, which is the highest ground in Mansfield, a view is obtained such as few inland towns furnish.

In 1864, Mr. Storrs became desirous that a school should be established in Mansfield of a higher grade than the district school. By his earnest solicitations and liberal aid, Mr. Edwin Whitney, of the Reform School in Providence, was induced to open a boarding and day school in the north parish in 1865. Mr. Whitney was well adapted for the work, and the school started with every prospect of success, but before the close of the first term it was broken up by a fire, which destroyed the principal's dwelling. Mr. Whitney built anew, but before the house was ready to be opened for scholars he offered it, with the farm, to the State, for use as a soldiers' orphans' home. Mr. Whitney had been prevented by physical disqualification from volunteering, and said that, as he could not offer himself to his country, he must do something that should be of service to the common cause. The State accepted the gift, and so the Connecticut Soldiers' Orphans' Home was established in Mansfield.

The population of the town is 2,154.

Vernon, incorporated in 1808, was first settled by sons from East Windsor and Bolton. The eastern part of the township is crossed by a range of mountains, forming the eastern boundary of the Connecticut Valley. The considerable streams are the Hockanum and the Tancanhoosen, which supply water to many mills and factories. Rockville, the principal manufacturing village, obtains its water-power from the Hockanum. It contains nine woolen mills, three cotton mills, a silk factory, machine shops, and various other industrial establishments.

A cotton factory was in operation in this town shortly before the year 1800. In 1811, Peter Dobson erected machinery for spinning cotton in Vernon. He conducted the business of cotton manufacturing for fifty years, and in connection with his family for nearly seventy years. The business is still continued in the vicinity.

The war of 1812 created a necessity for making cloth for soldiers. Our ports were blockaded, and all trade outside the States cut off. A piece of cloth from a tailor's bench was shown Mr. Dobson. Closely examining it, he found the warp cotton and the filling woolen yarn. He then made a jack and jenny for spinning wool, having seen similar machines in England. In a short time the facilities for spinning wool for filling, and cotton yarn for warps, produced a cloth called satinet. This cloth was blue mixed for soldiers' wear, and was made in a variety of colors. Satinets were made in Vernon from the first until 1841. The first cassimeres in Rockville were made in the New England mill, burned soon after its construction, and rebuilt in 1841-2.

The population of Vernon is about 7,000.

Stafford, on the Massachusetts line, and incorporated in 1808, was settled in 1719 by Robert White and Matthew Thompson from England, Samuel and John Warner from Hadley, Mass., David and Josiah Blodget from Woburn, Daniel Colburn from Dedham, and others from towns in Connecticut and Massachusetts. The first minister, Mr. Graham, was settled in 1723. There are several minerals in the town, of which iron ore is the most important. The ore which is principally used is the bog ore, and is of an excellent quality. In 1779, John Phelps and others built a blast furnace on a large scale. Hollow-ware, cannon, cannot-shot, and a great variety of patterns for manufactures and description of machinery were cast. In 1796 another large furnace was erected, and from that time until 1820 an immense business was carried on. Since the latter date the demand has been too great to be supplied from the ore-beds, and pig-iron has been used for machinery castings everywhere. The locality of the old furnace was called Furnace Hollow, and it is the post-office name to-day. But the blast furnace is gone, and also the business of former years. Stafford Springs and Foxville contain six large factories, and several of lesser importance. The mineral springs in Stafford in former years acquired considerable celebrity. The Indians made the white settlers acquainted with the virtues of these springs, when, in 1719, this region was first settled. It had been their practice from time immemorial, to resort to the springs in warm weather, and plant their wigwams around them. It is said that in 1766 the springs were carefully examined by Dr. Joseph Warren, who then had thoughts of purchasing the land on which they rise, with a view of establishing himself upon it. Subsequent events transformed the physician into the soldier, and Dr. Warren fell in the first great struggle of the Revolution—the battle of Bunker Hill. Dr. Willard afterwards put the plan of Dr. Warren into operation, by erecting a large hotel for the accommodation of patients and others.

Stafford Springs contains four churches and several banks. The New London and Northern Railroad passes through the place. Total number of churches in the town, eleven. About five years since a large reservoir in the northern part of the town gave way. Dams and mills were destroyed, and at the Springs, six large dwellings, a church, factories, stores, a bank, etc., were swept away, and two men, standing on the steps of the church, were drowned. Staffordville, Hydeville, and West Stafford, have important manufactures. The entire town has a population of about 4,500.

Coventry was first settled about the year 1700, by Nathaniel Rust and others. In the spring of 1709, a number of persons, principally from Northampton and Hartford, moved here, and two years later the town was incorporated. The township was given by Joshua, sachem of the Mohegans, to a number of legatees in Hartford. These conveyed their right to William Pitkin, Joseph Talcott, William Whiting and Richard Lord, to be a committee to lay out the township and make settlements therein.

A stream called the Skungamug runs through the town, and, uniting with other streams, forms the Hop River. Lake Wangumbog, two miles in length, is an important feature of the landscape.

Coventry will ever be remembered as the birthplace of Capt. Nathan Hale, the patriot and martyr. He was the son of Richard and Elizabeth Hale, and was born June 6, 1755, being the third in descent from Rev. John Hale, the first minister of Beverly, Mass. Nathan Hale graduated at Yale in in 1773, with high honor, and for a brief period taught school at East Haddam and New London, with great success. His parents intended him for the ministry, but, on the Lexington alarm in 1775, he wrote to his father, saying that sense of duty urged him to sacrifice everything for his country, and soon after entered the army as lieutenant, but was soon promoted to be captain. He served with credit in the vicinity of Boston, and in September, 1776, when in New York, he with an associate, planned and effected the capture of a British sloop, laden with provisions, taking her at night from under the guns of a man-of-war. After the retreat of the army from Long Island, when it was important to understand the plans of the enemy, Capt. Hale answered Gen. Washington's application for a discreet and faithful officer to enter the enemy's lines and obtain intelligence. Passing in disguise to the British camp, he made full drawings and memoranda of all the desired information, but on his return was apprehended and taken before Gen. Howe, by whom he was ordered for execution the next morning. He was denied a Bible and the aid of a clergyman; the letters he had written to his father and sisters were destroyed, and he was hanged, saying with his last breath: "I only regret that I have but one life to lose for my country."

In November, 1837, an association was formed for the purpose of erecting a cenotaph that should fitly commemorate the life and services of Hale. The day on which it was formed was the anniversary of the evacuation of New York, and twenty Revolutionary soldiers were present. It was not, however, until 1846, that the monument was completed. It is of Quincy granite, and bears for one of its inscriptions the dying words of the youthful hero.

A romantic and tender interest attaches to the last utterances of Alice Adams, to whom Hale was betrothed. She married William Lawrence of Hartford, and for many years had in her possession a minature of Hale, besides numerous letters and his camp book. She died Sept. 4, 1845, at the age of eighty-eight. The last words of Mrs. Lawrence were "Write to Nathan."

Coventry has produced many men of eminence. Among them may be mentioned Harlan Page. It has a population of 2,043.

Hebron began to be settled in 1704. Among the earliest settlers were Samuel Curtiss, Timothy Phelps, Stephen Post, Jacob Root, William Shipman and Benoni Trumbull, who came from towns on the Connecticut River.

Hebron was made a distinct town in 1707. The earliest church was organized in 1717. The first pastor was the Rev. John Bliss, who became the occasion of the establishment of an Episcopal church in Hebron, by his own conversion to Episcopacy in 1734.

The second pastor of the Congregational church was the Rev. Benjamin Pomeroy who, like many of the best ministers of the Colony in that day, was one of the "New Lights," or promoters of the revivals that spread through Connecticut in the years immediately following his settlement in 1735.

The notorious Rev. Samuel Peters, of Connecticut "Blue Laws" fame, was a native of this town and a Tory. A mob of about 300 assembled in August and again in September, and made known their determination to obtain from him satisfaction for his published slanders, and the acknowledgment of his errors. He met them arrayed in official robes for protection. But the exasperated mob had as little respect for these as for the wearer, and seizing him violently, to the damage of his garments, they carried him to the Green where he was forced to make a confession previously prepared for him, and then he was set at liberty. After this he went to Boston, from whence he wrote to his mother, in a letter that was intercepted, that six regiments were now coming from England, and sundry men-of-war. "So soon as they come, hanging work will go on and destruction will first attend the sea-port towns; the lintel sprinkled and the side posts will protect the faithful." A few days later he sailed for England, where he published the famous history of Connecticut, which has served by its Munchausen stories to preserve the name of the author from oblivion.

A second ecclesiastical society was incorporated in 1748, and called Gilead. It was stated to the first pastor of the Gilead church, as an encouragement to settle there, that there was not a drunkard in the parish, and not a prayerless family, the result of revivals under the ministry of Dr. Pomeroy.

John S. Peters, M. D., LL.D., governor of Connecticut in 1831 and 1832, was a native of Hebron. And so was William A. Palmer, at one time governor of Vermont; and also Erastus Root, who was once lieutenant-governor of New York.

Inasmuch as Hebron gave birth to the author of Peters' "History of Connecticut," it was fitting that the historical balance should be restored by the production of another history of Connecticut by Rev. Benjamin Trumbull, D. D., another son of Hebron, and one of her most honored children.

At the commencement of the present century, Hebron was probably at the height of its prosperity. The population of Hebron in 1880 was 1,243.

Somers, situated in the northwest corner of the county, was originally a part of Enfield, and both were comprehended within the limits of the ancient town of Springfield. The first settlers of Enfield were from Springfield. In May, 1683, these first settlers petitioned the General Court of Massachusetts for a new township, asking that the limits of the town extend ten miles east from the Connecticut River. The grant inclosed the present town of Somers. These parties respected the Indian title, and paid the Indians £25 for the land covered by the grant. The Indian chief Totatuck alienated all right except that of hunting and fishing. This purchase was in 1688.

The first settler of Somers was one Benjamin Jones, of Welsh descent. He adopted the Indian fashion of making Somers a summer residence, returning into Enfield to spend the winters. But for five years he was alone, and singular in this way of living. In 1713, others began to come in from Enfield to make a permanent settlement. Among these first settlers were men bearing the names of Kibbe, Pease, Sexton, Root, Chapin, Parsons and Woods, nearly all of whom have lineal descendants in Somers. Of those who were in Somers in 1730 most were from Enfield. The remainder were from Springfield, Northampton, Longmeadow, Pomfret, and Wallingford. In 1734 the General Court of Massachusetts incorporated the town by the name of Somers. It is said that Gov. Belcher asked that the town receive this name in honor of Lord Somers. It continued under the jurisdiction of Massachusetts until 1749, the year in which the Connecticut court passed the resolution, declaring that the towns south of the Massachusetts line were entitled to the privileges of the Connecticut jurisdiction.

Eight of the first settlers of the town were constituted a church, the 15th of March, 1727, and on the same day the Rev. Samuel Allis was settled as pastor. Four years after a meeting-house was built, where all the inhabitants of the town could sit at once on the sills.

The third pastor of this church was Mr. Charles Backus, who was ordained and settled in a pastorate which became distinguished, and was terminated by his death in 1803. Dr. Backus was, according to the testimony of Prof. Woods of Andover, who studied theology with him, one of the ablest extemporaneous preachers of his day. He became noted as an instructor in theology, and nearly fifty young men sought his instruction. Among them were Leonard Woods and Dudley Field.

Somers was prompt, like all eastern Connecticut, to respond to the alarm of war in 1775. News of the battle of Lexington, June 19, reached the town the day following. A Mr., afterwards Captain Chapin of Somers, wrote in his diary that very day: "When the news of the fight reached Somers, the militia were ordered to meet at the meeting-house, and about fifty enlisted for the relief of their brethren in and near Boston. Emory Pease was chosen captain. Friday the 21st, at about nine o'clock, we set out on our march to Boston by way of Wilbraham and Palmer." Captain Pease's alarm company reached Cambridge and paraded on Monday at 4 P. M.

Somers is mainly a farming community. The town lies for the most part at the base of the hills of Tolland County, and in the more level and fertile region of the Connecticut Valley.

There has also been manufacturing of different kinds in the town. About 1830, Mr. Ebenezer Clark commenced the manufacture of straw bonnets. It is said that it was the first establishment of the kind in the State. The braiding of the straw and the sewing of the braid into bonnets gave employment not only to many of the women and girls of Somers, but to many in adjoining towns. Not far from this time another firm began to make straw bonnets and palm-leaf Shaker bonnets. The palm-leaf was put out into private families all over Tolland County, where it was woven into sheets. These sheets were returned to Somers, where they were cut up and made into Shaker bonnets, which were worn extensively in New England, and were sent in large quantities to the South.

There was in 1825 a small establishment for making satinet in Somers. About 1836 a satinet factory was built in Somersville.

L. E. Pease, a native of this town, and a descendent of one of the original settlers, was secretary of state for Connecticut for several years.

The population of Somers in 1880 was 1,242.

Tolland has been the county-seat of the county of Tolland from its organization. In 1715, a petition of some inhabitants of Windsor to the General Court to make a town of what is now Tolland, states that "several families are already there." The petition was granted, and a town called Tolland incorporated the same year.

The historian of Tolland—Hon. Loren P. Waldo—says that this region was the summer resort of Indians whose home was nearer the sea-coast. Snipsic Lake contains in its name a memorial of the Indians.

The names of Joseph Benton and Joseph Baker occur among the first settlers, and also of Nathaniel Grant, Joshua Loomis, Joseph Mather, Hezekiah Porter, Shubael Stearns, Joshua Willes, Henry Wolcott, William Eaton, Joseph Slafter and Thomas Stoughton.

The war for Independence was generously supported. Like other towns of eastern Connecticut, Tolland began to enlist a company the same day that news came of the beginning of hostilities in 1775 at Lexington. A company of ninety-eight was formed, which served near Boston. Judge Waldo, in his history of Tolland, says: "Several times almost the entire active male population was absent in the army, and ordinary work on the farms was done by female hands. I heard a venerable lady, daughter of one of the Revolutionary officers of Tolland, relate that she and her younger sisters frequently yoked the oxen, and harvested the crops with their own hands."

The first church of Tolland was organized, it is supposed, and the first minister ordained, in June, 1723. This minister was Rev. Stephen Steel, who continued pastor until 1758.

Rev. Nathan Williams, grandson of Rev. John Williams of Deerfield memory, was second pastor of this church. He was its sole pastor for nearly fifty-three years.

The fourth pastor of this church was Rev. Abram Marsh. He was installed in 1813 and continued in the pastorate until 1868. So for a period of one hundred and forty-five years the Congregational Church of Tolland had had but four settled ministers, and during all those years there had been but fourteen months' vacation in the office.

In 1791 the Methodists succeeded in establishing a church in Tolland, and in 1794 they built a house for public worship.

In 1807 a Baptist church was organized.

Satinet, cotton-batting, cotton-yarn and thread have formerly been to some extent manufactured in Tolland.

The business of tanning and currying leather had been carried on near the village for many years before 1840. About that time Mr. Moses Underwood purchased the property and continued the business successfully for several years, when he and one of his sons engaged in manufacturing belts in connection with the business of tanning leather. The Underwood Belting Company, formed in 1875, have increased this business and have erected more commodious and extensive buildings, furnished with expensive machinery.

From about 1836 to 1845, the manufacture of silver spoons and the frames of silver-bowed spectacles was successfully carried on in Tolland.

Loren P. Waldo was born in Canterbury, Windham County, Feb. 2, 1802. Mr. Waldo was educated in the common schools of his native town, and commenced teaching in a common school before he was fifteen years of age. He was admitted to practice in Tolland County in September, 1825. He was State's attorney twelve years; represented the first congressional district in Connecticut in the thirty-first Congress of the United States; two and one-half years was commissioner of pensions at Washington city; and eight years a judge of the Superior Court of the State of Connecticut. It is doubtful if any other lawyer has ever resided in the town of Tolland who will live longer in the memory of its sons and daughters and be held in more grateful affection by them than Judge Waldo, by reason of the deep interest he has always manifested in their welfare, and because of his faithful "Early History of Tolland," on which he spent much time and careful research. Mr. Waldo's home was in Tolland from 1830 to 1863.

William Wallace Eaton, who was a member of the United States Senate, was born and reared in the town of Tolland, and is a lineal descendant of William Eaton, one of the pioneer settlers of the town.

Tolland was at its zenith of prosperity in the early part of the present century. Judge Waldo says: "These principal mail routes have been turned from Tolland in consequnce of the building of the railroads, so that while other places have been benefited by those improvements, this town has been a sufferer." Its population in 1880 was 1,169.

Willington. — Early in 1720 a company of eight men from different towns in western Connecticut purchased a tract of land containing 16,000 acres of the colonial governor for £150. This tract was called Wellington.

A Congregational church was organized, probably some time in 1728, for on Sept. 11, 1728, Mr. Daniel Fuller was "ordained pastor of ye Church of Christ in Wellington. It is quite probable that the church was organized the same day. They had no meeting-house at that time, and the ordination services were held at the house of Mr. John Merrick, one of the original settlers.

Mr. Fuller died of small-pox in the thirty-first year of his ministry and sixtieth year of his age. He was interred in the old burying-ground on Willington Hill, which he himself gave to the town.

Willington was not backward in doing its part for the defense and welfare of the Colonies during the Revolutionary period. Thirty men went at once from Willington on hearing of the Lexington battle. And early in the Revolutionary war a company of fifty men went from the town under the command of Capt. John Parker.

There were brave women as well as brave men in those days in Willington. One fall, during the war, several soldiers returned to their homes to see about provisions for their families, and to cut and get up wood for the winter. A Mr. Sanger came home with two of his sons for this purpose, but his patriotic wife urged him to return at once with his boys to the army, and leave the care of the family to her. He complied with her request; and she and her daughters husked the corn, threshed the rye, felled trees in the woods, yoked the oxen, and hauled to the door the winter's supply of fuel for the fire. Mrs. Sanger was not an exceptional woman; there were other wives and mothers in Willington as energetic and patriotic as she.

An eleven-year old boy, son of Rev. Gideon Noble, the second minister of the Congregational Church, went as fifer in one of the military companies from this town. It was thought that he would want to return home by the time he had reached New York, and his friends expected that he would return; but he continued with the company throughout the war. He was the pet of the soldiers, and he was so small that they often carried him on their shoulders while marching.

Abraham Weston, another Willington boy, went as drummer in the same company. He was only fourteen years old.

For many years after its settlement the business of the town was almost entirely farming, and has been mainly that always. About sixty years ago a glass-factory was built in the western part of the town, which was for a number of years a prominent industry.

About forty years ago Messrs. Dale & Co. erected a silk-mill on Fenton river, in the southeast part of Willington, and a little village soon grew up around the mill, which went and still goes by the name of Daleville. For a few years a large business was done there, but changes occurred and the enterprise ceased. For a number of years that neighborhood was so nearly deserted that it strongly reminded one of "Goldsmith's Deserted Villages." Within a few years this property has been purchased by another company who are now manufacturing beaver cloth in the old silk-mill, and the village again has the appearance of activity.

Not far from the time that the silk factory was established at Daleville, Messrs. Elisha Johnson, Origen Hall, Otis Dimmick and others formed a company for the manufacture of cotton spool-thread, in the southwest part of the town. It was one of the first establishments of the kind in the United States. For a number of years the works had lain idle, when, at the commencement of the late war, Gardiner Hall, Jr., & Co. purchased the property and commenced manufacturing thread again in the old mill. This part of Willington has been greatly changed and improved within a few years. This village goes by the name of "South Willington," and it is now altogether the most flourishing part of the town.

For many years after the organization of the town the Congregational church was the only one in Willington. But during the latter part of the second minister's pastorate, a Baptist church was organized in the north part of the town, and a meeting-house was erected.

Several years later another Baptish church was organized on Willington Hill. After the fourth pastor of the Congregational church—Rev. Hubbel Loomis—had filled the pastorate to the acceptance of his people twenty-four years, his doctrinal views underwent a change, and he became a Baptist. Mr. Loomis was a man of education, talent and strong influence, and was greatly beloved by his people, and soon brought nearly one-half of the church and society over to his views; and so the Baptist church was formed on the hill, and a meeting-house was soon erected near the Congregational church. The Baptists in the north part of the town united with this church, and worship in the old Baptist house was abandoned. In 1878, this church celebrated the fiftieth anniversary of its orgnaization.

There has also been for many years a Methodist church in the northeast part of the town.

The Congregational church established a Sunday school in 1815, which, it is said, is the oldest Sunday school in Tolland County.

Willington claims as one of its most distinguished sons, Rev. Jared Sparks, a Unitarian clergyman, a voluminous historical and biographical writer, and president of Harvard College from 1849 to 1852. He was born May 10, 1789, and died at Cambridge March 14, 1866.

Elias Loomis, professor of natural philosophy and astronomy in Yale College, and author of several valuable text-books, is a native of Willington, and son of Rev. Hubbel Loomis.

The population of Willington in 1880 was 1,086.

Columbia lies above the valley of Hop River, which forms its northern boundary. It is by considerable climbing that one mounts from this valley to the broad, level tract on which the village is situated. This is a very pleasant street and presents an agreeable picture of what the centre of an ancient farming-town becomes, where the chief and only business is farming, and there has come to be a cluster or street of farmers' houses more closely together than in other parts of the town, with the meeting-house, the house for the entertainment of travelers, the store, the parsonage, and the doctor's office nestled among the white-painted, green blinded, and sometimes vine-embowered dwelling-houses.

For eighty-eight years after its separate organization as an ecclesiastical society, Columbia was a part of Lebanon, and was called the Second Ecclesiastical Society of Lebanon. This part of Lebanon went by the name of Lebanon Crank. This ecclesiastical society was constituted in 1716, and continued the second society in Lebanon until 1804, when Columbia became a distinct town. Although it remained in its minority, so to speak, through the eighteenth century, it nevertheless became widely known as an ecclesiastical society, and its independent history really dates back far beyond the time of its organization as a town. For, besides its due quota of fathers and sons and brothers given to the cause of national independence, the events of which Dr. Wheelock was the central figure and moving spirit, have given to Columbia an eminent name among the towns of Tolland County.

In the Revolutionary war it counted only as a part of Lebanon in all its relations to the commonwealth of Connecticut. At least sixty-four persons went into active service from this parish. And of these, fourteen were killed or died in the army. The soldierly spirit was not exhausted in this generation. During the war of 1812 the people of the town of Columbia were quick to respond to the call for the defense of New London. There is an accredited tradition, the Rev. F. D. Avery, of Columbia, tells us, that as soon as the news of the burning of New London reached the place, at the hour of some religious service, Mr. Brockway, the pastor of the church, started off with his long gun and deacons and parishioners to assist in doing battle with the enemy.

In the civil war eight of this town's soldiers died in the service.

The Congregational Church, which has been from the first to this day the only church in Columbia, was organized in 1720, and on the same day Samuel Smith was ordained pastor.

The third pastor was Eleazer Wheelock, eminent for his activity and his sympathy with the Great Awakening of 1742 and the following years, and for his interest in the education of Indian youth.

This interest was awakened by the coming to him one day in December, 1743, a young Indian sachem named Samson Occum, soliciting instruction. Occum proved so apt a scholar that Mr. Wheelock took up the project of training Indian youth to become missionaries among their own people. To encourage this enterprise Mr. Joshua Moor, of Mansfield, gave a lot of land near the centre of the parish. A school-house was built, the frame of which is still preserved in the frame of the present school-house on the green.

The school was fairly started in 1754. Indian youth from the Delawares, Mohawks, and other tribes, resorted hither to obtain an education. White students were also received into the school in numbers about equal to the Indians. Sometimes there were more than twenty in the school. Many of the Indians became teachers in their tribes. Occum only became an ordained minister. But several of the white students went to college and became missionaries among the Indians. And here in Lebanon Crank, says Mr. Avery in his centennial sermon, were ordained first in Connecticut, missionaries to the heathen.

Mr. Wheelock's school was sustained and the missionaries were supported by appropriations from the General Courts in Connecticut and Massachusetts, and by funds from England to the amount of £7,000, of which the king gave £200, and from the Scottish Society for propagating Christian knowledge. In acknowledgment of Mr. Moor's generous donation, Mr. Wheelock called the school "Moor's Indian Charity School."

Out of Samson Occum's application to Mr. Wheelock for instruction grew Dartmouth College; for the government of New Hampshire invited Mr. Wheelock to remove to Hanover to establish a college in that place. He consented to do so, and in 1770 took his family and school to Hanover. The funds contributed in England to the Indian school were intrusted to a Board, of which the Earl of Dartmouth was the president. And from this circumstance, although the earl himself was opposed to the removal of the school from Columbia, the new institution was called Dartmouth College.

The situation of Columbia has made it for the most part a farming town. There has been, however, for over forty years, a cotton-mill at Hop River, which has grown in recent years under the proprietorship of W. Curtis Jillson, into its present thriving condition. It now goes by the name of the "Hop River Warp Manufacturing Company." It has been for several years the chief manufacturing industry of the town. Previous to this there was a carding-mill near that place.

There was also in former years considerable business in the town in the manufacture of cheap woolen hats. Fur hats were also made here at one time, on a small scale.

Hon. Dwight Loomis of Rockville, who was elected representative to Congress from the first congressional district of Connecticut, in 1859, and re-elected in 1861, was born and reared in Columbia.

The population of the town is about 800.

Union.—The first settlement was made in 1727 by William McNall, John Lawson and James Shearer from Ireland. The town was incorporated in 1734.

In 1738 the first meeting-house was erected in the town, and the same year the Congregational church was constituted, andthe Rev. Ebenezer Wyman was ordained pastor. The ordination services were held in a private dwelling, as the meeting-house was not sufficiently complete at that time for this purpose. It appears that the Puritan element was, almost from the first, well represented by settlers who came from some of the oldest Puritan towns of New England, notwithstanding Union's pioneer settlers were Scotch-Irish from the north of Ireland, and were probably Scotch Presbyterians of the John Knox and Covenanters' stamp.

Union ranks among the smallest towns, both in area and population in the county—in fact in the State; but its history shows that it has contributed its full quota to the advancement and prosperity of the republic; 146 persons from this town served in the war of the Revolution; and in 1774 the total population of Union was only 514.

Union is chiefly a farming community, but the soil is hard to till and unproductive, compared with some portions of the county. The thriftiest of pine and hemlock trees grow here. They are indigenous, and formerly they were to be found in every part of the town. It is said that Union has produced more pine and hemlock lumber than all of the rest of Tolland County. The lumber business has been, and still is an important industry of the town. Thirty years ago, or more, the domestic manufacture of boots and shoes was carried on to a limited extent.

Mashapaug Pond, covering 800 acres, with its clear waters overshadowed with evergreen trees, is an attractive feature.

The nearest railroad station to Union is at Stafford Springs, about six miles from the centre of town.

Among some of the distinguished men who originated in Union was Jesse Olney (1798-1872), at one time a popular school-teacher in Hartford, the author of a number of valuable school-books, and for several years comptroller of the State, and Rev. Charles Hammond, LL.D., widely known as the principal of Monson Academy, Mass. Mr. Hammond was born June 15, 1813, and died November 7, 1878.

In 1880 the population of Union was 539.

Bolton is situated on the western brow of the hills of Tolland County. The scenery from some of the hills is exceedingly beautiful.

Settlements began to be made in Bolton about the year 1717, by two or three different parties, coming from Windsor, Wethersfield, and Hartford. It was made a distinct town in 1720. As was the universal custom in the towns of the Colonies, immediately after settlement, Bolton's first care was to establish the regular public worship of God. There is a record that Jonathan Edwards preached there in 1722, and received a call to settle. In November, 1723, the following record is entered, in his handwriting, upon the town records: "Upon the terms that are here recorded I do consent to be the settled pastor of the town of Bolton. Jonathan Edwards." Mr. Edwards' appointment to a tutorship in Yale College seems to have broken up this arrangement.

Mr. Thomas White, the first settled pastor of this people, was ordained and installed in 1725, and the church was probably organized at the same time.

Rev. George Colton, the second pastor of this church, was installed in 1763. He died in 1812. Mr. Colton was distinguished for his eccentricity and piety. He is said to have been six feet and seven inches in height, and he was familiarly called the *high* priest of Bolton. It is said that he published in rhyme, from his pulpit, his own marriage banns.

Two companies went from Bolton on the Lexington alarm in 1775—one of thirty-five men, and one of twenty-eight.

When Dr. Samuel Peters, rector of the Episcopal church in Hebron, was mobbed for being so outspoken in defense of the arbitrary acts of Parliament, and for his false representations, a large number of Bolton men were present and took part in forcing a recantation from him.

From an early period in the present century, the principal occupation of the town, aside from farming, has been the quarrying of flag-stone. The stone is a bright, light gray, a species of slate, and is very strong and enduring. More stones for flagging purposes have been sent out from these quarries than from any other in the State. About 1812 this stone was used considerably for gravestones.

Fifty years ago, Mr. Duthon Avery of this place carried on the cabinet-making business quite largely for a country town, and people from all the towns in the vicinity used to go there for household furniture, coffins, etc. Mr. Avery took in farmers' produce in exchange for his goods.

The following copy, from one of Mr. Avery's old day-books, exhibits the manner of trafficking in those days, and some of the old-time prices:

Phineas Carver, Dr.

To a Coffin for your Child	67
" " " Mother	4 50
" " " Wife	4 50
To Cambric for Shroud	50

Credit.

By a Saddle.
" Mending wagon harness.
" ½ day's work mowing.
" forty-five and a half pounds of beef at 6c.
" Eight pounds & six ounces cheese at 4c.
" Making two wagon harnesses.

The late Hon. Julius L. Strong, a member of Congress in 1869, was a native of Bolton.

The population of the town in 1880 was 512.

Andover is the youngest town in Tolland County. As a distinct parish, however, it is much older than the county, having been incorporated as a second ecclesiastical society in May, 1747. The territory of the new parish was taken from the three towns of Hebron, Coventry and Lebanon. This parish, Dr. Sprague thinks, was called Andover because the original settlers were from Andover, Mass. It consisted of sixty-eight members, called "householders."

At an early date it was voted that a committee of four "go forthwith and see out for a preacher to preach the gospel in this society." Mr. Samuel Lockwood was ordained and installed as pastor of the church, Feb. 25, 1749.

His ministry continued till his death in 1791, and during the whole of this period the parish seems to have been in a state of great and growing prosperity. In 1790, the degree of Doctor of Divinity was conferred upon him by his *alma mater*, Yale College. This Congregational church of Andover had the common experience of long pastorates in the early period of Connecticut Congregationalism. When its one hundredth anniversary came, its fourth pastor was then serving the twentieth year of his pastorate.

Andover was not incorporated as a town until 1848. Its civil history previous to this year is therefore in part that of Hebron.

The chief manufacturing industry has been the making of paper. The business is now entirely farming.

Among the sons of Andover was William B. Sprague, D. D., a distinguished minister, and an author of various works.

The population of the town in 1880 was 428.

Ellington was originally a part of the township of East Windsor, called the Great Marsh. It was not until about seventy-five years after the settlement began on the east side of the Connecticut River, that any settlers located themselves in the part now called Ellington. The present town includes what was formerly known as "Equivalent Lands." This tract of 7,250 acres was granted by the General Court, in 1716, to the town of Windsor, as a recompense for a loss by that town of some 7,000 acres of land in the adjustment of the boundary line between Connecticut and Massachusetts.

Rev. John McKinstry, the first minister of Ellington, was educated in Scotland, and settled here in 1733. The principal settlers came from Scotland and the north of Ireland. Ellington is largely a farming town, and tobacco is raised to a considerable extent. The western section is well supplied with water-power. The Windermere factory produces cassimeres and broadcloths.

The population of the town in 1880 was 1,569.

WINDHAM COUNTY.

In 1726, ten towns in the northeast corner of Connecticut, previously included in the counties of Hartford and New London, were erected into the county of Windham. Union and Woodstock were subsequently added; Mansfield, Coventry, Lebanon, Union and Columbia taken away; and several of the original towns divided. Sixteen towns—Woodstock, Thompson, Putnam, Pomfret, Brooklyn, Killingly, Sterling, Plainfield, Canterbury, Eastford, Ashford, Chaplin, Hampton, Windham, Scotland and Voluntown—form the present Windham County. Its average length is about twenty-six miles and its breadth nearly nineteen miles. Its area comprises a little less than 553 square miles.

The greater part of this tract of country prior to English settlement was included in Nipnet—the Fresh-water country—the inland region between the Atlantic coast and the Connecticut River. It was sparsely occupied by the scattered tribelets or families of Nipmucks or Nipnets, although the land east of the Quinebaug was also claimed by Narragansets. The northern part of this contested strip was Mahmunsqung—the Whetstone country. Land now included in the towns of Sterling, Plainfield, and Canterbury was the Quinebaug country, and its residents were known as Quinebaugs. The tract west of the Quinebaug River, and north of the Quinebaug country, was Wabbaquasset—the mat-producing country.

Acquittimaug of Wabbaquasset is the first Windham County inhabitant of whom we have record. In the winter of 1630-31, news came to this people that a company of Englishmen had come to the Bay who were in great want of corn, and would pay a good price for it. The fertile hills and valleys of the future Woodstock were already noted for their large production of this aboriginal staple. With each a bushel or more of corn upon their backs, Acquittimaug and other Indians toiled through the wilderness to the infant settlement at Boston, and were joyfully welcomed by the needy colonists. Acquittimaug lived about ninety-five years after this incident, and when, in extreme old age, he visited Boston, he was welcomed and generously entertained by some of the chief dignitaries of the Massachusetts Colony.

The Windham County territory became known to the English with the first settlement of Connecticut. It lay directly in the route from Boston to Hartford, a part of that "hideous and trackless wilderness" traversed by the first colonists. A rude track, called the Connecticut Path, obliquely crossing what is now Thompson, Woodstock, Eastford and Ashford, became the main thoroughfare of travel between the Massachusetts and Connecticut colonies. Yet for fifty years no settlement was effected within the limits of the county, and the aborigines remained in undisputed possession of the territory. They were subject clans of little spirit or distinctive character. Their number was small. A few families occupied the favorable localities, while large sections were left vacant and desolate. Large tracts were burned over every year and kept open, to furnish pasture for deer. Game and fish abounded in wood, lake and river. The principal rivers, lakes and hills bore the names that still distinguish them. An Indian trail, known as Nipmuck Path, ran south from Wabbaquasset to the sea-shore. The Greenwich Path crossed eastward from the Quinebaug to Narraganset. A few rude forts were built and maintained in various localities.

As the Mohegans increased in power, they laid claim, under various pretexts, to the greater part of this territory. The timid and peace-loving Wabbaquassets readily acknowledged allegiance to Uncas, and "paid him homage and obligations and yearly tribute of white deer-skins, bear-skins and black wolf-skins." With the Quinebaugs Uncas was less successful. His right to their allegiance was disputed by the Narragansets. Pessacus, alias Moosup, brother and successor to Miantonomo, asserted his right to the Quinebaug country, affixing his name to the largest branch of the Quinebaug. For many years the land was in contention, the distracted inhabitants yielding homage to whichever chieftain chanced to be in the ascendency. Tradition tells of various bloody rencontres and one distinct battle between the natives.

While the Indians east of the Quinebaug were thus contending, those on the west were yielding to better influences. The most noteworthy incidents of Windham's aboriginal history were connected with the ministry of the great Indian apostle, John Eliot. Young Indians, trained by him at Natick, went out as missionaries into the Nipmuck wilderness. The simple and tractable Wabbaquassets hearkened willingly unto the Gospel thus presented and many were persuaded to unite in church estate, and assume some of the habits of civilization. They observed the Sabbath, gathered into villages, and built wigwams, the like of which were seen nowhere else in New England. Thirty families were gathered at what was called Wabbaquasset Village, now in the south part of Woodstock; twenty families at Myanexet, on the Quinebaug, in or near the north part of Woodstock; and twenty families of Nipmucks at Quinnatisset, now Thompson Hill. These villages and churches were under the care and guidance of Sampson, a hopeful, pious and active young man. In 1674 he was encouraged and strengthened by a visit from Mr. Eliot, who, with Maj. Daniel Gookin, magistrate over the Praying Indians, came to confirm the churches, settle teachers over them, and establish civil government. They found peace, order and a friendly welcome in each of the praying villages. Mr. Eliot preached in Myanexet, and gave them John Moqua for their teacher. "A sober and pious young man of Natick, called Daniel," was appointed minister for Quinnatisset. At Wabbaquasset, where he passed the night, Eliot was warmly welcomed by the teacher, Sampson, and entertained in the spacious wigwam of the sagamore. On the following morning, Sept. 16, 1674, a great meeting was held in Wabbaquasset Village. All the Praying Indians from the different villages were there, and many others. An opening religious service was conducted by Mr. Eliot, and then a "court" was held by Maj. Gookin, establishing civil government among the natives. The teacher Sampson was approved as their minister, and Black James of Chaubongagum installed over them as constable. Having thus settled religious and civil institutions, Mr. Eliot and his friends bade adieu and journeyed homewards, greatly pleased with the progress of Christianity and civilization among this tractable and friendly people. Seventy families had been reclaimed from heathenism.

These hopeful prospects were soon blighted. The Narraganset war swept away the results of years of missionary labor. The villages were destroyed, the churches broken up, and the Praying Indians relapsed into savages. The Nipmucks east of the Quinebaug joined the Narragansets; the terrified Wabbaquassets left their pleasant homes and planting fields and threw themselves under the protection of Uncas at Mohegan. No battle or skirmish occurred during the war within Windham County territory, but it was repeatedly traversed and ravaged by scouting and foraging parties. Great quantities of corn and beans, stately wigwams, the like of which had not been seen, and the several forts were all demolished. The close of the war found the Nipmucks almost annihilated. Those that were left sought refuge with distant tribes. The Wabbaquassets remained for a time at Mohegan. The aboriginal inhabitants of the future Windham were scattered or destroyed, and their territory left to English occupation.

The first English proprietor within Windham County territory was Governor John Winthrop, of New London, who, in 1653, secured from Hyems and Massasshowett a grant of the Quinebaug country. The validity of this conveyance was extremely doubtful. The grantors were renegade Narragansets, exercising a delegated authority, with no legal title to the land conveyed. The General Court of Connecticut, however, "allowed the governor his Indian purchase at Quinebaug, and gave him liberty to erect thereon a plantation;" but the Indian troubles prevented settlement. After the restoration of peace, the Massachusetts government opened negotiations with the remaining Nipmucks, and February 10, 1682, secured a deed of the whole Nipmuck country, allowing to the Indians a five-mile reservation. A full half of this reservation was immediately made over by them to Governors Joseph Dudley and William Stoughton, who had served as commissioners in the transaction. Dudley's fine farm was laid out in the Quinebaug Valley, and was afterwards included in the towns of Thompson and Dudley. Five thousand acres at Quinnatisset, embracing what is now Thompson Hill and its vicinity, were conveyed to Stoughton, laid out in farms, and sold the following year to Robert Thompson and Thomas Freak, of England. Tracts of land in Quinnatisset were also granted by the Massachusetts government to other proprietors.

Connecticut's share of Windham County territory was mostly appropriated by Uncas and his representatives. To his son Owaneco was assigned the whole Wabbaquasset country and rights in the Quinebaug country. This chieftain was a drunken, worthless fellow, of no stability or force of character. Swarms of greedy land hunters now gathered around him, eager to obtain possession of his land upon any pretext. Conscious of his own inability to manage his great possessions, Owaneco yielded to the persuasions of his friends and accepted the younger James Fitch of Norwich as his guardian.

The whole Wabbaquasset country was formally conveyed to him in 1689. The landed interests of Windham County were thus to a great degree vested in the hands of one individual, destined to play an important part in its settlement and development.

Towns.

The first white inhabitant of the present town of Windham (population 8,000), was one John Cates, an English refugee, hiding, according to traditional report, from the spies of Andros. In the autumn of 1688, he found his way into this desolate wilderness, and passed the winter in a cave or cellar, dug out by the hands of his faithful negro. With the restoration of peace and charter government in 1689, Cates came out of his hiding-place, and purchased a tract of land. The second reported settler was Jonathan Ginnings. He was soon followed by Joshua and Jeremiah Ripley of Hingham, Mass., May 12, 1692, the plantation was granted the liberty of a township, to be called Windham, and June 12, a town government was organized. Only fifteen citizens were then reported, but their number increased rapidly. The great size of the town occasioned its first serious difficulty. A controversy ensuing in regard to the location of the church, resulted in a division of the town in May, 1703, the north part of Windham being formally erected into the town of Mansfield. A church had previously been formed, December 10, 1700, and Mr. Samuel Whiting ordained as its pastor. A meeting-house in Windham Green was completed in 1703.

The first settler in the northeast section, now Hampton, was David Canada, a reputed Welshman. Many sterling Massachusetts families settled in this vicinity on Appaquage Hill and River. The difficulty of attending public worship at Windham Green led these northern settlers to ask for society privileges, and in 1717 a religious society was there organized. This section was known as Canada Parish, and also as Windham Village, and a church was gathered there in 1723. A third religious society was set off in 1732, in the southeast section of the town, known as Scotland Parish, and a church organized in 1735.

Windham Green continued to increase in influence and importance as the seat of town government and business centre of a large section. A Court of Probate was established here in 1719, Capt. John Fitch, judge. In 1726 Windham was made the shire town of the newly constituted Windham County. The first Court of Common Pleas was held June 26. Timothy Pierce of Plainfield was appointed judge. A jail and state house were soon erected, and the town soon received a fresh impetus. Iron works were now established at Willimantic Falls, and other manufactures. The First Church of Windham was particularly flourishing at this time. A very remarkable religious awakening had been enjoyed during the last years of Mr. Whiting's ministry. His successor, Mr. Thomas Clap of Scituate, was a young man of uncommon administrative ability, who brought the whole population under stringent watch and discipline. Every head of a household was connected with the church, either by profession of faith or owning the covenant. Family prayer was observed in every household, and every child consecrated by baptism. Profane swearing was but little known, and open violation of the Sabbath very rare. In 1739 Windham was compelled to resign her distinguished minister to the presidency of Yale College. He was succeeded by Mr. Stephen White, a young man of very dissimilar character.

It was about this time that Windham's famous "Frog Panic," more widely known than any event in its early history, occurred. War between England and France was imminent. Indians were alert and turbulent, ready to join in the first outbreak. One night the residents of Windham Green were aroused from their slumbers by the most appalling and unearthly sounds—an indescribable hubbub and tumult, that seemed to fill the heavens and shake the earth. Some thought it an earthquake; some thought the Day of Judgment was at hand. Others seized upon the more natural, but hardly less appalling, explanation that an army of French and Indians was marching upon them. Consternation and terror fell upon all, and the night was passed in anxious suspense, not to say frantic lamentation. The morning dawned at length, and brought a ludicrous solution of the mystery. The unearthly clamor and uproar had been produced by a chorus of frogs, excited in some mysterious way to a preternatural activity. This story of Windham's tragic alarm flew all over the country, with innumerable additions and exaggerations. It was sung in song; it was related in history; it served as a standing joke upon every native of Windham. A letter to President Stiles fixes the date of this incident as prior to July 9, 1754.

The military spirit for which Windham was always noted found ample exercise during the French and Indian war. Many of its citizens served with distinction in numerous bloody campaigns. Public affairs and political issues engrossed more and more of their attention. No people were filled with more patriotic fervor, and more ready to engage in the great struggle for American liberties. They responded to the first summons from Boston by renouncing the use of all imported articles not absolutely essential. At a fashionable wedding in 1768, bride and guests wore home-spun, and all the refreshments were home-made. As agitation went on, the Windham boys were foremost in opposition to imposts and Tories. When the port of Boston was closed, Windham's instant offering of a small flock of 258 sheep was the first succor received by the distressed Bostonians. Throughout the long Revolutionary struggle she was equally ready and faithful. Dyer, Elderkin and Wales served day and night in Connecticut's Committee of Safety. Gray and Elderkin make powder in their mills at Willimantic. Huntington made the first gun turned out of an American workshop, and repaired the wretched firearms carried by the common soldiers. Hundreds of brave men periled their lives in camp and battle, sustained and encouraged by the prayers and sympathy of thousands of Windham women, as patriotic and devoted as themselves.

With the establishment of independence, Windham entered upon a new era of growth and prosperity, her citizens engaging with such spirit in various business enterprises that she was reported "to exceed any inland town in the State in trade and merchandise." A vast amount of produce was raised and sent to market. Special industries were developed in different neighborhoods. Experiments were made in silk raising and manufacture. In 1791 Windham issued its first newspaper, "The Phenix," or "Windham Herald," printed by John Byrne, which attained extensive circulation throughout the country. Before 1800 the first post-office was opened, John Byrne postmaster. An academy had also been opened. The venerable Stephen White died in 1793, after a ministry of fifty-two years. He was succeeded by Rev. Elijah Waterman, a young man of great energy, active in promoting new measures and public interests. Foremost among Windham's public men of this generation was Zepaniah Swift, one of the ablest lawyers in Connecticut.

In 1819, a bill was passed, transferring the courts of Windham County to the town of Brooklyn. Windham had previously lost more than half her original territory by the formation of new towns. To the loss of prestige and position was now added a transference of business interests from the Green to the Willimantic—the younger settlement attaining leadership.

Plainfield (4,000)—The settlement of this town was contemporaneous with that of Windham. The beautiful valley of the Quinebaug, with its open hill-slopes and bountiful yield of corn, offered great attraction to settlers, especially as its Indian inhabitants, though very numerous, were most tractable and friendly.

Timothy and Thomas Pierce, Thomas Williams, Edward, Joseph and Benjamin Spalding were among the east-side settlers. Major Fitch, Samuel Adams, Elisha Paine and others settled on the west side. In 1669 the Quinebaug Plantation was invested with town privileges. The Governor, Fitz John Winthrop, gave the new town the name of Plainfield. The first care of the town was to call a minister, Mr. Joseph Coit, of Norwich, who held religious services statedly in private houses.

In consequence of the difficulty of crossing the Quinebaug River in winter and during high water, for the purpose of attending meeting, the town, in October, 1703, was divided, the territory west of the river being erected into the township of Canterbury.

The tranquility of Plainfield was most grievously disturbed by controversies growing out of the great awakening of 1740. A pleasing feature of the revival was its effect upon the surviving Quinebaugs, who were "not only filled with knowledge of ye way of Salvation," but reformed in their ways of living and abstained from drinking. Dissenting from some of the doctrines and practices of the established church, and especially from the payment of the minister by rate or tax, the new converts, after a time, organized as a separate church. Mr. Coit was now old and infirm. A majority of the town refused longer to pay their assessments for his support. The settlement of his successor was followed by a most bitter and protracted contest, demoralizing churches and town, and "separating very friends and brothers." After a generation of strife and contention, the churches finally happily united in the choice of Rev. John Fuller, of Norwich, all parties agreeing that the ministry should thenceforth be supported by voluntary contribution, without tax or coercion. This same controversy prevailed nearly throughout the county, distracting and prostrating many of even the most prosperous churches on the territory.

Throughout the Revolutionary period Plainfield was active and prominent.

Plainfield Academy was established during this period. In 1778 Ebenezer Pemberton, of Newport, was secured as its rector. Scholars came in large numbers from Providence, New York, New London and other places. For many years this academy enjoyed a high reputation under such distinguished teachers as Dr. Pemberton, John Adams, Benjamin Allen, Zechariah Eddy, Timothy Pitkin, Calvin Goddard, Eliphalet Nott, Rinaldo Burleigh, and many others. Dr. Joel Benedict, who succeeded Mr. Fuller in the pastorate at Plainfield, a man of high character and uncommon attainments, and Dr. Elisha Perkins, one of the most noted physicians and surgeons of his generation, were among the distinguished citizens of this town.

Plainfield embraces within its limits the flourishing manufacturing villages of Central Village, Moosup and Wauregan.

Canterbury (1,300)—The western part of the Quinebaug Plantation, when endowed with town privileges 1703, had but few inhabitants, but these were men of character and position, well fitted to manage the affairs of the town. Maj. Fitch was long "the great man" of all the surrounding country, and his Peagscomsuck homestead, a very noted establishment, a rendezvous for land speculators, civil and military officials, and hordes of idle Indians. Here courts were held, military expeditions organized, and whole townships of land bartered away. Maj. Fitch was for a time one of the most prominent men in Connecticut, and had great personal and political influence; but his immense land operations, and his own violence and lack of judgment, involved him in very serious complications and quarrels. The claims of Fitch and other large land-owners delayed the growth of the town. "All the good land upon the Quinebaug" had been monopolized by these voracious "land-grabbers," and for a considerable period but few persons succeeded in establishing settlements. Town records are lacking till 1717. Previous to this date a meeting-house had been built, a church organized, and Mr. Samuel Estabrook ordained as minister. Mr. Estabrook remained in charge of the Canterbury church till his death in 1727.

Canterbury was the scene of a remarkable ecclesiastical controversy, growing out of the memorable great awakening, to which reference has already been made. A majority of the church had become what were termed New Lights—opponents of the established or "standing order" church. The Rev. James Cogswell, a candidate for settlement over the Canterbury church, was strenuously opposed to the new measures. The civil and ecclesiastical authorities, professing to have become alarmed at the ungovernable fanaticism of the revivalists, determined upon the revolutionary, unconstitutional, uncongregational, and hence utterly unauthorized measure of settling the candidate of the minority. This flagrant violation of the rights of the majority not unnaturally excited widespread indignation, while the bold and persistent championship on the part of the latter of the rights of the majority and of pure Congregationalism, in opposition to the arbitrary measures and assumptions of the authorities, elicited much admiration and sympathy, and was the occasion of the organization of many societies on an entirely independent basis.

The persecution visited upon this new movement significantly indicates the temper of the times. Elisha and Solomon Paine, the acknowledged leaders of the revival party in Canterbury, were fined and imprisoned; their nephews, from Yale College, for presuming, while at home in vacation, to attend the religious services conducted by their uncles were expelled. One Obadiah Johnson, an old and respected citizen, when chosen a representative of the town to the General Court by a fair majority, was expelled from his seat in the House for being a member and officer of one of these separate or independent organizations.

After the lapse of many years, and the discontinuance of this exciting and distracting controversy, these "separate" societies either became extinct, or were finally resolved into regular Congregational churches.

Mr. Cogswell remained in charge of the Canterbury church till 1771. Among many pupils received into his family were Naphtali Daggett, afterwards president of Yale College, and Benedict Arnold. The western part of Canterbury was incorporated as Westminster Society in 1770, and a church organized the same year. Rev. John Staples was ordained as its pastor in 1772, and continued in charge till his death in 1807.

The most noted citizen of Canterbury during the Revolutionary period was Moses, son of Capt. Aaron Cleveland, who entered early upon the practice of law, and also engaged in extensive business enterprises. He was agent for the Connecticut Land Company, that settled the Western Reserve, Ohio, and selected the site of the city of Cleveland, which was named in his honor.

"Master John Adams," a very successful teacher, principal for many years of Phillips Academy, Andover, was another noted son of Canterbury, and won his first laurels in his native town, where he opened a high school in 1796. Among many Canterbury youth, distinguished in after life, who were pupils of Master Adams, was John Hough, professor at Middlebury College. Ebenezer Fitch, first president of Williams College, was also a native of this town.

In 1833, Canterbury was brought very prominently into notice in connection with the colored school opened by Miss Prudence Crandall. Under the patronage of leading men of the town, Miss Crandall had previously established a young ladies' school, which had been handsomely sustained. The introduction of a young colored girl gave great offense to the parents of her other pupils, who threatened to withdraw their daughters. Finding that she could not instruct both white and colored together, Miss Crandall decided in favor of the latter, and, after counseling with friends in regard to the matter, threw open her school "for young ladies and little misses of color." Indignant at what they deemed a breach of good faith, the former patrons of Miss Crandall made use of "every argumentative effort to convince her of the injustice and impropriety of the proposed measure." But having decided upon it from supreme conviction of duty, nothing could change her resolution. Personal insults and violence and legal injunctions were alike ineffectual. At length a vehement petition from Canterbury procured the enactment of the celebrated "Black Law," by which all persons were forbidden to establish a school for the instruction of the colored persons not inhabitants of the State, or teach in any school, or harbor or board any colored person attending such school, under very heavy penalties. Undismayed by this opposition and persecution in most annoying forms, Miss Crandall went calmly on with her school, supported by her own indomitable spirit, and the smypathy and material aid of prominent Abolitionists. Arrested upon charge of breaking the newly enacted law, Miss Crandall suffered herself to be carried to jail for a night, to awaken public sympathy and indignation. A final trial was held before the Court of Errors, July, 1834, when the court reserved its decision, and the suit was quashed for alleged defects of information. During all this time the greatest excitement raged in Canterbury and the adjoining towns. Failing in their efforts to break up the school by legal process, the opponents of Miss Crandall resorted to more systematic violence, and, after an ineffectual attempt to set the house on fire, broke in the windows with iron bars, and so seriously damaged it that repairs were deemed impolitic, if not impracticable.

Woodstock (2,700).—The first settlement within the limits of the present Windham County was made in Woodstock. By a mistake in the southern boundary line of the Bay Colony, the territory now included in Woodstock and Thompson was long held by Massachusetts.

The first settlers of the town were emigrants from Roxbury, Mass., and hence its original name of New Roxbury. Among the settlers at Plain Hill were Thomas and Joseph Bacon, James Corbin, Benjamin Sabin, and Henry Bowen.

When the French settlement at Oxford was destroyed by marauding Mohawks, its fugitives found refuge in the New Roxbury plantation. Great apprehensions were felt at other times of a rising of the Wabbaquassets. During these days of trial, the women and children might have been seen gathered into garrisons with but a single man to guard them and "hold the fort," while the other men under arms tried to carry on their out-door labor. In 1690 the colony was accorded town privileges, and granted the name of Woodstock, and during the same year Mr. Josiah Dwight, of Dedham, engaged in the work of the ministry. A meeting-house was completed in 1694, and a church soon afterwards organized though the date cannot be ascertained. From an isolated frontier town, Woodstock developed into a flourishing business centre. The most prominent citizen during this period was Captain John Chandler. All important commissions and negotiations were intrusted to him. He was the first and long the only representative sent to General Court, and was superintendent of the Wabbaquasset Indians. No man was more concerned in the settlement of Windham County. He owned large tracts of land in Killingly, Pomfret and Ashford. Nearly every town in Windham County was laid out by him, and he was held in high repute by the Connecticut Government. When Massachusetts' south boundary line was rectified in 1713, it was agreed that she should retain jurisdiction over the towns she had settled, an arrangement which for a time gave entire satisfaction; but after the death of Colonel Chandler and other town fathers, the new generation were led to desire transference to the government of Connecticut, where taxes would be lighter and greater privileges accorded. The change was subsequently made and the first town meeting under the jurisdiction of Connecticut was held on Woodstock Hill, July 28, 1749.

During the Revolution, Charles C. Chandler, a rising lawyer, was very active on the Committee of Correspondence; Samuel McClellan was much engaged in civil and military affairs, serving in the northern army, leading out the militia again and again, and paying them from his own purse when the treasury was empty. After the close of the war he was made general of the fifth brigade.

At the special request of Washington and Putnam, the church at Woodstock Hill yielded their beloved pastor, Rev. Abiel Leonard, LL.D., to officiate as chaplain of Putnam's own regiment. His eloquence and patriotism made him a great favorite in the army, and he continued to serve with much fidelity and acceptance until his most untimely and lamented decease in August, 1777. Another distinguished son of Woodstock, Gen. William Eaton, the conqueror of Tripoli, began his military career during the Revolutionary war in the company of Capt. Dana of Ashford.

With the restoration of peace and prosperity, Woodstock felt the need of greater educational privileges, and through the active instrumentality of Rev. Eliphalet Lyman, successor of Mr. Leonard, an academy was established at Woodstock Hill in 1802. Its first preceptor was Thomas Williams of Pomfret. He was succeeded by an array of teachers more or less celebrated, under whom the Academy maintained a good reputation.

Woodstock is becoming famous as a summer resort, vieing with Brooklyn and Thompson in this regard. Elmwood Hall and Woodstock Common are widely noted. Their publicity is mainly due to the enterprise and public spirit of Mr. Henry C. Bowen, publisher of the New York "Independent," who, being a native of Woodstock, made it his summer home, and who has done much for its improvement and adornment. Through his efforts and liberality, and the generous co-operation of his fellow-citizens, the old Woodstock Academy is placed on an assured basis, with an elegant new academy building, and an ample endowment. His last and perhaps greatest achievement is the opening to the public of Roseland Park, a beautiful pleasure-ground on the border of Woodstock Lake. The old military and election parades, and other rollicking festivites of the olden time that formerly furnished the chief diversion of the populace, have been outgrown. Mr. Bowen has proposed to meet the higher and varied demands of the present generation by creating this delightful park, which, with its musical concerts and many provisions for innocent recreation, promises to be a place of great public resort. Woodstock has already suprised the world with its monster mass-meetings and unique Fourth of July celebrations, bringing together, on these occasions, some of the foremost men of the nation.

Pomfret (1,500)—The settlement of this town was closely connected with that of Woodstock. On May 1, 1686, 15,100 acres of wilderness land were conveyed to several gentlemen from Roxbury, Mass. The first settler was John Sabin (June 22, 1691). This sturdy pioneer, during the Indian wars, rendered most important service by "standing his ground," protecting the frontier, and engaging the surrounding Indians as allies of the English. After the restoration of peace, settlement began in earnest. Mrs. Esther Grosvenor took possession of her allotment in 1700. Philemon Chandler, of Andover entered soon after upon a right purchased of Ruggles. Dea. Benjamin Sabin of Woodstock, with six sons, removed to the Mashamoquet settlement in 1705. These settlers experienced comparatively few hardships. The soil was good and easily subdued. Smooth hills, mostly bare of trees, yielded a coarse rank grass, so that cattle could forage for themselves through the winter. Woodstock afforded them mills, market, and religious privileges, men, women, and children toiling over the rough ways every Sunday to "Mr. Dwight's meeting-house." A grist-mill was set up on Bark-Meadow Brook by James Sawyer in 1709. A military company was organized in 1710. In May, 1713, town privileges were accorded, and it was also ordered "that the said Massamugget shall be called Pomfret."

A church was organized October 26, 1715, and Mr. Ebenezer Williams of Roxbury was ordained its pastor.

The most conspicuous event of Pomfret's early history was the destruction of that "old she-wolf," so famous in legendary story. Other Windham county wolves had succumbed to the prowess of hunters, but this "pernicious animal" found refuge in an almost inaccessible ledge of rock and forest in the south part of Pomfret, and feasted at pleasure upon the richest flocks and herds of the county. Combination and private effort failed to effect her capture. Wary and wise she outwitted all her pursuers, and continued for many years an intolerable nuisance. A slight snow-fall in the winter of 1743 enabled some hunters to trace her to the vicinity of her lair, and a dog belonging to Mr. John Sharpe tracked her into a den or cave, tunneling between the rocks down into the depths of the earth, and engaged with her in fierce combat. A young son of Mr. Sharpe followed on and gave the alarm. People gathered from all the farms around and used every possible means to rout the wolf from her hiding-place. Her first assailant was withdrawn from the cave badly disabled, and no other dogs would enter. Late at night it was remembered that a young farmer in Mortlake, one Israel Putnam, had a bloodhound of superior strength and courage, and the dog and his master were called to the rescue. His coming brought matters to immediate crisis. The obscure young farmer of 1743 was very like the brave "Old Put" of '76. Not a moment was wasted. The wolf must be mastered at any hazard. If she would not come out to them they must go in to her. Dog and negro refused to go, but Putnam was ready for the onset. With a rope fastened round his body and a blazing torch in his hand, Putnam crawled down the black icy passage until he could see the glaring eye-balls of his adversary, and with one dexterous shot dispatched Pomfret's last wolf, and made himself famous.

The west part of Pomfret was incorporated as Abington Society in 1749. A church was herein organized, January 31, 1753, and David Ripley of Windham was ordained as its minister. A meeting-house was completed the same year. Pomfret was distinguished during this period for intelligence and intellectual activity, eleven young men from this town being contemporary collegiates in 1757-59. Not only a most distinguished general, but many brave officers and men represented Pomfret in the Revolutionary struggle. Lieut. Thomas Grosvenor and a picked company of Pomfret boys were among the defenders of Bunker Hill.

Pomfret maintained a leading position in the county for many years. Dr. Waldo gained here a high reputation for medical skill. Dying suddenly in 1794, he was succeeded in practice by a young pupil and fellow townsman, Thomas Hubbard, who achieved even greater distinction than his master ere he was called by Yale College to occupy a high place in her surgical department. His contemporary, Dr. Jonathan Hall, was also very noted and popular, and his sons and daughters were shining ornaments of that polite and cultivated society which distinguished Pomfret above her sister towns, and made her a favorite resort for Newport and Providence families.

Richard Adams was the first white settler within the limits of the present town. Isaac Allen and Edward Spalding soon followed. These settlers were left for some years unrelated to any town, a few isolated families surrounded by a wilderness. In 1724, Richard Adams granted a parcel of land for the setting up of a school-house, and Daniel Cady granted another tract for "a convenient place to bury ye bodies of the dead among us." In 1731, parish privileges were accorded, and a society erected out of parts of Pomfret, Canterbury and Mortlake.

The Mortlake Society, as it was commonly called, organized a church and built a house of worship, and on September 24, 1735, ordained Ephraim

Avery of Truro, for its minister. The Rev. Mr. Avery was succeeded in the pastorate of the church by Josiah Whitney of Plainfield, who was ordained February 4, 1756. The widow of Mr. Avery, after a second marriage and widowhood, became the second wife of Col. Israel Putnam. In 1767, Putnam removed from the Whiteshire farm-house to Brooklyn Green, and opened a house of public entertainment. Through all the Stamp Act agitation, and other pre-revolutionary movements, he was the popular leader; and this Brooklyn tavern became one of the most noted rendezvous in eastern Connecticut. As a private citizen he was equally alert and active, ever ready to serve town, church and parish in any capacity.

During the whole Revolutionary period, Brooklyn was conspicuously prominent. Putnam was a host in himself. The opening of hostilities at Lexington called him from the plough to the saddle, and, until disabled by paralysis, he gave his whole time and energies to the patriot cause. The town and parish sustained him by constant co-operation and sympathy.

Brooklyn (2,300) was incorporated as a town in May, 1686. Various improvements were now set on foot, and the town took a leading position in all public affairs. The most important event occurring for many years during this period, was a controversy concerning the nature and persons of the Trinity, which resulted in church and society division, and the organization of the first Unitarian church in Connecticut. Dr. Whitney remained in charge of the Orthodox church, aided by colleagues, till his death in 1824, aged ninety-three years. The secular energies of the town during this period were mainly devoted to the struggle for a change of county-seat. After many years of sectional agitation, the civil administration of Windham County was transferred to Brooklyn Green, near the geographical centre of the county.

The first bank in Windham County was established in Brooklyn in 1822. In various reforms and aggressive movements, Brooklyn now took the lead. Samuel J. May, the well-known philanthropist and reformer, pastor of the Unitarian church, was active in all reformatory movements. The Windham County Agricultural Society, formed in 1820, now held its annual fair at Brooklyn. In 1830, Brooklyn Academy was incorporated and enjoyed for many years a large share of patronage. After 1840, newspapers and some other business interests were transferred to Danielsonville; but, though a little aside from railroads, Brooklyn has maintained her energy and vitality, and gains in wealth and population.

Thompson (2,300).—This town was not incorporated till 1785, but its record begins more than a century before that date, when twenty families of "Praying Indians" gathered on Quinnatisset hill-top and received a Christian teacher from Mr. Eliot. The first known white settler here was Richard Dresser of Rowley. Sampson Howe of Roxbury followed the next year. Samuel Converse of Woburn, with five sons, purchased land south of Quinnatisset Hill in 1710.

The first society meeting was held on Thompson Hill, July 9, 1728. A church was organized January 28, 1730, and Marston Cabot of Salem was soon after ordained its pastor. A Baptist church was organized in 1773, and a meeting-house built on what is now called Brandy Hill. The town was incorporated in May, 1785.

The transference of travel from turnpike to railroad, greatly affected Thompson, with other hill-top villages, and carried business away to other centres; but the town in general has maintained its early standing, and has ever been distinguished by thrift, order and public spirit. The old Congregational Church has been especially noted for the permanence of its ministry. The Rev. Daniel Dow, ordained April 20, 1796, celebrated the fiftieth anniversary of his settlement in 1846, and continued to officiate till the day of his death, in August, 1849.

Killingly (7,000).—The first white settler within the limits of the future town was Richard Evans, of Rehoboth, who, in 1693, made a home in the wilderness, three miles east from Woodstock. Peter Aspinwall, sent by Woodstock to cut through the cedar swamps to make a way to Providence, settled east of the Quinebaug about 1700. James and Joseph Leavens, of Woodstock, gathered turpentine for Woodstock traders in this section, and soon after joined the settlement, the latter marrying the daughter of Capt. John Sabin, of Pomfret, she receiving a beautiful valley farm for her marriage portion. These early settlers were favored by government oversight and protection, and in 1708 were allowed town privileges.

Though emigrants now came in more rapidly, money was scarce. The border position of the town made it particularly accessible to tramps, vagabonds and roving Indians. The large number of roads made requisite by the size of the town was very burdensome, especially as population was so scattered that nearly every household had to have a way of its own. Meantime these difficulties of travel, in roundabout ways, over rocks, and through swamps "to mill and to meeting," often became the occasion of society division. Hence the building of the meeting-house on Killingly Hill in 1746, the South Society occupying the house on Breakneck.

Killingly Hill, after the building of the meeting-house in 1746, was recognized more and more as the head and heart of the large township, the place for town meetings, trainings and public gatherings. Among its early residents were Rev. Aaron Brown, Noah, son of Justice Joseph Leavens, and Dr. Thomas Moffat, the first known physician of the town. John Felshaw, father and son, maintained a popular house of entertainment at the northern extremity of the hill for more than half a century. During the revolutionary troubles many substantial families from seaboard towns found refuge in Killingly, and were numbered among its most valued citizens.

A church was formed in West Killingly in 1801, and Westfield Parish organized. A thriving village grew up in this vicinity, which became a noted social and business centre. Its first physician was Dr. Hutchins. Rev. Roswell Whittemore succeeded Rev. Gordon Johnson in the pastorate of the church in 1813, and retained the office for thirty years. Other villages grew up on Five-Mile River and Whetstone Brook, which furnished many manufacturing privileges. Though it declined somewhat in importance after the removal of the town centre, Killingly Hill still furnishes a pleasant place of residence. Rev. Elisha Atkins served as pastor of the church from 1784 to 1839, and was greatly esteemed. In 1855 the north part of Killingly was incorporated into the new town of Putnam.

Among the most brilliant and promising of the sons of Killingly were the Rev. Joseph Howe, and Manasseh Cutler, one of the founders of the Ohio Company, very active and prominent in the opening and settlement of the Northwest Territory. Through his influence some of the best of Killingly youth joined in the first emigration to the distant territory, and many substantial families sought homes in the far West.

Voluntown.—The old town of Voluntown, which for many years embraced what is now Sterling, was, with Killingly, part of the Whetstone country, and was granted about 1700 by the General Court of Connecticut to volunteers in New London County who had served during King Philip's war. The roughness and barrenness of the land discouraged settlement, and it was long feared that the scattered inhabitants would never be able to establish religious worship. Several families of Scotch-Irish Presbyterians, however, purchased volunteer's rights in 1721–22, and aided greatly in building up the town and establishing religious institutions. Town government was organized June 20, 1721. A meeting-house was erected near the centre of the long, narrow township; and October 15, 1723, a church was organized. Rev. Samuel Dorrance a graduate of Glasgow University, licensed to preach by the Presbytery of Dumbarton, received a unanimous call to the pastorate, and after a strong opposition from dissenting inhabitants, who feared that Presbyterianism was a cloak for Popery and heresy, he was formally ordained minister of the Voluntown church and township.

Mr. Dorrance remained in charge of the Voluntown church till 1770, though suffering much from the disaffection of his people and the difficulty of obtaining a comfortable support. He died November, 1775, aged ninety years. The church was greatly weakened not only by dissension, but by emigration. Presbyterianism finally declining, a Congregational church was organized in 1779.

Several cotton-manufactories have been put in operation in the southwest part of Voluntown, greatly stimulating its development and improvement.

Ashford (1,000), so called on account of the great number of its ash-trees, was first settled in 1710. John Mixer, the first emigrant to these parts, settled on Mount Hope River, on the site of the present Warrenville. The road from Boston to Providence passed near his residence. John Parry of Marlborough settled soon after near the site of the present Eastport Village. A town organization was effected in 1715. About this time William Ward sent in search of a minister, to serve for a quarter of a year, and was so fortunate as to secure one for a quarter of a century—Rev. James Hale of Swansea, a most faithful and worthy man.

At this date Ashford contained about forty families. A church was organized Nov. 26, 1718. The First Baptist church in Windham County, now extinct, was formed in this town in 1743, and Thomas Denison ordained its pastor.

Ashford's position on a great public thoroughfare of travel brought her prominence and prosperity, especially during the Revolutionary days, when soldiers and even armies traversed her highways. "Clarke's tavern" still bears the name of many an illustrious guest upon its ancient windows. Washington spent at least one Sabbath here. Many of her own sons distinguished themselves greatly during the war. Thomas Knowlton and his brother Daniel, after gaining valuable experience in the French war, took the field at once in favor of American liberties. The regiment sent by Windham County upon the Lexington alarm, was placed under command of Thomas Knowlton. The services rendered by Knowlton at Bunker Hill, Boston, Long Island and Harlem, where his valuable life was offered up in sacrifice, will never be forgotten by American patriots. Daniel Knowlton was equally brave and devoted, serving throughout the war. Capt. James Dana, second under Knowlton at Bunker Hill, was almost equally forward and meritorious. John Keyes, Daniel Marcy—indeed, the thirty Ashford boys who fought at Bunker Hill, and saved the retreating provincials from destruction—deserve perpetual gratitude and commemoration.

The opening of the Boston and Hartford Turnpike in 1798 increased business and travel through Ashford, and contributed to its growth and importance. These prosperous days have been succeeded by isolation and decay. The opening of railroads left the old town far from business centres and markets, with no great farming or manufacturing facilities.

Eastford (900).—The incorporation of the eastern section of Ashford was delayed till 1777, when, notwithstanding the scarcity of men and means, society and church organization was initiated. Andrew Judson, pastor elect, Benjamin Sumner and others, united in church fellowship Sept. 23, 1778. Capt. Benjamin Sumner was long one of its most prominent citizens. The present Congregational house was erected in 1829, Benjamin Bosworth, Esq., purchasing the former building. In removing the old house from the hill-site, a chain snapped off, whereupon the workmen demanded "treat," which was refused by Esquire Bosworth, who had just joined the new Temperance Society. Men and oxen at once "struck" and left the old meeting-house suspended, till Mr. Darius Matthewson of Pomfret, president of the County Temperance Society, came to the rescue with a band of good temperance men from Abington, and accomplished its descent without a single drop of liquor.

A woolen-manufactory was established in Eastford Village about the year 1816. In 1847 Eastford was made a town.

Nathaniel Lyon was born at Ashford July 14, 1819, graduated at West Point in 1841, and served in the Florida and Mexican wars. At the outbreak of the civil war he was in command of the arsenal at St. Louis, and broke up a camp of secessionists established by the governor, C. F. Jackson. Jackson then assembled a force at Boonesville, where he was routed (June 17, 1861) by Lyon. In the battle of Wilson's Creek, while attempting to hold his position against the united forces of McCulloch and Price, after having been twice wounded, as he was leading into action a regiment whose colonel had just fallen, he was himself shot in the breast and killed on the spot, Aug. 10, 1861. His funeral at Eastford, where, by his own request, his remains were buried beside his honored parents, was the most remarkable ceremonial ever witnessed in Windham County. Gen. Lyon bequeathed $30,000, nearly all his property, to the government, to aid in the prosecution of the war.

Putnam (6,000) is pre-eminently the modern town of Windham County. Its central site and great water-privilege have indeed long been occupied. For one hundred and fifty years the Great Fall of Quinebaug has run its grist-mills, and carried on malting and dyeing. In the days of old Capt. Cargil (1760-98) these mills were very celebrated, and residents of the four adjacent towns resorted to them on needful occasions. When Rhode Island capitalists began to look outside their little State for cotton-factory locations, a keen eye marked this spot, and active hands soon reared and put in operation the first successful cotton manufactory in Connecticut.

It was at the opening of the Norwich and Worcester Railroad in 1839, that this place started on a new career of progress. The fine geographical position and great manufacturing facilities of the location were at once recognized, and people from all the surrounding towns hastened to take advantage of them. Great factories, stores, churches, and dwelling-houses, sprung up as if by magic, and soon the gathering population felt the need of town organization.

In 1849 they asked for a distinct township, taking parts of Thompson, Killingly, Pomfret and Woodstock. Against great and determined opposition, the incorporation of Putnam township was secured in July, 1855. In less than a quarter of a century, the place has far outstripped some of her more venerable elders, and won a place among the leading towns of Connecticut. With the spirit and resolution of her heroic namesake, she has grappled with every obstacle. The great fire of 1877 swept out her business centre, but the burnt district was long since filled up with more substantial buildings, and business is flowing on with redoubled briskness and energy. The junction of the two railroads passing through the county, and convenient access from all the neighboring towns, make Putnam the railroad and business centre for a large section of country. New stores and warehouses are continually opening to meet the increasing demand. Very many branches of manufacture are now carried on, besides the mammoth cotton-factories that are ever in motion. The population of the village increases at a rapid rate.

Putnam has been remarkably fortunate in the high character and public spirit of her leading business men, who have ever been ready to aid in needful improvement, and labor earnestly for the best good of the town. Five school buildings have been erected, and an admirable high school is in successful operation. "The Putnam Patriot," an enterprising weekly journal, was established in 1872. The religious interests of Putnam have been carefully guarded. Baptist, Congregational and Methodist churches, formed at an early day, are accommodated with convenient and even elegant houses of worship.

Willimantic.—The village of Willimantic owes its development to the establishment of cotton manufactories. Soon after 1820 several manufacturing companies were formed, and eligible privileges secured by Rhode Island capitalists and residents of the vicinity. Half a dozen well-conducted cotton-factories were soon in operation, and population quickly gathered around them. The site, like that of Putnam, formed the natural centre for a number of prosperous towns, and business flowed to it from a wide extent of country. Baptist and Congregational churches were organized and provided with houses of worship before 1830. In 1833, the west side of Windham, on both sides of the Willimantic, was incorporated as a borough. Its steady, healthy growth has been greatly quickened by the opening of the New London Northern and Hartford and Providence railroads, and still farther stimulated by the completion of the Air Line route, making it a place of much business and importance. Maintaining its connection with Windham, but reversing previous relations, it became in time the *head* of the mother town, administering the town government and probate office, and absorbing much of its business vitality. Its population has been drawn largely from its immediate vicinity. The energy and public-spirit of the citizens of Willimantic are attested by its convenient town building for the accommodation of public offices, its substantial school-houses, its numerous and handsome church edifices, its finely graded streets and costly bridges, its tasteful private residences, and general aspect of thrift and prosperity. Its various manufactories are carried on with much spirit. Its cotton, woolen and linen goods are well known in market, and Willimantic thread is sold throughout the civilized world. "The Willimantic Journal," established in 1848 by John Evans, has been sustained for over thirty years, and has greatly aided the improvement of the village.

Danielsonville also owes its origin to manufactures. The Danielsonville Manufacturing Company was the second formed in Windham County, and the village dates back to 1810. For many years its growth was limited to the demands of the factory, until the opening of the Norwich and Worcester Railroad brought quickening growth and expansion. From river to depot, and onward to Westfield village, and east, west, and south into the surrounding country, it was soon built up with houses, stores, and public buildings. The three villages, of Westfield, Danielsonville, and East Brooklyn were united in 1850 in the borough of Danielsonville, and instituted local government. It has gained steadily in business and population, and is now a wide-awake and flourishing village, its central position in the county giving it additional influence and importance. "The Windham County Transcript," established in 1848 under the management of J. Q. A. Stone, has done much in awakening county feeling, improving public morals, and stimulating growth and improvement in every direction.

The remaining towns of Windham County are Chaplin (600), so called from its first settler, Benjamin Chaplin, Jr., incorporated in 1822; Sterling (1,600), named for Dr. John Sterling, who presented a public library to the town; Hampton

(800), incorporated in 1786, and Scotland (600), whose first town meeting was held July 4, 1857.

The most remarkable family reared in Scotland was that of Nathaniel Huntington. His sons, Enoch and Joseph, received collegiate education, and became distinguished ministers. Jonathan, without scholastic education, filled an honorable position as physician and preacher. Samuel, during his apprenticeship at coopering, studied law, and became an eminent lawyer, a signer of the Declaration of Independence, president of the Continental Congress, and governor of the State. He married the daughter of the Rev. Ebenezer Devotion, long the respected pastor of the Scotland church; retained through life his affection for his early home, and left a bequest to the Scotland Society.

Another noted son of Scotland was James L. Kingsley, who filled for many years a professorship at Yale College.

Hon. Chauncey F. Cleaveland of Hampton, an able jurist and statesman, has been very active and influential in public life, and was for four years governor of the State.

HARTFORD.

HARTFORD, a port of entry, the capital of Connecticut and of Hartford County, is situated on the west bank of the Connecticut River, at the head of sloop navigation, fifty miles from its mouth. It is built for the most part on elevated ground, and its site is eminently picturesque and healthful. Main street, a wide avenue, has many imposing business blocks, notably the large granite buildings of the Charter Oak and Connecticut Mutual Life Insurance companies, and the massive brownstone Cheney block. The granite structure of the Hartford Fire Insurance Company, and that of the Phœnix Insurance Company, are worthy of important mention. Bushnell Park, a neatly laid-out inclosure of forty acres, lies in the central part of the city. The Park, or Little River, emptying into the Connecticut at Dutch Point, is spanned by several substantial bridges. Two bridges cross the Connecticut at this place—one for the New York and New England Railroad, and the other a highway bridge. The river, at an ordinary stage of water, is about 1,000 feet wide.

The new capitol, unquestionably one of the most satisfactory public buildings in the country, occupies an elevated site in Bushnell Park, in full view of passengers arriving in the city by railroad. The first state-house in Hartford was erected in 1719. In 1783, during the celebration of the declaration of peace, it was damaged by fireworks, and was rebuilt in very modest style. The edifice now standing on Main street, and which was vacated by the State when the new capitol was finished, was completed in 1796, and is now the property of the city of Hartford. In 1871 the Legislature made an appropriation for the erection of a new capitol.

The building, which was completed in 1879, at an expense, including the site, of more than $3,000,000, is in the modern secular Gothic style, at once massive and ornate, and is constructed of white marble, quarried at East Canaan, Conn. The extreme length of the structure from east to west is nearly three hundred feet, and the average breadth 106 feet. It is two and a half stories in height, with a mezzanine story between the first and second floors, and the roof is of the mansard pattern. In the centre of the building is a twelve-sided tower, surmounted by a dome, terminating in an open lantern, on which stands a colossal ideal figure in bronze, by Randolph Rogers, representing the Genius of Connecticut. The total height from the ground to the top of the crowning figure is 257 feet. In the interior polished granite of different colors alternates with white marble, producing a most agreeable effect. The staircases and halls are ornamented with paintings and statues, including an original portrait of Washington by Stuart, painted in 1800. The legislative halls are very elaborately finished in gold and colors, and the various offices are replete with every elegance and convenience.

In Bushnell Park are bronze statues of Israel Putnam, by J. Q. A. Ward, and of Dr. Horace Wells, by T. H. Bartlett. The new buildings of Trinity College are situated on the summit of a rocky ledge, about one mile south of the former location. The site is an admirable one, affording most attractive views in either direction. The architecture is the early French Gothic, and the two structures already completed form the central portion of the western side of the main quadrangle. The college grounds contain about eighty acres, and will be improved under the direction of Frederick L. Olmsted, well known in connection with the wonderful transformation of Central Park, New York. Trinity College was founded in 1826, and was originally known as Washington College. The faculty is composed of fifteen members, the Rev. Thomas R. Pynchon, D. D., being president. The average number of students is one hundred. The college library contains about 20,000 volumes.

The Theological Institute of Connecticut has lately removed to its new buildings, a short distance west of the High School building. This seminary, first established at East Windsor in 1834, has taken high rank among similar institutions, and through the liberality of its friends, notably the late James B. Hosmer, is enabled to greatly extend its usefulness.

The American Asylum for Deaf-mutes is pleasantly situated on what is known as Lord's Hill, near the principal railroad station. It was founded in 1817 by Rev. T. H. Gallaudet and Laurent Clerc, and is the parent of all similar institutions in the country. The average number of inmates is two hundred and thirty.

The Old Men's Home, endowed by the late C. H. Northam, is the latest accession to the benevolent institutions of the city, and a monument to his liberality.

The public schools of Hartford are unexcelled by any in the country. The high school, which has acquired an excellent reputation will occupy an imposing brick building, costing $250,000. The grammar school, founded by Edward Hopkins in 1657, and incorporated in 1798, and limited to thirty-five pupils, forms the preparatory classical department of the high school.

A neat brick edifice in the western part of the city was the headquarters of the Chinese Educational Commission, founded largely through the exertions of Yung Wing, a graduate of Yale, and formerly a member of the Chinese embassy at Washington. The object of this commission was the education of young men for positions under the Chinese government. The candidates were selected in China by competitive examination, and upon their arrival in this country, were placed in carefully-selected families, and entered the city schools. Some of their number obtained the highest honors in the public schools, in the face of severe competition.

The Hartford Orphan Asylum, some years ago removed to its spacious new building, a short distance west from the capitol. This building is of brick, in the modern English style, and contains a memorial dining-hall, elaborately finished in oak. About one mile south of the capitol are located the admirably-adapted buildings of the Retreat for the Insane, an institution which has had almost unparalleled success in the treatment of lunacy. Near by is the Hartford Hospital, a model institution of the kind.

The Wadsworth Athenæum building, on Main street, contains the Watkinson Free Library of Reference, having over 30,000 carefully selected volumes; the Hartford Library, of nearly the same number of volumes; the rich collections and library of the Connecticut Historical Society, and a valuable gallery of paintings and statuary.

There are thirty-six churches in the city, many of them models of tasteful architecture. The Church of the Good Shepherd, erected by Mrs. Samuel Colt as a memorial of her deceased husband and children, is regarded as one of the finest ecclesiastical edifices in the country. The Roman Catholic Cathedral, now being erected, and nearly finished, will be an ornament to the city. The Catholics have several large schools, that connected with the convent of Mt. St. Joseph having an established reputation as an educational institution for young ladies.

The Hartford Female Seminary acquired great celebrity under Miss Catherine E. Beecher, who was its principal for several years, and under its present management retains much of its former prestige.

Hartford is a centre of the insurance business of the country. The assets of the various insurance companies—fire, marine, life, accident, and steam-boiler, are in the rough, $150,000,000. The capital, properly speaking, cannot be even roughly approximated, because most of them are mutuals, with no capital at all except the accumulations from business; the stock companies are a small minority, and their nominal capital bears little relation to their business. There are thirteen banks with a capital of $11,000,000; and also seven savings banks and trust companies, with deposits of $15,000,000. Sixty-four manufacturing companies, representing a capital of $20,000,000, have their principal offices in this city, although many of their works are located elsewhere.

The principal manufacturing establishment in Hartford is the works of the Colt's Fire-arms Manufacturing Company. This extensive factory is situated on the river meadow, just south of the mouth of Little River. The site was subject to overflow from the river, and Col. Colt protected it by building an embankment or dike, about two miles long, inclosing some one hundred and twenty acres of land, at a cost of $80,000. The buildings are of Portland stone and brick, and the floor contains an era of nearly seven acres. February 5, 1864, a large part of the works was destroyed by fire, causing a loss of $2,000,000; but they were immediately rebuilt. Portions of the shops are now leased to different parties, and a variety of articles are manufactured on the premises, including the celebrated Gatling gun, the invention of Dr. R. E. Gatling, a resident of Hartford; sewing-machines lawn-mowers, gold and stock indicators, conductor's punches, etc. In addition to the manufacture of Colt's improved fire-arms, the company are also sole producers of Baxter's steam engines. The works have a capacity for the employment of several hundred hands.

The leather-belting manufactory of P. Jewell & Sons is one of the most extensive establishments of the kind in the world, consuming weekly the hides of a large herd of cattle. Smith, Bourn & Co. are extensive manufacturers of harness, collars, saddles, etc. The Pratt & Whitney Manufacturing Company are manufacturers of machinery, fine tools, etc. Near their establishment are the works of the Weed Sewing Machine Company. The Plympton Manufacturing Company, the United States Stamped Envelope Works, which has the contract for envelopes for the United States, testing the utmost capacity of a large factory, requisitions for several million envelopes being sometimes received in one day. The Hartford Engineering Co., the Billings & Spencer Co., the Hartford Machine Screw Co., Batterson's New England Granite Works. The Cheney Brothers' silk manufacturing company have a factory here, employing some 200 hands, in addition to their extensive works at South Manchester. The publishing of subscription books is an important branch of Hartford industry, and several extensive printing establishments are located here. That of the Case, Lockwood & Brainard Company is scarcely surpassed in the country.

The main water supply of the city is from four reservoirs in West Hartford, which are fed from small streams and springs, having a total capacity of 1,200,000,000 gallons. There is also a pumping-engine on the river, which supplies the lower part of the city in times of drouth. The city has a paid fire department and a fire-alarm telegraph. Its railroad facilities are ample, it being on the through line from New York to Boston, and about midway between the two cities. The New York and New England Railroad has been completed to the Hudson River, giving Hartford a new route to the West. By its connections at Millerton and Canaan, the Connecticut Western line affords a convenient route to western Massachusetts and Albany, while the Connecticut Valley brings the seashore within easy reach. The Connecticut Central furnishes a route to Springfield. The New York, New Haven and Hartford line has extensive construction and repair shops at this point. During the season there is a daily line of steamers to New York.

The Opera House is one of the most commodious and best-appointed places of amusement in New England, its seating capacity being equal to that of the largest metropolitan theatres. There are also several large halls, well adapted for lectures, concerts, etc.

There are many elegant private residences in the city. Armsmear, the home of Mrs. Samuel Colt, is surrounded by extensive and beautiful grounds, laid out with great taste, and ornamented with statues and fountains. The conservatories are of great extent.

Cedar Hill Cemetery, incorporated in 1865, lies about three miles south of the capitol, and contains 268 acres. It is laid out upon the lawn system, without fences, and is rapidly developing into a beautiful "city of the dead." There are many elegant and tasteful monuments in this cemetery, the most noticeable being that of Col. Colt.

The population of Hartford in 1880 was 42,551. Assessed valuation, $46,992,000. Probably a fair estimate of the total wealth of the city, invested here or elsewhere, would be $175,000,000.

Thomas Hooker, the first minister at Hartford, and one of the most prominent men in the early history of Connecticut, was born at Markfield, Eng., in 1586, and studied at Cambridge; was a popular preacher in London, but espoused the Puritan doctrines, and was compelled to leave the country; went to Holland, and thence to Newtown, now Cambridge, Mass.; accompanied the first settlers to Hartford, where he died July 7, 1647. In conjunction with John Cotton, he wrote a book on church discipline, and a number of his discourses were published in England. A selection from his works, with a memoir by the Rev. E. W. Hooker, was published in Boston in 1849.

Edward Hopkins was born at Shrewsbury, Eng., in 1600; settled in Hartford in 1639; was deputy governor or governor of the Colony from 1640 to 1654; returned to England, where he died in 1657. By his will he devised £1,000 for the establishment of a grammar school in Hartford, which is still in existence as the preparatory classical department of the high school.

George Wyllys, a native of Warwickshire, Eng., settled in Hartford in 1638, and was deputy-governor and governor in 1641 and 1642. He died March 9, 1645. His son Samuel, born in 1632, died in 1709; graduated from Harvard in 1653, and was a magistrate from 1654 to 1684. Hezekiah, son of Samuel, was secretary of the Colony from 1712 to 1734, and was succeeded by his son George, who graduated from Yale in 1729. He resigned in 1795, and was in turn succeeded by his son Samuel, who resigned in 1809, making ninety-eight years during which the office of secretary had continued in this family. Samuel Wyllys was born in Hartford, Jan. 15, 1739, and died there June 9, 1823. During the Revolutionary war he served with marked ability, and attained the rank of colonel. He was subsequently appointed major-general of militia. The Wyllys mansion, in front of which stood the famous Charter Oak, was, until quite recently, one of the landmarks of Hartford.

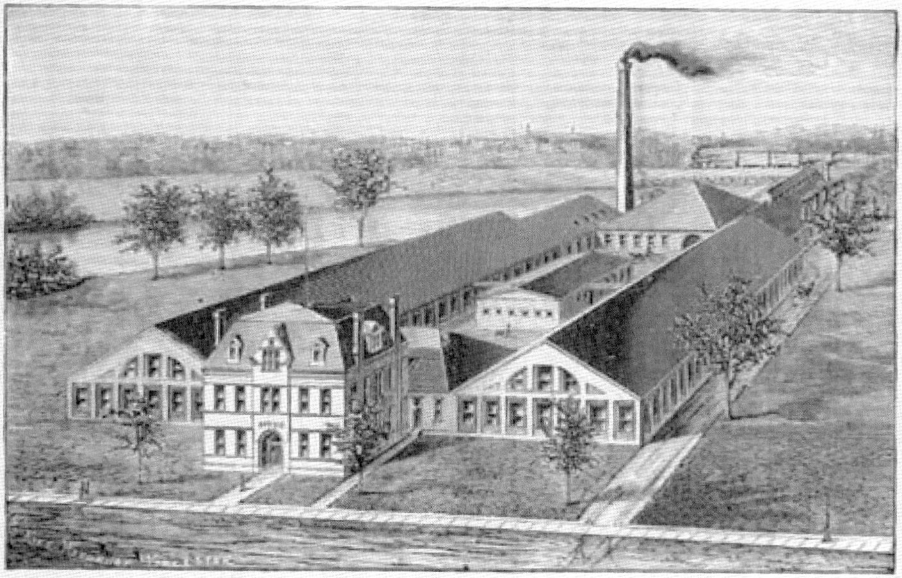

WORKS OF THE HARTFORD MACHINE SCREW CO.

John Talcott, one of the original settlers of Hartford, was born in England; died at Hartford, July 23, 1688. His son, Maj. John Talcott, held various positions of trust, and rendered distinguished service in the various wars against the Indians. Joseph Talcott, son of John, was governor of the Colony from 1725 to 1741.

John Trumbull, LL.D., was born in Watertown, Conn., April 24, 1750, and graduated at Yale in 1767. In 1781 he located in Hartford, where, in 1782, he published his celebrated epic poem of "McFingal." He was a clear and pungent satirist, and, in conjunction with Joel Barlow, Dr. Lemuel

Hopkins and Col. Humphreys, wrote a series of essays entitled "American Antiquities," which attracted great attention. He was State attorney for Hartford from 1789 to 1795; a member of the legislature in 1792 and 1800; judge of Superior and Supreme courts from 1801 to 1819; removed to Detroit, Mich., in 1825, where he died May 10, 1831.

Jeremiah Wadsworth was born in Hartford in 1743. He was an intimate friend of Gen. Washington, and the first meeting between that officer and Count Rochambeau took place in Wadsworth's mansion. He was a member of the convention for the ratification of the Constitution, and six years a representative in Congress. He received honorary degrees from Dartmouth and Yale colleges. He died April 30, 1804. His son Daniel Wadsworth was the founder of Wadsworth Athenæum, which occupies the site of the family mansion.

Dr. Lemuel Hopkins—born in Waterbury, June 19, 1750, a graduate of Yale and a physician of high repute—was best known as a writer of poetry and humorous prose. He was one of a celebrated coterie of literary men known as the "Hartford Wits." He died April 14, 1801.

Theodore Dwight, born in Northampton, Mass., Dec. 16, 1764, was a prolific writer on political subjects. He was a representative in Congress in 1806 and 1807, and secretary of the Hartford Convention. He died June 11, 1846. His son Theodore, born March 3, 1796, killed by a railroad accident Oct. 16, 1866, was the author of a history of Connecticut, a gazetteer of the United States, and many other successful works. He was a finished scholar, and a member of many learned societies.

Isaac Toucey, LL.D., born at Newtown, Conn., Nov. 5, 1796, was for many years State attorney for Hartford County; a representative in Congress from 1835 to 1839; governor of Connecticut in 1846 and 1847; attorney-general of the United States, in 1848 and 1849; United States senator from 1852 to 1857, and secretary of the navy during the administration of President Buchanan.

Gideon Welles, born in Glastonbury, Conn., July 1, 1802, like Mr. Toucey, was for many years a leading democratic politician. In 1826 he became one of the proprietors of the Hartford "Times," and assumed the editorial management of that journal. Being opposed to the extension of slavery, he identified himself with the Republican party at its organization, and in 1861 succeeded his townsman, Mr. Toucey, as secretary of the navy, a position which he retained until 1869, when he retired from public life and returned to Hartford, where he died Feb. 11, 1878.

Thomas H. Gallaudet, LL.D., was born in Philadelphia, Dec. 10, 1787. He graduated at Yale in 1805, and, entering Andover Theological Seminary, was licensed to preach in 1814. He became interested in the education of deaf-mutes, and on his return from a visit to Europe in 1816, he was accompanied by Laurent Clerc, a deaf-mute, who had been a pupil of the Abbe Sicard, with whose aid Dr. Gallaudet established the American Asylum at Hartford, the parent institution of the kind in the country. He remained in charge of the asylum until 1830, when he was appointed chaplain of the Retreat for the Insane, which office he held until his death, Sept. 9, 1851. He was the author of several religious books for the young. Mr. Clerc retired from

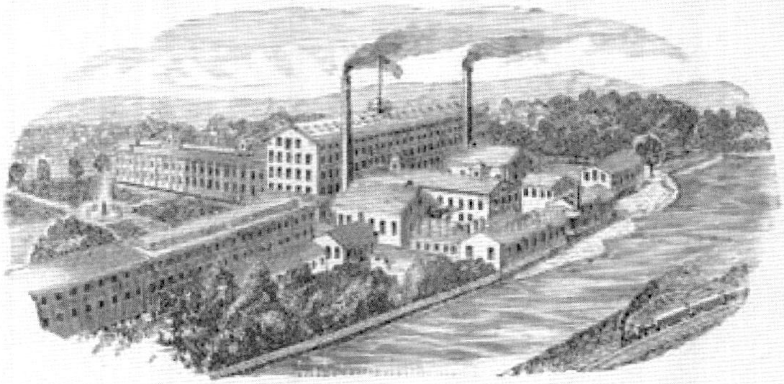

WORKS OF THE WEED SEWING MACHINE CO., HARTFORD.

the asylum on a pension in 1858, and died July 18, 1869.

Horace Bushnell, D.D., born in Litchfield, Conn., in 1802, was pastor of the North, now Park, Congregational Church in Hartford from 1833 to 1859. He was a preacher of great power and eloquence, and distinguished as an essayist, and was the author of numerous popular moral and religious works. He died Feb. 17, 1876. Three days before his death the common council of the city passed a preamble and resolution, giving to the public park the name of Bushnell Park, in recognition of his earnest efforts to secure this beautiful resort for the city.

Lydia H. (Huntley) Sigourney was born in Norwich, Conn., Sept. 1, 1791. In 1814 she opened a select school in Hartford, and in 1819 married Charles Sigourney, a merchant of that city. She early manifested great ability as a writer of both poetry and prose on religious and moral subjects, and her name has become a household word throughout the entire country. She died June 10, 1865.

Samuel Colt, inventor of revolving fire-arms, was born in Hartford, July 19, 1814. When fifteen years old he ran away to sea, making a voyage to the East Indies before the mast. He took out his first patent for revolvers in 1835. In 1837, the Florida war having created a demand for revolvers, Mr. Colt laid the foundation of the immense works at Hartford, the capacity of which was gradually increased until 1,000 finished weapons were produced each day. He was also the inventor of a powerful submarine battery. He died Jan. 10, 1862, leaving a very large fortune.

Thomas C. Brownell, D.D., born at Westford, Mass., Oct. 19, 1779, graduated at Union College in 1804; entered the ministry of the Episcopal Church in 1816; was consecrated bishop of Connecticut in 1819, and removed to Hartford. He was instrumental in founding Trinity College in 1824, and was its first president, resigning in 1831. He was also prominent in connection with literature. He died Jan. 13, 1865.

J. Hammond Trumbull, LL.D., born at Stonington, Conn., Dec. 20, 1801, and graduated from Yale in 1838, is a distinguished philologist, especially in the aboriginal dialects of New England. He has published a work upon the Blue Laws of Connecticut, and is a frequent contributor to our best periodicals. His brother, H. Clay Trumbull, now editor of the "Sunday School Times," was for many years a resident of Hartford, and occupied the position of New England secretary of the American Sunday School Union. He won great distinction as chaplain of the Tenth Connecticut Regiment during the late war.

Joseph R. Hawley, born at Stewartsville, N. C., Oct. 31, 1826, a graduate of Hamilton College in 1847, commenced in 1850 the practice of law in Hartford. In 1857, adopting the profession of a journalist, he became editor of the Hartford "Evening Press," an organ of the Republican party. An outspoken and earnest opponent of slavery, at the outbreak of the war in 1861 he was one of the first to volunteer. He rendered distinguished service, winning, meanwhile, rapid promotion to the different ranks of colonel, brigadier-general and brevet major-general of volunteers. Mr. Hawley was governor of Connecticut in 1866, president of the Republican convention at Chicago in 1868, and representative in Congress from 1872 to 1875, and is now United States Senator. He was president of the Centennial Commission in 1876, and to his exertions the great success of the Exposition was largely due. He was again elected to Congress in 1878.

Other eminent names associated with Hartford are Thomas Day (1777-1855), a distinguished jurist, and president of the Connecticut Historical Society; John M. Niles (1787-1856), founder of the "Hartford Times," jurist and author, and at one time postmaster-general; James H. Ward (1806-1861), a naval officer; Horace Wells (1815-1848), the discoverer of nitrous oxide as an anæsthetic; Thomas H. Seymour (1808-1868), a lawyer by profession, member of Congress, a gallant officer in the Mexican war, governor of the State and minister to Russia; William B. Franklin, a major-general in the war of the Rebellion; and Marshall Jewell, formerly governor of the State, minister to Russia and postmaster-general, who died on February 10th, 1883.

Prominent among the natives of Hartford, who have attained distinguished positions, may be mentioned Generals Alfred H. Terry, Robert O. Tyler and Griffin A. Stedman; Frederick E. Church, the artist; and Thomas S. Preston, Roman Catholic prelate and writer. Many well-known literary people have resided in Hartford during a portion of their lives. Among these may be noticed Dr. M. F. Cogswell, S. G. Goodrich, Noah Webster, George D. Prentice, John G. Whittier, Lewis G. Clark, Catherine E. Beecher, Rose Terry Cooke, Robert Bonner, William H. Bradley, Mary A. H. Dodd, Jonathan W. and Tryon Edwards, Charles A. Goodrich, E. C. Stedman, and Joseph Trumbull. The directory of the city at the present time includes the names of Samuel L. Clemens (Mark Twain), Charles Dudley Warner, Harriet Beecher Stowe and her husband, Professor C. E. Stowe, who are all permanent residents. The Rev. Dr. Joel Hawes, who was the pastor of the Centre Congregational Church for nearly fifty years, is widely known through his published "Lectures to Young Men," which has reached a circulation of more than 100,000 copies.

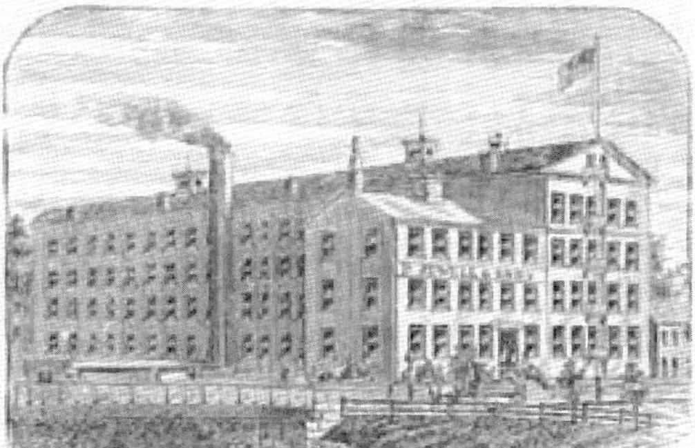

P. JEWELL & SONS' LEATHER BELTING FACTORY, HARTFORD.

HARTFORD'S INSURANCE INTERESTS.

The Ætna Insurance Company.—The Ætna is the largest fire insurance company in the United States, and is probably greater in point of capital and assets than any similar organization in the world. The annual statement, published on January 1st, 1883, shows an actually paid up capital of $4,000,000, while its gross assets are stated at more than five millions in excess of that sum, or, to be exact, at $9,054,610.58. The Ætna began business in 1819, and, according to tradition, in a peculiar way. The only company then doing insurance business in Hartford had for secretary a gentleman whose relatives resided in Wethersfield, and who was accustomed to take from Saturday noon to the same hour on Monday to visit them, leaving the office closed and would-be insurers to await his return. The inconvenience of this state of affairs provoked displeasure and discussion, resulting in the determination to form another company, whose doors should be open and whose officers should be on duty during business hours. Such was the inception of the Ætna. The reason for the selection of the apt title of the company is buried among the unknown things of the past, but, doubtless, its sponsors had in view "the eternal fitness of things," for while it has been steadily in eruption its foundation is as solid now as ever. The Ætna was started by subscription, a small part of which was in cash, by far the greater portion in notes. The makers of these expected that the earnings of the company would be great enough to warrant dividends sufficient to pay their balances, and that they would, therefore, not be called upon to meet the liability by further advances of cash. In this they were disappointed, for shortly after the organization of the company the conflagration in Mobile occasioned such great losses that it became necessary to call on the reserve. This caused such consternation that many of the stockholders got rid of their stock at any sacrifice, some of them going so far as to surrender their certificates to anybody who would assume the obligations of the notes. A few of the stockholders retained their courage and their stock, and by so doing enabled the company to weather the storm and laid the foundation of the large fortunes many of them afterwards enjoyed. Commencing in 1812, with a capital of $150,000, the Ætna advanced in 1822 to a capital of $200,000; in 1846 to $250,000; in 1849 to $300,000; in 1854 to $500,000; in 1857 to $1,000,000; in 1859 to $1,500,000; in 1864 to $2,500,000, and in 1866 to $3,000,000. In 1871 the Chicago fire called on the resources of the company to the extent of $3,782,848.10, and in one day the capital was marked down a million and a half, but the stockholders immediately subscribed the amount necessary and the capital was restored to three millions. The following year was again marked by disaster in the shape of the great fire in Boston, which involved the company in losses aggregating $1,604,348.50, compelling another reduction of the capital, this time by one-third, or one million dollars. This amount, like the other, was at once subscribed and the capital again restored. From 1872 until 1881 the capital of the company remained at three millions, being increased in the latter year by the addition of another million, continuing it the largest of any Fire Insurance Company in the United States. In the sixty-four years of the existence of the Ætna it has paid in losses the enormous sum of $54,660,000, and yet, such has been the admirable management of affairs that in 1883 it can boast of assets to the amount of nearly ten millions, and a surplus over its liabilities so great as to be an absolute guarantee against disaster even of the magnitude of the great conflagrations through which it has heretofore triumphantly passed.

The first President of the company and one of its incorporators was Thomas K. Brace. His Presidency continued uninterruptedly until 1857, when he was succeeded by Edwin G. Ripley, he serving until 1862. In that year Thomas A. Alexander became President and in 1866 Lucius J. Hendee, the present incumbent, was elected. Mr. Hendee was elected Secretary of the company in 1861, holding the office until his election to the Presidency, at which time, also, Mr. Jotham Goodnow was chosen to the vacancy, and Mr. William B. Clark, formerly Secretary of the Phœnix Fire Insurance Company, was appointed to the Assistant Secretaryship of the Ætna. Both these gentlemen have retained their offices continuously since and are the incumbents.

The present Directors of the Ætna are a body of men whose names inspire universal confidence and who are representatives of a vast amount of individual wealth. They are as follows: Roland Mather, Gustavus F. Davis, Drayton Hillyer, Walter Keney, Charles H. Brainard, William F. Tuttle, Lucius J. Hendee, Francis B. Cooley, William R. Cone, Henry E. Russell, Nathaniel Shipman, Asa S. Porter, Austin C. Dunham, James A. Smith and Morgan G. Bulkeley. E. J. Bassett is the General Agent and J. C. Hilliard, T. P. Stowell, W. C. Goodrich and James F. Dudley, Special Agents.

The building owned and occupied by the Ætna Insurance Company as well as by the Ætna Life Insurance Company and the Ætna National Bank, is situated on the easterly side of Main street near the Wadsworth Athenæum, opposite the City Hotel and in close contiguity to the business centre of Hartford. It is of brown free-stone and is four stories in height. It is an unpretentious but solid structure, and in the latter respect a fitting home for the company.

The Ætna was one of the first companies to recognize the importance of extending its agencies, and by an energetic use of its opportunities it became and has continued the leading agency company of the United States. The history of the Ætna Insurance Company compels admiration for the methods and men that worked its remarkable success.

The Connecticut Mutual Life Insurance Company.—The Connecticut Mutual Life Insurance Company stands, with a single exception, at the head of the list of the life companies of this country as regards assets, and is among the best in point of stability. It is one of the five whose history is coeval with that of life insurance, and one of the few that have demonstrated the theory of "the survival of the fittest." It was in the year 1846 that Dr. Guy R. Phelps took the initiatory steps towards the formation of a mutual life insurance association, and it was in the same year that he, with a few friends, applied to the Legislature of Connecticut for a charter for the company that was to be purely mutual in its character. In May of that year the charter was granted, and the document was, perhaps, one of the most peculiar of its kind that ever saw the light. No capital of any kind was required, and no minimum of applications fixed as a condition for commencing business. No limits of territory hampered the strides of the infant corporation, and its liability was of the most vague description. The company was authorized to take promissory notes or other obligations for part or whole of the premiums. In case the funds in hand at any time were insufficient to pay the losses, these notes were to be assessed for the deficiency, and if the assessment was not paid in sixty days, the policy was forfeited and the company could proceed to collect by law. The company might "receive notes or other securities for premiums in advance from persons intending to receive its policies, for which such persons may be allowed a sum not exceeding six per cent. per annum. And said company may negotiate the same for the purpose of paying claims only."

As strange to those of our day were the provisions concerning the distribution of the profits. Each member was to be yearly charged with his proportion of the losses and expenses, according to the premiums paid, and credited with his share of the premiums earned, less losses, expenses and profits from investment. The difference was to be credited to the member, but to be held liable for future losses, until the net profits amounted to two hundred thousand dollars, after which any excess was to be applied to the redemption of the certificates issued.

Ten years later the charter was amended so as to allow the directors to adjust and pay the dividends at their discretion and power was granted to issue non-participating policies. Care was taken that the effect of external influences should be as small as possible, and centralization of power was provided against by a clause limiting the term of office to four successive years. Edson Fessenden, E. P. Pratt and Guy R. Phelps, or any two of them, were to call the first meeting. After the trifling difficulty of obtaining a charter had been disposed of, the real labor of the infant corporation began. It was found to be impossible to induce persons to insure their lives in a company without any tangible capital or assets or financial responsibility, and to remove this disability and gain the confidence of the community was the first step necessary to success. In order to accomplish this desirable end, it was resolved to solicit from the prominent and wealthy citizens of Hartford a guarantee fund of fifty thousands dollars for the protection of policy-holders until the business and income of the company should warrant a dependence on its own resources. This it was found difficult to do, but after earnest and protracted effort, the late Thomas K. Bruce, then President of the Ætna Fire Insurance Company was induced to lead the subscription, his example being quickly followed by other leading citizens until in a short time the required sum was guaranteed and the company started on its prosperous career.

The company organized with Mr. Eliphalet A. Bulkeley, as President, and Dr. Phelps, as Secretary. The latter made an extensive tour of Europe for the purpose of studying the different modes of life insurance, and on his return applied the results of his investigations to the conduct of the company, with gratifying success. Mr. Bulkeley remained as President of the company until January, 1848, when he was succeeded by Mr. James Goodwin who held the office until 1866, when he resigned, remaining out of office for three years, and being re-elected in 1869, on the death of Dr. Phelps, who had filled the office in the mean time.

In three years from the organization of the company its membership numbered over six thousand and two years later its assets reached a million dollars. So extraordinary was the success of the company that in the succeeding year this sum was doubled, and it took the rank it has since maintained among the leading life insurance companies of the world. For many years the Connecticut Mutual was the prominent champion of the credit system, and by its rapid growth, contributed largely to the extensive adoption of that method among the younger companies, and it was among the first to break in upon the time-honored custom of the British companies in declaring reversionary bonuses, and substitute therefor the method of annual dividends applicable to the payment of premiums.

Another of the salient features in the conduct of the company's business, and one which provoked favorable comment and discussion, was the investment of its funds in Western securities, from which a larger return of interest could be earned than in those nearer home. This excess was more than four per cent. above the rate assumed in its calculations, enabling the company to cancel to a corresponding extent the credit obligations of its members.

In twenty years from the incorporation of the company, in 1865, the accumulated fund amounted to nearly ten millions of dollars; it had paid to policy holders three millions in dividends and four millions in losses, and this unexampled rate of increase has kept its steady pace up to the present, the annual statement published January 1, 1883, showing gross assets to the amount of nearly fifty-two million dollars, with liabilities about five million dollars less.

In 1869 the company began the erection of the building now occupied by its office and other insurance and financial institutions, and in the following year it was completed and utilized. This is one of the finest business edifices in New England and will stand for centuries a monument to the energy and foresight of the founders of the Connecticut Mutual.

In 1866, at the time Dr. Phelps was elected to the Presidency, Mr. Woodbridge S. Olmstead was chosen Secretary. In 1871, Mr. Olmstead was appointed Vice-President and Treasurer, and Mr. Jacob L. Greene, now President of the company, was elected to the vacancy.

In March, 1878, Mr. Goodwin died, and Mr. Greene was selected to fill the Presidency, a post he has since administered with marked ability.

The present officers of the company are: Jacob L. Greene, President; John M. Taylor, Secretary; William G. Abbot, Assistant Secretary; Daniel H. Wells, Actuary; Elisha Risley, Superintendent of Agencies.

Of these gentlemen it can be said that they are among the most prominent and able insurance men in the country, and of their company that it is what it claims to be—thoroughly reliable.

The Ætna Life Insurance Company.—In the year 1820 the Ætna Insurance Company of Hartford obtained from the Connecticut Legislature an amendment to its charter authorizing an increase of its capital stock to the sum of $150,000, for the purpose of creating an "Annuity Fund," and authorizing it to issue annuities and insurance upon lives. The fund set aside was to be liable for no other debts or hazards of the Ætna Insurance Company.

In the year 1850 it commenced business, and certain directors were delegated to manage the affairs of the "Annuity Fund," and Eliphalet A. Bulkeley, Vice-President of the Ætna Insurance Company, was selected as the Chairman of the Managing Directors of the "Annuity Fund," and John W. Seymour was chosen Actuary.

But very little business was transacted by the "Annuity Fund" Department until the year 1853, when the General Assembly granted an amendment to the charter, incorporating the shareholders of the "Annuity Fund" as a separate and distinct organization, under the name of the Ætna Life Insurance Company. The separate organization was completed in July of that year by an election of the following directors:

E. A. Bulkeley, Austin Dunham, H. Z. Pratt, L. C. Ives, M. Howard, John Warburton, R. Mather, S. L. Loomis, J. W. Seymour, W. H. D. Callender. The following officers were elected: President, Hon. E. A. Bulkeley; Secretary, J. W. Seymour; Consulting Physician, H. A. Grant, M.D.; Examining Physician, G. W. Russell, M.D.

In 1855 Samuel Coit was chosen Secretary. In 1856 J. W. Seymour was elected Vice-President. In 1857 John Warburton was chosen Vice-President in place of Mr. Seymour. In 1858 T. O. Enders was elected Secretary in place of Mr. Coit. In 1860 S. L. Loomis was elected Vice-President to fill the vacancy caused by the death of John Warburton. In 1863 Austin Dunham succeeded to the Vice-Presidency upon the death of Mr. Loomis. In 1867 H. W. St. John, the company's present Actuary, was appointed to that position. In 1872, following the death of the company's first President—Eliphalet A. Bulkeley—T. O. Enders, the Secretary since 1858, was elected to fill the vacancy caused by the death of Judge Bulkeley; and J. L. English was elected to succeed Mr. Enders as Secretary. In 1877 W. H. Bulkeley was elected Vice-President to fill the vacancy caused by the death of Austin Dunham. In 1879, T. O. Enders having declined a re-election as President, Morgan J. Bulkeley, the present President, was elected his successor. W. H. Bulkeley having retired from the position of Vice-President, which had not before been an active executive office, J. C. Webster, then Superintendent of Agencies, was chosen Vice-President, and is the present incumbent.

To the year 1861 all contracts for insurance, written by the Ætna Life, were upon the non-participating or proprietary plan. During that year the company commenced the insurance of participating policies; and since that date it has continued to issue policies under both systems. During the first seven years after the establishment of the Participating Department, the company issued policies upon the then popular method known as the premium note plan. In 1868 it adopted plans of insurance which required the payment of the full premiums in cash. In the year 1870 it abandoned wholly the insurance of premium note policies. Under the cash system its business has been conducted to the present time. In 1878 the capital stock of the Ætna Life was increased to $750,000, which amount has been fully paid up in cash.

January 1, 1883, the Ætna's assets were $28,102,886.79. Its surplus above its liabilities, calculated upon the most rigid standard, viz., that of four per cent., was $4,418,123.68. Upon the basis of four and one-half per cent., the standard of New York and most other States, its surplus was estimated at $6,000,000.

Hon. E. A. Bulkeley, the first President of the Ætna Life and father of the present incumbent, was one of the incorporators, and the first President of the Connecticut Mutual Life Insurance Company of Hartford. To T. O. Enders, the successor to Judge Bulkeley and the Ætna's second president, is due great credit for the remarkable growth and the present financial standing of the Ætna Life. Commencing with it as its secretary, in the year 1858, he continued as its active official until the year 1879, when he declined a re-election as president.

The present directors of the Ætna Life are: T. O. Enders, Gurdon W. Russell, Leveret Brainerd, A. R. Hillyer, W. H. Bulkeley, James Campbell, M. G. Bulkeley, S. G. Dunham.

Hon. Morgan G. Bulkeley, the present President of the company, was born in East Haddam, Conn., December 26, 1837. Early in life he engaged in mercantile business in Brooklyn, N. Y. In 1872 he returned to Hartford and organized the United States Trust Company (now the United States Bank), and for a considerable time was its president. In 1880 he was elected Mayor of Hartford, receiving the largest majority ever given a candidate for that office. At the expiration of his term he was re-elected. He is a director in the Willimantic Linen Company, in the Hartford Silk Company, the United States Bank, and the Ætna Fire Insurance Company. He was elected a director of the Ætna Life in 1872, and its president in July, 1879.

J. C. Webster, Vice-President, was born in Kingfield, Me., May 24. 1839. He commenced with the Ætna Life in the spring of 1864, as its local agent in Concord, N. H. Subsequently he was made its State Agent, and in April, 1873, was appointed Superintendent of Agencies, which position he occupied until elected Vice-President in July, 1879. He is one of the directors of the Hartford Trust Company.

J. L. English the Secretary was born in Woodstock, Vt., October 1, 1843. He commenced with the company as clerk in the Home Office in the year 1867. Was elected secretary in the year 1872, and has occupied the position since.

H. W. St. John, the Actuary, was born in Newport, R. I., April 4, 1834. He completed his education in the Scientific Department of Yale College, commenced with the Ætna Life as its Actuarial Adviser in the year 1867, and has continued with it in that capacity ever since.

Gurdon W. Russell, M.D., Consulting Physician, was born in Hartford, Conn., April 10, 1815. He was graduated at Trinity College in 1834, and the Medical Institute of Yale College in 1837. He has been in practice in Hartford continuously since. Upon the retirement of Dr. Grant, in the year 1854, Dr. Russell took charge of the Medical Department of the Ætna Life and has since continued as the company's Adviser.

The Hartford Fire Insurance Company.—This Company, the oldest in Hartford and fourth in the country in capital, was incorporated in 1810, although history tells us that fire risks were written in the name of the Hartford Insurance Company as long ago as 1794. It is not claimed, however, that the "Hartford" as at present constituted had an existence prior to the date of its incorporation in 1810, and hence its history goes back only to that time. The original capital was $150,000, and as was the custom in those days, the greater part of it was in notes subject, of course, to collection for the payment of losses in case the small percentage of paid-up capital should be insufficient to meet demands.

The first President of the Hartford was General Nathaniel Terry, who was succeeded in 1835 by Eliphalet Terry, of the firm of E. & R. Terry, then a leading house here. The company had not been succeeding very well. Energy and advertising were not so common then as they have shown themselves to be since, and it was the custom, if a large loss was met, to drop the agency and retire from business in the locality, instead of following the present and better plan of paying the claim with all the promptness which a careful investigation will warrant and making fame from the transaction and profit from the loss. At the same time that Mr. Terry was chosen President an entire change was made in the working officials of the company, with a view of infusing new life and bringing its affairs out of the lethargic state in which they had so long remained. Mr. James G. Bolles, then a dry goods merchant and many years later President of the North American Company, was chosen Secretary and Mr. C. C. Lyman, a lumber merchant was made Assistant Secretary. The latter gentleman held his office for forty-three years, declining all promotion and retiring in 1878. The first six months of the new management in 1835, were very successful and a dividend was about to be declared when the great New York fire of that year occurred. This deferred the dividend, but gave the business of the company a fresh and lively impetus. Secretary Bolles and E. D. Morgan, later Governor of New York, recently deceased, who was then a director, went down to that city, opened an office amid the ruins and did a very brisk business at good rates. The losses were all paid inside the stipulated sixty days and the reputation and credit of the company was at once established on the firm basis it has since maintained. It was in that year that the company began spreading out its agencies, and it reached as far west as Cleveland, Ohio. In 1846 the St. Johns, Newfoundland, and Nantucket fires made large inroads on the resources of the company, but all losses were promptly paid at the time, as indeed they have ever been since. In 1854 the capital of the Hartford was increased to $300,000; in 1857, to $500,000, and in 1864, to $1,000,000. At this latter figure it remained until 1871, when the great losses sustained at the Chicago fire compelled a reduction of one half. This state of affairs was of very brief duration, however, and the deficiency of $500,000 was at once subscribed by the stockholders and the capital restored to the old figure. The losses sustained by the Hartford in the Chicago fire amounted to $1,968,225.32, nearly twice the amount of its capital, and the promptness with which the misfortune was met and the necessary funds subscribed, speaks volumes for the energy, foresight and honesty of the gentlemen composing the association. In 1877 the capital was still further increased by the addition of $250,000, and the annual statement published on January 1st, 1883, shows gross assets to the amount of $4,337,280.56, with a surplus as to policy-holders of $2,608,240.77, and a net surplus of $1,358,240.77. Following Mr. Terry in the Presidency, in 1849, came Hezekiah Huntington, with whom were also Samuel and Frank Huntington in the direction of the company at the same time. Mr. Timothy C. Allyn succeeded Mr. Huntington in 1864, and he, in 1867, was succeeded by Mr. George L. Chase, the present incumbent. Among the prominent insurance names that have been connected with the company may be mentioned A. F. Wilmarth of the Home of New York; C. B. Bowers, afterwards President of the City Fire; George M. Coit, now of New York; J. D. Browne, afterwards President of the Connecticut Fire, who were secretaries. Mr. D. W. C. Skelton, now Secretary of the Phenix Fire, and General L. A. Dickinson, for a time local agent of the Ætna, were also graduates from the office of the Hartford. The present President, Mr. Geo. L. Chase, is one of the oldest underwriters in the country, having commenced about the year 1847 with a Mutual Company in Massachusetts. Afterward removing to the West, he was connected with the New England Insurance Company. Subsequently he formed an arrangement with the Hartford, where he remained for a number of years prior to being called to the Presidency of the company. The Hartford, under his management, has been eminently successful and prosperous. The present Secretary of the company, Mr. C. B. Whiting, is an underwriter of wide experience, and was for some years secretary of the National Board. After leaving that position he was, for about ten years, connected with the Home, of New York, and was subsequently with the Fire and Marine, of Springfield, Mass. Mr. P. C. Royce is the Assistant Secretary, and brings to his duties a thorough knowledge of the insurance business, gained in a long experience with various companies. The directors for 1883 are as follows: Geo. L. Chase, Charles Boswell, Henry Keney, Calvin Day, C. C. Lyman, E. B. Watkinson, Jonathan B. Bunce, James J. Goodwin, Jacob L. Greene. All of these gentlemen are otherwise and prominently identified with the business interests of Hartford, and their names are a guarantee of the soundness of any institution with which they are connected. The Hartford owns a beautiful Quincy granite building on the corner of Pearl and Trumbull streets, centrally located and an ornament to the city, an illustration of which will be found on page 93. It is a general insurance centre, containing the offices of the Connecticut Fire and Continental Life Insurance Companies.

The Hartford dates its existence from the inception of Fire Insurance in this country, and can truthfully claim to occupy a position at the top.

The Phœnix (Fire) Insurance Company

(See illustration, page 89.)

—This standard company was incorporated in 1854, the first informal meeting taking place in a workroom in the rear of the store of the late Lyman Stockbridge, No. 264 Main street, and the formal organization in the rear office of the late Wm. H. Imlay, in the building known as Union Hall, then standing on the present site of the building of the Connecticut Mutual Life Insurance Company, corner of Main and Pearl streets. This room was used as the office of the company until December, 1854, when it was removed to No. 275 Main street, remaining there until December, 1862, and removing thence to Hill's Block, No. 333 Main street. In August, 1872, the company laid the foundation of the elegant and spacious building now occupied (an illustration of which will be found elsewhere in this volume), and in November of the following year the business was transferred to it and permanently located. The building is distinguished for the severe simplicity of its architecture and the solidity of its construction and furnishing, and is, perhaps, in those respects, typical of the character of the organization to which it owes its existence. Everything that a thorough knowledge of the business and a keen foresight as to the possibilities and probabilities of its growth could suggest was employed in planning and building the edifice, and it stands now, as it will a hundred years hence, a monument to the energy and probity of the men who gave to the world the "Phœnix." The cost of land, building, furniture, etc., amounted to somewhere in the neighborhood of $125,000, an investment the wisdom of which has been thoroughly demonstrated by the rapid and steady increase in the value of the property.

On the 21st of June, 1854, the subscription to the capital stock was opened, and $100,000 were immediately forthcoming. On that day the company was organized and the following-named gentlemen were elected directors: Chester Adams, John A. Butler, Elisha T. Smith, Edwin T. Pease, Ralph Cheney, Erastus Smith, William Faxon, James C. Walkeley, Joseph Merriman, Nathan M. Waterman, Samuel B. Beresford, Lyman Stockbridge, and Nathaniel H. Morgan, the latter gentleman being chosen President, and Mr. Henry Kellogg, the present incumbent of that office, being elected Secretary.

Five days later the subscriptions were reopened and the capital stock was increased to $200,000, with one hundred and three separate subscriptions. About ten per cent. of this stock was paid in cash, the remainder being secured by stock notes, indorsed, guaranteed and protected to the full satisfaction of the directors and the security of the policy-holders.

The first policy ever written by the "Phœnix" was issued on June 29th, 1854, and was in favor of Mr. Elihu Geer, the well-known printer and publisher at Nos. 10 and 12 State street, and covered his furniture, wearing apparel and library. On June 16th, 1859, the capital stock was again increased, this time to $400,000, and on April 7th, 1864, it was still further increased to $600,000. At this figure it remained until December 1st, 1871, when, at a special meeting of the stockholders and in consequence of the great losses at the Chicago fire, it was voted to reduce the capital stock to $300,000, and at the same meeting the subscription books were re-opened, and, such was the confidence of the stockholders in the management of the company, the entire deficiency was immediately subscribed and the capital restored to the old sum. This action, coming so promptly at such a disastrous time, did wonders for the reputation of the Phœnix, and in a moment placed it in the position it now so firmly occupies as one of the essentially reliable insurance organizations of the country.

The next increase of capital stock occurred in July, 1876, when $400,000 were added, making a grand total of $1,000,000, and still further enhancing the reputation and business of the company. For five years the figures representing a million of dollars stood unchanged as representing the capital stock, but at the expiration of that period, in July, 1881, the rapid growth of the volume of insurance carried by the company induced yet another increase. This time it was not considered sufficient to add to the capital by the hundred thousand dollars, but at one stroke it was increased to $2,000,000, at which figure it remains to-day. Up to February 25th, 1856, the business of the company had been transacted on an actual cash capital of ten, twenty and thirty per cent. of the real capital, the latter two figures being represented by accrued dividends credited on the stock notes, only ten per cent. of the amount having been actually paid in, although, as the result proved, the notes were as good as the cash itself. At this time, and in consequence of inimical and aggressive legislation in several States, requiring that the capital stock of companies doing business within their borders should be actually paid up in cash, the Board of Directors demanded from the stockholders payment of the remaining seventy per cent. on their stock, and fixed the limit for such payment on March 28th. Before that date every dollar was paid, and the capital stock of the Phœnix became what it has since remained, absolutely cash. Not alone has the capital stock of the Phœnix increased in an almost marvelous degree, but the other assets have kept time until the latest annual statement (January 1st, 1883,) gives the entire assets, inclusive of the capital stock, at $4,446,208.31.

The month of October, 1871, marked the only thing that ever looked like a crisis in the affairs of this Company. In that month the great conflagration in Chicago, as well as the lesser calamities of the forest fires in Wisconsin and Michigan, involved the Company in an aggregate loss of $987,395.96, or a little more than one hundred and sixty-four per cent. of its capital stock, the great impairment of which it became necessary to meet by subscriptions of actual cash. How well and promptly this was done has heretofore been noticed.

The Phœnix Insurance Company is remarkable for the safe and conservative methods of its business and for the fact that it relies on legitimate insurance at reasonable, yet remunerative rates. It acts on the wise principle that the assured can only be so when they themselves pay a safe premium, and that it is far better to be sure than hasty. Hence cheap insurance cannot be found with it, and hence sensible people are with its patrons.

The present officers of the Phœnix are: President, Mr. Henry Kellogg; Vice-President, Mr. Asa W. Jillson; Secretary, Mr. DeWitt C. Skelton; Assistant Secretary, Mr. George H. Burdick. Of these gentlemen it is unnecessary to say anything save that "their works do follow them."

The Travelers' Insurance Company.—To Mr. James G. Batterson, the well-known contractor, builder, and monumental sculptor, the people of this country are indebted for the introduction and practical working of general accident insurance. While in Europe he familiarized himself with the workings of accident insurance, and upon his return organized the Travelers' Insurance Company, with a paid-up capital of $500,000, which, in 1875, was increased to $600,000. A charter was procured on the 17th of June, 1863, and business was begun in April of the next year. The first written policy, for $5,000, was issued to Mr. Batterson, the President of the company. Mr. G. F. Davis was elected Vice-President, and to him belongs the credit of the construction of the company, as it now stands, prominent, unique and successful, after nineteen years of operation. The company was incorporated with power to insure "persons against the accidental loss of life or personal injury sustained while traveling by railroad, steamboat, or other mode of conveyance." Subsequently the charter was amended by including authority to make "all and every insurance connected with accidental loss of life or personal injury sustained by accident of every description." The organization of this company awakened a general interest in casualty insurance of all kinds. There is no country in the world where the people travel more than in America, and as our civilization rapidly develops with the wonderful increase of population, there are new combinations and an advancing complexity of relations which calls for a new indemnity in the form of a general casualty insurance. The Americans are a rapid, reckless people, largely at the mercy of corporations, and more liable to accidents of all sorts than any other. The new system of insurance comes not a day too soon. The success of the Travelers' was assured from the start. Two years later no less than eleven other companies started as competitors, but the Travelers' had secured the established trade, and very soon it was without a rival, as all the others abandoned the field. The original business of the Travelers' was limited to accident insurance. Along with the general accident policies, which included weekly compensation in case of injury, short-term tickets were issued for the special benefit of railroad travelers, and sold at the principal ticket-offices throughout the country. In eighteen months from the time of beginning business, over 27,000 policies were in force, giving an annual income of half a million dollars, and insuring $85,297,500. In 1866 a life department was added with the most encouraging results. Early in the same year it was decided to form a distinct corporation for the prosecution of the railroad ticket business. Experience had shown that this was so entirely a distinct branch of the business as to require a uniform system throughout the country. The Railroad Passenger Assurance Co., of Hartford, was therefore organized, with a capital of $500,000, and Mr. Batterson was made the president of the new enterprise. In a short time the new company rivaled its chief progenitor in the measure of its success. Afterwards, however, its business was again consolidated with that of the Travelers', and it ceased to have an independent existence, the Ticket Department of the Travelers' taking its place. This company enjoyed the advantage of the fact that the benefits of its protection was continually brought before the attention of the public. The disasters taking place in all parts of the country, when of any magnitude, seldom failed to furnish a member of this company in the list of sufferers. Thus, for the railway disaster at New Hamburgh, this company paid out $20,000; for Angola the same sum; to the victims of the Metis disaster, $12,000; for the Ashtabula disaster, $25,000; for the Newhall House, $17,000; with large sums to single individuals, in all parts of the country, who met with accidents. These are but a few examples, in the course of nineteen years, out of 1,300 death losses paid, to which are to be added 87,000 claims for disabling injury. As compared with similar insurance companies in other countries, the Travelers' appears to the greatest advantage. In twenty years the oldest and largest company in England had insured but 100,000 people, while in five years the Travelers' had insured 150,000 persons, and paid losses of nearly a million dollars, ranging from $1 to $10,000 each.

On the first of January, 1883, the records of the Travelers' showed that one person in every ten of its accident policy-holder has been paid under a claim for death or injury by accident. On its books were the names of nearly 85,000 of these recipients of cash benefits, the amounts making an aggregate of over $5,400,000. The company's tatement on that date showed assets of $6,667,394.40. The total liabilities amounted to $4,992,095.20, leaving a surplus as regards policy holders of $1,675,299.20. 103,121 policies were written in the accident department alone during the year 1882, a gain of 5,557 policies over 1881, and an increase in premium over the same year of $134,562.79. In the life department, too, 13,443 policies were in force, of which 2,042 had been written during the year, all on the non-participating cash plan. Down to the present time the number of accident policies written is about 850,000, and of life policies in force there are about 13,500. The number of accident claims paid in 1882 was 15,503, amounting to $750,572.36. The total losses paid by both departments since the foundation of the Travelers' are about $8,000,000. The officers of the Travelers' are James G. Batterson, President; Rodney Dennis, Secretary; John E. Morris, Assistant Secretary; George Ellis, Actuary; Edward V. Preston, Superintendent of Agencies; J. B. Lewis, M. D., Surgeon and Adjuster. The Board of Directors includes some of the foremost names in Connecticut, the late Marshall Jewell having been one almost from the start.

The Scottish Union and National Insurance Company, and The Lion Fire Insurance Company of London.—M. Bennett, Jr., Manager; James H. Brewster, Assistant Manager.—The Scottish Union and National Insurance Company, of which Mr. Bennett is the United States Manager, has been in operation nearly sixty years and is one of the strongest of foreign companies. It has a subscribed capital of more than twenty-one millions of dollars, a portion being paid up and all being in such a shape as to be liable for the claims of policy holders. The sum immediately available for the payment of losses amounts to over fourteen millions, while the entire assets are far in excess of that sum, being stated as $33,041,045, inclusive of the capital stock. Since its organization it has received premiums amounting to nearly $17,000,000, paid in losses more than $9,000,000, and, in dividends to its stockholders, between $5,000,000 and $6,000,000, besides issuing new stock to the amount of $275,000. Its stock sells at $400, per share on a par value of $100. Among the one hundred and sixty-six home and foreign companies reporting to the New York Insurance Department, there are but seven which have so large a paid-up capital as the Scottish Union and National. The company, in February, 1883, had invested in the United States the sum of $1,031,210.46, and could show a gain in the net assets in America, for the preceding year, of $212,087.30.

The Lion Insurance Company, although not as great a corporation as the Scottish, is held in equal esteem by insurers and bears as good a reputation as any company doing business in the United States. Its subscribed capital is $5,000,000, of which $1,250,000 are paid up. It has invested in America $748,760.63, and shows a gain in its net assets in this country, for the year 1882, of $105,243.16. This company is also under the management of M. Bennett, Jr., assisted by Jas. H. Brewster, and numbers among its Trustees for the United States, Julius Catlin, Jr., of New York, Francis B. Cooley of Hartford, and Rodney Dennis also of Hartford and Secretary of the Travelers'.

Mr. Bennett, the Manager of these two companies, is a native of Bristol, R. I., and forty-two years of age. He graduated at Brown University, Providence, R. I., in the class of '60, as a civil engineer, the university conferring upon him, in September, 1860, the degree of A. M. He was an officer of the Connecticut Fire Insurance Company for about twenty years, the last eight of which he filled the presidency, during that time bringing that company from No. 56 to No. 10 in point of net assets in the list of eighty-six American companies doing business in New York. On April 28, 1880, Mr. Bennett was elected president of the National Board of Fire Underwriters, an office he holds up to the present writing. In October of the same year, he severed his connection with the Connecticut, and established the United States Agency of the companies he now represents. A great deal is said for the executive and business ability of Mr. Bennett, when it is stated that the business he manages now requires the services of more than thirty clerks, as against a total force of only seven, two years ago. Mr. Bennett is also prominent in local insurance matters, and is regarded as an authority, particularly by the insurance journals, to a number of which he is a valued and graceful contributor.

Mr. James H. Brewster, assistant to Mr. Bennett in the management of these companies, is a native of Coventry, Conn., born in 1845. He was bred to the insurance business, having been connected with the Connecticut Fire for seventeen years, a great part of which he was assistant secretary. His connection with that company was severed simultaneously with that of Mr. Bennett, and his appointment to his present position was made at the same time. He also is regarded as an authority on insurance matters, and is esteemed as a thorough-going business man and a genial gentleman.

Of the Scottish Union and National and The Lion Insurance Companies and their managers it can be truly said that they stand in the front rank.

The Hartford Steam Boiler Inspection and Insurance Company.—This company was incorporated at the last session of the General Assembly in 1866, the first directors being T. C. Allyn, Henry Kellogg, R. W. H. Jarvis, F. W. Cheney, S. H. White, J. A. Butler, E. N. Kellogg, C. M. Beach, J. B. Bunce, R. D. Hubbard, E. T. Smith and Daniel Phillips, of Hartford; R. Battell, of Norfolk, Conn., and George Crompton and H. H. Hayden, of Worcester, Mass. Mr. Enoch C. Roberts was elected President, and Mr. H. H. Hayden, Secretary, the date of their election being November 10th, 1866. Very little business was done in the first year, and in October, 1867, Mr. Roberts resigned the presidency, and **Mr. J. M. Allen**, the present incumbent, was elected in his stead. Mr. Allen, who was at that time the Supervising General Agent of the Security Insurance Company of New York, brought to the administration of the affairs of the new enterprise a thorough knowledge of insurance in all its branches, and an energy and far-sightedness that have gone far toward the success his company new enjoys.

The inception of this enterprise grew out of the frequent explosions of boilers throughout the country, and the uncertainty of the security guaranteed by inspections by municipal and State officers, many of whom were appointed, not for their mechanical skill and knowledge, but through merely political influence and as a reward for party services. It was thought that a corporation which assumed a liability in connection with its work, thus having a pecuniary interest in each boiler inspected, would make a more thorough and searching examination, and, at the same time, inquire into the causes of boiler explosions, and the means of preventing such terrible accidents. The company entered upon its work with the determination to fully accomplish the object foreseen and desired by its projectors. All boilers under its care are carefully inspected annually, and quarterly visits of inspection are made besides. Steam gauges are tested, safety valves adjusted and weighted, boiler connections carefully examined, and information given relative to setting and management; all with a view to economy in the use of fuel, and safety to life and property.

Since the accession of Mr. Allen to the Presidency, the business of the company has steadily and rapidly increased, until, on January 1, 1883, it had in its care and insured about 17,000 boilers located in most of the manufacturing districts of the United States. The business of the company was originally to inspect boilers, and if satisfactory, to insure the owner against loss by explosion. This has grown with time so that at the present it not only inspects and guarantees boilers against damage by explosion, but furnishes the assured with advice and information relative to the construction of new boilers, their setting and management; furnishes specifications for boilers, settings, chimneys, boiler-houses, etc., all of which are the outcome of long experience and research, and are advised with a consistent regard for the safety and economy of the insured and a careful outlook against risk of loss by the company. So far, indeed, does the protecting care of this organization extend, that even the water used in various sections of the country is carefully analyzed in a laboratory constructed for that purpose, and the deductions so obtained are transmitted to the insured, together with advice as to how to treat the water, based on these conclusions. In addition to all this, the company issues a monthly paper, called "The Locomotive," in which is much information relative to the management of steam boilers; monthly reports of the inspectors; list of explosions, so far as they can be obtained, and other valuable information. This paper is sent to the policy-holders free of charge. This is the pioneer company of its kind, and as experience is one of the essential factors of safety and success, it may be safely said to be the leading company of the kind in the world.

Since Mr. Hayden, there have been two secretaries, his immediate successor being Mr. Theo. H. Babcock, now business manager for the company in New York State, and whose office is at No. 285 Broadway, New York City. Mr. Babcock was succeeded by Mr. J. B. Pierce, formerly Secretary of the North American Fire Insurance Company of Hartford, who has filled the office continuously since, and is the present incumbent. The capital of the company is $250,000, and its officers and directors are as follows: President, J. M. Allen; Vice-President, W. B. Franklin; Secretary, J. B. Pierce. Directors—J. M. Allen, President; Lucius J. Hendee, President Ætna Fire Insurance Company; Frank W. Cheney, of Cheney Bros., Silk Manufacturers, Hartford and New York; Charles M. Beach, of Beach & Company; Daniel Phillips, of Adams Express Company; Geo. M. Bartholomew, President Holyoke Water Power Company; Richard W. H. Jarvis, president Colt's Patent Fire Arms Manufacturing Company; Thomas O. Enders, late President Ætna Life Insurance Company; Leverett Brainard, of The Case, Lockwood & Brainard Company; Gen. Wm. B. Franklin, Vice-President Colt's Patent Fire Arms Manufacturing Company; Geo. Crompton, Crompton Loom Works, Worcester, Mass.; Thomas Talbot, Ex-Governor of Massachusetts, Lowell; Newton Case, of The Case, Lockwood & Brainard Company; Nelson Hollister, of State Bank, Hartford; Chas. T. Parry, of Baldwin Locomotive Works, Philadelphia; H. C. Robinson, Attorney, Hartford, Conn. These names guarantee the entire solidity of the company.

The Hartford County Mutual Fire Insurance Company.—For over half a century the Hartford County Mutual Fire Insurance Company has been familiar to the people of Connecticut, where it is justly regarded with pride as one of the stable and honestly administered institutions of the State. It was incorporated in 1831, and has never had occasion to make an assessment on the insured. It is a purely mutual company, and the number of policies in force amounts to 14,297. Its business is confined to the safe and conservative State of Connecticut, and as no manufacturing or business risks are taken, it is eminently safe as an insurance company. Its policies cover damages by lighting, and it makes a specialty of insuring dwellings and farm property. The amount at risk now insured in this company is $23,167,677.48, while the total amount of losses paid since its organization is $478,164.61. The present cash assets of the company are $229,[illegible].61. The guarantee fund is all invested in good State, municipal and railroad stocks. Most of the policies are written for three years. The office is at No. 321 Union street. The officers are as follows: William F. Sugden, President and Treasurer; James L. Howard, Vice-President; William A. Erving, Secretary; Directors, Julius Catlin, James L. Howard, Marcus DeForest, Elisha Johnson, Watson Dewey, William F. Sugden, George Sexton, William A. Erving, Thomas Sisson, James Lockwood.

The Connecticut General Life Insurance Company.—This company was organized in 1865, upon the petition of Edwin D. Tiffany, who was joined by Messrs. Henry C. Deming, John C. Palmer, Jonathan B. Bunce, George S. Gilman, Ebenezer N. Kellogg, John A. Butler, Henry J. Johnson and George D. Jewett as original stockholders and incorporators. The charter of the company, passed at the May session of the General Assembly in 1865, provided for a capital stock of not less than $500,000, to be increased at the pleasure of the company to $1,000,000. In the May session of 1873 permission was granted the company to reduce its capital stock to not less than $125,000, and early in the following year the Directors availed themselves of the permission and reduced the capital to $250,000, and in 1880 it was again reduced to $150,000. The business done by this company is apparently conducted on a safe and conservative basis, the latest annual statement, published January 1st, 1883, giving the gross assets at $1,390,440.77, and the liabilities about three hundred thousand dollars less than that sum. The executive officers are Thomas W. Russell, President, and Frederick V. Hudson, Secretary. Both gentlemen, as well as the directors of the company, stand high in the insurance world, and command the confidence of the community.

The Charter Oak Life Insurance Company.—This company was incorporated in May, 1850, and commenced business October 1, of the same year, with a capital of $200,000.

The first President was Hon. Gideon Welles, who was, during the war, Secretary of the Navy. The first Secretary was Mr. Samuel Colt. Since the time of Mr. Welles the following-named gentlemen have held the office of president of this company in the order of their succession: Alfred Gill, J. C. Walkley, E. R. Wiggin, Marshall Jewell, G. M. Bartholomew.

The present officers are G. M. Bartholomew, President; Charles E. Willard, Secretary.

Directors—G. M. Bartholomew, J. M. Allen, E. J. Bassett, W. E. Baker, Elisha Carpenter, C. S. Davidson, Wm. Faxon, J. Goodnow, Geo. E. Hatch, S. R. McNary, C. G. Munyan, D. W. C. Skilton, Joseph Breed, W. A. M. Wainwright, D. L. Bartlett, Wm. Franklin, T. A. Logan, S. W. Robbins, I. A. Sheppard, Clapp Spooner, and W. L. Squire, well-known residents of Hartford, Baltimore, New Haven, Cincinnati, Philadelphia, and Bridgeport.

This company owns and occupies one of the finest insurance buildings in America, situated on the main thoroughfare of the city of Hartford. It is of granite; built in 1869; is six stories in height and 94 x 172 feet in area.

The annual statement, published on December 31, 1882, shows assets amounting to $6,049,363.73, and a total liability of $5,577,029.05, thus leaving a surplus in favor of the policy holders of $472,321.68. The statement also shows that since the reorganization of the company, a period of four and one-half years, there has been paid to policy-holders the sum of $4,691,568.25.

The Phœnix Mutual Life Insurance Company.—This company was incorporated in 1851. Its offices are located in the Connecticut Mutual Life Insurance Company's Building, corner of Main and Pearl streets. The first policy was issued September 11, 1851, since which time they number 105,101. The total amount of premiums received up to January 1, 1883, was $31,931,805.35, while the total payments for death claims and endowments were $10,987,228.02. The total for dividends, surrenders, etc., was $10,783,675.05, and the amount paid policy holders, $21,770,903.07. The surplus at 4½ per cent. (New York standard) is over $1,300,000, and the gross assets over $10,500,000. The original corporators were Barzilla Hudson, Benjamin E. Hale, James B. Hosmer, Thomas S. Williams, Francis Gillette, Francis Parsons and Edson Fessenden, and the original name was The American Temperance Life Insurance Company.

In the May session of the Legislature, 1861, the name of the company was changed to the Phœnix Mutual Life Insurance Company, which change took effect in July of that year.

The names of the present officers are: President, Aaron C. Goodman; Vice President, Jonathan B. Bunce; Secretary, John M. Holcombe; Consulting Physician, A. W. Barrows, M. D. The Board of Directors are Edson Fessenden, George W. Moore, Newton Case, Aaron C. Goodman, Jonathan B. Bunce, Charles S. Goodwin, Drayton Hillyer, James Nichols, John C. Parsons and John M. Holcombe, all well-known gentlemen connected with the industrial and financial world of Hartford.

National Fire Insurance Company.—The National Fire Insurance Company of Hartford began business in November, 1871, having been incorporated in May, 1869. The capital stock of this company, all cash, is one million of dollars; the funds reserved to meet all liabilities amount to $269,155, while the net surplus over capital and all liabilities is $464,125. The assets of this company, in bonds and stocks, have a par value of $327,325, while the market value is $1,083,815. The cash controlled by this company on the 1st of January, 1883, amounted to $163,749, mostly on deposit in Hartford banks. The total assets amount to $1,733,281. Mr. Mark Howard is the President and Mr. James Nichols the Secretary. Any one who will study these figures must become convinced that the National Fire Insurance Company does business on a safe basis, and possesses ample funds to meet all probable losses. Its funds are safely invested in United States and city bonds, and in railway and bank shares. It has now been so long in business and has conducted its affairs with such good judgment, that it has won the entire confidence of the community.

The State Mutual Fire Insurance Company.—This mutual fire insurance company was incorporated in 1867. The original incorporators and officers were: Ralph Gillett, President; F. A. Brown, Caleb Clapp, Albert Keney, F. K. Fox, S. T. Wolcott, Newton Carter; J. Cross, Jr., Secretary. Of this number, Messrs. Brown, Clapp, Keney and Carter, have since died, while the same officers of the company have continued as such up to the present time.

The present directors are Ralph Gillett, Willis Thrall, Aner Sperry, Roswell W. Brown, William W. House, E. L. Cook and Isaac Cross, Jr. The company takes risks of the safer class only, and strictly on the mutual plan. Damage by lightning is paid when the building is not burned. The company has been in operation sixteen years and has issued and renewed over 18,000 policies. All losses and expenses are paid to date. The company have added largely to its cash surplus yearly since organization, and have nearly $100,000 assets for the security of the policy holders.

The Orient Fire Insurance Company.—In the matter of capital the Orient Fire Insurance Company ranks with the first fifteen or sixteen in the country. There are more than two hundred companies doing business in the United States with less capital, hence this is one of the large concerns. The Orient has a cash capital of one million dollars, all paid up, and assets of $1,395,404.18. The Orient was organized in January, 1872, with a paid-up capital of half a million of dollars. The City Fire Insurance Company, which had but a quarter of a million of dollars capital, and was unable to meet the losses caused by the Chicago fire, took the charter of the Orient, and thus secured its first hold upon business through the agencies formerly used by the City Company. Early in the existence of the Orient Company the Boston fire caused a loss of $170,000. This blow was met by reducing the original capital of half a million dollars to $350,000 Up to 1881 the total losses paid by this Company amounted to over a million and a half of dollars. Now, with a prosperous business and total cash assets of $1,395,-404.18, this Company is able to meet all losses that it may encounter. The Company has its offices in the Hartford Insurance Company's building, and is doing an extensive business. The offices are: President, S. C. Preston; Secretary, Geo. W. Lester; Vice-President, Newton Case; Directors, David Gallup, Newton Case, G. M. Bartholomew, Wm Boardman, Daniel Phillips, Fred. B. Foster, Selden C. Preston, Leverett Brainard, Chas. J. Cole, Wm. H. Bulkeley, Geo. S. Lincoln, James Campbell.

Hartford Life and Annuity Insurance Company.—The Hartford Life and Annuity Insurance Company, organized in January, 1866, has gained a wide-spread popularity, and has done a large business at a very slight cost to members. This company claims that the old line system of insurance is out of the reach of the large class who most need life insurance protection, since it is a luxury people in moderate circumstances cannot afford to enjoy. This company introduced the safety fund system, which is distinct in its features from all other assessment plans. This fund, on the first of January, 1883, deposited in Security Company, amounted to $139,883. It is held in trust, and invested in U. S. Government bonds, the income of which is to go to the members, while the entire fund is pledged for the full payment of their claims. Each year has witnessed large additions to the actual number of certificates in force in this safety fund. The idea of the fund is simply an assessment insurance, a plan which is now indorsed by some of the best actuaries and writers on life insurance. It is co-operative insurance, about the only form of co-operation which has become popular in this country. If a man of forty years of age wishes to get insured, say for $10,000, according to the safety fund system, he pays an admission fee of $40, and the fee for the medical examination; also annual renewable expenses of $30. For the safety fund deposit a member will have to pay once $10, for every $1,000 certificate, or $100 for a certificate of $10,000. There is also a table of graduated assessment ratios for death losses for every $1,000, which runs from 65 cents at twenty-one years of age, to $2.68 for sixty years of age, or $1.12 at forty years of age. An investment upon this system is much more economical than after the old plan, as it is claimed, every investigator can demonstrate for himself. The Life and Annuity Insurance Company now has assets amounting to $1,114,304, while its total liabilities are but $805,661, yielding a gross surplus on policy-holders' account of $308,642. The total death claims paid under the safety fund system amount to $311,000. The officers are: President, F. R. Foster; Vice-President, H. A. Whitman; Secretary, Stephen Ball; Medical Examiner, Dr. I. W. Lyon; Superintendent of Agencies, H. P. Duclos. Some of the leading merchants and manufacturers of Hartford and vicinity are in the board of directors.

Mutual Benefit Life Company.—The Mutual Benefit Life Company, incorporated in 1869, insures at absolute cost; has no vast accumulation of members' money; makes every man his own banker; pays no big stock and cash dividends to stockholders, and has the common interest of the company and members at heart. The total assets of this company on the 1st of January, 1883, were $122,946, while the liabilities were but $24,052, leaving a surplus for the protection of members of $98,894. The amount paid for death and accident claims in 1882 was $72,125. The president is A. R. Goodrich; Vice-President, J. H. Welch; Secretary, De Witt J. Peck The following gentlemen are directors: Hon. A. R. Goodrich, Treasurer State of Connecticut; Hon, Geo. G Sill, Ex-Lieut.-Governor State of Connecticut; John H. Welch, M. D., Med. Examiner; Seymour Bunnell, Contractor Colt's Armory; Hon. Carlos Smith, Ex-State Senator New Haven; Hon. Jeffrey O. Phelps, Capitalist, Simsbury; Hon. Charles W. Barnum, of Barnum, Richardson & Co., Lime Rock; C. H. Russell, Merchant; G. D. Goodrich, Druggist.

The Continental Life Insurance Co., of Hartford, Conn., has a record of nearly twenty years of successful business. Its nineteenth annual statement, dated January 1, 1883, shows its surplus as $453,783.57. During the year 1882 the increase in number of policies was 43 per cent.; increase in amount of new business 50 per cent.; increase in number of policies in force 116; increase in amount of insurance in force, $311,189; ratio of assets to liabilities, 122 per cent. The following named gentlemen are its officers and directors: James S. Parsons, Wm. M. Hudson, J. S. Welles, Lyman B. Jewell, A. S. Winchester, Robert E. Beecher, Thomas Ramsdell, Ansel Arnold, J. Griffin Martin. James S. Parsons, President; Robert E. Beecher, Secretary.

The Connecticut Fire Insurance Company of Hartford, Conn., was incorporated in 1850 with a perpetual charter. Its office is in the fine granite structure of the Hartford Fire Insurance Company. The company are soon to build a home of their own, which will be one of the striking buildings in Hartford. The cash capital is $1,000,000, and the cash assets on January 1, 1883, were $1,781,626.50. The list of officers and directors embrace some of the most reliable business men in Connecticut. They are as follows: J. D. Browne, President; Charles R. Burt, Secretary; L. W. Clarke, Assistant Secretary. Directors: Julius Catlin, Henry T. Sperry, Henry C. Robinson, Alfred E. Burr, John R. Redfield, Rodney Dennis, Julius Catlin, Jr., William J. Wood, Franklin G. Whitmore, T. W. Russell, J. D. Browne, D. R. Howe, Robert Allyn.

MERCANTILE AND MANUFACTURING.

The Colt's Patent Fire Arms Manufacturing Company.—History has failed to record the name of the original inventor of fire-arms, yet evidence appears conclusive that the idea was first conceived from an accidental experiment of Berthold Schwartz, a monk at Mayence, who discovered in about the year 1320, that when confined and set on fire, gunpowder had an immense expansive force, by which means heavy bodies could be propelled a given distance with great rapidity.

Without following the history and development of this idea in detail from the time of Edward III. of England, who reigned in 1327, down through succeeding centuries, we will come at once to the discussion of the Colt's Patent Fire Arms Manufacturing Company of this city, which was founded by Colonel Samuel Colt in 1852. See illustration on page 91.

The history of this company is similar to that of most great enterprises, and is built on a series of failures which served as stepping stones to a great success.

Colonel Colt's first business enterprise was the Patent Arms Company in 1836, at Paterson, N. J., which expended capital to the amount of $300,000 and was forced to suspend operations in 1842. His second was at Whitneyville, Conn., where he completed his first contract to furnish arms for the United States Government and shortly after he established the nucleus of *his own* manufactory, now the Colt's Patent Fire Arms Manufacturing Company, at Hartford, the business of which has been from that day to this, a constant success and which has resulted in the completion of the most perfect establishment for the manufacture of fire-arms that exists in this or any other country. This grand scheme, so brilliantly planned and so successfully carried out is a towering evidence of the vast conceptions of their author and his extraordinary executive abilities in perfecting them.

The grounds purchased on which to erect the buildings contained about 250 acres, and the buildings occupy about 500 x 500 feet of space, the average height being three stories. The company as now organized has a capital of $1,000,000 with liberty to increase it to $1,500,000.

The following are the present officers: President, R. W. H. Jarvis; Vice-President, Gen. W. B. Franklin; Secretary and Treasurer, Hugh Harbison; Superintendent, Horace Lord; Engineer, E. L. Murphy.

Since the war, when the facilities of the works were taxed to their utmost in manufacturing arms for the Government, parts of the works have been leased to other parties, manufacturing companies and others, the company reserving the eastern armory which is 500 x 60 feet in size and four stories in height, with a connecting building 300 feet long and three stories high, for their own immediate business, where 700 men are employed in the manufacture of double barreled breech-loading shot guns, of all calibers, breech-loading revolving pistols, Gatling and other machine guns, Baxter steam engines, disc engines, Gally's Universal printing presses, electric machines, rapid Telegraph machines, hand drills, etc., etc. A part of the works embraces an iron foundry where first-class castings are produced. Mr. Richard W. H. Jarvis, the president of this company is a brother of Mrs. Samuel Colt, and was born in Portland, Conn., about fifty-five years ago. He is a graduate of Trinity, and previous to his presidency of this company was a lawyer in New York City.

General William B. Franklin, the Vice-President, is a native of York, Pa., and fifty-nine years of age. He is a graduate of West Point, and up to 1861 was an Engineer officer. He figured conspicuously in the war of the Rebellion as a Brigadier and Major General, during which time he was in the command of the Sixth and Nineteenth Corps. At the close of the war he became identified with this company and has been a resident of Hartford since. He has been Adjutant-General of Connecticut and otherwise actively interested in the military, social, political and financial affairs of his adopted State. Mr. Hugh Harbison, the Secretary and Treasurer, is a native of Hartford, about fifty years of age. He is a well-known and long-established citizen, and has been interested in mechanical pursuits for many years. Mr. Horace Lord, the Superintendent, is a native of Massachusetts, and about sixty years of age. Of Mr. E. L. Murphy we have no record save that he is one of the most skillful engineers and master machinists in America.

In this connection a brief sketch of the founder of this company, Col. Samuel Colt, would perhaps be appropriate. He was born in Hartford, July 19, 1814. He acquired the rudiments of an English education, and at ten years of age was transferred to the factory of his father (who was a manufacturer of wool, cotton, and silk goods, of which last article he established the first factory in New England). He finished his education at Amherst, Mass. His curiosity was deeply aroused to see distant lands, and upon the impulse of the moment, he ran away to sea, shipping before the mast for Calcutta. Returning delighted with his experience, he consented to a short apprenticeship again in the manufactory of his father, where he learned the leading principles of chemistry, a science of which he was very fond, and which he turned to good account soon after as a public lecturer for two years, traveling in the United States and Canada. Though at that time but a youth of seventeen or eighteen years of age he made a profit of from $5 to $50 per night, to say nothing about the knowledge he gained of men and the country.

All of these profits, beyond those required for the supply of his daily wants, were sedulously devoted by the youthful adventurer to the prosecution of that great invention which has since extended his renown throughout the civilized world. His life was wholly devoted to the invention, perfection, and manufacture of fire-arms, in which his career was unexampled. He died in the early part of 1862, leaving a large fortune and a business, the first of its class in the world.

Joseph G. Lane (successor to J. W. Danforth & Co.), Importer and Wholesale Dealer in Groceries and Liquors, 222, 224 and 226 State street.—One of the largest and most enterprising wholesale grocery and liquor houses in this State is that of Jos. G. Lane, at Nos. 222, 224 and 226 State street. It was originally established in the year 1834 by J. W. Danforth & Co., Mr. Lane succeeding to the business in August, 1875. The commodious brick building occupied by Mr. Lane is stored from basement to attic with one of the largest stocks carried by the business firms of Hartford. While there is a full line of groceries and grocers' sundries the great bulk of the stock, as well as of the business of the house, is in liquors, in which trade Mr. Lane covers an extensive territory, employing a large force of resident and traveling salesmen, as well as a number of clerks, porters and other assistants. Besides being the agent for Robert Smiths' Philadelphia India Pale Ale, Mr. Lane makes a specialty of the manufacture of Farwell's Old-fashioned Cherry Bounce, Cherry Brandy and Cherry Rum, a list of beverages that has attained to great popularity throughout New England and the other parts of the country to which his trade extends. Mr. Lane was born in Plymouth, Luzerne county, Pennsylvania, in 1845, and received his education in the schools of Indiana, in which State his early life was passed. He arrived in Hartford in February, 1862, and has resided here ever since, winning for himself a high position in the business world and a cordial recognition of his pleasing social qualities.

Wenk & Brockway, Merchant Tailors, Dealers in Ready-Made Clothing and Gent's Furnishing Goods, 132 State Street.—The custom or merchant tailors of every city are justly entitled to consideration and recognition as among the important branches of commercial industry.

Their work leaves its impress on our every-day life and goes far towards influencing our fellow-mortals in making up opinions in reference to one another. Shakespeare said of dress: "Costly thy habit as thy purse can buy, but not expressed in fancy; rich, not gaudy; for the apparel oft proclaims the man."

Among the oldest and representative merchant tailors is the house of Messrs. Wenk & Brockway, situated at No. 132 State street.

Fifty-eight years ago the business was established by Mr. Robert Buell, who was the fashionable tailor for our grandfathers, in their youthful days.

Succeeding him came the firm of Buell & Clark, in 1850. In 1866 Mr. Clark was fortunate in making an alliance with Mr. J. H. Wm. Wenk, who had won his way to the front rank as a cutter, and the firm was called Franklin Clark & Co., which continued until 1878, when Mr. Clark retired, and a former clerk, Mr. C. H. Brockway, joined with Mr. Wenk, making the firm, as it stands to-day, Wenk & Brockway.

The store occupied is 20 x 50 feet, and is fitted with every modern convenience for the prosecution of the business.

Spacious show windows afford ample room for the display of rare suitings and choice importations as well as samples of their productions, in the shape of business and dress suits, overcoats, trousers, etc. The stock of cloths, cassimeres and suitings is one of the best in the State, a large proportion being of their own importation; the trade for which they cater requiring the best in quality and style. A comparatively small stock of the better grades of ready made clothing is kept for the convenience of old customers as well as new. An important adjunct is the Gents' Furnishing Goods Department, a factor in the business of the house. In the formation of this firm circumstances seemed to have favored it. Mr. J. N. Wm. Wenk had for many years enjoyed a first class reputation as a merchant tailor, both as a cutter and a business man, and brought these factors in the formation of the new firm in 1878. He is a native of Germany and came to Hartford about thirty-two years ago, since which time he has been daily adding to his reputation.

Mr. Ulysses H. Brockway is a native of Lyme, Conn., and the business manager and financier of the house, bringing to it the experience of nine years with the firm who preceded this. His extended acquaintance and correct business methods have contributed not a little to their well-known success.

His first experience in the stern duties of life was as a boy on a farm, in his native town, where he was afterwards educated at the village high school, coming to Hartford in 1867, and was clerk for the firm which preceded him, never changing his business or employers. Both gentlemen rank high among the experienced merchant tailors in Hartford.

William Spencer, Livery Stable, 70 State Street.—Among the livery establishments of Hartford, that of William Spencer deserves especial mention in this work as being one of the largest and in every way a representative of the best class of such establishments here.

His stables are located at No. 70 State street, in the rear of Exchange Bank, and near the United States Hotel. They are complete in every particular, and are arranged in a manner that affords the greatest convenience in every department.

The business was established thirty-nine years ago in this city, since which time he has enjoyed an uninterrupted and solid reputation.

During these thirty-nine years he has only changed his location three times, being at one place twenty-three years, and removing to his present location in 1878.

For a long time he was proprietor of the United States Hotel stables.

Riding or driving, single or double teams, can always be secured here, and a specialty is made of furnishing carriages for weddings, parties, balls, drives, funerals, etc., twenty-five horses being kept for these purposes.

Mr. Spencer is a native of East Hartford, Conn., and was born in 1818.

Prompt and reliable, he long ago established himself in the confidence of the public, and is highly respected and esteemed as a courteous gentleman and honorable citizen.

Watrous & Higgins (Chas. F. Watrous and Chas. Higgins), Foreign and Domestic Fruits, Nuts, Confectionery, Tobacco, Cigars, etc., No. 82 State Street—This business was established about twenty years ago by S. W. Gregory, who built the building known as Gregory's Building, a portion of which is occupied by the firm. The house of Watrous & Higgins succeeded to the business in 1880, their immediate predecessors being Smith & Emmons. The store is 25x80 feet in size and is stocked with a full assortment of fine fruits, nuts, confectionery, cigars, tobacco, etc. The trade is principally local and among the better classes and has grown from a small beginning until it ranks among the largest in the city. Mr. Watrous is a native of Hartford and is about forty years of age. He has been identified with the business and other interests of his native city for many years and enjoys the universal esteem of his fellow citizens. Mr. Higgins was born in Glastonbury, Conn., in 1822. During the war he enlisted in the Twenty-seventh Connecticut Infantry, a nine months' regiment, and was so badly wounded at the battle of Fredericksburg as to incapacitate him for further service. Like his partner he enjoys the entire respect of the business and social community.

This house has the reputation of being among the best in its line in the State.

W. H. Brainard, Trunks, Bags, Ladies' Satchels, etc., No. 434 Main Street.—This business was established in 1864, at its present location, by Mr. W. H. Brainard, who has been a practical trunk maker from boyhood. He manufactures trunks, bags, and ladies' satchels, and makes a specialty of making sample trunks for commercial travelers and others to order. Several skilled workmen are employed by him in the prosecution of his business. Mr. Brainard was born at Portland, Conn., in 1838, and came to Hartford in 1845. He received an excellent education in the public schools of his native State.

He is an active worker, and enterprising and thoroughgoing business man and one of the most sociable men in Hartford. By diligence, industry, and perseverance he has earned a first-class connection and built up a profitable and reliable business.

C. E. Bishop & Co., Manufacturers of Ladders, etc., corner Capen and Main streets.—The name of Bishop is largely identified with the manufacturing of ladders for fire departments, painters, masons, carpenters, farmers, and others.

Connecticut, Massachusetts, and Rhode Island are represented in the manufacture of this specialty by four brothers. In addition to ladders they also manufacture basket-seat chairs, wood eave troughs, step-ladders, Whiteners' horses, boys' clipper sleds, snow shovels, clothes horses, and revolving clothes-drying machines; particular attention being paid to the manufacture of painters' stage ladders, ladder hooks, etc.

The business history of these brothers extends back to 1857, when C. E. Bishop, who is now located in this city, started with his brother, Hiram R. Bishop, the manufacture of ladders in Charlestown, Mass. In 1861, C. E. Bishop sold out his interest to his brother and removed to Providence, R. I., where a large and prosperous business in the manufacture of ladders was built up, which was sold out to another brother, Henry C. Bishop, the same being now conducted under the name of A. M. & L. E. Bishop in that city. In 1872 Mr. C. E. Bishop came to Hartford, where the reputation of the Bishop ladders, chairs, etc., had preceded him, and where he found but little trouble in building up a business, the largest of its kind in the State, if not in New England.

His establishment covers a large area, including several buildings. Most of his business is conducted in the States of Connecticut, Massachusetts, and New York, where eight teams are kept constantly running over regular routes.

His productions have been exported to California, Cape of Good Hope, and Florida, but a near-by trade is mostly solicited.

One of his greatest specialties is the portable extension fire-escape ladder for fire departments. For fire-escapes there is nothing in use to equal them. One to extend fifty feet can be raised and lowered by one man of ordinary strength, and can be extended to any distance required within its capacity, which is within one hundred feet (in two sections).

His chairs have an enviable reputation, particularly for hotels and office use.

Mr. Bishop rejoices in the possession of an elegant dwelling, recently erected near his manufactory, in which he resides, and where he dispenses that hospitality so proverbial with the Bishop family.

The United States Stamped Envelope Works, No. 1 South Ann Street.—It may be of interest to the great public to know that all the stamped envelopes and newspaper wrappers used by the United States Government are made in Hartford by the United States Stamped Envelope Works, Mr. M. S. Chapman, Superintendent. The proprietors of these works are the Plimpton Manufacturing Company of Hartford, and the Morgan Envelope Company of Springfield, Mass. The establishment embraces a brick building, 45x110 feet in size, and four stories in height, with basement, together with an L 50x30 feet, same height. In addition to stamped envelopes and newspaper wrappers, are made all the official envelopes used in the Postal Department of the United States. The number of people employed is one hundred and fifty, and the capacity is 1,300,000 envelopes and wrappers per day; the production at present being about 900,000.

The works were established here in 1874, since which time the increase in production has been about eight per cent. yearly.

The products are shipped direct to the post-offices by orders from the officials at Washington. The process of manufacture is quite interesting.

The Billings and Spencer Company, Machinists and Machinery Manufacturers, Lawrence cor. Broad streets.—The Billings and Spencer Company of Hartford, Conn., the pioneers of drop forgings, as a regular and successful business, was organized in 1869, and in July, 1872, received from the Legislature of the State of Connecticut, a special charter of incorporation, conferring very favorable privileges, the capital stock being $150,000, with liberty to increase the same to $300,000.

In March, 1877, the company reduced its capital stock to $125,000.

Its manufactory is located between Lawrence and Broad streets, in the western part of the City of Hartford, and near the geographical centre of the city, occupying a front of 312 feet on Lawrence street, and 179 feet on Broad street.

Its main factory is three stories high, covering an area of 40 by 130 feet, with engine and boiler rooms. The forge shop is 82 by 100 feet. There are also several smaller buildings connected with the business of the company on the premises.

As a specialty, the drop forging business is followed by very few concerns in the world, and there are none in the United States making in any comparison the amount and variety made by this company.

The manufactory is supplied with machinery and tools of improved make and description. In the forge shop are twenty-five drop hammers, ten presses, one atmospheric and four tilt hammers. The machine shop is furnished with lathes, planers, upright drill-machines, die-sinking machines, and a variety of special machines for use in manufacturing the several kinds of tools produced by the company.

A full description of the almost endless variety of drop forgings, cannot be given in this limited space. Upwards of 2,000 different articles for parts of guns, pistols, sewing machines, special machinery, machinists' tools, sewing-machine shuttles, are among the drop forgings. A large variety of goods are also put upon the market in a finished state by the company, among which may be mentioned the following, viz: Billings' patent screw plates and dies, tap and reamer wrenches, lathe dogs in twelve sizes from ⅜ to 4 inches, Billings' adjustable pocket wrench, Barwick wrenches, screw drivers from best tool steel, thread cutting tools, Billings' improved double-action ratchet drill with sockets for using Morse taper shank twist drills, or the old-fashioned square shank drills, five sizes Packer ratchet drills, about forty varieties of sewing-machine shuttles for the different makes of sewing machines in this country and Europe, combination pliers, Billings' patent breech-loading single-barrel shot gun, Spencer's patent recapper and uncapper for shot-gun shells, Billings' patent drop-forged and cold-pressed sewing machine shuttles, and all descriptions of steel and iron drop forgings for adjustable machine, chuck and track wrenches, machine handles, thumb screws, thumb nuts, hexagon and square head bolts, chuck pinions and jaws, Spanner wrenches, carriage spring heads, chuck rings, coal breaker teeth, picker teeth, threshing machine teeth, locomotive spring link-keys, saw sets and swedges, nut crackers, bit-brace jaws, valve stems, button hole cutters, vise jaws, tap wrenches, beater arms, parts of guns, pistols, sewing machines and machinery generally.

The officers of the company are: President, Chas. E. Billings; Treasurer, Lucien H. Holt; Secretary, Eben H. Stocker. The company employ 100 men, and its entire buildings are heated by steam and lighted by gas. Medals were awarded to this company at the Vienna and Centennial Exhibitions for variety and excellence of productions, and quite an export trade in shuttle forgings is transacted with England, Germany and other foreign countries.

Mr. Charles E. Billings, the President and Superintendent, is a native of Wethersfield, Vermont; born in 1835. He learned the trade of a machinist with the old Robbins & Lawrence Co., of Windsor, Vermont, and came to Hartford in 1867 to reside permanently. During the war he was here temporarily as a contractor in Colt's Armory and in Ilion, N. Y., where he had a forging contract at the Remington Armory. On his return to Hartford in 1867 he was Superintendent for the Weed Sewing Machine Company for three years, directly afterwards commencing the foundation of this business. He is a director in the Berryman Steam Heater Company, and is one of the representative manufacturers of this city.

At Rocky Hill, Conn., he manufactures, on his own account, patent belt clamps, belt awls, machinists' clamps, and surface gauges. He is the exclusive manufacturer of Gardner & Millers' patent belt clamp, and has made new and improved patterns of them. This apparatus has proved itself indispensable to every establishment using belts six inches wide and upwards, and will soon pay its cost in saving of time in lacing belts quicker and better than any other way, and avoids any necessity or excuse for injuring a wide belt by putting it upon the pulleys after it is sewed.

Mr. Lucien H. Holt, the Treasurer, was born in Wellington, Conn., in 1820, and has been a resident of Hartford since boyhood. He was at one time a well-known flour dealer here. In early life he learned the trade of a jeweler, and for seven years has been a representative of this company.

Mr. Eben H. Stocker, the Secretary, is a native of Hartland, Vermont; born in 1846, and has been in Hartford ten years, at first in a mercantile line, and later as secretary of this company.

The Billings & Spencer Company have an international reputation for superiority and variety of productions, and is one of the first-class manufacturing establishments of which Hartford and Connecticut are justly proud.

The Pratt & Whitney Co., Manufacturers of Machinery of Superior Quality.—This company, whose productions are the wonder and admiration of all skilled mechanics, and whose reputation is as great in Europe as in America, was organized in July, 1869, and has a capital of $500,000.

The officers are—President, Francis A. Pratt; Secretary, R. F. Blodgett; Treasurer, Wm. A. Healy; Superintendent, Amos Whitney.

As manufacturers of machinists' tools, gun and sewing machine making machinery, forging machinery, machinery for threading bolts, tapping nuts, etc., etc., they stand pre-eminently at the head. The history of this establishment, like most others of similar magnitude, represents slow and steady growth, and more or less discouragements; but the factors in it were such that no obstacles seriously impeded its progress or prevented its ultimate success.

It was about twenty-three years ago that Messrs. F. A. Pratt, Amos Whitney, and Monroe Stannard began together the manufacture of machinists' tools, etc., in a small way in this city. Marked business ability, mechanical skill, energy and ambition were the motive powers in the enterprise. Their motto was quality, and their ambition perfection. From year to year the business grew and flourished. With reputation came increased business that necessitated more capital and more facilities. In 1869 the present company was formed, with a capital of $350,000, which has since been increased to $500,000.

The works are on the north bank of Park River, a branch of the Connecticut, about ten minutes' walk from the Union Passenger Depot, and can be seen from the cars of the New York, New Haven and Hartford and the New York and New England Railroads. A branch track connects with the main lines of these roads. The building is built of brick, with brown-stone trimmings, is 225 x 45 feet in size, and four stories in height, containing 40,500 square feet of floor area.

A building 146 x 42 feet, three stories high, and containing 18,000 square feet of floor area, is used mainly for heavy machine work. The forging shop is 175 x 42 feet, and the main foundry building 120 x 60 feet, with numerous wings.

The entire establishment covers, in all, about two acres. There are ten fires in the forging shop, a 1,200-pound steam hammer, a 60-pound atmospheric hammer, three drop hammers, a cushioned tilt hammer, two trimming presses and a patent power shear.

The foundry has a pickling and cleaning house, 48x40 feet, three large annealing ovens, for softening small castings, a room for core making, with ovens of large capacity. There is also a crane of fifteen tons lifting power, and another of ten tons for lighter work, two McKenzie cupolas, known as Nos. 2 and 4 of this celebrated make, and a large McKenzie blower. The machine shop has 250 lathes, seventy planers, thirty drilling machines, thirty milling machines, 6 screw machines, 6 gear and rack cutters, and 3 large boring mills.

As a whole this vast equipment is valued at about one half million of dollars. Automatic sprinklers, with powerful pumps, should the ordinary city supply of water fail, are a protection against fire. All the rooms are heated by steam and lighted by gas or electricity. Western Union and Mutual Union Telegraph offices are part of the company's facilities for transacting business, and the number of employees is 660.

Mr. Francis A. Pratt, the President, is a native of Vermont. He has been identified with Hartford for about thirty years, during which time he has represented his ward in the City Government as alderman and member of the City Council. He is a director in the Pratt & Cady Co., and otherwise interested in the mechanical industries of his adopted city. Several successful machinists and machinery manufacturers owe their mechanical success to him and his company.

A noted manufacturer in Belgium wishing to give his son a thorough education in the manufacture of fine machinery, sent him to this country in the fall of 1882 to make an exhaustive investigation into the better class of establishments in America to that end. After visiting several manufactories he decided in favor of the Pratt & Whitney Co., where he is now preparing himself to superintend the 700 workmen employed in his father's establishment.

Mr. William A. Healy, the Treasurer, is a native of Windham County, Conn., and about sixty years of age. He learned the trade of a shoemaker and went west to Cincinnati, Ohio, where he was interested in the Syracuse Salt and Coal Co. He has been a resident of Hartford about fifteen years. He is a director in the American National Bank, the Dime Savings Bank, Washburn Car Wheel Co., Hartford Steam Heating Co., Billings & Spencer Co., and other manufacturing companies in his adopted city.

Mr. Roswell F. Blodgett, the Secretary, is a native of Hartford, Conn., and forty years of age. He was educated at that excellent educational institution, the Hartford High School, and has been with this company since 1866. He is President of the Blodgett & Clapp Co., located at No. 51 Market street, in this city.

Mr. Amos Whitney, the Superintendent, is one of the gentlemen from whom the company takes its name, and, as above mentioned, is one of its projectors. He was born at Biddeford, Maine, and is about fifty years of age. He has been a resident of Hartford thirty or more years, and the position he holds is a sufficient indication of his skill as a master machinist. Like the other officers of this company, he is a part of the earnest, active, successful business world of the Capital City, and largely interested in its institutions.

Mr. Monroe Stannard, the Superintendent of the department of special machinery, with Messrs. Pratt & Whitney, was one of the original owners of these works. He was born in New Marlboro, Mass., and is fifty-seven years of age. The reputation of the company's tools for exactness and convenience and elegance is due in no small degree to the inventive genius of Mr. Stannard.

Mr. Edward G. Parkhurst, the Assistant Superintendent of the works, is, like Mr. Healy, a native of Windham County, Conn., and fifty-two years of age. He has been a resident of Hartford for over twenty years. His fellow citizens have elected him to represent them from the Second Ward as a member of both branches in the city government, honors which were thrust upon him rather than sought for, as he is essentially a business man of rare executive ability.

The Pratt & Whitney Co. acknowledge no superior in the manufacture of machinery. Their productions, without particularizing, go to all parts of the civilized world; and if the sojourner in Hartford should leave its establishment out of his route, he can tell one but little about manufactures of superior machinery.

N. P. Hough & Co., (Successors to H. J. Johnson), Wholesale Dealers in Provisions, Nos. 95 to 105 Allyn Street.—The firm of N. P. Hough & Co. succeeded in September, 1880, to one of the oldest and largest provision businesses in New England. Their immediate predecessor was Mr. H. J. Johnson, the successor of the house of Moore & Johnson, which house had followed that of Porter & Moore, who established the business about thirty years ago on Commerce street. In the extensive warehouses occupied by this firm are stored immense quantities of hams, bacon, pork, dried beef, lard, cheese, fish, etc., from which large shipments are made daily to all parts of New England and to portions of the Middle States. This house makes a specialty of Johnson's celebrated hams and breakfast bacon, a line of goods that has won a high reputation for excellence and evenness of quality. The packing for the firm is done in Chicago, where it can be done to greater advantage than at this place, and employs a large force of men.

Mr. Hough is a representative New Englander, having been born in Essex, in this State about thirty-seven years ago. Since his settlement in Hartford, about eighteen years since, and up to the present, he has steadily won his way as a business man and in the respect of his fellow-citizens, first, as assistant cashier of the Phoenix National Bank, a position he occupied for a long time, and latterly at the head of his present business.

C. K. Hubbard, Watches, Clocks, Jewelry, etc., No. 150 Asylum Street—Among the oldest and best known establishments of this kind in the State of Connecticut, is that of Mr. Hubbard, centrally and eligibly located in the Allyn House block on Asylum street. Mr. Hubbard has a well-earned reputation for the excellence of his wares and the fidelity with which work intrusted to him is performed. Hence, his business is prosperous and steadily increasing. Mr. Hubbard was born in Saulsbury, Conn., in the year 1822, and has lived in Hartford since the establishment of his present business in 1856. His trade in watches, clocks, etc., is only limited by the confines of the State, while his repairing work has its specimens in all parts of the country. In 1840 Mr. Hubbard removed from his native place to Ashley Falls, Mass., where he remained for some years, going thence to Falls Village, in which place he was in business for nine years prior to settling in Hartford. In early life Mr. Hubbard was apprenticed to and learned the trade from his father, but he abandoned its pursuit for the more congenial occupation he is at present engaged in. In person and manners, Mr. Hubbard is calculated to please, and a long-continued business career, distinguished by urbanity and fair-dealing, has won for him a fair measure of success. Mr. Hubbard is regarded as one of the representative men of Hartford.

Dwight, Skinner & Co, (Drayton Hillyer, Henry C. Dwight and Wm. C. Skinner), Wool, No. 107 Allyn Street.—This firm are the successors to the business of the widely known wool firms, Hillyer & Bunce and H. C. Dwight & Co., under which latter title it was known from 1879 to May 1, 1882, when Mr. Skinner was admitted and the present designation adopted. The business of the firm is general dealing in wool, and in that respect it stands among the largest houses in New England, while it can, undoubtedly, be classed as among the leading houses in Connecticut, its transactions amounting to over a million dollars annually. The specialty of this firm is scoured wools of all grades, the preparation of which is effected at the Anchor Scouring Mills at Windsor Locks, an establishment owned and run by the firm, and giving steady employment to forty of the sixty men in their service.

In this particular the operations of the firm are far in excess of those of any of their competitors. A peculiar process of extracting burrs from wool is the property of the firm and is used only in their mill. The ramifications of the trade of Dwight, Skinner & Co. are only limited by the number of woolen mills in the United States, to all of which they are constantly shipping their scoured wools.

Captain Dwight, of the firm, is a native of Massachusetts, forty-one years of age, and has passed most of his business life in Hartford. During the war of the Rebellion Captain Dwight served his country as Captain in the Twenty-seventh Massachusetts Volunteers and won an enviable record. Since his advent in Hartford he has been selected by his fellow citizens to represent them in the City Council and Board of Aldermen, serving in both bodies for several terms. He is a director in the American National Bank and the Mechanics' Savings Bank, and holds the important position of Street Commissioner, the duties of which are discharged with great satisfaction to the people.

Mr. Hillyer, the senior partner of the firm, is a native of Connecticut, about sixty-five years of age, and has been in business in Hartford for more than forty years. He has been for many years a director in the Ætna Insurance Co., and is also a director in the Hartford National Bank.

Mr. Skinner, the junior and the youngest member of the firm, was born in New York State, and is twenty-eight years of age. Prior to his joining this house as partner he was connected with the well-known house of Keneys & Roberts, where he acquired the knowledge of business and the correct methods of trade for which he is generally esteemed.

This firm, collectively and individually, ranks high among the very foremost in Connecticut.

N. Palmer & Co. (F. C. Clark), Manufacturers of Oak-tanned Leather Belting and Dealers in Belt Leather, Manufacturers' Supplies, etc., No. 302 Asylum Street.—This business, one of the largest of its kind in New England, was established in 1859 by Messrs. N. Palmer, George Aspinwall and J. Ward Fuller. In 1869 Mr. Palmer died and the business was conducted by the remaining partners until 1875, when Mr. Fuller retired from the firm. In 1878 Mr. Clark entered the firm, and on the death of Mr. Aspinwall, in 1880, he assumed the sole proprietorship, retaining the old firm name of N. Palmer & Co. The manufacture of leather-belting and other articles, as well as the trade in manufacturers' supplies, is carried on in a large salesroom and workshop, occupying almost an entire floor of the spacious building at No. 302 Asylum street, and gives employment to a force of about a dozen workmen, besides the necessary clerks and salesmen. The business is the outgrowth of a very small beginning, and amounts at this time to a figure in the neighborhood of $60,000 a year, distributed as regards locality all over the New England States and sections of New York, and, to a less extent, throughout the country. In addition to the manufacture of belting and the sale of manufacturers' supplies, the house supplies the entire country with a patent lubricating axle washer, said to be the best thing of its kind ever invented. It is manufactured from leather which undergoes a treatment by a chemical solution that renders it impermeable to moisture and non-sensitive to the action of heat or a dry atmosphere, while it acts as a lubricant to the axle. It also acts as a deadener of sound, and as it retains its virtues through all seasons, it is never superseded until actually worn out. Besides this the house makes a specialty of polishing-leather, for polishing steel, and is the sole agent in Connecticut for the American Jacket Fire Hose, made of a knitted fabric and lined with rubber, an article in extensive use and great favor with Fire Departments, manufacturers, and others. Mr. Clark was born in 1849, in Windsor, Conn., and has resided in Hartford since 1866. He is a type of the New Englander who rises by his own exertions from a humble beginning to a foremost place in the business world. At the age of thirteen years he commenced his life's work in a cotton mill, going thence to a woolen mill, and subsequently to the grocery and provision business, finding in these varied employments the business experience necessary for the successful conduct of the establishment of which he is now the proprietor and director.

A busy life has left him but little time to enjoy the pursuit or gain of office, yet in one particular he has been prominent. For fourteen years he has been actively connected with the State military forces, and has enjoyed the honor of being elected a lieutenant in the crack corps known as the Governor's Foot Guard.

Mr. Clark stands high among the well-reputed business men of Connecticut, as well as in Hartford's best society.

S. N. Hart, Carriage Manufacturer, Nos. 39, 41 and 43 Albany Avenue.—The City of Hartford, probably, has a larger proportion of wealthy people within its limits than any city of the United States, and hence, the industries which go to supply the wants and luxuries of that class are peculiarly prominent and numerous. In no place in the world is the custom of keeping private carriages so general, nor can there be found elsewhere such a prevailing excellence in style and manufacture. In the best work of carriage-making, remarkable for elegance of finish and originality of design, combined with lightness, strength and durability, Mr. S. N. Hart is the most noted manufacturer in Hartford. The business was originally established in January, 1853, on Church street, by Balch & Hart, Mr. Hart succeeding to the entire business some years later. The building on Albany avenue, at present occupied by Mr. Hart, is three stories in height, with a frontage of 84 feet and a depth of 160 feet, accommodating the four departments of the business, in which there are employed from twenty-five to thirty workmen, whose weekly pay-roll aggregates about $400. Mr. Hart builds all kinds of family carriages, sulkeys, coaches, wagons, trucks, rockaways, phaetons, buggies, etc., and enjoys the reputation of turning out some of the finest work ever seen in New England or elsewhere. The stock carried in this establishment averages in value about $20,000, while the annual business amounts to five times that sum. It is a generally conceded fact that Mr.

Hart stands at the head of his line of business in Hartford and, in fact, in the entire State.

Mr. Hart is a native of New Britain, and came to Hartford at the age of seventeen; he is about seventy-three years of age, and is justly regarded as one of Connecticut's solid and reliable business men, a respected citizen and a just and liberal employer.

D. A. Spear, Florist and Seedsman, No. 242 Asylum Street.—Mr. Spear established himself as a florist and plant grower on Wethersfield avenue in 1861, continuing there until 1867, when he relinquished the business of growing and entered the store business at his present quarters, his goods being largely supplied from the prominent nurseries in the vicinity of Hartford. Mr. Spear's spacious store is stocked with a large assortment of birds, fishes, cages, fancy baskets, plants, floral designs, etc., while a large greenhouse in the rear produces and shelters a great variety of the rarer plants, exotic flowers, ferns, etc. Mr. Spear is among the original florists in Hartford, and his trade has extended among the better classes to so great an extent that his yearly sales can be counted far up among the tens of thousands. In the matter of artistic floral decorations for weddings, parties, etc., Mr. Spear does a large business, and, in that particular, is regarded as at the head of the trade. Mr. Spear was born in Canada, just across the line from Vermont, in the year 1848. He has resided in Hartford since 1861, and has won a business and social standing of the first order.

P. H. Dunn.—Manufacturer and Dealer in Monuments, Headstones, etc., No. 104 Albany Ave.—The rapidly increasing business of Mr. H. Dunn is a pleasing evidence that strict attention to business and invariable fair dealing, will bring its own reward. Mr. Dunn established himself in his present location in 1877, and since that time his business has so largely increased that his force of workmen is constantly employed in getting out the fine work for which he has become justly noted. Mr. Dunn is a native of Connecticut, having been born in Middletown on December 22, 1852. Among the specialties of Mr. Dunn's factory are monuments, headstones, and marble, granite and brown stone fences. The cemeteries in Hartford and vicinity bear numerous evidences of his skill, while many of the palatial residences here and elsewhere are surrounded by the beautiful evidences of his handiwork. Mr. Dunn is himself a practical and skilled workman, having learned his trade at the works of J. G. Batterson.

For so young a man, Mr. Dunn commands a large business, and its rapid and steady growth promises to place him in the front rank of his trade long before he shall have attained middle age.

E. W. Sage & Co., Wool Pullers, Dealers in Hides, Tallow, Calf and Wool Skins, Nos. 64 and 66 Albany Avenue.—This business was started about 1850, by Elisha E. Sage, father of the present proprietor, since deceased, and has grown from insignificant proportions until it has reached its present volume of about $100,000 a year. Mr. Edwin W. Sage succeeded to a partnership in the firm in 1871, the other interest being represented by the estate of his father. While this house does a large and growing business in the purchase and sale of hides, tallow, etc., its specialty is "wool pulling," a process by which sheep skins are denuded of their wool and that commodity, as well as the skin itself, made ready for market. In this particular the firm does the largest business of the kind, theirs being the only wool-pulling establishment in Hartford or its immediate vicinity.

Mr. Sage was born in East Hartford in 1851, and has lived in the city since he was two years of age, growing to merit the esteem of business men and the cordial liking of an extensive circle of acquaintances and friends. In 1880 he was elected a councilman from the Seventh Ward, and during his term of service demonstrated his capacity and integrity to the complete satisfaction of his constituents.

P. Jewell & Sons, Manufacturers of Leather Belting, corner of Hicks and Trumbull Streets.—The oldest, largest, and best-known manufactory of leather belting in America is that of P. Jewell & Sons, corner of Hicks and Trumbull streets. The house was founded by Mr. Pliny Jewell in 1849. The Yankee idea of conveying power by leather belts was of slow growth, but in time it was generally approved, both in this country and Europe. The use of leather belts rapidly increased, and the business of manufacturing them grew in proportion. In a short time the elder Mr. Jewell had admitted his four sons—Marshall, Pliny, Charles H., and Lyman B.—into partnership, with the firm name of P. Jewell & Sons, which has remained ever since. The factory is an imposing brick building, 185 x 44 feet, five stories high, with an L three stories high. Here the belts are manufactured from the leather in the rough, which comes direct from a large tannery in Michigan, with a capacity of tanning 50,000 hides a year. These belts are now found in general use throughout the United States, and large quantities are exported to Europe. See illustration, page 161.

The Jewell brothers were born at Winchester, N. H., and the family had been tanners for five generations. The boys were taught the art of tanning by their father, and therefore had the best preparation for making a success in the new business. The family traces back to Thomas Jewell, who lived in Boston as early as 1639. Pliny Jewell, the founder of the house, died in 1869, at the age of seventy-two. His son, Pliny, was born September 1, 1823, and was educated in "the little red school" house of those days. He is a director in several banks and insurance companies in Hartford. Marshall Jewell, the second son, was born October 20, 1825, and died February 10, 1883, aged fifty-seven years and four months. He received a common school education, and at the age of eighteen years had mastered the trade of tanning. In 1847 he learned telegraphy, and had charge of offices, and was superintendent of lines, until 1850, when he went into partnership with his father. From 1852 to 1857 he traveled throughout the country, extending the business of the house. He visited the Old World in 1859, '60, '65, '66 and '67, including

Europe, Asia, Africa, the Holy Land, and the Paris Exposition. In 1868 he began his political career, and was three times made Governor of Connecticut. In 1873 he was appointed United States Minister to Russia. He negotiated the trade-mark treaty with Russia and discovered the process of making the scented Russian leather. Since that time Russian leather has been made in America equal to any. On the 1st of September, 1874, he became Postmaster-General in the cabinet of President Grant, retiring July 14, 1876. He negotiated the postal treaty with Canada. In 1880 he became chairman of the Republican National Committee, and did much good and efficient work for the party, of which he was an enthusiastic member. The business connections of the late Governor Jewell were very extensive, and proved him to be a prompt, energetic, far-seeing man. He was one of the original directors of the Phoenix Fire Insurance Company, director of the Travelers' Insurance Company, director of the Hartford Bank; president of the Charter Oak Life Insurance Company, a director in the Weed Sewing Machine Company, Peerless Wire Mattress Company, Connecticut School of Design, etc., president of the United States Telephone Company, a member of the Union League and University Clubs, New York City; a Knight Templar, an honorary M. A. of Yale College; owner of the new belt road around Denver, Colorado, a partner in the large dry-goods house of Charles Root & Co., Detroit, and interested in a large number of manufacturing and railroad projects throughout the country.

He was given to historical research, and was an officer in the New England Historico-Genealogical Society. His residence on Farmington avenue, Hartford, has become historic for its hospitality. The untimely death of Governor Jewell, in the prime of life, was widely lamented.

Lyman B. Jewell, the third brother, was born in 1827, August 29th. Charles A. Jewell was born March 29, 1841, and educated at the Hartford public schools. The three surviving brothers now carry on the business of manufacturing belts, and are also interested in the Jewell Pin Company, which manufactures brass and adamantine pins. This company was incorporated in 1881, with a capital of $60,000, and the late Marshall Jewell was the President. Mr. Charles A. Jewell is the Treasurer, and Mr. Charles L. McIntosh the Secretary. The factory stands in the rear of the belting works, and consists of two buildings, each eighty by twenty-five feet, two stories high. Thirty-seven hands are employed, producing annually 1,500, of 180 packages in a case.

Mr. Charles L. McIntosh was born in Columbia, Connecticut, and is thirty-two years of age. He has resided in Hartford about thirteen years and was formerly the bookkeeper and private secretary of Governor Jewell. Mr. F. B. Wesson, the superintendent of the pin factory, was born in Hartford in 1850. He was educated in the public schools, and was formerly in the dry-goods business.

Paul F. Schneider, Gun and Locksmith, Dealer in Guns, Pistols and Sporting Goods, Fishing Tackle, Cutlery, Locks, Keys, and Optical Goods of every description, No. 222 Asylum Street.—One of the best selected stocks of miscellaneous hardware, guns, cutlery, optical goods and sporting articles to be found in Hartford is contained in the establishment of which this sketch treats. Mr. Schneider, who is a practical gun and locksmith, does a large share of the repairing business of the city and an extensive trade among those sportsmen who desire fine and reliable guns and other articles for their use. In the specialty of optical goods, this store has few equals and no superiors in Hartford or the surrounding country. Mr. Schneider began his business career in 1870 at No. 16 Mulberry street, with practically no capital, and has progressed so favorably that he now carries a large and valuable stock, all of which is clear of debt. The business extends to all parts of the State, the store being in close proximity to the railroad depot, and, therefore, commanding a large share of the country trade. The present location has been occupied since 1879, and has proven itself in every way a satisfactory one.

Mr. Schneider was born in Saxe Coburg, Germany, in 1830, and arrived in America in 1852, making his home in Hartford, where he has remained ever since, and where he has attained to a thoroughly good standing in business and private life.

T. R. Shannon & Co., (successors to Shannon & Marwick), Drugs, etc., No. 143 Trumbull Street.—Among the absolute necessities to the well being of a city or town, there is nothing of more importance than a well-regulated and largely-stocked drug store, where the physician and patient can send their prescriptions in the absolute certainty of having them properly compounded, and where money can be expended for the various articles that go to make up the adjuncts to the business, with a satisfying sense that a *quid pro quo* is rendered. Among such houses that of T. R. Shannon & Co. stands preeminent. Established about twenty years ago by Dr. J. F. B. Butler, the business was succeeded to in 1873 by Mr. Albert Pitkin, and in 1878 by Messrs. Shannon & Marwick, the latter withdrawing from the firm on July 15, 1882. The business, small at first, has been extended by the energy, enterprise and fair dealing of its various conductors, aided by a thorough, practical knowledge of the details of all its branches, until now it stands among the foremost in point of volume and in the very front rank as regards character.

Mr. Thomas R. Shannon, the present head of the house, was born in Londen, New Hampshire, on May 10, 1853, and lived in Portland, Maine, the greater portion of his adult life. He is a graduate of the College of Pharmacy of Massachusetts, at Boston. As a business man his standing is high, while his social qualites are such as to make his circle of friends a very large one.

W. L. & H. E. Pitkin, Manufacturers of Sterling Silverware, No. 174 Pearl Street.—At No. 174 Pearl street is the new and handsome building used by Messrs. W. L. & H. E. Pitkin, manufacturers of sterling silverware and platers of plated ware. For fifteen years past this firm has occupied one of the Jewell buildings, but increasing business compelled them to remove into larger quarters, which removal occurred on the 1st of January, 1883. The business was established in 1858, on the site of the old Yale building, and succeeded to a business left by Mr. O. D. Seymour, who has retired, and Mr. H. J. Sawyer, who is deceased. Mr. Seymour was the successor of the well-known William Rogers' Co. He afterwards became the Collector of Hartford.

Mr. W. L. Pitkin was born in East Hartford, in 1830, and learned the trade of silversmith of Walter Pitkin, in the same town. At one time he went upon the road selling goods, and found he could command enough trade to keep his establishment running. He now employs ten hands, keeps two men on the road, and manufactures from $30,000 to $40,000 worth of goods a year, besides plating 100 dozen knives and forks a day. The specialty of the house is flat ware, in solid silver, and this has such a reputation that it is sought for throughout the country. Mr. Pitkin is a member of temperance organizations, a Congregationalist, etc., but being wholly devoted to business, has never sought office. His brother, H. E. Pitkin, born in 1832, is his partner. This firm makes a cleaning and polishing powder, known as Silver Detersive, which holds the ware clean for a long while after it has been applied.

James Campbell & Co.—Manufacturers of Harness Trimmings, Nos. 39 and 41 Trumbull Street.—One of the numerous manufacturing establishments in Hartford, whose productions go to make up a variety, is that of Messrs. James Campbell & Co., situated at Nos. 39 and 41 Trumbull street. The business was established in 1836 by Mr. Edwin Bolles, in the rear of the "Times" office, on Main street, and was removed to its present location about thirty-five years ago. In April, 1879, Mr. James Campbell, under the firm name of James Campbell & Co., succeeded to the business. The works comprise three rooms, the largest 25x75 feet in size, where from twenty-five to forty people are employed in the manufacture of finely finished rosettes, ornaments, saddle nails in silver, nickel and gold, and harness trimmings generally. The productions are sold by agents in all parts of the country, principally in the western states, extending to California and Oregon, where they have an enviable reputation.

Mr. James Campbell is a native of Hartford, born in 1846, and was a workman in this establishment for twenty years previous to his becoming proprietor. The productions of this house rank high in the trade, and for ornamentation and finish are not excelled

Farris Music Store, Wholesale and Retail Dealers in Music and Musical Instruments, No. 178 Asylum Street, Allyn House Block.—The oldest and one of the most thoroughly stocked music stores in the State of Connecticut is the one whose designation forms the title line of this sketch. The business was started in 1851 by Mr. John Farris, who still retains his place at the helm, and conducts the steadily increasing trade of the house. While one of the branches of the business is the sale of pianos and organs, in which the justly celebrated J. P. Hale piano is the staple, it is subordinated to the trade in the smaller instruments, such as violins, guitars, banjos, band instruments, flutes, accordeons, strings, bridges, and, in fact, all the instruments, accessories, and tools needed by musicians, as well as sheet music in great variety, song books, etc. The two spacious show windows of this establishment present a variety of musical goods not to be found elsewhere in this State, and to be found in few places in the entire country. Mr. Farris feels a pardonable pride in his large and carefully selected stock of old and rare violins, and claims that in his specialty, the manufacture of banjos, he excels the world, a claim which is borne out to a considerable extent by the numerous indorsements from professionals and others in his possession.

Mr. Farris is a native American, having been born in Coventry, R. I., in 1826, removing thence to Hartford on January 1, 1850.

In addition to his music business, Mr. Farris is interested, as treasurer and manager, in the Hartford Boltless and Noiseless Thill Coupling Company, manufacturers of a deservedly celebrated device, the character of which is indicated by its name. Besides these, he is the patentee and owner of Farris patent safety straps and button for use on carriages in connection with the coupling. Mr. Farris bears a high reputation among business men, and in social life is regarded as an acquisition to any circle.

William Toohy.—Auctioneer and Manager of Real Estate Sales, No. 182 Asylum Street—The subject of this sketch, although not a native of this country, may from his long residence here and his thorough identification with the interests of this city and State, be justly regarded as a representative American. In 1861, Mr. Toohy started his present business and has continued with unvarying success until he can point with pride to the fact that in the twenty years of his business career more than five millions of dollars' worth of property have passed from seller to purchaser through his hands, with perfect satisfaction to the interested parties and a reasonable profit to himself. Mr. Toohy's large wareroom is filled with an immense stock of furniture and house-furnishing goods, from among which the bargain-seeking housewives of Hartford and vicinity are continually making selections, delightful alike to the eye and to the scanty purse. It is not too much to say that in the business of selling real estate at auction, Mr. Toohy has practically a monopoly, his business in that line extending not only throughout Hartford and its environs, but all over the State of Connecticut.

In person, Mr. Toohy is what a man should be who depends for success in business on personal contact with the public. Of an imposing and magnetic presence and with that peculiar gift of eloquence so essential to his peculiar calling, backed by indomitable energy and unquestioned integrity, he has placed himself in front of the front rank and has won for himself the undoubted right to be called the first auctioneer of the State. Mr. Toohy's family connections are more than ordinarily good, one of his brothers, a leading lawyer in San Francisco, having been lately chosen a Judge of the Superior Court in that city.

C. T. Marston & Co., Lumber Dealers, No. 54 Morgan Street.—Among the oldest established lumber dealers of New England may safely be classed the firm of C. T. Marston & Co., the business of which dates back for fifty years or more, when it was established in a modest way by Mr. Stephen Marston, the father of the present proprietor. In 1880 the son succeeded to the business at the death of the father. A large and varied stock of all kinds of lumber and timber is to be found in the extensive yards, and hundreds of houses in Hartford have been built by lumber shipped by this house. Two yards covering an area of eight acres are necessary to store the lumber in stock and the business done amounts to upwards of $300,000 per year.

Mr. Charles T. Marston is a native of East Hartford, born in 1842. He has represented his native town as State representative in the legislature with honor to himself and his constituents. Mr. Marston's large business is managed in most of its details by Mr. C. A. Atkins Jr., who has been connected with Mr. Marston since 1869, having thoroughly mastered all the minutiæ of the business. Mr. Atkins has risen step by step to the position he now occupies as manager and buyer for the house, by the exercise of those qualities of honesty and shrewdness for which the better class of New England's sons are noted. He was born in Mansfield, Conn., in 1852, but has resided in Hartford for a large part of his life. He is looked upon as a rising man and one who is sure to make his mark.

Associated with Mr. C. A. Atkins Jr., in the carrying on the business and attending to the numerous details in the yard is Mr J. R. Atkins, a brother of much promise who, although here but a few years, has already won the entire confidence of the trade, and is a valuable assistant in the management of the firm's affairs. He is a native of Mansfield, Conn., where he received his education.

The Hartford Courant.—The oldest newspaper of continuous publication in the United States is "The Courant," of Hartford. It was established by Thomas Green, and the first number appeared October 29, 1764. From that day to this there has been no break in its files, a complete set of which is preserved in the fire-proof room in the new and handsome office on State street. This paper is older than the United States, and gives a history of the country from its birth. When the Stamp act came, this paper was filled with letters from the people in opposition to British oppression. From that day on it has been a representative medium for expressing the wishes of the public. It has discussed war with England; the declaration; the Confederation; the Constitution; and the amendments; participated in every Presidential election, and taken an interest in every important event in the history of the Nation and the State. For generations it has been a welcome visitor in the houses of Connecticut, and has widely circulated throughout the country. The growth of families and industries can be traced in its columns. The City of Hartford has become what it is since the first number was issued. At that date Indians occupied most of New England, and the Mississippi Valley was hardly known. Such a journal can boast a history, a patronage, and the confidence of the community, as rare as it is valuable. Some of the incidents of its career are especially interesting. At the close of the year 1775, it being impossible to obtain paper, the proprietors built for themselves a paper mill, and called upon their lady friends to be "very careful of their rags." This was the beginning of the paper manufacture of East Hartford and Burnside. Letters from Ethan Allen and Israel Putnam have appeared in its columns. The paper has changed ownership fourteen times. It belonged to the Goodwin family from 1778 to 1836. From 1770 to 1778, Mrs. Watson, the widow of Ebenezer Watson, conducted the paper, probably the first woman in America who ever engaged in this business. In the fall of 1837, Mr. John L. Boswell established the "Hartford Daily Courant" in connection with the old "Connecticut Courant." In 1850 Mr. Wm. Faxon, who learned the printer's trade as an apprentice in the office, became a partner with Mr. Boswell. He afterwards became the Assistant Secretary of the Navy. In 1867 the paper passed into the hands of Hawley, Goodrich & Co., the present owners. Among those who once were type-setters in the office, are Robert Bonner, of the "New York Ledger," and Alfred E. Burr, editor of the "Hartford Times." In 1856 a paper called the "Evening Press," was established, that the city might have a republican journal. A year later Mr. Joseph R. Hawley, a young lawyer, became one of the proprietors. In 1860 Mr. Charles Dudley Warner became assistant editor. On receipt of the news of the firing upon Sumter Mr. Hawley enlisted, being the first volunteer from the State. In 1867 the "Press" was consolidated with the "Courant," and ceased to exist. The present members of the firm, each equal partners, are Gen. Joseph R. Hawley, William H. Goodrich, Charles Dudley Warner and Stephen A. Hubbard. Gen. Hawley, when not engaged in public duties, is the editor-in-chief. In his absence those duties devolve upon Mr. Warner. Mr. Hubbard is the managing editor. The "Courant" now occupies a large and handsome building, which was finished in 1880. It is as handsome as any newspaper office in New England, outside of Boston. It stands on the north side of State street, facing the old State-house square and the new Government buildings. The house is five stories high, 117 feet by 47, modern gothic in style, and executed in red brick and mortar, relieved by bands of diaper brick, moulded brick belt courses, and deep window openings spanned by hard brick arches. The inscription "1764, Connecticut Courant, 1880," in terra cotta is built in the brick-work over the windows on the second story. The engraving of the establishment on page 87 will give a better idea of its outside appearance than any letter-press description. The interior of the building is a complete newspaper and printing establishment, from the engine and Hoe's double cylinder press in the basement to the composing-room on the fifth floor. The business and editorial rooms are elegantly fitted up, and the establishment is provided with telephones and telegraphs, connecting it with every part of the entire world. The "Courant" building stands on historic ground. At the old number of 66 State street, where the new structure stands, no less than twenty-eight newspapers and magazines have been published during the past 115 years. This spot has been a centre for the radiation of information, and is the place where the Republican party of Connecticut was rocked in its cradle. Anti-slavery and temperance have been preached from this place for many years, and at this center pure literature has found its inspiration. The insurance business of Hartford, now the first and foremost in America, began on this spot February 8, 1794, the date of the first policy issued. From 1831 to 1835 the Post Office was in the same building with the "Courant," and Gov. Oliver Ellsworth had his office on the same site. Of the success, fame, stability, prosperous growth, and able editorial management of the "Courant," it is almost unnecessary to speak. The first issue was a small sheet, fourteen by eight inches, the present "Courant" is a sheet thirty by forty-six inches, folding in the middle, and containing as much matter as a common-sized book of 400 pages. It is a live, well edited newspaper, of such age and wealth that it can afford to discuss all subjects impartially, with dignity and conservatism. It has gained wisdom and vigor from age and experience, and as its editors are men who have had an extensive practical experience of life, on the field, in politics, in business, in the world of letters and society, they know what they are writing about, and, therefore, command the confidence and support of the public.

Gen. Joseph R. Hawley, the managing editor, was born in North Carolina in 1826. He was educated at the Hartford grammar school, at Cazenovia, N. Y., and at Hamilton College, where he graduated in 1847. He began the practice of law in 1850, and in his office organized the Republican party. In 1861, as soon as the news came of the firing on Sumter, he enlisted for three months and went to the war as captain in the First Connecticut. He re-enlisted, and was made Lieutenant-Colonel of the Seventh Connecticut, under command of General Alfred H. Terry. He was at Charleston, Pulaski, Morris Island, Fort Wagner, James Island, Pocataligo and Chester, also at Richmond and Petersburg. He became a Colonel in 1862, a Brigadier-General in 1864, and a Major-General in 1865. In 1866 he was elected Governor of Connecticut. In 1868 he presided over the Chicago Republican Convention. In 1872 he was elected to Congress, and re-elected the next year. He passed 1876 in Philadelphia as President of the Centennial Commission. In 1879 he was again sent to Congress, and is now a member of the Senate.

Mr. Charles Dudley Warner was born in Pittsfield, Mass., and graduated at Hamilton College in 1851. After graduating he wrote for the magazines and published the "Book of Eloquence." Having studied law with Daniel S. Dickinson, of Binghamton, he practiced for three years in Chicago. In 1860 he was called to Hartford as assistant editor of the "Press," and has remained ever since. He is the author of "My Summer in a Garden," "Saunterings," "Back Log Studies," "In the Levant," "Mummies and Moslems," "Being a Boy," "In the Wilderness," and other works.

Mr. Stephen A. Hubbard had been a printer in Amherst, Mass., and in New York. He became connected with the "Press" in 1861. In 1853 he established the Winsted, Ct., "Herald," and was associated with E. C. Stedman, the poet. Mr. Hubbard became one of the owners of the "Courant" when the "Press" ceased to exist.

Mr. Wm. H. Goodrich is the business manager of the "Courant," and has been connected with it since 1851 as compositor, foreman, publisher, owner and manager.

N. G. West, Druggist and Apothecary, No. 815 Main Street.—Mr. West is a native of Bristol, R. I., born in 1843, and previous to his residence in Hartford a member of the firm of Buffington & West. He established himself here in 1875, and for a time was at No. 795 Main street, after which he removed to his present central location.

Mr. West was in the army as clerk in the Post Commissary Department, stationed most of the time at Warrenton, Va. He was obliged to resign after a long and arduous term of service, on account of sickness occasioned by his constant attention to duty. Mr. West's residence in this city during the past seven years has familiarized the people with him so favorably that he was elected a member of the city government as Councilman from the seventh ward in the spring of 1882, on the Democratic ticket.

As a reliable compounder of physicians' prescriptions and as a large retail dealer in pure, fresh drugs, medicines, physicians' appliances, toilet articles, perfumery, soaps, etc., Mr. West stands second to none, as his success in business largely testifies.

Frederick Ellsworth, Wholesale Dealer in Flour, Cotton Seed Meal, etc., No. 44 Market Street.—The wholesale flour-house of Mr. Frederick Ellsworth, which is located at No. 44 Market street, was established many years ago by Mr. W. K. Holt, who died in 1880.

In 1876, the firm of Holt, Ellsworth & Co., succeeded Mr. Holt, and in 1879, the business was assumed by Mr. Ellsworth alone, who conducts a large trade, extending throughout the State and adjoining country.

The stock comprises, flour, cotton seed meal, linseed meal, and fertilizers, a specialty being made of Oliver's chilled plow, for which he is an agent.

Mr. Ellsworth is a native of East Windsor, Conn., where he was born in 1833. He was educated in the public schools, and came to Hartford in 1869. He was a Commissioner in the Provost Marshal's Department during the war, where he discharged the duties of that office with fidelity and ability. He is a live business man, genial, easy to approach and affable in conversation, facts which have done much in winning the success which is so generally accorded him.

R. P. Judson, Proprietor Charter Oak Butter Store, Bakery and Meat Market, No. 466 Main Street.—The well-known store named in honor of the historical charter oak, was established by Mr. A. Judson, the father of Mr. R. P. Judson, in 1876. The stock consists of fresh made and superior bread, plain and fancy cakes, pies, biscuits, rolls and the celebrated New England doughnuts. In the butter and cheese department are the finest grades of butter and cheese, selected from the best dairies of this and New York State. The meat market has a large assortment of meats, game and poultry. The store is neat and attractive in appearance, convenient in its appointments, and well adapted for the large business conducted. The baking department is provided with everything necessary for the business, and special attention is given to supplying weddings and parties with everything necessary to their pleasure, in the best manner.

Mr. R. P. Judson is a native of Bethlehem, Conn., born in 1850, and for some years previous to 1876 was a well-known business man in New Haven. Since his settlement in this city he has succeeded in building up a profitable business, amounting to $50,000 yearly. He is a progressive and wide-awake business man, a resolute believer in quick sales and small profits, and controls a first-class trade, which is daily increasing.

John S. Russell, Grocer, No. 646 Main Street.—It is a matter of history that more than half a century ago one of the centrally-located business stands in the then village-like city of Hartford was the general store of Chester Adams, the site of the present store of Mr. John S. Russell, the subject of this sketch.

Generation after generation has "bartered" at this stand; the traditional green doors, and the ancient cellar porch have given away to more modern conveniencies; but the reputation of the place inherited from son to son still holds good.

The successor to Chester Adams was James M. Adams, who continued from the year 1863 to 1869, when Hiram W. Adams conducted the business for one year, selling out to Byron P. Soper, who occupied the stand for two years—1870-1. On the expiration of the year 1871 Mr. Hiram W. Adams again assumed the responsibilities of the business, who again sold out to Byron P. Soper. Messrs. Russell & Barnes succeeded Mr. Soper.

The present proprietor was connected with it as Russell & Barnes in 1878, who so continued till Nov. 1st, 1882, when he assumed the business, purchasing it of his partner. The present amount of stock carried is varied, and the volume of business done large. Mr. Russell is a native of Cromwell, Conn., from which place he came to Hartford some years since. He is an enterprising business man and deserves the large patronage which this desirable location has always commanded since the days of Mr. Adams, and to which the affable manner and native politeness of Mr. Russell has largely contributed.

The Herold Capitol Brewing Co., Brewers of Extra Fine Lager Beer, Nos. 54 to 66 Bellevue St.—The railway traveler from Hartford to Springfield will notice on the left, soon after he emerges from the tunnel, the imposing buildings of this company, which was incorporated in 1879 with a capital of $15,000, half of which is paid into the treasury. The officers are J. A. Miller, President; Julius Huebler, Secretary; Charles Herold, Treasurer. This business was established over twenty years since, with limited capital and under adverse circumstances by the present treasurer of the company, Mr. Chas. Herold, after whom the company is named. The grounds cover about three acres. There are three buildings, one of them a very imposing one. The specialty of this company is the brewing of extra fine lager beer for bottling, a reputation for which extends throughout New England and the adjoining States. Since the establishment of this brewery by Mr. Herold, the prejudice of the community against beer drinking is not so marked, and as a legitimate result, and owing to the excellence of the beer of this company, the business of bottling has increased many fold, as is attested by the enormous increase in the production of this company to eight thousand barrels yearly.

Mr. J. A. Miller, the President, is a native of Prussia, and was captain of the Germania Guards in this city.

Mr. Julius Huebler, Secretary, is a native of Saxony and a prominent business man here. Mr. Charles Herold, the Treasurer and ruling spirit of this company was born in Coburg. Being a practical and experienced man, and having a high standard for their productions, the result is an enviable notoriety, extending far beyond the trade of Hartford.

Jacobs & Forbes, Importers and Jobbers in Crockery, China, Glass, Silver, Tin and Woodenware, No. 412 Main Street.—This firm is an illustration of "a union of hearts and a union of hands" from boyhood. It was formed in 1870, and established at No. 606 Main street, and enlarged, it taking in 608 to 614, and moving to their present location, 412 Main street, in 1881. Their store is centrally located in the midst of the rush and bustle of the retail trade, on the principal business thoroughfare of the city. The stock consists of a large variety of plain and ornamental crockery, china and glassware, solid silver and plated ware, tin and woodenware. The record of the firm and how it was formed, the good feeling always existing from boyhood between the members, shows how two friends, having confidence in each other's honesty and ability, unconsciously unite their forces and, like this prosperous firm, never sever them. The two were boys together and worked at the same bench as apprentices to the gun trade in Colt's armory.

Mr. Henry M. Jacobs is a native of Columbia, Conn., born in 1843, educated at an academy, and came to Hartford in 1860. In addition to being a member of this firm, he finds time to attend to the business of a contractor as member of the firm of Howe & Jacobs, at Colt's armory. He served his country by being detailed to work on guns at the armory, instead of using them at the front.

Ellery S. Forbes was born at East Hartford in 1840, was educated at the East Hartford Academy and at the then well-known and popular school of

Mr. Sol. Phelps. He has always resided in and been identified with his native town and enjoys the confidence and respect of the entire community, as has been shown in his election to represent them in the State Legislature during the session of 1880-81.

Both gentlemen are well-known, active, efficient and successful business men, of unusual social and business qualifications.

E. M. Dickinson, Dealer in Leaf Tobacco, No. 230 State Street.—Chief among the industries for which Hartford is noted is the dealing in leaf tobacco.

The stranger will observe, on a walk through the business center, the number of houses dealing in this important production.

Among the younger and most enterprising dealers is Mr. Eliada M. Dickinson, whose office is at No. 230 State street, where he has been established since 1877.

Mr. Dickinson's advent in this trade was as agent for Mr. C. Taylor, with whom he learned and mastered its details, after which he entered it on his own account. He was born in Marlboro, Conn., in 1854, and educated at the Providence Conference Seminary, East Greenwich, R. I.

Although a comparatively young man in the tobacco trade of Hartford, he is one of the most progressive. He is highly esteemed and is recognized as a most excellent citizen.

Joseph W. Baker, Flour and Provisions, No. 212 State Street.—This business was established by Mr. Joseph W. Baker at its present location in May, 1882. He deals in the best brands of Flour, from the principal markets of the West, South and East, and also is a pork packer and provision dealer at both wholesale and retail.

Mr. Baker was born at Windsor, Conn., in 1830, and was first identified with Hartford as a business man in 1860. He was educated in the public schools of his native town at first, and after at Wilbraham, Mass. He employs about seven competent assistants in the prosecution of his business, which extends throughout the city and adjacent country.

He resides in and is identified in many ways with his native town, although his business connections are wholly with this city.

In Windsor he was selectman of the town during the years of 1877, '78 and '79, inclusive. His religious tendencies are shown in his occupying the positions of superintendent of the Sabbath-school, and treasurer of and chorister in the Windsor Congregational church.

Reliable and trustworthy in all matters, Mr. Baker has by over twenty years of an active life secured the confidence of the public as a thoroughly conscientious business man and citizen.

A. Blumenthal & Son (I. Blumenthal), Dealers in Draught, Coach, Driving and Farm Horses, No. 629 North Main Street.—The firm of Blumenthal & Son is probably the largest of its kind in Connecticut, transacting a yearly trade amounting to about $40,000, and dealing all over the State. Their extensive premises at No. 629 North Main street consists of three stables, a large sales-yard, and an office where there are sold or exchanged an average of 500 horses a year. The elder Mr. Blumenthal, the founder of the business, was born in Germany, in the year 1812, and remained in his native country until he was 33 years of age, when he came to America. Two weeks were spent in New York, after which he located in Hartford, where he has resided for a continuous term of thirty-six years. His first business venture was as the proprietor of a grocery store at the corner of Front and Temple streets. This was continued for some years and until Mr. Blumenthal entered his present business, about 20 years ago. Mr. Blumenthal, who was the third native of Germany to make his residence in Hartford, has the reputation of being a thoroughly honest business man, who has the interests of his adopted city at heart, and who has done much for its advancement. He was one of the gentlemen who organized at their own expense the celebrated military company known as the Seymour Light Cavalry. He is the father of a large family, all of whom have become celebrated for their musical talent and its exercise in the cause of charity.

Mr. Isaac Blumenthal, the son, is a native of Hartford, born in 1855, and has lived here all his life, entering early into his father's business and becoming a thorough master of its details. As a business man he has won success as well as reputation, and bids fair to be a worthy successor to the good name of his father. In politics, like his father—who has refused tempting offers of political preferment—he is only active to the extent of supporting the best men. As a prominent member of the Governor's Horse Guard, and in social life generally, he is regarded as a pleasant associate.

Buckley & Griffin (John Buckley and Daniel J. Griffin), American and China Tea Company, and Importers and Wholesale Dealers in Wines, Liquors, etc., Nos. 475 and 477 Main Street. —The firm of Buckley & Griffin was formed on February 1, 1882, and succeeded to a business established about fourteen years ago by the late M. C. Needham, who died about five years since, and whose estate continued the business until its purchase by the present firm. The premises occupied by the business of this house consists of two stores and basements at Nos. 475 and 477 Main street, each about 20 x 75 feet in size. The northernmost of the stores is devoted to the wholesaling and retailing of teas, coffees, flour, canned goods, spices, and other high-class groceries, while in the other is transacted a wholesale and retail trade in wines, liquors, etc., especial attention and prominence being given to the wholesale branch. The trade of the house extends throughout Connecticut and into Massachusetts, and some of the other New England States, giving employment to three traveling salesmen, in addition to the nine people employed about the premises. The stock carried by the firm amounts in value from $15,000 to $20,000, and the annual business to $100,000. A feature of this business, and one not often found among mercantile houses, is an invariable rule to purchase for cash only, thereby rendering necessary the employment of a much larger capital than is usually embarked in houses of like size and character.

Mr. John Buckley, the senior partner, is a native of Ireland, and is about forty-five years of age. He came to this country when but a boy and has been a resident of Hartford for more than thirty years. For many years, and up to the time he entered his present business, he was a partner in the railroad depot restaurants in New York, Bridgeport and Hartford, a business in which he won a wide acquaintance, an enviable business reputation and an ample fortune.

Mr. Daniel J. Griffin is also a native of Ireland, and is thirty-four years of age. He has resided in the United States for eighteen years, four years of which were spent in New York City, and the remainder, with the exception of three years passed at the Yale Law School, in Hartford. He was in mercantile life some years prior to entering the law school, as well as in the office of Hon. Henry C. Robinson, of Hartford, where he pursued a course of preparatory study. Subsequent to his term at Yale he practiced at the bar in Hartford for three years, relinquishing the practice of his profession to re-enter the more lucrative walks of business.

This firm occupies a position in the front rank of Hartford's business houses, and its members are universally esteemed and respected.

Brown & Gross, Publishers, Booksellers and Stationers, Nos. 77 and 79 Asylum Street.—The history of this well-known and long-established house is closely allied to the literary record of Hartford and the State of Connecticut. In 1835, when the city was comparatively a village and Trinity College was on the site now occupied by the Capitol building, Mr. F. A. Brown embarked in the business of a bookseller on State street. Later the business was removed to Main, corner of Asylum street. Since 1838 the business has been conducted under the firm names of Brown & Parsons and Brown & Gross, as successors to F. A. Brown, the founder. The latter firm has been known to the reading public as publishers and booksellers since 1858.

Mr. F. A. Brown died Feb. 13th, 1880, at the ripe age of seventy-three. For many years he was an important factor in the educational world of Hartford, and for a long time was Town and City Treasurer. His store was the resort of the lovers of books, and his influence can never be estimated. In 1869 the business was removed to the present location at 77 and 79 Asylum street. The premises are 30 x 70 feet, with basement. The present members of the firm are Mr. Wm. H. Gross and Mr. Leverett Belknap, who transact business under the name of Brown & Gross. As publishers they have a well-earned and widespread reputation in school and college text-books, of which the following are the most prominent: Alcestis of Euripides, Antigone of Sophocles, Electra of Sophocles, Gorgias of Plato, Prometheus of Æschylus; all with notes by President Woolsey of Yale; Swift's Natural Philosophies, Robbin's Outlines of History, Connecticut State Register, Connecticut Civil Officers, Catalogue of the Connecticut Volunteer Organizations in the Service of the United States, 1861-65; Hollister's History of Connecticut, etc., etc. As booksellers and stationers they are probably the largest in Hartford, if not in the State.

Mr. William H. Gross, the senior member, is a native of Hartford. Previous to becoming a member of this firm he was clerk in the publishing houses of Wm. James Hamersley and of Messrs. A. S. Barnes & Co. in New York. Mr. Leverett Belknap, the junior member, is also a native of Hartford, born in 1851. He became identified with this house when a boy of thirteen, and a partner in 1880. As publishers of educational books they surpass all others in the State, and enjoy the entire confidence of the public.

E. S. Kendall & Co., Proprietors of the "Hub" Clothing House, No. 141 Asylum St., opposite Allyn House.—Among the larger and more enterprising clothing houses in Hartford is that of E. S. Kendall & Co., at No. 141 Asylum street, corner Trumbull street and opposite the Allyn House. The business was established in 1873, at No. 358 Main street, by Jordan, Clark & Co., of Boston, and was removed in 1874 to Nos. 13 and 15 Asylum street, and in 1878 to its present location. Mr. Kendall succeeded to the proprietorship of the business in 1880, since which time, by careful attention to the wants of the public and liberal and judicious management and advertising, he has succeeded in forcing it to the front rank of the clothing houses of the Capital City. The store, one of the most pleasant and eligibly located in the city, is 35 x 110 feet in size, and, with a basement of like dimensions, is stocked with one of the most complete and extensive assortments of gentlemen's clothing, boys' clothing, etc., to be found in this section of the State. This house is one of a great system of clothing houses extending throughout New England and the West, and has exceptional advantages in the matter of procuring the better classes of goods at the most reasonable prices.

Mr. E. S. Kendall is a native of Massachusetts, and has resided in Hartford since 1873. During his residence here he has won the respect and confidence of the community, and for his house a first class business reputation.

I. B. Davis & Son, Manufacturers of the Berryman Patent Feed Water Heater and Purifier, and the Economic Patent Tank Feed Pump, Cushman Street.—The business of this firm was established in 1872 by the senior member, Mr. I. B. Davis. One year after its inception the business was removed to the two-story building now occupied by them on Cushman street, which is 135 x 42 feet in size, with an L, 30 x 30 feet, and a boiler-house adjoining. A 60-horse power engine of the Conway patent furnishes the motive power, and about thirty people are employed.

This house manufactures the Berryman patent feed water heater and purifier and the Economic patent boiler and tank feed pump, both of which have an extended reputation. The heater and purifier is universally acknowledged by engineers and all who have it in use to be the most perfect device ever discovered for heating and purifying the feed water for steam boilers with exhaust steam.

The Economic patent boiler tank feed pump, patented by Mr. I. B. Davis in 1879, is, as the name implies, an economical method, whereby water is supplied to steam boilers.

Illustrated circulars explain in detail the full advantages and give a long list of patrons, which are found in nearly every State in the Union.

Mr. Davis is a native of Oxford, New Haven County, Conn.; born in 1817. He was educated to the trade of a mason builder, and conducted that business at Seymour, Conn., till 1854, when he removed to Cincinnati, Ohio, where he was a steamboat builder and agent of the Syracuse Coal and Salt Company.

While there he made several improvements in the working and models of the Ohio river boats. He introduced a balanced rudder and revolutionized the models of the boats, whereby 700 tons could be transported as well as 400 tons, and with the same power.

The climate not agreeing with him, he was obliged to sever his valuable business connections, which he did in 1866, when he left there, in the opinion of his physician, to die. But the bracing atmosphere of his native hills resuscitated him, and to-day he is a fine specimen of a healthy man. In 1881, he admitted his son into partnership, since which time, the firm has been I. B. Davis & Son.

John O. Davis, the junior member, was born in Seymour, Conn., October, 1854. He received a preliminary education at Cheshire Academy, which was afterwards completed at the Yale Scientific School. He was, previous to becoming a partner with his father, a clerk for P. Jewell & Sons, in this city.

This house and its productions are known in every State in the Union, and at home it ranks with the best of its class, and its members among the representative citizens of Hartford.

John D. Fisk & Co. (J. D. and Chester D. Fisk), Dealers in Boots, Shoes and Rubbers, Leather and Findings, No. 375 Main St.—The boot, shoe, leather and findings business now carried on by Messrs. John D. Fisk & Co., at the Boston Shoe Store, No. 375 Main street, was established about forty years ago by J. W. Eldridge and Son, who continued it until January, 1880, when they were succeeded by the present proprietors and Mr. Holaday, the latter withdrawing from the concern in April, 1882. The firm occupies a spacious store and basement, doing a general retail business in boots, shoes, rubbers, etc., on the main floor and a jobbing trade in leather and findings down stairs, the whole amounting to $50,000 per annum with a rapid and steady increase from month to month over that average. Four salesmen are employed in the store, while a number of skilled workmen turn out large quantities of fine work, the making to order of which is the specialty of the firm, and in which line, it is claimed, they do the most extensive business in Hartford.

Mr. John D. Fisk, the senior partner in the concern and father of his associate, is a native of Williamstown, Vt., born in 1826. When quite young he moved to Malone, N. Y., where he resided until 1859, occupying a prominent place in its society and holding for several years the office of Town Clerk. From Malone, Mr. Fisk removed to New York City, and was for twenty years and up to the time of his removal to Hartford, with the well-known boot and shoe jobbing house of Nathaniel Fisher & Co., nine years as salesman and eleven as partner. Since his advent in Hartford Mr. Fisk has won the confidence and esteem of the community, and is now universally acknowledged as one of its substantial business men.

Mr. Chester D. Fisk was born in Malone, N. Y., in 1859, and resided in that place until his father removed to New York. For three years prior to his arrival here he was a clerk in the employ of the firm of which the senior Mr. Fisk was a member, and in that time gained the experience which is of such service in his present business.

The house is regarded as one of the rising business houses in Connecticut.

A. Squires & Son (Alvin Squires and Elisha B. Squires), Wholesale Oyster and Provision Dealers, Proprietors of The Putnam Phalanx Market, Nos. 33 to 43 Market Street.—The general provision and oyster business of A. Squires & Son, located on Market street, near State, is the largest of its kind in Hartford, and compares favorably with any in the State. The premises have a frontage of 175 feet and a depth of about twenty-five feet. Here, in addition to a very large retail business in meats, etc., there is carried on the business of pork-packing and the wholesaling of oysters. This firm are the originators and owners of a patent can for the transportation of oysters from any distance, and having retained the entire right in the patent have been enabled to control the market in oysters supplied in cans and refrigerators. These they bring from Chesapeake Bay and other places and deliver all over New England, guaranteeing them to be in as good condition when delivered as they were when opened. The business was established in 1867 by the elder Mr. Squires, the younger gentleman entering the firm in the year 1871. In addition to the large force of assistants employed by the firm to do the work of their trade, there is a boiler and engine used for running machinery for the preparation of sausage and mince-meat, vast quantities of which are made and sold daily.

Mr. Alvin Squires was born in Berlin in this State, in 1821. He was for many years in the steamboat business on the Connecticut River and Long Island Sound, and was commander of the steamer "Mary Benton," running a mail line on Chesapeake Bay, in the employ of the Government during the late war. During his residence in Hartford Mr. Squires has occupied several public positions, notably as a member of the Common Council, to which body he was elected in 1871–2, serving his constituents in an able and thoroughly satisfactory manner. He is also prominent in the historical military organization known as the Putnam Phalanx, in which he holds the office of Quartermaster.

Mr. Elisha B. Squires is a native of Hartford, born in 1850, and has resided here all his life. He is an active and respected member of the Masonic fraternity, and is the youngest man in the State who has attained to the thirty-second degree in that organization. He is looked upon as one of the rising young business men of Hartford, and a pleasant factor in its social life. The rise and growth of this house is a salient feature in the business history of Connecticut, and a pleasing evidence of what honesty and industry can accomplish.

W. H. Abelle, Dealer in Fancy Groceries, Teas, Coffees and Flour, No. 474 Main Street.—This business was established by Abelle & Lyman. The present proprietor, Mr. W. H. Abelle succeeded in September, 1881, since which time he has developed a business of no mean magnitude. Occupying a position at the corner of two thoroughfares and carrying a large and fine stock he offers unusual inducements to the public. The store is large and attractive in appearance, and in its arrangement affords every opportunity to display, in his usual artistic manner, the specialties of his trade. His customers are found in all sections of the city and in most of the surrounding towns. Mr. Abelle is one of the young, energetic business men who, as a rule, carve a name and a place for themselves wherever they are. The amount of business transacted exceeds $50,000 per annum. Mr. Abelle is a native of Franklin, Conn., born in 1848. His name is another in the list of successful young men who come to Hartford to win their way to ultimate success.

Wm. Boardman & Sons [Established 1841], Wholesale Dealers in Fine Teas, Pure Coffees and Spices, Tobaccos, Cigars and Grocers' Sundries, No. 304 Asylum Street.—In 1841 Mr. William Boardman, the senior member of the present firm, established himself in his present business in Wethersfield, continuing there until May, 1850, when he removed to Hartford, and with his son, Mr. William F. J. Boardman, established a house at No. 12 Central Row. In 1853 Mr. Thos. J. Boardman was admitted to the firm and removal was had to their store, No. 109 State street, which had been purchased by the firm, and fitted up with a steam engine of large capacity, the latest and most approved machinery added, and otherwise increasing the facilities for business. They remained at that location for about fifteen years, removing thence to No. 205 on the same street, still keeping the old store as a manufactory, and finally, in 1872, to the building on Asylum street, which they built of Portland freestone the year previous, and which is still the property of the firm. This building is a structure that is characterized as one of the most beautiful and commanding buildings in the city of Hartford. It is 52½ feet front and 100 feet deep, five stories high, and containing on the ground floor two stores, one of which is used by the firm. Besides the store, there is a basement where much of the stock is handled, and on the second and third floors are large store-rooms containing the surplus that attends a business of this kind. In the rear of the main building is a three-story brick factory, 40x60 feet in size, where the special brands of coffees are roasted and ground, as also their pure spices, for which the firm is noted. The stock carried averages about $35,000, while the annual business foots up to the very respectable figure of $350,000. In the store and factory there are employed an average of fifteen hands, most of the work being done by machinery. A complete assortment of the latest improved patterns being driven by an engine of twenty-five-horse power, supplied by a sixty-horse power boiler, which also performs the duty of hoisting, and heating the building.

This house is the oldest in the manufacturing line in New England, with a single exception, and ranks among the foremost. Its trade covers a wide extent of territory, but is chiefly in New England and New York.

Mr. William Boardman is descended from a long line of Connecticut ancestors, extending as far back as the year 1636, sixteen years after the landing of the Pilgrims at Plymouth Rock, and the same year that Roger Williams fled from the persecutions of his Massachusetts brethren, and found a welcome among the hospitable dwellers of the wilderness, in what is now the State of Rhode Island.

About this time the ancester of Mr. William Boardman, Mr. Samuel Boardman, emigrated to this country from England. Judge Royal R. Hinman, in his catalogue of the first Puritan settlers of the Colony of Connecticut, says: "Few of the first settlers came with a better reputation, or sustained it more uniformly through life, than Mr. Samuel Boardman."

Mr. William Boardman was born in Lenox, Berkshire County, Mass., in 1805, and moved to Wethersfield, Conn., with his parents when he was quite young. He was a printer by trade, serving his apprenticeship in the office of the Hartford "Times."

Mr. Boardman associated himself with Mr. William Faulkner, and under the firm name of Messrs. Boardman & Faulkner commenced in 1828 the publication of the Norwich "Republican," now the Norwich "Bulletin." It supported General Jackson for the Presidency, and was the second Jackson paper in the State. It had a fair circulation, and politically and financially was a success.

At the close of the first year he retired from the business, selling his interest to his partner and returned to Wethersfield.

In the year 1832, he, with Mr. Alfred Francis, engaged in the printing business in Wethersfield, where they published, by subscription, the Life and Correspondence of Thomas Jefferson, by Mr. B. L. Rayner, which was well received and had a large sale.

In addition to the printing and publishing business he found time, with others, to form a joint stock company for the manufacture of "Holbrook's School Apparatus," which they carried on by State Prison labor. He was president and treasurer of the company and had entire management of it until other business interests became so extensive that he was obliged to sell out and retire. He also assisted in organizing the Comstock, Ferre Co., a corporation for the growing and importing of every variety of garden seeds, which has a world-wide reputation. He was a stockholder and director in this company until he came to Hartford, at which time he disposed of his interest in the same.

Mr. Boardman is one of the oldest men in active business in the State of Connecticut, and is a fitting example of what a poor boy, without many opportunities can do in the great battle of life. Success seems to have crowned all enterprises with which he has been connected. Perhaps this is due in a great measure to his moral stamina—to a principle never to violate his promise or agreement but to fulfill each to the letter. This has resulted so that his credit in the financial world has always been of he best and his name has never come in dispute ith the business community

In Hartford he has occupied—as in other communities—prominent position, having been a Member of the Legislature and County Commissioner, besides being director in the old Hartford County, Bank, the Hartford Life and Health Insurance Co. the Orient Fire Insurance Co., and the Merrick Thread Co. of Holyoke, Mass. Other public positions have worn his name with honor, and he is universally regarded as an honorable business man and a worthy citizen.

In reviewing the history of this busy life, it will be observed the direct and indirect influence Mr. William Boardman has exerted in the literary, political and financial world. As one of the founders of the Norwich "Republican," now the "Bulletin," he was largely instrumental in the election of General Jackson to the Presidency.

It may safely be said that he was the pioneer in the great subscription book publishing business of which Hartford is the recognized centre.

He was foremost in the establishment of the great seed house of Comstock, Ferre & Co., whose name is known to every farmer's boy in America; and last, but not least, the founder of the oldest and largest coffee and spice house, with a single exception, in New England.

Mr. William F. J. Boardman is a native of Wethersfield, born in 1828. He has resided in Hartford since 1850, and was selected in 1863 to represent the citizens of the Third Ward in the Common Council, a position which history credits him with having filled with marked ability and thorough honesty. As one of the directors of the State Bank, he applied to its affairs the same administrative ability and sagacity that has characterized the conduct of his own business and which has tended so largely to its success.

Mr. Thomas J. Boardman is also a native of Wethersfield, and was born in 1832. Like his brother, he came to Hartford in 1850, and made it his permanent residence. He is also a member of J. W. Starkweather & Co., large lumber dealers, in this city. Close application to business has left him neither the time nor the desire to enjoy the honors and suffer the cares of political life, and he has, therefore, no salient point for the historian save the fact that among the many respected business men in New England he stands without a superior.

E. M. Roberts & Son. Dealers in and Manufacturers of Solid Silver and Plated Ware, No. 68 Market Street.—It is a recognized fact that the skill, progress, and refinement of a community are represented in its productions.

This is shown in ancient and modern history. The architecture of the ancients never was improved, the art of the old masters was never equaled, the blades of Damascus yet rank as the best.

In the new world we are fast arriving at the standard of the old in most matters, and for excelling them in others.

In no production do we excel more than in the manufacture of solid silverware here in this city, the richest of its size in America, noted for its educational advantages, and the refinement of its people, we should, as a natural sequence, expect the finest productions, requiring the best artistic skill of its educated artizans.

The growth of the solid silver and plated ware manufacturing interest in and about Hartford, for the past twenty-five years, has been surprising.

The amount of capital employed and the number of people engaged at that time were comparatively small. To-day that industry ranks among the first in the State.

One of the pioneers was the house of J. O. & W. Pitkin, who for a long time prosecuted the business at East Hartford. With them Mr. E. M. Roberts, the senior partner of the firm of which we write, learned his trade, and on the dissolution of the firm was a partner with Mr. John O. Pitkin as successor. It is not generally known that these pioneers are still alive and well. Mr. John O. Pitkin counts his years at eighty-five, and resides on his farm at Coventry, Conn., and his brother, Mr. Walter Pitkin, is a resident of Washington, D. C.

The apprentice and afterwards partner, conducted the business at the old place till it was destroyed by fire in 1879, when the business was removed to Trumbull street in this city. Finding the place too small to accommodate their increasing business, they removed on May 1, 1880, to their present location, when the present firm of E. M. Roberts & Son was founded, and where spacious floors and every convenience is afforded, and in the centre of business, near to the principal promenade and the larger hotels.

Here they manufacture the most elegant and costly designs possible of solid silver and plated ware, as well as transact an extensive business, as gold, silver and licensed nickel platers.

The processes through which their wares go is indeed interesting.

The solid silver used in the business comes in fifty-ounce bars. It is first melted into moulds, and rolled down to a required thickness; a dozen sets of spoons being the outcome of the fifty-ounce bar. The silver as moulded is, after a process of splitting, "struck up" in a die, giving shape to the article desired. Filing and stoned, the article is then ready for the burnishing, this latter being done, however, with solid silver and best plated work, polishing only being considered sufficient for the inferior grades of plated ware. From the burnisher or polisher the ware goes to the etching department, where the elegance and artistic finishing is done.

The word, sentence, or design, to ornament the ware is first engraved on steel or copper plate, an operation, by the way, very expensive. Ink is then run into the engraved parts the plate heated and put through a press where impressions are made on small strips of paper. The transfer of these papers is again transferred to the ware, which is soon after varnished by a secret process that washes away the ink, and forms the letter or design.

The various processes through which an article is put are very interesting. The result is elegant silver and plated ware, lasting for generations.

Mr. E. M. Roberts, the senior member of the house, is a native of East Hartford, Conn, and is sixty-three years of age. He has for many years applied himself to this business, the choice of his youth, in which he takes the keenest interest. No fertile fields of the West have enticed him away from his native town and his chosen pursuit, and he has been content to remain in one vocation, with one ambition, to manufacture and excel in the production of solid silverware.

That he has been successful is attested by the large business done by the firm, which is driven to the utmost to fill its orders.

Mr. Roberts still resides in Hartford, where he has earned by an upright life of probity and Christian example, the entire confidence of his fellow-citizens, and ranks among the oldest and most reliable silver workers in New England.

The active business and financial manager is the son, Mr. Joseph W. Roberts, a native of East Hartford, and twenty-four years of age.

Like his father, who established the house, he was educated to the business in the manufacturing establishment of the company, and now has general superintendence over its affairs. He pays strict attention to business, takes a pride in keeping up a uniform standard in the wares turned out, and the trade finds him a prompt and reliable person with which to form business relations.

Mr. Wallace N. Kenyon, the junior member, was born in New Britain, Conn., in 1854.

Upon his taste and discrimination as etcher, the firm mostly depends for the decoration of its wares. In addition to the etching for the firm, they have contracts with several large silver plate manufacturers in New England and the West for whom they do the etching, which is not only done by Mr. Kenyon on gold and silver, but on steel, ivory, and pearl.

The history of Mr. Kenyon is similar to many of our successful merchants and manufacturers. His father died when he was a babe, and he was left to battle with the world's stern realities.

From that time to this, without financial aid, he has worked his way up, and became a member of one the oldest and most reliable houses in their line in the Union. He possesses a thorough knowledge of his business, and is recognized as one of the most skilled etchers in the country.

While the trade of the house is mostly in Boston, it has customers in New York, the larger cities of the great West, and other commercial centres, where it ranks artistically and financially as among the first silverware manufacturers in America.

James G. Welles & Co., China, Glass and Earthenware, No. 27 Asylum Street.—The business of this house dates back to 1820, when Mr. Peter Morton was a well-known merchant at the corner of State and Front streets. During the past three-score years and three the house has continued uninterruptedly its successful career, but under different heads and management, and always a leading one to the present day.

In 1832 the house was known as Messrs. Bergh & Boughton. In 1840 Mr. Bergh retired and went to New York City, Mr. Boughton continuing till 1842, when Mr. Charles Mygatt assumed the business. In 1843 it was Mr. John S. Gray, and in 1846 Mr. James G. Welles, the present senior proprietor. Soon after it was Messrs. Welles & Goodwin, until 1856, when Mr. Goodwin retired and Mr. James G. Welles was again sole proprietor until 1862. In that year the house removed its business to No. 27 Asylum street, where it has since continued for more than twenty years. At the same time a brother, Mr. Charles B. Welles, was admitted a partner, and the firm name made Messrs. James G. Welles & Co., which continued till July, 1882, when a new company was formed under the same name, a silent partner being admitted, which arrangement still continues. The store is located in the centre of business, and is one of the largest and finest of its class in the State. Two large plate-glass show windows ornament the front, and the stock contains all of the imported novelties usually found in first-class stores of this nature. A large basement below is used as a sales and store room.

While the business is mostly retail, quite a wholesale trade is done with the towns in the State.

Mr. James G. Welles is a native of East Hartford ; born in 1821. He was educated at the East Hartford Academy and has been a well-known merchant here for forty-four years. During his long residence in Hartford he has taken active interest in its institutions. For several years he was Captain of the Governor's Foot Guard, in which organization he takes great pride. He has been a member of St. John's Episcopal Church for forty years, thirty of which as a warden and vestryman, and is also treasurer of the Widows' Home. He long ago established himself in the confidence of his fellow citizens, and is one of Hartford's representative men, noted for his interest in benevolent institutions.

Charles Teske & Co., Practical Watchmakers, Inventors and Manufacturers of the Mathematical Watch Regulator, for American and Foreign Watches, No. 214 Asylum Street.—The State of Connecticut is remarkable in the fact that within her borders can be found a greater number of skilled workmen and inventors than in any other State in the Union of like dimensions. Prominent among these may be mentioned Mr. Charles Teske of the above-named firm, the subject of this sketch, whose constantly growing business is a conclusive evidence of his skill and reliability. As a watchmaker and repairer, Mr. Teske is without a superior and a large proportion of the finest time-pieces owned in Hartford and vicinity find their way to his store where the mistakes of less able workmen are rectified. While Mr. Teske does a large business in the regular line of his calling, he has a specialty which bids fair to make his name a household word among watch owners and to result in that wealth which is the common aim. This specialty is the manufacture and sale of a simple yet effective device for the close regulation of watches, and is known as Teske's Patent Watch Regulator. This regulator can be moved the ten thousandth part of an inch with a common pin used by the owner. It was invented by Mr. Teske some years ago, and is covered by patents issued in 1874, 1875, and 1881. It is manufactured on the premises in a workshop containing a large number of expensive lathes, dies, punches, tapping machines, etc., the power being supplied by an improved water motor. The manufacture of these regulators is personally superintended by Mr. Teske, and about a half dozen skilled workmen are constantly employed. This invention, at once simple and effective, commends itself at sight and is already meeting with a large sale in all parts of the country, besides having been adopted by the Hampden Watch Company of Springfield, Mass., who give it their unqualified indorsement, not only by applying it to their watches, but by certificates of merit granted to the inventor.

Mr. Teske is a native of Prussia, where he was born in 1847. He came to America in 1869, and located in Albany, whence he removed successively to Balston Spa, Saratoga, and Hartford, arriving here in 1877, and immediately establishing himself in business. He has occupied his present location about two years, in which time he has succeeded by the faithfulness and excellence of his workmanship and the sale of only first-class goods, in building up a connection of which he may be justly proud. Mr. Teske stands in high repute with the business community and is looked upon as one of the progressive men of Hartford.

Arthur H. Eddy, Sole Manufacturer of the Mather Dynamo-Electric Machine, No. 68 Market Street.—The average New England mechanic is by nature an inventor. Statistics show that more patents are applied for by natives of New England than from any other locality in the United States. Hundreds of establishments having for their central figure a patent, are yearly started in this section of the country, and it is from these small beginnings grow the large representative establishments, occupying immense buildings, employing thousands of people, and necessitating millions of money to conduct them.

The history of the house of Mr. Arthur H. Eddy shows how, from an idea worked out by one of these inventors and protected by a United States patent, advances already a new process, making it still more useful and valuable. We refer to the Mather dynamo-electric machine for plating and electrotyping, manufactured by Mr. Eddy. The advantages of the dynamo-electric machine for plating and electrotyping are so decided that they have led to the introduction of a large number of machines for that purpose. The Mather dynamo-electric machine is an improvement on all others invented.

The manufacturer occupies one floor, 135 x 30 feet, in the large brick building at No. 68 Market street, for assembling and finishing machines, and in addition, he is designer and builder of special electric apparatus. Mr. Eddy was born in New Britain, Conn., in 1857, and after a preparatory course in the public schools of his native town, he attended the Rensselaer Polytechnic Institute at Troy, where he took a special course as draughtsman and mechanical engineer, after which he was two years at the Corliss Steam Engine Works, Providence, R. I., and two years at a large establishment in this city. This experience gave him a practical education that is now showing financial results in his present business.

Previous to December 1, 1881, the date of his establishment here, he was for one year in charge of the Connecticut Telephone Exchange, a position he filled with honor and fidelity. It was here that he made a study of electricity, for which his previous training had more generally fitted him. His career is a fitting example for other young men to follow, for he has earned an enviable reputation as one of the most successful young mechanical engineers and reliable business men in Hartford.

H. R. Gridley, Dealer in Doors, Windows and Blinds, also Paints, Oils and Glass, No. 88 Market Street.—For many years this stand has been known in connection with the door, sash and blind trade. The first man who was indentified with it was Mr. Richard Josyln, who, in turn, was succeeded in 1878 by the present proprietor, Mr. H. R. Gridley. The location is one of the most central in Hartford, one block from State street, and one from Main street, at No. 88 Market, corner Temple street. The stock, which is stored in a large, imposing building, consists of doors, windows, blinds, fine inside shutters and blinds, glass, oils, paints, colors, putty, etc., a specialty being made of hardwood work.

Mr. Gridley is a native of Berlin, Conn., having been born in the year 1830.

After a thorough education in the schools of his native town, and later at Westfield, Mass., he came to Hartford in the year 1848.

For more than twenty years previous to 1878 he was a well-known hardware merchant in this city, during which time the extended acquaintance formed has proven of great advantage in the prosecution of his present business.

His reputation for reliability has contributed in no small degree to his well-merited success.

Carpenter & Bartlett (W. O. Carpenter and E. S. Bartlett), successors to Henry Albro & Co., Dealers in Paper-stock, Rags, Metals, Waste, etc., No. 190 Front street.—About forty-five years ago, Mr. Nelson Hollister, founded the business now carried on by Messrs. Carpenter & Bartlett and conducted it till the year 1867, when he disposed of it to Mr. Henry Albro. In 1871 Mr. Carpenter became a member of the firm of Henry Albro & Co., and was followed eight years later by Mr. Bartlett, who for two years had been in the waste business at No. 75 Ferry street. In May, 1882, Mr. Albro died and Messrs. Carpenter & Bartlett succeeded to the entire business.

The history of Mr. Albro is so full of point and example, that it is thought well in this connection to give a brief outline of it.

He was born in Eastford, Conn., in 1833, and up to his twentieth year received no education, being debarred from attending school by the fact that he was almost helplessly an invalid. Determining to do something in life, Mr. Albro at this period began studying on his own account, and learned, besides the necessary business knowledge, the trade of shoemaking. We next find him with a horse and wagon traveling from place to place and buying rags, paper, etc., laying the foundation for the great business he left at his death. The first record of his appearance in the business circles of Hartford was as senior member of the firm of Albro & Morey, paper-stock dealers on Morgan street. This continued about one year, when Mr. Albro purchased Mr. Morey's interest and carried on the business on his own account until the change which made the firm William McCrone & Co. In 1866 Mr. Albro left Connecticut and established himself in business at Rock Island, Illinois. Here he remained only a short time, returning to Hartford in 1867 and purchasing the business of which this sketch treats. At this time Mr. Albro's capital amounted to only about $2,000, and his first year's business reached only about twice and a half times that figure. From 1867 to 1882, the business advanced with such rapid strides that in the latter year the books of the firm showed transactions to the amount of $250,000 and the further fact that about $100,000 capital is now invested.

Personally, Mr. Albro was remarkable. He suffered all his life with an incurable lameness and the lack of many of the advantages of early training, yet, notwithstanding these serious drawbacks he made a name, a place and a fortune of which the most favored of mortals might be proud. As a counselor to the young business man and an adviser of his fellows he was especially gifted and sought after, and it was rarely the case that results did not attest his excellent judgment. In East Hartford, where he passed his later life, the respect and confidence of his fellow citizens were shown by selecting him as a Justice of the Peace, an office that he filled with dignity and ability. He was also prominently connected with the schools, and labored hard in the interests of the early education which had been denied in his own case.

He passed away full of honor and riches and left behind him a name as spotless as the snow, a memory as sweet as summer roses are, and a void in business and social life not easily to be filled.

The business done by Messrs. Carpenter & Bartlett is the largest general business of the kind in the State. There are some other houses who transact more business in some one of the specialties, but as general dealers in paper stock, cotton and woolen rags, old metals, waste, etc., this house undoubtedly takes the lead. The building owned and occupied by the firm runs from Front street through to Charles street, and is 45 x 186 feet in size and has four floors crowded with baled and unbaled stock and the seventy men and women employed in sorting, grading, sacking, receiving, shipping and baling the immense quantities of merchandise handled by the house. In the rear of the building is a large iron yard, with about 160 feet of sheds, where tons of iron are being constantly received from all parts of the country and shipped to the foundries and machine shops in Hartford and vicinity. The business is divided into five departments, each with its superintendent, while the members of the firm themselves superintend the whole. Most of the work done here is necessarily performed by hand, and a walk through the establishment discloses nothing in the shape of machinery, save an immensely powerful press, in which an astonishingly great quantity of rags or paper is compressed into a surprisingly small bale. Besides this there are numberless scales, ranging from the great "Howe," of eight tons, in the yard, where loaded teams are weighed, through all sizes of platform and balance, down to the old-fashioned steel yard, used when the business was in its infancy. Most of these are used in the business of the house, but they serve the needs of others, Messrs. Carpenter & Bartlett being "City Weighers" by appointment of the Common Council. One of the peculiarities of this business is that all purchases are strictly cash, while the sales are made on time, as in other establishments. This, it will be seen, renders the employment of large capital necessary, and it is believed that in this respect Messrs. Carpenter & Bartlett lead all their associates.

Mr. William O. Carpenter was born in Eastford, Conn., in 1845. He remained there until he was twelve years of age, attending the public school. His education was finished in the Danielsonville Select School, after leaving which place he became a school teacher, and taught for two terms in Putnam and Sterling. Seeking more active business he came to Hartford and secured employment driving an express wagon. One year later found him employed as foreman in the flouring mills of W. B. Willard, Esq., where he remained for six years, leaving to accept an appointment on the police force. Here he remained for two years, and having managed to accumulate a few hundred dollars, bought into the firm of Henry Albro & Co., and began the building of the good fortune that has since attended him. Mr. Carpenter resided in East Hartford for some years, and was constable of that place for a long time.

Mr. Edwin S. Bartlett is a native of Woodstock, in this State, born in 1844. He remained at home until 1862; when he joined the ranks of the Eighteenth Connecticut Volunteers, a regiment raised in New London and Windham counties, enlisting for three years. He was taken prisoner while under General Sigel in the Shenandoah Valley, and imprisoned in Lynchburg, Danville and Andersonville, respectively, being paroled from the horrors of the latter place permanently disabled for service and weighing but seventy-five pounds. After spending some months in the Dale United States General Hospital at Worcester, Mass., he was so far recovered as to be able to come to Hartford and enter the Bryant & Stratton Business College, from which institution he graduated an accomplished bookkeeper and business man. He found employment as bookkeeper in the lumber yard of H. C. Burgess, and subsequently with W. T. McLean, dealer in paper stock. In 1866 he bought Mr. McLean's business and continued it until 1871, when, in company with Mr. Albro, he purchased the paper mill at Windsor Locks. This enterprise was given up by the firm in 1874, and Mr. Bartlett returned to Hartford and engaged in the waste business on joint account with Henry Albro & Co. This he continued until 1879, when the businesses were consolidated and he became a member of the firm. Mr. Bartlett resided for some years in East Hartford, where he was active in school matters, and in East Windsor from 1871 until two years ago, occupying the responsible position of Town Auditor for several years.

The history of the house of Carpenter & Bartlett, and of its predecessor, Henry Albro & Co., as well as the personal history of the individual members, is full of pleasant suggestion as to the possibilities of energy and honesty, and furnishes an example for the aspiring young men of to-day to follow.

S. Maslen & Co. (Stephen and James Maslen), Monuments, Grave Stones, Mantels, Grates, etc., No. 352 Asylum Street.—The flourishing business conducted by this firm was established in 1869 by Williams & Cook, at the corner of Maple avenue and Congress street, and was purchased a year later by Mr. Stephen Maslen. In 1873 Mr. Maslen's brothers, James and John, were admitted to co-partnership, the latter's interest being purchased by the present members of the firm in 1882, in August of which year the business was removed to the quarters it now occupies. The warerooms on Asylum street consists of two floors, each 23x80 feet in size, where all the finer work, such as sculpture and ornamenting, is done, and where the goods are exposed for sale. In the rear of the store is a large yard, in which a portion of the rougher work is accomplished and which is used for storing the large stones used in the building of monuments. The specialty of this firm is the manufacture of monuments from all kinds of stone, in the preparation of which they have from forty to fifty men engaged at the quarries in Quincy, Mass., Millstone, Conn., and Westerly, R.I. The annual volume of business now transacted by S. Maslen & Co. amounts to about $40,000, the trade having almost doubled within a year. This is confined almost entirely to Hartford and its immediate vicinity, although orders are received and filled for more remote localities. Among the many beautiful monuments that adorn the cemeteries of Hartford can be found numerous specimens of the Messrs. Maslen's handiwork, the chief of them being, perhaps, the elegant monument to the memory of ex-Governor Thomas H. Seymour, erected at Cedar Hills Cemetery in 1881, great crowds of people attending its dedication. The monument is Egyptian in style, 33 feet in height, about 50 tons in weight, and in its artistic finish reflects great credit on the firm who executed it.

Mr. Stephen Maslen was born in England in 1845. He arrived in America in 1863, and almost immediately began the study of the business of which he is now a master in all its branches. Boston and Worcester were the scenes of his earlier labors, and it was in the former city that he attained to a knowledge of the finer branches of sculpture, the results of which are conspicuous in the work turned out by this firm.

Mr. Maslen has resided in Hartford for about twelve years, and has been prominently identified with church matters, first as a committeeman at the South Baptist church and subsequently, for four years, as precentor at the Centre church, and in the same capacity for one year at the Asylum Hill Congregational church.

Mr. James Maslen, like his brother, is a native of England, and was born in 1843, arriving in America in 1861. He is a practical man in his business, having learned it in Boston, where he resided until about ten years ago, when he removed to Hartford. He has been for seven years, and is still, superintendent of the Sunday School Mission in Parkville, where he has done much for the advancement of the interests of religion.

Both gentlemen are good examples of the success which is sure to follow a life of probity and Christianity.

James Ahern, Practical Plumber and Gas Fitter, Dealer in all kinds of Plumbing and Gas Fitting Materials, No. 280 Asylum Street.—The plumbing and gas-fitting establishment of Mr. James Ahern, situated at No. 280 Asylum street, is probably one of the finest and most completely stocked of any of its kind in New England, and is the headquarters of a very extensive business.

Mr. Ahern began business in Hartford in 1868, locating himself at No. 272 Main street, where he remained until May 1, 1882, when the demands of his growing business compelled his removal to the elegant and roomy premises he now occupies.

The volume of business transacted yearly by Mr. Ahern amounts to $25,000 or $30,000, and requires the assistance of from twelve to sixteen workmen, the latter number being largely augmented in the busy season.

The premises occupied by this business consist of a lofty ceiled store and workshop extending from Asylum street through to a small street in the rear, where all goods are received and shipped. The store, including the workshop, has a frontage of twenty-five feet by a depth of ninety feet, and is stocked with a full line of plumbers' and gas fitters' materials, pipe, fixtures, etc., besides a large and elegant assortment of the latest designs in gas fixtures from the manufactory of Mitchell, Vance & Co., of New York, for which house Mr. Ahern is sole agent in Hartford County.

In the workshop—a model of its kind—there is to be found everything in the way of materials and tools that is required for any part of the plumbers' and gas fitters' business. Neatly arranged along the sides are numberless compartment shelves, containing every kind and size of fittings for gas and water known to the trade, while on the benches may be found a complete assortment of fine tools of every description used in the business. In the centre of the shop stands a machine driven by steam power and used for cutting and threading iron pipe. This machine saves much time and labor, and is so absolutely accurate in its operation that the tightness of the joints made by it can be relied on with perfect assurance.

In the basement there are stored immense quantities of cast and wrought iron pipe, fittings, etc., and there is no contract so large or varied in its nature that Mr. Ahern is not prepared to fill from his immediate stock.

The trade of this house is not confined to Hartford, but extends to other portions of the State, many of the finer residences outside the city having been fitted by Mr. Ahern. This extent of business is due in great measure to the fact that Mr. Ahern is one of the few in his line not content with being merely a "practical" workman, but who has studied the scientific and sanitary aspects of the trade to such advantage and with such earnestness of purpose that he is recognized not only as the leading plumber in Hartford, but as a scientific sanitarian who uses his knowledge in his work, and for his customers' benefit. In fact, Mr. Ahern has so thoroughly mastered the principles of sanitary science as applied to his particular calling that he has been enabled to issue a pamphlet on the subject of "Common Sense Plumbing," which treats of the subject with admirable clearness, and reflects credit on its author, while it conveys a vast deal of useful information.

Mr. Ahern is about forty-three years of age, and, although not a native of America, can be justly regarded as a representative American, having lived in this country since his boyhood, most of the time in Hartford, where he has won for himself an enviable place among the business fraternity and the good will of a great number of personal friends and acquaintances. He is a progressive business man, a desirable citizen, and enjoys the very honorable distinction of being a "self-made man."

George W. Williams & Co. (Charles S. Williams and D. Carleton), Wholesale Druggists, Dealers in Grocers' Sundries, Chimneys, Burners, Kerosene Oil, Matches, etc., Nos. 206 and 208 State, corner Front Street.—New England, and particularly Connecticut, is prolific of history, not only in the general sense, but as regards business houses whose inception dates back to the earlier part of the present century. Prominent among these is the house whose designation forms the title line of this sketch and whose history commenced when the century was in its first quarter.

In the year 1825, fifty-eight years ago, when Hartford was but the infant shadow of her present self, and when State and Front streets were the centre of the growing city, Mr. Isaac D. Bull commenced, in a modest way, the sale of drugs in a small store, occupying the corner where the present business is located. After conducting the store for a few years, Mr. Bull disposed of the business to Mr. George M. Welch, who continued it until 1854, when he was succeeded by Messrs. George W. Williams and Horace A. Hall, who began the wholesaling of drugs and the manufacture of the specialties for which the firm is famous, operating under the style of Williams & Hall. In 1861 Mr. Hall died and Mr. Williams succeeded to the entire business, changing the firm name to George W. Williams & Co., under which title the business is still conducted. In 1880 Mr. Williams retired from active mercantile pursuits, and the business passed into the hands of his son, Mr. Charles S. Williams, and Mr. D. Carleton, the present proprietors, who, in view of the wide celebrity attached to the old firm name, decided not to change it.

From Mr. Bull's modest beginning to the present immense trade and prosperity of the house was a long step, and one that was not taken without effort. There has been in the business career of this establishment none of that sudden and ofttimes evanescent glory that attends the manufacturer of nostrums and the cure-alls of the nation, until it raises them to a giddy height and leaves them gazing in the black abyss of ruin their unfounded claims have dug for them; but the rise has been of that leisurely and steady nature that is characteristic of the well-grounded business, and that almost invariably waits on intelligent and energetic effort, when it is backed by unswerving honesty and a never-failing excellence of product.

This great and growing business requires for its transaction the two buildings known as Nos. 206 and 208 State street, their combined frontage being in the neighborhood of one hundred feet, while the depth and frontage on Front street is half that figure. Each of the buildings is four stories in height with basement, and it will be seen that ten floors, each about fifty by fifty feet in size, are occupied. In the building numbered 206 is the office and counting room on the first floor, the second and third floors being used as a manufactory, laboratory, bottling-room and packing department, while the basement and upper floor are used for the purposes of storage. In No. 208 the lower floor is used as a salesroom, while the basement and three upper floors contain a large proportion of the immense stock carried by the firm. The number of assistants employed in the office, salesrooms, factory and warehouses average about twenty, although in the busier seasons it is found necessary to employ additional help. In addition to these there are a number of traveling salesmen whose sales form a considerable item in the business transacted.

While this house is known as a wholesale drug house, and while they carry an extensive stock and do a large trade in drugs, by far the greater proportion of their business is in the specialties which they own and manufacture. Among these, perhaps, the most important is the widely known and justly celebrated "Williams' Jamaica Ginger," "Williams' Flavoring Extracts," and "Williams' Essences." Besides these, the firm are the sole owners and manufacturers of "Chinese Cologne," the "New England Cough Remedy," "Skinner's Liniment," "Newell's Pain Reliever," "Globe Perfumes," "Dean's Insect Powder," as well as perfumed writing inks, hair oils of all kinds, liquid bluing, sewing machine oil, and other articles too numerous to mention. In addition to these, there is a full line of grocers' sundries, chimneys, burners, kerosene oil, matches, and kindred articles.

In the extent of territory covered by its business this house is second to none in New England, and probably stands at the head of the list, for the reason that its manufactures are used all over the country, and find sale in other countries as well.

Mr. Charles S. Williams, the senior partner in the firm, is a native and representative New Englander, born in Manchester, Connecticut, in 1844. After completing his education he entered his father's store and acquired the later and practical business education the fruits of which are so apparent in his business life. He is a thorough master of all the details of formula and manufacture in the specialties of the house, and is thus enabled to keep them up to the standard of excellence on which they won their reputation.

Mr. Carleton is also a New Englander, having been born at Thetford, Vermont, in 1846. After acquiring a common-school education he went to work on a farm, and remained at that vocation until his majority, when, his father having left him about $200, he took that sum and entered the Hartford Business College, where he acquired a thorough knowledge of bookkeeping and business forms. He entered the service of George W. Williams & Co. about twelve years ago as bookkeeper, rising rapidly to a confidential and managing position in the house, and, finally, in 1880, becoming a partner. Mr. Carleton's success in life is due solely to his own exertions, and stands as a shining example for the young men of the country.

The history of this house is a pleasant proof of the certainty with which probity and energy will win their way, and that honesty in representation and action is "good policy."

Paul Link, Hartford Steam Brewery, No. 110 Albany Avenue.—Twenty-five years ago the beverage now so widely kown as lager beer, and so extensively used throughout the entire country, had scarcely been heard of, except by those of our citizens who were born in Germany, or those who had enjoyed the then somewhat uncommon distinction of having traveled in Europe. Since that time the taste of the American people has been educated up to a liking for this pleasant and harmless drink, and now the establishments for its manfacture are numbered by the thousands, and find location in almost every city and town of any consideration, save where prohibitory laws forbid its sale. The Hartford Steam Brewery is one of the outgrowths of the comparatively recent taste for lager beer, and is one of the many growing industries in which excellence of goods commands a constantly increasing patronage. This brewery was established about the year 1858 by Charles Herold, Sr., who conducted it until 1866, when it was purchased by Paul Link, Sr., father of the present proprietor. When Mr. Link died in 1874, his son had not attained his majority, and the administrators of the estate leased the property to Mr. George Sichler for four years. Meanwhile young Mr. Link passed three years in Europe, perfecting himself as a practical brewer, the study of which profession he commenced while yet a lad, under the tutelage of his father.

On his return from Europe, Mr. Link spent some time in the breweries of Cincinnati, whence he removed to New York, and entered the service of the well-known brewing firm, George Ringler & Co., from whose establishment he graduated with a full and practical knowledge of his business. At the expiration of Mr. Sichler's lease in February, 1879, Mr. Link assumed charge of the brewery, and has conducted its affairs up to the present with such success that his yearly sales now amount to about 5,000 barrels, with the prospect of doubling that number within a few years. The premises occupied by this business are located on the corner of Albany avenue and Centre street, and consists of a brewery, ice-house, stable, dwelling-house, saloon, and the necessary out-buildings. The ground covered has a frontage of 125 feet on Albany avenue, by a depth of 200 feet on Centre street. The ice-house, one of the finest of its kind in Hartford or vicinity, has a capacity of 1,000 tons and is filled from the pond near the city, of which Mr. Link has a long lease, and which, even in the most moderate winters, yields a good supply. The average number of hands employed in this business is ten, a greater force being required in the busy summer seasons. These are assisted in their work by a engine of fifteen-horse power, supplied by a boiler of like capacity. The product of this brewery has attained an excellent reputation in Hartford, to which place Mr. Link has confined his trade, and is chiefly remarkable for its purity, life and flavor.

Mr. Link, although born in Reading, Penn., may be considered as a native of Hartford, having resided here since he was only a year old. He was born on the 29th of April, 1858, and is one of the progressive young business men of the State.

Lester L. Ensworth, Iron and Steel Carriage Materials, etc., No. 104 Front Street.—The establishing of this house dates back to 1801, when David Watkinson & Co. inaugurated it. After some years the house succeeded to Ezra Clark & Co., who in turn gave way to Clark & Co., and in September 1, 1881, the present proprietor, who was a member of Clark & Co. for twenty years, assumed the business.

The stock carried is one of the largest in the State. It consists of iron, steel, anvils, vises, bolts, springs, nuts, rivets, fire brick, spokes, rims, hubs, wheels, shafts, and carriage trimmings of every description.

A large building, built especially for the display and storage of the goods dealt in, is one of the features of completeness that strikes the attention of the visitor.

The business when established in 1801 was of inferior dimensions, but each successive firm has largely developed its trade, so that now, as it stands, it is one of the most extensive establishments in its line to be found in New England.

Mr. Lester L. Ensworth, personally, is one of those men having a commanding presence, possessed of a quiet dignity and rare executive capacity. He is a native of Hartford, educated here, and prominently identified with its history during the past twenty years. He was born September 4, 1842, and has been prominently identified with the iron and steel trade since a young man. He was a member of the City Council of Hartford during the sessions of 1879, '80 and '81, and is a director in the First National Bank of Hartford. As a Hartford production, by birth, education, business and social training, he will compare more than favorably with other representative men of the Western and Southern cities.

E. Habenstein, Caterer and Proprietor Elite Restaurant No. 269 Main Street.—One of the largest and most popular restaurants in Hartford is the establishment of Mr. Edward Habenstein, located at No. 269 Main Street. The growth of this business illustrates what application and a thorough knowledge will do for those who try.

In 1870, Mr. Habenstein was an employee in this city, but with an ambition to achieve success as a business man. In 1871, he succeeded to the business of a Mr. Williams, then a baker on Broad street, where he did a thriving trade in a small way, supporting a wagon, which delivered bread, cakes, and ice cream of his own make, to the best families in that vicinity. The increase of business necessitated his removal to larger quarters, and in 1873 he hired a store in the Union Hall Building, where he had an ice cream restaurant in addition to the baking, and where also he laid the foundation for his future success as a fashionable caterer. Here he continued till 1879, when he moved to his present location, which is one of the most central in Hartford.

The store is 20 x 106 feet in size, with a basement so desirable for restaurants, and is fitted and furnished in the most elegant æsthaetic manner. The store front is ornamented with large plate-glass show windows, in which are exhibited rare specimens of the baker and confectioner's handiwork. On either side of the front part of the store are expensive show-cases stored with all the delicacies usually found in first-class establishments of this kind. The back part of the store is furnished with an expensive carpet, real lace curtains, large mirrors and fashionable furniture generally, for the accommodation of one hundred and twenty-five guests dining at one time. With the drawing of the heavy lace and other curtains this part of the establishment can be secluded from the other, affording a suitable banquet hall for a large company.

The stained-glass windows ornamenting the rear part of the restaurant are a feature in its general appearance.

A regular dinner is served here every week day from 12 to 3 P. M., which is appreciated by ladies and gentleman of the city as well as those in town from neighboring villages.

In addition to the duties attending this business, Mr. Habenstein conducts the restaurant at the Capitol during the sessions of the Legislature, where his daily patrons are the Governor and other dignitaries of the State. In addition to the business of a restaurant and café, he has acquired an extended reputation as a caterer for weddings, parties, balls, etc. In this specialty he ranks as the largest and most popular in Connecticut. The finest of imported china, silverware, table linen and other accessories to the amount of thousands of dollars are owned and brought into requisition in carrying out the details of an order given for a small party up to that numbered at one thousand, and in any part of the State.

The business done as a caterer is very large, and it is safe to say that in this specialty he is the largest in the State.

Mr. Edward Habenstein is a native of Saxony, and thirty-eight years of age. He came to this country when a boy, at the age of nine years. He served seven years as a baker in Utica, N. Y., and the next seven as a confectioner in the establishment of a famous New Yorker, thus familiarizing himself with every detail of the business he is now pursuing. During his career as a business man he has been ably seconded by his wife, who has largely helped to make, instead of marring his fortune. She is an active worker, and superintendent of the various departments of the business, particularly that of catering.

During the past few years this establishment has catered for fully one thousand of the largest and most brilliant receptions in Connecticut.

He is now building a two-and-a-half story cottage at Watch Hill to be used by him during the summer seasons for a restaurant and the retailing of his celebrated ice cream.

In less than thirteen years, from a humble baker on a street in the suburbs, he has the satisfaction of knowing that he has the finest ladies and gents' café in Hartford, and is regarded as one of the most popular caterers in New England. From the proceeds of the constantly growing business he has built an elegant residence, which is a credit to him and an ornament to the city.

His career is a marked illustration of what can be done, and the success that can be won by industry, perseverance and merit.

Hartford Optical Company, Manufacturers and Dealers in Optical Goods, No. 144 Asylum Street, Allyn House Block.—This company, the only one of its kind in Hartford or the immediate vicinity, was founded in January, 1881, by Mr. Wm. T. Stevens, who remains as manager. The store of the company is stocked with a large assortment of optical goods of every variety. Conspicuous among which is the largest assortment of spectacles and eye-glasses to be found in the State. The specialty of the company is the manufacture of these goods to order, this branch being personally attended to by Mr. Stevens, whose abilities in that line have won for the house a widespread and flattering reputation. The company are fortunate in the fact that they have a connection with Dr. John A. Stevens (brother of the manager), a resident physician, widely known as a specialist in diseases of the eye.

In repairing optical goods, as well as watches and other pieces of delicate mechanism, the workmen employed by the company are unexcelled, and this fact goes far towards the rapid enhancement of the already considerable business. The trade of the company is not entirely local, but extends all over New England, and to a less extent throughout the United States. Mr. Stevens, the Manager, is a thoroughly scientific optician, and in this fact, doubtless, lies the secret of the success already achieved by the company. He is a native of Prestonholm, near Scotland, and is about thirty-one years of age. He can be classed almost American, as he has been in this country ever since his second year. Mr. Stevens has been a resident of Hartford about two years, the earlier portions of his life having been spent in the West and South; Chicago, Cleveland, and Chattanooga. He is generally spoken of as a reliable and energetic business man and a complete master of his profession.

C. F. Nichols, Manufacturer of Paper Boxes, No. 68 Market Street.—The extensive paper box manufactory, now carried on by Mr. C. F. Nichols, at No. 68 Market street, was established in 1850, by E. Tucker's Sons, who ran it until 1879, when Mr. Nichols became its owner by purchase. After assuming the ownership of the business, Mr. Nichols continued it for about a year in Boardman's building on Asylum street, removing thence to No. 428 Asylum street, and in February, 1883 to his present commodious quarters.

The premises now occupied consist of two full floors, one of which is 26 x 100 and the other forty feet wider in size, where employment is given to between fifty and sixty hands, a large proportion of whom are girls and young women. An engine and boiler on the premises drives a number of the unique machines used in the trade, and there is daily turned out thousands of paper boxes, chiefly for the use of manufacturers of silk twist and silver ware, and for jewelers and druggists, these departments being the specialties of the factory. The trade done amounts to from $12,000 to $15,000 per annum, and is increasing in such ratio as to warrant the belief that the lapse of two or three years will see those figures doubled. Mr. Nichols' manufactures find sale chiefly in Hartford and adjoining towns, although, in some cases, shipments are made to more remote points.

Mr. Nichols is a native of Bennington, Vermont; born in 1836. He remained in that place only until he was three years of age, when his parents removed to Belchertown, Mass., where he resided until 1851, removing thence to Springfield, Mass. In this latter place he was engaged for five years as a confectioner, a business he likewise followed for a time in Hartford before entering the paper box factory of E. Tucker's Sons, where he acted as foreman until he purchased the business in 1879. Mr. Nichols was for three years Captain of the First Company of the Governor's Guard and afterwards Captain of the Veterans of that organization for one year, the term being limited by the constitution. At the present writing he occupies the position of Lieutenant of the Veterans and is one of the most popular members of the corps.

Mr. Nichols' standing in the community is first-class, and in social circles he is highly esteemed.

The Wm. Rogers Manufacturing Company, Plated Nickel, Silver and White Metal Table Ware, No. 67 Front street.—All over the United States, and throughout many other parts of the civilized world, the name of Rogers has become associated with a peculiar trade-mark upon the best class of plated table ware. This trade-mark is like the eagle stamp upon a coin—it is an absolute warrant of genuineness. Many imitators and counterfeiters have sprung up from time to time, but like the counterfeiters of coin they have neither succeeded in deceiving nor escaping detection, and to-day the Rogers Manufacturing Company of Hartford is in almost exclusive possession of the field which the excellence of their goods has won. The inception of this great industry was in the year 1847, when Mr. William Rogers, father of Mr. F. Willson Rogers, Secretary of the present company, commenced the manufacture of plated ware on a comparatively small scale. The unusual excellence of the wares put on the market by Mr. Wm. Rogers rapidly augmented the business, and in 1865 it was deemed expedient to form the Wm. Rogers Manufacturing Company and enlarge the facilities for manufacturing. In 1872 the company was incorporated and the factory was removed to the works now occupied and which embrace four full floors, each 50x175 feet in size, and give employment to one hundred and twenty-five hands. The machinery used in the work is of the most expensive and improved patterns and is so economical in its operations that the one hundred and twenty-five hands employed are enabled by its aid to turn out a quantity of work that under the old system would have required the services of nearly three times that number. The salesroom of the establishment is on the ground floor of the factory building, and is filled with a wonderfully complete assortment of the celebrated ware made by the company, each piece of which bears the talismanic trade-mark which guarantees its excellence. Some idea of the remarkable growth of this industry may be gained from the fact that in 1878 the entire volume of business amounted to something like $90,000, there being seventy-five hands employed; while in 1882, with an increase of fifty hands—such has been the improvement in machinery—the business reached to nearly a half a million. Besides the employees in the factory proper, there is a large force of clerks and salesmen; eight of the latter being constantly employed on the road, visiting and making sales in every State and Territory in the Union. The business, as originally started, now embraces the manufacture of table cutlery, the company having consolidated with the Rogers Cutlery Company in 1879.

Mr. William H. Watrous, President and Treasurer of the company, is a native of Hartford, about forty-two years of age. He learned the trade of silver plating with Mr. William Rogers, founder of the original house, who was a practical man and superintendent of the business until his decease in 1873. Mr. Watrous has grown from boyhood in the business, and has filled a number of positions of trust and responsibility elsewhere, having been overseer for Rogers & Bros. in Waterbury, then in the Ames Manufacturing Company, of Chicopee, Mass., and afterwards with the Strong Manufacturing Company, of Winsted, Conn. Upon the formation of the present company, Mr. Watrous took charge of the plating department, and it is largely due to his skill that the goods of the house have maintained their supremacy in the market. When the rebellion broke out, he was one of the first to offer his services, and served as first lieutenant in a Connecticut regiment, going first for three months, and subsequently for the nine months' term.

Mr. F. Willson Rogers is also a native of Hartford, and was born in 1851. After completing his education, he learned the jewelry business, but left it to enter the Rogers Cutlery Company, of which he was made secretary in 1878. On the consolidation of the two companies in 1879, he was appointed secretary of the present concern, a position which he has held ever since. He is regarded as a shrewd and energetic business man, and a worthy successor to the good name left by his father.

The Wm. Rogers Manufacturing Company are the undisputed leaders in their busines in the United States.

Charles F. Sweet, Proprietor of Star Knitting Mills, Manufacturers of Children's Underwear, No. 133 Sheldon Street.—The establishment of this industry dates from June 1st, 1881, since which time its growth has been as surprising to the public as it has been gratifying to its projector. The mill occupies one floor of the building at No. 133 Sheldon Street, 150 x 40 feet in size, and employs about fifty people, most of whom are girls. The goods manufactured embrace all qualities of merino and cotton underwear for children exclusively, no men's or women's goods being made. Mr. Sweet purchases his yarns on the outside, but aside from that fact the mill is a complete knitting mill, all the other processes, such as cutting, washing, weaving, making up, trimming, etc., being done on the premises. The business now done reaches to the very satisfactory figure of $60,000 a year, while the prospect of largely adding to that sum is very flattering. Most of the goods made here are disposed of in other States by Mr. Sweet's agents, who are Iselin, Neeser & Co., No. 339 Canal street, New York, and Charles P. Lincoln, No. 312 Chestnut street, Philadelphia.

Mr. Sweet was born in Albany, N. Y., in Oct. 1849, and came to Hartford about five years ago, taking the position of manager of the Glastonbury Knitting Company at Glastonbury, a position he retained for three years and until the time he embarked in business for himself. He is thoroughly practical in his calling, having been in the business for sixteen years, the greater portion of which was spent in the mill of Benjamin A. Sweet, his father, at Albany, where he worked in and mastered the details of every department. This experience with his father, who, besides being a mill-owner, is one of the largest wool dealers in his section, has been of such value that Mr. Sweet is enabled to turn out the very best qualities of goods at reasonable prices, and to find a ready market for the products of his mills.

Mr. Sweet bears an enviable reputation in the business community, while his social qualities are such as to command the cordial respect and liking of his associates.

Smith, White & Co. (Edwin J. Smith and Frank G. White), Importers and Men's Outfitters, Manufact rers of the "C. & S." Shirt, Nos. 65 and 67 Asylum Street.—In every city of the United States will be found one house and firm that occupies a leading position in its line and stands head and shoulders above its fellows, both in enterprise and the amount of business done. In Hartford, the house of Smith, White & Co. occupies such a position in the men's furnishing goods trade. This business was established by Mr. Edwin J. Smith, of the present firm, in 1871, next door to the present stores, to which removal was had in 1878. Mr. Smith was joined in 1873 by Mr. W. E. Covey, and from that time up to January, 1883, when Mr. Covey withdrew, the firm was known as Covey & Smith. On Mr. Covey's withdrawal, Mr. Frank G. White became a partner in the house, and the present designation was adopted. The premises occupied by this business consists of an elegant and spacious store, 100x24 feet in size, with basement of like dimensions, and a second floor 40x 24, in which is stored and displayed one of the finest stocks in New England, valued at from $20,000 to $40,000, according to the season. The business, which is both wholesale and retail, and gives employment to a number of traveling agents in Connecticut, Rhode Island and Massachusetts, amounts to about $100,000 per annum, a large portion of the trade being in the celebrated "C. & S." shirt, manufactured and sold at wholesale and retail by the firm. Some of the specialties of the house are: Dent's gloves, Allen, Solly & Co.'s underwear, fancy goods from the well-known London house of Welch, Margetsin & Co., Fownes Bros.' gloves, McIntosh's rubber coats, Knight & Petch's house garments, Klock's French goods, Charles Guvé's noted French hosiery and underwear and other articles of the higher grades, all of which are imported direct from the manufacturers in Europe and elsewhere and procured by personal selection, Mr. Smith visiting England and the Continent every year for that purpose, and to select the later novelties in furnishing goods and artistic bric-a-brac to be found in the markets of the old world.

An idea of the character of the business transacted by this house may be gained from the statement that in addition to the regular trade of a furnishing goods house, they deal in such articles as house robes from Japan; candlesticks, vases, card receivers, inkstands, smoker's sets, and thermometers in bronze from Vienna; portfolios, jewel caskets, work baskets, flower stands, stamp cases, glove and handkerchief sachets, in silk and plush, from Paris; besides an endless variety of dressing cases, toilet sets, embossed and hand painted fans, card cases, robes, rugs, silk umbrellas, walking sticks, traveling bags, portmanteaus, and a thousand other things of use and ornament.

Mr. Edwin J. Smith, th senior member of the firm is a native of Washington, Litchfield County, Conn., born in 1844. He has resided in Hartford for about nineteen years, fifteen of which have been passed in his present business. During a portion of the war of the Rebellion he was a Sergeant in the Twentieth Connecticut Volunteers, and participated in the battles of Chancellorsville, Gettysburg, Lookout Mountain, Cassville or Fort Dallas, Peach Creek, and Atlanta, and was with General Sherman in his famous "March to the Sea." He was at one time a member of the City Council and at present is Fire Marshal and Commissioner, an office he has held for six years, and in which he has given entire satisfaction to the people of Hartford. Mr. Smith keeps up the memory of his military life by membership in the City Guard, and is Quartermaster of the Veterans of that organization.

Mr. Frank G. White was born in North Adams, Mass., in 1856, and has resided in Hartford since boyhood. His education was acquired in the public schools here, his graduation from the high school occurring in 1874. His business career began in the old Bee Hive, where he was engaged as clerk until its destruction by fire, after which he entered the service of Gemmill, Burnham & Co., with whom he remained until he assumed a partnership in his present business.

The firm of Smith, White & Co. bears a first-class commercial reputation and its individual members stand high in the esteem of the public.

Seth Belden & Son (James S. Belden), Proprietors of the Bolton Flagging Stone Quarry at Bolton, Tolland Co., Conn., office No. 69 Commerce Street.—About the year 1830, Mr. Seth Belden succeeded to the stone business of Mr. Apolus Sweetland, who had been established for a number of years, and who dealt principally in brown stone for building purposes. This branch of the business was carried on by Mr. Belden until 1850, when the quarrying and sale of flagging for sidewalks was begun, that gradually overshadowing the other department of the trade, until at the present it has become almost the exclusive specialty of the concern. In 1856, Mr. James S. Belden, son of the founder of the house, was admitted to partnership, and the firm has since been known by its present title. The quarry owned by this firm is situated at Bolton, Conn., about sixteen miles from Hartford, on the New York and New England Railroad. The stone is largely admixed with mica, and is especially valuable for sidewalks. The quarry is on a ledge, which is in no place more than 200 feet wide, and has been worked for a distance of three miles. Its great depth—about eighty feet—renders the employment of costl machinery an absolute necessity for extracting the rock, and most of the work is accomplished by its aid. The first working of this quarry dates back about seventy-five years, during which flagging has been shipped from it to all parts of New England, and in a number of cases as far south as New Orleans and Washington, a portion of the flagging in front of the National Capitol being composed of Bolton stone, as well as all of the corridors in the Eastern Penitentiary in Philadelphia.

The yards of the firm, at the corner of Commerce and Potter streets, are 350 x 200 feet in size, and there is a stock carried of about $10,000, while the yearly volume of business reaches nearly four times that sum.

Mr. Seth Belden was born in Middletown in 1812, and although he has reached the age of seventy years is active in business. He has resided in Hartford since 1827, and has filled a prominent place in her history, having been at various times a member of the city government, a director in the Farmers' and Mechanics' Bank, and United States Pension Agent under President Pierce. He is a practical stone-cutter by trade, and has never followed any other business.

Mr. James S. Belden is a native of Hartford; born on July 25, 1840. His education was obtained in the public schools here, and his business learned with his father. He was a member of the Common Council for three terms, 1866, 1867, and 1868, and is credited with having served his constituents with marked ability and honesty. He is Secretary and Treasurer of the Hartford Cement Tile Company, a description of which will be found elsewhere.

This firm and its constituent members are regarded as thoroughly reliable.

O. D. Woodruff & Co. (O. D. and J. E. Woodruff), Hatters, Furriers and dealers in Trunks, Bags, Furnishing Goods, etc., No. 355 Main Street.—As far back as the year 1840 a gentleman named Avery established himself in the hat and fur business in Hartford, and laid the foundation of the prosperous house whose title forms the head-line of this article. In 1845 he was succeeded by Messrs. Strong and Woodruff, which firm continued for thirty-three years and six months, terminating on September 10, 1879, by the withdrawal of Mr. Strong, the entrance of Mr. James E. Woodruff, and the adoption of the present firm name. The business done by this house embraces a trade in hats, furs, trunks, bags, gloves, gentlemen's furnishing goods, etc., a specialty being made of the manufacture of fur garments, in which line the house is among the largest in the State. The premises occupied are situated on the westerly side of Main street, north of Asylum street, and consist of a store and basement, each 20x135 feet in size. There are employed from twelve to twenty hands in the various departments of manufacture, while three or four salesmen attend to the wants of the numerous customers. The trade of the house extends to all parts of the country, although the bulk of it is done in the State of Connecticut.

Mr. Orrin D. Woodruff, the senior partner, was born in Canton, Conn., in 1820, and has lived in Hartford since childhood. For forty-nine years he has been in his present location, eleven years as clerk and the remainder as proprietor. The citizens of Hartford know him as a thoroughly reliable business man and a worthy member of the community.

Mr. James E. Woodruff is the son of the senior member and has been a partner in the house about three and one-half years. He is a native of Hartford, Conn.; born in 1844. Like his father, he has resided here almost his entire life, and for fifteen years was engaged in the dry-goods business with the firm of C. S. Weatherby & Co., for whom he acted as manager during the last three years of his service. He bears a first-class business reputation and is universally esteemed.

Charles King, dealer in Stoves, Furnaces, Ranges, Hollow and Tin Ware, Nos. 497 and 499 Main Street.—The establishment of the large stove and tinware business, now carried on by Mr. Charles King at Nos. 497 and 499 Main street, dates back to about forty-five years ago, when Mr. William J. Phillips started in a smaller way in a store located on Main street, some distance south of the quarters now occupied. The business remained in its original location until fourteen years ago, when it was removed to the more commodious premises in which it is now carried on. In February, 1872, Mr. King purchased the stock and good-will of the business, and has conducted it up to the present with unvarying success. The store is 26 by 125 feet in size and contains a very large and complete stock of stoves, furnaces, ranges, hollow and tin ware, etc., and is the headquarters in Hartford of the celebrated "Good News" range, the Argand base burner and the Burtis furnace, all of which are the specialties of the house. In the rear of the store is a three-story brick building where is stored the surplus stock and where is manufactured the tinware necessary for the jobbing and retail trade carried on. An average of seventeen hands are employed, the number varying with the season. The annual trade amounts to about $30,000, for the prosecution of which a stock of $10,000 worth of goods is carried. A branch house at Unionville, under the management of Mr. H. K. Vosburgh as agent, disposes of goods amounting to nearly $10,000 in value, annually.

Mr. King was born in Chicopee, Mass., in 1825, removing to Hartford when he was but seven years of age, and residing here continually ever since. His education was acquired in the public schools, and at the age of fifteen years he entered the service of T. Smith & Co.—now Smith, Bourn & Co.—the well-known manufacturers of saddlery and harness, with whom he remained as clerk and partner for a period of thirty-three years. Mr. King is active in church and charitable matters, having been a deacon in the Windsor Avenue Congregational Church since its formation, and is generally regarded as one of Hartford's best citizens.

The Weed Sewing Machine Co., Capitol Avenue, west of Broad Street.—The second largest manufacturing establishment in Hartford, in amount of capital, men employed and volume of business done, is The Weed Sewing Machine Co., the illustration of which adorn these pages. The capital is $600,000, all paid in.

The first plant was in the rear of the old Post-office on Main street, corner Grove. This was in 1867, the year the company was incorporated, and the first president was Mr. John S. Niles.

Outgrowing the old location, they moved into a portion of the works of Messrs. Pratt & Whitney, and in 1871, having bought the plant of the Sharp's Rifle Co., they removed to their present location, which is a pleasant walk of about ten minutes from the Union Station, or five minutes from the State Capitol, which is on the same avenue.

The fame of the Weed Sewing Machine Co. has been pushed to every part of the civilized world by its productions. The name Weed is a household word in America, known in connection with sewing machines. The latest and most perfect specimen of a sewing machine produced by them is "The Hartford," named in honor of the city. It is a machine designed for family use and for light manufacturing. On this machine ball-bearings are used, for the first time in sewing machines, the patent for which is the sole property of this company. They also produce a machine for manufacturing called the General Favorite, or "G. F." Machine, turning out, of both models, about 100 per day. The production of sewing machines, is only a part of their business. They manufacture all the celebrated Columbia bicycles and tricycles, the leading article of the kind, in the United States, forgings for agricultural implements and steam machinery, as well as a number of other sewing machines for companies not having works of their own, the McKay twin needle machine and others. Some idea of the size and capacity of these works is shown in the fact that their floor room covers five acres, and the motive power is supplied by a 250-horse power engine.

The illustration of the works of this company, which will be found on page 160, shows them as seen from the cars of the N. Y., N. H. & H. and the N. Y. & N. E. Railroads on the opposite side of the river. The Weed Sewing Machine Company is one of which Hartford boasts as one of the chief industries of the city.

P. Fay, Marble and Granite Worker, No. 8 Maple Avenue.—One of the most enterprising marble and granite-working establishments in Hartford is that of Mr. P. Fay, which was inaugurated at its present location, No. 8 Maple avenue, in the year 1879.

The salesroom, which is stocked with a number of very artistic and expensive mantels, ornamented with mirrors, tile, etc., is triangular in shape and 40x60 feet, fronting on two streets. Adjoining this is the office, while in the rear is a storeroom and workshop where from eight to ten people are kept busy in manipulating granite and marble into monuments, headstones, tablets, marble and slate mantels, grates, fenders, plumbers' slabs, cabinet slabs, etc., etc. He also deals in encaustic tiles for floors, and art tiles of all kinds, together with a full line of granite monuments, tablets and headstones. He also furnishes estimates for all kinds of foreign and domestic granite and does a business of about $15,000 per annum.

Mr. Fay is a native of New York City, born in 1839, and has been identified with Hartford since 1877. On the breaking out of the war he enlisted in the Fifth New York Artillery, in which he bore the colors of that famous fighting organization for six months, an act which gained him the shoulder-straps of a First Lieutenant. With his command he was in the hard-fought battles of Winchester, Gettysburg, the two engagements at Harpers' Ferry, and Cedar Creek, in the latter engagement of which he was captured and taken to Libby Prison, where, through the influence of a Confederate lady to whom he had extended a great favor when she was within the Union lines, he was saved from going to Andersonville, from which place he probably would never have returned alive.

Mr. Fay has, during his residence in Hartford, made a name and a place for himself in social and business circles. He is Commander of the Nathaniel Lyon Post 2, G. A. R., Department of Connecticut, in which organization he takes great interest. He is known as a reliable and persevering business man.

H. E. Patten, Dye Works, Carpet Beating and Cleaning Establishment, No. 37 Wells Street. —Among the various trades that go to make up the great and ever-increasing comfort of our advanced civilization, there are many deserving the praise of the lover of ease and cleanliness, and first among them is that which, without trouble to or personal attention from the owner, takes his half-worn clothing, gloves, feathers, carpets, etc., and in a wonderfully short space of time and with marvelous completeness, restores them to almost their pristine brightness, or adds to them other and more pleasing hues. Chief among these promoters of household happiness is Mr. Henry E. Patten, the successor to a business established in 1825 by Messrs. T. & J.

S. Parker, and sold by them to Mr. George Gilbert, by him to Mr. George Smith, and by his estate, in 1873, to the present proprietor, who started on May 1, 1855, as a workman in the establishment he now owns. The premises in which the operations of this extensive business are conducted are located on the south side of Wells street, No. 37, below Main street, and consist of four floors, in addition to a large dye-house situated in the rear of the main building. The structure has a frontage on Wells street of forty-five feet, and runs back to the Park River, a distance of seventy-five feet, the rear portion of the building being almost twice the width of the Wells street front. A large engine of twenty-five horse power, and a boiler of like capacity, furnish power and steam for the different machines and processes used in the business, the number of skilled workmen varying from twelve to twenty-five, according to the season. This establishment is by far the largest of its kind in Hartford, and, with perhaps one exception, the largest in the State. The building, as well as the one adjoining it on the east, is the property of Mr. Patten, both being among the most valuable business property in the city, and in a location where the enhancement of values is rapid and steady. The building not occupied by Mr. Patten is rented for model and machine shops, brass foundries, etc., and presents a scene of unusual manufacturing industry.

The business done by Mr. Patten embraces a wide range and includes the dyeing, cleaning and repairing gloves, flannel, blankets, feathers, table and piano spreads, woolen goods of all descriptions, silks in all colors, and other articles too numerous to mention. Gentlemen's garments are cleaned or dyed and repaired without ripping, while feather beds, pillows and bolsters are renovated by a process peculiar to the establishment. Perhaps the most extensive branch of the business is the cleaning of carpets by a machine designed by Mr. Patten, and a process known as the "wet process," by means of which the original colors are restored in all their brightness, and all dirt, moths, etc., effectually removed. Besides these machines there are two others of approved patterns for the ordinary work of beating carpets, both of which, as well as the one first mentioned, are in constant operation.

Mr. Patten is a native of Stafford, Tolland County, Conn., and was born in 1835. Up to his twentieth year he was engaged in the usual pursuits and pastimes of boyhood and youth, a great portion of the time being spent in acquiring an education, which he did at academies in Wilbraham, Mass., and Westfield, Conn. On May 1, 1855, he came to Hartford and immediately entered, as workman, the business that in later years brought him to his present elevated position in the world of trade, and won for him the comfortable income he now enjoys. Mr. Patten is a notable member of the company of self-made men of New England, and deservedly enjoys the hearty esteem of his fellow citizens.

T. Sisson & Co., Wholesale Druggists, No. 259 Main Street.—One of the oldest, largest and most extensive wholesale drug houses in the State of Connecticut is that of Messrs. T. Sisson & Co., located at No. 259 Main street. The foundation of the business dates back to 1822, when Messrs. Lee & Butler kept a drug store just north of the old stone bridge on Main street, removing to the present location in 1836.

For over thirty years the firm remained as it was in 1822. In 1855, the innovation of a new member was added, and the name made Messrs. Lee, Butler & Co. Three years later, in 1858, the firm became Messrs. Lee, Sisson & Co., in 1865, Messrs. Sisson & Butler, and in 1881, Messrs. T. Sisson & Co., the present proprietors.

The business stand, which has been a landmark on the business thoroughfare of Hartford for forty-seven years, is four stories in height, 30 x 60 feet in size, with an L.

The stock carried is, of necessity, very large, as their trade extends throughout the State, and to many points in New England. In addition to drugs, they carry a large stock of patent medicines, paints, oils, glass, and manufacturers' supplies. Twelve assistants, besides the members of the firm, are necessary for the prosecution of the business, which is very large and extended.

Mr. Thomas Sisson, the senior member, is a native of West Hartford, Conn., and fifty-four years of age. He has been a clerk and proprietor in this house for forty-one years, learning the drug business with it. He is closely identified with the benevolent and financial institutions of Hartford, being Treasurer of the Retreat for the Insane, director in the Connecticut Mutual Life Insurance Company, Hartford County Mutual Fire Insurance Company, First National Bank and Dime Savings Bank. From a boy he has won his way to being the head of one of the largest drug houses of the State, and is generally noted for his financial success and his many deeds of charity and benevolence.

Mr. Geo. P. Chandler, the next member of the firm, is a native of Saxton's River, Vermont; born in 1844. He learned his business in Greenfield, Mass., and has been in Hartford since 1865, and a member of the firm of Messrs. T. Sisson & Co. since 1871, which is a sufficient guarantee of his social and financial standing.

Mr. Fred. H. Chapin, the junior member, is a native of Lafayette, Indiana, but from boyhood has been a resident of this city, where he was educated at the Grammar and High schools. He is thirty years of age, and for fourteen years has been connected with the house, and since 1881 as one of the proprietors. He is also a special student in astronomy, and, in connection with Mr. C. P. Howard, of the firm of J. L. Howard & Co., has a very fine observatory and telescope for use in this study.

The wholesale drug house of Messrs. T. Sisson & Co. is a representative one, well-known, long-established, and is one of the few which has pursued the even tenor of its way for so many years and preserved its financial standing untarnished, adding, in the meantime, to its magnitude and capacity.

Dwight Slate, Builder and Designer of Machinery, No. 262 Main Street.—In the year 1835, Mr. Slate commenced the manufacture of machinery in Stafford, Connecticut. After an experience of ten years, he moved, in 1845, to Windsor Locks, where he became the senior member of the firm of Slate & Brown, manufacturers of cotton and other machinery.

It was at this time that the Mexican war was in progress, and Colonel Sam Colt had a contract with the United States Government to furnish one thousand of his revolvers, the barrels and cylinders of which were made by Slate & Brown, and used by Colonel Walker's regiment in Mexico. This was the first thousand pistols of Colt's patent used by the Government, and was the pioneer of many which followed.

During the business career of Slate & Brown at Windsor Locks they acquired an extended reputation for the manufacture of cotton machinery, counting among their patrons, the Palmer Company, Thorndike Company, Otis Company, Cordis Company, and other large establishments. They furnished, in 1845, the machinery for two mills belonging to the Otis Company, Ware, Mass.

In 1850, on account of ill health, Mr. Slate sold out his interest to Mr. Brown and removed to Augusta, Ga., where he, through the inducements of Mr. Wm. M. De Antignac, President of the Augusta Manufacturing Company, took the management of the Augusta Machine Works, which turned out freight and passenger cars and saw mills. Mr. Slate while there turned out the heavy castings for No. 2 cotton mill of the Augusta Manufacturing Company, and was consulting mechanic in the purchase of the machinery for the same, saving the company not less than $100,000 by having it purchased in New England instead of being made in Augusta. The wise advice of Mr. Slate has been recognized by members of that company in more ways than one since that time. Most, if not all, of the cars for the several railroads in the vicinity of Augusta were made at the Augusta Machine Works. Those of good credit began to make their own after a time, while those of poor credit continued as customers, which crippled the finances of the company, and Mr. Slate withdrew, and purchased a tract of land bordering on the Ohoope River, in the southern part of the State, and embarked in the lumber business. His near neighbor in the same business was Mr. Harmon Rowley, a native of this State, but now one of the richest men in Augusta, Ga. Selling his interest in Georgia, Mr. Slate returned to Connecticut, and during the war was a contractor at Colt's armory in this city. In 1866 he was a designer of machinery at the Pratt and Whitney Company, in Hartford, remaining there as such till 1872, when he embarked in business again as a designer of machinery, producing designs for the National Screw Company, American Paper Barrel Company, National Stove Company, and others.

His present establishment embraces one entire floor of a large building, situated in the business centre, and about thirty-five men are constantly employed. The business done aggregates about $45,000 per annum.

The machinery turned out at this establishment is of most every kind, a specialty being made of machinist's tools, upright drills, milling machines, marking machines, grinding machines, etc., most, if not all, being of his own design and invention.

One of his machines is called a Sensitive Drill, adapted for drilling three-eighth inch holes and under. He claims that there is nothing in the market like it, and that it will break less drills and drill faster than any drill-press made. A number of prominent manufacturers in New England and the West are using this drill with entire satisfaction.

Slate's Combination Grinding machine, is another invention of his. It is adapted for sharpening, by grinding, long-shanked, spiral, straight-toothed and taper reamers; milling machine cutters with spiral, straight, beveled, radical or disc teeth. It is in great demand for its accuracy, rapidity and general handiness.

Slate's Patent Cutting-off Tool is another design of his. The material and workmanship of all of his work is of the best and possess the qualities of accuracy, rapidity and durability. The machines and tools designed and manufactured by Mr. Slate are found in stock at the machinery depots of E. P. Bullard, No. 14 Dey Street, New York; W. A. Davis, No. 134 Pearl Street, Boston, Mass.; Hill, Clarke & Co., No. 36 Oliver Street, Boston, Mass.; Wardell & Hinckley, No. 14 South Canal Street, Chicago; W. A. James, No. 275 South Canal Street, Chicago, Ills.; J. H. Kerrick & Co., Minneapolis, Minn.; Bowman Machine Company, St. Louis, Mo.; Warner & Swasey, Cleveland, Ohio.

In 1871 Mr. Slate invented a water heater for steam boilers which is said to be the best made, brings the highest price, and is sold all over the world. He is also the originator of an Automatic Screw Machine that points one hundred screws per minute, a number of which are now in progress to fill an order recently received.

An Automatic Gear Cutting Machine and a Taper attachment for a Lathe are also his designs.

The number of his designs and inventions, the value placed upon them by those using and controlling them, the manufacturing establishment of his own of no mean proportions, all contribute to his well-won reputation as an originator and skillful designer.

Mr. Slate is a native of Gill, Franklin Co. Mass., and sixty-six years of age. He left his native town when a youth of sixteen, and has been identified with Connecticut most of the time since. His first venture in the business world was at the age of nineteen, since which time he has been an active worker, designing, inventing and manufacturing machinery. Mr. Slate is by nature an originator and a thorough machinist. The products of his ideas and designs have made several men and one or more incorporated companies rich. He takes much interest in the industries of his native State and is director and consulting engineer for the E. Horton & Son Chuck Co., of Windsor Locks.

The productions of his establishment are exported to England, France, Germany and Belgium, where his name is well known.

Prof. Noah Cressy, M.D., V.S., Ph. D., Veterinary Surgeon, No. 36 State Street.—In no department of physical science is there to be found more of pretense and chicanery than in the practice of the majority of the self-styled veterinary surgeons, and it is, therefore, a grateful task to record the history of an honorable exception to the rule.

Noah Cressy, is a native of Rowe, Mass., and is about forty-four years of age. His earlier education was obtained at Shelbourne Falls Academy and the University of Vermont. He graduated from the Berkshire Medical College, from which institution he holds the degree of Doctor of Medicine. After his graduation he attended a number of terms as a student of comparative anatomy in the scientific department of Harvard College, going thence to the Montreal Veterinary College, where he obtained his V. S. degree. Dr. Cressy practiced medicine for ten years before he decided to confine himself to the veterinary branch of the science and won for himself an enviable reputation as a practitioner.

As a professor of veterinary science at the State Agricultural College at Amherst, Mass., the doctor especially distinguished himself, and as a lecturer throughout New England did much to educate the masses to a knowledge of the needs and proper treatment of animals. So marked was his success that the University of Vermont took public recognition of it by conferring upon him the degree of Doctor of Philosophy (Ph. D.). Besides these titles and distinctions, the doctor enjoys the further distinction of having been the first State veterinary surgeon ever appointed, that event occurring in 1872, when Governor Marshall Jewell, of Connecticut, addressed to him the following: "Dr. Noah Cressy, State Veterinary Surgeon. Dear Sir:—In view of the prevalence of the epizootic among horses, and the general want of knowledge among our people, and also in view of your past experience as a veterinary surgeon, and your recent visit to New York and examination of the disease as it there appeared, I hereby authorize and direct you to visit the principal places in this State where the disease has broken out and give such advice and assistance as the exigencies of the case may require, giving such previous notice of your visits as circumstances may permit."

The communication was acted on, and it is admitted on all sides that the doctor's labors in this connection were productive of great good to the people and of much popularity to the governor. The consequent expenses were allowed by the Legislature, without dissent, and it is believed that Governor Jewell was largely indebted for his reelection to the favorable sentiment created among the agricultural portion of the community by his liberal action as regards the services of Dr. Cressy and the benefit derived from that gentleman's teachings.

Dr. Cressy has been established in Hartford since 1880, and in a comparatively short space of time has formed a connection in his profession unexcelled by any practitioner elsewhere and far greater than that of any of his immediate neighbors. He is the owner of the finest collection of works on veterinary science to be found in America, besides one of the very few complete sets of the "Veterinarian" on this side of the Atlantic. In addition to attending to the duties of his profession, the doctor finds time to fill the editorial chair of the Hygienic and Veterinary Department of the "National Live Stock Journal," published in Chicago, a position to which he was appointed in July, 1882, and thus pleasantly introduced:

"We take much pleasure in being able to announce that we have made arrangements with Prof. Noah Cressy, M.D., V.S., Ph.D., of Hartford, Conn., to edit the 'Hygienic and Veterinary Department' of *The Journal*. Dr. Cressy is well known as a talented and interesting writer on veterinary matters, and an able practitioner. His lectures and addresses have frequently been published in pamphlet form, and have attracted a great deal of attention. It was with his advice and assistance, as State Veterinarian for Connecticut, that the commission appointed to stamp out pleuro-pneumonia in that State performed such thorough work."

In a later issue *The Journal* says:

We have been much gratified by the flattering notices, in our New England exchanges, of Dr. Noah Cressy's engagement as editor of the "Veterinary" department. Prominent men in the East have also written us in very complimentary terms of his abilities, both as a writer and practitioner.

Dr. Cressy, ten years ago, took an advanced position among professional men, on the subject of experimental research on the nature and prevention of diseases among animals, and has since then persistently urged the importance of this on public institutions of learning. In view of this, he has reason to feel proud of the compliment paid him at the agricultural college of his native State, Massachusetts, where he has been professor of veterinary science, by the establishment of an experimental station, and the adoption of the very means he has advocated so long. We shall expect to hear of good results from these investigations.

From all the evidences at hand it is safe to venture the assertion that Dr. Cressy stands in the very front rank of his profession, and that he is far in advance of the majority. In Hartford, as elsewhere, he is regarded as a cultivated scholar, an honorable gentlemen, and a desirable accession to the ranks of professional men.

W. H. Post & Co., Household Art, Artistic House Furnishing, Carpets, Paper Hangings, Curtains, etc., Nos. 428 and 430 Main Street.—Statistics show that the City of Hartford is the richest according to size in the Union. Her citizens for some years have disputed with those of Providence Rhode Island, on this point, but the United States Census of 1880 settled it in favor of this the Capitol City. The stranger within her gates is impressed with the evidences on every hand of wealth, culture, education and refinement.

It is no wonder, then, that in such a city there should be a demand for household art decorations and artistic furnishing, which has been recognized and supplied by Messrs. W. H. Post & Co., who formed a partnership and commenced business in April, 1881. It is too much the ambition of a certain class of dealers to provide the cheapest article instead of the best at the lowest possible price, and it is always a great satisfaction to make note of any establishment whose projectors' aim is to revolutionize this practice, and, instead, give a "quid pro quo" for the patronage they invite and receive.

The intelligence of the customers of Messrs. W. H. Post & Co. will permit nothing else. The homes of the best families of Hartford and of the State show this in the quiet and substantial elegance of their furnishings and the dignified appearance of their surroundings. Such a policy, the best in all departments, is especially to be commended in the manufacture and sale of anything that so directly concerns our happiness, for the luxuries of the last generation are now the necessities of this.

More than twenty-five years ago, Mr. W. H. Post went into partnership with Mr. C. C. Talcott for the prosecution of the dry-goods, carpet and paper hanging business, under the firm name of Talcott & Post. Their business was very successful and their sales increased from year to year, until April, 1881, when they found it necessary to have more room, and they decided to separte their departments. Mr. Post had for some years devoted himself principally to the carpet and house furnishing department, so that this seemed to be his favorable opportunity to devote himself entirely to his favorite specialty, and the result was the formation of the new partnership of Wm. H. Post & Co. Mr. E. S. Yergason, who for twenty-two years had been in the employ of the old firm was admitted as junior partner. The spacious store Nos. 428 and 430 Main street, owned by Mr. Post and his former partner, is one of the most desirable locations for such a business in the city. The stores are fitted up in a most elegant manner, everything being in unison with the object of their business. Expensive plate-glass windows adorn the front, affording a flood of light so essential to persons selecting those delicate shades of color belonging to the more expensive carpets curtains and art decorations, of which a large stock is necessary to meet the demands of their special class of customers. The proprietors are aided by a corps of experienced salesmen selected especially to cater to the demands of their trade. It is too often the case that one gravitates to our larger cities for large stocks to select from, but this house has such an extensive following that everything found in New York or Boston can be duplicated here. The novelties of Paris, London and Vienna are drawn upon by the agents of this firm, that their customers may know at once the prevailing artistic furnishings in the old world as well as in this. In short, no effort which a lifelong experience can suggest is spared to produce household art in all its phases, to the entire satisfaction of all interested.

No house in the State carries a larger stock of household art goods, ranks higher in an artistic point of view, or has a more extensive trade than W. H. Post & Co.

Mr. W. H. Post, as above recorded, was a member of the firm of Talcott & Post for many years, during which time he earned the reputation of a progressive and substantial business man, a well-earned reputation he still preserves with every evidence of even yet attaining a higher rank, if possible, in the estimation of the people. He is a native of the State, by birth and education, and a product of the educational system of Connecticut for which it has been so long famous. Born in Hebron., Conn., April 1, 1834, he came to Hartford in 1850, where he has since resided.

The junior member of the firm, Mr. E. S. Yergason, was born in Windham, Conn., September 10, 1840, and is also a graduate from the public schools of the State. His training has been in keeping with his chosen pursuit and in consonance with his artistic instincts, which contribute in a great degree to the success of the house of which he is a member.

He served his country as a member of the Twenty-second Connecticut Volunteer Infantry and participated in all the battles and followed the flag of that famous historic organization through victory and defeat, and was present at the final grand review of the armies at Washington.

The business of the house amounts to half a million dollars annually. Finally, this establishment is a representative one, found only in such cities as Hartford, and reflects great credit upon the artistic tastes of the proprietors, who rank high among the most successful and substantial business men in this section of the State.

Dwight H. Buell, Fine Watches, Diamonds and Jewelry, No. 823 Main Street.—In 1851, the subject of this sketch, then a lad just entering his teens, began his business life in the service of Mr. Thomas Steele, with whom he learned the watch-making and jewelry trade, and all the other details necessary to the conduct of such an establishment as the one which now owns him as head. At the early age of twenty-one years Mr. Buell became a partner with Mr. Steele, remaining such for about nine years. In 1867, Mr. Buell left the old house, and, associating himself with Mr. Charles J. Wood, established the firm of D. H. Buell & Co., occupying the premises where he is at present located. After a short term of partnership, the firm dissolved, Mr. Wood withdrawing and Mr. Buell continuing the business in his own name up to the present. The store occupied by Mr. Buell is one of the most eligibly located in the city, it being on the westerly side of Main street, about four doors north from Asylum street, and within a very short distance of the Post-office, City Hall, banks, insurance offices, and other institutions, and in the very centre of the trading district. It is provided with a very elegant plate-glass front, while its interior is fitted up in the most tasteful and expensive manner. Six assistants are employed in the various departments of the business, which, although general in the jewelry line, is especially large in the specialties of fine watches and diamonds, large quantities of those articles being annually sold over an area of territory embracing many distant points. In the matter of watches, Mr. Buell has a reputation second to no dealer in the country, his custom being to keep and sell the finer descriptions, such as the Waltham and the Vacheron & Constantin, the latter being from the celebrated Swiss firm of that name, and for whom Mr. Buell is the agent. Besides these, there is a very large stock of other makes of watches, jewelry, silver and plated ware and bronzes, besides an unusually large and varied assortment of diamonds and other precious stones, selected with care and by the aid of a long experience. In short, it is probable that the stock carried by Mr. Buell embraces a larger variety of fine goods than can be found elsewhere in the city.

Mr. Buell is a native of Litchfield, Conn., where he lived until he was seven years of age, removing thence to Watertown, where he spent eight years, from there coming to Hartford to learn his trade. He is regarded as an energetic and successful business man, his claim to the title being proven by the fact that his first year's business in his present location amounted to over $100,000. Mr. Buell is held in high esteem by his fellow-citizens, having been on more than one occasion solicited to accept office, an honor he invariably declined, that his entire time might be devoted to his business.

Charles T. Stuart, Photographist, No. 275 Main Street.—The City of Hartford is in many respects fortunate, possessing as it does more of wealth, culture, and refinement than any other city of like size in the country. Not the least of its advantages lies in the fact that in the person of the gentleman whose name heads this sketch, there is within its borders the most skillful and enterprising photographic artist in the State, and one who has no superior in the world. The gallery in which Mr. Stuart produces those gems of art which have made him famous, was established about twenty-six years ago by Mr. S. C. Waite, who continued it until May, 1889, when Mr. Stuart purchased it. The premises consists of two floors, each 30x50 feet in size, besides a large room above the operating-room where the printing of pictures is done. On the lower of the two floors is an elegantly furnished reception and show room and an apartment devoted to the use of the retouchers and finishers. The operating room is on the floor above, and is one of the most complete in its way to be found in the United States. All the apparatus is of the very highest style and cost, Mr. Stuart being of the opinion that good work can only be made with good tools. In the matter of furniture, scenery, and other adjuncts to the production of first-class pictures, the gallery is notable, there being a more than ordinary large assortment of these articles, so large, indeed, that their cost has swelled the amount of capital invested in the business to about $12,000. In the year prior to Mr. Stuart's purchase of the gallery, there was a business amounting to between seven and eight thousand dollars, the largest ever done in Hartford up to that time. Under Mr. Stuart's management, and as a result of his skill, the business immediately took an upward tendency, his first year producing in the neighborhood of $15,000, his second year adding another $5,000, and the present year promising to swell the increase in still greater ratio. Like Miles Standish, Mr. Stuart believes that "if you want a thing well done, you must do it yourself," and hence gives his personal attention to the operating department, making all of the sittings himself. The specialty of his business is "the instantaneous process" with which he is enabled to catch a pleasant expression and a natural one, before the sitter becomes weary and unconsciously assumes a rigid stare, as is often the case with the old method. Children and animals are thus brought within the scope of the camera with as much certainty of good results as attends the process of the adult human. While Mr. Stuart is not alone in the application of this important discovery, he is the only artist in the city who uses it habitually, and the only one who seems to be willing to incur the extra expense and labor involved in its use. The "instantaneous process" can be applied in a light where it would be useless to attempt to make a picture in the ordinary way, and it is therefore a saving of time to sitters who would otherwise be compelled to wait for favorable weather. Not only in this respect is Mr. Stuart alive to the necessities of his profession, but in every direction where improvements are suggested he can be found experimenting and adopting the better methods. An element of his success is undoubtedly to be found in the fact that he entered his profession from pure love of it, that sentiment growing with his experience and giving him an advantage only possessed by the true artist. In the matter of elegant borders, double printed pictures, beautiful interiors, scenery, etc., Mr. Stuart is far ahead of the majority of photographers and is the equal of any in the world. The business of this gallery requires the services of ten assistants, who are engaged in the different departments of printing, re-touching and finishing. The greater portion of the business is among the *élite* of Hartford, although there is a large country trade.

Mr. Stuart began the study of his profession with Mr. C. H. Williamson, the celebrated photographic artist of Brooklyn, N. Y., and continued it with others eminent in the business. He practiced for ten seasons among the fashionables at Long Branch, for one season at Cape May, and for several seasons made sittings at the U. S. Military Academy, West Point; Vassar College, Poughkeepsie; Princeton College, Princeton, N. J.; and photographed the classes of '79 and '80 at Yale, and the classes of '80 and '81 at Trinity. Mr. Stuart is the possessor of an elegantly-engrossed testimonial from Yale College, the only one of the kind ever issued by that or any like institution of learning. It reads as follows:

"To Mr. Charles T. Stuart, Greeting:—In addition to the favorable testimony given by the picture committee of 1879, we desire to give an expression of our approbation of the manner in which Mr. Charles T. Stuart has performed his work as photographer of '80, and to cordially recommend him as a skillful artist and a courteous gentleman. C. W. Haines, Jay W. Seaver, W. H. Sherman; Picture Committee of Yale, '80."

In addition to this, Mr. Stuart has many other testimonials to his skill, the most important among which, perhaps, are the hundreds of specimens of his handiwork that adorn the walls of his gallery, each a living and incontrovertible proof that he stands in the foremost phalanx of the great column of photographers, and high upon the list of the few who can be called artists.

J. R. Barlow, Bookseller and Stationer, No. 232 Asylum Street.—Among the numerous stationery and bookselling establishments in Hartford that of Mr. Joseph R. Barlow, at the above location, is worthy of especial mention. A pleasant and commodious store, eligibly located on the line of travel from the railroad depot, and in easy distance from the residences of Hartford's best people, is one of the chief factors of the success which attends this growing business. Mr. Barlow established himself in his present quarters in 1875, and by strict attention to the wants of the public, aided, doubtless, by his large private connection with the better people of the city, he has succeeded in building up a business of no mean proportions. Besides dealing in goods that are strictly in the line of the stationery and book business, Mr. Barlow carries a large stock of novelties, articles of *verts*, etc., from which selections can be made with pleasure and profit. One of the features of the business is a circulating library, the extensive patronage of which is indicative of the superior literary taste of the people of Hartford. This store is regarded as the headquarters of the *élite*, most of its patrons being of that class. Mr. Barlow is a native of Massachusetts, having been born in Boston in 1847. He has resided in Hartford for twenty-six years, of which period ten years and three months were spent in the employ of Mr. Abraham Rose. He is particularly distinguished for his musical talents, and has been organist of Trinity Church for about five years.

Mr. Barlow is regarded by the business community as one of its most upright members, and by his customers and large circle of friends as a social acquisition.

R. G. Waterous & Co. (W. J. Benton), Hatters; Furs, Robes, Trunks, Bags, etc., No. 5 Asylum Street.—This business was established about seventeen years ago in Hartford, by Mr. Waterous, who had been previously engaged in the same line for many years at Bridgeport. The original location was on the corner of Main and Asylum streets, removal being had to the present location in 1877. The store is 25 x 70 feet, with a basement of similar dimensions, in both of which are contained large stocks of hats, caps, ladies' furs, robes, blankets, gloves, bags, trunks, etc., and where employment is given to three salesmen, as well as to the necessary bookkeepers, porters, etc. The trade of the house is largely retail, but extends outside of Hartford, the name of "Waterous the Hatter" being well known throughout the State for fair dealing.

Mr. Richard G. Waterous is a native of Albany, N. Y., about fifty-six years of age, and has been long and favorably known as one of Connecticut's most enterprising business men.

Mr. W. J. Benton was born in Hartford in 1850, and has been in his present business since early manhood, and is regarded as a rising man.

H. B. Beach & Son (H. L. Beach), Boiler Works. Manufacturers of Marine and Stationary Boilers, Plate and Sheet Iron of every Description and Design, No. 135 Grove Street.—The firm of Messrs. H. B. Beach & Son are the legitimate outgrowth and successors to a long line of ancestors, all more or less prominently identified with the manufacturing industries of Connecticut, Ohio, New York and New England. Going back to 1755, we read that Colonel Benjamin Hanks was born in September, 1755, at Mansfield, Conn., and that he in 1778 established himself in the clock and watch business at Litchfield, Conn. In 1785 he returned to his native town and established a foundry for bells and brass cannon. He died in 1820 at West Troy, N. Y., where he had, in 1808, established his third son Julius in the same business. Julius was succeeded by Mr. Andrew Meneely, who married Philena, eldest daughter of Rodney Hanks, brother of Colonel Benjamin Hanks, and who was a graduate of Julius' works, succeeded to his business in 1826, making church bells a specialty. He continued this business till 1851, when he died, leaving the business to his two sons, E. A. & G. R. Meneely, who continued it under the firm name of Andrew Meneely's Sons until 1863, when they changed it to E. A. & G. R. Meneely.

Returning to Connecticut, we find here Messrs. Alpheus & Truman Hanks bought out the foundry business of Goodwin, Dodd & Gilbert in the fall of 1820, and took possession of the same in 1821.

Alpheus was a brother and Truman a second son of Colonel Benjamin Hanks, heretofore mentioned, and was a member of the firm of Hanks, Gurley & Co., founders in Troy, N. Y., which place they left to enter business in Hartford, Conn. The firm continued till the death of Alpheus Hanks, in December, 1831, when Truman continued the business till September, 1834, and sold out to his sons Lucien B. & Edwin R. Hanks, they conducting it under the firm name of L. B. Hanks & Co. until March 1836, when they sold out to Truman Hanks, Horatio Fitch and Edwin R. Hanks, who conducted it under the firm name of Hanks, Fitch & Co., until March, 1839, when the other partners sold out to Mr. Truman Hanks, who then admitted one of his former apprentices, Mr. Samuel Woodruff, as partner, and a brother-in-law of Mr. Woodruff, Mr. Charles Wygatt, and the business was conducted under the firm name of Woodruff & Co., Mr. Hanks being an invalid and confined to his house by paralysis. In 1831, Lucius B, the eldest son of Truman Hanks, and his friend Jonathan S. Miles, who married Maria, eldest daughter of Alpheus Hanks, emigrated to Cincinnati, Ohio, and established the Cincinnati Iron Foundry, which afterwards was known as the Niles Works. In 1846, George L. Hanks, in connection with Niles & Co., established a bell and brass foundry in Cincinnati, Ohio. He died in 1859, and the establishment passed into other hands

In September, 1842, Truman Hanks and Samuel Woodruff bought out Charles Mygatt, and under the name of Hanks & Woodruff continued the business of the Hartford Iron Foundry until September, 1845, when Mr. Hanks retired, leaving his interest in the hands of his son-in-law Mr. Henry B. Beach, now senior member of the firm of H. B. Beach & Son. In 1846 Mr. Hanks died. In 1845 Mr. H. B. Beach and Mr. Samuel Woodruff formed a copartnership under the firm name of Woodruff & Beach, which in 1853 was merged into a joint stock company under the name of the Woodruff & Beach Iron Works, which went out of business November 2, 1871, the Hartford Foundry and Machine Company succeeding. In 1872, Messrs. Beach & Co. (brothers of Mr. Henry B. Beach), in connection with Messrs. Hilyer & Bunce, caused to be organized the Hartford Foundry and Machine Company, with a capital of $75,000 and leased to them the works and machinery except the boiler department, which had passed into the possession of Messrs. H. B. Beach & Son. The Hartford Foundry and Machine Company closed and wound up their business on the expiration of their lease in 1880. The works then remained idle until January, 1881, when the Hartford Engineering Company was organized, which still continues.

Returning to Messrs. H. B. Beach & Son, we find them as successors to the Woodruff & Beach Iron Works in the boiler department, actively engaged in the manufacture of the very superior and celebrated "Rheutan" tubular and water front marine and stationary boilers which it is claimed are not surpassed if even equaled by boilers of any kind now made in this country.

From their long experience in steam engine building, they fully understand all requirements necessary for a complete, well-made, reliable and economical boiler, and as their aim is to do the best work in all respects, they have selected the "Rheutan" as their specialty. The rapid increase of their business can only be a reliable proof of the correctness of their judgment.

The shop occupied by this firm is necessarily but one story in height, but the lack of space above is compensated by the area of ground covered, it being 200 feet square. Here is manufactured all the different kinds of marine and stationary boilers, plate and sheet-iron work produced elsewhere, while the specialty of the firm demands most of the time of more than forty skilled workmen, as heretofore mentioned. This specialty is a patent water-front tubular boiler, claimed and conceded to be one of the best things of its kind ever manufactured in this country, being simple in construction, with a constant circulation of water through all parts, made of the best material known to the trade and in consonance with the best accepted methods of workmanship. This boiler, the invention of Mr. G. H. Rheutan, Superintendent of the works, has a water-front which is a part of the boiler itself and forms a support for the front end, obviating to a great extent the use of masonry. The chief points of excellence in this boiler are safety, additional heating surface, its capacity for being readily cleaned, and its saving of fuel, in which latter respect it is claimed to be about one third cheaper than any other boiler made. That these claims are well founded, is attested by numerous testimonials and the fact that they are in use in nearly all of the great manufacturing and other establishments of Connecticut and the neighboring States, among which may be mentioned the following:

Weed Sewing Machine Co., Hartford, Conn., four boilers; Hartford Machine Screw Co., Hartford, Conn., three boilers; American Screw Co., works at Hartford and at Providence, R. I., two boilers; Hartford Engineering Co., Hartford, Conn., one boiler; Pratt & Whitney Co., Hartford, Conn., one boiler; Billings & Spencer Co., Hartford Conn., one boiler; Hartford Steam Heating Co., Hartford, Conn., one boiler; I. B. Davis & Son., Hartford, Conn., one boiler; John W. Gray & Co., Hartford, Conn., one boiler; Hartford Manilla Co., Hartford, Conn., works at Burnside, Conn., three boilers; A. Dunham's Sons, Poquonnock, Conn., three boilers; Hartford Paper Co., Poquonnock, Conn., three boilers; E. N. Welch Manufacturing Co., Forestville, Conn., three boilers; E. N. Welch Manufacturing Co., Bristol, Conn., two boilers; Bristol Manufacturing Co., Forestville, Conn., two boilers; Bristol Brass & Clock Co., (rolling mill), Forrestville Conn., two boilers; Greenwoods Co., New Hartford, Conn., one boiler; Union Mfg. Co., North Manchester, Conn., two boilers; Medlicott Co., Windsor Locks, Conn., one boiler; Hendey Machine Co., Torrington, Conn., one boiler; Fenwick Hall, Saybrook, Conn., one boiler; Williams Bros. Manufacturing Co., Naubuc, Conn., one boiler; Yale Lock Co., Stamford, Conn., six boilers; Stanley Rule & Level Co., New Britain, Conn., one boiler; Platt Bros. & Co., Waterbury, Conn., one boiler; Toy, Bickford & Co., Simsbury, Conn., two boilers; Johnson & Co., Uncasville, Conn., one boiler; Charles Parker Co., Meriden, Conn., two boilers; Hunter & Shiland, Essex Junction, Vt., one boiler; Grant & Bogert, Flushing, L. I., one boiler; Newburgh Steam Mills, Newburgh, N. Y., six boilers; Harmony Mills, Cohoes, N. Y., one boiler; C. T. Raynolds & Co., New York, N. Y., one boiler; Garner & Co., New York, N. Y., boiler; Nonotuck Silk Co., Florence, Mass., two boilers; American Hosiery Co., New Britain, Conn., one boiler; Bridgeport Organ Co., Bridgeport, Conn., three boilers; White Paper Co., Suffield, Conn., two boilers; Waterloo Woolen Co., Waterloo, N. Y., one boiler; Waterbury Manufacturing Co., Waterbury Conn., one boiler; Waterbury Clock, Co., Waterbury, Conn., one boiler; Hazard Powder Co., Hazardville, Conn., two boilers; Peter Adams, Buckland, Conn., one boiler; Allyn House, Hartford, Conn., one boiler; Brush Electric Co., Cleveland, Ohio, one boiler.

Mr. Henry B. Beach, the senior member of the firm, is of the well-known Connecticut family of that name, and was born in Hartford in 1817.

Mr. Henry L. Beach, the great grandson of Col. Benjamin Hanks, mentioned in the commencement of this sketch, and the junior partner of Messrs. H. B. Beach & Son, was born in Hartford in 1842. In the war of the Rebellion he served as an officer of the Sixteenth Connecticut Volunteers, a three years regiment. On his return he entered his present business.

The name of Beach is an honored one in Hartford, the father of the senior member of the firm having been for fifty years the president of the Phœnix Bank, transmitting to his sons and his sons' sons, a name second to none in the lustre of integrity and a reputation they have maintained with dignity.

Hart, Merriam & Co., House-furnishing Goods, Carpets, Paper Hangings, Dry Goods, Bedding, etc., No. 364 Main Street.—The house of Hart, Merriam & Co. is one of the oldest as well as the largest in New England. One of the present firm, Mr. Sugden, has been connected with it for forty years, having entered the employ of Catlin & Co., the originators of the business, in 1843. Five years afterwards Mr. Sugden became the owner of an interest in the house, and, until 1865, the style of the firm was Sugden & Co. In that year Messrs. Hart & Merriam joined forces with Mr. Sugden and the firm adopted its present designation. The premises occupied by this firm consist of a store and basement, each 50 x 250 feet in size, where can be found in stock and on sale the most complete assortment of dry goods, carpets, paper hangings, feathers, linens, beddings, etc., to be found in the State. This stock is probably the equal, in size and variety, to any in New England; and it is scarcely too much to say that there are few houses in the United States that excel Hart, Merriam & Co. in that respect. Their magnificent stock of carpets finds a fitting place of display in their spacious carpet-hall—an apartment 50 x 100 feet in size—their dry goods, linens, bedding and other articles for house furnishing are kept and shown in the front of the spacious store, while the basement is made the receptacle of the very large surplus of stock, an idea of the magnitude of which may be gained from the fact that one item of it alone, is stated at 145,000 rolls of wall-paper, in the sale of which article they stand second on the list of all the houses in New England.

Mr. William E. Sugden, the senior member of the firm, was born in Middletown, Conn., in 1821, and came to Hartford in 1843 to enter into the service of the firm of Catlin & Co., of which he afterwards became a member, and which the present firm succeeds. From that time to the present Mr. Sugden has attended to the financial interests of the house and has won for it and for himself an enviable place in the business world. Added to the cares of his immediate business, Mr. Sugden has those pertaining to the office of president of the Hartford County Mutual Fire Insurance Company, and director in the National Exchange Bank. Mr. Charles R. Hart was born in New Britain, Conn., on June 17, 1840, and obtained his education in the high and normal schools in that city. He came to Hartford in 1857, entering his present business four years later and becoming a member of the firm of Sugden & Co. one year prior to the formation of the present house. Mr. Hart deservedly enjoys the esteem and respect of the business and social world, and has had his merit recognized by three consecutive elections to a seat in the City Council, an office in the administration of which he displayed the same traits of ability and integrity that have distinguished his business career. He was one of the original members of the select military organization known as the City Guard and has done much to further the interests of that body. In other lines of business Mr. Hart holds a prominent place, while the social circles of Hartford find in him a welcome member.

Mr. Lent B. Merriam is a native of West Hartland, Conn.; born on October 7, 1836. His education was obtained in the Wesleyan Academy at Wilbraham, Mass., where he remained until his nineteenth year, when he entered the service of Mr. Norman Adams at Winsted, Conn., as clerk, remaining there for two years. In 1857 he began his business career in Hartford as salesman for Messrs. Talcott & Post, a position he retained for eight years and until he entered the firm of which he is now a member. Mr. Merriam's business connections have extended beyond the immediate circle of his house to the transportation business of the State, he being a director in the Connecticut Western Railroad Company, and Chairman of its Executive Committee. Mr. Merriam has taken an active part in the government of his adopted city, and has been honored by being elected for five terms to a seat in the Common Council, in which body he held the very important position of Chairman of the Committee on Claims, doing good service and winning a high reputation for probity and sagacity.

All the members of this firm enjoy the thorough confidence of the community, and the house is looked upon as a representative in its line.

M. O'Flaherty, Druggist, Capitol Avenue Drug Store, No. 117 Main Street.—The flourishing drug business now carried on by the gentleman whose name heads this sketch, was established in its present location about seven years ago by Mr. J. D. Smith, and conducted by him until September, 1878, when the present proprietor succeeded to it. The store is eligibly situated on the corner of Main street and Capitol avenue, in the Hotel Capitol building, and in easy reach of the residences of the wealthier classes of Hartford's citizens, to whom is due the larger portion of the trade. The premises are 25x80 feet in size, and are fitted, furnished and stocked in the most complete manner and at a large expense. The proprietor is a practical and accomplished pharmacist and druggist, and prescriptions are insured correctness under his personal supervision.

Mr. O'Flaherty is a native of Holyoke, Mass., born in 1850, and educated in the public schools. In his profession he stands in the front rank.

G. D. Goodrich & Co. (Dr. A. Goodrich and Dr. Noah Cressy), Veterinary Drug Store, No. 36 State Street.—Famous as is New England for the development of new ideas and the adoption of improvements, it has hitherto been impossible to disprove in her behalf the saying: "there is nothing new under the sun." To the firm whose designation forms the head of this article belongs the credit of being the first to demonstrate the fact that sayings which have passed into proverbs are not always incontrovertible. That there is something that will confirm this assertion was proven in November, 1881, by the establishment of the only purely veterinary drug store ever established in this State, or—so far as history or tradition inform us—in any other State. This store, situated on State street, adjoining the United States Hotel and opposite the City Hall and Post-office, is about 25 x 50 feet in size, and has in connection with it the office of Dr. Noah Cressy, the distinguished veterinarian, who, besides practicing his profession, is a partner in the firm, and whose prescriptions go towards creating a large portion of the business. The purpose of this establishment is the furnishing of absolutely pure drugs and other articles for the alleviation and cure of all the pains and diseases to which horses, cattle, and other domestic animals are subject, with the same care and attention to detail and quality bestowed in like matters affecting the human race. No patent cure-alls, no infallible nostrums, no mysterious mixtures compounded from the traditional recipes of the unlearned country doctor, cumber the shelves of the store, nor are they supplied. But, in their places, in addition to the line of regular drugs, are a number of preparations from the formulæ of Dr. Cressy, the demand for which is so great as to compel their manufacture in large quantities, that the time that would be otherwise consumed in putting up the numerous prescriptions can be saved. Among these preparations may be mentioned three types of condition powders for horses; the first for general debility; the next for coughs, colds, lung diseases and distempers; and the last for the various skin affections to which the animal is subject. The liniments, colic mixtures, worm medicines and other preparations put up in quantities have attained a wide reputation and sale, and have become the standards of such articles over a wide extent of territory. In addition to those already mentioned, there are medicines for all types of disease that touch the domestic animals, from the valuable and stately racer to the less valuable house dog, and from him to the comparatively insignificant but still valuable chicken.

In short, the wants of the ailing animal are thoroughly provided for, and the Veterinary Drug Store is the monument that marks a great rise in the elevation of the conditon of man's best friends—the domestic animals.

Mr. George D. Goodrich is the son of the well-known Dr. A. R. Goodrich, formerly State Comptroller and at present State Treasurer. He was born in Vernon, Conn., on August 4, 1850, and has made that place his home all his life. His education was finished at the Connecticut Literary Institution at Suffield, after leaving which he entered his father's office and began the study of the drug business. From 1873 to 1877 he served under his father as chief clerk in the State Comptroller's office, and at the expiration of his term purchased the Charter Oak Drug Store on Central Row, Hartford, conducting it until September, 1882, when he sold it out in order to give his undivided attention to his present business.

Mr. Goodrich was tax collector for one term in his native town, and served for five years as captain on the staff of Brigadier Generals W. Randall Smith of Norwalk and Stephen R. Smith of New Haven, performing, for the greater part of that time, the duties of major, as brigade commissary.

Mr. Goodrich is a practical druggist, and enjoys not only the reputation of being the first and only one to establish himself in his peculiar line, but is regarded as an honorable and rising business man and a cultivated gentleman.

The personal history of the other members of the firm will be found under their appropriate heads.

Billings & Hitchcock, Manufacturers of Knit Goods, No. 1189 Broad Street.—This business was established at Springfield, Mass., by Capt. H. R. Billings in 1879, and was removed to this city March 1st, 1882, at which time the present firm of Billings & Hitchcock was formed. They manufacture silk and woolen hosiery and mittens by hand machines, employing about thirty persons. The building occupied is 90 x 32 feet in size and one story in height.

Most of the productions of this factory are sold through the commission house of Messrs. Kibbe, Chaffee, Shreve & Co., Nos. 71 and 73 Worth Street, New York.

Capt. Henry R. Billings is a native of Windsor, Vermont, born in 1837. For several years he was a contractor at the Weed Sewing Machine Co., having learned the machinist trade in his native town. He was a member of the First Connecticut Regiment, and later of the Twentieth Connecticut, enlisting in the latter regiment as private and returning as captain of Company D.

Mr. Marcena Hitchcock is a native of Lebanon, New York, and is fifty years of age. He has been in Hartford since 1866, most of the time, as now, a contractor at the works of the Weed Sewing Machine Co. He is also a practical machinist, wood-worker and inventor. The firm has a good financial standing and its productions are of the best.

George Sichler, proprietor Hartford Gambrinus Brewery, Park, corner Lawrence Street.—The Hartford Gambrinus Brewery, situated at Park, corner Lawrence street, George Sichler, proprietor, is the latest accession to the list of breweries in Connecticut, and is of the most modern construction. The largest building is 100 x 45 feet in size, and four stories in height, the brewery proper is 35 x 36 feet, five stories, and these with a restaurant and residence adjoining, comprise the establishment owned and occupied by Mr. Sichler. The buildings are built of expensive pressed brick, ornamented with granite and present an imposing appearance. The production is about 25,000 barrels of lager beer per year. As is usual with first class brewers, Mr. Sichler takes great pride in his horses and teams, which are used in his business. The trade extends to different points in the State and the productions of the Gambrinus Brewery are well known to Connecticut people.

Mr. Sichler was born in Wurtemberg, Germany, in 1840. He learned the trade of a brewer in his native town and came to America in 1867. For several years he was a brewer in New York City coming to Hartford in 1876 and carried on business on Albany avenue, for four years before building in his present location.

Mr. Sichler is known to the public as an honorable business man, and to the trade as a capable and intelligent brewer. His establishment contributes largely in the supply of a refreshing beverage, the consumption of which the recent industrial census shows has increased more than fifty per cent during the last decade.

A. S. Cook, Manufacturer of Machinery, Colt's West Armory.—This manufacturing establishment is one of the many in Hartford which has developed quite an export trade for its products. The business was established in 1869, and its gradual and substantial increase since that time, is complimentary to the financial ability and mechanical skill of the proprietor.

In the growth of most businesses of any magnitude, there is sometimes felt the immediate use of capital, which too often is supplied by some capitalist, to the detriment of the originator, and instead of labor and capital going hand in hand, the former is controlled by the latter, and what at first gave brilliant promise to the inventor and projector results in a bare existence, while the capitalist reaps the main reward.

Not so with Mr. A. S. Cook. He has made haste slowly but surely, until now the premises occupied by this flourishing business embrace an area of 60 x 200 feet in Colt's West Armory, while he employs from fifty to seventy-five, and indirectly one hundred men, according to the demands of his business. While, in a general sense, he is a manufacturer of machinery, he makes a specialty of manufacturing machinery for the making of wood screws, tire bolts, stove bolts, lag screws, and rivets, and is also manufacturer of Stephens' patent parallel vise and special machinery.

In the manufacture of vises Mr. Cook is a marked instance of business success. He has brought into his service workmen of a high order, and not only requires a large number, but gives them constant employment. The invention is the most obvious advance in the economy of vises yet discovered. It is the embodiment of simplicity and effectiveness, and is so marked an improvement on anything of the kind yet discovered that its introduction to popular use is only a matter of time.

The requisitions made on Mr. C. for this article are surprising. It is evidently meeting a necessity long felt and general. To meet this demand a strong force is constantly engaged. But this is by no means all or even the largest part of his business. He manufactured a complete outfit of screw machinery for the Russell & Erwin Manufacturing Co., of New Britain, Conn., and furnished them a complete set of patterns and drawings for the same. Such of these powerful machines for heading the blanks, as he now has finished, present the appearance of great durability and immense strength. They cannot fail to perform well the hardest tasks that may be assigned them in their future combats with the cold iron. They are creditable exhibitions of the skill and enterprise of this successful manufacturer, and must meet the highest approval of the wealthy company who are to employ them.

The following-named companies are also furnished with a complete outfit of screw machinery made by Mr. Cook: Wardell & Hinckley, Chicago, Ill.; The Massachusetts Screw Co., Holyoke, Mass.; Syracuse, N. Y., Screw Co.; Philadelphia, Pa., Screw Co.; Atlantic Screw Works, Hartford, Conn.; Dominion Bolt Co., Toronto, Canada; Dayton Screw Co. (of which Mr. Albert G. Angell, formerly of the American Screw Co., Providence, R. I., is president), Dayton, Ohio. A factory in Berlin, Germany, was also supplied, sending to the latter city men to put the machinery in operation. Sweden and other countries have also machinery made at this establishment.

The facilities of Mr. Cook enable him to undertake any large contracts for machinery of any kind, as he has completed his arrangements to meet the most diverse requirements. Mr. A. S. Cook is a native of Sandwich, Carroll Co., N. H., and about sixty years of age. He has been a resident of Hartford for over thirty years. He learned most of his trade in Lowell, Mass., finishing it with Mr. A. Pratt, president of the Pratt & Whitney Co., of this city, since which time he has been in his present business—the manufacturing of machinery. In the various departments of the business, Mr. Cook is assisted by his two sons, who have grown to manhood, with him, and, like the father, are practical machinists. Mr. M. F. Cook is thirty-one years of age, and has charge of the planing department.

Mr. John F. Cook, the youngest, is twenty-eight years of age, and has charge of the office. Both are natives of Hartford and graduates of the high school.

Mr. A. S. Cook is a member of the city council of his adopted city, and enjoys the distinction of being the only manufacturer of wood and coach screw machinery in the world.

The Hartford Sanitary Plumbing Company, Manufacturers of the Hartford Glass Water-Closet, Nos. 68 to 86 Market Street.—There is no department of sanitary science that has received so much attention of late years as has the subject of the construction of water-closets, with a view of removing the objectionable features that render the ordinary closet a nuisance to the senses of sight and smell, and what is infinitely worse, absolutely dangerous to health and life. Hundreds of inventors have busied their brains in devising plans for preventing the deadly sewer-gas from gaining an entrance to our dwellings, and some of the hundreds of consequent inventions have been more or less successful, the majority, however, serving no other purpose than to increase the evil they were designed to ameliorate. The absolute solution of this vexatious problem was left to the Hartford Sanitary Plumbing Company, the patentees and manufacturers of the Hartford Glass Water-Closet, an article which has won for itself an immense sale and the unqualified indorsement of the sanitarians of the country.

This closet is manufactured in the highest style of metallic work and on a principle never heretofore used. It consists of a metallic shell, lined with blown opaque glass, with automatic air-tight valves and hermetically closing traps. The glass lining is smooth and non-absorbent, covering the whole interior and preserving it continually in a state of absolute purity and sweetness. The valves are so constructed that they cannot be opened by pressure from the sewer, and all the parts of the discharge being of equal size all deposits are carried off by the action of an unbroken column of water. In short, the construction of the closet is so perfect and simple that it explains and commends itself at once.

The company was incorporated in 1880, with a capital of $60,000. The officers are: Robert E. Day, President; R. W. Farmer, Secretary and Treasurer; H. S. Lord, Superintendent.

Mr. Day is a well-known citizen of Hartford, where he fills a number of important positions in the business world. He is president of the Hartford Security Company and is director in the leading banks and insurance companies.

Mr. Farmer is a member of the well-known banking firm of Hubbard & Farmer, and has been State Auditor for ten years.

Mr. Lord, Superintendent of the company's business, is a native of Lyme, Conn., and was born in 1839. His advent in Hartford occurred in 1862, since which time he has served as clerk in the Allyn House for six years, and as a traveler for the house of Rodgers Brothers of Waterbury and for the William Rodgers Manufacturing Company of Hartford.

T. Steele & Son (T. Sedgwick Steele), Importers and Dealers in Watches, Jewelry, etc., No. 407 Main Street.—Hartford, the Capitol City of Connecticut, is celebrated for its wealth, its culture, its educational facilities, its churches, its insurance and banking institutions, the enterprise of its business men, and for many other things too numerous to detail. Perhaps one of the chief items in the list of its characteristics is the widespread and intelligent love of the beautiful and artistic among its residents, a taste that finds expression in the many and expensive objects of art adorning their homes. It has been said that love of the artistic is inborn in those who possess it and that it cannot be acquired by any one unfortunate enough to lack it at birth. While this may be, and doubtless is, true to a certain extent, the statement can be qualified by the equally positive assertion that latent tastes may be cultivated, and natural instincts fostered from their original crudeness to a condition wherein cultured intelligence softens the rough edges of unthinking enthusiasm to the smoother delights of enlightened discrimination. That there must be leaders and teachers in every upward movement is a truth that proves itself, and that there must have been such in the development of the taste that has made Hartford the art centre of provincial New England is equally obvious. Among these leaders and teachers the names of Messrs. Steele & Son occupy prominent positions, awarded by the public and conceded by their competitors.

As long ago as the year 1836, the elder Mr. Steele established himself in the jewelry trade, by the purchase of the business of J. O. & W. Pitkin, located at No. 340 Main street. Mr. Steele had as partner Mr. Crocker, the firm being known as Steele & Crocker up to 1842, when the latter gentleman died. From that time until 1866 Mr. Steele conducted the business on his sole account, his son, Mr. T. Sedgwick Steele, being admitted to partnership in that year and the present firm designation adopted. From the time of the entrance of the younger gentleman as a member of the firm may be dated the ever-increasing excellence in art matters that has culminated in placing the house in the proud position it now occupies in that respect. In 1875 it was found that the old quarters were inadequate to the needs of the business, both in a mercantile and artistic sense, and removal was determined on. Immediate steps were taken towards the fitting and furnishing of the new store, and it was decided that in those essentials it should be second to none in New England, and superior to any in Hartford or the entire State. How well that decision bore its fruit may be learned by an inspection of the palatial quarters now occupied, where the beauty-loving eye is surfeited with the dazzling *ensemble* of rosewood and marble, of fret and fresco, of plate-glass and tapestry, of velvets and carving, of jewels rare and metals bright and the unequaled collection of tasteful and expensive objects of art, culled from the markets of the older countries by master hands, whose labor was a work of love.

In December, 1875, the new store was ready for occupancy, and the business was transferred to it, the younger Mr. Steele being then the sole proprietor, his father having passed from earth only a short time prior to the removal. From that time until the present Mr. Steele has labored to elevate and maintain the standard of taste in art matters, with the gratifying success heretofore indicated.

The advantages enjoyed by this house are perhaps greater than those of any similar establishment between New York and Boston, for the reason that their agency at Geneva, Switzerland, enables them to import direct, thus saving a considerable percentage in prices, and bringing the later styles of goods before the public much earlier than can be done by houses depending on the jobbers in other American cities.

Mr. T. Sedgwick Steele, the proprietor of this magnificent temple of the arts, is a native of Hartford, and was born on June 11, 1845. From an early age he has shown that love of the beautiful in nature and art which has culminated in his present leadership in matters of taste, and which has done so much for culture in his native city and State. Not only as a lover and judge of art is Mr. Steele conspicuous, but as one of its practical exponents he has won merited distinction, chiefly as a painter of still-life pieces, a number of which have found places "on the line," at the New York National Academy of Design and the Brooklyn Art Academy. With the pen Mr. Steele is as ready as with the brush, and the columns of many newspapers and magazines have been enriched by his articles on the hunting and fishing regions of Maine, Lake Superior, Florida and other places through which he has journeyed. His latest contributions to current literature are in the form of two books, entitled "Paddle and Portage," and "Canoe and Camera," respectively. These works are the outcome and description of the author's experience in northern Maine and New Brunswick, in which almost unknown country he made a number of canoe tours. The illustrations, which are both numerous and artistic are from photographs made by Mr. Steele himself, whose knowledge of the camera and its uses is as thorough and as practical as is his knowledge of the uses of the brush and pen.

With these lighter and more pleasing labors, Mr. Steele combines the sterner pursuit of the surveyor, having compiled and published the latest and most complete map of the head waters of the Aroostook, Penobscot and St. John's rivers, embracing portions of Canada and New Brunswick. Mr. Steele is Secretary of the Connecticut School of Design, an institution in which his influence has been felt. His love of the athletic side of life is evidenced by his annual canoe tours and the fact that he is an active member and President of the Connecticut Bicycle Club.

In conclusion, it is safe to say that the house of T. Steele & Son is the leading jewelry house outside of Boston, in New England; and of its proprietor, that he enjoys well-merited and universal esteem.

William H. Kelsey & Co. (Wm. H. Kelsey, Jr.), Merchant Tailors, No. 283 Main Street.—The elegant and spacious store of William H. Kelsey & Co., merchant tailors, is situated on the corner of Main and Pearl streets, and is one of the finest of its kind in Hartford. It is 20 by 100 feet in size, with an extensive plate-glass front on both streets, affording unusually great facilities for the display of the first-class goods and the fine workmanship for which the house is noted. The business was established about twenty years ago by the elder Mr. Kelsey, the firm of Kelsey, Carpenter & Hitchcock succeeding him. Another change, some years later, made the firm Kelsey & Hitchcock, and on February 1, 1882, the final change took place by the admission of Mr. W. H. Kelsey, Jr., and the present firm name was adopted.

Mr. William H. Kelsey, Sr., is a native of Clinton, Conn., born in 1826. He moved to Hartford when a young man and commenced at once to learn the business in which he has won high repute. He is prominent in church and charitable matters and is one of the officers of the Asylum Hill Congregational Church.

Mr. Wm. H. Kelsey, Jr., is a native of Hartford, born in 1854. He acquired his education in the public and high schools here and his knowledge of his business from his father, with whom he has been as clerk and partner for about six years.

The firm has an excellent standing in the mercantile world and its members enjoy the hearty esteem of their fellow citizens.

Charles S. Goodwin & Son, Dealers in Boots, Shoes and Rubbers, No. 277 Main Street.—This house is the oldest retail boot and shoe house in Connecticut, and, with perhaps one exception, the oldest in the line, either wholesale or retail. It was established in 1804 by Mr. John Goodwin, father of the senior member of the present firm and grandfather to its junior. From the founder, the business descended to an elder son, John H. Goodwin, who carried it on in his own name for several years, and afterwards under the firm name of John H. Goodwin & Co. In 1865 Mr. Charles S. Goodwin assumed entire proprietorship and continued the business until 1881, when his son and present partner was admitted to the firm, and the designation, C. S. Goodwin & Son, adopted. The store at No. 277 Main street, now occupied by the firm, is a pleasant and commodious one, being about 22 x 60 feet in size, with very high ceilings and desirable show windows. The stock carried ranges from $7,000 to $8,000 in value, and the business done is in the usual mercantile proportion. The history of this business contains, perhaps, more of the direct history of one family than any other of its line in Hartford, or indeed in the State. For more than seventy-five years it has been carried on at the same location, and always by members of the Goodwin family, embracing three generations. The first successor to the founder of the house was Mr. John H. Goodwin, who entered it when but fourteen years of age, and who, in his time, carried on a manufacturing, wholesaling and retailing trade, the first two features having been subsequently dropped. He was for many years a director in the Phœnix Mutual Life Insurance Company, and otherwise prominent in the community until 1873, when, at the age of sixty-three years, he passed away, respected and lamented by his fellow citizens.

Mr. Charles S. Goodwin, of the present firm, is a native of Hartford; born in 1819. He is also a director in the Phœnix Life, and is otherwise conspicuous in the business world.

Mr. Charles L. Goodwin, son of the last named gentleman and junior partner in the firm, is a native of Hartford; born in 1858. His education was acquired here, as well as the knowledge of business. The firm enjoys the thorough confidence of the community and its individual members universal respect, as well as the distinction of being partners in the oldest house in direct line of succession in this section of the State.

The Hills Archimedean Lawn Mower Company, No. 274 Main Street.—One of the many manufacturing establishments which have contributed greatly to the reputation which Connecticut has as a manufacturing State is The Archimedean Lawn Mower Company of this city, whose works comprise a part of Colts' Armory, with an office at No. 274 Main Street. The business was inaugurated many years ago by Messrs. Sawyer, Brewer, Bassett & Co., who conducted business at first in this city and later at Birmingham, Conn.

In 1871, this company bought what is known as the Hills patent, and were organized with a capital of $100,000, and the following-named officers: President, Mr. Ebenezer P. Miner; Vice-President, Mr. Henry K. Morgan; Treasurer, Mr. Francis P. Cooley; Secretary, Mr. John R. Redfield.

The works at Colts' Armory comprise three floors, each 60 by 100 feet, where from 75 to 100 people are employed making four kinds of lawn mowers, adapted not only to the wants of this country but Russia, England, France, Germany, Australia, New Zealand, and other foreign countries, to which about one-half of their productions are exported. The mowers made by this company have been awarded the highest praise wherever exhibited. At the principal exhibitions of the world the number of medals won is no less than twenty-four, including a gold medal at Hamburg, Germany, and medals at the World's Fair at Vienna, and at the Centennial at Philadelphia. So popular are they that they have become celebrated throughout all civilized countries, and are recognized as the most perfect and desirable lawn mower ever made.

The officers of the company are all well known residents and men of financial standing in Hartford.

The President, Mr. Ebenezer P. Miner, is a native of Groton, Conn., born in 1837, educated in the public schools of the State, and has been identified with this city since 1862, where he was a prominent dry goods dealer for ten years prior to assuming the office of president of this company.

Mr. Henry K. Morgan the Vice-President is a retired capitalist here, director in the Pratt Street Savings Bank, Phœnix Fire Insurance Company, Weed Sewing Machine Company, and interested in several of the benevolent institutions here, the Hartford Hospital, and others of like nature.

Mr. Francis B. Cooley, the Treasurer, is president of the National Exchange Bank, and at one time the head of the great dry-goods house of Messrs. Cooley, Farwell & Co., Chicago, which he established.

The Secretary, Mr. John R. Redfield, is cashier of the National Exchange Bank, and well known in financial circles.

The sales of the company amount to $150,000 per annum, and their productions stand in the front rank, and have a reputation second to none.

Honiss & Abbe, Fresh Fish, Lobsters, etc., No. 183 State Street.—This business is one of the oldest in its line in Hartford. It was established by Mr. Frank G. Oakes about fifteen years ago. Later it was Oakes & Abbe, who were succeeded by Mr. L. G. Abbe, the present firm taking possession in the spring of 1882.

In addition to dealing in all kinds of fresh fish, lobsters, clams, etc., they make a specialty in the season of dealing at wholesale in the celebrated Connecticut River shad, which they send throughout New England and adjoining States.

The senior partner, Mr. Thomas Honiss, is, in addition to his interest here, proprietor of the wholesale and retail oyster depot at No. 30 State street, under the United States Hotel, where he has been in business for a number of years. He is forty-seven years of age and represents his ward as Councilman in the city government.

Mr. L. G. Abbe is a native of East Windsor, Conn., born in 1839. He served his country as a member of the Twenty-second Connecticut Regiment during the war of the Rebellion. He was later postmaster in the town of Waterbury from 1871 to 1876, and was agent for the Naugatuck Railroad and Adams Express Co. for five years, and also school committee in the same community. Both houses are representative in their line and do an extensive business in this city and adjoining States.

Seidler & May, Furniture Dealers and Manufacturers of Patent Sofa-Beds, Nos. 14 and 16 Ford Street.—In 1868 Mr. George N. Seidler, the senior member of the firm of Seidler & May, established this extensive business, which has since grown to be one of the largest in the State. In 1869, a year later, the firm was made Seidler & May, under which name it still continues at Nos. 14 and 16 Ford street, opposite the new State Capitol. Their business consists of dealing in all kinds of furniture, mattresses, spring beds, mirrors, feathers, etc. They are also manufacturers of furniture to order and their patent sofa-bed, which received the highest award—a medal and diploma at the Centennial. It opens easily without having to be removed from the wall, and makes a good, comfortable bed for constant use. The fact of it being made in sections precludes the wear on the covering of the sofa, when used as a bed, making a much more durable sofa, it is claimed, than where you have to use both seat and back to sleep upon. It was patented Dec. 7, 1875, and its sales since that time have contributed not a little to the unusual success of the house.

The premises occupied by Seidler & May, consist of a building five stories in height 39x116 feet in size, including the basement. The show-rooms and office are particularly pleasing and business-like. In addition to the other specialties they manufacture a reclining chair which has met with much favor from the public. About twenty-five employees are engaged and a very large business done in the city and with the surrounding country.

Mr. Geo. N. Seidler is a native of New York, born in 1835, and since 1854 has been in the furniture business.

Mr. Charles May is a native of South Hartwick, Otsego County, N. Y., born in 1839, and has been in this line of business since 1869.

The house, though not as old as some others in years, excels in its facilities and ranks among the first in Connecticut as to character and amount of business done.

The Hartford Woven Wire Mattress Company, No. 175 Pearl Street.—This company was incorporated in 1868, with $60,000 capital. It has the following-named officers: President, George Roberts; Treasurer, W. J. Myers; Secretary, Henry Roberts. The directors are the above-named officers, S. T. Woolcott, Charles Green and W. L. Matson. The manufactory and office are located at No. 175 Pearl street, where four floors of a spacious brick building are occupied, and sixty people employed.

More than thirteen years' use of the woven wire mattress has demonstrated its usefulness in families, hotels, asylums, hospitals, etc. The company has agents in thirty-three cities, and commercial travelers are employed in every State in the Union. The company publishes an illustrated twenty-five-page circular, which shows the designs and describes in detail the different makes.

The company is the largest manufacturers of woven wire mattresses in the Union, and its productions are protected by patents.

The officers and directors are some of Hartford's successful men and well-known citizens.

Hartford Wire Works, F. H. Crosthwaite, Manager, No. 247 Asylum Street.—The business of the Hartford Wire Works was established by Mr. J. Henry Martin in the year 1870. At that time, as at the present, he was a contractor at the county jail, hiring convict labor. Happening, one day, to be in a florist's place, he was attracted by the wire designs there on exhibition, and conceived the idea of manufacturing them.

To that end, he experimented at first with a few of the inmates at the county jail, and ultimately had a number at work with gratifying results.

The office and salesroom, at that time, was located on Trumbull street, which were removed to the present location, No. 247 Asylum street about four years ago.

For some years Mr. Crosthwaite was a partner with Mr. Martin, but on the removal of the business to this number he purchased it, and now conducts it as sole proprietor.

All kinds of florist's wire designs are manufactured; also, spark-guards and fenders, window-guards, office-railing, wire-cloth, fencing, etc.; a specialty being made of patent window-screens.

The premises occupied consist of two floors, 26 x 65 feet in size. The first floor is used as an office and salesroom, the other as a manufactory for window-screens. The other goods are made at the county jail, where about fifteen people are engaged in this pursuit.

The history of the wirework business in Hartford is full of non-success for those who were engaged in it, no less than five concerns having started and failed in a few years, leaving the Hartford Wire Works alone in possession of the field.

Mr. F. H. Crosthwaite is a native of London, England; born in 1852. He has resided in Hartford since a boy, where he was educated in the public schools, and has been in this business for ten years. The establishment is one of the largest of its class in the State, and its productions find a market in New York and other large cities.

Chas. F. Hurd & Co. (C. F. Hurd and Moses Mellen), Importers and Dealers in Crockery, China, Glass and Plated Ware, etc., 231 and 233 Main Street.—About the year 1840, the business now carried on by Messrs. Chas. F. Hurd & Co. was established on the opposite side of Main street by a Mr. S. P. Kendall, he being joined some years later by Mr. A. R. Skinner. The firm of Kendall & Skinner was dissolved, the latter gentleman continuing the business on his own account until purchased by Mr. Hurd of the present firm. In 1878 Mr. Moses Mellen purchased an interest in the business and the present designation was adopted. Thirty-three years ago the business was removed to the store now occupied, which is one of the finest in the city. It is 25 x 85 feet in size, and has two very spacious and elegant plate-glass show-windows in which are displayed specimens of the large and varied stock of crockery, china, glass, and plated ware, etc., carried by the firm, who are importers and wholesale and retail dealers in those articles. In addition to the store proper, there are several lofts in different localities used for storage of the surplus stock and a large packing room in the rear of the store. The business done by this house is very large and rapidly growing, it having trebled in five years.

Mr. Charles F. Hurd is a native of Connecticut about thirty-nine years of age, and has resided in Connecticut the greater portion of his life. He is universally respected and esteemed, and is looked upon as one of the leading business men of the Capitol City.

Mr. Moses Mellen was born in Boston, Mass., and is about thirty-nine years of age. He has resided in Hartford since his connection with the firm, and has won the entire confidence of the community. During the war of the Rebellion, Mr. Mellen served his country as a member of the Forty-fourth Massachusetts Infantry, coming home with a good record.

The house of Charles F. Hurd & Co. is classed among the leading houses in Connecticut.

L. B. Goodman, Wholesale Dealer in Boots, Shoes and Rubbers, No. 147 Asylum Street.—One of the oldest among the old established shoe houses in Connecticut is the one at present conducted by Mr. L. B. Goodman, at No. 47 Asylum street. In 1838 the firm was known as Whitney, Hills & Rising, in 1842 it was Hills & Rising, six years later, Hills, Risang & Childs—Mr. Goodman having then risen from a clerkship to a partnership—in 1858 it became Hills & Goodman, about nine years later it was changed to Goodman & Hills, and in 1871 Mr. Goodman assumed the sole proprietorship, retaining it up to the present. The premises occupied by Mr. Goodman consist of two floors, each 22 x 110 feet in size and stocked with a very large assortment of boots, shoes, rubbers, etc., in which articles there is done an extensive wholesale and jobbing trade throughout the State.

Mr. Goodman is a native of West Hartford; born in 1820. Prior to attaining his majority he was clerk in the grocery business, but subsequently to that event entered his present business and has remained in it since. In addition to carrying on the affairs of his house, Mr. Goodman has at times been connected with the banking business as director, but was compelled by the growth of his own business to relinquish all outside matters and devote his entire time and attention to those affairs.

In the commercial world the name of L. B. Goodman stands high and its bearer is universally respected.

Henry Meyer, Dealer in Furniture, No. 175 Main Street.—Among the retail furniture stores in Hartford deserving of mention is that of Mr. Henry Meyer, who first commenced business on Mulberry street in 1876, removing to his present location in 1878. The store now occupied at No. 175 Main street is 20 x 75 feet, and in addition there are three floors and an L for workshops and warerooms, in which six workmen are employed.

The stock consists of furniture of every description, upholstery goods and bedding, and all the many goods usually found in such establishments.

The location is central, being on the line of the principal business thoroughfare and in the midst of the retail business of the city.

Quite a business is done in the manufacture to order of fine furniture, and the repairing of the same, for which Mr. Meyer has an excellent reputation.

Mr. Henry Meyer is a native of the northern part of Germany, born in 1831. He has been a citizen of this country for about thirty years and a resident of Hartford for nineteen years. He served his adopted country during the war as a Sergeant in the famous Berdan Sharp Shooters, and was attached to Porter's Corps.

During his residence here he has built up a good trade and acquired the reputation of a careful, conservative business man and a highly respected citizen.

Clayton H. Case, Jeweler, No. 335 Main Street.—The very elegant jewelry establishment of Mr. Clayton H. Case, or, as he is more frequently called, Captain Case, is situated on Main street, a few doors from Asylum street, in one of the most eligible business locations in Hartford. The store, the largest in the city used for the jewelry business, has a plate glass front about 20 feet in width, while its depth is about four times that figure. Twenty-five feet of apartment is partitioned off for a workroom, leaving the depth of the salesroom at fifty-five feet. Mr. Case employs an average of eight workmen, and does a considerable business in manufacturing as well as an immense trade in watches, his stock of which is unequaled in size and variety by any similar establishment in Hartford and by few in the State. Mr. Case carries an extensive stock of silverware, jewelry and diamonds, the value of which reaches the neighborhood of $40,000. The establishment of this business dates from the year 1868, when Mr. Case began in a small way at 553 Main street, remaining there for three years, and being forced to seek a larger store at No. 10 Asylum street. Here he remained for nine and one-half years, and in September, 1880, was again forced by his rapidly growing business to remove, taking the commodious store he now occupies.

Mr. Case is a native of Connecticut, born in Hartland, in 1840. He has been a resident of Hartford for about fifteen years, the early part of his life having been passed in his native place, and in Barkhamsted, New York, and California. He entered the service in 1861 as a member of the Tenth Connecticut Volunteers, serving one year in that organization. In 1864 he joined the Fourteenth Regulars, in which organization he remained for three years, two of which was spent among the Indians. At the expiration of his term of service he returned to New York, coming thence to Hartford and entering at once into business. Shortly after he settled in Hartford he became a member of that historical corps known as the Putnam Phalanx, and in 1868 was elected to the captaincy, a position he has held consecutively up to the present and through five successive terms. Mr. Case enjoys the entire respect and confidence of the community, and is one of few business men who have built themselves up from the smallest to the largest.

Allen Brothers (Albert L. & Irving W. Allen), Dealers in Choice Groceries, etc., No. 103 Main Street.—The business of the Messrs. Allen Brothers was established by them at their present location, No. 103 Main street, in the year 1880.

The premises consist of a store 25 x 100 feet, well stocked with choice groceries, fruits, wood, willow and stone ware, etc. The amount of business done amounts to $30,000 per annum, in which the services of two clerks are required.

Both of the proprietors have been in the grocery business in the city previous to commencing here. They are both natives of Canterbury, Conn., and came to Hartford in 1871.

Mr. Albert L. Allen is thirty-five years of age, while his brother, Irving W., is thirty-two, and were successful farmers in their native town before coming to Hartford to reside. They are classed among the most active and enterprising young business men in the Capitol City.

Linus T. Fenn, Furniture, No. 205 Main Street.—It may not be generally known that this business was established in 1811, and has continued uninterruptedly on the same site since that time.

The founder, who built so well, was Mr. Daniel S. Dewey, who was succeeded by the firm of Messrs. Elton & Deming. The senior member of the firm, Mr. Elton, was the preceptor of Mr. Fenn, the present proprietor. In 1873, Mr. Fenn was promoted from a position in the house to be a partner, and the firm became Deming & Fenn. In 1877, four years later, the sign of Linus T. Fenn was hung on the outer walls where it has since remained, a recognition of the success of the proprietor who has grown from the boy to the man, from an employee to the proprietor of one of the oldest and largest furniture establishments in the State of Connecticut.

The premises now occupied for this constantly increasing business have long since outgrown their original dimensions. Situated at No. 205 Main street, on the corner of Mulberry and opposite the Athenæum, it extends down the latter street 200 feet, and embraces two whole buildings, comprising six floors. The front of the store has a fine display of elegant furniture, and in the rear, besides display and store rooms, are also workshops, where from twenty to thirty skilled workmen are kept busy in the manufacture and repairing of furniture.

Every conceivable kind of furniture for the rich and for the poor is to be found in these warerooms, including parlor, chamber, dining-room and library suites.

Two elegantly appointed double teams, the finest for the purpose in Hartford, are engaged in the delivery of furniture in the city and surrounding villages, where the name of Fenn is synonymous with furniture.

Mr. Linus T. Fenn is a native of Plymouth, Conn., and fifty-two years of age. He came to Hartford when a youth of seventeen, since which time this business has felt his influence in some capacity. His career is a fitting example to every youth who desires to achieve success without having it thrust upon him.

Commencing at the beginning, Mr. Fenn has mastered all the minutiæ of his business, and stands without a peer in Hartford, in his special line, the architect of his own fortune.

Scott & Co., Fine Art Dealers and Frame Manufacturers, No. 8 Mulberry Street.—One of the new enterprises which were started during the year 1882, in Hartford, for the public's favors, is that of Messrs. Scott & Co., who embarked in business in June of that year, at No. 8 Mulberry street, which is a store 20 x 30 feet in size with basement, near the corner of Main street. The general appearance of the establishment is suggestive of success. The proprietors manufacture and deal in mirrors, pictures, frames, paintings, engravings, stereoscopes, views, and make a specialty of all styles of gold frames for framing large oil paintings, water colors, fine engravings, etc.

Mr. P. Scott and Mr. R. A. O'Gorman are practical men in their business, pleasant and courteous, deserving all the success which they have achieved since their association has commenced.

L. Tiffany & Co. (Lucian Tiffany and E. W. Clark), Machinists and Manufacturers of Light Machinery, No. 31 Wells Street.—One of the busiest and most prosperous among the machine shops in Hartford, is that of L. Tiffany & Co., at No. 31 Wells street. The present firm was established on April 1st, 1881, Mr. Tiffany having previously conducted the business on his own account for many years. The shop is quite a spacious apartment, and contains the usual assortment of lathes, drills, planes, punches, presses, etc., found in establishments of this kind, and finds room and employment for an average of six workmen besides the proprietors, who are both practical machinists.

The manufacture of light machinery, repairing and jobbing, and the renovation of mowing machines and lawn mowers form the principal part of the trade of the concern, which extends to the outlying towns and amounts to about $10,000 per annum.

Mr. Lucian Tiffany was born in Southbridge, Mass., and is sixty-nine years of age. For forty years he has been a resident of Hartford, most of that time engaged in his present business. He is a thorough master of his trade and is universally respected as a citizen.

Mr. E. W. Clark is a native of Boston, Mass., twenty-eight years of age. He has resided in Hartford for fifteen years, during which time he learned the trade of machinist, becoming a member of the firm as above stated. He is a first-class mechanic, and, like his partner, has an excellent reputation in the community.

Edwin W. Kenyon, Dealer in Tea, Coffee, Sugar, Spices, etc., No. 433 Main Street.—About ten years prior to 1883, Messrs. Degnan & Quinn started in the tea, coffee and spice trade at the location on Main street, near Church, now occupied by Mr. Kenyon, their successor, who purchased the business on March 22, 1880. The store has a commanding front of thirty feet, its depth, inclusive of the store-house and packing room is about eighty feet. A general wholesale and retail trade in teas, coffees, sugars, spices, etc., is done, extending in its scope throughout Hartford and many of the adjoining towns. The specialty of the establishment is the sale of teas and coffees, the finer and medium brands of which are to be found here in great variety and quantity. Four assistants and two delivery wagons are employed in the business, which on an average stock of $5,000, reaches a volume of about $40,000, with indications of a large and steady increase, it having been doubled by Mr. Kenyon since its purchase from the original proprietors.

Mr. Kenyon was born in Enfield, Conn., in 1853, but has resided in Hartford since infancy. His education was acquired in the public and high schools here, and his early business experience in the service of the Colt Manufacturing Co., where he was bookkeeper for the ten years preceding his entrance into his present business.

In the business and social circles of Hartford, Mr. Kenyon is regarded as a rising man and a citizen of undoubted worth.

The Hartford Hammer Co., Cushman Street.—In the western part of the city, on and near Capitol avenue, there are a number of manufactories which have located there within a few years, comprising some of the largest in Hartford.

Prominent among these establishments is the Hartford Hammer Co., which was incorporated in 1881, with a capital of $20,000 and the following-named officers: President, Samuel L. Way; Secretary and Treasurer, Geo. W. Rogers. The premises occupied consist of one building, 50 x 100 feet in size and two stories in height, and the number of men employed is thirty.

The specialty of the company is the manufacture of solid cast steel machinists' riveting, nail and horse-shoers' hammers, in which they are the second largest in America.

All hammers are made of a superior quality of cast steel, and the handles of the best selected hickory. They are thoroughly tested at the factory. They are of an improved shape and superior finish. Their eye is so constructed as to give greater strength to surrounding parts and allow hanging the hammer to suit any taste. They have an elongated socket, which gives greater bearing to the handle than the ordinary trade hammer, and improves the appearance as well as being of great advantage in its use.

They employ commercial travelers in different parts of the United States and do quite an export trade.

Mr. Samuel L. Way, the president of the company, is a well-known and long-established wholesale and retail hardware dealer in this city, where he was born in 1833, and, like his father before him, is closely identified with the mercantile and manufacturing interests of Hartford.

Mr. Geo. W. Rogers, the secretary and treasurer, is a native of Hartford, born in 1845, and has since his majority been engaged in mechanical pursuits, and during the war was an engineer in the U. S. Navy.

The productions of this company rank high with the trade, and "Hartford Hammers" are a guarantee of reliability and artistic finish.

The Charter Oak City Shirt Co., Manufacturers of Shirts, Collars, Cuffs, etc., No. 42 Union Place.—The inception of this industry which takes its name and trade-mark from the historic tree that figured so largely in the history of Connecticut, dates from the year 1859, when H. Griswold & Co. began the manufacture of shirts, etc., on Asylum street. The original firm was succeeded by C. A. Griffith & Co., who gave place to Case & Rathbun, they being succeeded by McCullough & Robertson, and then by Covey, Smith & McCullough, and they by the present joint-stock company, which was formed in 1882, Mr. W. E. Covey, being chosen President, Mr. John H. Burr, Secretary and Treasurer, and Mr. John McCullough, Superintendent. The premises occupied are in the elegant brick building corner of Union place and Allyn street, and consist of two floors, each 50 x 150 feet in size, where there are employed an average of from fifty to sixty hands. Thirty sewing machines, run by steam, are in constant operation, and the goods turned out are numbered by the hundreds of dozens per month. The company make a specialty of custom-made shirts, and their trade in this line, as well as in the other branches, extends all over New England and portions of the Middle, Western and Southern States, amounting in the aggregate to about $50,000 per annum. In the basement of the building and in connection with the factory is situated a steam laundry where, in addition to the company's work, there is done a general laundry business of from $12,000 to $15,000 per year. This factory is the largest in Hartford and one of the largest in the State, and its trade is increasing to such an extent as to warrant the belief that a few years will place it at the very head of the list.

Mr. J. M. Burr, the president of the company, is a native of Torrington, Conn., and is well known in the business circles of the State. Mr. John H. Burr, his son, the secretary and treasurer, is also a native of Torrington, and is about twenty-two years of age, having been in the company since its organization.

Mr. John McCullough, the superintendent, was born in Pottsville, Penn., in June, 1844, and has been in the business of manufacturing shirts since boyhood. He has resided in Hartford about twenty years, and is thoroughly esteemed by all who know him.

Abner Church, Manufacturer and Dealer in Hemp, Flax and Cotton Rope, etc., Manufactory and Office, No. 33 Morgan Street.—The manufacture of rope is one of the oldest industries in Hartford.

The first record we have of it is of one Everett Benjamin, who was located at No. 46 Morgan street, and of whom the father of Abner Church, the subject of this sketch, learned his trade, and succeeded to the business in 1789.

When a boy of ten years, Abner commenced to learn the business of his father, James Church, and for eleven years was a faithful apprentice and assistant. In 1837 he succeeded in turn to the business, still remaining at the old stand, where he continued till November 7, 1882, when he removed to No. 33 Morgan street, where he has a new building erected for his constantly increasing business. At East Hartford he owns a rope-walk 900 feet in length, where is produced a larger part of his stock. Besides manufacturing hemp, flax and cotton rope, lines, twine, and rope belting, he deals largely in tar, pitch, rosin blocks, scrap iron, metals, etc., doing a business amounting to $40,000 per annum.

That Mr. Church is fond of old faces is attested by the retaining in his employ the same assistants for nearly thirty years. It is claimed, that previous to his removal on November 7, 1882, that this business was the oldest in the State with one continuous existence in the same family and at the same location.

Mr. Church is one of Connecticut's most reliable citizens. He has been honored by the people by electing him as alderman in the city government from the Sixth Ward, and in 1861 was a representative to the State Legislature. In both positions he represented his constituents with honor and fidelity.

E. B. Farnham, Dealer in Coal, No. 253 State Street.—The history of the coal business in Hartford would not be complete if the name of Mr. Elias B. Farnham was omitted from the list. It was in 1859 that he was first connected with the business as bookkeeper for Mr. M. Lord. In 1861, he embarked in business on his own account, on the opposite corner from that on which he is now located. In 1863, he removed across the street to No. 253 State, where, for twenty years, he has built up a substantial reputation. His yards contain a stock of sufficient magnitude to meet all demands from his numerous customers, at short notice and on the most reasonable terms. The site of Mr. Farnham's office and yards is indentified with the early commercial history of Hartford.

Mr. Wm. H. Imlay, for a long time kept a store here, and held extensive business relations with people throughout the State. On making excavations, not long since, an old fashioned, imported fire poker was unearthed, which is now in use by Mr. Farnham, and which he exhibits with much interest as a relic of more than fifty years ago, and the one used by Mr. Imlay, who long since passed away. Mr. Farnham sells about 12,000 tons of domestic coal yearly, and makes a specialty of the Franklin coal, claimed to be the best in the world. He is a native of Connecticut, and has spent most of his busy life in Hartford. In 1861, he was captain of the first military company which drilled for the war, and spent much money in his effort to keep them together till they could be mustered in. It was in this company that Gen. Hawley drilled as private, and it is with much interest that Mr. Farnham relates the attending circumstances. Later he was appointed Captain of Marines in the Navy, but declined, prefering the solid and substantial life of a successful coal merchant to that of a roving life at sea. He is a man of rare executive ability, quick in action, of good business qualifications, and one possessing the respect and esteem of a large circle of acquaintances.

Andrew R. Hull, Dealer in Meat, Poultry, Game, Fruit and Vegetables, etc., No. 70 Market street.—The meat and fish market of Mr. Andrew R. Hull, which is located at No. 70 Market street, was established in its present location by that gentleman in 1881.

He deals in meat, poultry, game, fruit, vegetables, fish, oysters, clams and lobsters, and delivers the same to his customers without extra expense throughout the city.

His market is centrally located, expensively fitted up with all the modern conveniences now found in first class establishments of this kind, including a cosey office, modern refrigerators, etc., etc.

Previous to embarking in business for himself he served an apprenticeship as a butcher in this city, where the large acquaintence he made was of great benefit to him when he embarked in business for himself.

Mr. Hull was born November 3, 1842, in Cheshire, Conn., and came to Hartford in 1859.

He was a member of the Twelfth Connecticut Infantry, participating in all the battles in which that veteran regiment was engaged up to that of Winchester, Va., October 19, 1864, where he was shot in the head and in the report of the Adjutant-General was announced dead. The ball went in near the eye and passed diagonally down coming out in the neck, a very serious wound which kept him sick for two years. He is an active member of the Tyler Post, G. A. R., of this city, and one of the best-known marketmen in Hartford. By diligence, industry, and perseverance he has earned a first class trade, and is using every honorable means to advance and extend it.

James H. Ashmead & Son., Gold Beaters, No. 41 Trumbull Street.—It was in 1839 that Mr. James H. Ashmead established this business in Hartford. He continued alone till 1867, when he took his son, Mr. Robert H. Ashmead, into partnership, thereby forming the firm of J. H. Ashmead & Son, and at the same time removed to their present location. The premises occupied are two floors, each 60x25 feet in size, and twelve people are employed. The feature of the business is manufacturing gold foil for dental purposes, of which they are the largest producers in New England. They also make gold leaf for gilding. In contrast to most gold beaters, this firm makes a specialty of refining gold, taking nothing for granted as to quality. In the manufacture of their gold foil and leaf they start right. This process of manufacture and principle of business was one of the cardinal maxims of the founder, and which has done much towards making the name "Ashmead" synonomous with purity, in the trade.

Mr. James H. Ashmead was a native of Germantown, Pa., born in 1810. He learned his trade in Philadelphia, and came to Hartford to reside in 1836. He some years ago was an alderman in the City Government. He died December, 1880.

Mr. Robert H. Ashmead was born in Hartford, in 1844. He learned his trade of the father, and, as above mentioned, became a partner in 1867, and conducts the business as sole owner, under the name of J. H. Ashmead & Son.

The business of this establishment extends in a wholesale way throughout the United States and to many parts of Europe. It is the second oldest of its class in America.

Olds & Whipple (Alfred H. Olds and Frederick H. Whipple), Hot-Air Furnaces, Ranges, Stoves, Agricultural Implements, Fertilizers, etc., Nos. 164 and 166 State Street.—In 1858, Messrs. Backus & Barstow, who conducted, at that time, a stove store in Norwich, Conn., saw in the growth of Hartford an opening for their business. In the spring of that year, they opened a store at Nos. 164 and 166 State street, in this city, under the charge of Mr. Charles Allen as agent. For a time, the business was conducted as above, when Mr. Allen purchased it. The successors to Mr. Allen were Allen & Willard, who conducted it until September, 1872. Mr. C. L. Willard was the next proprietor, and remained so till November, 1877, when the present gentlemen, Messrs. Olds & Whipple, assumed the proprietorship. After five years of successful effort, during which time a business aggregating $63,000 per annum was built up, they, in February, 1882, bought the stove business of Mr. R. D. Allen, who was located at 168 State street, next door, and consolidated it with their own. The venture proved a success, as shown in the increase of business done in 1882, which amounted to $82,000. The premises necessary for the prosecution of the business consists of two buildings at numbers 164, 166, and 168 State street, each three stories with attic, in height, and 40 x 80 feet; also several storehouses in different parts of the city. The business is divided into three departments—1st. Stoves, Furnaces and Ranges; 2d. Agricultural Implements; 3d. Fertilizers.

In the stove, furnace and range department are found a large stock of every conceivable style of stoves and heaters for the parlor, kitchen or office. They make a specialty of Boynton's furnaces, Barstow's wrought-iron furnaces and Gold's hygean and health heaters. About fourteen experienced workmen are found necessary in this department.

In the agricultural implement line they are agents for the Champion mowing machine and the Mudgett hay feeder, horse rakes, Wiard's chill Plow, and Kemp's manure spreaders.

As dealers in fertilizers, they make a specialty of the Quinnipiac fertilizer, manufactured at New London, Conn., and the Castor pumice made in St. Louis, Mo.

Mr. Alfred A. Olds, the senior member of the firm, is a native of Danielsonville, Conn., and thirty-one years of age. After receiving a preliminary education in the schools of his native State, and a thorough course in a business college of this city, he commenced his business life in an insurance office, from which he graduated to learn his present business.

Mr. Frank H. Whipple was born in New Braintre, Mass., in 1856. He was educated in the public schools and at a business college in Poughkeepsie, N. Y., coming to this city on the formation of the firm of which he is now a member.

It is safe to say that for so young a firm there is not a house in the city that excels them in growth, credit, and volume of business done.

Conservative, yet enterprising; cautious, yet bold, they have won their way unobtrusively to the first rank in the commercial world of their adopted city, and fully deserve the liberal patronage which they now enjoy.

Kibbe & Robinson (Elbert S. Kibbe & Charles P. Robinson), Wholesale Grocers, Provision Dealers, and Commission Merchants, Nos. 232 and 234 State Street.—Occupying a conspicuous position among the wholesale grocery houses of Connecticut, the establishment of Kibbe & Robinson is worthy of more than a passing notice in this volume, both on account of the high commercial standing of the gentlemen who compose the firm and on account of the extended scope of their operations. Some years ago this business was carried on under the firm name of Kibbe, Wadsworth & Miller, they being succeeded by Kibbe, Bolles & Co., who in turn gave place to Kibbe & Robinson, the present firm, in March 1, 1882. The building occupied by this firm is a spacious, substantial and elegant edifice, and is an ornament to the business section of the city. Its internal arrangements impress the visitor with the idea that a large and prosperous business is transacted within its walls and a cursory view of the immense stock of merchandise is calculated to confirm that impression. The commodious and elegantly fitted counting room, with its crowd of busy clerks, together with the admirably arranged salesroom with its force of energetic and affable salesmen present a sight of rare activity and are in themselves proof of the immense business transacted. In addition to this the firm has a large railroad warehouse on Windsor street running through to the track of the New York, New Haven and Hartford road to and from which shipments are directly made and received.

The trade of this house is not confined by the limits of the home State, but extends in various directions and over a large territory.

Mr. Kibbe, the senior partner and the younger man of the firm, was born in East Long Meadow, Mass., in 1854, and has lived in Hartford since 1868. Mr. Robinson is a native of Connecticut, born in the town of Scotland in 1854. He received a good education in the public schools there and in Hartford, in which latter place he took up his residence when he was just 18 years of age.

Both members of the firm occupy high positions in business and social life and the firm is looked upon as being one of the representative young business houses of Hartford.

Horace H. King, Dealer in Boots and Shoes, No. 495 Main Street.—In April, 1846, Mr. Hollis T. Chapin, in company with Mr. Horace H. King, established the boot and shoe business now carried on by the latter gentleman, and located it next door to the store now occupied. Six years later the firm, then known as Chapin & King, purchased the building in which the store is now situated and moved their business into it. The firm continued until 1873, when Mr. Chapin died, his interest reverting by purchase to Mr. King, who has since conducted the business on his sole account. The store is 24x65 feet in size, and is well-stocked with boots, shoes, rubbers and the other articles that go to make up the merchandise of a first-class establishment of its kind. The trade, which is entirely retail, is confined to Hartford and the immediate vicinity, but is of large and satisfactory proportions. For many years subsequent to the establishment of the business the firm engaged in manufacturing, but the introduction of machinery and the construction of large factories induced them to abandon that branch, which they did about ten years ago.

Mr. King is a native of Lyme, Conn., and was born in 1822. He resided in that place until he was twenty-one years of age, learning there the trade of practical boot and shoe maker. He came to Hartford in 1843, and after working as journeyman in a small shop for about six months, purchased the business, continuing it until he entered into partnership with Mr. Chapin. Mr. King is regarded as one of the safe business men of the Capitol City.

Edward J. Cusick, Brass Founder, No. 33 Wells Street.—It was some years ago that Mr. W. C. Marshall carried on the business of a brass founder in this city. Later he was succeeded by Mr. Edward J. Cusick, on Trumbull street, in 1864. The constantly increasing business necessitated his removal to the present location at No. 31 Wells street, in April, 1880. The foundry is situated in the rear, overlooking the Park river, and is built of brick. It is 40 x 60 feet, and is one of the largest and most complete establishments of its kind in Connecticut.

He manufactures railway work, machine work, ship work, spikes and rudder braces, babbit metal, red metal, yellow brass, and is the only foundry in Connecticut which furnishes dry sand work.

All of the business is done in the office situated on the street, and about seven people are employed in its details. The amount of business exceeds $30,000 per annum. A large part of the works is engaged in the manufacture of brass valves for several of the large establishments in and about this city.

Mr. Cusick is a native of New Haven, forty-three years of age, and has been a resident of this city about sixteen years.

His establishment is the largest of its class in Hartford, and its productions have an enviable reputation among the large manufacturing concerns in the State.

Fred. Kingsley, Proprietor of The Popular Market, No. 272 Asylum Street, corner Ann.—The finest, largest and most expensively fitted market in Hartford is undoubtedly "The Popular Market" at the corner of Asylum and Ann streets, of which Mr. Fred. Kingsley is the proprietor. Mr. Kingsley started in business in 1872 on the opposite side of Asylum street and continued there until the demands of his rapidly and steadily increasing trade forced him to seek the more roomy premises he now occupies. His traffic is mainly among the better class of Hartford families, and hence, his stock of meats, vegetables, fruit, poultry, etc., is selected with unusual care. So well has Mr. Kingsley earned for his market the title "popular," that his yearly trade, which is almost entirely a retail one, amounts to the very respectable figure of $75,000.

Mr. Kingsley is "native and to the manor-born," and is about forty-one years of age. In business circles he enjoys an enviable reputation, while his social qualities have won him hosts of friends.

A. W. Ramsdell, Dealer in Flour, Grain, Feed, and Hay, No. 608 Main Street.—The business of Mr. Ramsdell was first established on January 1, 1882, as A. W. Ramsdell & Co., which so continued till May of the same year, when he succeeded to the business alone. A profitable business in flour, feed, grain and hay has been built up against strong competition, thus demonstrating the successful business qualifications of Mr. Ramsdell. He was born in Pequonock, Connecticut, in 1858, and for so young a man can be considered a good example for the average youth who come to Hartford to seek their fortune. Mr. R., by uniform politeness and attention, has achieved a success which can be pointed to with great satisfaction.

E. D. Williams, Cigars and Tobacco, Manufacturer of the Paul Murphy, Pearl Queen, Windmill, Nutmeg, and "555" Brands of Cigars, No. 555 Main Street.—Among the popular establishments for the manufacture of cigars and the sale of other articles for the comfort and pleasure of the smoker, the store of Mr. Williams is rapidly taking a place in the front rank.

Mr. Williams began his business in a small way in 1875, at No. 4 State street, and remained there until November, 1, 1882, when his rapidly increasing trade compelled him to seek the more commodious quarters he now occupies. Mr. Williams' special brands of cigars have attained such popularity that he keeps constantly employed a half dozen skilled workmen in their manufacture. His trade is largely wholesale, many of the saloons and cigar stores in Hartford selling only the brands manufactured by him. Mr. Williams is a native of Brooklyn, Conn., and his birth dates from November 1, 1835. He came to Hartford in 1858, and was for sixteen years identified as salesman and partner with the wholsale and jobbing tobacco house of J. D. Burnham & Co. Mr. Williams is a representative man in his line, and enjoys the fullest esteem of the community.

S. G. Moses, Sportsmen's Goods and Druggists' Sundries, No. 587 Main Street.—Mr. Stephen G. Moses, the subject of this sketch, is one of the oldest and best known business men in Hartford, having been in the drug business in that city for a period of thirty-five years. Up to the year 1881 Mr. Moses conducted the large drug store at No. 605 Main street, now owned by Messrs. Goodrich & Rapelye, running his present establishment as an adjunct. Mr. Moses' retirement from business in 1881 was caused by illness, but with recovery came the longing to re-enter active life, and its result, the present business.

Mr. Moses is a native of Simsbury, Conn., and was born in 1818. He has lived in Hartford, for about fifty years, during which time he has attained to an enviable reputation as a thorough and reliable business man. During his busy life he has had but little time or inclination to seek or serve in office, and was never induced to accept such burdens except in the year 1877, when he served one term as Water Commissioner. Mr. Moses is one of Hartford's respected citizens.

Bingham & Dodd, Engravers and Lithographers, No. 80 State Street.—The general business of engraving and lithographing now conducted by Messrs. Bingham & Dodd, at No. 80 State street, was established about the year 1844. The present firm was formed in 1859. The premises comprise one floor 50x100 feet, where four power presses and twenty people are employed. Large quantities of work for insurance companies, manufacturing establishments, and show people are daily turned out here.

Mr. John H. Bingham was born in New York city, in 1831, and Mr. Wm. H. Dodd in Hartford, in 1826.

Both gentlemen have long been identified with Hartford, where they have built up a business, one of the largest of its kind in the State, are regarded as a reliable and representative firm, and their establishment is a credit to the industries of the city.

Peerless Wire Mattress Co., Manufacturers of Woven Wire Mattresses of every Description, No. 287 Sheldon Street.—It goes without saying that New England is the home of inventions.

In Hartford there are large and small establishments which are producing the inventions of a busy brain, each of more or less benefit to mankind.

The Peerless Wire Mattress Co. of which we write produces a mattress which enables thousands to say with great satisfaction,

"Tired nature's sweet restorer,
Balmy sleep."

The company was organized in February, 1880, with a capital of $5,000, which was increased in February, 1882, to $10,000, with A. A. Hunt, President; E. W. Fuller, Secretary; H. P. Hitchcock, Treasurer; and the following gentlemen as Directors: Governor Marshall Jewell, A. A. Hunt, H. P. Hitchcock, C. A. Jewell, and E. W. Fuller.

The building occupied for the manufactory and office is 138 x 40 feet, one story, and the number of people employed averages about twenty. The wire mattresses manufactured by this company are made under the patents of Mr. John Farnham, the original inventor of woven wire mattresses, and are claimed equal if not superior to any manufactured. Only the best quality of steel-tempered, double-tinned wire and thoroughly-seasoned, hard wood lumber is used; the aim of the company being to put upon the market a mattress that has strength, durability and beauty combined, which will compete with any manufactured sucessfully as regards price, for the same quality of goods.

Two non-adjustable styles are made, called the Peerless and Pefection, respectively, while the adjustable is called rightly the Excelsior, as it is claimed to be "the handsomest bed in the market."

A very superior cot for sea-side cottages, hotels, and other places is very handsome and luxurious, being very strong and light, weighing only twenty-eight pounds, and when folded can be put away in a very small space.

Most of the trade of this company lies in New England and New York State, with a considerable export trade in Spain, Cuba, Jamaica, Chili and other warm countries.

Mr. Asa A. Hunt, the president, is a native of Coventry, Tolland County, Conn., and was educated at Williston, East Hampton, Mass., and became a resident of Hartford in 1868. In addition to attending to being president of this company, he carries on an extensive retail coal business here, which was established about four years ago.

Mr. Edgar W. Fuller, the secretary, is a native of East Haddam, and has been in Hartford since 1867. He is thirty-four years of age.

The treasurer, Mr. Henry P. Hitchcock, is a native of Farmington, and about forty-two years of age. He was educated at the Wilbraham, Mass., Academy, and was formerly of the firm of the well-known clothiers and merchant tailors in this city, Messrs. Kelsey & Hitchcock. He has been a member of the city government of Hartford, and occupied other trusts of a public nature.

The officers and directors of this company rank among the best known and most influential of Hartford citizens, and its productions are recognized as among the best if not superior to any of its class now before the public.

Ludlow, Barker & Co., Dealers in Pianos, Organs, Sheet Music, Musical goods, etc., Nos. 153 and 155 Asylum Street.—Mr. Ludlow Barker, the subject of this sketch, established himself in the music business in Hartford in 1850, and located at the corner of Main and Pearl streets, whence he removed to the store he now occupies about thirteen years ago. The premises now occupied are 50x40 feet in size and are among the most pleasant and eligibly located in the city. The business done is probably the most extensive in its line in Hartford, or perhaps in the State of Connecticut, and embraces music and musical goods in every variety, especial prominence being given to the Chickering, Hazelton, Haines Brothers, Ivers and Pond's, and Hardman pianos, and the Mason & Hamlin organ, Mr. Barker having sold the latter instrument for upwards of twenty-five years. Other lower priced pianos and organs are also sold. Besides these there is a full assortment of musical instruments of all kinds and the annual sale of violins, guitars, banjos, flutes, accordeons, drums, etc., forms a business of itself, larger than the entire trade of some of the other houses in the same line in Hartford. The house claims to carry the most extensive stock and largest variety of sheet music, foreign and domestic, in the State, a claim that inspection seems to verify. Barker & Co.'s Musical Journal is a sixteen-page monthly devoted to musical matters and containing a vast deal of information regarding the profession as well as copies of the latest music.

Mr. Ludlow Barker is a native of New Brunswick, about fifty years of age. He has been a resident of Hartford for thirty-three years and has always been identified with his present business. He is a practical as well as theoretical musician, having been a professor of music and piano tuner before entering business here. He is leader of the Hartford Male Chorus, and has been an organist in this city for nearly thirty-six years. The last ten years at the Centre Church, the richest and one of the oldest church organizations in the State of Connecticut. In business as well as in private life, Mr. Barker is highly regarded, and it is due to him to say that much of the musical taste for which Hartford's people are noted, is due to his earnest efforts and admirable example. Mr. Barker's son, W. L. B. Barker, has been with him as assistant for the past ten years, and thoroughly understands the business.

W. H. Lathrop, Wholesale and Retail Grocer, Dealer in Foreign and Domestic Fruits, Teas, etc., Nos. 314, 316 and 318 Asylum Street.—This business was begun in 1867 at No. 119 Pearl street, under the firm name of Dow & Lathrop. About four years thereafter Mr. Lathrop purchased Mr. Dow's interest and continued the business at the old stand until 1877, when he moved to his present commodious and elegant stores on Asylum street.

The premises occupied by Mr. Lathrop consist of a store and basement, each 30 x 100 in size and running through from Asylum street to the small street in the rear. The business done requires a stock of groceries, teas, fruits, liquors, etc., amounting to about $10,000 in value, and reaching a yearly volume of $75,000, with a steady increase. The trade of the house is both wholesale and retail and reaches far along the lines of all the railroads running out of Hartford, its bulk, however, being transacted in the city. An average of six assistants are employed, except in the holiday seasons when the force is increased to meet the demands of the brisker trade. Mr. Lathrop does a very large trade in fruits, and in this particular his shipments take a very wide range, extending to all parts of the New England States.

Mr. Lathrop is a native of Coventry in this State, born in 1845, and has lived in Hartford most of the time since 1861. In early life he learned the trade of bank note printer, being employed in that business both in Hartford and New York, in which latter city he was for some time in the service of the Continental Bank Note Company.

Mr. Lathrop has earned and enjoys the entire respect of his business associates and patrons as well as the cordial liking of a large circle of personal friends.

Francis & Co., Importers and Dealers in Hardware and Metals, No. 343 Main Street.—The establishment of the house of Francis & Co. dates back to 1799, when Mr. C. Sigourney laid the foundation of the business, which was succeeded to by Francis & Gridley, and in 1867 by Francis & Co. The firm formerly consisted of Messrs. William and F. A. Francis, but in 1880 the latter gentleman withdrew, and the business has since been carried on by Mr. William Francis, the old firm name being retained. The stock consists of a general assortment of hardware, tools, cordage, metals and wire, the latter article being manufactured to order. The trade of the house, which is both wholesale and retail, is located in Hartford and its vicinity, and is one of the largest in the hardware line in the city. The premises occupied are on Main street, near Asylum street, and within a short distance from the Post-office and City Hall, in the heart of the business portion of the city. The store is a spacious one, and, with the floor above and a large storehouse in the rear, affords room for carrying a very large stock.

Mr. Francis is a native of Hartford, born in 1824, and is a descendant of the old and well-known Connecticut family by that name. He has been in his present location since 1843, and has won and maintained an irreproachable business reputation.

C. A. Wright, Artists' Materials, No. 197 Main Street.—The founders of this house were Messrs. Wright & Burnham in the year 1837. Later it was Mr. William L. Wright, the father of the present proprietor, who conducted it up to the year 1860, since which time the son, Mr. Charles A. Wright, has carried on the business. The father died in 1871. For many years the business was conducted on Central Row, and was removed from there to the store next to the present location, and to No. 197 Main street in August, 1882.

The premises are 18 x 50 feet in size, and the stock consists of artists' materials in every variety, English tube paints, artists' canvas, and brushes, water-colors, pencils, fine colors of every description, wax flower materials, crayons, pastels, engineers, and architects' supplies, paints, oils, glass, varnishes for painters and decorators, etc., etc.

In addition, a general business is done in house and sign painting, from four to fifteen people being engaged, according to the season of the year.

Mr. C. A. Wright is a native of Hartford, and forty years of age. He has always been identified with this business from boyhood, and does a safe and lucrative trade.

H. C. Judd & Root (H. C. Judd, J. H. Root, C. H. Owen and L. A. Barbour), Commission Wool Merchants, corner Allyn and High Streets.—The very extensive wool commission house of H. C. Judd & Root dates its formation from the year 1869, when Messrs. Henry C. Judd, Judson H. Root, E. H. Owen and G. Wells Root entered into a copartnership and laid the foundation of what is now one of the largest houses of its kind in New England, and the only commission house of any magnitude in the State of Connecticut. In 1872 Mr. G. Wells Root withdrew from the firm, and in 1881 Mr. E. H. Owen was removed by death, his place as special partner being filled by his son, Mr. C. H. Owen, of the present firm, who, with Mr. L. A. Barbour, constitutes the special branch in the concern. The premises occupied by the firm prior to the completion of their new building, was at No. 90 Asylum street, where three large floors and a basement were used for sales and storage. Besides all this space the needs of the business required most of the room afforded by several large warehouses situated in different localities in Hartford. All this has proven insufficient, and in the spring of 1883, the firm removed its business to their elegant new six-story building on the corner of High and Allyn streets, one of the largest and most costly business structures in Hartford. The building has a frontage on High street of 93 feet, while that on Allyn street is 141 feet, there being seven stores on the ground floor, three of which, as well as the entire upper part of the building, being designed for occupation by the firm.

The selling trade of the house covers a large area of territory, and although immense quantities of wool are consumed within a radius of twenty-five miles from Hartford, the trade of the house is not confined to that section, but reaches to other points in New England and the more remote Middle States. Some idea of the business done by this house may be gained from the fact that the annual business requires the handling of seven millions of pounds of wool, amounting in value to about two and one half million of dollars.

Mr. Henry C. Judd is a native of Northampton, Massachusetts, and has resided here more than forty years. He is now about fifty-five years of age. In the business world he occupies a prominent position, and in addition to the affairs of his house finds time to attend to the duties of director in various financial and insurance institutions, among which is the Hartford Bank.

Mr. Judson H. Root is a native of Hartford, born in 1840. He has been in the wool business for twenty-two years, eight of them being spent in learning its minutiæ and the other fourteen in building up a business for himself and partners, the magnitude of which is indicated by the figures mentioned in this article. Mr. Root is a director in the Mercantile National Bank and the Hartford Sanitary Plumbing Company, and is otherwise identified with the business and financial interests of his native city.

Messrs. Owen and Barbour, the special partners in the concern, are recognized as among the leading citizens and are men of considerable weight in the commercial world.

George S. Burnham & Co., Dealers in Paints, Oils, Glass, etc., No. 22 Central Row.—Fifty-eight years ago was in 1826. On January 1, this year, the business of which Col. Geo. S. Burnham is now proprietor was established by his father, George Burnham, Esq., and his successors conducted it up to January 1, 1869. He died October, 1868, at the age of sixty-nine years. For thirty-three years he was a prominent merchant in Hartford, in the same line of business which is now conducted by his son. The premises occupied are 22 x 110 feet, and in addition to dealing in a large stock of paints, oils, varnishes, window-glass, brushes, painters' supplies, etc., a number of men are kept busy as painters, glaziers and grainers in different parts of the city, and surrounding country.

Col. Geo. S. Burnham, the proprietor, claims the proud distinction of being the first man in the State of Connecticut to enlist for the suppression of the Rebellion. He is a native of Hartford, born in 1828, and has been clerk and proprietor at this location for thirty-five years.

It was on April 15, 1861, the day that Lincoln's proclamation for seventy-five thousand men was issued, Col. Burnham was sitting in the office of the "Daily Post" when it was received. He immediately went to the office of J. D. Williams, Adjutant-General of the State, and enlisted. A company was formed, and he elected captain of the first volunteer company organized in Connecticut that was independent from any military organization.

Although elected Captain and recognized by the State as such, by orders from the Adjutant-General, he did not receive his commission. Events crowded thick upon each other in the rush for war, and when the First Regiment Connecticut Volunteer Infantry was organized, of which Dan. Tyler was made Colonel, Captain Burnham was commissioned Lieut.-Colonel April 29, 1861, and on the same day, Joseph R. Hawley, then First-Lieutenant in Rifle Company A, and now United States Senator from the State of Connecticut, and editor of the Hartford "Courant," was promoted to the Captaincy. On the promotion of Colonel Dan. Tyler, May 10, 1861, to a Brigadier-Generalcy, Lieutenant-Colonel Burnham was promoted to the Colonelcy of the regiment, came home with it, and was mustered out July 31st of the same year.

On the organization of the Twenty-second Connecticut Infantry for nine months' service he was commissioned as Colonel and came home as such after ten months' service. Later he was made City Clerk, and in April, 1864, he was again called to the service as Captain and Acting-Quarter-Master, United States Army, until September 1, 1865, when he returned to Hartford, and accepted the position of Town Clerk. Previous to the war he was in command of one of the numerous independent military organizations of which Connecticut has been so long famous.

Colonel Burnham is well-known throughout the State in social and business circles, and history records him as foremost to respond to the call of his country in her hour of adversity.

Willis Thrall & Son, Hardware, No. 10 Central Row.—One of the best known hardware stores in Hartford is the establishment of Messrs. Willis Thrall & Son, who started in business at this location in the year 1858, afterwards removing to Asylum street, where they were for several years, returning to their original place about ten years ago. The store is located directly opposite the new Post-office and City Hall, at No. 10 Central Row, and is one of the most central business stands in Hartford. It is 20x80 feet, and is stocked with all of the varieties of hardware, a specialty being made of joiners' tools. The business, which amounts to about $25,000 per year, extends throughout the city and to adjoining villages.

Mr. Willis Thrall is probably the oldest hardware dealer in active business to be found in the State. He is a native of Vernon, Conn., and was eighty-two years of age January 14, 1383. In his early life he was a manufacturer of wood screws, and later acquired an extended reputation as the publisher of a valuable map of the United States. He has always been a resident of this city from early manhood, where he is highly esteemed as a gentleman of the old school, for which Hartford is so generally noted.

Mr. Edward B. Thrall, the son and junior member, is forty-six years of age and a native of Hartford. He has always been an active, undemonstrative business man, pursuing the even tenor of his way, careful and conservative in business, spontaneous in his friendships, and taking rank as a valuable acquisition to the social and business world.

The firm enjoys good credit and stands high in the estimation of the public.

Allyn, Blanchard & Latimer, Steam Coffee and Spice Mills, and Wholesale Dealers in Teas, Coffees, Spices, Tobacco, Cigars, Grocers' Sundries, etc., Nos. 34–38 Market Street.—The history of this firm illustrates how a large profitable business by a representative house grows and develops from a comparatively small beginning.

It is twenty-seven years since the senior partner, Mr. O. H. Blanchard, conducted the business of a retail grocer at No. 203 State, corner Front street. After a profitable business for several years, he, in 1866, became a member of the firm of Park, Fellows & Co., which continued till the year 1878, when the firm name was changed to Allyn & Blanchard.

In February, 1881, Mr. Latimer was admitted, making the firm name Allyn, Blanchard & Latimer. The premises occupied for their extensive business consists of an imposing building five stories in height, 85 x 33 feet, at Nos. 34, 36, and 38 Market street, with coffee and spice mills in the rear, three stories in height, 25 x 20 feet. The large stock carried consists of the best grades of teas, coffees, spices, tobaccos, cigars, and a large line of grocers' sundries.

Their steam coffee and spice mills are one of the largest and most complete in New England, and the reputation of the goods produced extends to adjoining States.

A large wholesale trade is conducted in every State in New England, a corps of commercial salesmen being a factor in this result.

Mr. O. H. Blanchard is a native of Centerville, N. Y. Born in 1834, and came to Hartford when he was twenty-two years of age. He is and always has been one of the most active, hard working men in the trade. Our reporter found him with overalls on, acting as a porter in the rush and hurry of active business. This hearty co-operation in all the departments has done much toward the success of the firm.

Mr. Noyes B. Allyn is a native of Ledyard, Conn. Born in 1838, on September 29. He was educated at that well-known educational institution, the Providence Conference Seminary at East Greenwich, R. I.

He, previous to his settling in this city five years since, was in business at New York, and at Middletown, Conn., where, at the latter place, he built up the largest retail grocery business in the State, aggregating in one year $280,000.

Later, he was cultivating his farm in the town of Ledyard, Conn., from which he was sent as a representative to the Legislature. He is a man of rare executive ability, quick of perception, active, and enterprising—all factors in the unexampled success which he achieved in Middletown, as before mentioned.

Mr. Richard R. Latimer was born May 25, 1831, at Montville, New London County, Conn. He was educated at Colchester, Conn., and for fifteen years previous to his connection with this firm, was a traveling salesman for the old wholesale grocery house of W. R. Mitchell & Co., in New York. During that time he built up a business in New England which has probably never been excelled by any other wholesale grocery representative. On the retirement of W. R. Mitchell & Co. from the trade he became a resident of Hartford, and a member of this firm. As made up, this house possesses all the elements of the success which they have attained. Straight-forward and honorable business men, they are to be highly recommended for the vigor with which they prosecute their business. The mercantile community recognize their merit and give substantial encouragement which years of persistent toil and honest effort have brought forth.

Gemmill, Burnham & Co. (John Gemmill and Edgar F. Burnham), Importers and Tailors, Manufacturers of Fine Ready-made Clothing, Nos. 64, 66 and 68 Asylum Street.—The finest store in the city of Hartford devoted to the sale of clothing is that occupied by the firm of Gemmill, Burnham & Co., and situated on Asylum Street within a minute's walk from the Court-house, Post-office and the business centre. The building, which was erected in 1882, is the property of the firm and was built with a view of accommodating their business. It is an elegant structure of brick with a frontage of thirty-seven and a half feet by a depth of eighty feet, and is three stories in height. All this space is occupied, the ground floor as a salesroom, the second floor by the custom department and the top floor as a manufactory. On each side of the building are alleyways, and numerous windows opening thereon from all its sides render it one of the lightest and most pleasant business edifices in the country. The immense plate-glass show-windows are probably the largest in Hartford and were constructed at a great expense. The interior finishing is all in unpainted ash, producing an effect at once pleasing and elegant. The business of this firm gives constant and profitable employment to about seventy-five people, the majority of whom are engaged in the manufacturing department making a class of fine goods for the ready-made trade that has won for the house the reputation of being the producers of the most stylish ready-made clothing to be found in the State. In addition to this there is a very large business in the custom department the needs of which compel the employment of a large number of skilled workmen and the carrying of an immense stock of fine goods, large quantities of which are directly imported by the house, on favorable arrangements with European manufacturers, to whom Mr. Burnham makes periodical visits. The trade of the house extends throughout the surrounding country, but is largely local and among the better classes of Hartford's citizens. While all branches of the business are given due attention, a specialty is made of the manufacture of ready-made clothing, after the same models used in custom work and by the same workmen, and it is claimed that the stock of this house comes nearer the prevailing styles, and is better in finish than that of any similar establishment in the State. This business was established in 1871, by the present firm, their quarters being on Asylum street, about eight doors above their present location. Here they remained until 1882, when their rapidly growing business and the impossibility of renting such premises as they needed, compelled the erection of their present quarters.

Mr. John Gemmill was born in Suffield, Conn., and is about forty-three years of age. He has resided in Hartford for twenty-five years, and was one of the patriotic citizens who shouldered muskets and went forth to do battle for their country. Mr. Gemmill served for three years in the Sixteenth Connecticut Volunteers, holding the position of orderly sergeant, and earning a very creditable record as a soldier. On his return from the war he joined the City Guard, and is now a member of the veteran corps of that organization. Mr. Gemmill is active in religious and charitable matters, and is one of the deacons of the South Baptist Church, enjoying the hearty esteem of its members, as well as of the community in general.

Mr. Edgar F. Burnham is a native of Willimantic, Conn., and was born in 1849. He has been a resident of Hartford for about eighteen years, all of which time has been spent in the clothing business. He was elected a member of the Common Council from the Seventh Ward in 1880, and in the two following years was sent from the same ward to the Board of Aldermen, in both bodies serving with zeal the interests of his constituents and the good of the community. Mr. Burnham is prominent in the Masonic Order, being a member of Washington Commandery, Knights Templar, and of St. John's Lodge. Like his partner, he is highly regarded in business and social life, and enjoys the distinction of being a member of the largest purely retail clothing-house in the State.

J. W. Starkweather & Co., Lumber Dealers, No. 25 Front Street.—For more than twenty years a large number of the citizens of Hartford and surrounding towns have drawn their supplies of lumber from the well-known yard of which Messrs. J. W. Starkweather & Co. are now the proprietors. The originator of the house was Mr. J. G. Chase, who came from Springfield, Massachusetts, in 1860, and embarked in the lumber business at the present location. In 1863 Mr. J. W. Starkweather, who was not yet of age, became the bookkeeper for Mr. Chase, with whom he continued until 1878, when Mr. Chase retired and the business was purchased by Mr. Starkweather, who continued sole proprieter till 1881. The rapid increase of the business necessitated more capital, which was furnished by Mr. T. J. Boardman, of William Boardman & Sons, the well-known and long-established tea, coffee and spice house of this city, who, in the above-named year, became a partner.

The yards cover an area of 300x160 feet and the stock carried is valued at about $50,000. It consists of hard and soft wood lumber, shingles, lath, timber, Michigan pine, spruce, hemlock, Southern pine, flooring, ceiling, mouldings, whitewood, ash, cherry, white oak, red oak, butternut, black walnut, mahogany, curly maple, Spanish cedar, with all kinds of sawed and turned work done to order. The trade extends to the neighboring villages and cities.

The growth of the business since Mr. Starkweather bought it in 1878 has been steady and reliable. The business for 1882 was over 400 car loads, or 4,250,000 feet of lumber. The history of this business illustrates what a poor boy with a good constitution, strong character and earnest effort can do in the battle of life.

Mr. Starkweather, the main partner, is a native of Hartford and thirty-eight years of age. He was educated on a farm and afterwards at the Hartford High School, from which excellent institution of learning he graduated.

In the possession of the lumber business he was particularly favored—one of those tides in the affairs of men which he took at the flood and has led on to fortune. Opportunity alone was not the cause of his present success, but the possession of those traits of honesty and a correct business training enabled him to make the most of the opportunity, and are the reasons for his present standing in the business world. By an honorable and straightforward course he arose from an assistant to be the proprietor of the business which he now so successfully conducts; from comparative obscurity he has arisen to prominence as a leading and representative man in the lumber business of his native city and is truly the architect of his own fortune.

The A. D. Vorce Company, Importers and Dealers in Oil Paintings, Water Colors, Etchings, Engravings, etc., No. 276 Main street.— The artistic taste and the love of art in a community is generally shown in the number and completeness of its art stores.

The stranger in Hartford cannot fail to be impressed with evidences of wealth and refinement which are illustrated by the art galleries, where are on exhibition selections from the best artists in this and other countries. The largest and best known of these art stores is that of The A. D. Vorce Company, located at No. 276 Main street.

The business was established by Messrs. Glazier & Co. in the year 1858, who were succeeded by Messrs A. D. Vorce & Co., which, in 1880, for the convenience of the two partners, was incorporated, under its present title, in April, 1880, with a cash capital of $15,000. The premises embrace a store twenty-five by one hundred feet, in the rear of which is an art gallery with a double skylight, while adjoining is a picture frame factory, where are produced some of the very best gilt and bronze frames for framing oil paintings, water colors, etc., known to the trade, at which six skilled workmen are kept constantly employed.

The specialty of this company is the collection of rare and expensive oil paintings of the French and German schools, etchings, engravings, rare metals, Oriental and Continental porcelains, *bric-a-brac*, curios from Japan, etc., all of which they import under the direction of Mr. A. D. Vorce, who ransacks Europe and Oriental countries yearly to select for his art gallery the most rare and valuable works which the past ages have produced.

No art establishment east of New York equals in their collections the display of rare works to be found in the The A. D. Vorce Company's art gallery of this city, and Goupil is the only one in the metropolis who ranks with them.

Mr. Allen D. Vorce, the art critic and active member of the company, is a native of Penn Yan, N. Y., and forty-six years of age. For twenty years of his life he has been identified with art matters, and during his business residence in this city has been regarded as an able and conscientious connoisseur in art matters. The homes of the more wealthy Hartford citizens bear witness to this, as well as those of other cities. Previous to his engaging in art matters he was a banker in the service of the Government under Chase, Fessenden and McCullough respectively. The issue of the '81's, 5.30's and 7.30 bonds, amounting to hundreds of millions, passed through his hands during this important period in the nation's history, from 1861 to 1865.

Mr. Silas W. Robbins, the other member of the company, is a native and resident of Wethersfield, and sixty years of age. His interest in this company is not so much for financial gain as it is to help the development of art in Hartford and vicinity. He is largely identified with the interests of Hartford and Wethersfield. At the latter place he has a large fancy stock farm, and expensive barns, where are to be found the largest herd of imported cattle in New England. He is also at this place the main partner in the great seed house of Messrs. Johnson, Robbins & Co., whose name is a familiar household word in every farmer's home in America. In Hartford he is a director in the City National Bank, and for nearly thirty years has been a director in the American National Bank of this city. The A. D. Vorce Company rank among the first art dealers in America.

Alonzo White, Paper Dealer and Stationery, No. 12 Central Row.—When Hartford was a village and long after, the business of the surrounding country centered at Central Row, in which the paper and stationery store of Mr. Alonzo White is now located. The Row is as central now as of yore, but the business of the city and country has extended up and down Main and Asylum streets and intruded itself even into side streets, leaving Central Row, opposite the new Post-office and the City Hall.

The business which Mr. White now conducts was established by his uncle, Mr. Cyrus White, twenty-three years ago. Seven years later Mr. Alonzo White bought the establishment in which, during that time, he had been a valuable assistant, and soon after removed his business to Asylum street in 1869, where he was for seven years, and then to State street, and after nine years he returned to his present location where he has now been five years.

The store is 23x100 feet and is arranged for the prosecution of a large business.

The stock carried embraces all the different kinds of fine and coarse writing and wrapping paper, twines, paper bags, etc., used by merchants, stationery printers' supplies, etc., etc.

The business extends throughout the State and New England, a commercial traveler being kept on the road for that purpose. In addition to the wholesale trade a large retail trade centers here, the result of twenty-three years' acquaintance.

Mr. White is a native of Franklin, Franklin Co., Vermont, and is forty-one years of age. He has been a resident of Hartford for over twenty years, and during his business career has built up a reputation of which one ought be proud, and as a progressive and thoroughgoing business man he has no superior.

Horace W. Stetson, Dealer in Fresh and Salt Meats, Vegetables and Poultry, No. 142 Main Street.—In every city there are well-known business men who have always been identified with a special line of business and located for a long time in one place.

The years come and go but the familiar face still is seen going the rounds and attending to the active duties of his chosen pursuit.

It is perhaps not too much to say that Mr. Horace W. Stetson is a representative of this class in Hartford.

As long ago as 1848 he became known at the Franklin Market at 142 Main street, and the intervening years have added to his acquaintance a host of customers who at that time were not born.

The Franklin Market is a well-known business stand, centrally located and very popular with the representative citizens of this city.

Mr. Stetson occupies one-half of the same, which includes about 25 x 30 feet. It is furnished with all the latest improvements usually found in a first-class establishment of this kind, including an extensive ice-house and a cosy office. Three competent assistants and two delivery teams are kept busy supplying his numerous customers which are found in all parts of Hartford. Whatever is to be had in his line is sure to be found at his place, fresh and salt meats, vegetables, poultry, game, and all delicacies in their season.

Mr. Stetson is a native of Lisbon, Conn., and was born in 1821. He has been a resident of Hartford since 1845, and from early manhood has been in his present business. He is a stockholder in more or less of the numerous incorporated companies for which Hartford is noted, and is closely identified with its welfare, as a property holder and merchant.

The esteem in which he is held by his fellow citizens was shown in his election to represent them one term as alderman, and two terms as councilman in the city government of Hartford.

George S. Lincoln & Co., Proprietors Phœnix Iron Works, Nos. 54 to 60 Arch Street.—The history of this establishment is closely identified with that of Hartford. Founded by the late Levi Lincoln, father of the present proprietors, it has grown from comparative insignificance to one of the largest, as it is the oldest, of its class in the State.

In 1834 the facilities for transportation and the number of population were not as great as at the present day, and as a consequence the "comparative insignificance" of the Phœnix Iron Works in those days reflected more credit perhaps on its founder than on the present owners.

To establish a business like this fifty years ago required much practical experience, executive ability and force of character.

Levi Lincoln was by nature an inventor, his active mind grasped the principles and possibilities of an invention, and shaped it to active practical results. He and William Rogers experimented in the discovery of electro plating. In an old directory published by Messrs. Jocelyn, Darling & Co., of New York, in 1832, a record is made of the Hartford Card Manufacturing Company, of which Levi Lincoln was the agent. They made sheet and filleting cards for cotton and wool, also card setting machines. He invented a card setting machine which consisted of the sheet card and the setting of the teeth therein by machinery, a great saving of time and money. Previous to the using of this valuable invention, it was the custom of the wives and children of the farmers surrounding to insert these teeth by hand, thereby earning considerable money, which constituted in the aggregate quite an income. This invention of Mr. Lincoln's did away with all this, and one more important step made towards the manufacture of cotton and woolen goods in this country. Mr. Lincoln was also the inventor of the first machine for the manufacture of hooks and eyes, which he made for the Norths at New Britain, Conn., who, by the way, were enabled by the inventive genius of Mr. Lincoln to be the pioneers of that business in America, if not in the world.

In a cursory review of the life of Mr. Lincoln one is impressed with the amount of good a man can do even during a short life. It is too often that, in the rush and hurry of this generation, we forget the memory of those who by their inventive genius have done so much for our comfort and happiness. It is the province and agreeable duty of the historian to record the acts and approximate the results of such a life as Levi Lincoln.

On his death the business was so arranged that his sons George S. Lincoln and Charles L. Lincoln succeeded and the firm of George S. Lincoln & Co. has since been one of the best known in New England.

In "Webb's New England Railway and Manufacturers' Statistical Gazetteer" which was published in 1869, the Phœnix Iron Works was classed as one of the representative manufacturing establishments. Since that time it has rather added to its capacity and extended reputation. The works face on Parks River and Arch Street and comprise six large buildings, embracing an area of two acres used as machine shops, foundry, etc., etc., and fitted with all the latest and most approved appliances known to the trade.

They make a specialty and pride themselves on the manufacture of the latest designs of architectural iron work, consisting of building fronts, columns, lintels, girders, vaults, jail doors, shutters, railings, balconies, fire-escapes, etc. They also make large quantities of machinists' tools and Lincoln's molasses gates, the latter being an indispensable article for and used in every retail grocery in the country, which is also an invention of Levi Lincoln, improved and repatented in 1848 by the sons.

The architectural beauty of hundreds of stores and building fronts in our New England cities is largely due to the artistic productions of this firm, they having furnished the ironwork for most of the prominent public and private buildings in the State and for many outside of it. The average number of skilled artizans employed is about 115.

The senior member of the firm, Mr. George S. Lincoln, while he was born in Boston has been a resident of Hartford since 1826, at which time he was eight years of age. He has grown with the city and its institutions.

He represented his ward as alderman in the City Government for eight years and for twenty-three years has been a director in the Hartford Bank, also director in the City Fire and Orient

Insurance companies. For several years he was an active member of the State military forces, serving as Brigade Major on the staff of General Waterman.

Mr. Charles L. Lincoln, the junior member of the firm, is also a native of Boston, born in 1825, and came to Hartford when he was three years of age. Like his brother his ambition has been to enlarge and perfect the immense business, the germ of which was left to them as a legacy by the father. He occupies the responsible position as director in the Mechanics' Savings Bank and is also a director in one or more of the horse railway companies of this city.

The Messrs. Lincoln are well known throughout New England and rank among the ablest business men of to-day; and in Hartford among her leading citizens, representative manufacturers and promoters of its best interests.

St. John Appo, Draper and Tailor, No. 254 Main Street.—Among the more prominent merchant tailors of the Capitol City who have done much towards shaping the city's fashions in the matter of dress is Mr. St. John Appo, whose chambers are located at No. 254 Main street, "Times" Building, and who first embarked in business at No. 266 Main street, in the year 1879, removing to his present location in the spring of 1881. The premises embrace a part of the second floor, and are 30 x 100 feet, and well adapted and arranged for the business.

The stock consists of cloths of every description for suitings, etc., piece goods of all kinds, cassimeres and vestings, a specialty being made of imported English woolens, of which Mr. Appo is a direct importer.

The services of thirteen skilled workmen are employed, and the amount of business done amounts to $20,000 per annum.

Mr. Appo is a native of Philadelphia and thirty-three years of age. He came to Hartford in 1871, and previous to 1879 was cutter for the house of Saunders, another artistic merchant tailoring establishment in Hartford. The family of Appo had its origin in a French colony of Hindoostan. Mr. St. John Appo's grandfather was a Brahmin, a man of birth and education, and took high rank in his native country, where he was converted to Christianity by the French Jesuit priests, an act which exiled him from his native land. This was during the time of the first French Revolution. He left Hindoostan in a French ship, was captured by an English cruiser and taken to Portsmouth, England. Here he found friends, in a to him new country, and adapted himself to the circumstances which surrounded him by learning the art of confectionery. He married in England and soon after embarked for America, and settled in Philadelphia, where he lived and died.

His youngest son (William) was the father of the present Mr. Appo. He was sent in early life to Hayti, where he received a military education was a prominent officer in the Haytien army, and an intimate friend and associate of the President of the Republic, John Peter Boyer.

During one of those petty insurrections which are often occurring in the West Indies he became involved and again an Appo was exiled, thus illustrating the old adage that life and history repeat themselves. The numerous medals that he received for bravery are still in possession of the Appo family. Mr. Joseph Appo, a brother of Mr. St. John Appo's father, was at one time a resident of Jamaica, and was the first man to import manila grass into the United States for the purpose of rope making. His sister married Mr. Frank Johnson, a famous musician of the day in Philahelphia and a leader of Frank Johnson's Band, a very popular musical organization, bringing the whole town on the streets when it made a parade. After his return to America, Mr. William Appo adopted the musical profession, following it till he died. In the latter part of his life he was instructor of singing in the public schools of the City of New York. His son, William Appo, Jr., was an officer in the Thirtieth N. Y. Volunteers during the war of the Rebellion, and was killed at the battle of the second Bull Run.

Few families there are whose history embrace so much of romance and adventure, covering such a wide range, and full of such daring and interesting situations.

The subject of this sketch, in contrast to his ancestors, has made himself prominent in business pursuits while they were so in a military, religious and professional sense.

He is regarded as *au fait* in matters pertaining to dress, and a valuable acquisition to the social and business circles of Hartford.

H. N. Jones & Co. (Henry N. Jones and Fanklin Lewis), Manufacturers and Dealers in Sash, Doors and Blinds and Dealers in Paints, Oils, Glass, Colors, and Plate-Glass, No. 162 Main Street.—The door, sash and blind manufactory of Messrs. H. N. Jones & Co. was first known under that name in the year 1879, at which time the firm was formed, and the premises and machinery formerly used by Mr. K. Joslyn at Manchester, Conn., for the same purpose, rented. The factory, at 162 Main street, Hartford, embraces one floor, 80 x 120 feet, of the building, where are employed, on an average, sixteen skilled workmen turning out doors, sash, blinds, mouldings and other work of a kindred nature—a specialty being made of hardwood work of all kinds. In addition to their factory, they have a store at No. 150 Main street, where is kept on hand a large stock of paints, glass, oils, colors—a specialty being made of plate-glass.

Mr. Henry N. Jones is a native of Glastonbury, Conn, and is forty-five years of age. He has been identified with the door, sash and blind business for sixteen years, previous to which he was a carpenter and builder, on quite an extensive scale. Mr. Franklin Lewis was born in Manchester, Conn., in 1824. For twenty-eight years previous to 1879, the time which he became a partner with Mr. Jones, he was engaged in other pursuits.

The firm are rated as able business men, reliable dealers, and enjoy the confidence and respect of the entire business community.

Hamlin Pump Co., Manufacturers of Hamlin's Patent Elastic Rubber-Bucket Pump, No. 20 Potter Street.—There are pumps and pumps. After years of experiment and invention, it has been demonstrated that the rubber-bucket pump, for general use, is the most simple and effective of any. The records of the Patent Office in Washington, show that twenty-three separate patents have been issued to parties who have a claim to a rubber pump. The Hamlin Pump Co., of this city, after many years of experience and carefully studying the use of the same, has at last succeeded in producing an expansive rubber bucket, which makes their pump the best in the market.

The company was incorporated in 1879, with a capital of $10,000, and Gov. George S. Gill, as President, and Mr. Richard E. Rose, as Secretary and Treasurer. The company occupy a one-story wooden building, 150 x 70 feet, situated at No. 20 Potter street, which is supplied with all the improved machinery necessary for the manufacture of pumps and packing cases, the latter being turned out in large numbers.

It is not generally known that the original inventor of a rubber-bucket pump was a native of Vermont, and the patent granted about forty years ago. Since then it has been improved upon and perfected. The Hamlin Pump Co. producing the latest and best results. Their pump is the most simple and durable, having the only expansive bucket which can be expanded as much or little as may be desired by the parties using it, without opening the chain, and without the use of tools. The drip is cut in the thin edge of the rubber, allowing the water to all drain out to prevent freezing. Finally, its advantages over all others is, that it throws a constant stream of water, it purifies the water by keeping it in motion, the water is drawn from the bottom of the well and is always fresh, the tube does not wear, the wear of the bucket is replaced by its self-expansion, and last, but not least, every bucket is guaranteed satisfactory. A fifteen-horse power engine furnishes the motive power for the factory. Commercial travelers are kept busy throughout New England, Eastern New York, and New Jersey, establishing agencies for the sale of this pump, and the number of manufacturing establishments using it are many. The Willimantic Linen Co. has twenty-five, Windham Manufacturing Co., twelve; Warren Cotton Mills, ten; Ponemah Manufacturing Co., twenty-two; while the Hazard Powder Co., P. Jewell & Sons, and numerous other establishments, school-houses, hotels throughout the surrounding country are using them with entire satisfaction.

They can be put in wells of any depth, the deepest as yet being eighty-four feet. A five-eighth-inch bucket will pump thirty-two gallons a minute, and the largest size, four-inch bucket, 200 gallons, both with slow or hand motion.

Gov. George S. Gill, the president of the company, is a well-known lawyer in Hartford, and was Lieutenant-Governor of the State under Governor Ingersoll.

Mr. Richard E. Rose, the secretary and treasurer, is a native of Hartford, and forty-two years of age. He was, previous to investing in this company, a prominent music dealer in this city, giving up that business on account of his health. He was a member of the Twenty-fifth Connecticut Volunteers during the war of the Rebellion, serving at first as a private, and later offered a lieutenancy, a position he could not fill on account of a wound received in battle. The origin and foundation of the company is due to him, and the practical results achieved are very flattering to his ability as an organizer and successful business man.

G. A. Hayden, Dealer in Fresh, Salt and Smoked Meats, Poultry, Game, Vegetables, Oysters, etc., No. 134 Main Street.—One of the oldest meat markets in the city of Hartford is that of which Mr. Geo. A. Hayden is proprietor. It was first known in that connection in 1851, when it was opened by Mr. A. L. Sisson, who retired from active business in the year 1880.

On September fifteenth of that year the present proprietor took possession, since which time he has had an unexampled career of prosperity.

The premises are centrally located and are 30x 110 feet, with every modern convenience for the successful prosecution of his business.

In the front part of the market is a cozy office, where the bookkeeper is engaged, while in the rear is Mr. Hayden's private office.

One of the largest refrigerators for retail trade in the State, holding five tons of ice, is conspicuous and has a capacity for holding twenty carcases of beef at one time.

All kinds of fresh and salt meats, smoked meats, poultry, game, vegetables and fish are dealt in, a specialty being made of oysters at wholesale and retail.

Ten competent assistants are employed in the sales and delivery of stock, with the aid of two delivery teams.

Mr. Hayden is a native of Hartford, and thirty years of age. From the time he was twelve years of age he has been in active business for himself, conducting the sale of fish and oysters at his present location as an adjunct to his predecessor's meat business. As before-mentioned, when he bought out Mr. Sisson in 1880, he combined the two which he has since conducted so successfully.

Mr. Hayden belongs to an old and well-known family. He is a nephew of General Wm. Hayden, who was a man of note in his day, and whose name figures conspicuously in the history of the events of fifty years ago.

Mr. Hayden is a good illustration of what an enterprising young man can do in the battle of life, as he has one of the largest businesses in its line in the city, enjoys good credit, and is deservedly respected by all with whom he comes in contact.

Edward H. Judd, Engineer and Machinist, Nos. 18 and 22 Mechanic Street.—In the year 1870 this well-known house was established by Messrs. Sawtelle & Judd, at its present location. After an uninterrupted success for ten years, the senior member, Mr. Sawtelle, died in 1880, and in 1881 Mr. Judd succeeded to the business. He is a well-known mechanical engineer, master mechanic and manufacturer of all kinds of complicated machinery requiring the experience of an educated mechanical engineer.

The works comprise the ground floor of the substantial brick building situated at Nos. 18 and 22 Mechanic street, 150 x 200 feet, and the business done amounts to $30,000 per annum. Hamilton's Independent Air Pump and Condenser for steam engines is built here, and mill work and castings of all descriptions are furnished, a specialty being made of engine repairing, and dealing in A. S. Cameron's steam pumps, for which he is the agent. The details of the business requires the work of about twenty skilled artizans.

Mr. Edward H. Judd is a native of New Britain, Conn., and forty five years of age. He came to Hartford in 1850, since which time he has been prominently identified with its interests. The esteem in which he is held by his fellow citizens has been shown in electing him to represent them in both branches of the City Government of Hartford, was a water commissioner, also a commissioner in the City Fire Department. From his residence of several years in Hartford, and the leading part he has always taken in his endeavors to promote the wellfare of his adopted city, he has gained a prominent rank in the list of her representative professional and business men.

Leonard Bailey & Co., Manufacturers of Patent Adjustable Iron Bench Planes, Try Squares, Bevels, Copying Presses, etc., No. 133 Sheldon Street.—This well-known establishment to the hardware and stationery trade was founded in the year 1875 by Mr. Leonard Bailey, who transacts business under the firm name of Leonard Bailey & Co. The premises occupied comprise one floor 150 x 40 feet, and the number of people employed is twelve.

The specialty of the house is the manufacture of mechanics' tools, try squares, bevels, patent adjustable iron bench planes, spoke shaves, box scrapers, etc.

The tools are made under the direct supervision of Mr. Leonard Bailey, the original inventor, and are fully warranted.

The reputation of Mr. Bailey as an inventor of mechanics' tools is well known. His latest and most successful invention is that of a new style copying press, which will, as soon as made more public, supersede all other copying presses in the market. The water dish and brush, which accompanies all other presses, are with this done away, and better results are produced with the Bailey press with less time and trouble than with others.

In the plane department no less than thirty-seven different styles of planes are manufactured, besides several styles of box scrapers, spoke shaves, etc.

The suggestive name of Victor is given to all of the planes made here, and they are claimed to be the most simple, compact and practical adjustable plane ever yet produced, and the natural outgrowth and result of a quarter of a century's exclusive experience of Mr. Bailey in the production of patent planes.

All opportunities for the improvement of these tools have been sought, and no device that could add to their usefulness has been neglected, and it is the rigid policy of the house to produce nothing but the best goods, keeping the quality at the highest attainable point of perfection, and selling at a low, but reasonable profit.

The productions of this establishment are, and have been for many years, exported to Russia, Germany, Great Britain, East and West Indies, and other foreign countries, where they are recognized as standard in the trade.

Mr. Leonard Bailey, the inventor, is a native of Hollis, N. H., and fifty-six years of age. Previous to his becoming a resident of Hartford, he resided in New Britain, Conn., Boston, Mass., starting in business at Winchester, Mass., twenty-eight years ago. He is regarded as a most successful inventor and business man, two qualities which are rarely combined in one person, and his numerous inventions are found in every hardware store in America.

G. W. Woolley & Son (Geo. W. Woolley and Geo. H. Woolley), Furnishing Undertakers, Dealers in Undertakers' Supplies, and Manufacturers of Coffins and Caskets, No. 164 Main Street.—The name of Woolley has long been known in connection with the business of undertaking—longer perhaps than any other name in Hartford. It is just forty years since Mr. Geo. W. Woolley embarked in this business. W. P. Woolley, his brother, associated himself a few years afterwards, and it was carried on uninterruptedly till the year 1870, when Mr. William P. Woolley retired, and Mr. Geo. H. Woolley, a son of Mr. Geo. W., was admitted, and the firm name changed to Messrs. G. W. Woolley & Son.

In addition to the business of furnishing undertakers, they do an extensive business as dealers in undertakers' supplies, and are also well-known to the trade as manufacturers of coffins and caskets, keeping twenty-five people at work producing the latter.

The establishment embraces three large buildings, and the motive power for the manufactory is furnished by a forty-horse power engine.

Commercial travelers represent them in many of the New England States, where most of their trade lies.

Mr. Geo. W. Woolley, the senior member of the firm, is a native of Glastonbury, Conn., and was sixty-one years of age, February 22, 1883. He has long been identified with church matters, being vestryman and warden for many years of St. John's Church. He is one of Hartford's oldest citizens, and is endeared to all for his many social qualities and for his fund of sympathy which always responds to those bereft of relatives and friends. As in most pursuits, undertakers are born, not made, and this well-known fact applies in the case of Mr. Woolley, and has done much towards his achieving preferment in his chosen pursuit.

Of late years the details of this business has been left to the care of the junior member of the firm, Mr. Geo. H. Woolley. He is a native of Hartford, and is thirty-seven years of age. He received a liberal and preparatory classical education at the Brookfield Academy with the intention of entering college, but one of those tides in the affairs of men carried him at once into the business world, for which he fitted himself at a commercial school in his native city, and received his early business education in the American National Bank. For a time he was a resident of a Western State, resuming his residence about the time he became a partner with his father. For the last four years he has made a study of the art of embalming, in which he takes great interest.

The firm are well-known, long-established, and preserve the excellent reputation for reliability and financial success, the foundation of which was so long ago commenced by the senior member.

John Otis, Moulding and Planing Mill, Manufacturer of Pine and Hardwood Mouldings, No. 133 Sheldon Street.—The extensive moulding business of Mr. John Otis was established by that gentleman at its present location about six years ago, and has grown from modest dimensions until the business transacted now amounts to about $30,000 annually, and gives employment to ten people. The planing and moulding mill occupies the greater portion of a building 225 x 24 in size. Here are manufactured all the different patterns of pine and hardwood mouldings known to the trade, and here, also, the great steam planing machines turn out vast quantities of dressed lumber for the numerous lumber dealers of Hartford and vicinity. The large steam engine which drives the numerous planers, saws, moulding machines, etc., is kept constantly busy, and the mill presents a scene of unusual activity and business bustle. The office, in its fitting, is a model of the carpenter's skill, and is a fitting place in which to transact so large a business. In addition to the cares of his own business, Mr. Otis has the management of the extensive manufacturing property in which his works with others are situated, he being the agent for the American Screw Company, who are its owners.

Mr. Otis is a native of New York, about forty-five years of age, and has resided here for over fifteen years. Since his advent in the business world, he has been unusually successful. From a business requiring comparatively but little capital, he has established one of large dimensions which ranks among the first in the State.

A. C. Hills, Dealer in Flour, Grain and Feed, Hay and Straw, No. 126 Main Street.—On March 1st, 1875, Mr. Augustus C. Hills established his present business at No. 126 Main street, where he has since enjoyed a large degree of prosperity. In addition to his office and salesroom, which is 30x125 feet, he has a large storehouse in the rear and one on the line of the N. Y., N. H. & H. Railroad.

The amount of business done in flour, grain, feed, hay and straw amounts to about $175,000, and the trade extends throughout the city and to the surrounding villages.

Mr. Hills is a native of East Hartford, Connecticut, born in 1845, and for eleven years has been identified with his present business, previous to which he was a well-known grocer in Hartford.

He is essentially, and always has been, a thorough business man, without ambition for political honors, but was prevailed upon to represent his fellow citizens, on the Republican ticket, as a member of the City Government from the third ward in 1876-7, which he did with honor to himself and to his constituents. Later he declined further political preferment as alderman, finding it necessary to give his entire attention to his growing business.

W. F. Whittelsey & Co., Merchant Tailors, Men's and Boys' Fine Ready-made Clothing, Nos. 34, 36 and 38 Asylum Street.—Mr. W. F. Whittelsey, doing business under the firm name that heads this article, is probably the oldest in his line of business in Hartford, and perhaps in the State of Connecticut. The store occupied by him is on the ground floor of a building owned by the Allyn estate, and known as Whittelsey's Block, and is about 40 x 70 feet in size. The trade is entirely retail, and consists largely of custom work, although there is carried a stock of ready made goods amounting in value to about $40,000. An average of fifteen people are constantly employed, the larger portion being engaged in the manufacture of custom work in a large room located in the second story of the building. Mr. Whittelsey originally established himself in business about forty years ago, being then located on Mulberry street, moving thence to Main street. After carrying on business in these locations for some years, he sold out and went to Sandusky, Ohio, remaining there for three years. He then returned to Hartford, and re-established himself in business on State street, where he remained for eight years, removing thence to his present quarters about twenty-two years ago.

Mr. Whittelsey is a native of East Windsor, Conn., and was born on November 4, 1822. He came to Hartford when he was fifteen years of age, and after serving for two years as clerk in a grocery store, apprenticed himself to the firm of H. S. Larkum & Co., then prominent in the clothing trade, going into business for himself at the expiration of his term of apprenticeship. Although frequently solicited to become a candidate for office, Mr. Whittelsey has persistently declined, preferring to give his undivided attention to his growing business. He is regarded as one of the most solid merchants of Hartford, and is universally respected.

R. P. Kenyon & Co., Manufacturers and Jobbers in Hats, Caps, Furs, etc., No. 337 Main Street.—The house of R. P. Kenyon & Co. was established in 1874, by Mr. R. P. Kenyon, who does business under the firm name at the head of this notice. For four years prior to going into business on his own account, Mr. Kenyon had been a member of the firm of Stillman & Co., and had been in the employ of their predecessors, Messrs. Daniels & Priest, from boyhood. The store occupied as a salesroom by Kenyon & Co., is situated on the northerly side of Main street, near Asylum street, and in close contiguity to the business centre of Hartford. It is 20 x 85 feet in size, but forms only a portion of the space occupied by the business, there being besides a basement almost the entire size of the building, a two-story factory in the rear, and two floors of a large building on Asylum street, known as Whittelsey's Block, where the wholesale stock of hats are stored, and from whence they are sold and shipped. In addition to the three or four salesmen constantly on the road, Mr. Kenyon employs an average of sixteen men, and from ten to sixty girls, according to the season. The business is both wholesale and retail in hats, Mr. Kenyon being the sole local agent for Dunlap of New York, and Christie of London, the celebrated hat manufacturers, while the trade in the finer classes of furs is probably the largest in Hartford or its vicinity. The extent of territory covered by the operations of this house embraces all the New England and many of the adjacent States, and the yearly volume of business foots up to about $200,000. Mr. Kenyon makes a specialty of fine furs, making an annual visit to Europe to secure the high class of goods demanded by his trade. This house carries a stock of from $40,000 to $60,000, and is the only jobbing concern of its class of any size in the State of Connecticut.

Mr. Kenyon is a native of Plainfield, Conn., and was born in 1847. In 1864 he entered the navy as Paymaster's Clerk, and served in that capacity until 1867. On his return home in that year he stopped in Hartford, taking a course in the Bryant & Stratton Business College, after which he entered the service of Messrs. Daniels & Priest, working himself from the position of errand boy to the enviable position he now occupies in the business world. Mr. Kenyon has been for ten years a member of the Putnam Phalanx, in which time-honored organization he now holds the position of Sergeant-Major. He is one of Hartford's leading business men.

Smith, Northam & Co. (James A. Smith, Chas. H. Northam, E. V. Mitchell), Flour, Grain and Feed, No. 129 State Street.—The business carried on by this firm was established in 1855, as an agency for a Bridgeport flouring mill. The original firm was W. Hawes & Co., they being succeeded in 1860 by Hawes & Smith, in 1866 by Smith, Northam & Robinson, and finally, in July, 1882, by Smith, Northam & Co. Since its inception this business has grown from an agency with annual sales of about $75,000, until it is now the leading grain business in New England. The new mill, the largest meal mill in the country, lately erected on Windsor street, has a capacity of about 6,000 bushels of meal per day, about twelve car loads, and is furnished with all the latest improved machinery and appliances for the lightening and expediting labor. So complete, in fact, are these, that four men are enabled to unload, grind, sack and reload a car of corn in two hours. The warehouse, adjoining the mill, is situated between the tracks of the New York, New Haven and Hartford and the New York and New England Railroads, thus enabling the firm to ship goods direct from the warehouse, saving the trouble and expense of teaming. Cars are unloaded by machinery, and everything that is possible to be done by the aid of steam is so accomplished. It is frequently the case that an order for an assorted car load of grain, meal and feed is filled in fifteen minutes after its receipt. Besides the immense business done at the warehouse, the firm delivers to any station in New England car loads of grain, from 300 to 500 of which are constantly on the road, moving annually more than 5,000,000 bushels of grain, about 15,000 tons of bran, middlings and rye feed, and nearly 100,000 barrels of flour. This extraordinary business is the outgrowth of a fair beginning and a result of energetic business methods and fair dealing.

Mr. James A. Smith, the senior member of the firm, was born in Glastonbury, Conn., about forty-four years ago, but has lived in Hartford since 1850, being educated in and graduating at the high school here. He is a director in the Ætna Insurance Co. as well as in the Phœnix National Bank.

Mr. Charles H. Northam is a native of Washington Village, R. I., born on March 9th, 1842. He has resided in Hartford for a long time, and is justly regarded as one of her leading citizens. Mr. Northam's education was finished at Suffield, a short time prior to his entering active business life.

Mr. E. V. Mitchell, the junior member of the house, was born in Sangerville, Me., and is twenty-eight years of age. He has been a partner in the house only since July, 1882, but was connected with it about eight years in a confidential capacity. Mr. Mitchell is a graduate of the Framingham, Mass., high school, also Bryant & Stratton Business College in Boston, and demonstrates in his business the benefits to be had in that admirable institution.

The firm of Smith, Northam & Co. stand in the very first class as regards extent and credit.

Lester, Pope & Co. (Henry and C. H. Lester and F. B. Pope), Interior Decorators, No. 42 Asylum Street.—The firm of Lester, Pope & Co., interior decorators, at No. 42 Asylum street, is one of the youngest in its line in Hartford, but has already won its way to a large and profitable business which is increasing in such rapid ratio as to warrant the belief that a very few years will see the house among the foremost in its line. The firm was formed and the business established on the 15th of September, 1882, and, owing to the long connection of all the partners with the trade in other houses, sprang at once into favorable and profitable notice. The members of the firm, save the senior partner, are practical men, and with their assistants are able to turn out a large quantity of work in their line. The staple of their stock consists of wall-paper, shades, draperies, lambrequins, rugs, ornaments of all kinds, etc., while the finer grades of carpets are sold by sample. All interior furnishing is done and a specialty is made of supplying everything needed for comfort and elegance, taking a house from the builder and rendering it to the owner completely finished in all the details of furnishing. Mr. Henry Lester is a native of East Hartford, about sixty-three years of age, and has resided in Hartford since his birth.

Mr. C. H. Lester, his son, is a native of Hartford, and was born in 1844. He has been in the present business for eighteen years, most of that time with the house of Hart, Merriam & Co., and is regarded as one of the best and most tasteful workmen in the business.

Mr. F. B. Pope was born in Woodbury, Conn., and is about twenty-six years of age. He has been resident in Hartford since boyhood, and, like Mr. Lester, served a long term with Hart, Merriam & Co. The house is well regarded in business circles and promises to have a prosperous future.

Chauncey B. Boardman, Hack, Livery and Sale Stables, No. 104 Main Street.—It is something more than twenty-five years ago since Mr. C. O. Gilbert started a livery stable at this location. After a time it was Messrs. Gilbert & Co., and then again Mr. Chas. O. Gilbert.

In 1860, Maj. C. B. Boardman inaugurated a similar establishment on State street, removing from there to his present location in 1875, purchasing the stock and good-will of the same from Mr. Gilbert, and combining the two establishments, made the business one of the largest of its class in the State.

The stable has from thirty to thirty-five horses for livery and hack purposes, and from ten to fifteen boarders.

Quite a business is transacted in the sale and exchange of horses, which is one of Mr. Boardman's specialties.

There is, probably, no other stable in the city which runs as many hacks as this, the number being thirteen.

Mr. Boardman is a native of Hartford, and forty-three years of age. He has since a youth taken great interest in military matters, having enlisted in the First Governor's Horse Guards as far back as the year 1855. His zeal and energy have been illustrated in the fact that, from that time to this, a period of nearly thirty years, he has never missed a training or parade, an appreciation of which is shown in his being elected major, an office he has held for thirteen years.

Major Boardman started in life as a carpenter and builder, having served an apprenticeship to that end, but his love for horses led him into this, his life pursuit, in which he is classed as one of the most popular in Hartford.

He has been an alderman and member of the City Council from the Fourth, now the Eighth Ward, of his native city, which is one of the evidences of the popularity he enjoys among his fellow-citizens.

A. H. Tillinghast, Dealer in Choice Groceries, Provisions, etc., No. 93 Main Street.—One of the most extensive, well-known and reliable retail groceries in Hartford is that of Mr. Alva H. Tillinghast, located at No. 93 Main street.

The business was established by Mr. Henry B. Rhodes, in the adjoining store, and purchased by Mr. Tillinghast April 1st, 1868, who continued in the same place till three years since, when he removed to his present location. Both of these stores are old business stands of thirty years record. No. 93 Main street is 22x75 feet in size, and contains a large stock of choice groceries, provisions, fruit, wood, willow and stone ware, the sales amounting to $50,000 per annum, requiring the service of four experienced assistants.

Mr. Tillinghast is a native of Plainfield, Connecticut, and fifty years of age. He has been a resident of Hartford since 1864, and for four years was well known in insurance circles, which business he conducted. Previous to this he was a successful merchant in Attleboro, Massachusetts, which place he left on account of ill-health. He is well-known in church circles and a prominent member of the South Church, in the welfare of which he takes much interest.

Charles Soby, Fine Cigar Manufacturer, No. 349 Main Street.—The largest cigar manufactory in Hartford, and, with two exceptions, the largest in the State of Connecticut, is owned and operated by Mr. Charles Soby, at No. 349 Main street. This business was established by Mr. Soby in 1875, at No. 106 Asylum street, where he remained for three and a half years, removing thence to No. 64 on the same street, where he remained for four years, and on April 1, 1882, to the elegant quarters he now occupies.

Besides his store, which is about 20 x 50 feet in size, Mr. Soby occupies a portion of the second story of the building, where the stripping of tobacco leaves is accomplished and a large factory in the rear where the cigars are made. An average of thirty skilled cigar-makers produce the million cigars that are made yearly in this establishment, and the services of about a half dozen girls are required in the stripping department. Mr. Soby's trade is both wholesale and retail, and extends to various parts of New England as well as, in a lesser extent, to portions of the Western States.

The choice brands of cigars for which Mr. Soby has become famous are retailed by drug stores and the better classes of hotels, and are in such active demand that an enlargement of the factory and the working force will soon become an absolute necessity. Among the more prominent of the favorite brands made are: "Elegantes," "Henry Clay Conchas," "Speckled Beauties," "Hazel Kirke," "Sports," "Old Bachelors," "Blue Ribbon," "Old Mill," "Seal of Connecticut, Regalia," "Seal of Connecticut, Opera," and others too numerous to mention. Private brands are made to order, and many leading houses have their cigars made at Mr. Soby's factory.

Mr. Soby is a native of Suffield, Conn., born in 1854. He has been a resident of Hartford since the establishment of his business, and has won his way to a first class position in the mercantile world. He is a practical cigar-maker, and it is largely due to his capable supervision that his goods meet with the ready and extensive sale accorded them.

Edward B. Dix, Hatter and Furrier, No. 347 Main Street.—The business now carried on by Mr. Edward B. Dix was established about twenty years ago by his uncle, Mr. C. R. Dix, and was continued by him until 1878, when the present proprietor succeeded him. The business is among the largest in the retail line in the city and is carried on in a store about 20x60 feet in size, eligibly located on the westerly side of Main street, in the very midst of the business section and on the fashionable promenade. Three salesmen, besides a number of workmen and girls are employed, and the seal sacques, dolmans and other furs turned out have won an enviable reputation among the better classes of Hartford's society. Mr. Dix also does a large trade in hats, making the finest grades a specialty. Mr. Dix is a native of Newington, Conn., and was born in 1857. He has resided in Hartford for the greater part of his life and bears the reputation of being one of its worthy and pushing business men.

The Hartford Chemical Works, Manufacturers of Lavine, 30 Union Place.—The word "Lavine" has obtained such a world-wide celebrity that no history of the manufacturing industries of the State of Connecticut would be complete without a somewhat detailed account of the place where it was manufactured, and a sketch of the men who has done so much to lighten the labors of thousands of weary men and women throughout the civilized world.

The factory where this admirable substitute for soap and other cleaning agents is prepared is situated in Union Place, opposite the railroad depot, and occupies an elegant five-story and basement brick building, in which all the different processes of mixing, drying, labeling and packing are performed, and whence issues the vast amount of pictorial and other advertising, for which the enterprising proprietors expend thousands of dollars yearly. Here also are made all the paper boxes used for packing "Lavine," the improved machinery known as the Cleveland Paper-box Machines being used for that purpose. Beginning with the basement, we find a huge boiler of sixty-horse power, furnishing steam to a large stationary engine of about the same capacity, which drives, in addition to the numerous and complicated machines used in the business, a patent safety elevator, running from basement to garret. In the front of this floor is the tool, pipe and machine shop, where are stored the various implements and parts of machines necessary for repairs and the new work which is being constantly done to meet the demands of the increasing trade. On the ground floor is the office, salesroom and packing room, in the latter of which is contained much of the machinery for making boxes as well as for filling them. In the salesroom are piled, tier upon tier, thousands of cases of "Lavine," their great number attesting the claim of the manufacturers that they are already making and selling more than one million pounds of "Lavine" per annum. The machinery for making the boxes for packing the one-pound packages of the preparation is operated by a boy and girl, and turns out with astonishing rapidity the complete boxes at the rate of 6,000 per day. The upper floors are used for mixing—a process which is a secret—drying and boxing, in which departments a large number of hands are given constant and profitable employment.

The growth of this business from its comparatively recent start in 1879, and its ramifications embracing, as they do, not only the United States, England, South America, Australia, and all parts of the civilized world, where an easy attainment of cleanliness is deemed desirable, prove the truth of the old saying "good wine needs no bush," although Mr. Gillett has provided his "wine" with a very considerable "bush" in the matter of extensive and judicious advertising.

Mr. Gillett, the creator and supervising spirit of this great business, is a native of Ellington in this State, and is still a young man, having first seen the light in the year 1846. He has made Hartford his home for about thirty years of his life, and has grown to be favorably known in the business and social communities. During the war of the Rebellion he served in the Paymaster's Department of the navy for two years, resigning his position when the war was practically at an end, and thereafter embarking in the manufacture and wholesaling of spices and grocers' sundries, a business he continued until August, 1882, when the growth of the Lavine interest compelled him to dispose of the other branches to Messrs. Allyn, Blanchard & Latimer, and give his entire attention to his specialty.

Mr. Gillett was a member of the City Council in 1873, and in that capacity won the hearty respect of his constituents and the public, a respect he continues to enjoy and merit.

The sudden rise of this industry is a pleasing proof that its founder is prominent among those of whom it is said: "They are wise, for they knew their opportunities."

Since the above was put in type, this business has been changed from an individual to a corporated enterprise under the name of the Hartford Chemical Company, with a capital of $30,000, and the following-named officers: President, A. B. Gillett; Secretary and Treasurer, Roswell W. Brown.

Mr. Brown is a native of Hartford, and about forty years of age. He has been for years first selectman in the Hartford Town Government, and is a well known successful business man. The change in the business administration was necessitated on account of the rapid growth of the sale of Lavine which extends to every State and territory in the Union.

The Hartford Machine Screw Company, Capitol Avenue.—The most recent addition to the more important manufacturing establishments in Hartford, is The Hartford Machine Screw Co., the works of which were built in 1880. They are situated in the neighborhood of the Weed Sewing Machine Co., The Pratt & Whitney Co., The Billings & Spencer Co., and others, with them forming a *coterie* of successful establishments, which are the back bone of the manufacturing industries of the Capitol City. The company was incorporated July, 1876, with a capital of $100,000 and has the following-named officers:

President and Treasurer, G. A. Fairchild; Secretary, Daniel Morrell; Superintendent, C. M. Spencer.

These works are the result of the inventions of Mr. C. M. Spencer, the superintendent, and are the largest of their class in the world. (See illustration p. 159). They are built of brick in the form of a hollow square, and cover about 45,000 square feet of surface. This company have now in operation from 300 to 500 automatic screw machines with which they are enabled to produce more uniform results than by hand machinery. With these machines are manufactured all of the better grades of machine screws, from the smallest watch screw to the largest screws, used in mill work, together with a great variety of fancy turned work used in the construction of guns, pistols, sewing machines, clocks, shears, etc. The mechanical departments are a model of neatness and completeness. The business offices are finished in ash, elegantly furnished, and the whole plant has an unconscious atmosphere of stability and success.

The machines which produce such wonderful results have been adopted by some of the largest sewing machine companies and gun manufacturers, and are giving daily entire satisfaction. The practical workings of the inventions of Mr. Spencer, so far as these machines are concerned, have been of recent date, and the results have been immediate and more than satisfactory. The attention of manufacturers in this and foreign countries, where the company is fully protected by patents, have been attracted to this company and its processes and products. So much interest is excited in the minds of inventors and others interested in machinery that visitors are entertained daily and hospitality shown to all who wish to inspect the works.

Mr. G. A. Fairfield, the President, is a native of Lansingburg, N. Y., born in 1834, and has been a resident of Hartford for twenty-five or more years. He was formerly a contractor at Colt's Armory and later, president and superintendent of the Weed Sewing Machine Co., and was the first man in their employ. He invented the "F. F." or Family Favorite machine, "G. F." or General Favorite, and "M. F." or Manufacturers' Favorite. Before the war he was employed by the American Machine Works in Springfield, Mass., making drawings and machinery for the manufacture of guns at Harper's Ferry, Va., which were afterwards burned. At one time he was engaged in the manufacture of fire arms at Windsor, Vt., in connection with the Robbins & Lawrence Co., who were filling large contracts for the English Government during the Crimean war. He was selected by the United States Government to write up the history of sewing machines for the Vienna exhibition.

He was a member of the city government of Hartford for two terms and is a director in the Mechanics' Savings Bank, Cedar Hill Association and other institutions in his adopted city, as well as president of the Western Automatic Machine Co. of Elyria, Ohio.

Mr. Daniel Morrell, the Secretary, is a native of Canajoharie, N. Y., and forty-six years of age. He is a retired capitalist and for many years was a member of the well-known brokerage firm of David Groesbeck & Co., New York. He has been a resident of Hartford for about seven years and takes but little interest in the business world.

Mr. C. M. Spencer, the Superintendent, is a native of South Manchester, Connecticut, born June 20, 1833. In addition to his interests here, he is one of the founders and a stockholder in the Billings & Spencer Co., the works of which are situated near by. His first ventures in mechanical pursuits were with the Cheney Bros., silk manufacturers. He is probably one of the most prominent and successful inventors in America. He is the inventor of the celebrated Spencer rifle, which is perhaps his most successful effort. It is a new repeating shot gun and rifle and is said to be the most rapid gun ever produced. A company is now being formed for their manufacture, to be located at Windsor, Conn.

The automatic screw machine, the patents of which are owned by this company, are a mechanical wonder, and the works of The Hartford Machine Screw Co. are a model of elegance and architectural beauty.

The Hartford Manila Company, No. 1 South Ann Street.—The works of this company are situated at Woodland, in the town of East Hartford, on the Hockanum river, two and a half miles east of the New York and New England Railroad Station. The office is at No. 1 South Ann Street, in this city. The company was incorporated in 1881, with $100,000 capital, and the following-named officers: President, M. S. Chapman; Vice President, H. J. Wickham; Secretary, C. H. Wickham; Treasurer, L. B. Plimpton. The works produce about six tons of Manila paper daily; about one-third of which is used in the United States Stamped Envelope Works in this city, of which the president of The Hartford Manila Co., Mr. M. S. Chapman, is superintendent. He is a native of East Haddam, Conn., and forty-four years of age. He has been a dealer in and manufacturer of paper and envelopes for the past twenty years, commencing his business career as a commercial traveler for the Plimpton Manufacturing Company of this city, of which he is now vice-president. He resides in South Manchester, which town he represented in the Legislature in 1881. In addition to his interests here he is a director and large owner in the Kanawha Wood Pulp Company, at Parkersburgh, W. Va.

Although a business man in Hartford, his home is as above stated.

Mr. H. J. Wickham, the vice-president and General Superintendent, is a native of Manchester, and about forty-six years of age. He is a practical machinist, and inventor of the machinery now used in making stamped envelopes and newspaper wrappers.

Mr. C. H. Wickham, the secretary, is a son of the vice-president of the company, born in Manchester, and about twenty-three years of age.

Mr. L. B. Plimpton, the Treasurer, is also president of the Plimpton Manufacturing Company, one of the largest envelope manufactories in this country. As will be seen, the principal customer of this company is the United States Stamped Envelope Works, in which its principal officers are financially interested.

The Hartford Daily Times, Burr Bros. (A. E. Burr, F. L. Burr & W. O. Burr), Publishers, No. 254 Main Street.—On the first day of January, 1883, sixty-six years had passed and left their impress on the history of the "Times." Sixty-six years ago, on January 1, 1817, Mr. Frederick Bolles issued the first number of the "Hartford Weekly Times," edited by Mr. John M. Niles, who afterwards attained to national celebrity as United States Senator, and as Postmaster-General during the Presidency of Martin Van Buren.

The "Times" was established in the interest of what was then known as the "Toleration" party, and advocated principles nearly akin to those it maintains to-day. In 1827 Mr. Bolles was succeeded by Norton & Russell, as publishers, and in

1829, by Mr. John Russell, who still ran the paper as a weekly, and in the same general tone as regards politics. In 1841 Mr. A. E. Burr succeeded to the proprietorship, and began the publication of a daily, issuing in the afternoons. Under Mr. Burr's control the paper has always been distinctly Democratic in politics, and early won for itself a foremost place among the Democratic journals in New England. Mr. Burr continued as sole proprietor of the "Times" until 1878, in which year the present firm was formed by the admission of Messrs. F. L. and W. O. Burr, his brother and son, respectively.

In circulation and influence, the "Times" stands on an equal footing with the best and largest papers published in New England, excelled in the former respect by few and the latter by none. This journal is a living proof that consistent honesty coupled with ability will win respect for a newspaper, and that respect is the first essential to the foundation of its influence. The head of the firm, Mr. A. E. Burr, under whose sole proprietorship the foundations of the paper's present prosperity and influence were laid, has never been else in politics than a consistent and outspoken Democrat, refusing office and emolument for himself, but laboring with zeal and patience to elevate the good men of his party to the rule of the State, and his party itself to power in the nation. It is, perhaps, not too much to say that the result of the Fall election of 1882, in Connecticut, was largely due to the Messrs. Burr and their paper.

The "Times" is published every afternoon excepting Sundays, and is delivered by carriers and sold by newsboys and dealers in Hartford, and sent by mail all over the United States. It has a particularly large circulation in its own State, and is looked upon as the leading Democratic paper of Connecticut.

About forty people are constantly employed, and it is a matter of general knowledge that the "Times" office retains its employees for very long terms.

Mr. A. E. Burr, the senior partner, is a native of Hartford, born on March 27, 1815. He received the rudiments of his education in the public schools, the intermediate course in private schools, and the finish in the printing office. He is a practical printer and newspaper man.

Mr. F. L. Burr is also a native of Hartford, and was born on December 27, 1827. His education was acquired in the same manner as that of his elder brother, and he is likewise practical in all branches of newspaper work.

Mr. W. O. Burr, the junior member of the firm, like his seniors, is a native of Hartford, his birth occurred on September 27, 1843. He is a practical printer and newspaper man.

The success of the "Times" is proved by the fact of its already great circulation and influence, and is emphasized by the recent addition of one of Hoe & Co.'s web-perfecting presses, of the latest improved pattern, with a capacity of 12,000 double sheets per hour, and an enlargement of the paper to an eight-page daily.

William J. Tolhurst, dealer in Groceries, Provisions, Meat, Fish, Vegetables, etc., No. 55 Maple Avenue.—The largest grocery store and meat market combined, in the western part of the city, is that of Mr. William J. Tolhurst, located at No. 55 Maple avenue, corner of Retreat street.

The business was established about the year 1859, long before it had reached its present proportions, and before this part of the city had become so thickly populated. The first gentleman to show his enterprise in the establishing of this house was Mr. Lyman M. Bacon; next, the firm was Messrs. Bacon & Rowley, then Mr. William R. Rowley, and on July 1, 1879, the present owner became proprietor.

The location is all that could be desired; situated on the line of horse cars, a prominent corner, and facing two streets, it commands the attention of the public going either way.

The premises are 150x60 feet in area. The front is used as the grocery department, where is carried a large stock of teas, coffees, dried fruits, spices, canned goods, sugars, farinaceous goods, soaps, candles, salt, crackers, brooms, brushes, pails, etc., while in the rear is the meat and fish market, where all kinds and varieties of meat, poultry, game, vegetables and fish are found in abundance. To transact this large retail business requires the services of seven employees and two delivery wagons, the sales amounting to about $50,000 per year.

Mr. Tolhurst is a young but experienced business man, thirty-two years of age, a native of Headcorn, England, and a resident of this country since he was a few months of age. He spent most of his boyhood on a farm near Middletown, Conn., and came to Hartford in November, 1863. Since that time he has been identified with the grocery and meat business, and for five years previous to 1879 was a member of the well-known firm of Messrs. Barrows & Tolhurst, in this city. He is a progressive and popular merchant, with a first class trade which is constantly increasing.

Hartford Cement Tile Co., Manufacturers of Tile, Chimney Tops, etc., No. 69 Commerce Street.—Prominent among the many industries of Connecticut and peculiar in its line is the one whose name heads this article. The company was incorporated on March 14, 1873, with a capital of $10,000, and immediately began, on a large scale, the manufacture of the durable and beautiful tile and chimney tops, the excellence of which has won a wide reputation and an extensive patronage. Mr. John R. Hills, the well-known builder, is President of the company, while the Secretaryship is in the able hands of Mr. James S. Belden, of the firm of Seth Belden & Son; dealers in flagging stone, at whose office the business of the company is transacted. The goods manufactured by this company find a ready market, and many of the finer buildings in Connecticut and other States are adorned with them. An average of about eight men are given constant and profitable employment with a prospect of largely increasing the force in the near future.

Holcomb & Sperry (J. R. Holcomb and E. K. Sperry), Manufacturers and Dealers in Brushes and Feather Dusters, No. 177 Asylum Street.—The firm of Holcomb & Sperry, brush and duster manufacturers and dealers, are the successors to Messrs. C. L. W. Baker & Co., whom they succeeded in

1872. The business has been in its present location since its establishment, and has grown therein from a very small beginning to among the leading industries of the State. The premises occupied consists of three floors, one in front and two in the rear, where there are employed from twelve to thirty-five people, the number varying with the season. All kinds and varieties of brushes and dusters are manufactured here, a specialty being made of machine and scratch wire brushes, the trade in which latter articles is chiefly confined to this house. While the factory turns out quantities of goods for the New England trade, by far the greater portion of the business is done in the West, where the firm's traveling salesmen are constantly engaged and where many thousands of dollars' worth of the celebrated Holcomb & Sperry brushes are annually sold, those goods being especially prominent in California and the other extreme Western States and territories.

Mr. J. R. Holcomb is a native of Elizabethtown, N. Y., born in 1827, and has been a resident of Hartford since 1850. In its society and business he has held a prominent place, having been a member of the Common Council for four years, and an active member of the old Governor's Foot Guard, in which historic organization he was a lieutenant and is now a veteran. In the Masonic fraternity he is an old and prominent member, and has held all the offices possible to hold. He is now a Knight Templar, a member of the Grand Commandery, and Deputy Grand Commander. Before entering his present business he was junior partner in the old "Bee Hive" dry goods store, and in that business laid the foundation of the very excellent commercial reputation he now enjoys.

Mr. E. K. Sperry is a native of Hartford, and forty three years of age. He is of the well-known family of that name, who have been prominent in the history of Connecticut for many years, one brother having been mayor of New Haven, and another postmaster in the same city.

During the administration of Mr. Lincoln he held the appointment of United States Consul for Barbadoes, W. I., and its dependencies.

George Marchant, Harness, etc., No. 109 Main Street.—The harness and saddle business of Mr. George Marchant was established at No. 86 Main street sixteen years ago.

In 1876 he removed to No. 109 Main street, which is his present location.

He manufactures and deals in harness, saddles, bridles, collars, whips, brushes, combs, fly nets, etc., and makes a specialty of dealing in the celebrated vacuum oil blacking. He does a small but safe business, employing three workmen, and turning out superior work. Some of the sets of harness used in the most stylish turnouts in Hartford are evidence of his handiwork.

Mr. Marchant is a native of Braghlang, Sussex, England, born in 1837. He came to America in 1852, and to Hartford, learning his trade here in the same year, and where he has since enjoyed an enviable reputation as a good workman and excellent citizen.

A. O. Dole, Grocer, No. 72 Park Street.—As a city grows, the demand for stores from which the surrounding inhabitants get their supplies increases, and is supplied as made. One of these representative stores relying entirely on the immediately surrounding trade is that of which Mr. Augustus O. Dole is proprietor, located at No. 72 Park street, corner Hudson. It is 18 x 50 feet in size, and stocked with a well selected assortment of first-class groceries, in which the sales amount to $15,000 per annum.

Mr. Dole, the proprietor, is a native of Buckland, Franklin County, Mass., born in 1844. Previous to his locating here in June, 1881, he was a successful and well-known commercial traveler.

During the war he served three years in the Thirty-seventh Massachusetts Infantry, and most of that time was a clerk in the Sixth Corps' Hospital, where he was instrumental in securing the names and preserving the identity of thousands of the killed and wounded, which but for him would have been lost forever. Modest and undemonstrative in his methods, he has achieved that success which true merit always wins.

J. J. Poole & Co., Wholesale and Retail Dealers in Anthracite and Bituminous Coal, No. 278 Main Street.—Mr. J. J. Poole commenced business in Hartford, under the style of J. J. Poole & Co., on the first of July, 1876, succeeding to the old-established trade of G. B. Linderman & Co. The business done is both wholesale and retail, the latter predominating, and is the largest of its class in the city.

The office is centrally located on Main street, while the yards, which have a storage capacity of 5,000 tons, are located on Commerce street, embracing the numbers from 172 to 180, inclusive. While all descriptions of coal are handled and sold, the house makes a specialty of the celebrated "Sugar Loaf" (Lehigh) coal, of which there are annually many thousands of tons passing through their hands, and which has attained a very high reputation in Hartford and the surrounding country where the trade of the house extends.

Mr. Poole is a native of Baltimore, Md., and has been a resident of Hartford since 1876. He is regarded as an energetic and reliable business man, and as a desirable acquisition to the mercantile community.

The Hartford Evening Post, Nos. 23, 25 and 27 Asylum Street.—Hartford supports two evening papers, "The Post," which is Republican in politics, and "The Times," Democratic.

"The Post," which has a weekly edition called "The Connecticut Post," was established in 1856, by Mr. J. M. Scoville. The present proprietors of both papers is The Evening Post Association, with Mr. H. T. Sperry, President and managing editor, and Mr. J. A. Spaulding as Secretary, Treasurer and business manager. The Evening Post Building is an imposing structure situated in the centre of business on one of the principal thoroughfares. It is 40x70 feet in area, four stories in height, with an annex for press room and composing room 40x40 feet, two stories, the whole premises being of brick. The demands of the business necessitate the constant employment of forty-two men and twenty-seven boys as carriers during the afternoon. The circulation of "The Evening Post" in the surrounding cities and villages is very large, while the number of carriers employed in a city of 45,000 people indicates the extent of its circulation in Hartford.

Mr. H. T. Sperry, the president and managing editor, has been engaged on "The Post" for twelve years. While seeking to ignore all political preferment, he was at one time member of the city government of Hartford. He was born in Hartford, and is forty-seven years of age.

Mr. J. A. Spaulding, the secretary, treasurer and business manager, was born in Killingly, Conn., forty-nine years ago, and has been connected with "The Post" for nearly five years. He is well known as an experienced journalist, having been proprietor of the Killingly (Conn.) "Transcript" for five years, the Webster (Mass.) "Times" for seven years, the Rockville (Conn.) "Journal" for eight years, and the Worcester (Mass.) "Press" for five years.

With an existence of over twenty-five years "The Post" has done great service to the Republican party. Its influence is felt in every section of the State, where its circulation is rapidly increasing.

The Tunxis Worsted Co., Worsted Yarns and Tops, No. 66 State Street; Mills at Poquonock, Ct., and

The Dunham Hosiery Co., Hosiery, Zephyrs and Yarns, No. 66 State Street; Mills at Naugatuck, Ct.—This city is the centre for the manufacturing districts surrounding it. Nearly every water-power is the site of a mill of some kind, with the houses of the superintendent and operatives in close proximity; the whole forming a good sized village. The headquarters are generally in Hartford, where the owners live, and from which they communicate their orders by telephone.

Among the most important manufacturing establishments are The Tunxis Worsted Co. and The Dunham Hosiery Co., who have their headquarters at No. 66 State street.

The first-named was incorporated June 21, 1880, and has a capital of $160,000, and a surplus of $60,000. The officers are: President, S. G. Dunham; Treasurer, A. C. Dunham; Secretary, Henry Osborn.

The mills, two in number, are situated at Poquonock, Conn., about twelve miles from Hartford, on the Farmington river, one of the best water powers in Connecticut; the number of feet fall being nine feet eight inches, and six feet three inches, respectively. The capacity of the establishment is 200,000 pounds of raw wool per month, the manufacture of combed tops and fancy colored worsteds being made a specialty.

The combs here were patented by Mr. Samuel Metcalf, and are not excelled or duplicated in the United States.

The officers of the company speak in a very complimentary manner of the Risdon Turbine Wheel, made at Mount Holly, N. J., which is in use here. About three hundred people are employed in the manufacture of worsted yarns and tops, which have an extended reputation with the trade.

In the same office, at No. 66 State street, is the headquarters of The Dunham Hosiery Co., which has for its officers the same gentlemen who are officers of The Tunxis Worsted Co. The Dunham Hosiery Co. was incorporated June 21, 1880. The capital stock is $42,500, with a surplus of $30,000. The officers are: President, Austin C. Dunham; Treasurer, Samuel G. Dunham; Secretary, Henry Osborn.

The establishment, which consists of one mill, is located on a tributary of the Naugatuck river at Naugatuck, Conn., and the company are successors to Messrs. Theo. Lewis & Co., who made fancy cassimeres. About two hundred people are employed in the manufacture of shirts and drawers, of which 21,000 dozen are turned out annually; also manufacturing 60,000 pounds of zephyr yarns per year.

In addition to a National Turbine Wheel a steam engine is relied upon at intervals. The sales agent for both The Tunxis Worsted Co. and Dunham Hosiery Co. is Mr. A. S. Haight, No. 48 Howard street, New York.

The Messrs. Dunham are the sons of Austin Dunham, Esq., who was one of the pioneers in establishing large and successful industries in different localities in Connecticut. He established, in 1870, the business to which The Tunxis Worsted Co. succeeded. He was the originator and projector of The Willimantic Linen Co., and prominently identified with the leading banks and insurance companies of his native State. He died in the year 1877, leaving behind him as a heritage to his sons a name that is gratefully spoken by thousands, and that stands at the head of a long list of Connecticut's pioneer philanthropic manufacturers.

Mr. Austin C. Dunham, president of one of the above-mentioned companies and treasurer of the other, is a native of Hartford, Conn., and about fifty-two years old. He is a graduate of Yale, in the class of 1854; a director in the Ætna Fire Insurance Co., The Travelers Insurance Co., The Exchange National Bank, The Willimantic Linen Co., president of the Rock Manufacturing Co. of Rockville, Conn., and largely interested in real estate, and other matters identified with the interests of his native city.

Mr. Samuel G. Dunham is an officer in The Tunxis Worsted Co. and The Dunham Hosiery Co., being president of the former and treasurer of the latter. He is also a native of Hartford, and thirty-three years of age, a director in the Ætna Life Insurance Co., the Phœnix National Bank, the United States Bank, and the Rock Manufacturing Co. of Rockville. He learned the business of manufacturing from his father, and is one of Connecticut's representative citizens.

Mr. Henry Osborn, the secretary of both companies named in the title lines of this sketch, was born in Willimantic in 1847, and received his education in the public schools of his native town. He has also been connected with the Dunhams, directly and indirectly, for the past seventeen years.

The companies above named are conspicuous among the reliable and well-known establishments which go to make up the reputation Connecticut enjoys as a manufacturing centre.

Way & Co., Importers and Wholesale Dealers in Hardware, Cutlery, Agricultural Implements, etc., No. 344 Main Street.—It is a well-known fact that repetition is advertising. The French claim that an advertisement is seen seven times before it is read, and read many times before it is indelibly fixed in the memory of the reader. If this is so, the name of the hardware house of Way must be unusually familiar to the present generation of Hartford people.

More than half a century has passed since George M. Way embarked in the hardware trade. From the year 1831 to 1883 the sign of "Way Hardware" has been conspicuous on the main thoroughfare of Hartford, one being synonymous with the other. After a long life of business activity and probity, he died in October, 1882, the business passing to Samuel L. Way, his son, who conducts it under the firm name of Way & Co.

The store is conspicuous for its originality of interior construction; the ceilings are very high, and openings through the several floors, around which are railings, offer an uninterrupted view from the ground floor to the upper story, a pleasing contrast to most hardware stores in this and other cities.

The stock consists of all kinds of hardware, cutlery, agricultural implements and tools, manufacturers' and mechanics' supplies, iron, steel, wooden ware, etc., etc., which are sold at both wholesale and retail, the trade of the house extending throughout the State, and particularly among the large class of manufacturing establishments which cluster in and around Hartford.

The main store and salesroom is located at No. 344 Main street, three stories in height; this, with a four-story building directly in the rear, and one on a side street, comprise the buildings devoted to the trade.

Mr. Samuel L. Way, the proprietor, is a native of Hartford, born in 1833. He is one of the most enterprising and progressive merchants of the Capital City, and his long experience has made him familiar with every detail of the business.

Pond & Childs, Booksellers and Stationers, No. 301 Main Street.—For several years previous to 1860, Mr. Charles G. Geer and Mr. DeWitt C. Pond were conducting book stores on their own accounts and in different localities in this city. In that year they formed a co-partnership under the name of Geer & Pond, and located in the old Post-office building at No. 256 Main street. Mr. Geer died in 1874. Mr. Pond has been in the book business for over twenty-five years, and is well known as a *connoisseur* in such matters. On the death of Mr. Geer, Mr. Edward C. Hamlin became a partner, and the firm was called Pond & Hamlin, which continued till 1876, when Mr. Hamlin died, the business in the mean time having been transferred to its present location, December 1, 1875. Soon after the death of Mr. Hamlin, and in 1877, Mr. Charles R. Childs became a member of the firm in the place of Mr. Hamlin, and the name changed to Pond & Childs, which has since continued.

The store is located in the Phœnix Bank Building, a marble front structure and one of the finest buildings in the State. The store proper is 35x90 feet in size, and a general business in books, stationery, newspapers, and periodicals is conducted, necessitating the employment of four clerks.

Mr. DeWitt C. Pond is a native of Poultney, Rutland County, Vermont, born in 1824, and has been a resident of Hartford since 1850. He learned the trade of a jeweler, but his love for literature and of books led him into the business which has proven so profitable to him. His long residence here has identified him closely with the interests of the city and its institutions.

He has served two terms as a member of the City Council, five years as alderman, representing the Second Ward, and is now President of the Board of Aldermen.

He is also an active worker in the Congregational Church, and has been a member of the Governor's Foot Guard—both *active* and a *veteran* member—since 1860.

Mr. Charles R. Childs is a native of Springfield, Mass., born in 1846, and has resided in Hartford thirty-four years, where he received his education, previous to 1877, when he became a partner with Mr. Pond.

The house of Pond & Childs do a large retail business, and its members rank among the city's most respected citizens.

Pitkin Brothers & Co., Iron Founders, Steam Engineers, Contractors and Manufacturers of Steam Engines, Boilers, etc., No. 152 State Street. —The history of this house is closely identified with the history of the manufacturing industries of Hartford, and is one of the oldest in its line in New England.

It was first, Bidwell, Pitkin & Co., in 1849, at which time the business was established. In 1859 the firm was changed to Pitkin Bros. & Co., and has so continued up to the present. During the past thirty-three years the business and reputation of the house has extended through Canada and to every State east of the Mississippi River, the business amounting annually to $300,000.

The establishment consists of the following described buildings, situated at No. 152 State Street, viz.: A one-story building 100x20 feet, a five-story building 200x60 feet, and a one-story boiler and workshop 100x100 feet. They employ about seventy-five skilled artisans in the manufacture of steam engines, boilers, heating apparatus, all descriptions of plate work, steam, water and gas pipe and fittings. They are also steam engineers and contractors for anything under that head.

Mr. Albert P. Pitkin, the senior member of the firm, was born in Hartford fifty-four years ago, and after serving at his trade, was one of the original founders of the house.

He is one of the leading representative business men of his native city and a director in the Farmers and Mechanics' Bank.

Mr. Norman T. Pitkin was born in Hartford forty-nine years ago, and after a thorough preliminary education and the mastering of the profession of steam engine builder, he became one of the firm, with his brother. He has always been, like his brother, a steady-going, conservative business man, refusing all opportunities for political advancement, and seeking only to enlarge and perfect the already extensive business acquired by his firm.

Mr. Charles A. Pitkin, the junior partner, is also a native of Hartford, and is forty-two years of age. He is and has been for several years a resident of San Jose, Cal. The members of this house, individually and collectively, rank among the first of New England representative manufacturers and as leading representative citizens of Hartford.

The Blodgett & Clapp Co., Importers and Dealers in every description of Iron and Steel, Nos. 47, 49, 51 and 53 Market Street.—History does not record to a certainty who established the house of The Blodgett & Clapp Co., iron and steel dealers at Nos. 47, 49, 51 and 53 Market street in this city. The first name on record, as proprietor, is that of Mr. Philip Ripley, who was dispensing iron and steel in 1790, as successor to some one, of whom there is no mention. It is safe to say, that the house is as old, if not older, than the Constitution of the United States, and would have been justified in celebrating its centennial in conjunction with the Union in 1876. Owing, no doubt, to the inherent modesty of the present officers, who were at that time, members of a firm which the present company succeeded, they did not.

They will certainly be perfectly justified in celebrating their centennial most any year now, and if when 1890 arrives they do not honor Philip Ripley for leaving a business card to posterity, so that historians can write of the house to a dead certainty, we shall be sorry that we ever went into their history at all.

After Philip Ripley, came Ripley & Cone; Ripley, Roberts & Co.; Ripleys & Talcott; E. G. Ripley & Co.; R. G. Talcott & Co.; R. F. Blodgett & Co.; Blodgett & Clapp, respectively, and on January 1st, 1880, The Blodgett & Clapp Co., the present proprietors, came into possession, as an incorporated company, with Mr. R. F. Blodgett, President; Mr. J. O. Phelps, 3d, Treasurer; Mr. J. B. Clapp, Secretary.

Their office and principal salesroom occupies a three-story building 125x50 feet, with an L. Several buildings are employed for storage purposes in different parts of the city.

The stock consists of every description of iron and steel, nails, chains, bolts, nuts, anvils, vises, springs, rivets, fire brick, spokes, rims, hubs, wheels, shafts, and every description of carriage materials. The business done amounts to $150,000 per annum.

The officers of the company rank among the progressive business men of Hartford, and are largely identified with its manufacturing interests. Mr. R. F. Blodgett, the President, is a native of this city, where he was educated in its public schools. He is forty years of age, and secretary of the Pratt & Whitney Co., a very extensive manufacturing establishment in Hartford, to which he gives most of his time.

Mr. J. O. Phelps, 3d, Treasurer, is a native of Simsbury, Connecticut, and twenty-seven years of age. Although much younger than the other officers of the company, he is looked upon as a true representative of such a house as this of necessity must have.

The Secretary, Mr. John B. Clapp, is a native of Wethersfield, Connecticut, and forty years of age. He also is an educational product of the public schools of the State. During his active business life he has found time to represent his ward for two years in the City Council of his adopted city. He was also port warden for one year, and a member of the board of fire commissioners for nine years.

During the war he enlisted as a private in the Sixteenth Connecticut Volunteers, serving with honor and bravery, and came home as brevet captain and assistant adjutant-general.

The gentlemen who are the officers of The Blodgett & Clapp Co. are liberal and progressive in all affairs for public good, of excellent judgment, and enlarged experience in financial matters and of men.

Geo. P. Bissell & Co., Bankers, No. 307 Main Street.—The oldest and largest private banking house in Hartford, if not in New England, is that of Geo. P. Bissell & Co., in the handsome marble building at No. 307 Main street, near Asylum street, and in the very centre of the business district. The house was established in 1854, and has been for twenty-nine years in business in one location, and under one firm name and management. During all this time it has done an immense business, has met with no reverses, been uninfluenced by financial panics, and has never put the interests of its customers in jeopardy. It buys stocks, discounts commercial paper, allows interests, furnishes letters of credit, and has a safe-deposit vault. Mr. Bissell owns the building in which the bank is situated. At the foundation of the business, he had for partners, Calvin Day and D. F. Robinson. The latter gentleman has since died, and Mr. Day has retired. Mr. Albert H. Olmsted is now the partner. He was born in Hartford forty-five years ago, is wholly devoted to business, and neither seeks nor has held any public office. Col. George P. Bissell was born at Rochester, N. Y., fifty-five years ago, and has resided in Hartford for the past thirty-five years. During the war he was the commander of the Twenty-fifth Connecticut Regiment, and during the administration of Governor Jewell, was Paymaster-General of the State. He is a director of the Insane Retreat, and executor and trustee of the H. A. Perkins' estate. For many years he has taken a prominent place in all public enterprises in the city and State.

Beach & Co. (George Beach, J. Watson Beach, Charles M. Beach), Nos. 209 and 211 State Street.—The organization of this reputable house dates back to in 1836, when Messrs. George Beach, Sr., and George Beach, Jr., were the first partners.

In 1849, the present firm of Messrs. Beach & Co. was formed, and is composed of Mr. George Beach, Mr. J. Watson Beach and Mr. Charles M. Beach, who conduct the business of manufacturing dye stuffs, and the importing of chemicals, dye woods, etc.

The manufactory, which is situated on Potter street, in this city, is a three-story building 200 x 65 feet, fully supplied with all of the most improved machinery, necessary for the production of ground dye woods. The salesrooms at Nos. 209 and 211 State street, consist of a three-story building 40 x

65 feet, with one in the rear four stories, same dimensions.

The business is one of the most extensive in New England, as it is one of the oldest.

The thousands of manufacturing establishments tributary to this city, contribute to the large sales of this house. About twenty-five people are employed, and the amount of business done per annum exceeds one million of dollars.

Mr. George Beach, the senior member, is a native of Hartford, and about seventy years of age. He has held several important trusts during his busy life, among which was the office of State Senator.

Mr. J. Watson Beach was born in Hartford in 1824, and besides attending to many of the active duties devolving on a member of a house having such extensive connections, he has found time to be prominently identified with the manufacturing and financial interests of his native city. He is president of the Mercantile National Bank, president of the extensive Weed Sewing Machine Company, and director in other incorporated institutions too numerous to mention.

Mr. Charles M. Beach is a native of Hartford, and fifty-six years of age. Like his brothers, he is conspicuous in the business circles of the State. He is president of the Home Woolen Mills Company, and a director in the Phoenix National Bank, Phoenix Fire Insurance Company, Connecticut Mutual Fire Insurance Company and Steam Boiler Insurance Company.

There is, probably, not a firm in the State doing such an extensive business, whose members are so largely and actively interested in its financial and manufacturing industries as Messrs. Beach & Co.

The Case, Lockwood & Brainard Company, Printers and Bookbinders, corner of Pearl and Trumbull Streets.—This business, now grown to vast proportions, and to a position among the leading printing and bookbinding houses of the United States, was established in 1836, by Newton Case, Edwin D. Tiffany, and Alanson D. Waters, under the firm name of Case, Tiffany & Co. Their office was provided with eight Wells' hand presses, one Ramage press, and a considerable quantity of type, there being few stereotype and no electrotype plates at that time. Shortly after their establishment the firm purchased an Adams press, of the first patent, which for more than two years was run by hand-power.

In 1838, Mr. Waters retired from the firm, and Leander C. Burnham was admitted. At this time, the largest printing office in the State, owned by Philemon Canfield, was offered for sale, and Case, Tiffany & Co., effected its purchase. This office was equipped with five power and nine hand presses, a large amount of type and a steam-engine. In order to unite the two establishments, the premises on the corner of Pearl and Trumbull streets, known as the "old jail" was leased for the purpose. This building, erected in 1793 for a county jail and tavern, required many alterations to adapt it to the business. In April, 1838, the firm commenced operations in their new quarters and three years later purchased the property. In 1848, Mr. Burnham died, and the remaining partners continued the business at the old stand until 1850, in which year they erected a building on Trumbull street, south of the old corner structure, the main part being 50 x 64 feet, five stories high. In the basement was placed a new engine, and a portion of the building was fitted up for a bookbindery. In 1853, James Lockwood and Albert G. Cooley, were admitted to the firm. In 1857, Mr. Tiffany and Mr. Cooley both retired, and the business was conducted by Messrs. Case and Lockwood as Case, Lockwood & Co. On the 1st of January, 1858, Leverett Brainard was admitted as a partner.

It had been apparent to the firm for several years that the constantly increasing business must of necessity be accommodated in more commodious quarters; and it was decided that the "old jail" building must be demolished and a new building erected on its site. Accordingly, in 1865, a brick building was erected just west of the old one on Pearl street, to be occupied during the work of demolition and construction.

Early in the spring of 1866 the last stone of the "old jail" was removed. Work on the new building was immediately begun, and in April 1867, it was ready for occupancy. On the 1st of January, 1868, the firm name was changed to represent the three partners—Case, Lockwood & Brainard. After six years of business under that name, the firm organized, under a charter granted by the Connecticut Legislature, "The Case, Lockwood & Brainard Co.," dating from January 1, 1874. In 1875 an important addition was made to the establishment by the admission of the "Hutchings Printing House" entire. This house had acquired a reputation for good work, and was well equipped in the departments conducted. The consolidation, while permitting the continuance of any style of work peculiar to that establishment, naturally proved an advantage to its former customers, who were alike benefited by the enlarged facilities afforded, and the experience of the older house.

The building at present occupied by the Case, Lockwood & Brainard Co., is of brick, with brownstone trimmings. It is one hundred and thirty-five feet long by forty feet wide, exclusive of an L containing stairways, elevators and closets—and five stories high, besides the basement. All kinds of printing, as well as electrotyping, bookbinding, and other branches of the business are carried on. Hundreds of thousands of pounds of type, as well as book and job presses in inconceivable variety and in great number, together with all the machinery used in bookbinding and for other purposes give employment to nearly three hundred persons, and turn out work that has placed the name of the Case, Lockwood & Brainard Co., at the very head of the list of printers, not only in Connecticut, but throughout the entire country.

The Kellogg & Bulkeley Co., Lithographers, No. 175 Pearl Street.—It is rare that a lithographic establishment so large as this is found in a city the size of Hartford. The cause of its growth is found in the demands of various insurance companies and manufacturing establishments in and around this city.

It was over a half century since Messrs. E. B. & E. C. Kellogg commenced the lithographic business from which this company grew. To be exact, it was in 1831, and the place, No. 245 Main street. Establishments did not grow as fast in those days as in this. The facilities were not as many and the demand so great. But the firm improved every opportunity and grew with the city and State. In 1868 the firm was changed to Messrs. Kellogg & Bulkeley, and in 1870 new and larger quarters were found in their present location, an incorporated company formed with a capital of $33,000 and the following-named gentlemen elected as officers: William H. Bulkeley, President; Wallace T. Fenn, Secretary and Treasurer. The premises occupy two floors of a substantial brick building at No. 175 Pearl street, 125x40 feet in size. A large business as lithographers, steam printers and wood engravers is done, a specialty being the manufacture of metallic show cards in colors, and gold-leaf agency signs, in which they are one of the first in the country. The officers and directors are some of the representative men of Hartford.

The president is Gen. Wm. H. Bulkeley, one of the city's leading dry goods dealers. General Bulkeley is a native of East Haddam, Conn., and was born on March 2, 1840. He is a descendant of one of the oldest of the ancient families of New England, the founder of which in this country was the Rev. Peter Bulkeley, a distinguished Non-Conformist divine who was compelled to seek refuge in America with the Puritans, and who settled in Concord, Mass., in 1634. Since that time the history of the Bulkeley family has been a part of the history of New England. When the subject of this sketch was but seven years of age, his father, Hon. Eliphalet A. Bulkeley, a prominent lawyer in his time, then holding the office of school fund commissioner, removed to Hartford and continued his residence here until his death, which took place a few years since. General Bulkeley acquired an education in the schools of Hartford, after which the young man entered the employ of Thatcher, Goodrich & Stillman, then one of the leading drygoods houses in Hartford. In 1857 he went to Brooklyn, N. Y., and a few years thereafter established himself in the dry goods business on Fulton street, in that city, conducting it successfully for about six years. In 1868 General Bulkeley returned to Hartford and organized this company, of which he has always been president. He has been vice-president of the Ætna Life Insurance Company, and is now a director in that organization, besides holding a similar position in the Orient Fire Insurance Company, the American National Bank and the United States Bank. For five years he was a member of the Common Council, serving one year as vice-president and one year as president of that body. He has served for three terms as a member of the Board of Street Commissioners, and in the election of 1880 was chosen Lieutenant-Governor of the State on the Republican ticket, an office he filled with rare ability and with thorough satisfaction to his constituents. General Bulkeley's war record is a creditable one, he having been one of the first as a member of the Brooklyn City Guard, Co. G, 13th Regiment of the New York State National Guard, to respond to the first call for troops. After a service of four months in that organization, General Bulkeley organized Co. G, of the 56th N. Y. S. N. G., and was engaged in the Pennsylvania crisis of 1863. During the New York riots the regiment was ordered home, and at the subsidence of that trouble was disbanded. General Bulkeley is an active member of the Grand Army of the Republic and of the Army and Navy Club, as well as of other associations purely civic in their character. He is one of the few men whose lives go to make up the real and interesting history of the State, and is eminent in the class who can point with pardonable pride to their records and their standing with their fellow citizens.

Mr. Wallace T. Fenn is a native of New Haven, born in 1848, and has been a resident of Hartford since 1865, and secretary and treasurer of this company since its formation.

He was a member of the City Council from the Second Ward in 1880-81, and is commissary on the staff of Col. L. A. Barbour, of the First Regiment Connecticut National Guard.

To his rare executive ability and financial management is due in no small measure the success of this company.

The New York Sewing Machine Co., Manufacturers of the New York Sewing Machine.—There are sewing machines and sewing machines. The latest candidate for public favor is the New York Sewing Machine, which is manufactured in this city at Colt's West Armory. The company was incorporated in 1881, with a capital of $100,000, and the following-named officers: President and Treasurer, Hon. E. A. Wilkinson, of Newark, N. J.; Vice-President, Mr. R. W. Lundy, of New York City; Secretary, Mr. T. C. Woodward, of New York City; Superintendent, Mr. J. B. McCune, of Hartford.

The aim of the company is to produce the best that money and skill can procure. Special and standard machinery of the most approved kind has been purchased to insure perfect construction. The machines are manufactured upon the interchangeable system, each machine in detail being a complete duplicate of the original perfected model; an important feature, as it saves the trouble of sending machines a great distance for repair, and being without its use often for many days, and also cost of repairs.

The company claim for their machine a superior beauty of design, elegance of finish, and that it is the most beautiful and elegant sewing machine of the day. In its details it differs materially from other machines, and its simplicity is at once apparent.

The premises occupied by the factory of this company is 200 x 60 feet, and the number of employees is from fifty to sixty. The salesroom and office is at No. 42 East Fourteenth street, New York, where all the business of the company is conducted.

NEW BRITAIN.

New Britain is situated in Hartford County, about ten miles southwesterly from Hartford, on the line of the New York and New England Railroad. It has been a city since 1870, and a borough since 1850. The city proper comprises about three quarters of the town of New Britain and contains about seven-eighths of the population, which is estimated at between seventeen and eighteen thousand for the entire town, it having grown since 1880, from a census enumeration in that year of 13,978 and of only 3,029 in 1850. The government of the town and city are two distinct organizations, the former being composed of three selectmen, a town clerk, town treasurer, and town comptroller, three assessors, a board of relief, school committee, justices of the peace, constables, etc., while the city is governed by a mayor, and a common council, consisting of four aldermen and sixteen councilmen, one of the former and four of the latter being elected annually from each of the four wards comprised in the city. The city officers are: city clerk, treasurer, collector, auditor, street commissioner, city attorney, and sealer of weights and measures. There are also the board of water commissioners, consisting of three members; the board of sewer commissioners, three members; and the board of street commissioners, six members. The police department consists of a chief and five regular patrolmen, assisted by quite a large force of specials, many of whom are uniformed and do regular duty, the larger proportion, however, being employed as watchmen in the various manufacturing establishments of the city. The fire department embraces a chief and one assistant, with a working force of one hundred men, all of whom are paid by the city, which is also the owner of the apparatus, consisting of one steamer, six hose carriages and one hook-and-ladder truck. The water supply of the city is obtained from Shuttle Meadow Lake, two and a half miles southwest from the city, the works being the property of the people. Water is furnished to families at a cost of about $4 per year, while manufacturing establishments are charged according to the quantity used. The gas company, a private corporation, furnishes a good quality of illuminating coal-gas at a charge of $2.50 per thousand feet. There are about eighteen hundred dwelling-houses in the city, as well as a very large number of business structures, manufactories, etc., the assessed valuation of real estate being in the neighborhood of $5,000,000. The streets in the central portions of the city are macadamized, the work having been begun about four years ago. Something more than a mile of macadamizing has been done since the beginning, and the annual outlay has been $10,000. About thirty-three thousand feet of brick and tile sewers carry off the drainage of the city, the main sewer being eight feet in diameter, and emptying into a brook in the northwestern part of the town. These have cost $200,000, of which $70,000 have been paid in cash, the remainder being in the shape of a bonded indebtedness. The poor of the city are taken care of by the town, a few being permanently located at the town-farm, the majority being assisted with temporary relief at their homes. There are nine churches in the city, of which one is Adventist, two are Baptist, two Congregational, one Episcopal, one Methodist, one Roman Catholic and one Universalist. The schools of the town occupy ten buildings, employ about forty teachers, and range from the primary to the high-school grade. There is also the St. Mary's Parochial school, attached to the Roman Catholic Church of that name, which has an attendance of from nine hundred to one thousand pupils daily. The State Normal School is also located here, the new building being far toward completion. The manufacturing industries comprise a very large number of extensive establishments, the most of which are devoted to the production of some form of hardware. There are two banks, one national and one savings; three hotels, the Strickland House, the Humphrey House and the City Hotel, and a number of secret and benevolent societies, clubs and social organizations. The post-office has not yet attained to the dignity of a carrier system, but is otherwise satisfactory. Four newspapers are published, "The Herald" being the only daily. Among the notable buildings here may be mentioned the South Congregational Church, said to have the largest membership of the churches in New England; the Masonic Hall, Odd Fellow's Hall and the recently constructed opera house, pronounced the most beautiful of its kind to be found in New England, outside the larger cities. A complete telegraph system, telephone lines, electric fire-alarm, and the other conveniences of modern civilization are all enjoyed here, and the constant whirr of machinery, giving employment to a very large proportion of the population, is a satisfactory evidence that prosperity walks hand in hand with thrift. The traveling facilities afforded by the New York and New England Railroad are supplemented by a branch of the New York, New Haven and Hartford Road, which connects with the main line two miles away, and furnishes communication with the outside world almost hourly. The situation of the city is beautiful in the extreme, being about 130 feet higher than the track of the New Haven Road and occupying a natural amphitheatre among the surrounding hills, which in the gentler seasons wear robes of many-tinted flowers and of emerald green, in charming contrast to the smoky factory region that environs it about and makes the beauties of its setting the more apparent. New Britain can be justly classed among the prosperous and pleasant places with which Connecticut abounds.

From the early days, when brass andirons were made here, and carried on horseback over the hills to Albany, and when the first tin-ware made in the country was carried from house to house in a basket, manufacturers have ever rendered New Britian a place of world-wide reputation. One can but admire the energy and perseverance of those men who have converted a dreary swamp into one of the most important industrial cities in the country. The amount invested in manufactures is about $7,000,000.

Elihu Burritt, "the learned blacksmith," was born in New Britain, December 8, 1811. He received only a common school education; but while devoting himself to his trade he acquired several ancient and modern languages, and became renowned as a scholar and reformer. He died March 7, 1879.

Ethan A. Andrews, LL.D., was born in New Britain in 1787, and graduated at Yale College in 1810. He studied law, and practiced for several years. In conjunction with Prof. Solomon Stoddard, he published a Latin grammar, which has passed through some seventy editions. He also issued several other popular works of instruction in Latin He died March 25, 1858.

John Smalley, D. D., born in Lebanon, Conn., June 4, 1734, was settled over the First Congregational Church in New Britain, April 19, 1758, where he remained until his death, June 1, 1820. He was one of the most celebrated New England divines of his day.

The Stanley Works (Established 1843), Manufacturers of Wrought Iron Butts, Strap and T Hinges, Door Bolts, Handles, etc., Myrtle Street.— The great success of American manufacturers is largely due to the use of machinery specially adapted to the rapid and perfect performance of certain specific work. While the manufacturers of the old world are content to follow in a rut as old as their trade, performing some tedious part of their work by the slow process of hand labor, the genius of the American mechanic prompts him to devise a machine which will accomplish better results and thus materially improve the quality, as well as greatly cheapen the cost of his productions.

The Stanley Works are an illustration of what has been done by inventive genius, of the triumph of mind over matter, bringing practical results in the shape of improved productions and wealth to the proprietors. These works are among the oldest and largest of their class in the world, and their prosperous career furnishes a fitting commentary on the many advantages New Britain possesses as a manufacturing point, and is of itself the most fitting evidence of the high quality of the goods they have made. As a producer of builders' and cabinet hardware, this establishment stands pre-eminently above all competitors. It is forty years since Mr. F. T. Stanley, now president of the company, began the manufacture of bolts, with a few workmen, in a small shop in this city. It is from this small beginning has grown the great works, covering an investment of about half a million dollars, and with 500 people as operatives.

The company was incorporated in 1852, with a capital of $30,000. The chief business at that time was the manufacture of strap and T hinges. The business of manufacturing wrought iron door bolts was added in 1857. In 1866, the business was still further increased by the addition of a complete line of wrought iron butts, and since then other articles

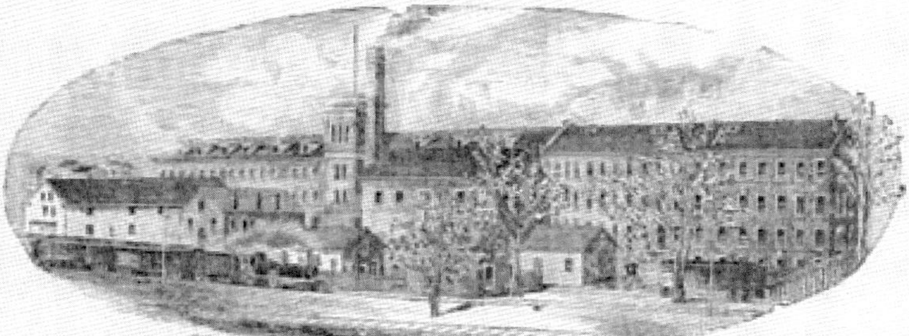

THE STANLEY WORKS, NEW BRITAIN CONN.

of builders' and cabinet makers' hardware have been added.

It has been the province of The Stanley Works to take the primitive iron hinges, as made forty years ago, invent machinery for the manufacture, design new styles, and bring the standard up to a point commanding the patronage and admiration of the trade.

The company's new works were erected in 1871. The buildings are mainly of brick, consisting of the main building three stories in height and 325 x 40 feet in area, an engine and boiler house 65 x 40 feet, and a storehouse 108 x 35 feet, and other smaller buildings necessarily found in large establishments.

The company own tracks connecting with the New York and New England, and the New York, New Haven and Hartford Railroads, enabling them to ship direct from their own yards in car lots, and to receive in the same manner the raw material in any quantity. The arrangement of the works is such that the iron goes in at the western end, and on its journey eastward passes through the different processes necessary until it arrives at the eastern end ready for shipment in a finished production.

In building their new works, and knowing the imperfections of the old, every detail was attended to, to facilitate the manufacture of goods, and every move gives an indication that the projectors knew by experience the advantage of "Heaven's first law."

In the prosecution of the business no false economy is a factor. Liberality and excellence better explains their motto. Liberality towards their customers and employees and excellence in their productions.

This is, perhaps, better illustrated in the complete system with which their wares are packed, labeled and prepared for the market, nothing being omitted that will make them more acceptable and valuable to their customers.

The iron used has to be of the best, and the inventive genius of several iron mills is continually striving to produce a superior iron, knowing that, if successful, the patronage of the Stanley Works is assured. Over 400 different sizes of iron and iron wire are carried in stock, and orders are given to replenish the same several months in advance.

A 150-horse power Brown engine furnishes the motive power and a complete system of hydrants and a fire pump are ready for immediate use for fire purposes. They are connected with an independent set of pipes, and with the city waterworks. So that in the event of a failure of either source the other may be used.

The lower floors of the building are laid in concrete, all other floors are five inches thick, with thresholds raised and pipe holes scuppered, allowing the flooding of either floor without damage to the others. A system of Brush Electric lights furnishes the illumination for the works run by the company.

In the spacious yards, which have a capacity for a long train of cars, there are buildings for pickling iron, and fire-proof buildings for japanning, bronzing, nickel plating; boiler room with extra room for new boilers where required, carpenter shops, etc.

By a visit to the workshops one sees hundreds of busy workmen and scores of intricate machines, each bent on the particular duty assigned. The endless variety of processes through which a piece of iron goes cannot be in detail explained here, but true economy seems to be the pervading idea, as nothing goes to waste. We say economy, for that, after all, is liberality and excellence. In the tower are stored the expensive dies used, which are doubly protected from fire with a system of sprinklers connected with a stand pipe extending to the top. The toilet conveniences for the help have been neatly arranged, a thoughtful foresight greatly appreciated. It must not be inferred that this great establishment has grown to its present proportions without experiments and failures, without battles fought and won. While, in a financial sense, they stand as they always have A1, they have arrived at their present mechanical excellence by a series of experiments, some successful, some otherwise, but wherever a mechanical failure was made it was turned as a stepping stone to success. With the English and the Germans they have hotly contested the field for superiority, till they have driven their productions out of the market, and the wares of the Stanley Works not only go to all parts of America, but intrude themselves to the doors of our foreign friends not only in England and Germany, but to all parts of the civilized world.

The officers of this company are:—F. L. Stanley, President; H. Stanley, Vice-President; Wm. H. Hart, Treasurer; William Parker, Secretary.

The works, an illustration of which will be found on page 243, are completely equipped with all the latest and most improved machinery and appliances of every character that can expedite and cheapen the production of their goods, with a capacity of turning out fully 106,000 butts and hinges each day, besides large quantities of door bolts, miscellaneous hardware and wrought iron specialties. A catalogue containing over 300 illustrations will be sent on application.

The improved machinery has been for the most part made on the premises. The New York warehouse is at No. 79 Chambers street.

The company and its officers have an international reputation. The first, as the representative of its class; the second, as gentlemen widely known in the business world as men of worth, experience, character and integrity.

Russell & Erwin Manufactuing Company, Myrtle Street.—The large and world-wide known manufacturing establishment of Russell & Erwin, situated on Myrtle street, was founded by the brothers Stanley, two enterprising inhabitants of this city. In 1830, Wm. B. Stanley, Henry W. Clarke and Lora Waters opened a machine shop, which was bought by Fredk. T. Stanley in 1833. He produced the first plate locks made in America. In 1835 the concern passed into the hands of F. T. & W. B. Stanley, and even then had acquired a wide reputation. This was also one of the first establishments in the State to employ steam power, and the first engineer was Westell Russell, afterwards the Sheriff of Hartford County. In the latter part of the same year, Mr. Emanuel Russell, Mr. Smith Mattison, and the firms of F. T. & W. B. Stanley, and T. & N. Woodruff, all of New York, purchased a large lot of land, and formed a company for the manufacture of locks, the name being Stanley, Woodruff & Co. In 1839 the Woodruffs, W. B. Stanley, and Emanuel Russell retired, and the business was conducted under the name of Stanley, Russell & Co., the new partners being Henry E. Russell and C. B. Erwin, the latter coming from Booneville, Lewis County, N. Y. In 1841 the firm was changed to Mattison, Russell & Co., F. T. Stanley retiring, and John K. Bowen taking his place. At this time a warehouse was established in New York City. The death of Mr. Mattison caused the firm name to be changed to Russell, Erwin & Co., which, in July, 1850, was dropped for that of Russell & Erwin, and so continues to the present day. On the 1st of January, 1851, the Russell & Erwin Manufacturing Company was formed with a capital of $200,000, which was increased to half a million in 1864. The business now done by this house amounts to millions of dollars annually, and the company has independent warehouses in New York, Boston, Philadelphia, Chicago, San Francisco and Baltimore, and the articles it manufactures are sent all over America, Australia, China, South America, and Europe, a branch house having been established in London. Three enormous buildings are used by this company, all of which are run to their fullest extent.

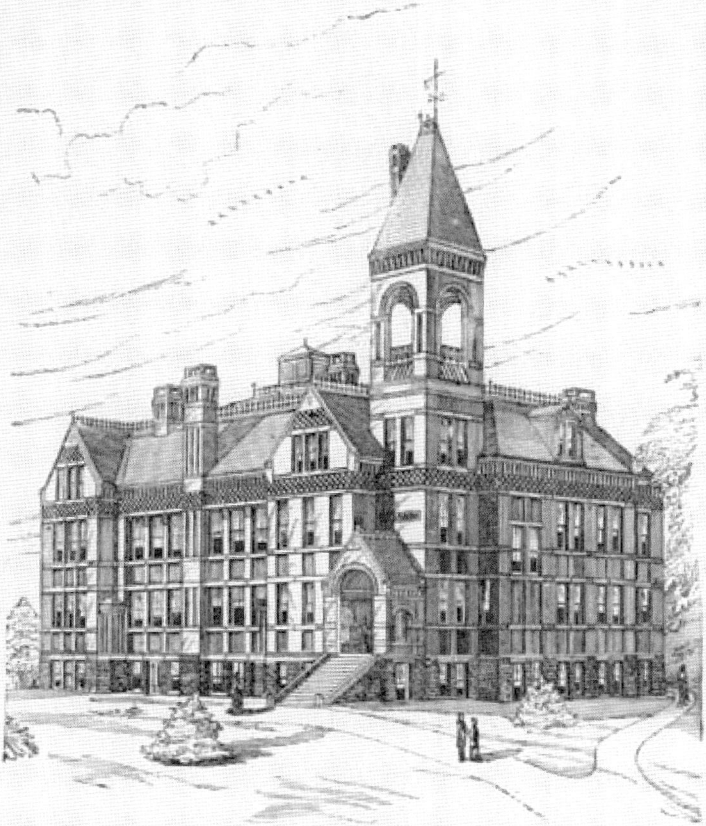

THE NEW STATE NORMAL SCHOOL BUILDING, NEW BRITAIN, CONN.

P. & F. Corbin, Hardware Manufacturers, New Britain—Philip and Frank Corbin and Edward Doen united in partnership in May, 1849, with but a small capital, some $600, to begin the manufacture of various articles of hardware. Horse power was used to drive the machinery, and besides the firm, but one was employed. Owing to the energy and business capacity of those engaged, the experiment proved a success. In November, 1849, the name of the firm was changed to Corbin, Whiting & Co., and in 1851, Mr. Whiting having retired, the name became P. & F. Corbin, which it still remains. In 1854, the company was incorporated with a capital of $50,000. In 1865, the capacity of the manufactory was increased. The foundry was made 40 x 225 feet, the main building 156 x 44 feet, four stories high, with a wing 24 x 40. A new brass foundry was built, 30 x 200 feet. A small army of persons is employed in this huge fabric, and an enormous amount of iron, brass and lead is consumed each year. The success of the establishment is largely due to Mr. Philip Corbin. The goods manufactured include builders', cabinet, undertakers' and miscellaneous hardware, locks, butts, latches, coffin-handles, etc. The company has a warehouse in New York.

The American Hosiery Company, Park Street, New Britain.—The American Hosiery Company was organized in 1868 by an association of capitalists, at whose head was Mr. John B. Talcott, whose long experience as a manufacturer enabled him to so plan the establishment and to adopt such machinery and processes as would enable them to make goods which should rank second to none in the world in respect to quality and finish. The buildings originally erected for the use of the company are two handsome brick edifices, running parallel with each other, connected in the middle by another building running at right angles. The front building is five stories high and is surmounted by a massive mansard roof, which gives it an imposing appearance. The company also erected, in 1881, their new mill, No. 3, which is fifty feet longer than the former main building, and is built in the same thorough and substantial manner. In this mill are located the offices of the company—a commodious and pleasant suite of rooms. The utmost thoroughness in general and in detail has been observed in the erection of these buildings, and they are an instance of successful architectural effort as well as of great stability. They are provided with the most approved defenses againt fire, such as double windows, a network of sprinkling pipes, and a system of automatic sprinklers, by means of which any floor may be instantly flooded with water. In addition to these, hydrant pipes run through all the buildings, with hose attached, ready for service. The company ordered the most improved machinery from England, and had it built with special reference to their service. This was supplemented by some portions which were built by themselves. It is evidently the most perfect machinery for the purpose to be found, and the superiority of the goods attests its admirable action. A specialty is full fashioned or regular made goods, in gentlemen's shirts and drawers, in ladies' vests and drawers, misses', children's and boys' vests, pantelets, drawers and union suits, ladies' and misses' hose, gentlemen's half hose, gentlemen's double-breasted shirts, etc., etc. These are made both in scarlet and white goods, of which every fibre is of the finest cashmere wool. Some idea of the variety of these goods may be gained from the fact that nearly five thousand different sizes and kinds are made, including qualities from the lightest gauze and gossamer to the very heaviest fabrics. The carding and spinning of wool and merino for knitting purposes has long been a business of itself in England, the yarn being sold to the knitting establishments, and it is a fact highly creditable to American enterprise, as exhibited by this pioneer company, that they are actually spinning the yarns and manufacturing them into underwear which rivals the most noted European manufactures. The clear, handsome color noticeable in the manufactures of this company is attributable to the fact that a living spring of the purest water exists on the premises, affording a copious supply for the purposes of bleaching, rinsing, etc., etc. The machinery is driven by a magnificent engine of 250-horse power, built by C. H. Brown & Co., of Fitchburg, Massachusetts, and steam for the engine and for heating, scouring, etc., is furnished by five boilers, aggregating 300-horse-power capacity. Employment is furnished to 1,000 persons, and it may be mentioned as a remarkable and gratifying instance, that at no time since the mills were started, have they been stopped for a single day on account of dull times, but they have been running on full time constantly, and a portion of each year have been compelled to run overtime.

The American Hosiery Company is represented by Henry Stanley, President, John B. Talcott, Treasurer, and E. H. Davison, Superintendent. They have an office and extensive salesrooms at Nos. 108 and 110 Franklin street, New York.

As an instance of successful effort on our own soil, this company is certainly an encouraging example, and shows conclusively that by the use of those means which have given our foreign goods so high a standing, we can ourselves compete and achieve results which will contribute not only to the wealth but to the industrial progress of the country.

Mr. Henry Stanley, president of the company, is a native of New Britain, and is largely interested as a stockholder in many of its manufactories, but not actively engaged in them.

Mr. John B. Talcott, Treasurer, and the controlling spirit of the concern, is a native of West Thompsonville, Conn., born in 1824. His education was begun in the public schools of Hartford and continued in Yale College whence he was graduated in 1846, taking the honors of the salutatory. Returning to Hartford, he began the study of law with Francis Fellowes, Esq., paying his expenses by acting as Clerk of Probate for Judge Mateson, and hearing Latin recitations in the Hartford Female Seminary for about a year and a half, when, recommended by the Yale Faculty, he received an appointment as tutor in Middlebury College, Vermont, to fill a vacancy caused by the resignation of Professor Twining. At the end of a year, Mr. Talcott again returned to Hartford and was admitted to the bar, expecting to make the law his profession, but being tendered an appointment as tutor in Greek at Yale College, accepted it, and remained three years, meanwhile continuing his law studies. At the expiration of his term of service at Yale, he was offered and accepted a partnership with Major S. J. North, in the then flourishing hook-and-eye and knitting business, and has ever since been a resident of New Britain.

He was Treasurer of the New Britain Knitting Company for fourteen years prior to the organization of the present company, and in that position displayed the same able methods of management that characterize his operations now. Mr. Talcott is interested as stockholder and director in other New Britain companies, and is president of the New Britain Institute, and director in the New Britain Savings Bank and the City National Bank of Hartford. He entered the City Council in 1866, and was elected Alderman in 1877–78 and '79, and mayor in 1880 and '81. During his six years identification with municipal affairs he manifested a characteristic thoroughness and a conscientious regard for the best interests of the city, and while Mayor his judicious and economical management of the city finances elicited the admiration and hearty thanks of the taxpayers. Mr. Talcott is a man of broad and liberal views, of clear and decided opinions, a close observer of public affairs. His studious habits have made him familiar with the best literature, and extensive travel in Europe has supplemented the learning obtained from books. In all the relations of public, business and social life Mr. Talcott has been without reproach, and he deservedly enjoys the respect and the confidence of the community in which he lives, and of everybody who knows him.

Mr. E. H. Davison, Superintendent, is a native of Brooklyn, Conn., born in 1841. He has been a resident of New Britain since the organization of the company, and has held the office of superintendent from the commencement. His aptitude for the industrial and mechanic arts is in part inherited from an ancestry which has been prominent in these pursuits. His education and experience have made him familiar with all the details incident to the manufacture of textile fabrics and the operations of this large establishment.

The Landers, Frary & Clark Manufacturing Company, employing more than five hundreds hands, are proprietors of the Ætna Cutlery Works, and also of a large manufactory of hardware. The salesroom in New York is at No. 298 Broadway.

wood bench planes, bevels, gauges, etc. The line of carpenters' tools made is very extensive, and they are so superior to other tools of the same kind that they win their way on their own merits. The number of rules alone manufactured at this establishment embrace over ninety different styles. The officers of this company are: Henry Stanley, President, who was born in New Britain; Mr. F. N. Stanley, Secretary; and Mr. C. L. Mead, Treasurer and in charge of the store at No. 29 Chambers street, New York.

Mr. F. N. Stanley was a member of the Thirteenth Connecticut Regiment during the war, and saw much service in Louisiana, and under Sheridan in Virginia. The Stanleys, and those associated with them, are live business men, who keep fully abreast of the times, know what the market needs, and are fully able to meet its requirements. They are among the most substantial citizens of the town.

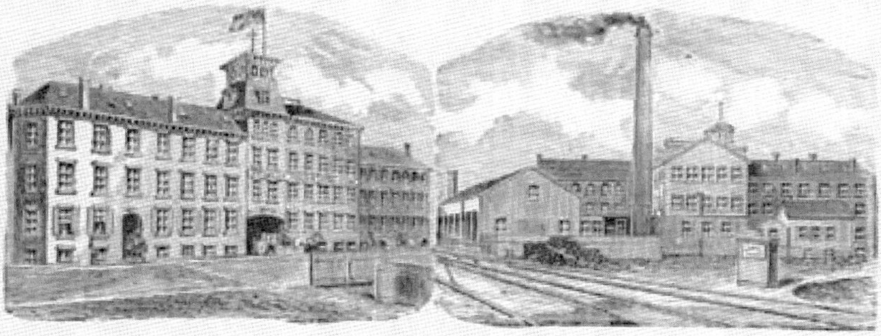

STANLEY RULE AND LEVEL CO., NEW BRITAIN CONN.

Stanley Rule and Level Co., Manufacturers of U. S. Standard Boxwood and Ivory Rules, Bench Planes, etc. The enormous establishment of the Stanley Rule and Level Company, which is one of the great and leading manufactures of this place, was organized upon its present basis in 1857, and at that time united several branches of business, which previously had been carried on separately. Some thirty-eight or forty years ago the business was begun under the firm name of Hall & Knapp. From that day on it has steadily grown with the growth of the country, until it is a representative manufactory in the list of American industries. The capital in 1857 was $50,000, in 1867 it had been increased to $200,000, and is at present $300,000. The main building is of brick, 300 x 40 feet, and four stories high. Two additions have been made, each 150 x 20 feet; half a dozen other smaller buildings complete the establishment. Altogether from 375 to 400 hands are employed, and the goods made find their way to all parts of the civilized world. Three steam engines are used, with an aggregate of 300 horse power, and the production amounts to $500,000 a year. The leading articles manufactured are boxwood and ivory rules, levels, try squares, patent iron and

Churchill, Lewis & Co. (William W. Churchill, Charles M. Lewis, Fredk. Wessel), Manufacturing Jewelers, No. 53 Main Street.—The city of New Britain enjoys the distinction of being, not only one of the most important centres for the manufacture of special lines of wares, but the quality of the goods made here stand unrivaled in the market, and their reputation for fine quality is established beyond question. The ability and enterprise which has secured this important result, can be trusted to so guard and preserve it that the position that New Britain now occupies as a manufacturing centre is well assured for the future. The same care which has built up her trade and reputation will be fully exerted to hold and extend it. Among the houses which have contributed in no small degree to this result, is Messrs. Churchill, Lewis & Co., manufacturing jewelers, whose works are located at No. 53 Main street.

The commencement of this business dates back previous to 1820, when Mr. William B. North founded it. Later, Mr. William A. Churchill, father of Mr. William W. Churchill, was made a partner, and the firm called North & Churchill. As near as can be ascertained, this change was made previous to the year 1838, for we find that in that year he died, and Mr.

Churchill conducted the business under his individual name till about the year 1848, when Mr. James Stanley, a former apprentice in the establishment, was made a partner, and the firm called Churchill & Stanley. This arrangement continued for a time, when Mr. D. C. Pond, at present a merchant in Hartford, and then an apprentice, became a member and the firm name changed to Churchill, Stanley & Co. Soon after, the firm of Warner & Lewis, who had been in the same kind of business in New Britain, dissolved and became members of the firm of Churchill, Stanley & Co., on the retirement of Mr. Pond in 1853. After a few years, Mr. Warner retired, and, in 1863, Mr. Stanley. For some time previous to this date, Mr. E. B. Dana had charge of the New York office of the firm and on the retirement of Mr. Stanley, as above noted, became a member, and the firm name was changed to Churchill, Dana & Co., which so continued till 1871, when he retired and Mr. W. W. Churchill and Mr. Fredk. Wessel were admitted and the firm's name changed to its present style, Churchill, Lewis & Co.

The building occupied is prominently and centrally located on the main street, is two stories in height and 40x90 feet in area. Thirty skilled jewelers are employed in the manufacture of the finest class of solid gold jewelry, in bracelets, sets, rings, etc. Tiffany and other representative houses are among the customers of this establishment.

Of Mr. Wm. B. North, the founder, there is but little positive information, only that he died as above stated. Mr. William A. Churchill, his first partner in this business and his successor, was about sixty-four years of age when he died. He was a prominent member of the First Congregational Church, one of the principal movers in its erection, and a prominent man in the community.

His son, Mr. William W. Churchill, is not personally identified with this city, but represents his firm in New York, where he has resided for several years. The office is at No. 692 Broadway. Mr. C. M. Lewis is a native of New Britain, born in 1816, and has been a jeweler for fifty years, commencing at the trade when but sixteen years of age. He is a member of the First Congregational Church.

Mr. Fredk. Wessel was born in New York City in 1846, and has been a resident of this city for sixteen years. All products of this house are from their own original designs, executed by Mr. Wessel. He is a practical jeweler and designer, and a member of the first Congregational Church.

This establishment makes the most elegant and expensive designs of solid gold jewelry, have preserved and maintained their credit for over sixty years, and stand at the head, as they are the oldest, of the manufacturing jewelry establishments in America.

The Strickland House, Main and East Main Streets, New Britian.—The Strickland House is the largest hotel in the city, centrally situated at the corner of Main and East Main streets, in close proximity to the Opera House, Masonic Hall, Burritt School, etc. It is a large, four-story brick structure, with fifty rooms for guests. The dining hall is on the second floor and is very pleasantly situated with windows on three sides. The hotel possesses a bar, barber's shop, etc., and guests are well looked after. Mr. William Hill, of Hill's Mansion House, Easthampton, Mass., is the proprietor, and Mr. T. R. Hill, formerly of the Creighton House, Boston, is the polite and genial manager. This hotel is the headquarters for the traveling public, and is within easy walking distance of the depot.

Moses S. Austin, Plumber, Gas and Steam Fitter, Nos. 62 and 64 Church Street.—Mr. Austin's success is an illustration of what a thorough knowledge and correct methods will accomplish in the business world.

First he apprenticed himself to a master workman in the plumbing, gas and steam fitting line, and, unlike many half-starved, poor plumbers, he served out his time, perfecting himself in every branch of the business. For fifteen years he worked at his trade, always commanding the highest wages; for his services were eagerly sought after. Finally, in 1878, with the capital earned by his honest endeavors, he launched out into the business world, and for the first time looked upon the sign over his door "M. S. Austin, Plumber, Steam and Gas Fitter." What had so long been the dream of his life had in that year become a reality, and has since continued an evidence of his executive ability as a business man.

The store occupied is 18x100 feet in size, and is stocked with a complete line of articles pertaining to the plumbing, gas and steam fitting departments.

In the rear is a storeroom and a tile yard, where are kept sewer pipe of the original Akron make, for sewer connections, of which he makes a specialty, and which he is prepared to take contracts for laying. Mr. Austin also takes contracts for fitting up houses, stores, manufactories, churches, and public buildings with gas, water pipes, fixtures, etc. Some idea of the extent of his business can be inferred when the reader is informed that from twenty to fifty men are employed, according to the season.

In 1874 he built the New Milford, Connecticut, water works, and in 1881 laid the sewers for the town. In 1882 he laid over one mile of sewer pipe in New Britain. With his long and successful career he is ably qualified in every respect to contract for public water works and to do all kinds of sewerage work, and it may truthfully be said has the best record and facilities of any in the city.

Mr. Austin is a native of Suffield, Connecticut, born August 14, 1844, and has been a resident of this city since 1868, where he enjoys a large acquaintance, and is proprietor of one of the oldest and largest establishments of its class in New Britain.

The New Britain Herald, No. 320 Main Street, New Britain.—The New Britain "Herald" was started on the 3d of April, 1880, by

Adams Brothers, at No. 203 Main street. It was purchased by a joint stock company in September of the same year. The company included many of the most prominent business men in town. Among them—Adams Brothers, C. B. Erwin, D. N. Camp, H. E. Russell, Jr., Henry Stanley, Mitchell & Hungerford, A. J. Sloper, A. P. Collins, William Parker, R. L. Webb, O. B. Chamberlain, J. H. Minor, C. E. Woodruff, and others, numbering in all about forty. It was run as a strong local campaign paper for the Republican party during the fall of 1880. The paper was afterwards bought out by C. E. Woodruff, the secretary of the company. The New Britain "Times," a weekly, published by Maloney & Loughrey, was purchased in July, 1881, and consolidated with the "Herald," that paper being furnished to subscribers of the "Times" after that date.

A semi-weekly edition, published every Tuesday and Friday, was started on the 10th of January, 1882, but was finally merged into the daily "Evening Herald," which first appeared on the 2d of December, 1882. A weekly edition, the New Britain "Herald," is also published on Fridays. The "Tunxis Valley Herald," is also edited and published by Mr. Woodruff. This circulates mostly in Unionville and Collinsville, and is published on Thursdays. Mr. Woodruff is a very industrious, enterprising young man, and his growing business soon induced him to take a new office.

The editorial and printing rooms of the papers he now publishes are situated on the first floor of the Railroad Block, at No. 320 Main street. They are elaborately fitted up with black walnut desks for reporters, telegraph, telephone, etc., and with private offices for the editors. The papers published are filled with local news and circulate largely in the city. The large share of advertising patronage which they have, shows better than anything else the estimation in which they are held by the community. The "Evening Herald" is the only daily paper published in New Britain, and keeps its readers well informed regarding the news of the world.

J. A. Lewis, Photographer, No. 125 Main Street.—Thirty years or more ago when Daguerreotypes were first introduced in this country, a Mr. Judson, who still resides in New Britain, opened a picture gallery at what is now No. 125 Main street, which is now occupied by Mr. John A. Lewis as a photographer, and as successor to Mr. J. B. Davidson, who started here in 1880. December 1, 1882, he sold his business to Mr. Lewis. The premises consists of four rooms 25 x 40 feet in size, where all the appliances and accessories necessary for a business of this nature are found.

Mr. Lewis' specialty is artistic photography in all its branches, together with portraits in ink, crayon and water colors.

He was born in Naugatuck, Conn., in 1856, and has been a resident of this city for about three months, where he is building up a lucrative business complimentary to his ability as a photographer and a business man.

John A. Williams, News Depot, No. 35 West Main Street, New Britain.—Next door to the Post-office, between it and the bank, at No. 35 West Main street, on the north side of the public square, stands the granite building occupied by Mr. John A. Williams' bookstore and news depot. This is one of the most popular places in the city, and is constantly thronged with men and women, searching for the latest magazines, New York, Boston, Hartford and Springfield papers, for the freshest books issued by the publishers, for the latest styles in stationery and cards.

A circulating library is connected with this establishment, as well as an art department, where can be found the newest engravings, oil paintings, bas-reliefs, frames, etc. This depot is to New Britain what Brentano's is to New York. The selling of literature is a congenial occupation for Mr. Williams. He was a teacher when nineteen years of age and with his love of literature he became a dealer in it, commencing with only $120 as capital. His business now amounts to $20,000 per annum. His knowledge of books, of men and the world, together with his urbanity and faculty of keen repartee, has won the confidence and patronage of all the town. He is about thirty-three years of age, a native of Stonington, and popular wherever known.

J. M. Belden, Dealer in Lumber, Coal, Flour, Feed, Garden Seeds, Fertilizers, Potatoes, etc., No. 167 Main Street.—Mr. Belden is an illustration of the active successful New Englander. The commencement of his business dates back to the year 1865, when he was nineteen years old, at which time he was a wholesale dealer in potatoes, a business he has since continued up to the present time. The wholesaling of potatoes by the car load for so many years extended his acquaintance to all parts of the State. The name of Belden was a synonym for potatoes as it was for honesty.

The average business man would have branched out and added other departments long before Mr. Belden, but his motto was to make haste slowly. In addition to dealing largely in potatoes, he was for twelve years a truckman here, in which business he had several horses and trucks engaged. In 1876 he sold out the trucking business. He was thirty-five years of age, in that year, and he saw his opportunity—"That tide in the affairs of men which taken at the flood leads on to fortune,"—and bought the flour and feed business of Tubbs & Bartholomew. A few months after, moving into his present store at No. 167 Main street, which is the general office of the different branches of business which he represents. In 1868 he started a grist-mill at Chestnut street, corner Bigelow, which has one set of stone, run by steam, where corn and feed only are ground. In 1879 the sale of fertilizers was made a feature of the business, of which he sells large quantities to the farmers in the Connecticut Valley. After systematizing this new branch of his already extended business, he added another, the coal and lumber business, in 1880. The yards for these are situated adjacent to the railroad track, off of Meadow street, near the gas-house, a track connecting with the main line of the N. Y. & N. E. R. R. The yards have a capacity of 1,200 to 1,500 tons of coal and a large amount of lumber. Three to four delivery teams are run in the coal department, while in the lumber a profitable business is transacted. In 1881 the business of dealing in garden seeds was added, and in 1882 building materials. From the time he purchased the flour and feed business of Tubbs & Bartholomew in 1876, up to the present, he has, one after another, carefully and methodically added department after department till now it is one of the largest in New Britain.

Mr. Belden is a native of this city, and thirty-seven years of age. He, contrary to Horace Greeley's advice to young men did not go West, but has always been identified with his native town or city, where he enjoys an enviable reputation for promptness and reliability, and is highly appreciated by a large circle of friends for his many business and social qualities.

John Hanna, Monumental and Building Works, Dealer and Worker in Granite, Marble, Freestone, etc., No. 207 East Main Street.—This business, the largest of its kind in this section of the State and the only one in New Britain, was established by Mr. Hanna in 1858, and has been conducted by him from an unpretentious beginning to its present large proportions. The premises occupied consist of about an acre of ground, on which there are a workshop and office, the former being 35 x 110 feet in size. From twenty-five to thirty skilled workmen are given employment, and the annual business done ranges from $20,000 to $30,000. All kinds of stonework, from laying flags for sidewalks to the construction of the most costly building or imposing monument in marble, in granite and in freestone, are done here and the buildings of New Britain as well as the cemeteries in the vicinity, for a radius of twenty miles around bear many evidences of the skill and industry for which this establishment is noted.

Mr. Hanna is a native of Ireland, fifty-one years of age. He has been in this country thirty-five years and in New Britain since the establishment of his business in 1858. He is a practical stone and marble worker, having thoroughly mastered his trade in New York City. His record in New Britain is first-class, and his reputation as a business man is second to none.

Fahy Brothers (Edward H. and Thomas W.), Gentlemen's Furnishing Goods, Hats, Caps, Trunks, Bags, etc., No. 413 Main Street.—This, perhaps, the youngest firm, in years and in business, to be found in New Britain, began their commercial career in February, 1882, in the store on Main street, one door south of the Strickland House Block. The store is 20x42 feet in size, and is well supplied with a stock of the articles mentioned, and amounting in value to about $4,000. In the first and only year of their business, the sales amounted to about $12,000, and the ratio of increase was so great as to warrant the belief that the succeeding annual statement will show figures greatly in excess of that amount. Two assistants are employed and the indications point to an increase of the force in the very near future.

Mr. Edward H. Fahy is a native of Hartford, twenty-five years of age, and resided in his native city until he commenced business here, being employed by a book concern and afterwards as a civil engineer. Mr. Thomas W. Fahy is also a native of Hartford and is twenty-two years of age. He is a machinist by trade and was formerly an adjuster of sewing machines for the Weed Company.

The firm has a good business reputation.

The New Britain Observer, No. 308 Main street, New Britain.—The New Britain "Observer," the Democratic organ of the city, has its office at No. 308 Main street, where it occupies the second floor of a fine building, and is published every Tuesday evening. It is chiefly devoted to local news, of which it gives all the best, served in an attractive form. Its editorials are sharp and pointed. The "Observer" was started in 1876 by Mr. R. J. Vance, who was born in New York City on the 15th of March, 1854, and was educated in the common schools of that city, and also in the high school of New Britain. In 1875 he paid a visit to Europe. In 1877 he ran for the Legislature and was defeated. In the spring of 1878 he was elected City Clerk, and has held the office since. He is at present a member of the Democratic State Central Committee.

New Britain Lumber and Coal Co., Dealers in Lumber, Coal, Flour, Grain, Feed, Sash, Doors, Blinds, Box Shooks and Manufacturers' Supplies, Park Street, east of Railroad Crossing.—The New Britain Lumber and Coal Company, incorporated in 1871, succeeded in that year to the business of Giddings & Strong. That firm had been in existence since 1857, and were the successors to Anderson & Alling, who had founded the business ten years previously. The company has a capital of $20,000, and does a general business in coal, lumber, sash, doors, blinds, flour, grain, feed, box-shooks, manufacturers' supplies, etc. The office is on the corner of Park street and the track of the N. Y. & N. H. Railroad, the yards immediately adjoining having a frontage of eight hundred feet on the line of the road and covering an area of about three acres. The storehouses for grain, sash, doors, etc., together with the lumber sheds and other necessary buildings aggregate about 1,000 feet in length, and contain vast quantities of the articles mentioned. Some idea of the growth of this business may be gleaned from the fact that in the first year of the company's existence the sales amounted to but $70,000, while in 1882, in the item of lumber alone, there were sales of more than 5,000,000 feet. This, supplemented by the disposal of 7,000 tons of coal and large quantities of the other merchandise dealt in, brought the volume of that year's business to the very satisfactory figure of $220,000, and left the company in a position to anticipate an annual increase in like ratio as that from 1871. This company leads all other dealers in their line in New Britain, and bids fair to maintain the position its fair dealing and commendable business methods have won.

Mr. Henry P. Strong, President of the company, is a native of Woodbury, Conn., and is about sixty years of age. He has been for many years identified with the De Forest & Hotchkiss Company, of New Haven, and is well-known throughout the State as a leading business man, having been in business in Derby, Bridgeport and New Britain. He is a large owner of real estate in New Britain, and has been prominent in her government as town agent, selectman, city councilman and member of the Board of Relief.

Mr. Frederick G. Platt, the Treasurer, is a native of Middlebury, Conn., and is about thirty-five years of age. He has resided in New Britain since 1871, and has won an enviable position in business and social circles.

Mr. Albert N. Lewis, the Secretary, is a native of Naugatuck, aged about thirty-five years. He also has lived in New Britain since the formation of the company and has been its secretary from the first. Like his assistant officers he enjoys the merited esteem and confidence of the community.

The New Britain Record, No. 287 Main Street, New Britain.—This paper was established in 1857, by Mr. L. M. Guernsey, under the name of "The True Citizen." He published it until 1865, when Mr. J. N. Oviatt became the proprietor, and changed the name to the "New Britain Record." In 1868 Mr. Samuel Baker became a partner, and the firm name of Oviatt & Baker was continued until January 1, 1880, when Mr. Samuel Baker became the sole proprietor. In March, 1881, Mr. F. W. Baker bought the paper, and became its editor. The publication office is at No. 287 Main street, and the paper appears every Friday morning. It is printed on a Potter large cylinder press, run by steam, and is the Republican organ of the city. Mr. Baker was born in Hartford. He is a young man, and at one time edited a paper in Iowa, but was obliged to abandon that State on account of the malaria. He makes a sprightly, newsy and interesting paper, and has a fair show of patronage.

J. P. Curtiss, Dealer in Flour, Feed, Grain, Coal, Wood and Ice, near City Buildings and Passenger Depot.—Although this house has been in existence since 1876, it has gained such a prominent position in the business world of New Britain as to mark its proprietor a man of superior enterprise and business ability.

The business was established by Curtiss & Douglass in the year above stated and in the present location. For over five years Mr. Curtiss has been the sole proprietor. A large business is transacted in flour, feed, grain, coal, wood and ice. The feed mill and store are in one building, which is 62 x 32 feet in size, and two stories in height, with an L 28 x 68, one-story. One set of stone is run, and the number of employees averages from ten to fifteen people. Three ice wagons are run during the warm season. Most of the coal is sold direct from the cars, although a yard is used for storage when required, which is one of the largest in the city. Mr. Curtiss is a native of Bristol, Conn., born in 1832, and has been a resident of New Britain for seventeen years. First as a machinist and table-knife maker for one of the large establishments here, and later in this business.

He was a member of the Fifteenth Connecticut Infantry during the war of the Rebellion, and is active in the Grand Army Post here.

Reuben W. Hadley, Groceries, Meats, and Provisions, 283 Main Street.—This business, probably the largest of its kind in New Britain, was established in 1863, in its present location, by Mr. Charles Bassett, who continued it until 1875, when he disposed of it to Messrs. Schultz & Sanders. This firm lasted only a few months and Mr. Bassett resumed proprietorship of the business, retaining it until March, 1876. In that month, Mr. Reuben Hadley, the present proprietor, purchased the stock and good will, and began to lay the foundation of his present prosperous trade. The premises occupied by Mr. Hadley consist of a store and basement, each 20 x 75 feet in size; a large storehouse in the rear of the store, and several smaller apartments on the outside, used for the keeping of extra stock, one of the outside rooms having a storage capacity of two to three car-loads of flour, a quantity he keeps constantly on hand. The stock consists of a general assortment of staple and fancy groceries, meats, provisions, crockery, etc., with an average value of $12,000. The business, requires the services of eight assistants, and extends far into the adjoining country, its annual volume exceeding $100,000. In the matter of flour alone, the business is more than ordinarily extensive, an average of one car-load of that staple being sold by Mr. Hadley every month. Mr. Hadley is a native of England, born in 1843, and has been in the United States since his seventh year. The family originally settled in Winsted, where Mr. Hadley's father was one of the Winsted Shovel and Tongs Company. In 1858, Mr. Hadley came to New Britain to work in the factory of Russell & Erwin, where his father had a contract. Here he continued until 1863, when he went to Yonkers, New York, to take a contract with the Star Arms Company, remaining there until 1866, when he returned to Russell & Erwin's. In 1874, he formed a copartnership with Mr. Ambrose Beatty, now Mayor of New Britain, and made his first venture in the grocery business. This partnership lasted for a year and nine months, and shortly after its dissolution, Mr. Hadley entered upon his present business. Mr. Hadley has been prominent in civic and military matters in New Britain, especially so in the latter particular, having been commander of the first section of the Light Artillery, and afterwards captain of Company D of the 1st Regiment of Infantry. Since his resignation of the latter office in 1878, Mr. Hadley has declined office, either civic or military, the demands of his rapidly growing business requiring all his time and attention.

Mr. Hadley is known throughout the section in which he lives as a clear-headed, reliable business man, and as one of the most reputable of New Britian's citizens.

ROCKVILLE.

Situated in the town of Vernon, Tolland County, Ct., is eighteen miles from Hartford, and twenty-four miles from Springfield. It is noted as a picturesque, beautiful, healthy place, the seat of numerous large manufacturing interests, and a population of some 7,000 intelligent, well-to-do people, the most of whom own the houses in which they live. Situated in a beautiful recess, among pleasantly rounded hills, closed in on three sides, its streets are wide, macadamized, and well shaded with fine elm trees. The Hockanum River, as a water power, early attracted the attention of manufacturers, and the first attempt at wool carding was made about 1794, by John Warberton, who came from England. Spinning was begun in 1811 in two mills of 192 spindles each; stocking yarn was made, which was sold to peddlers for domestic manufacture. The weaving of woolen cloth began in a small way a year later. In 1824 the town had five hand looms and two power looms. In 1827 the satinet factory made 200 yards a day, and population began to increase. In 1833 there were sixty sets of machinery, all making satinets, and a small cotton mill was running. The population of Rockville, in 1858 was about 500. The first meeting-house was dedicated in 1839. The post-office was opened in 1841. In 1871 the village had a population of 4,500. The Methodist church was built in 1865, at a cost of $65,000. The town now has some fourteen mills, six churches, two newspapers, two opera houses, gas, and water works, telephone exchange, two parks—Central and Fountain—five school buildings, a large number of stores of all kinds, four banks, a paid fire department, and an excellent hotel known as the Rockville House. Altogether it is a pretty and enterprising place, with all the modern improvements.

The Rockville Aqueduct Co., organized in 1847, and reorganized as a new company in 1866, has Mr. Geo. Maxwell for President, and J. C. Hammond, Jr., Secretary and Treasurer. The water is drawn from Snipsic Lake—Indian name of Shenipsit—one-half mile east of the village. This lake was a favorite resort for the Indians of the vicinity, who held their councils, ceremonies, and war-dances on its borders. Even to this day many arrow-heads, spears, and other implements are found on its shores. The lake is now a favorite pleasure resort during the summer season. The water-works cost over $50,000, and consists of the main pipe, fourteen inches in diameter, and seven miles of mains, which run through the village. The supply of water is equal to the demands of a population of 40,000. The lake contains some 600 acres, and is the source of the Hockanum River, which gives the motive power to the numerous factories in the village. The natural pressure of the water gives a head of from 60 to 279 feet, which forces a stream over the highest spire in the village, and supplies the many private and public fountains with which the town is adorned. The office of the Aqueduct Co. is in the post-office building, where also is the office of the Rockville Railway, the officers of the two companies being the same. This railway is four and three-quarter miles in length and connects at Vernon with the N. Y. & N. E. R. Road. The road was built by subscription in 1862-3, and was operated by the original company for five years, when it was leased to the Hartford, Providence & Fishkill R. R., and later to the New York and New England. The building of this road increased the value of property fifty per cent. Before it was built it required eighty horses to do the hauling for the mills. The Connecticut Central Branch, seven miles in length, began operations in 1876. Towards the building of this road Vernon and Rockville contributed $60,000. There are fourteen trains daily on the two roads.

The town and village was well represented in the war of 1859-65, having one company in the Fifth Connecticut, one in the Fourteenth, one in the Sixteenth Regiment, altogether from three to four hundred men having entered the service of their country.

Rockville is more than a representative New England village, and there are few, if any, which surpass it in beauty and natural attractions, in its water-power and genuine facilities for manufacturing, in the size and reputation of its establishments and their productions, in the intelligence of its people, and for a place to make and save money and enjoy life.

Belding Bros. & Co., Manufacturers of Machine Twist, Sewing and Embroidery Silks.—Among the most interesting objects in Connecticut, and certainly the most interesting in its own vicinity, is the sewing silk and twist mill of Belding Bros. & Co. on Main street. The business carried on here is the outgrowth of a very small beginning, and its immense proportions are the direct result of the energy, enterprise and honest methods of its originators, the Belding Brothers.

The foundation of this and the other establishments now owned by Belding Bros. & Co. was laid in 1860 by Hiram H. and Alvah N. Belding, now vice-president and secretary, respectively, of the present company, who started from their home in Belding, Michigan, on a tour through the West, peddling, from house to house, sewing silks purchased for them by their brother, M. M., who was then residing at their common birthplace, Ashfield, Mass. This peddling rapidly assumed the shape of a large business, and, in a year after their start, the Belding Brothers had extended the scope of their traffic, until it required the services of several teams and wagons, and embraced the larger part of the jobbing trade of the section in which they were operating. Three years after their start they established a house in Chicago, and in the same year were joined by their brother, Milo M., who took charge of that agency, retaining it for a year, and then removing to New York, where he has since remained. In the same year the brothers formed a copartnership with E. K. Rose, and taking the first floor of what was then known as the Glasgow Company's thread mill, at Rockville, began manufacturing for themselves. Three years later, the business had grown to such an extent that more room became absolutely necessary, and the erection of the main building of the present mill was begun. Before the completion of the building, and owing to some disagreement, the brothers dissolved partnership with Mr. Rose, and hiring several small mills, in various localities, continued their outside business. Meanwhile, Mr. Rose had formed a company known as the Rose Silk Company, and started operations in the new mill. At the expiration of ten months from the starting the Rose Silk Company failed, and operations ceased. During all this time the business of the brothers had been increasing in a wonderfully rapid manner. Mill after mill had been added to their resources of manufacture, and the establishment of agencies in the larger cities had followed each other in like ratio. In 1869 it was decided to concentrate the manufacturing branch of the business, and the mill now occupied, which had stood idle for about two years, and since the failure of the Rose Company, was purchased. Some four years afterwards the brothers established the immense mill, now owned by them, at Northampton, Mass., and, subsequently, those at Montreal, Canada, and San Francisco.

The principal agencies of the firm are located in New York, Boston, Philadelphia, Chicago, Cincinnati, St. Louis, San Francisco and Montreal, and the smaller agencies all over the country.

The mill in Rockville, of which this is a sketch, consists of a main building of brick, 145 x 42 feet in size, four stories in height, with a stone basement, and an "L" recently constructed, also of brick, with stone foundation and basement, 62 x 50 feet in size and of the height and general appearance of the main building. In the rear of the main structure is the dye-house, a one story brick, one hundred feet long by about thirty-five feet in breadth. The power for running the mill is supplied by a thirty-four foot breast wheel, turned by the waters of the Hockanum river, which has its source in the beautiful Snipsic Lake situated in the hills about one mile above. In addition to this wheel, and rendered necessary by the recent enlargement of the capacity of the mill is an elegant "Buckeye" engine of eighty-horse power, used for running a portion of the machinery and fed from two boilers, each of eighty-five horse power capacity, which perform the further duties of furnishing steam for the dyeing and for heating the buildings. Among the machinery used in this establishment there are thirty-three "winders" used for winding the thread from the skein as imported; sixteen "doublers," the use of which is indicated by the title; eight "cleaners" for cleaning and removing obstructions, imperfections and impurities from finished silk; one hundred and fifty "spoolers" for winding finished silk on spools for market; eight "stretchers" for stretching and evening the silk; fifty-four "spinners" for making the thread; seven "reels" for winding the silk into skeins and measuring into desired lengths, and a number of other smaller and ingenious contrivances, among which are machines for winding embroidery silk on cards; for winding the exact amount of knitting silk required upon each spool; for braiding the celebrated "Martin" fishing lines and for stamping the firm's label on the ends of spools. Among the machinery peculiar to this establishment and worthy especial mention is the contrivance for cleaning finished silk. This is the invention of Mr. Elisha J. Martin, an attaché of the mill, the patent being owned by Belding Bro's & Co., and one other silk manufacturing concern. This machine does the work formerly done at a cost of two cents per ounce at an expense of less than that figure per pound. This, it will be seen, is an immense saving, and probably goes far towards assisting this company to turn out their superior goods at prices that enable them to sucessfully compete with their rivals in trade. Another invention, and one used only by this company, is a dial attachment to the "spoolers" used in winding the heavier grades of twist, by which the exact number of yards on each spool is determined, which number is plainly marked on the blank end of the spool, and warranted correct. This, it is believed, is done only by Belding Bro's & Co.; and the fact that a customer is enabled to know exactly how much he is getting for his money has doubtless done much towards the great success achieved. The "stretchers" for evening the silk consist of two copper cylinders, about six feet long and twelve inches in diameter, revolving horizontally, around which the threads are wound. The upper cylinder revolves seven times while the lower is making six turns. In connection with this machine it is interesting to note that the company purchased a half interest in the patent some years ago, paying therefor $8,400, and that since their purchase they have sold to other manufacturers more than $100,000 worth of rights to use the invention.

This mill gives employment to about 550 people within its walls, to say nothing of those employed on the outside as agents, salesmen, and in other capacities. About 5,000 pounds, net, of finished silk are shipped weekly to the various agencies, whence it is sent to all parts of the civilized world.

Up to 1882 the business was conducted by the firm of Belding Brothers & Co., but in that year it was decided to incorporate as a company, and to that end application was made to the Legislature for a special charter, allowing the retention of the firm name. This was granted, and under the new charter Mr. Milo M. Belding was made President and Treasurer, Mr. Hiram H. Belding Vice-president, Mr. Alvah N. Belding Secretary, and Mr. D. N. Belding, another brother, in charge of the Cincinnati agency, a Director.

Mr. Milo M. Belding, president and treasurer of the company, was born in Ashfield, Mass., and is about forty-eight years of age. Until he reached his majority he lived on his father's farm, beginning directly afterward the sale of jewelry for W. M. Root, of Pittsfield, Mass., and, when his brothers established the silk business, buying their silk for them. When the Chicago agency was established he took charge of it and remained about one year, when he went to New York, where he has since remained as financial man of the concern and buyer of raw silk.

Mr. Hiram H. Belding, vice-president of the company and one of the founders of the business, is also a native of Ashfield, and is two years younger than his brother Milo. He lived at home until about twenty-one years of age, and, like his brother, was engaged in the sale of jewelry. With his father and brother Alvah, he went to Michigan, where the three cleared up a farm in a locality where there is now a thriving town named after the family—"Belding."

A year afterwards the two brothers started out peddling silk, with the success already detailed. When Milo M. retired from the Chicago agency, Hiram H. took charge of it and has retained it to the present, conducting its business from comparatively nothing up to a sale in 1882 of $700,000.

Mr. Alvah N. Belding, secretary of the company and manager of the Rockville Mill, the youngest of the three brothers prominent in the business and one of its founders, was, like his partners, born in Ashfield and is forty-two years of age. When he was seventeen years old he moved with his father to Michigan, as before detailed, and when only twenty years of age he started with his brother Hiram on the peddling tour, which has resulted in the vast business now owned and controlled by Belding Bros. & Co. He has resided in Rockville since 1869, and has always had the management of the mill here, and until a year ago that of the Northampton Mill, a duty he was compelled to relinquish, owing to the rapid growth of the interests here and the impossibility of one man attending to both establishments. In 1882 the people of his town sent him to the Legislature, giving him 754 votes out of a total of 901 polled. Re-election was offered, but declined, on account of the cares of his immediate business. He is a director in the People's Savings Bank, and is otherwise prominently identified with the financial and social interests of the village.

The history of the rise of Belding Bros. & Co. from the modest start without capital, save native energy and honesty of purpose, followed through the twenty years that have brought them to the very front of the silk manufacturers of the world; using hundreds of thousands of dollars invested in mills and machinery and stock; owning and controlling three of the largest mills in America, one of which is the largest in the world, together with the smaller one in California; giving employment to more than a thousand people; turning out more and better sewing silk than any other manufacturer in all the world, and doing an annual business of over $2,500,000, is not only interesting in itself, but serves to point a moral, and as an inciting example to the youth who believes that honest effort is sure to win success.

The Hockanum Company, Manufacturers of Fancy Cassimeres and Worsted Coatings for Men's Wear.—One of the oldest and most important of the manufacturing establishments in Rockville is that of the Hockanum Company, whose organization dates back to May 31, 1836, when the first meeting was held. The original incorporators were: Lebbeus P. Tinker, President; Alonzo Bailey, Secretary; Austin Holt, Agent; Ralph Talcott and Bickford Abbott. The original capital was $7,500, which was soon afterwards increased. The establishment comprised two buildings, 40 x 40 feet each in size, and two sets of machinery were run, manufacturing satinets. That was nearly fifty years ago. The old buildings have been replaced by larger and more elegant structures. The original incorporators have passed away; new faces, advanced ideas, expensive machinery, and a higher standard of excellence for the productions, have taken the place of those of 1836, and a new impetus and a modern business atmosphere pervades the whole establishment. The main mill, adjoining which is the office, was built about the year 1849. The basement is of brick; the remainder of the structure of wood. It is 36 x 200 feet in size and three stories and attic in height. In 1873 an extension of fifty feet in length was added, so that at present the length of the building is 250 feet. In 1881 a brick mill was erected, west of the original building, which is 50 x 116 feet in size, and of the same height as the main building. A few rods below is the old Saxony mill, now owned and run by this company, which is 120 x 34 feet in size, and is two stories high, with basement and attic, the basement being of brick and the other parts of wood. An elegant business office adjoining the first-named mill was built in 1880, and is a model of convenience and artistic furnishing. Although there are but ten sets of machinery run, by the use of worsted yarn the capacity of the mills is equal to double that number. The finer grades of cassimeres and worsteds are turned out here and in such quantities as to give employment to 325 people. Two water powers are monopolized, the number of feet fall being eighteen and twelve, respectively. In addition two engines, one of eighty and the other of sixty-horse power, are made use of.

The selling agents are Messrs. Pomeroy & Plummer, of Nos. 61 and 63 Leonard street, New York.

Mr. George Maxwell, the President and Treasurer, has been a resident of Rockville since 1844. He was born in Charlemont, Mass., in 1817, and was first identified with this village as a country merchant. Later he was bookkeeper for the *old* New England Company, and has been a manufacturer since 1846. In 1858 he was appointed agent and treasurer of the Hockanum Company. At that time the company ran but three sets of machinery, and it was at that time also that the change was made from the old style satinets to the modern all-wool fancy cassimeres and worsteds, the standard being elevated until the productions of the Hockanum Company rank among the best in the market. In 1869, Mr. Maxwell was elected president and treasurer, and has continued in those offices up to the present. He is also president of the New England Company, a neighboring manufacturing establishment; vice-president of the Rockville National Bank, and is otherwise largely interested in the institutions and industries of his adopted town. He was a Representative in 1871 and a Senator in 1872, and has been otherwise shown honor by his townsmen.

Mr. George Sykes, the Manager, is a native of Huddersfield, England, born in 1840, and has been a resident of this country since boyhood. He has been in charge of the manufacturing of goods for this company since 1866. He is a director in the Hockanum Company, the New England Company, and the Hartford Engineering Company, and is a thorough master of his business.

The Hockanum Company is one of those well-known and long established business associations which are in no need of praise. It has maintained its credit for nearly half a century, not only in a financial sense, but in the class of goods turned out, and its conservative yet enterprising methods have won deserved success.

Its officers and directors rank among the most respected and influential of Connecticut's representative men.

White, Corbin & Co., Envelope Manufacturers and Paper Dealers.—This industry was established in 1855 by Messrs. White & Corbin and so continued till 1866, when a former clerk, Mr. Wm. H. Prescott, was admitted, and the firm became White, Corbin & Co. In the commencement a patent machine for gumming, folding and cutting envelopes was invented, of which they availed themselves, commencing with one and adding others from time to time, until the present, when the capacity of the works is 2,000,000 envelopes per day. About two years ago they purchased the largest and most substantially built structure for manufacturing purposes in Rockville, and soon after occupied it. This afforded them more room and greater facilities, and is, probably, the largest and most extensive building occupied for the manufacture of envelopes in America. It is built of brick, with a tower in the centre, and is 200 x 50 in size, four stories and basement, containing 45,000 square feet of floor area. The water at this power has a fall of eighteen feet. A thirty-seven horse power turbine wheel and a one hundred and twenty horse power breast wheel are used, and one hundred and fifty persons are employed.

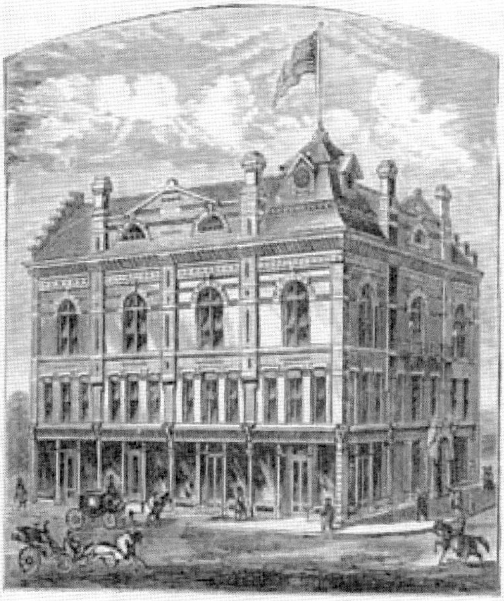

THE HENRY BUILDING, ROCKVILLE, CONN.

Mr. Cyrus White, the senior member of the firm, is president and treasurer of The White Manufacturing Company in this village, an account of which the reader is referred to in another column for detailed mention of Mr. White.

Mr. Lewis A. Corbin is a native of Thompson, Conn., and is about fifty-eight years age. He has been a resident of Rockville for about thirty years, and was originally a mason builder here. Several of the mills, stores and residences are evidences of his skill in this direction. He is president of the Connecticut Button Company, and has taken great interest in the welfare of the town, in the government of which he has served as assessor and selectman.

Mr. William H. Prescott was born in London, N. H., in 1840, and came to Rockville twenty-three years ago as a clerk in this establishment. As above mentioned, the firm recognizing his correct business methods and general capacity admitted him as a full partner in 1866, and he is now the financial and general manager of the business. He is a director in the First National Bank of Rockville and the White Manufacturing Company, both of this village.

White, Corbin & Co. enjoy the reputation of being the largest manufacturers of envelopes in the world.

The White Manufacturing Co., Manufacturers of Domestic Ginghams and Dress Goods, Rockville, Conn.—The White Manufacturing Company was incorporated in 1870, with a capital of $170,000, and has the following-named officers: President and Treasurer, Cyrus White; Secretary, George C. Rice.

About three hundred and fifty people are employed in the manufacture of domestic ginghams and dress goods. The number of spindles, which will show the capacity of the mills, are ten thousand. The selling agents are Messrs. Joy, Lincoln & Motley, New York and Boston.

There are three mills in this establishment, and three water powers with the following feet fall, respectively: twenty and one-half, thirty-two and forty-three feet. The buildings are built of brick and stone, and the establishment is the largest in the number of hands employed, and the only one manufacturing ginghams and dress goods in Rockville. Previous to 1869 it was run as a thread mill.

Mr. Cyrus White, the president, secretary and principal owner, is a native of Richford, Vermont, born in 1814. On his advent in Rockville, forty-five years ago, he was twenty-six years of age. He was at that time the possessor of a good trade, that of a blacksmith, which he afterwards followed here for twenty-four years. His frugal habits, business tact and general capacity soon made themselves felt; and, from an obscure youth, he has won his way to the position of one of the first and most influential manufacturers in his adopted village. His first venture as a manufacturer was as a machinist and iron-founder; later, he, with Mr. Corbin, founded the house of White, Corbin & Co., in this village, the largest manufacturers of envelopes in America, of which he is one third owner. In 1870 he retired from active business, content with his accumulations, but was forced to utilize manufacturing property of which unexpectedly he became possessed, and the White Manufacturing Co. was the result. Mr. White is largely interested in the industries of Rockville. He is president of the Smith-Heltsizer Manufacturing Co., a new manufacturing establishment recently started in this village. He is one of the firm of L. C. King & Co., merchants; is the proprietor of White's Opera-house, the popular play-house of Rockville, and otherwise interested in the institutions of his adopted town.

Mr. George C. Rice, the secretary, is a native of Worcester, Mass., born in 1849, and has been a resident of Rockville and secretary of this company for seven years.

The productions of The White Manufacturing Co. rank high with the trade, and their sale is limited only to the confines of the continent.

The New England Company, Manufacturers of Worsted Goods and Cassimeres for Men's Wear.—This well-known manufacturing establishment is a legitimate successor to the *old* New England Company, whose organization dates back to the year 1836. The present company, on its incorporation in 1879, adopted the name of the old, and has so continued to the present time. The capital is $80,000, and the officers are as follows: President, Geo. Maxwell; Secretary and Treasurer, A. Park Hammond; Superintendent, B. F. Mellor.

On the organization of the new company, they bought the mills and water power, and have since taken a high rank in the production of worsteds and cassimeres for men's wear, in which they aim to excel.

Nine sets of cards, forty-six broad looms and 175 operatives are employed.

The fall of water at this power is twenty feet, and a 24 by 16 breast wheel, supplemented by a seventy-five horse power engine, is used for motive power.

The selling agents are Pomeroy & Plummer, Nos. 61 and 63 Leonard street, New York City.

The president, Mr. George Maxwell, is a native of Charlemont, Mass., and about sixty-six years of age.

He has been a resident of Rockville for over thirty-five years—first, as a merchant, then as bookkeeper for the old New England Company, where he learned the business in which he has since taken a front rank. In addition to discharging the duties of principal officer of this company, he is president and treasurer of the Hockanum Company, a neighboring manufacturing establishment in this village, the information about which and its officers will be found in another column.

Mr. A. Park Hammond, the secretary and treasurer, was bred and born on the hills of Vernon, the town in which the village of Rockville is situated, and is forty-seven years of age.

He was educated at the Polytechnic Institute, Troy, New York, after which he learned the mysteries of manufacturing woolen goods with the old New England Company, of which Mr. Allen Hammond, his father, was founder in 1836. The father was, in his day, like the son in this, a prominent manufacturer in Rockville. He died in 1864, at the age of sixty-three years.

During the war of the Rebellion, A. Park Hammond was a captain in the Fourteenth Connecticut Regiment, and later represented his native town in the Connecticut Legislature. With the exception of four years spent in the West, he has been a resident of the town in which he was born and where he is a worthy representative of a family well-known and long identified with its earlier history.

Mr. Benjamin F. Mellor, the superintendent, was born in Woonsocket, R. I., and is about thirty years of age. He learned his trade of the Harris Manufacturing Company in that enterprising village, which is accredited with the honor of being the pioneer in this country in the manufacture of fine cassimeres for men's wear. He has been a resident of Rockville for four years, and is one of the promising manufacturers of New England. The New England Company is one of the larger establishments which go to make up the extended reputation which Rockville has as a manufacturing centre, and is an important factor in its continued success.

The American Mills, Manufacturers of Fancy Cassimeres and Meltons for Men's Wear. —The most imposing manufacturing establishment in Rockville as seen from the business centre is the American Mills, which were built in 1847. That same year the company, with the same name, was incorporated, with a capital of $100,000.

The first meeting of the directors was May 18, 1847, at which there were present Pheneas Talcott, President; Nelson Kingsbury, Secretary, Treasurer and Agent, of Rockville; D. H. Arnold of New York, Calvin Day of Hartford, and Isaac Hacker of Philadelphia. The present officers are, Calvin Day, President; Charles Seymour, Treasurer, of Hartford; E. J. Smith, Secretary; C. N. McLean, Agent, of Rockville.

The mill is 200x40 feet in size, and six stories in height. The first two are built of stone, and the remainder of wood. Fifteen sets of machinery, fifty-five broad looms, are run, and two hundred and sixty people employed in the manufacture of fancy cassimeres and meltons. A forty-two feet and two and one-half inches breast wheel is used to furnish the motive power, and the goods are sold at their own store at No. 89 Worth street in New York.

The president and treasurer, as before mentioned, are residents of Hartford, and representative men in that city.

Mr. E. J. Smith, the secretary, is a native of Tolland, Tolland County, Connecticut, born in 1815. He has been a resident of Rockville for thirty-six years, during which time he has been connected with this company. He is auditor of the Rockville Savings Bank and a well-known and respected citizen.

Mr. C. N. McLean, the agent, was born in Manchester, Connecticut, in 1850, and is comparatively a new accession to the business and social life of the village. He was formerly in the wool business and is well-calculated to satisfactorily represent the interests of the company as agent.

The American Mills are an important manufacturing interest here, and its productions have assisted in giving Rockville an enviable reputation as a centre for the manufacture of fine cassimeres, worsteds and meltons for men's wear.

Rockville Warp Mills, White and Colored Warps, Henry Adams, Proprietor.—Nearly a mile in a northeasterly direction from Rockville Post-office, in a most charming location, and surrounded by all the evidences of thrift, is the Rockville Warp Mill, of which Mr. Henry Adams is the proprietor. The business done here is the spinning and coloring of the cotton warp used by other manufacturers in the making of satinets and cassimeres.

The establishment of this mill dates back about thirty years, when Mr. Joseph Selden began the business, continuing it for eighteen years, when he was succeeded by the Adams Manufacturing Company, of which Mr. Adams was a prominent member. This company continued in business only about a year and a half, when, through troubles and other circumstances beyond its control, it was obliged to suspend. Indeed, so bad were its affairs that no creditor could be found who thought it worth while to sue for his claim, and Mr. Adams himself was obliged to procure the appointment of an assignee. As soon as the necessary legal formalities had been gone through with, the mill and its assets sold to satisfy judgments, etc., Mr. Adams found himself without means and staring the world in the face in a somewhat perplexed frame of mind. At this juncture, Mr. George Talcott, president of the First National Bank of Rockville, Mr. Milo W. Pember, wholesale cloth merchant, and Mr. A. N. Belding, of Belding Bros. & Co., silk manufacturers, all of Rockville, who had some interests at stake and who had unbounded faith in the honesty and capability of Mr. Adams, proposed to him that he should start the mill on his own account, they to furnish the funds. After some consideration the offer was accepted, and Mr. Adams stepped into the place he has since occupied, and in which he has not only repaid all advances, but has accumulated a competency for himself.

The mill, which is the first to take power in the Hockanum River and from that wonderful and beautiful sheet, Snipsic Lake, is of stone, the main building being 130 x 40 feet in size and four stories in height, with an L 40 x 30 feet in size, containing two floors.

In the mill there are 3,000 spindles, with a capacity of 4,500 lbs. of warp per week, giving employment to an average of seventy people. The machinery is run entirely by water-power, which is furnished by a forty-inch Leffell turbine wheel, fed by a fall of twenty-two feet, which can be enlarged to twenty-eight feet when necessary. A large steam boiler makes the steam used in scouring and dyeing as well as for heating the buildings. The products of the mill are wound upon what are technically termed "beams," and are shipped to different cassimere and satinet factories in New England, New York and New Jersey, the greater portion being used in the home State. The beams contain anywhere from 200 to 6,000 "ends" or threads, each from 1,000 to 20,000 yards in length, the number on a beam being regulated by the length of the thread. The amount of money invested in this business is very large, and the annual business is in the neighborhood of $100,000.

Mr. Adams, the controlling spirit and proprietor of this establishment, is a native of Great Barrington, Mass., born on May 20, 1838. At the age of ten years his family moved to South Adams, where his brothers now own a mill formerly run by his father and his uncle, Mr. John M. Seeley, now proprietor of the Housatonic Mills, and a State Senator in Massachusetts. Mr. Adams learned his business with his father and uncle, remaining there until he was twenty years of age, and going thence to the Indian Orchard Mills, where he continued for four or five years. From there he went with his uncle to Housatonic and assisted in building the two mills now owned and run by the latter at that place. From Housatonic the next and last recorded move was to Rockville, where he has remained since, steadily growing in favor and in fortune.

Mr. Adams is one of the few whose energy and perseverance has conquered fortune from disaster, and whose business and social records form a bright page in the State's history and furnish a shining example to struggling youth.

The Springville Manufacturing Co., Manufacturers of Union Cassimeres for Men's Wear. —This company was incorporated in 1833, with a capital which has since been increased to $24,000, and the following-named gentlemen as incorporators:

Chauncey Winchell, President; Alonzo Bailey, Agent; Christopher Burdick, Isaac L. Sanford.

With the exception of Mr. Winchell they have all passed away, he alone remaining, and still holds the office that he was elected to fifty years ago. His son, Mr. Cyrus Winchell, is Treasurer and Agent. The mill is built of stone and wood, four stories in height and 84 x 34 feet in size.

Three sets of machinery are run and fifty people employed in the manufacture of union cassimeres. The water-power at this mill has eighteen feet fall. The selling agents are John Slade & Co. and Whitman & Welch, in New York City.

Chauncey Winchell, the president, is probably the oldest gentleman doing business in the State of Connecticut. He was born on January 25, 1796, in Berlin, Conn., and removed to Rockville in 1829. He was a mill-wright, learning his trade in Manchester, Conn., previous to his removal here. During his long and active business life he has filled many responsible positions in the gift of the people. He was a member of the Legislatue as representative in 1853, and is now president of the Rockville National Bank. Cyrus Winchell, the agent and treasurer, was born in Manchester, Conn., in 1821, and has been identified with Rockville since 1829. He has always been a manufacturer and connected with the present company. He is vice-president of the People's Savings Bank, and was a Representative in the Legislature in 1876. The Winchells have been longer connected with the manufacturing industries of Rockville than any other family, and have lived to see it grow from a straggling hamlet to one of the important manufacturing villages of the State.

James J. Regan, Manufacturer of Woolen Flocks, Shoddy and Yarns.—This business was established in 1869 at the upper end of this village by the present proprietor. Outgrowing the original quarters, it was removed to Willington, Conn., about twelve miles east, from which place, after a term of five years, he returned to Rockville in 1875, and occupied a part of the premises once used by the old Florence Manufacturing Company. Mr. Regan's premises consist of six wooden buildings, having an average of three stories in height. Two large four-story wooden buildings situated in another part of the village are used for storehouses.

The water at this power has a fall of eighteen feet. A breast wheel is used in addition to a sixty-five horse power engine, which is kept in reserve for use in the dry seasons. About sixty-five people are employed in the manufacture of the finer grades of shoddy, woolen flocks and yarns, the first two of which he makes a specialty and counts among his customers manufacturers throughout New England. The weekly production is about 15,000 pounds of flock, 12,000 pounds of shoddy, and 1,000 pounds of yarn. The manufacture of clothing yarns is of recent date and it is the intention to soon commence the manufacture of woolen goods in addition to the present business.

The life of the proprietor illustrates what a thorough knowledge of a business, tact and business application will do for a man in the race for success. He was born of Irish parentage in Stone, in Staffordshire, England, in 1836, and came to America in 1848. For twenty-three years he has been a well-known resident of Rockville and vicinity, the first nine as an employee in the role of a woolen carder and spinner for one of the several woolen goods manufacturers for which the village is noted. During the years he has been a manufacturer he has built up one of the largest businesses of its class in New England.

He is ably assisted by his son Mr. Francis J. Regan who is superintendent of the works and a native of Rockville, twenty-two years of age.

The success of Mr. James J. Regan illustrates the possibilities afforded in America, even in New England, for a man to make and save money and enjoy life.

The Smith-Holtsizer Manufacturing Co., Manufacturers of Fancy Worsted Cloths for Men's Wear.—The latest accession to the manufacturing industries of Rockville is the Smith Holtsizer Manufacturing Co., which was incorporated in 1882, with a capital of $10,000, and the following-named officers: President, Cyrus White; Secretary and Treasurer, L. C. Smith. Although incorporated as above stated, business was not commenced till January 1, 1883. The premises occupied consist of a building 150x50 feet in size, five stories in height, and one half of another large building adjoining. The yarns used in the establishment are manufactured by other parties, leaving only the weaving and finishing to be done here, in which thirty persons are engaged. The selling agents are Case, Leeland & Co. in New York and Boston, and the goods made are fancy worsted cloths for men's wear.

The president, Mr. Cyrus White, is president and treasurer of the White Manufacturing Co., an account of whom will be found in another column. Mr. Louis C. Smith, the secretary and treasurer, is a native of South Hadley Falls, Mass., born in 1857. He was educated at the public schools and afterwards learned the business of a druggist in Lee, Mass. He has resided in Rockville for three years, where he was a prominent druggist previous to being identified with this company. The Smith-Holtsizer Manufacturing Co., although a new incorporation, gives promise of developing into an important factor in the industries of Rockville.

Eldredge & Adams (Joseph Eldredge and Thomas R. Adams), Rockville Marble and Granite Works, Mantels, Monuments, Table Tops, Slabs, etc., Office and Works, near Railroad Depot.—The only marble and granite works of any importance in Rockville is that carried on by the gentlemen whose names head this sketch. The business was established about twenty years ago by a German named Laubscher, who was succeeded in about three years by Mr. H. T. Bolles, the latter gentleman continuing it until February 1, 1881, when the present proprietors came into possession. All kinds of marble, granite, brown-stone, marbleized slate and other stones are worked, and the cemeteries in the vicinity bear many evidences of the firm's skill in monuments and grave-stones. Besides these are manufactured mantels, table-tops, plumber's slabs, and, in fact, anything that can be made of marble or stone. Six people are employed, two of whom are engaged for the greater part of the time in New Hampshire, quarrying and dressing the granite used here in the business. The business extends all over the State of Connecticut, and, to a lesser extent through sections of Massachusetts and Rhode Island. This firm own the buildings they occupy, which are situated directly alongside the railroad track, giving facilities for loading and unloading stone and marble at little expense, and superior to those of any other firm in the same business in the State.

Mr. Joseph Eldredge is a native of Willington, Conn., born in 1819, and has been a resident of Rockville about thirty years. Since his residence in the community he has been solicited to accept office, but has uniformly declined, preferring the quiet side of life and attention to his immediate business.

Mr. Thomas R. Adams, son-in-law to Mr. Eldredge, is a native of New Haven, about thirty-two years of age. He comes of an old family of stone-cutters, going back to his great grandfather, and is himself thoroughly practical in all branches of the business. He has resided in Rockville about eighteen years, sixteen of which were spent in the service of and in partnership with Mr. Bolles, the former proprietor of the business. He is regarded as a sterling business man, a master of his trade and a desirable citizen.

The firm of Eldredge & Adams is ranked among the best in its line in the State of Connecticut.

Heber Townsend, Pharmacist, Mr. Heber Townsend, the pioneer druggist of the village, began business at No. 2 Park place, in 1865, in what was termed the "Snipsic Block," under the firm name of F. B. Skinner & Co., of which Mr. Townsend was the junior member. In 1868, Dr. M. M. Townsend of Eckhart Mines, Md., purchased the interest of Mr. F. B. Skinner, changing the firm name to Townsend Brothers. In March, 1874, Mr. Heber Townsend took upon himself the entire business, Dr. Townsend retiring from the firm. The increasing demands of a flourishing business resulted in the moving away and rebuilding of the present magnificent four-story brick and iron block known as the Henry Building, "Townsend's Rockville Pharmacy," occupying the Park place and Park street corner. The store, as it now appears, is one, if not the finest, of its kind in the State, no pains or expense having been spared to make it first-class in every respect. Here can be found a select assortment of drugs and chemicals, and druggists' sundries, second to none outside of the large cities. It is centrally located, just opposite the Rockville House, and only two minutes' walk from the railroad, telegraph, telephone, and express offices, thus securing to itself a large share of the local trade and the patronage of the traveling public. It is here that the tickets for Henry Hall, which is directly over the store, and White's Opera House, are always put on sale. The facilities for serving customers with tickets are complete, as a "box-office" is situated at the rear end of the store, opening into the entrance of the hall above. The pharmacy is elegantly fitted up in white and Hungarian ash, relieved with native red cherry, marble counter-tops and floor, French plate-glass windows, Puffer's soda apparatus, chandeliers with electric lighting apparatus, comprise a few of the modern improvements, which, with steam heat throughout, makes this store an attractive place to do business in, as is proven by the constant and increasing crowds who visit it daily. Mr. Townsend has issued a neat and attractive business card, with a view of the

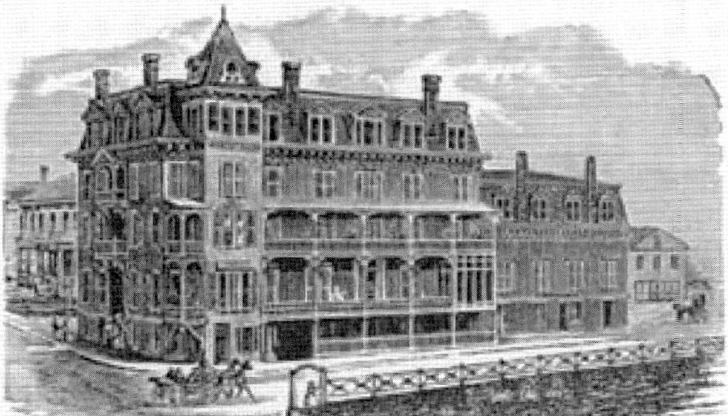

ROCKVILLE HOUSE, ROCKVILLE, CONN.

Henry Block on the outside—the inside containing a diagram of the seating arrangements, stage, etc., of the hall.

Mr. Townsend has compounded a number of popular preparations, the most celebrated of which are, Townsend's Hay Fever and Asthma Remedy, Cough Mixture, Throat Confection, Wild Cherry Bitters, and Dyspepsia Cure.

The First National Bank, Park Place. The First National Bank of Rockville was chartered February 24, 1863, with Mr. J. J. Robinson as the president. He served but a few months, and was succeeded by Mr. Clark Holt, who in his turn has been succeeded by Mr. George Talcott, who is now the President. The capital of the bank is $200,000, with a surplus of $40,000. The charter was renewed on the 24th of February, 1883, and has twenty years to run. For the past fifteen years it has occupied its present position under the Methodist Church, Park place. Mr. John H. Kite, born in Charleston, Mass., is the Cashier. The bank has pursued a prosperous and uneventful career, save the incident of 1875, when the cashier discovered that the famous Northampton bank robbers were making an attempt to rob the vault of this bank. This plan was frustrated, and a new and remarkably strong vault, as good as any in the country, was built. This contains the safes, which are provided with time locks and all the necessary safe-guards.

F. A. Randall, Bookseller and Stationer, and **Geo. W. Randall,** Dealer in Musical Instruments.—The largest and best known book store, with a portion of the establishment devoted to the sale of musical instruments, is that of F. A. Randall, at No. 3, in the fine and imposing Henry Building, facing the Public Square. For six or seven years the business was conducted on Main street, by F. Ziegler. Mr. Randall purchasing it January, 1881, and in the Fall of 1882 it was transferred to its present handsome and commodious quarters.

Mr. F. A. Randall is a young and energetic business man, having been born in Rockville, in 1861. He received his education in the public schools of the town, and early in life began business for himself. His store has quite a metropolitan air, and besides the large assortment of books in all branches of literature, one can find everything wished for in the line of fine stationery, school books and school supplies, as well as the weekly and daily papers from Hartford, Springfield, Boston and New York, and all of the latest magazines as fast as puplished.

In conjunction with the book store, Mr. Geo. W. Randall keeps a music store, with a good and large supply of pianos, organs and other musical instruments. The salesroom is some sixty by twenty feet, light and well adapted for the purposes for which it was intended.

Mr. Geo. W. Randall was born in Rockville, in 1857. He was educated in the village. He is a member of the order of the Knights of Honor, and treasurer and clerk of the St. John's Episcopal Church.

E. A. Kuhnly, Dealer in Stoves, Ranges, Furnaces and House Furnishing Goods.—It was twenty-five years ago since Messrs. Blackman & McCrary established the business now conducted by Mr. Edward A. Kuhnly. The immediate predecessor to Mr. Kuhnly was Mr. R. B. Chapman. Mr. Kuhnly, previous to doing business at his present location, was in the same business on the other side of the railroad since 1877, and moved here in March, 1882. The store is designated and known as No. 4 Exchange Block, situated in the centre of business. The premises are 50 x 23 feet in size and embrace four floors. A large stock of stoves, furnaces, ranges and house furnishing goods is carried, and five employees are kept busy in the plumbing, gas-fitting and roofing departments.

A specialty is made of the New Hub Range and the Boynton Furnace. The trade is not confined to Rockville, but extends to the villages of Vernon, Ellington, Tolland, Colton, Quarryville, Coventry, Windsorville and the surrounding country.

Mr. Kuhnly is a native of Greenville, near Norwich, Conn., born in 1848. For several years previous to 1877, at which time he came to Rockville, he was a resident of Hartford. He rejoices in having the largest assortment and doing the most extensive business of any in his line in the village, where he stands as the representative man of his class and worthy of the confidence of the community.

F. A. Severance & Co., Clothing, Hats, Caps and Gents' Furnishing Goods, No. 1 Exchange Block.—One of the largest dealers in clothing in Rockville is Messrs. Severance & Co., whose business was established in 1869 in a store under the Methodist Church, by Mr. F. A. Severance, the present proprietor, and since conducted under the above firm name.

After remaining about one year in the old location the business outgrew the original quarters and a removal to the present location was necessitated, which occurred in 1870. The store is 18 x 56 feet in size, and is stocked with the best quality and style of men's, youths' and boys' clothing, hats, caps and gents' furnishing goods. Two experienced assistants are required in the prosecution of the business, which extends to the country towns for miles around.

Mr. F. A. Severance is a native of Walpole, N. H., born in 1844, and was educated in the public schools. He has been a resident of Rockville since 1867, and is one of the thriving, enterprising merchants of the village, and ranks high in the commercial world.

Rockville National Bank, Park Place.—Close by the Second Congregational Church, at the southern end of Central Park, stands the neat brick and granite building of the Rockville National Bank. This bank was organized in 1855 as a State bank, with Mr. Allen Hammond as president. It became a National Bank in 1864. The second president was Mr. E. B. Preston, and he was succeeded by Mr. Chauncey Winchell, who is now the President. Mr. Geo.

Maxwell is the Vice-President, and Mr. E. C. Chapman, who has been with the bank since 1868, is the Cashier. The Directors are Messrs. Chauncey Winchell, George Maxwell, Isaac Chester, M. W. Pember, Ansel Arnold, J. N. Stickney, D. N. Kimball, Frank Grant, and E. C. Chapman. The capital stock of the bank is $300,000, with a surplus of $64,000. The deposits amount to $180,366. The total assets of this bank amount to $877,104. Of these there are in limited State bonds $312,000, loans and discounts, $477,612, and real estate and fixtures, $10,000. This bank has the confidence of the business community, and has connected with it some of the foremost men of the place.

Wilburt L. Talcott, Manufacturer of Cigars and Dealer in Tobacco and Smokers' Articles, No. 6 Market Street.—Mr. Wilburt L. Talcott, the only manufacturer of cigars in Rockville, who deals in other articles for smokers' use, established his business in 1873, the original location being at the Rich Place near the Town Farm, where he remained for three years, removing thence to Johnson's Block on Main street, and in 1878 to his present location. Mr. Talcott employs four skilled workmen, turning out about 100,000 cigars annually. Many brands are made, but especial attention is given to the "Henry Hall" and the "Snipsic" brands, on which Mr. Talcott's reputation is largely based. The trade is chiefly local, but the special brands find purchasers in many other parts of the State.

Mr. Talcott is a native of Vernon, born in 1853. For twelve years he resided in the West, most of the time in Cleveland, Ohio, where he learned the trade of cigar making. He returned here in 1873, since which time he has succeeded in building up the best business in his line to be found in the vicinity, and in establishing a thoroughly good reputation.

John Mulligan, Stoves, Furnaces, etc., White's Opera House.—The first large block of importance observed after leaving the railway station, which stands head and shoulders above the surrounding buildings, is a straw-colored structure known as White's Opera House. And the largest store in this block is Mr. John Mulligan's, a leading Rockville dealer in stoves, furnaces, ranges, tinware, etc. The business was established about one year ago, and has occupied its present commanding position something over a year. The storeroom is about 50 x 20 feet, and is well filled with such things as modern civilization demands for the kitchen. Even in stoves and ranges the fashion changes, and improvements are constantly being made. Here a specialty is made of the Magee range, which can be placed in the kitchen like a stove, and needs no brick-work. The small cooking-stove of a generation ago is unsalable, as housekeepers have discovered that the modern range will do the work much more satisfactorily. Mr. Mulligan also keeps the new and handsome parlor or sitting-room stove, with artistic tiles ornamenting the top; a stove far in advance of the old air-tight arrangement of our grandfathers. He was born in East Windsor twenty-eight years ago, and is a practical tinsmith and manufacturer, as well as dealer. Having a thorough knowledge of the business, with a first-class and extensive assortment of goods, his business success is readily accounted for.

The People's Savings Bank, Henry Building.—The People's Savings Bank, incorporated in 1870, began business in a small way and in small quarters, but constantly gaining the confidence of the public, until now it has a handsome office in the fine brick block known as the Henry Building. The total number of depositors, according to the annual statement, made October, 1882, is 755; the deposits amounting to $235,344.60. The total assets of the bank amount to $244,558.73. These consist, for the most part, of loans on real estate, always secured by first mortgage; loans on indorsed notes, and bank stocks in Connecticut. Mr. John W. Thayer was the first president. The present officers are: President, George M. Paulk; Treasurer, E. S. Henry; Directors or Trustees, George M. Paulk, Cyrus Winchell, Francis Keeney, E. S. Henry, Dwight Marcy, R. G. Holt, Frederick Walker, of Vernon; Asaph McKinney, of Ellington; E. C. Chapman, A. N. Belding, C. Fitton, Robert Patton, of Ellington, and Samuel Fitch, of Rockville.

The Tolland County Journal, Thomas S. Pratt, Editor and Proprietor.—The literary status, culture and business enterprise of a community are reflected in its newspapers. "The Tolland County Journal," the first number of which was issued by Mr. J. A. Spaulding, February 7, 1867, bears out this assertion. For five years this paper was ably edited by Mr. Spaulding, during which time he so established it that it won its way to its proper place, foremost in the front rank among the representative weekly newspapers in the State. Mr. Spaulding is now one of the editors and proprietors of the "Hartford Evening Post."

In January, 1872, Messrs J. N. Stickney & Company assumed the proprietorship of the Journal and continued its publication up to February, 1880, when it was sold to Messrs. French Brothers who continued it for a brief period. In May, 1881, the present editor and proprietor, Mr. Thomas S. Pratt, succeeded to the business. Mr. Pratt was born in South Adams, Mass., September 24, 1842, and finished his education at Pierce's Academy, at Middleboro, Mass. He brought with him to Rockville the result of many years journalistic experience as editor and proprietor of several newspapers in Massachusetts, the "Marlboro Mirror-Journal," the "Rockland Standard," the "Attleboro Advocate," and the "Mansfield News," the latter of which he still retains an interest in.

It is neatly printed, ably edited and is typical of the advanced business ideas of the cultured people of Rockville.

Rockville House, Claude Harvey, Proprietor, Main Street.—This handsome and admirably kept hotel stands at the corner of Main and Park Streets, commanding a fine view of the village, and remarkably convenient to the depot, post-office, banks, churches, etc. It contains fifty rooms, besides a large and handsome dining-room, a fine hall for dancing, 40 x 60 feet, a bar, office, barber's shop, etc. The rooms are nicely furnished, with good beds and well kept. The table is one of the best to be found at any New England hotel, well supplied with good food, admirably cooked. For pies, puddings, cakes, etc., it cannot be surpassed by metropolitan establishments, and the food set before the guest is tempting, and never stinted. The building is a large, four-story structure, surrounded with balconies and piazzas, and presents a home-like and inviting appearance. A hotel has stood upon this site ever since the village was founded, or for thirty-five years. It was first kept by Mr. Keeney and next by Col. Lay, father-in-law of the present genial and gentlemanly proprietor. Mr. Harvey has been the proprietor of the Rockville House for seven years. He is a native of Stafford, Conn., where he was formerly engaged in cotton manufacture, and subsequently in the stove and tinware business.

The Savings Bank of Rockville, Main street.—Beneath the large and handsome Methodist Church, facing the park, is the Savings Bank of Rockville. It occupies roomy and handsome quarters, and is the oldest and richest savings bank in the town. The total liabilities of the bank are $796,780.05, the whole amount of deposits being $758,053.97. The assets of the bank are the same as the liabilities, and consist for the most part of loans on real estate, loans on indorsed notes, and bank stocks in Connecticut and other States. The total number of deposits is 2,547, and the amount of their deposits is $758,053.97. During the year 1882 the income of this bank was $47,212.04, while the dividends declared amounted to $32,557.27. The bank was incorporated in 1858, and has the following gentlemen for officers: President, B. H Bill; Treasurer, Lebbens Bissell; Directors or Trustees, George Talcott, William Butler, J. S. Dobson, E. I. Smith, B. H. Bill, Lebbeus Bissell, G. W. West, H. L. James, A. R. Goodrich, and T. M. Durfee.

Charles F. Weeks, Carriage Manufacturer and General Repairer, Main Street, near American Mill.—Mr. Charles F. Weeks, whose establishment is situated on Main street, near the American Mills, is the largest manufacturer of wagons and carriages in Rockville, and does a greater business in a general way than any of his competitors. The business was established about 1873, and has grown to be one of the important industries of the village. The building occupied is 20 by 75 feet in size and two stories in height, the blacksmith and wood-working shops being on the lower floor, while the upper story is occupied by the paint-shop and trimming department. Ten men are given employment, and all kinds of wagons and carriages are here turned out in as good style and as cheaply as at any similar establishment in the State.

Mr. Weeks is a native of New Athens, Maine, born in 1839, and has lived in Connecticut thirteen years. His trade was learned in West Springfield, Mass., at the factory of Edson Clark, so celebrated for turning out fine workmen. Mr. Week's reputation as a business man is unexcelled, and his work gives entire satisfaction to his customers.

Tolland County Leader, Leader Building, Market Street.—The well-printed, large, eight-page paper known as the "Tolland County Leader," was established in February, 1879, with many odds against it, but with sufficient muscle and brain power, it has come into favor with business men, and has become an established institution. Inside of two years it was found necessary to enlarge the paper, and Mr. B. L. Burr, the publisher and editor, bought out the interest of his partner, Mr. Byron, and increased the size one-third. The "Leader," as all local papers should, makes a specialty of the news of the village and neighborhood, and besides giving good original and selected miscellaneous reading, supplies its patrons with a condensed account of the important news of the world at large. Mr. B. L. Burr, the editor, was born in the old town of Haddam, thirty-seven years ago. At the outbreak of the war he became a volunteer in the Sixteenth Connecticut Regiment, remaining with his command until after the Battle of Antietam. Major Robert L. Kellogg, author of "Life and Death in Rebel Prisons," was one of the officers of this regiment. For a year or two Mr. Burr was connected with the Springfield, Mass., "Union," his services having been sought on account of his ability as a local editor. He started a paper called "The Gleaner" previous to being employed on the "Union," and after having run it up to a good circulation, sold it out. The "Leader" Building is a handsome and commodious structure on Market street, near Main. Here Mr. Burr has his editorial rooms, library, printery, etc., and here he is connected by telephone and telegraph with the outside world. His paper has a fair share of advertising patronage, and is well-filled with local news. It appears every Thursday evening, at the rate of $1.50 per year.

Geo. M. Paulk, Lumber Dealer, Market Street.—Just off of Market street, on what is known as the "Brooklyn side" of the Hockanum River, is the large lumber yard of Mr. Geo. M. Paulk, which is the only depot in town for lumber. It covers an acre or more of grodnd, and being close by the railway station, is conveniently situated for receiving supplies. The lumber comes from Canada, Michigan, and the northern portions of New York State, Vermont and New Hampshire, and consists of pine, hemlock, spruce, in short, all the woods used in modern house building. In this yard can be seen large piles of lumber and timber, pine and spruce clapboards, shingles, lath, mouldings, brackets, etc. The house builders and carpenters of Rockville draw their supplies from this yard. The neat and comfortable offices of the yard are situated close by, and have telephonic communication with rest of the State. Mr. Paulk is one of the substantial and respected citizens of Rockville. He has been in the lumber business since 1869. Before that date he was a builder. He became a resident of Rockville in 1841. He was born in Tolland in 1820, and was educated in his native town. He has taken more or less interest in county politics, but of late years has not taken an active part and is now wholly devoted to business. From 1869 to 1878 he was the sheriff of Tolland County—three terms of three years each.

Mr. Paulk is president of the People's Savings Bank and director in the First National Bank. He owns a handsome residence, and takes a lively interest in all that concerns the welfare of the village.

Hodgson & Metcalf, Druggists (Pharmacy Hall), Orcutt's Block, No. 12 Main Street.—This new and enterprising firm are the direct successors to L. C. Smith, who for three years carried on the business originally established by Tracy & Peck, about the year 1866. On February 1, 1883, Messrs. Hodgson and Metcalf purchased the fixtures of the store from Mr. Smith, and putting in an entirely new stock, commenced to cater to the trade, so large a portion of which has already fallen to their share. The stock is large and complete, both in drugs and fancy goods, as well as in cigars, confectionery, etc., and the store, 20 x 80 feet in size, is one of the largest in the village.

Mr. J. Hodgson is a native of Lyme, Conn., born in 1854. Since boyhood he has been in the drug business in South Coventry, Conn.; Springfield, Mass.; Rockville, Willimantic, and again in Rockville, where he is known as a first-class druggist and pharamacist. He is a member of the Connecticut Pharmaceutical Society, in which body he is regarded as an acquisition.

Mr. W. A. Metcalf is a native of Vernon; born in 1857, and, like his partner, was brought up to his present business. He was a clerk for three years in the store of Sill Brothers, and previously for some time for Dr. Wilson. He is also a member of the Pharmaceutical Society, in good standing, and is universally regarded as a skilled and conscientious member of the profession.

The indications are favorable towards the complete success this young firm deserves.

The Rock Manufacturing Co., Manufacturers of Fancy Cassimeres.—The original incorporators of this company were Francis McLean, Geo. Kellogg, Ralph Talcott and Aaron Kellogg, and the date was 1828. The first meeting was held December 31st of that year, when the following-named gentlemen were chosen as officers: President, Francis McLean; Secretary, Geo. Kellogg, who was also Agent up to the year 1837, and again from 1846 till his death in 1870. At that time there were no large and spacious edifices filled with costly machinery as now, but instead, a small mill with machinery of the most primitive patterns, and a company with limited capital. The salary of the president was only $400 per annum, the secretary received $410, and was allowed the use of a house and garden for $60. The same house now rents for $250, and the salary of the officers—well, it is safe to record is more than what it was over fifty years ago. Since that time great improvements have been made, and much money expended in the building of new mills, and putting in the most modern machinery for the manufacture of the finest grades of fancy cassimeres possible in America.

The present officers of the company are: A. C. Dunham, President; H. L. James, Secretary and Treasurer; Crosley Fitton, Agent and Superintendent. The company's store is at No. 69 Worth street, where Geo. T. Cruttenden is Selling Agent. Twenty sets of cards, one hundred and thirty broad looms, and 350 people are employed. The establishment embraces three mills, and the fall of water at the three powers is sixty-eight feet each.

Austin Dunham, the father of the present president, was president of the company from 1873 to 1877, when the son succeeded. Previous to Austin Dunham was Allyn Kellogg, who was chosen n 1862. The main office of the company, together with the mills, occupy one of the most desirable locations in Rockville, on the main street opposite the village park and post-office, near the banks, and in the centre of business, it presents a scene of unusual activity noticeable alike to the citizen and stranger.

Mr. A. C. Dunham, the president, is a resident of Hartford. Mr. H. L. James, the secretary and treasurer, is a native of Connecticut, and about forty-two years of age. He has resided in Rockville since 1854. In early life he prepared to enter college, but gave up the purpose to enter immediately into the active pursuit of manufacturing, with which he has been connected for twenty-five years, with this company and at the Florence Mills, Rockville.

Mr. Crosley Fitton, the agent and Superintendent, is a native of England, and forty-four years of age. Previous to taking up his residence here, sixteen years ago, he resided in Vermont. In 1874 he was promoted to agent, succeeding S. D. W. Harris.

The productions of this company are recognized by the trade as equal to any imported, and are sometimes sold as such by merchant tailors. The diplomas and medals won at Vienna and Philadelphia attest the superiority and excellence of their fancy cassimeres.

TALCOTTVILLE.

A village of about two hundred inhabitants, situated on the main line of the New York and New England Railroad, eleven and one-half miles east from Hartford.

The Tankarooson, a tributary of the Hockanum River, furnishes the water-power or manufacturing purposes.

Talcott Brothers, Manufacturers of Union Cassimeres.—The moving spirits in this house, the reputation of which is national and its influence felt generally, were Horace W. Talcott and Charles Denison Talcott, known to the business and Christian world as Talcott Brothers. They, in 1856, after an apprenticeship to the business, purchased of Hon. N. O. Kellogg, the manufacturing village of Kelloggville, now known as Talcottville. The brothers were sons of Elijah and Florilla Talcott and born in Manchester, Conn., Horace W., in 1821, Charles D., in 1823. The former died June 16, 1871, the latter July 17, 1882. The father was a farmer and teacher, as occasion required; occupations which were followed by the sons before they learned the manufacturing business.

The manufacturing establishment as it stands to-day, is 160 x 34 feet in size and three stories in height, with two wings, eighty and ninety feet in length respectively, and two stories each, to which is added a picker-room forty feet in length, one-story, the whole having a frontage of 370 feet, in which there are 100 people employed, six sets of machinery and fifty-two looms.

The fall of water at this power is twenty-one feet. The agents in New York are C. H. & F. D. Blake.

The brothers' views were comprehensive and orthodox. Charity, Liberality and Christianity were their motive powers. No one in their employ was allowed to use intoxicating liquors. In doing this, as in every transaction, they meant to do good, knowing by repeated experiences that "Doing good is the only certainly happy action of a man's life."

They gave to the village a church, costing $31,000, which was erected in 1866. In 1880, a model school-house was erected at a cost of $4,500, and, in 1881, a library building, costing $10,000, which, like the church, were presented to the village. The library building is surmounted by a tower which is ornamented with a four-dial public clock.

Since the death of Charles Denison Talcott, the business has been conducted for the heirs of the estate by Horace Gardner Talcott, a son of Horace W., who has associated with him in the management and responsibility, Messrs. Samuel A. and Morris H. Talcott.

Mr. Horace Gardner Talcott is a native of Talcottville, born in 1847. After receiving an education at Andover, Massachusetts, and at Yale, he learned the manufacturing business in the establishment over which he is now general manager.

He is a director in the First National Bank of Rockville, and succeeds to the deaconship of the Congregational Church and superintendency of its Sunday-school.

Mr. Samuel A. Talcott, a son-in-law of Horace W. Talcott, is a son of Deacon Samuel Talcott, formerly of Gilead, Connecticut, has been associated with the company for nearly twelve years. The store is especially under his care.

Morris H. Talcott a nephew of the Talcott Brothers, and son of Deacon Elijah Hart Talcott, the oldest of the brothers, has had the care of the books for over eleven years.

The farm of over 300 acres is under the management of Lyman P. Talcott, the only surviving brother.

The Talcott family has an honorable record, extending back to 1558, and their lives are in keeping with the motto engraven on their coat of arms, "*Virtus sola nobilitas.*"

VERNON DEPOT.

Twelve and one-quarter miles east from Hartford on the New York and New England Railroad. The branch road to Rockville joins the main line here.

The Ravine Mills Company.—This company is the legitimate successor to Peter Dobson, the founder of the first cotton mill in the town of Vernon, and one of the first in America. He was co-worker with Samuel Slater, the father of cotton manufacturing in this country, and like him brought over from England plans from which he made the machinery that was used in the old mill that he built, and which is still standing, a monument to his energy and success.

The company was incorporated in 1873, and has the following-named officers:

President, James Campbell; Agent, Secretary and Treasurer, R. B. Parker. These two, with Lucius Parker, the father of R. B., are the three owners. Two mills are run by this company. The first called the Phœnix Mill, is situated on the Tankarooson River, a tributary of the Hockanum, and a few rods from the Vernon Depot. It was built in 1836, and for many years was run and owned by The Phœnix Mills Co., in the manufacture of cotton warps. In 1879, it was bought by the present company, who have since made here, seine twine.

The dimensions of the mill are 110 x 35 feet, three stories and attic, and two L's, 50 x 40 and 80 x 20 respectively, each two stories. The basement of the whole is of stone, the upper stories being of wood; and twenty-five people are employed. The fall of water at this power is eighteen feet. A Risdon turbine wheel is used, supplemented by a forty-horse power engine. The other mill is situated in a ravine, and is appropriately called The Ravine Mill, and was built of wood in 1873, on the site of a former mill built by Peter Dobson and his son, John S. Dobson, which was burned. The dimensions of the mill are 115 x 35 feet, three stories, and one L 100 x 25 feet. The stream is the Tankarooson, and the water at this power has a fall of twenty feet. A Victor turbine is used, supplemented by a thirty-horse power engine. About twenty-five people are employed in the manufacture of cotton warps and sewing twine.

Mr. James Campbell, president of the company, is a native of Vermont, and about seventy-two years of age. He resides in Manchester, a neighboring town, where he has resided since 1833. He began life as a farmer, then an insurance agent, and capitalist, and is president of the Manchester Warp & Yarn Co., and also of the Globe Mill Co., is director in the United States Bank of Hartford, and several insurance companies in that city. His capital was his head and hands when he came to Manchester and he is now the wealthist man in town.

Mr. Lucius Parker, the father of the agent, secretary and treasurer of the company, was born in Mansfield, Conn., in 1807, and is one of the pioneers in the manufacture of cotton goods in Vernon. He was a picker boy for Peter Dobson, and of him learned the business. His first business venture was at Coventry, Conn., where he conducted the Boynton Mills from 1837 to 1842, which were owned by the well-known family of that name, who were also manufacturers of woolen machinery. From there he removed to Hop River, Conn., where he bought and run the Hop River Warp Mills which he continued up to 1847, when he removed to Manchester to establish the Mutual Manufacturing Co., which is now called the Manchester Warp & Yarn Co., and in which he is a director. He also built and conducted the Pacific Knitting Mills in that town, where he still resides. From a poor picker boy he worked himself up to be the originator, owner and director of manufacturing establishments, and an honored and influential citizen of many years' standing. His son, Mr. R. B. Parker, was born in Coventry, Conn., in 1838, and has been in Vernon seventeen years. He learned the business of his father and, in 1873, established the Ravine Mills Co., of which he is agent, secretary and treasurer. He sells the productions of this Company and also those of the Manchester Warp & Yarn Co., of which he is also agent, secretary and treasurer.

The Parker family are largely interested in the manufacturing industries of Vernon and the adjoining towns, where it members are regarded as highly respected and thoroughgoing citizens.

The Vernon Mills Company, Manufacturers of Flocks, Shoddy and Wool Extracts.—This establishment is another of several built by Peter Dobson, and some fifty-five years ago.

It was run as a shoddy mill about fifteen years by Messrs. Dobson, White & Co. Mr. John S. Dobson, the senior partner, being the son of the founder. Later, it was carried on by Messrs. Hilliard & Smith under its present title, and so continued till February, 1882, when the present proprietor, Mr. Jesse E. Smith, assumed the business. Mr. John A. Smith is Agent and Mr. Julius A. Smith, Superintendent. The mill is 90 x 33 feet in size, four stories and attic, with L 40 x 20 feet, one story. There is also a picker-room seventy-five feet long, built of brick, and fire-proof. There are from twenty to twenty-five people employed, and the mill runs night and day, producing 10,000 pounds of shoddy and 9,000 pounds of flocks per week. The fall of water at this power, which is on the Tankaroocon river, is twenty-two feet. A turbine wheel and a forty-horse power engine, with a Pitkin boiler are used. The Smiths are natives of Rhode Island and Massachusetts, and previous to residing in this town were in Burrillville, R. I., and later, conducted the same business in Rockville, Conn.

MANCHESTER AND SOUTH MANCHESTER.

The town of Manchester is on the line of the New York and New England Railroad, 108.6 miles from Boston, 81 1-4 miles from Providence, and 8.7 miles from Hartford. A railroad about two miles in length, built and operated by Cheney Brothers, connects the two subdivisions of the town, North and South Manchester, the terminus at the former place being at the depot of the N. Y. & N. E. R. R., and at the latter place in close proximity to the extensive silk mills of that firm. North Manchester presents a thriving appearance, a number of manufacturing establishments being located here. The main street, running along one side of the railroad track, is well furnished with stores of various kinds, the most important of which will be found mentioned in detail elsewhere. The post-office, two hotels, the Coles House and the Clifton House, are also on the main street, and do their part towards the general appearance of business and bustle pervading the place. The churches and schools are numerous, the latter being especially noted for their excellence, while the former are well attended and have been productive of much good, notably in making the place a "no license" town, in which it is unlawful to sell intoxicating liquors. One newspaper, the *Manchester Saturday Herald*, established in 1881, is published weekly, has an uncommonly large circulation, and is ably edited.

South Manchester is deservedly credited with being the model manufacturing village in New England, and when that is said it means "in all the world." The growth and appearance of this place is due to the untiring energy and philanthropy of the Cheney Brothers, whose immense silk mills are the nucleus around which has clustered the most ornate and comfortable residences for operatives and other employees, as well as commodious churches, schools and other public buildings, their erection being due to the liberality of the firm. Nowhere in New England is the lot of the mill operative so happy a one, and nowhere in the world are the material and spiritual comforts so thoroughly looked after at so small an expense as in this modern arcadia. Magnificently constructed roads, fringed with stately elms and hardy firs and bordered with neatly laid and well-kept asphaltum walks, lead from place to place in the village, in the centre of which are the elegant buildings of the Cheney Brothers, whence all this beauty and comfort have emanated. A visit to Connecticut, if one desired to see its principal points of interest, would be incomplete were this charming spot omitted.

The Manchester Warp and Yarn Co., Manufacturers of Warps and Yarns, North Manchester.—This company was incorporated August 1, 1882, with a capital of $12,000 for the manufacture of cotton warps and yarns. The following are the officers and directors: President, James Campbell; Secretary, Treasurer, and Agent, R. B. Parker; Directors, James Campbell, Lucius Parker, R. B. Parker, and John Purtell. The mill is situated about three-quarters of a mile east of the Manchester Depot on a tributary of the Hockanum, and is 100 x 35 feet in size, three stories with two L's 25 x 50 feet and 30 x 20 feet respectively. The fall of water at this power is twenty-eight feet.

The officers of this company are also officers of the Ravine Mills Company in Vernon, to which the reader is referred for further particulars, under the head of Vernon Depot.

Robert P. Bissell, General Merchandise, North Manchester.—The general merchandise business conducted by Mr. Robert P. Bissell, at North Manchester, is a good evidence of what may be accomplished in a comparatively brief time by energy and correct business methods.

Mr. Bissell is, in every sense, the architect of his own fortune, having established his business himself, and having forced its growth, in less than three years, from the very smallest of beginnings, to an annual trade of $60,000. The trade done by Mr. Bissell embraces the sale of almost everything that can be needed, among which can be mentioned dry goods, groceries, flour and feed, meats, boots and shoes, hardware, crockery, paints and oils, teas, coffees and spices, fruits and vegetables, and, in fact, so long a list of articles that there is not space for its enumeration. The store occupied by this large and growing trade is forty by eighty feet in size, and, together with a basement of like dimensions, is stocked with full lines of the goods mentioned, their average value being in the neighborhood of $10,000. The upper story of the building is occupied by Bissell's Hall, a place of amusement, with a seating capacity of about six hundred, well furnished with stage, scenery, piano, seats, etc.

The business done by Mr. Bissell is not altogether local in its character, but is largely done through the surrounding country, his customers being served by teams, three of which he has constantly on the road, one being reserved for the delivery of orders in the immediate vicinity of the store.

Mr. Robert P. Bissell is a native of South Windsor, Conn., born July 9, 1856. He has resided in Manchester all his life. He graduated from the Normal School at New Britain, in the second class of 1875, and for five years thereafter taught school in Manchester and North Manchester, being for three years principal of the graded school at the latter place.

Mr. Bissell is the leading dealer in his line in North Manchester, and enjoys a first-class business and social reputation.

Fitch & Drake (Jasper A. Fitch and Levi Drake), General Merchandise, Main Street, North Manchester.—The firm of Fitch & Drake was established August 22, 1876, succeeding G. P. Babcock, who was one of the line of proprietors extending back for a period of about thirty years. The business has always been in the same location—on Main street, opposite the railroad depot—and occupies both floors of a two-story building 25x75 feet in size. The stock, which is general in its character and embraces dry goods, groceries, crockery, hardware, boots and shoes, tea, coffee, and spices, etc., is valued at about $7,000, the annual business being estimated at more than five times that sum, or in the neighborhood of $40,000.

Mr. Jasper A. Fitch was born in Andover, Conn., in 1843, and has been a resident of Manchester for about ten years. Prior to his advent here he was in the grocery business in his native town, and was its representative in the Legislature in 1870 and 1872. In Manchester he has been prominent in school matters, having been principal of the school for two years prior to entering his present business, and one of the visitors since that time. Mr. Fitch is also the local agent for Adam & Co's Express.

Mr. Levi Drake is a native of Tolland, Conn., thirty-six years of age, and has been a resident of Manchester sixteen years. He has followed the grocery business all his life, having formerly been a clerk and afterwards partner with Mr. Parkhurst, now of Parkhurst & Haynes, whose store is situated near the gingham mill. Mr. Drake has steadily refused public position, preferring to devote his time to the necessities of his growing business.

The firm has an "A 1" commercial reputation, and its members stand high in the community.

BUCKLAND.

The little village of Buckland, in the town of Manchester, Conn., is seven miles from Hartford, and thirty-four from Springfield, Mass. It contains a school-house, a depot, post-office, and is the seat of the Waverley paper mills of the Peter Adams Company, and the woolen mill of E. E. Hilliard & Co. The village was named after the Buckland family, which was the original proprietor of the land, and many members of which sleep in the old burying ground. It is on the line of the New York and New England railway, and has five trains daily going west, and four trains going east. Mr. H. G. Parker is the postmaster.

Peter Adams Company, Paper Manufacturers, Buckland, Conn.—The Waverley Mills of the Peter Adams Co., manufacturers of chromo, plate and lithographic papers, are situated in the village of Buckland, about one-half mile from the railway, in the romantic valley of the Hockanum. The mills are new, large and handsome brick buildings, having been recently entirely reconstructed.

Originally, there was a small wooden building, with but one paper-making machine. Now it has two fourdrinier machines, one of which is eighty-six inches in width. The establishment was formerly known as Mr. Goodwin's, but in 1863 was purchased by Mr. Peter Adams, a resident of Paterson, N. J., who is President of the company, which was incorporated in 1883.

The main office and warerooms are at 57 Murray street, New York.

Mr. James D. Pickles, the Superintendent of the mills, is of English birth, and a practical paper maker.

A new dam across the Hockanum gives a reservoir of forty-five acres in extent.

As pure water is essential to success in the manufacture of a fine quality of paper, great pains is taken to render the water used as pure as possible. It is filtered through charcoal and strained through sponges, before coming in contact with the cotton and linen rags from which the pulp is made. Thirty-five women are employed in the room where the rags are assorted. The mill is supplied with two Hartford Automatic Cut-off engines of 500-horse power, to be used in case the water power is insufficient. The production of the Waverley Mills is six tons per day, and of an extra quality of stock for the specific purposes which it is intended.

The office of the works is an artistic little building, standing in the maple-shaded grounds, fitted with a telephone, all the modern improvements, and adorned with pictures. Altogether this mill ranks as one of the best of its class in America.

INDEX.

INDEX.